Lure of the Sinister

Lure of the Sinister

The Unnatural History of Satanism

Gareth J. Medway

NEW YORK UNIVERSITY PRESS

New York and London

NEW YORK UNIVERSITY PRESS
New York and London

Library of Congress Cataloging-in-Publication Data
Medway, Gareth J.
Lure of the sinister : the unnatural history of Satanism /
Gareth J. Medway.
p.   cm.
Includes bibliographical references and index.
ISBN 0-8147-5645-X (cloth : alk. paper)
1. Satanism.   I. Title.
BF1548 .M43 2000
133.4'22'09—dc21   99-049577

New York University Press books are printed on acid-free paper,
and their binding materials are chosen for strength and durability.

Manufactured in the United States of America

10 9 8 7 6 5 4 3 2 1

To Rose Lopes, Ph.D. and Priestess-Hierophant,
with respect and gratitude.

Contents

Acknowledgments

I thank everyone who has helped me, wittingly or otherwise, with the preparation of this book. First, I thank Matthew Goulding, who unasked lent me his collection of materials relating to Satanism and was extraordinarily patient when it took me years to return it.

It was originally hoped that this study would be independent of any other, but this proving impractical, I exchanged information with Peter Ward, a barrister whose *The Satanic and Ritual Abuse of Children* is still regrettably unpublished, and whose help was invaluable. Margaret Jervis gave me access to important documents. Without Professors Jean La Fontaine and Ronald Hutton, this book would not have appeared at all.

Special thanks to Gavin Sneddon, for all kinds of reasons;

the same to Jocelyn Chaplin, Debbie Gallagher, and "Kitty," for fascinating interviews;

the same to Julie James and Janice Hellary, for their accounts of life in an independent Evangelical church;

the same to Jeffrey S. Victor, professor of sociology at the University of Jamestown, New York, and author of *Satanic Panic*, for sending me information;

the same to Michael Aquino and David Austen of the Temple of Set;

the same to various current and former members of the OTO;

the same to Gerald Suster of the Company of Heaven;

the same to Jules, for her anecdotes of life as a teenage Satanist;

the same, for various reasons, to Caroline Wise, Robert Hicks, Caroline Robertson, Mark McCann, Tania Hunter, John Roberts, Gaile McGonaghie, Mark Ye Morris, Spencer Woodcock, John and Paul of the Association of Autonomous Astronauts, John Rimmer and the late Roger Sandell of *Magonia*, Mark Pilkington, Andy Collins, Carl A. Wilkes, Muriel Renard, and the dedicatee, Rose Lopes.

Finally, I thank all those people who would rather I didn't mention them and who will, perhaps, claim not to know me.

Introduction

On Saturday, the fifth of June, in the year 1598, Loyse, the eight-year-old daughter of Claude and Humberte Maillat, of Coyrieres in south-western France, was struck helpless in all her limbs so that she had to go on all fours. She also began twisting her mouth about in a very strange manner. She continued thus for some weeks, until the nineteenth of July, when her father and mother, who judged from her condition that she was diabolically possessed, took her to the Church of Our Savior to be exorcised. The priest found that there were five devils possessing her, whose names were Wolf, Cat, Dog, Jolly, and Griffin.

When the priest asked the girl who had cast a spell on her—for it was thought that devils would enter into humans only at the instigation of a witch—she pointed out an old woman named Françoise Secretain.

None of the devils went out of Loyse that day; but they left her the next morning, after her parents spent the whole night praying for her. Soon, the family had told the story to officers of the law. Françoise Secretain, they said, had come to their house on the evening of the fourth of June, asking for lodging for the night. Humberte had reluctantly agreed. According to Loyse, when her mother had gone to arrange things for her guest, Françoise had come up to Loyse as she sat by the fire and had given her a crust of bread, which she had eaten. This crust, it was supposed, had been bewitched and caused the child's possession. The local judge, Henri Boguet, convinced by the girl's testimony, had Françoise Secretain seized and put into prison.[1]

For three days, Secretain refused to confess to anything. Far from acting like a witch, she played with a rosary continually and talked of God and the Virgin Mary, as if she was a pious woman. Then they put her in "stricter" confinement (this probably means she was manacled by her ankles) and threatened her with torture. Still she would not say any of the things demanded of her. But when they shaved her head (the usual preliminary to torture), she broke down and said just what they wanted to hear.

1

Yes, she had wished five devils on Loyse Maillat. Yes, she had given herself to the Devil: he had known her carnally, in the form of a dog or a cat or a fowl. Yes, she had often been to the witches' sabbat held near the village of Coyrieres; she would fly there on a white staff, placed between her legs.[2]

This was not enough for her interlocutors. If she had consorted with other witches at the sabbat, then she ought to be able to name some of them. Who were her fellow witches?

The first she named was Jacques Bocquet, known as "Fat Jack," who came from Savoy. He, too, was arrested. Françoise and Fat Jack named others, starting with Clauda Jamprost from the village of Orcieres, an "old and lame" woman. In turn, Jamprost named two more women from Orcieres, Clauda Jamguillaume and Thierenne Paget. These named others still, and in due course more than twenty people were arrested, ranging from old women to children aged younger than ten.

As soon as the news of the arrest of Secretain and Bocquet became public, an orphan girl known as Christofle of Aranthon (she herself did not know her own surname) announced that they had taken her to the sabbat by force. She, too, was arrested.[3]

Most of those incarcerated came to confess that they had been at the sabbat, had had carnal connection with the Devil, had conjured hailstorms by beating the surface of water with wands, and were given powders and ointments by the Devil, which they used to curse and blight their neighbors' cattle and crops. Four of them also confessed that the Devil had given them a special grease, which they used to turn themselves into werewolves.

In 1990, a girl from a family identified only as "W," on the island of South Ronaldsay in the Orkneys, made a number of alarming allegations. The girl, described as "very disturbed," had for considerable time refused to go to school and was being taught by a tutor provided by the Education Department. The girl implied that one of her younger brothers, "an immature boy who hadn't reached puberty," had been sexually abusing both herself and a younger sister. An elder brother, she said, had been doing the same.

On 31 October (ominously enough), the girl's case was discussed by the Children's Panel, and in consequence, the next day she was taken "into care" by the Social Work Department. It so happened that this was one day before her sixteenth birthday, after which they could not have acted.[4]

Five days later her younger brothers and sisters, seven in all, were also taken into care in the belief that they were "at risk." The social workers went to their school and removed them in front of the other children, and some of them struggled and tried to escape. One locked himself in the rest room and had to be tricked into coming out. Once in care, they were subjected to "disclosure therapy."[5]

During these "therapeutic" sessions, the children told horrific stories of bizarre sexual abuse, ritual dancing, and music, out of doors at night in an old quarry. Various adults were present, including one whom they referred to as "The Master." They said they were made to stand in a ring, and they appeared to be describing some kind of occult ceremony. Asked for the names of others present, they mentioned children who belonged to four neighboring families and identified "The Master" as the Reverend Morris Mackenzie, a local clergyman.

Accordingly, at dawn on 27 February 1991, nine more children were taken from their beds by social workers and police and flown to "places of safety" on the Scottish mainland. The police also searched their families' homes and removed many items: a paperback novel by Ngaio Marsh that had a picture of a goat on the cover, a photograph of woods on the island of Shapinsay, videotapes (of TV programs, as they realized when they watched them), and children's coats with hoods. The parents were driven to mainland Orkney for interrogation. The home of the Reverend Mackenzie was also searched, the police taking away the cloak that he used for funerals, a broken cross awaiting repair, and masks that were used in a Nativity play.[6]

Though these two cases are widely separated in space and time, certain parallels are at once obvious: an adolescent girl starts behaving strangely; this is attributed to a sinister cause; and whether it be "demonic possession" or "sexual abuse," some adult can be blamed for her condition. Others are taken into custody or "care" and pressured to give names of others still, and thus the whole affair proliferates. It is assumed that all those concerned have been present at some secret, midnight occult gathering, at which one's physical presence is taken to be proof of serious crime, and the mere mention of one's name is taken to be proof that one was there.

The old orthodox view of sexual offenses, as of a few hundred years ago, was set out at length in a massive 1700 work *De delictis, et poenis* (On crimes, and punishments), by Ludovico Maria Sinistrari, a former consultor to the Supreme Tribunal of the Inquisition in Rome. He graded "crimes against chastity" as follows:

1. Dubious consorting
2. Solicitation to vice
3. Fornication
4. Adultery

5. Ravishment
6. Incest
7. Rape
8. Violation of a nunnery [entering it with immoral intent]
9. Sacrilege with a nun [succeeding in the immoral intent]
10. Masturbation
11. Sodomy
12. Bestiality
13. Demoniality[7]

Part of the reason for this order was that the fundamental sin was the depositing of semen anywhere other than "the vessel for which it was intended." Thus, masturbation was a worse crime than, say, raping one's grandmother.

The lowest three categories followed logically: placing one's semen in the wrong vessel, as in sodomy, was even more sinful than masturbation. Bestiality was worse still, since a creature of a different species was involved. The greatest sex crime of all was demoniality, that is sex with demons, since demons were not even creatures of flesh and blood.

Thus, at witches' sabbats such as those that Françoise Secretain and the others were accused of attending, those present committed the *worst sexual crime possible* (by the ideas of the time) by having "carnal connection with the Devil." In the present day, child sexual abuse is considered the worst possible crime, and it is this that is the centerpiece of all allegations about Satanism.

Henri Boguet, the judge in the Secretain case, wrote a general account of wicked deeds of witches at their sabbats:

> Some have remarked that the place where the Sabbat is held is always conspicuous, and marked by large trees or Crosses . . . the Witches of Longchamois used to assemble in a meadow on the main road to Saint Claude, where one can see the ruins of a house; whilst . . . Jacquema Paget and Antoine Tornier reported that the Witches' Sabbat of Mouille was held in the courtyard of the Priory of that place.

> The Witches being assembled in their Synagogue, then, first adore Satan, who appears there, sometimes in the shape of a large black man, and sometimes in the shape of a goat; and to do him the greater homage, they offer him candles, which burn with a flame of a blue color, and they kiss him on the shameful parts of his behind. . . .

In the second place, the Witches dance, and do this in a ring, back to back . . . moreover there are demons, who assist in these dances in the form of goats, or of sheep. . . . Antoine Tournier said that when she danced, a black sheep took her by the hands with its feet, which were very hairy, that is to say rough and unpleasant.

The dancing over, the Witches turn to copulation, and in this the brother does not spare the sister, nor the father the daughter, nor the son the mother: just as the Persians had the opinion, that to be a great Witch and Magician, one should be the child of a mother and son. . . . I shall pass over and not dwell on all the other types of perversion, those abominations which led to the destruction of Sodom and Gomorrah, which they commonly engage in.

In the fourth place, having wallowed in the filthy pleasures of the flesh, the Witches fall to feasting and banqueting. Their banquets are composed of all kinds of meats. . . . But all the Witches are agreed that there is no taste at all in the dishes of which they eat at the Sabbat.

Having finished the banquet, they render to Satan an account of what they have done since the last assembly; and those are the most welcome who have caused the death of the most persons and cattle, who have cast the most spells of illness, and spoiled the most fruit—in short, those who have done the most mischief and wickedness. Others, who have behaved rather more humanely, are hissed and derided by all, are set apart to one side, and are generally beaten and ill-treated by their Master. . . .

It is at this point, that the Evil One makes a pact with his followers against Heaven, and plots to ruin the human race. He makes these wretched creatures again renounce God, Chrism and Baptism. They reaffirm their solemn oath, that they have made, never to speak of God, of the Virgin Mary, nor of the Saints except by way of mockery and derision. . . . He then exhorts them always to do evil, to harm their neighbors, to cause them illnesses, to kill their herds, and avenge themselves on their enemies. . . . He makes them swear solemnly never to accuse one another, and never to tell of anything that is done amongst them.

Concerning the Mass, which they celebrate at the Sabbat, I cannot write without horror; for he who is to say the Office, is dressed in a black cope with no cross on it, and after having put water in the chalice he turns his back to the altar, and in place of the Host, he elevates a slice of rape-plant colored black; and then all the Witches cry aloud, *Master, help us*. At the same time, the Devil pisses in a hole in the ground, and makes the Holy Water of his urine, with which he who says the Mass sprinkles his assistants, using a black aspergillium.

Finally Satan, having taken the form of a goat, is consumed in flames, and reduced to cinders, which the Witches collect, and keep for use in the performance of their pernicious and abominable designs.[8]

Boguet's contemporary Martin Del Rio offered other details:

So it is that the witches, once they have anointed themselves with their ointments, generally go . . . astride broomsticks or canes. . . . They arrive at the *Games of the Good Society* (as their conventicles are called in Italy) . . . where, illuminated by the fire, the Devil presides, evil and menacing, sitting on a throne, generally in the terrifying guise of a goat or dog. They draw near to worship him . . . some on their knees, some on their backs, others walking on their hands but managing to keep their faces upturned. There, with an offering of tapers made from pitch or babies' umbilical cords, they kiss his hind parts in homage. And to render the sacrilege absolute, they proceed to a travesty of the sacrifice of the Mass, using holy water and following the Catholic rite closely. . . .

Then they offer up their own children to the Devil . . . in 1458 a mother sacrificed three of her children. . . . It is said they even offer up their ejaculated semen, as did that most wicked sorcerer who had sexual intercourse with a woman in a church and mixed his semen with the holy oil. . . .

They appear at the banquet sometimes with the face uncovered, sometimes covered by a veil, cloth or even a mask. Frequently the familiar demons take their respective masked pupils by the hand and all those who are able perform together a grotesque rite; they arrange themselves back to back in a circle, hand in hand, and dance around tossing their heads in a frenzy . . . singing obscene verses in his honor and dancing to pipes and drums played by musicians under a tree. The devils intermingle with their disciples to such an extent that all kinds of ridiculous and unnatural acts take place.[9]

What goes on in modern Satanic rituals has been described at length in many newspapers, journals, and books and goes roughly as follows. The Satanic hierarchy is an international conspiracy seeking world domination; at the lower levels they are organized into temples and covens of thirteen. Satanic ceremonies, known as *sabbats*, are held in the middle of the night in barns, churches, churchyards, crypts, cemeteries, tunnels, caves, cellars, ruined abbeys, castles, derelict houses, or aircraft hangars; also in heath or woodland, on beaches, or in Satanic temples. Those present are either naked or wear robes and masks. A circle is marked on the floor. An altar has on it an inverted cross, candles, bowls, chalices, a dagger, and perhaps a sword. There are also books (of Black Magic rites) and sometimes a human skull or a goat's head. Also playing a part are drugs, alcohol, body paint, live insects, spiders, frogs, and snakes. Demons or Satan himself may appear, though sometimes after a series of therapy sessions the witness will conclude that he or she was really seeing a cult member dressed up. Poppets or curse dolls are used in some ceremonies. Live animals are used for perverted sex and for blood sacrifice; the rituals also involve blood, urine, feces and semen. Human sacrifices are common, the victims being in some cases fetuses, often the product of criminal abortions on female cult members made pregnant for the purpose (such women are called "breeders" or "broodmares"); unregistered babies; children, usually runaways who will not be missed; and adults, sometimes cult members who have stepped out of line. The victims are not merely killed but dismembered, and often, parts of them are eaten.

Children are taught the philosophy of Satanism: that Satan is more powerful than God and will ultimately triumph, and that Christ is Satan's enemy and must be spurned. They are taught to hate God, Jesus, the church and everything good. This cult mind-control technique ensures that members will acquiesce in the most abominable crimes. A girl's hands are held on the dagger by the high priest when the coven performs a human sacrifice, so as to incriminate her forever in the cult and to ensure that no one will turn state's evidence. Destruction of Christian symbols is common, as is desecration of graves and the use of Christian items, such as an altar, church candles, a crucifix, or a font for sacrilegious purposes, as well as desecration of the Host, which is used in the Black Mass, a parody of Christian services, such as the Catholic mass but with the name of Satan substituted for that of God and with prayers altered or read backward. Children are force-fed rotting meat, live maggots, or excrement.

Children are hired out to pedophiles; their abuse is filmed and distributed for commercial purposes or may be held for its blackmail value. Some members acquire great wealth through dealing in drugs, pornography, and violent "snuff" videos.

Remarkable efficiency is used by Satanists in covering their tracks: the bodies of sacrifice victims are incinerated or otherwise totally destroyed; the ritual sites are hidden or camouflaged. Satanists occupy leading positions in the establishment—politicians, judges, vicars, journalists, and TV personalities have all been named—as well as in the police force, which is why convictions never result from these crimes.

Given the remarkable similarity between the accounts of witches' sabbats and the gatherings of Satanists, two conclusions are possible. One, which has been advanced by such writers as Tim Tate in *Children for the Devil* and

Andrew Boyd in *Blasphemous Rumours*, is that there has been a continuity of diabolical practices through the ages. The other is that for the last few years we have been suffering a rerun of the old witch-hunts. Rather than make dogmatic assertions one way or the other, or argue on the basis of plausibility alone, I examine the nature of the evidence, the legal processes involved, the psychology of the subject, the people who are making the allegations, and the history of witchcraft and certain occult practices.

As the whole question of Satanism is indissolubly linked with religion, I feel obliged to declare my own theological position: I am a Pagan and a priest of Themis in the Fellowship of Isis. This prejudices me in advance, since I don't believe that Satan exists. Yet this view does not in itself suggest anything to me about Satanism, since in the same way, while I don't believe in Christianity, I have no doubt that Christians are real.

It has become common for certain people who pose as authorities on this subject to be referred to by their opponents as "experts," the quotation marks being intended as an insult. Such people will be mentioned here often, but it is a little unfair to condemn them in advance this way, so they will be distinguished with the upper case, as Experts. Likewise, those who claim to have survived abuse by Satanists will be called Survivors.

1

What Is a Satanist?

Words change in meaning. The *Oxford English Dictionary (OED)* records three distinct usages of *Satanism* from across the centuries. The first was found in a Catholic tract of 1565, referring to the Protestants: "Luther first brinced [brought] to Germanie the poisoned cuppe of his heresies, blasphemies, and sathanismes." It meant, evidently, a form of Christianity other than one's own. In a similar way, *Satanist* appeared in an Anglican work of 1559, where the Anabaptists and other unofficial sects were called "swarmes of Satanistes."

The second definition of *Satanism* in the *OED* is "writing of the Satanic school"—for instance, the poetry of Lord Byron.

So when did Satanism come to imply a conspiracy of diabolical orgiasts, as it does today? The *OED* is quite clear here: "[Definition] 3: The worship of Satan, alleged to have been practiced in France in the latter part of the 19th century." The first representative quotation is from a magazine article: "There are two sects, the Satanists and the Luciferists—and they pray to these names as Gods."

Since Satanism has now replaced witchcraft as the name for the great conspiracy of evil that is supposed to be all around us, it is important to consider its genesis. It is an importation of the French *satanisme*, and though for some reason most French dictionaries do not acknowledge that as a word (perhaps from purism), its origins can be clearly traced.

In April 1885, the Roman Catholic Church believed that it had secured an important convert. Gabriel Jogand-Pages, better known by his pen name of Léo Taxil, a leading light of the anticlerical movement, had gone to a priest saying that he had been moved by the Holy Spirit and had become reconciled to the church. Formerly editor of journals such as *The Mud-Slinger* and *Down with the Clergy!* he had also turned out a large number of anticlerical and pornographic books, including *The Debauches of a Confessor* and *The Pope's Mistresses*. As he admitted in his subsequent memoir, *Confessions of an Ex-Free-Thinker*, he had freely indulged in fraud and hoaxing: his anonymous *Secret Loves of Pius IX* had featured an imaginary privy chamberlain of that pope, named Carlo-Sébastiano Volpi, complete with fake signature. He had also forged a bull of excommunication (against himself) and taken in the ultrasocialist journal *La Bataille* by claiming to be a secretary to the archbishop of Paris, and writing a series of articles exposing nonexistent corruption in the church, such as an underground group of the Canons of Notre Dame who were conspiring to restore the monarchy.[1] Taxil now said he was determined to devote the remainder of his life to undoing the mischief of his former work.

Taxil's conversion became highly celebrated, and in June 1887, he was even received in audience by Pope Leo XIII[2] (whom he had previously accused of being a poisoner). His first book after his repentance was an exposé of Freemasonry, which the pope had condemned in a bull of 1884.

It should be explained that the church's fundamental objection to Freemasonry is its tolerance. To become a Mason, one is expected to declare a belief in God, but one's actual creed does not matter. Jews and other non-Christians have always been welcome (at least in English jurisdictions) and the appropriate holy book substituted for the Bible during the taking of the oath. The Catholic Church held that for Catholics to attend such gatherings with non-Catholics might prejudice their salvation; therefore Masonry, said the pope, like everything contrary to the church's teaching, must be the work of the Devil.

Normally, such accusations are meant to be understood only in general terms. Though Catholics have always believed the Reformation to have been inspired by Lucifer, if they entered a Protestant church, they would not actually expect to see the Devil called on by name. Yet Taxil suggested that it was literally true. He reproduced what he alleged was a secret lecture given to initiates, which concerned Hiram, the architect of Solomon's temple, around whose legend the Master Mason's degree is based. In this lecture, Hiram was said to have had a vision of a mysterious fiery figure who taught him a creed that was the inversion of Christianity. Adonai, or Jehovah, the God of the Old Testament, he depicted as a jealous tyrant, whereas Eblis (Arabic for the Devil) was an angel of light who governed a kingdom of liberty, whose residents dined on the fruits of the Tree of Knowledge.

The figure prophesied that Hiram's "offspring," that is, the Freemasons, would set humanity free: "They will establish throughout the world the cult of Fire. Your children, rallying to your name, will destroy the power of Kings and of all who minister the tyranny of Adonai"—in other words, the Catholic Church.[3] Taxil's book was so successful that it ran to four volumes.

Having come so far, one might next expect to hear hints of wild orgies, so common in conspiracy theories. But Masonic lodges admit only men, which would limit them to one particular type of sexual debauch.

Fortunately for seekers after the salubrious, it was soon revealed that there existed a secret inner group of Freemasons, called the Palladian Order, which was said to involve both men and women. Taxil's 1891 *Y-a-t-il des femmes dans la Franc-Maçonnerie?* (Are there women in Freemasonry?) gave texts of the crudely blasphemous Palladian rituals:

> *Grand-Master:* What is the sacred word of the Mistresses of the Temple?
> *Grand-Lieutenant:* Lucifer.
> *G-M:* Do you not tremble when you pronounce that name?
> *G-L:* The wicked and the superstitious tremble, but the heart of a Mistress of the Temple does not know fear. Holy, holy, holy Lucifer! He is the only True God.
> *G-M:* What is the work of a Mistress of the Temple?
> *G-L:* To execrate Jesus, to curse Adonai, and to adore Lucifer, &c.[4]

Included was a picture of the order's evil female chief, Sophie-Sapho. In the preface to this book, Taxil was able to cite letters of goodwill written to him by seventeen bishops, archbishops and cardinals.

It has often been claimed that the rank-and-file Masons, who joined in all innocence, know nothing of the secret doctrines and policy at the higher levels. On the face of it, there is little to support this view: Masonic lodges are for the most part autonomous in their management, and although the Grand Lodges do have authority over them, for example, being able to order changes in the rituals, these are generally matters of which every Mason will be aware.

Nevertheless, conspiracy theorists often insist that the "Scottish Rite" of Masonry secretly controls the rest. (Again, on the face of it, the chiefs of the Scottish Rite have authority over only the Scottish Rite.) In the 1880s the head of the Scottish Rite was Albert Pike of Charleston, South Carolina.

In 1891 in France, a pamphlet appeared, *The Existence of the Lodges of Women*, by "Adolphe Ricoux,"[5] which confirmed the views of Taxil (whom Ricoux commended warmly). Ricoux had managed to obtain a copy of "Secret Instructions" purporting to come from Pike, from which it appeared that the inner orders of Freemasonry were indeed involved in Devil worship. The true Masonic theology, according to Pike, was that there are two supreme beings who struggle for supremacy: Lucifer, the principle of intelligence and light, and Adonai, the principle of matter and death. Adonai, of course, is the Christian God. According to this theology, the soul comes from Lucifer but the body from Adonai, who attempts to seduce the soul. Most of the universe is freed from him, but the planet Earth and another planet called Oolis are still beneath his sway.

"Yes, Lucifer is God, and unfortunately Adonai is also God. For the eternal law is that there is no light without shade, no beauty without ugliness, no white without black, for the absolute can only exist as two Gods."[6] This was called the Luciferian creed; the word *Luciferian* was originally used by the Inquisition as a term of abuse for certain medieval heretics.

Pike also discussed "Satanism." As in England, where *Satanism* described Byron's poetry, in France this word had come to refer to decadent writers. The original Satanist, Charles-Pierre Baudelaire (1821–67), suffered bitter melancholy in his mid-twenties: his stepfather had cut his allowance to a minimum; he was pursued by creditors; and his mistress was unfaithful to him. It was in this spiritual torment that he began to call himself a Satanist and penned *The Litanies of Satan*:

> Bereft of praises, betrayed by despicable
> Fate, most handsome angel and most knowledgeable,
> O, Thou, Satan, take pity on my wretchedness.[7]

That someone could write like this was symptomatic of the weakening of the power of the church. But the Satanism of a poverty-stricken poet, moving from one lodging to another just before the rent was due, posed no serious threat to the world.

Yet the new disclosures of the 1880s and 1890s made Satanism into a widespread secret cult. Curiously, the "Instructions" criticized the Satanists, saying that they accepted Christian theology, merely worshiping evil rather than good. According to Pike, this was also a mistake, because Christian theology was all a grand error perpetrated by the evil principle, Adonai. "Thus, the doctrine of Satanism is a heresy; and the true and pure philosophic religion is the belief in Lucifer."[8] Thus, Freemasons ought to be Luciferians, not Satanists.

In 1892, a massive work, *Le Diable au XIXe siecle* (The Devil in the nineteenth century), started to appear in serial form. The book was based on the memoirs of a Dr. Bataille who had been a ship's surgeon in the French merchant navy. It was generally known that "Bataille" was really Doctor Charles Hacks, writing in collaboration with Léo Taxil and others.

The story began in the style of a horror romance. On a voyage to Ceylon, Bataille noticed an Italian passenger named Carbuccia who seemed inexplicably sad. Eventually, the doctor learned why: Carbuccia confessed to him that he was a Freemason and hence condemned to eternal damnation.

Bataille made the bold decision to infiltrate Masonry himself. He sailed to Naples, where he was able to obtain high Masonic grades in exchange for a fee of five hundred francs.[9] On his return to the Orient, he found that he was now welcome into all kinds of diabolical ceremonies. What he witnessed would have confirmed the worst fears of his most paranoid readers.

It appeared that the omnipresent Freemasons were in league with the Hindus, the Buddhists, the spiritualists, the English, and everyone else disliked by French Catholics. Furthermore, all these people, especially the English, openly worshiped the Devil. Bataille revealed the real identity of Taxil's "Sophie-Sapho" to be Sophie Walder, the daughter of a sinister Englishman named Phileas Walder.

Typical was Bataille's visit to the Hindu-English city of Calcutta, where the Freemasons took him to Mahatawala, a complex of seven temples on a rocky plateau outside the city. In each of these temples a different Satanic ritual was enacted. In the first temple, Bataille underwent the "Baptism of Serpents"; in the second, called the Sanctuary of the Phoenix, he witnessed the blasphemous "Marriage of the Apes," during the course of which the celebrant washed his hands in molten lead (the servants of darkness being capable of much that was impossible for Christians); in the third temple, consecrated to Eve, he said that what he saw was so obscene that he dared not print it; in the fourth, a Rose-Croix sanctuary, he watched while Indian girls danced and then dematerialized; fifth, in the Temple of the Pelican, there was a lesson in Masonic charity; sixth, in the Temple of the Future, a hypnotized girl tried unsuccessfully to divine what was going on in the Vatican; and finally, in the Temple of Fire, there was the usual human sacrifice.[10]

On a boat to Singapore, Bataille met a young Scottish woman, a Presbyterian, named Arabella D——. Now, according to Catholic theology, the Presbyterians are Socinian heretics; hence they are Gnostics, who are a type of Satanist. It was not so surprising, then, that when Arabella took Bataille to a Presbyterian church in Singapore, it transformed at the touch of a button into a Masonic lodge, where he witnessed the initiation of a mistress of the temple (the Palladian ceremony given previously in *Are there Women in Freemasonry?*). The climax was the desecration of the Host:

> A deathly silence fell on the assembly. The Grand-Mistress raised her voice and spoke in a metallic tone, her throat contracted: "The Priests say—This is your body. We say: it is the body of a traitor."

> . . . Then the Grand-Mistress raised the host, with an imperious gesture; but Miss Arabella had no need of encouragement; the dagger in her hand, she lashed out in rage at the host, crying out like a demon: "Holy, holy, holy Lucifer! Curses on Adonai and his Christ!"[11]

Bataille's accounts of the wickedness of the English must have helped boost the book's French popularity and sales. The Rock of Gibraltar, which Bataille visited, proved to be hollow and filled with infernal factories for making Satanic regalia and weapons to be used in a future war against Catholic nations.[12] He learned that the Palladian Order was the controlling body behind Freemasonry and every other type of Satan worship. It was based at Charleston, along with the Scottish Rite. Each Friday afternoon, Lucifer appeared there in person to give instructions to his disciples, which would be carried out by conspirators all over the world.[13]

The Devil in the Nineteenth Century, which ran to nearly two thousand pages, became one of the best-sellers of the decade. Soon others were jumping on the anti-Satanist, anti-Masonic bandwagon. Some of these authors were (unlike Hacks/Bataille and Taxil)[14] also violently anti-Semitic. Leon Meurin, archbishop of Port-Louis, published *Freemasonry: The Synagogue of Satan*, in which he argued that Freemasonry is based on the Kabbalah and that the Kabbalah is Jewish, which he considered proved his title. Other writers threw in their own pet obsessions. A certain Louis Martin combined anti-Masonry with anti-Semitism and Anglophobia, turning out such titles as *The English, Are They Jews?*, and *England Governs France by Means of Freemasonry*. The notorious *Protocols of the Elders of Zion*, which were forged in Paris at about this time, may well have been influenced by the Taxil affair.[15]

Catholic journals, in their zeal to combat the powers of darkness, published letters written by "Sophie Walder" and also by "Diana Vaughan," another high priestess of Lucifer. Photographs of Vaughan wearing Masonic vestments showed her to be a handsome young woman.

At this point came a curious hiccup. Among the anti-Luciferian publications that had sprung up was the *Revue du Diable*, which exposed a certain Mlle. Lucie Claraz, a wealthy spinster with a wide circle of distinguished Catholic friends, as secretly being the high priestess of a Luciferian sect. In consequence, she was excommunicated. She promptly sued for libel, stating in court that she was a devout Catholic. The editor of *Revue du Diable* made a novel defense: the existence of Devil worshipers, he said, was manifest nonsense. Since what the paper had alleged about Mlle. Claraz was thus impossible, no one could take it seriously, and it was not therefore libelous. The judge refused to accept this and awarded five thousand francs in damages, but the episode gave an indication of how far these promoters of stories about Luciferians and Satanists believed what they were saying.[16]

Unashamed, the public campaign continued. It was now revealed that there were factional splits among the Devil worshipers. Domenico Margiotta, another Taxil collaborator, related how orthodox Luciferians, including Diana Vaughan, had objected to the election of Italian politician Adriano Lemmi as grand master, because, they said, he was a Satanist. To prove the truth of this, Margiotta reproduced the English text of the dissenters' meeting, together with a French translation. It was written in an extraordinary style, including such sentences as: "Besides, he has laid a tax upon the poor italian lodges, which are obliged to pay, on pain of erasing, after three premonitions."[17] The accompanying French gave the last word as *avertissements*, which can mean either "warning" or "premonition." Obviously, here it meant "warning." Similarly, *radiation* could mean "erasing," but in this context should have been "expulsion." These kinds of mistake occurred all through the document, along with French habits such as writing "italian" in the lower case. It is hard to explain this, unless one supposes that this document was, in fact, written in French and then translated into English by a native French speaker using a French-English dictionary.

Next, it was disclosed that Diana Vaughan had fallen out with Sophie Walder and had come to Europe, where she founded the New and Reformed Palladium, a small number of copies of whose journal were actually available in Paris.[18] Clergymen, horrified by the blasphemous Luciferian creed being announced in their midst, prayed incessantly to Saint Joan of Arc for Miss Vaughan's conversion. In June 1895, Taxil was able to announce that, miracle of miracles, Vaughan had indeed become reconciled to the Catholic Church. The journal of the New and Reformed Palladium ceased publication, to be replaced at once by Diana Vaughan's serialized *Memoirs of an ex-Palladist*.

Miss Vaughan began her story by describing how she had attended one of the Friday seances at Charleston, South Carolina. Lucifer appeared in the form of a beautiful young man, seated on a diamond throne, and announced that he was appointing her as his high priestess. He gave her an army of spirits of fire, who took her to the Garden of Eden, defeated the angel guardians, and enabled her to enter. Inside, she mounted a huge white eagle, on which she flew off to the distant planet Oolis, the realm of Adonai. With Lucifer's help, she returned to Charleston by way of a volcano and the center of the earth (as in Jules Verne's *Journey to the Center of the Earth*, though here the center of the earth was implied to be hell). She herself claimed to be descended from the seventeenth-century English alchemist Thomas Vaughan, who, she said, signed a pact with Satan in 1645, occultism having run in the family ever since.[19]

In 1896 an anti-Masonic congress was held at Trent. By now doubters were appearing. The rationalists present refused to believe in the very existence of Diana Vaughan, since she was associated with supernatural events such as appearances by the Devil. "The Count H. C." read a paper in which he stated that he had tried to check some of the facts given in *The Devil in the Nineteenth Century* and found that they were totally wrong. A member of the Asiatic society of Bengal had written to him saying that there was no complex of seven temples on a plateau outside Calcutta and could not be, as the countryside was totally flat for one hundred miles around the city. He noted also that a picture given by Dr. Bataille, taken from the *Hong Kong Telegraph*, which Bataille said was of the mutilated body of a Masonic traitor, in fact showed a parricide executed by dismemberment in Canton.[20]

In England, Arthur Waite was also skeptical: he pointed out that parts of the ceremonies of the Palladian Order, supposed to have been written in the eighteenth century, were copied from the writings of Eliphas Lévi (1810–75), which Waite knew well since he had translated some of them into English; as for Leon Meurin, the account of "an authentic apparition of Satan" given in his *Freemasonry: The Synagogue of Satan* was quoted from *Blackwood's Magazine*, where it had appeared as fiction. Waite's attacks were noticed by Diana Vaughan, who retorted that he was a Freemason himself, who had translated Lévi for the use of his Luciferian compatriots.[21]

In November 1896, Dr. Hacks/Bataille gave an interview to *Verité* in which he frankly admitted the hoax:

> When the Encyclical *Humanum Genus* appeared, directed against the Freemasons as allies of the Devil, I thought that here was a way to make money out of the credulity and limitless stupidity of the Catholics. . . .
>
> Sometimes, when the fibs I perpetrated were a little too blatant, for example, the story of the serpent who wrote prophecies with his tail on Diana Vaughan's back, or the story of the Devil transformed into a young girl in order to marry a Freemason, and changing in the evening into a crocodile to play the piano, my collaborators, laughing till they cried, told me: "You must be more careful, my friend, you will spoil everything!" I replied to them: "Bah! Let it be! It will pass!" And it passed![22]

In April 1897, Taxil called a meeting at the Geographical Society in Paris, where, it was announced, Diana Vaughan would appear. Instead, he took the stage and himself made a speech:

> Reverend Fathers, Ladies and Gentlemen: I must first of all offer my thanks to my colleagues and the Catholic Press. Do not be angry, my Reverend Fathers, but laugh in your heart, in learning today that what has happened is the exact opposite of what you believed. Bataille is not a devoted Catholic, exploring the high Masonry of Palladism under a false nose. But on the contrary, he is a freethinker who, for his own edification, not out of malice, has entered your camp, not for eleven years, but twelve: and . . . it's your servant.
>
> I had two collaborators, two, no more: the one, an old friend of my childhood, to whom I gave the pseudonym Dr Bataille; the other, Miss Diana Vaughan, a French Protestant, something of a freethinker, a typist by profession. The one and the other were necessary to assure the success of the latest episode of this joyous obfuscation, which the American journals have called "the greatest mystification of modern times."
>
> At first the Freemasons were indignant: they could not foresee the outcome, which will be a universal roar of laughter.
>
> My first books on Freemasonry were a mish-mash of rituals with interpretations; each time that a passage was obscure, I explained it in a sense agreeable to Catholics who would see Lucifer as the Grand Master of the Freemasons.
>
> There were several books by authors who ran in the train of my marvelous revelations. The most extraordinary of these works was that by a Jesuit bishop, Monsignor Meurin, bishop of Port Louis, who came to see me in Paris and consult me. He got well informed!
>
> In my book *Are There Women In Freemasonry?* I created the personage of a Grand-Mistress of Palladism, one Sophia-Sapho, for whom I gave only the pretended initial of her name: W. To my friend the doctor, I gave the entire name in confidence. Sophie Walder, a myth! Palladism, my most beautiful creation, never existed except on paper and in thousands of minds! It will never return.[23]

After speaking for an hour about how he had created his "mystification," whose purpose had been to make fools of the Catholics, Taxil left hastily. Pandemonium broke out in the hall, and the police had to be called to break the meeting up. The churchmen present refused to believe that they had been duped and declared that Taxil had been "bought" by the Freemasons.[24]

Regenerating Satan

Satanism, then, was originally a nonexistent sect invented for a laugh and to sell books. (For some reason *Satanist* rather than *Luciferian* came into English currency.) The task would be much easier if it could be left at that and said that there never was such a person as a Satanist. Things are not so easy, however: in about 1935 a perfectly real Luciferian temple was founded in Paris.

Maria de Naglowska came from a Caucasian family that had been despoiled by the Russian Revolution of 1917. Part of her life was spent in Egypt. Her first disciples were recruited from Bohemian circles: models, art students, and "inverts," whose gatherings in the Montparnasse she called "Satanic Initiations." She taught them her own theology, in which the Trinity comprised Father, Son, and Sex, the last being the most important. "Sex confers Knowledge, that is to say Satan regenerated."[25] For this reason, her Luciferian doctrine was generally referred to as "the Third Term of the Trinity."

She described herself as a high priestess of love, and affirmed: "It is necessary that the Priestess of Love has a vocation, that is to say that she can give the same physical ardor to all males. It is not necessary that she should love them, esteem them or admire them individually, for in each man she must know how to love, venerate and adore the Perfect who must come. She offers her body in sacrifice, putting in the same devotion as a nun. . . . Me and my disciple Priestesses . . . emit benefic radiations which, in regenerating Satan, will bring about—when we have sufficient numbers—the happiness of humanity. We awake in each disciple the Knowledge, also called the fruit of the tree of good and evil, the one in the Garden of Eden."[26]

The inaugural meeting of the Luciferians was held publicly at a room in the Studio Raspail, 46 rue Vavin. A chart on the wall depicted "the ternary evolution of humanity"; another represented "the union of the sexes, and the nervous and magical influx which it brings about."

An altar had been erected up two steps. "Next to it, Maria de Naglowska is sitting in an armchair, wearing a gold robe and crowned with a diadem. Before her, with their backs to the public, the two candidates are standing in the shadows."

The high priestess rose and placed a silver chalice in the hands of each of the two male postulants. "It is the symbol of your fertilizing blood," she explained solemnly.

A canticle followed, sung by the choir of young men and women:

> Silently a gondola,
> Glides across the azure lake,
> Softly she advances,
> Rocking with pure dreams.

Some of the congregation joined in the chorus:

> With certain foot, advance
> Towards the shining altar,
> Neither signs, nor symbols,
> Show the truth so clearly!

Naglowska advanced before the two young men, who raised their chalices toward her. She blessed the symbolic wine: "By this sign, she says, the transformative power of the Female, which is in me, at the same moment most truly mixes with the primordial principle which is in you two, men."

Softly she returned to the altar and pronounced these words: "All ye, who assist at this preliminary Mass of Gold, hear me! The two elements, masculine and feminine, are now combined in me. I project them over all of you by a magical emanation."

The audience then appeared to feel the mysterious surge of the spirit flowing over them. The priestess, disrobing, majestically mounted the two steps to the altar and stretched herself out on it, her head at the west and her feet to the east. A silence fell. She remained still and quickly sank into a magical trance.

Then the first candidate approached her. He placed his chalice of blessed wine on her "sacred triangle" (as he called it) and in a firm and compelling voice made his profession of faith:

DECLARATION OF ADMISSION TO THE BAPTISM OF THE T.T.T.

I believe—for such is my will as a thinking and free man—in the doctrine of the Third Term of the Trinity, revealed by Maria de Naglowska, the High Priestess of the Temple of the Third Term.

I swear to strive by any means to illuminate myself, with the aid of a woman who knows how to love me with virgin love. I shall guard against losing myself with an impure woman. I will perform the Rite of Nature according to the teachings of the Third Term of the Trinity, which will not tolerate the unwholesome perverse vibrations, but very wisely counsels the man who respects himself to be the enlightened Lord, and not the slave of woman.

I will research with companions the initiatory erotic act, which, by transforming the heat into light, arouses Lucifer from the satanic shades of masculinity. I will devote myself to the art of writing, I propose to contribute in my future work to the glory of the Third Term and the magnificence of our Humanity.

I accept the baptism which is given to me at this time, with respect, joy, and knowledge.

Motto: "Towards Knowledge, through Love."

[Signed:] Frater LUG.

He took up the silver cup again. The second postulant placed his cup on the same intimate spot and read a similar declaration. Then the two newly baptized ones slowly drank the magnetized wine as the choir sang the refrain:

> In this living tomb
> I deposit my blood.
> I rebel against the Darkness,
> I aspire towards the Light.

The lights were turned up, and the high priestess slowly came out of her trance. She was assisted to dress, her gold robe and diadem sparkling under the electric lamps. Her eyes had "a prophetic fixity." Suddenly she burst out with joy, celebrating "the unseen Man, whom I have seen, who has been here: the Bridegroom is coming for his mystical Spouse, at the Dawn of the New Day!"

After washing the feet of her newly-born disciples, she proceeded to make a declaration: "We can now say that the Religion of the Third Term of the Trinity is effectively constituted. For a religion exists when he or she who carries the blessing gives the Baptism to at least two candidates. Before this first event, the Doctrine is without real life. It is brought into the world with this event. We hope that other candidates will now present themselves to be consecrated. In the meantime, the *preliminary Mass of Gold* will be celebrated every first and third Tuesday of the month, here, at the *Studio Raspail*."

"A final gracious action, and her friends and adepts follow Maria de Na-glowska to *la Coupole* (for *la Rotonde*, where she used to go no longer welcomes her, I don't know why); and the enthusiastic party carries on until an advanced hour of the night."[27]

Maria de Naglowska disappeared during World War II and was never heard of again; since she had Jewish blood, one can assume the worst. In the 1970s, however, there was a reemergence of French Luciferians, and they are said flourish in Paris at the present day.

The main point about this real Luciferian is that she was not practicing "evil for evil's sake," nor was she engaged in criminal acts. Most significant, she did not (as one might suppose) accept Christian theology, merely transferring her worship to the other side, but had her own metaphysical theories, which, even if one thinks them misguided, were undoubtedly sincere. It is quite different from the kind of views ascribed to Satanists by those who would root them out.

Satanic Churches

There is no need here to add much to the great weight of paper that has been filled with accounts of Anton Szandor LaVey and the Church of Satan.[28] LaVey (1930–98) was a born showman who worked in circuses and carnivals in his youth. It is impossible to say how many would-be Satanists there were in America in the 1940s and 1950s; however, none of them had organized themselves into orders. LaVey looked around for Satanic churches to join and could find none. He did acquire various books of "Black Magic," such as the *Grand Albert* and the *Sixth and Seventh Books of Moses*, and was disappointed; despite their sinister reputations, he found they were all written from a Christian viewpoint and dealt mainly in crude charms.

Most people would acquiesce in this situation, but LaVey was a doer: finding no Satanic orders and no texts of Black Magic that were to his taste, he created them himself.

He had already been holding regular Friday-night lectures on magic for some years when, in 1966, he founded the First Church of Satan in a blare of publicity. The philosophy and practices of the church were set out in *The Satanic Bible* (1969), which has now sold more than six hundred thousand copies. (Many of these have been bought by anti-Satanists, but there clearly has been a lot of interest in what he had to say.)

LaVey does not advocate evil in the sense of physically harming others, but he promotes devotion to Satan as "Self," which deserves to be worshiped and flattered. *The Satanic Bible* advises one to use magic to achieve one's selfish aims, for instance, cursing one's enemies to death; it specifically tells one not to commit physical crimes.

By the mid-1970s LaVey was finding it difficult to earn a living as a priest of Satan. He therefore stated in the church newsletter that, in future, all higher degrees of initiation would be available for contributions in cash, real estate, or valuable objects of art. Many of the priesthood were repelled by what they saw as hypocrisy, the very thing the church was founded to stand against. In June 1975, LaVey's Church of Satan experienced a mass desertion. On 21 June, Michael Aquino, a U.S. Army officer who had been in the church since April 1969, did a ritual to summon the Prince of Darkness for advice. The result was a piece of automatic writing known as *The Book of Coming Forth by Night*, in which Satan informed Aquino that, in future, he wished to be known by his "true name" of Set, and that he was appointing Aquino as LaVey's successor. Aquino therefore founded the Temple of Set, a nonprofit church in the State of California, of which he was the first high priest. To prevent a recurrence of "dictatorial" problems, the high priest is responsible to a corporate board of directors.[29]

Both the Church of Satan and the Temple of Set are law-abiding organizations. If this seems odd, bear in mind that most traditional sins and pleasures of the flesh are legal, however much they may be thought immoral. Nor is there any law against dressing in black robes and performing sinister rituals.

Over the past decade or so I have met a number of professed Satanists. Although it is difficult to generalize, I have found there to be broadly three types:

First are those who regard Satan as a personal friend. One such, who was described by a mutual acquaintance as an "alcoholic and drug addict," showed me a sketch of "The Boss," as he called him; curiously, his Satan looked just like the pictures of aliens used to illustrate abduction stories, except that he had horns and carried a guitar. Another adherent, who has been a regular glue-sniffer for many years, showed me a book of magic that was being dictated to him by his demon friends; it was called something like *The Book of Impossible Lies*. Satanists of this sort are most likely to be found in psychiatric outpatient departments.

The second type are serious, "religious" Satanists of the general type of LaVey and Aquino. At least some of these belong to the Temple of Set or to other Satanic orders, but not too many. The most recent (non-paranoic) estimate of the membership of Satanist sects in Great Britain put the total at only about one hundred.[30] This is probably too small, but the true figure is unlikely to be more than a few hundred. Most of them have a serious interest in the practice of magic, with a tendency toward the theatrical side.

The third type, who are by far the most common, are those sometimes called "dabblers." They can be found at hard-rock concerts or hanging around the Slimelight Club on Saturday nights wearing black clothes— black T-shirts from haute couturiers Man at C&A are essential Satanist dress—black lipstick, and occult jewelry bought in Kensington Market. Among other occult practices, they listen to records by Ozzy Osbourne or the Bollocks Brothers; watch Motley Crue videos, Hammer Horror films, and *The Addams Family*; make blasphemous remarks during "Songs of Praise" to upset Granny; walk in Highgate Cemetery during open hours; and recite the Lord's Prayer backward as a party piece. These Satanists eat jelly babies (gumdrops), dismember Barbie dolls, chop heads off flowers, paint demons on their skateboards, turn crucifixes upside down, start Aleister Crowley's *Magick without Tears* and give up after three chapters, torture the neighbors by playing bootlegs of The Damned, and give their girlfriends gold-plated necklaces from Camden Lock with the words "I tore this from the neck of a fresh corpse I disinterred last night, darling."

One thing that all three types have in common is their independence of thought: they are rebels against arbitrary authority. For this reason, they do not take kindly to authorities within Satanism itself. Anton Long, founder of a homegrown British Satanic group, the Order of the Nine Angles, quotes this conversation that he had at his introductory meeting with the Satanic mistress who initiated him:

> *Satanic Mistress:* What is it that you seek?
> *Anton Long:* Knowledge.
> *SM:* Are we what you seek?
> *AL:* Possibly.
> *SM:* And you are ready to serve—and obey?
> *AL:* No.
> *SM:* And you call yourself a Satanist?
> *AL:* Yes! I would rather die than submit! If I am to learn, it will be as an equal out of respect.[31]

Obviously, people of such an anarchic frame of mind do not sit easily within organizations, and Satanic orders are generally small. Furthermore, they are not obviously morally worse than anyone else. Satanism is usually a "me" religion, pursued for ego gratification and personal power. But these are the common values of contemporary society.

On the face of it, therefore, there is little to support popular anti-Satanist claims, since Satanism is neither widespread nor linked to crime. There is allegedly, however, a fourth type of Satanist: those who belong to tightly controlled groups, who sexually molest children as a policy, and who often perform regular human sacrifices undetected by the police. I have never met a Satanist of this type, nor do I know anyone who claims to have met one.

There is also a fifth use of the term *Satanist*, applying to those who do not call themselves Satanists but who have had that label given to them by critics. Certain hostile people fix the word *Satanist* arbitrarily on *all* occultists, even tea-leaf readers and spiritualist mediums (in much the same way that extreme Trotskyists used to denounce all other political groups as "fascists," from the National Front to the Labour Party). If one accepts such a broad definition, Satanism is indeed extremely widespread, but such use of the word is simply rooted in prejudice. It does not prove anything about Satanic crime. I may state here that I have personally attended hundreds of occult ceremonies (apart from those I have conducted myself), ranging from séances to Odinic witchcraft, and I have never seen any illegal acts occur, except occasionally some people smoke pot afterward.

Quite apart from the small-scale spread of Satanism, recent decades have seen a revival of witchcraft: since hostile studies have led to a lot of confusion on the subject, it must be emphasized that modern witchcraft normally has nothing to do with Satan worship. Today's witches are most often nature worshipers. The most common contemporary form of witchcraft is Wicca, a pagan magical religious system, a revival or reconstruction of prehistoric religion. Being pagan, Wiccans do not worship the Devil, for the simple reason that they do not believe that the Devil exists. Once or twice Wiccans have been arrested when performing naked rituals outdoors, but witchcraft in itself is perfectly legal and not a matter to concern the police.

Wicca and various other forms of Paganism such as Druidry are presently far more common than Satanism. Unfortunately, those who have been active in spreading recent scare stories about Satanism generally fail to notice or acknowledge any difference between these belief systems, which has often confused the general public.

It is true that the demarcations between these different groups are not normally absolute, and many of them are open; that is, membership in, for instance, a Druid order is considered wholly compatible with other religious affiliations (at least, as far as the Druids are concerned). So, while most witches are pagans, there also exist Satanic witches—and for that matter, Christian witches and Jewish witches—but these compound categories are small.

Contrary to popular belief, few occultists of any sort meet in groups of thirteen. The reason is one of simple practicality: to have exactly thirteen members, usually you will either have to include people whom you don't really want or exclude people whom you do want. If just thirteen people are invited to a particular gathering, then very likely one will phone at the last minute to say that he or she can't come because the dog is sick. Alternatively, they will all turn up, but someone will bring along a new boyfriend, girlfriend, or cousin Fred who is staying with the person and doesn't want to be left out. If there are ever exactly thirteen at a coven meeting, it is usually by a happy coincidence rather than design.

Long lists of occult societies, given by certain writers, are of little value if they give no indication of membership. Many occult orders are founded on paper only, because that is much easier than recruiting real members. Consider the SadoMasochistic Initiates of Thelemic Ecstasy (SMITE) document, which reads in part as follows:

> Do as thou art told shall be the whole of the Law
> Love is the Law, Love under Heel
> Motto: Vision through Submission
> Aim—that all in turn experience
> a) the loss of the illusion of Self by submission to others
> b) elevation to godhead, receiving adoration from others.
>
> *Rituals*
> . . . after banishing and concentration exercises—breathing, meditation, etc. . . . Choose sacrifice from members of group by lots. Sacrifice is beaten, bound and blindfolded. They are given the illusion of a journey down the Styx, they are reawakened as a god, given symbols of godhead and all pay homage. Banishment by laughter featuring everyone doing impressions of gibbons and orang-utans.
> Clothes. Combination of SM and occult.[32]

The SMITE document was written by a secretary at a well-known insurance firm during a lunch break. She managed to interest two of her boyfriends in the order, but nothing came of it, and the inaugural ritual, which was to have taken place in a corner of a nightclub in Putney, never happened. She is now going out with a clean-living Cambridge graduate. But it may be that her manifesto is still on a company disk somewhere and will one day be found, and a story will be sold to a Sunday tabloid about how this sinister cult is infiltrating city financial institutions.

The Pentagram

The five-pointed star is a very ancient symbol of health and good fortune and has been adopted by several religions. Today, it is used as a symbol of Paganism and, in particular, of witchcraft.

Originally, it was unimportant which way up the pentagram was drawn, and this remains the case when it is used as an Islamic symbol. However, the nineteenth century French magus Eliphas Lévi, who had the habit of presenting ideas that came from his own imagination as if they were ancient arcane doctrines, wrote in *The Key of the Mysteries* that the "five-pointed star of occult masonry" should have one point upright; when turned upside down, with two points up, it became "the hieroglyphic sign of the goat of Black Magic, whose head may then be drawn in the star, the two horns at the top, the ears to the right and left, the beard at the bottom." Lévi's disciple Stanislas de Guiata included an illustration of such a pentagram with a devil's head in it in his *Key of Black Magic* (1897).[33] Both Lévi and de Guiata might have been forgotten on this matter but for Maurice Bessy, who reproduced the de Guiata pentagram in his coffee-table *Pictorial History of Magic and the Supernatural*, whence Anton LaVey found it and took it as the symbol of his Church of Satan.

Festivals

Basically, there are no such things as Satanic festivals. The Church of Satan does tend to hold its biggest rituals at Walpurgisnacht (May Eve) and Halloween, but apart from that, there is nothing in the nature of an official calendar. Since Satanism is a selfish religion, many Satanists will take their own birthdays as festival days. In practice, they often use the calendar of eight festivals, which is actually of pagan origin:

Imbolc—2 February
Spring Equinox—21 March
Beltane—1 May
Summer Solstice—21 June
Lammas or Lughnasadh—1 August
Autumn Equinox—21 September
Samhain (Halloween)—31 October
Yule (Winter Solstice)—21 December

For want of other, accurate information, these eight festivals are routinely listed in anti-Satanist writing as being the "Major Satanic Festivals."[34]

Elements of Magic

One thing that witches, Pagans, and Satanists have in common is a belief that magic can work. Magic (often spelled "magick") may be defined as "attempting to effect something by noncausal means." Whole libraries have been written on the theory and practice of magic, but just a few techniques need be outlined here.

Black versus White

According to Dennis Wheatley: "By prayer, fasting, and mortification of the flesh, the Saints called down power in order that they might perform miracles to the glorification of God, and heal the sick. This, the use of Supernatural Power for good or *unselfish ends*, is WHITE MAGIC. The use of Supernatural Power for wicked or *selfish ends* is BLACK MAGIC. Such magic is of the Devil and can be obtained only by such sexual depravity and bestial rites as are described in the official reports of the initiation ceremonies of the Mau Mau."[35]

Wheatley does not say in which category he would place holy men who fast and then pray that God will strike their enemies with bolts of lightning; nor could those modern Pagans who perform debauched rites to heal the environment be easily classified by this scheme.

Though the terms *Black Magic* and *White Magic* go back hundreds of years, they were formerly more common on the continent than in England. The first example of *Black Magic* noted by the *Oxford English Dictionary* comes from 1871: "What with slavery and what with black-magic, life is precarious among the Wakhutu."[36] The term evidently came into fashion in Victorian times because the English usually encountered magic only in their colonies; thus it has racial overtones.

Witch-hunters normally mentioned these terms only to deny their validity; as an early seventeenth-century theologian put it: "White, as much as Black Magic, is nothing other than the operation of evil spirits."[37] Modern Christian anti-Satanists take the same view: "Many people say, 'I know Black Magic is wrong because that is from the devil, but White Magic is OK because it's the forces of goodness that are at work here.' This is a prime example of the deception of Satan. Both kinds of magic are from Satan."[38] Most magicians also reject the distinction, saying that magic simply raises power, which can be used equally for good or for evil purposes. Clearly, these labels have little meaning or value.

The Grimoires

Grimoires were the most popular type of "learned" magic in the sixteenth and seventeenth centuries, to judge from the large number of them that survive.[39] The best known of these is the *Goetia* or *Lesser Key of Solomon*, usually circulated in the version published by Aleister Crowley in 1904.

The principle is straightforward. The magician stands within a protective circle traced on the floor. By the use of words of power, he conjures up a demon into the "triangle," which is drawn outside the circle. The demon will be compelled to obey him and carry out whatever he commands. The *Goetia* lists seventy-two such spirits, for example:

> MARBAS–He is a Great President, and appeareth at first in the form of a Great Lion, but afterwards, at the request of the Master, he putteth on Human Shape. He answereth truly of things Hidden or Secret. He causeth Diseases and cureth them. Again, he giveth great Wisdom and Knowledge in Mechanical Arts; and can change men into other shapes. He governeth 36 Legions of Spirits.[40]

Another popular grimoire was the *Key of Solomon*, ascribed to the biblical king but actually a product of the sixteenth century. It gives elaborate instructions for the consecration of magical implements and the conjuration of the spirits, all of which was to be done by means of the Hebrew names for God. This is important as it shows that those who summoned demons retained a Judeo-Christian belief; indeed, they were instructed to lead pure and holy lives. Notice in particular that this method of commanding spirits is totally different from allegations about "pacts" and "Devil worship." A pact implies that the human and the evil spirit are equal; Devil worship implies that the evil spirit is superior; grimoires treat demons as potential slaves. Christian conjurers retained their Christian belief.

Circles of Power

This is the usual way of working magic in Wicca and other pagan groups. The coven form the circle with their bodies (it need not be marked on the ground) and invoke the power of the goddesses and gods into it. The power is then directed to whatever magical intention is wished for.

A circle of this type is different from those of grimoire types: in the latter, the circle is protective and the spirit outside of it; in the former, the energy is in the circle itself.

In anti-Satanist literature, circles are often mentioned, but it is seldom explained which type of circle is meant.

Blood Sacrifice

In ancient times, it was normal to offer a part of one's wealth to the gods. This could be done in different ways: gold and silver might be given to a temple in perpetuity, but since, for most people, wealth was measured in terms of herds and crops, these were generally offered in sacrifice. On a holy day, a cow, for instance, would be slaughtered and the choicest cuts offered to the gods, either by ritually burning them or by giving them to the priests to eat. The people would then feast on the rest. This is still done in some parts of the world.

The origin of human sacrifice is not known, but it may have come about because people were "wealth" in themselves, a large tribe being more likely to defeat its neighbors in battle. It seems that normally the victims were willing; indeed, the Aztecs had so many volunteers for human sacrifice that they had to start turning people away. Usually the victims had to be healthy adults, but children were sacrificed by the Carthaginians until they were defeated and destroyed by the Romans. Even two thousand years ago, though, human sacrifice had ceased in most places.

In the grimoires of the Middle Ages, the spirits who were to be invoked were sometimes given offerings similar to those made to the gods in pagan times. The *Key of Solomon* says: "When blood is to be sacrificed it should be drawn also from virgin quadrupeds or birds, but before offering the oblation, say: 'May this Sacrifice which we find it proper to offer unto ye, noble and lofty Beings, be agreeable and pleasing unto your desires; be ye ready to obey us, and ye shall receive greater ones.' . . . But when we make sacrifices of food and drink, everything necessary should be prepared without the Circle, and the meats should be covered with some fine clean cloth, and have also a clean white cloth spread beneath them; with new bread and good and sparkling wine. . . . Animals, such as fowls or pigeons, should be roasted."[41]

It should be borne in mind that, in those days, if you wanted chicken for dinner, you might have to wring the bird's neck yourself. Nowadays it comes plucked, beheaded, and wrapped in plastic, so it is possible to pretend it was never alive. People are far more squeamish these days about killing, and that includes most would-be practitioners of magic. In Iceland, where Odinism has survived (and is recognized as a religion by the state), it is said that the faithful offer "supermarket-packed legs of lambs" to Thor. In Britain, though magic and witchcraft flourish, animal sacrifice is virtually unknown. If sacrifices are made, they are normally in the form of wine and (ready-cooked) food. If a blood sacrifice is felt to be imperative, sometimes a magician may cut himself for the purpose, while women use their menstrual fluids.

Sex Magic

Anyone hoping to take part in an orgy would be better advised to join a swingers' club than a coven. It is true that certain rituals are based on the sexual act. One is Aleister Crowley's Gnostic Mass, in which the priest holds a lance and the priestess a cup. These obviously represent the genitals, and it is possible that Crowley intended actual intercourse to take place at the high point of the rite. If so, he was to be disappointed; though the Gnostic Mass is often performed, it is done with perfect decorum. Much the same is true of the Great Rite of Wicca: in theory it involves sex, but usually in practice only token motions are gone through. Sex rituals are not a complete myth, but they are far rarer than most people suppose, and when they do happen, the intercourse is usually between regular partners.

Enochian

This is one of several techniques popularized by the Golden Dawn, a British magical order that flourished at the turn of the century. It consists principally of a series of invocations or "keys," in a language that appears like gibberish:

> Micma goho Piad zir com-selh a zien blab Os Lon-doh Norz Chis othil Gigipah vnd-l chis ta-pu-im Q mos-pleh teloch. . . .

This language first appears in the manuscripts of Dr. John Dee (1527–1608), who was astrologer to Elizabeth I, among other things.[42] The English translation of the above is: "Behold, sayeth your God, I am a Circle on whose hands stand 12 Kingdoms. Six are the seats of living breath: the rest are as sharp sickles: or the horns of death. . . ." (Since some of these words, such as "vnd-l" are unpronounceable, the Golden Dawn taught an expanded form, with extra vowels added, in which the third key begins: "Micama goho Pe-Iad zodir com-selahe azodien biabe os-lon-dohe. Norezoda cahisa otahila Gigipahe; vaunud-el-cahisa ta-pu-ime qo-mos-pelehe telocahe. . . ." It is this version that is most often printed.)

Dee believed that "Enochian" was the language spoken in heaven. The magical system was so called because it was thought to have been taught by angels to the patriarch Enoch. Over the passing of many centuries, the original had degenerated into demonic magic, as flourished in Dee's time; the Enochian chants were supposed to be a restoration of the angelic purity of Enoch's time.

Anton Szandor LaVey, however, included the keys in his *Satanic Bible*, changing "your God" to "Satan" throughout the accompanying translation, plus "Heaven" to "Hell" where appropriate. LaVey has here pulled a fast one on his readers: Satanists who use the book think they are invoking Satan, but in fact, they are calling on the Christian God.

Mind Traveling

"Kitty" is a mild, inoffensive-looking Englishwoman of the blue-jeans-and-anorak brigade.[43] Friends often ask her to look after their pets while they are on holiday. Few people would guess that she is a lesbian sadist who practices large-scale destruction magic.

Kitty's magic is all done in her mind. She does not employ robes, incense, candles, runes, incantations, athames (ceremonial knives), circles, talismans, or disciples. Rather: "I was taught in the first place that you can take your mind anywhere, even if you're sitting in your armchair you can do works of malediction and death, you can heal, you can 'see.' That's a basic principle of magic. I could be just sitting here watching *Coronation Street.*"

She claims to have been "a party to" the forest fires that devastated parts of Australia in 1994. This was done by "an interface with atavistic creatures, like giant insects, who live southwest of Ayers Rock." Her collaboration with wholly supernatural beings in this makes her, as it were, an agent of destiny rather than merely a malevolent human.

"When I deal with things like earthquakes, natural disasters, all I'm doing is gathering up the energy that's around, and directing it. It's not involving any spirit, it's just pure energy." In the summer of 1993, she attended a magical conference at a hall in London: "There was colossal energy there, so I thought I'd take some of it." On this occasion, it went shooting off across the landscape, to the east, until it "ran out of land." She went home and looked at the map and found that it would have traveled to the edge of the continental shelf, by the northern part of Japan. A few days later there was a major earthquake in North Japan. "I've never liked the Japanese."

Why does she want to destroy other humans? "There's too many of them, they're a plague on the face of the earth, an overgrown parasitic force."

Whatever may be thought of the morality or the reality of Kitty's activities, there can be no doubt about their legality. Even if she were really responsible for widespread destruction in Australia and Japan, she did not do so by any "causal" method recognized by modern law. In the physical world, she may merely have been knitting in front of the television.

(And what about her sadism? She has wholly theoretical views on how men should be treated: "Any society that calls itself truly civilized would not countenance having undomesticated males about the place. All males who have either fulfilled their biological function or are not required to do so would be treated in the same manner as the cattle on your farm, or the dog on your hearth. They would be rendered civilized by the excision of the offending parts. The only exception is homosexual males, who would be encouraged to live amongst their own society, for their own pleasure.")

It was certainly common to do mind traveling centuries ago. Francis Perreaud, one of the less credulous demonologists, told a curious anecdote, which he said happened about 1595. A man in Echalens in the Pays de Vaux accused himself of crimes of witchcraft and demanded to be executed for them at once. Imprisoned in the castle of the town, he was visited by the bailiff, who told him that he could not believe the things he had confessed.

> On this the prisoner, who was disposed to die, replied calmly, that all that he had said and confessed was true, and that if he pleased, for proof of it, if permitted, he would kill the cows belonging to a neighbor whom he named, for which he needed his unguent-jar[44] and wand, which were in his house in a place he indicated. At this, the Bailiff wanting to satisfy his curiosity, resolved to go and find the wand and unguent-jar, resolving also in any case to pay whoever owned them for the cows. This wand and jar being carried and placed in the hands of the Witch, then in the presence of the Bailiff, of the Minister and of some others, he did all the ceremonies which all other Witches are accustomed to do with these instruments of Satan, after which he fell as if dead at their feet, without movement or expression, remaining thus for an hour or three quarters of an hour, after which he revived as if from death to life, or as from a very deep sleep. And being asked by the Bailiff, where he had been, he said that he had been and killed the cows of which he had spoken, and for which permission had been given. At once the Bailiff went to see if it was true or not, and he found that indeed the cows were dead, as he had said.[45]

It is typical of the uninformative nature of old witchcraft treatises that Perreaud fails to explain what it is that witches are "accustomed to do" with their implements; but the jar no doubt contained witches' "flying ointment," which is known from old recipes to have contained aconite and belladonna. These would not produce flight, of course, but they could cause a sensation or hallucination of flying.

Importantly, Perreaud recognized that witches' sabbats were purely mental events, though he still blamed Satan:

> It should not be thought strange if the Devil, who has much greater power than melancholic humour, works strange and horrible effects in the imagination of witches. Such are those which work at the time whilst they are asleep, that there often appear in their imagination forms, spectres, phantoms, figures sometimes cheerful, eating, drinking, singing, leaping, dancing, and lechering. . . . They often believe that they are physically present at their Sabbats and nocturnal assemblies, which only happen in their imagination, in which the Devil works in such a way that their memory on waking represents it to their exterior senses, so that they firmly believe that those things which Satan suggested have really happened.[46]

Copulation with devils may also have occurred as a purely mental event. According to the fifteenth-century *Malleus Maleficarum* (The witches' hammer):

> Witches have often been seen in fields and woods, lying on their backs, and naked up to the navel. And it appears from the disposition of their sexual organs, and from the agitation of the legs, that they have been copulating with Incubus demons which are invisible to the onlookers.[47]

That the crimes of witches were committed only in the mind, if at all, used to be well known, and witch-hunters used to have to explain it away. After all, it might be held to be unfair to burn someone at the stake for what they had only imagined they had done. Boguet declared that although *sometimes* witches went to the sabbat in spirit only, at other times they went physically. Furthermore, spirit travel "never happens except to such as have previously attended in person the Witches' Sabbat, and have already enlisted beneath Satan's standard."[48] So, if a woman said she was at the sabbat when in fact she had been sleeping peacefully in her bed, she was nonetheless worthy of incineration.

2

Why Worship Satan?

In 1620, when Antoinette Bourignon was four years old, she told her parents that she wanted to live in the country of the Christians. When they mocked her and said that Flanders, where they lived, was a Christian country, she said "that could not be, for *Jesus Christ* was born in a stable, and liv'd in Poverty, whereas they all love to have fine Houses, and fine Furniture, and much Wealth; and therefore she concluded they were not Christians, and that she would go into the Country where the Christians do live."[1]

Finding little satisfaction in this world, the child turned to God through prayer: "she from her Infancy had daily Conversation with God, he speaking inwardly to her Heart; and she thought this Divine Conversation was a thing common to all. Thus for Instance, remarking that her Father was surly to her Mother, and oft-times transported with Anger against her, after having endeavour'd to appease him by her childish Embraces, she would retire apart, and considering how hard a thing it was to be married to a troublesome Husband, would say to God, *My God, my God, grant I may never marry*, and she beg'd that instead of being married, *he would give her the Grace to become his Spouse*."[2] (Be patient, reader, the connection of all this with Satanism will become apparent.)

Since her father intended to marry her to a rich French merchant, she secretly made herself a hermit's habit. On Easter evening, having cut her hair, she put on the habit and slept a little, then went out at about four in the morning, taking with her nothing but one penny to buy bread for that day. But God said to her: "Where is thy Faith? in a Penny." So she threw it away, begging pardon of God for her fault.[3]

After some misadventures she went to live as a recluse in a little house in the churchyard of the village of Blatton. She lived there on and off for some years as a hermitess, returning to her family for periods. After her father's death, she was the sole heiress to the family estate, and God said to her, "Pursue your Right, take your Goods, you shall have need of them for my Glory."[4]

> Being one Day in the Street about her Affairs, a Man whom she knew not accosted her, and afterwards came to her Lodging, telling her there were multitudes of poor Infants made Orphans by the Wars, in great Want both as to Body and Soul, and that she might remedy this great Evil, God having given her Talents and Commodities to undertake so good a Work. . . . He told her He was call'd John S. Saulieu. . . . In *November*, therefore, 1653, about the 37th Year of her Age she undertakes the Care of a Hospital of Orphan Maids, founded by one *John Stappart* a Merchant in *Lisle*, some Twelve or Thirteen Years before. She found all Filthy, and in Disorder. She made all Clean, and put all in Order, and made a Rule by which all were alike as to Diet, Bed, Cloathing, and all other Accomodations.[5]

Such was her compassion that she took in many other girls, and the number increased to more than fifty, though the hostel had been founded only for ten or twelve. She employed her own goods to maintain them and her time to instruct them. They learned the Christian doctrine and some useful skills to gain their living with. And she brought things into such order that there was almost no trouble in governing this great family.

All was regulated from morning until night, without intermission. They rose precisely at five; after having spent half an hour in dressing and prayer, they learned to read and write until half past six, when they went to church; at seven they were set to work, with which they recited the common prayers; they breakfasted at eight and read some pious book; at nine they sang spiritual songs; the next hour they passed in silence at work; at eleven they repeated the catechism; they dined at noon, after which they took half an hour's recreation; and from one to eight they repeated all that they had done in the morning. When they had supped at eight, they went into the oratory to pray; after that, they lay down in silence, and all the lamps were put out at nine.[6]

"There was nothing of ill observed in their Comportment, but that some of them would not work willingly. Others were enclinable to Lying and to Thieving, for which they were Corrected, and many times with profit and amendment."[7] Local citizens became desirous to get their servant maids from this hostel, as the girls were honest and faithful.

One day, Saulieu proposed to Bourignon that they might marry and live together in virginity, that he might assist her in the cares of the house. She told him that marriage was not needful for that. Nonetheless, by degrees he revealed a great passion for her, so that in the end she was obliged to apply to the local magistrates for an order barring him from molesting her.

To prevent like dangers, Bourignon had the house shut up as a cloister, that no men might have occasion to come near her. This was done by the order of the bishop of Tournay. "She was now greatly comforted and in quiet, being out of the Hazard and Conversation of Men."[8]

About three years after the house was shut up, one of the girls, Belotte, of fifteen years of age, having done some fault, was shut up for a penance in the prison of the house. She was locked in behind three separate doors by the provisor of the house, who went to the market with the keys at her girdle. Yet within an hour the girl came into the workhouse where all the rest were. When Mademoiselle asked her how she got out, she said that a man had taken her out. After dinner Bourignon called Belotte, and the girl gave the same reply. Bourignon asked if Belotte knew the man. The teenager said she knew him very well; it was the Devil.

At this Antoinette Bourignon trembled, saying, "The Devil is a spirit not a man." The girl said: "He comes to me in the form of a man, and I calling him to help me when shut up, he opened the door and took me out." Bourignon asked her if she had known the man a long time. Belotte said yes, all her life; that her mother from her childhood had carried her to the sabbat of the witches, which is kept in the night; and that when she was a little child, this Devil man was a young boy, and he had grown up as she did, being always her lover, and caressed her day and night. Bourignon could not believe this, for she had never heard of such things.

Mademoiselle immediately sent for the three pastors, the overseers of the house, to whom the girl declared that she had given her soul to the Devil and denied God; that to confirm the gift, she had received a mark in her foot; that she had done this freely when twelve years of age, although long before this the lover had been entertaining her and had carried her to the sabbats of the sorcerers, which were held in great castles where they met to eat, drink, dance, sing, and do a thousand other "insolencies." Bourignon put the girl out of the house that very day, fearing lest the other girls should be corrupted.[9]

About three months afterward, as another girl of fifteen was going to be imprisoned for stealing, she said the Devil made her do it. She, too, was immediately put out of the house, that it might be purged of such persons.

But after three months more, another girl, this one eleven, was going to be whipped for the same fault when she said, "Do it not, and I will tell who made me do this evil." Bourignon took the child to her chamber, where the girl said it had been the Devil. The child explained that when she was young and had been playing with the girls of the town, they had told her that if she went with them, she would have good cheer and a lover. "The Lover came on a little Horse, and took her by the Hand, asking if she would be his Mistress; she consenting, was carried through the Air with him, and the other Girls, into a great Castle, where they had all sort of Feasting and Mirth, that she has been there ever since, Three or Four times a Week."

The pastors examined this girl and thought it not fit to put her out of the house until it was discovered whence this evil might arise. One of them, Peter Salmon, undertook to examine the child daily and to endeavor her conversion. He asked her one day if there were any others in the house like her; she said there were two who went with her daily to the sabbat. These two were called and spoken with separately, in private. They confessed that they were in covenant with the Devil and said there were yet two others of the witches in the house, and being asked to name them, each girl named two different girls. These, on being called, confessed, each naming two more different persons who were of the same crew—so that from two to four, from four to eight, it was discovered that all the thirty-two girls then in the house were bound to the Devil, of their own free will, having contracted with the Devil diversely: some through their fathers, some through their mothers, and some through playing with other little girls. This they declared to both Bourignon and the pastor, who put in writing all they said to him.[10]

> *A.B.* [Antoinette Bourignon] was in no little Perplexity to be shut up in a House, from whence she could not get out, with Thirty Two Persons who declar'd they had given their Souls to the Devil, and that she must eat and drink with them, or what they made ready. She propos'd to dismiss them by degrees, but then fear'd to be guilty of the Mischiefs they would do to others. . . . The Pastors thought it fittest to keep them; said there were Hopes they might be converted to God, having been engag'd to the Devil before the Use of their Reason, and promised to come every Day to admonish and exercise them, and pray for their Conversion. This was done for the space of Eight Months, in which the Girls made great shews of Conversion, by Tears, repeated Confessions, Prayers, and attending to the Admonitions given them, but without Sincerity. Their Hearts were wedded to the sensual Pleasures which the Devil gave them.

> Pastor *Salmon* wrote down their Confessions, they declar'd plainly they had daily carnal Conversation with the Devil, that they went to the Sabbath, where they eat, drank, danc'd, and committed other Sensualities. Each had their Devil in form of a Man, and the Men theirs in form of a Woman; that

they never saw more numerous Meetings in the City than at their Sabbaths, of People of all Ranks, Young and Old, Rich and Poor, Noble and Ignoble, but above all, of all sorts of Monks and Nuns, Priests and Prelates.[11]

"I asked them," wrote Antoinette,

if the *Admonitions, Exorcisms and Prayers of the Pastors*, did not take away the Power of the Devil, from holding them thus subjected to him? They told me that *the Devil Laugh'd at these Performances*; and that after the manner of a Monky he mimick'd the same Ceremonies that the Pastors did; when they Kneel'd down to Pray, the Devil kneel'd behind them, and with a Book in his Hand he babled out the same words; and when the said Pastors Preach'd, the Devil made behind them the same Gestures, and sprinkled about the Holy Water; and also Confess'd them as the Pastors did, imitating them in every thing in Derision and Mockery.

I told them that all these falsities would certainly bring them to Hell. Their answer was, that they very well knew it; and that they were assured to be Damned; but that the Devil promised them the same carnal and sensual Pleasures in Hell, that they took with him in this World.[12]

At this distance of time, it is not possible to tell if the girl Belotte had spare keys to the prison room, or if it was possible to exit by the window, or if there was some other natural explanation for her escape. But it is clear that the other girls were having hallucinations or lucid dreams. Bourignon did not say if it occurred to her to check the dormitories in the middle of the night to see if the girls were all there (though, since they were cloistered, they could hardly have gotten out except by supernatural means or in their minds alone). But she did notice that they all had a great appetite for their bread and butter at breakfast, even eating dry bread if it was given to them, which they would not have touched if they had just been feasting on dainties.

Reading through the story of Bourignon's girls, it is hard to resist concluding that their Diabolism was a reaction to their cloistered lives and the relentless Christianity of their days. Some people who take up a vegetarian diet find that they start to have dreams of sausages and steaks. Bourignon's orphans, singing hymns and reciting prayers as they worked (with only half an hour's break a day), crammed with piety, debarred the sight of men, found at last that some kind of compensatory mechanism in their brains took over and gave them nighttimes of wickedness and delight—so they thought. When their moral guardians tried to cure them with even more Christianity, they failed.

When Sister Jeanne of the Angels, the mother superior of the Ursuline convent of Loudun, was possessed by the demon Behemoth, "I felt a continual aversion against God. . . . Moreover, he gave me a very strange aversion to my profession as a nun, so that sometimes, when he was in my head, I tore up all my veils, and those of my sisters which I could find. I crushed them under foot, I ate them, cursing the hour when I had entered the cloister."[13]

In the sixteenth and seventeenth centuries, many nuns became possessed by devils, and this is most readily explained as a reaction to an all-encompassing regime of holiness. It must be remembered that women usually became nuns not out of religious conviction but to save their fathers the expense of finding them a dowry or because it was good for the family reputation.

Compared to a lifetime of prayer and penitence, possession could be a lot of fun, as can be seen in this account of the behavior of Sister Claire, also of the Ursulines of Loudun:

> She fell on the ground, blaspheming, in convulsions, lifting up her petticoats and chemise, displaying her privy parts without any shame, and uttering filthy words. Her gestures became so indecent that the audience averted its eyes. She cried out again and again, abusing herself with her hands, "Come on, then, fuck me!"[14]

One might expect that the church would disapprove of this sort of behavior, but very often the clergy encouraged it. Demonic possession was a miracle, as much a proof of the Catholic faith as any other miracle. The Loudun case is thought to have begun when some of the bored younger nuns started producing knocking sounds in the night for a joke, making out that the building was haunted. Their confessor, Father Mignon, then got the idea that certain political and other advantages could be gained by having a case of possession in the town, so he deliberately engineered it, and it went on for years.[15]

Another possessee, Madaleine Bavent of the convent of Louviers in Normandy, was eventually able to tell her story at length to her confessor. Madaleine asked readers of her autobiography "to distinguish what they thought real from what seemed to be hallucinations." No one has made much effort to do so, but here is an attempt.

At age thirteen, Bavent, an orphan brought up by her aunt and uncle at Rouen, was apprenticed to a dressmaker, but at sixteen she entered the convent at Louviers.[16]

Usually sisters devoted to God would only ever see one man, their father confessor. At Louviers, the chaplain was Father Pierre David, who, like a number of such priests, took advantage of his position to make the convent into his own private brothel. Instead of teaching the Bible, he instructed them from a book of his own composition: "He taught that one sin must, as it were, be cancelled and blotted out by another sin, so that we may at length achieve the perfect innocence of our first parents, who before the fall walked naked and unashamed."[17]

Accordingly, Madaleine was ordered to strip to the waist and communicate with her breasts exposed. "The most holy, virtuous, and faithful nuns were held to be those who stripped themselves completely naked and danced before him in that state, appeared naked in the choir, and sauntered naked through the gardens." The nuns were also encouraged to fondle one another and Father David. The nuns also made a huge phallus out of paste for their pleasurable usage.[18]

In 1628, Father David died and was replaced by Father Mathurin Picard and his assistant, Father Thomas Boulle. These two men took their vows of chastity more seriously than their predecessor had, and there were no more orgies in the convent.

Fairly soon, Madaleine was suffering sexual frustration, which turned into hysteria, which in turn started to give her hallucinations. One morning when she went to the grille to receive Holy Communion, as Picard gave her the wafer, she thought he hissed in her ear: "You will very soon see what is going to happen to you." Then, an "irresistible force or impulse drove me out into the garden, where I flung myself, feeling quite exhausted, on a pile of wood under a mulberry tree. And it was here that the Devil appeared to me for the first time, a demon in the likeness of a great black cat belonging to the house. He put his two front paws on my shoulders and with all his weight pressed his hindquarters on my knees, thrusting his hot muzzle right up to my mouth. His eyes blazed with fury, and I felt that he wanted to tear from me the Sacred Host. For nearly an hour I remained thus, half swooning, speechless, unable even to make the sign of the Cross, powerless to drive away this demon beast."[19]

As her hysteria grew worse, she started seeing this cat everywhere (no one else noticed it), and it now seemed to have an enormous phallus. It visited her in her cell and forced her to have coitus with it.

Eventually, she started flying to the sabbat. "I was always called up at night, and after I had been asleep for a while. . . . I at once arose in order to reply to the voice, which always appeared to be that of one of the nuns in the house. As soon as I reached the door I felt myself carried away." [20]

This sounds like what is now referred to as "lucid dreaming." But it cannot have been real, for Barent was locked inside her cell; eventually, at her request, a second lock was put on the door, but it did not stop her nightly travels, which clearly were not in the flesh.

She had already decided that Picard and Boulle were wizards and had bewitched her, so it was not surprising that they were there at the sabbat, along with the specter of Father David. Also present were various other priests and nuns whom she did not know, as well as half-bestial demons. The orgies that she thought took place were horrible rather than erotic. People would lie with demons and dine on human flesh. The priests read an irregular mass from a "Paper of Blasphemy." [21]

"One midnight, after we had made our public renunciation of good, a certain crucifix of no great size was produced ... every person present came forward and pricked it deep with a sharp knife." [22]

On one Good Friday, a woman brought to the sabbat her newborn babe. "It was decided that this innocent should be crucified, and before they fastened his tender limbs to the cross they stuck small Hosts on the places where his hands and feet would be pierced by the nails." [23]

Occasionally they went too far:

> One time a certain Priest brought a host, in order to burn it. This time Jesus-Christ appeared in the middle of their blasphemous assembly, and their rage was especially against him: but our Lord blasted the Priest, of whom there was not an atom left, with his divine wrath.

Another time a priest tried to injure the sacred blood by sticking a knife into it; this time both Jesus and the Virgin Mary appeared, and reduced three priests to cinders. [24]

Madaleine also signed, or thought she signed, pacts in blood:

> I give myself to thee with all my heart, devoting body and soul to thee. I worship thee as God, I renounce and revoke all the renunciations which I have ever made of thy power and thy works. [25]

Her nocturnal journeys continued for fourteen years, unnoticed. But when Picard died in 1642, Madaleine became more hysterical still, so that it seemed to others that she was possessed. This condition being apparently infectious, several others also showed the signs. Public exorcisms started to be held and attracted many spectators.

A series of unpleasant legal proceedings started and dragged on for years. Picard's body was disinterred and thrown into a sewer. As a result of legal action by his family, it was reburied decently, but subsequently it was reexhumed and defiled again. Father Boulle was burned alive. Madaleine Bavent herself was given solitary confinement for life in a small dungeon in the basement of the convent.[26]

A similar explanation must underlie the religious deviations of Aleister Crowley, who was brought up in the faith of the Plymouth Brethren. Since so much is written nowadays about Crowley's "Satanism," it is worth examining how it came about. As a child he attended a private boarding school in Cambridge for the sons of Brethren. Several anecdotes concerning this school suffice:

> A boy named Barton was sentenced to one hundred and twenty strokes of the cane on his bare shoulders, for some petty theft of which he was presumably innocent.
>
> Champney's [the headmaster's] physique being impaired, one may suppose by his excessive devotion to Jesus, he arranged to give sixty strokes one day and sixty the next.
>
> My memory fails—perhaps Barton will one day oblige with his reminiscences—but I fancy the first day came so near killing him that he escaped the second.
>
> On Sunday the day was devoted to "religion." Morning prayers and sermon (about 45 Min.) Morning "meeting" (1½ to 2 hrs.) Open-air preaching on Parker's Piece (say 1 hour). Bible reading and learning by heart. Reading of the few books "sanctioned for Sunday" (say 2 hours). Prayer meeting (called voluntary, but to stay away meant that some sneak in the school would accuse you of something next day) (say 1 hour). Evening prayer and sermon (say 30 Minutes). Preaching of the gospel in the meeting-room (1½ hours). Ditto on Parker's Piece (say 1 hour). Prayer before retiring (say ½ hour).[27]

After his father's death, Crowley's uncle, Tom Bond Bishop, stood *in loco parentis*. He was not one of the Brethren, but neither was he any more liberal in religion: "He devoted the whole of his spare time and energy to the propagation of the extra-ordinarily narrow, ignorant and bigoted Evangelicalism in which he believed. He had founded the Children's Scripture Union and Children's Special Service Mission. The former dictates to children what passages of the Bible they shall read daily: the latter drags them from their play at the seaside and hands them over to the ravings of pious undergraduates or hired gospel-geysers."[28]

It is not surprising that in such surroundings, one day the eleven-year-old Crowley "went over to Satan's side." It happened soon after his father's death, which may have been a trigger. Instead of wanting to become a shining light in Christianity, he was set on damnation.[29]

This was not an easy goal, for he still accepted the theology of the Plymouth Brethren. "I was opposed to an omnipotent God; and for all I knew to the contrary, He might have predestined me to be saved. No matter how much I disbelieved in Jesus, no matter how many crimes I piled up, He might get me in spite of myself."[30]

He had, however, heard of the sin against the Holy Ghost, which "shall not be forgiven . . . in the world to come" (Matthew 12:32, King James Version). If only he knew how to do that, he could be sure of being denied entry to heaven. Theologians have never been able to agree on what the sin against the Holy Ghost actually is, though they are unanimous that it cannot be forgiven. In Victorian England, it was widely believed that masturbation was the sin against the Holy Ghost.[31]

Crowley's sexual ignorance made this approach to damnation difficult for him:

> The reign of terror was so firmly established in the school that nobody dared tell me outright the nature of this sin . . . at last a boy named Gibson told me what action to make, but he did not tell me to what object to apply the process."[32]

Crowley wrote that he made "ill-directed" experiments; one can imagine the adolescent Aleister frantically frigging his thumb, then asking, "Am I damned now?"

Another idea for sinning came from the conflict between his mother's and his uncle's different branches of Christianity. As one of the Brethren, his mother was inclined to believe that her Evangelical brother was damned and, according to the rules of the sect, ought not to have associated with him at all.

Now, the Plymouth Brethren did as they believed the earliest Christians had done, so they held their prayer meetings in their homes, churches (a development of slightly later Christianity) being diabolical. This gave Crowley, who was racking his brains for some really abominable crimes to do, another idea: "In a moment of desperate daring I sneaked one Sunday morning into the church frequented by my uncle Tom on Streatham Common, prepared, so to speak, to wallow in it. It was one of the most bitter disappointments of my life!"[33]

By the time Crowley was twenty-two, his world had broadened, and he was an enthusiastic chess player and mountaineer. Having gone up to Cambridge, he spent much of his time reading, making up for the lost years when he was allowed almost no books apart from the Bible. At twenty-one he inherited his late father's estate, which came to £17,000—a considerable sum in those days, though by the age of forty he had squandered the lot.

But then he underwent a strange meditation that convinced him of the worthlessness of this world. He was left with an urge to "evoke the denizens of other planes." Supposing that all spirits were either good or evil, he still held that "the forces of good were those which had constantly oppressed me. . . . Since, therefore, it was my business to explore the spiritual world, my first step must be to get into personal communication with the devil."[34]

The booksellers Deighton Bell supplied him with a copy of A. E. Waite's *The Book of Black Magic and of Pacts*, a recently published compendium of the old grimoires. Like LaVey after him, Crowley was disappointed to find that though these books dealt with demons, they were written from a Christian viewpoint. But the work started him on reading occult literature generally, alchemy, the Kabbalah, and mysticism. In November 1898 he joined the Hermetic Order of the Golden Dawn, the only organization practicing ceremonial magic at that time.

The final result was that he came to found his own religion, known as Thelema or "Crowleyanity." The basis for Thelema was *The Book of the Law*, which Crowley said had been dictated to him by his holy guardian angel in Egypt in 1904. *Thelema* is Greek for "will," and the guiding principle was "Do What Thou Wilt shall be the Whole of the Law." The idea came loosely from Rabelais, whose novel *Gargantua* included an Abbey of Thelema, guided by "Do What Thou Wilt," which the French satirist had supposed would result in a much healthier and happier establishment than the real, gloomy monasteries. Crowley stated that by "will" he meant "True Will," that is, the will of one's holy guardian angel. There would be no trouble or harm in the world if everyone did as their guardian angel suggested.

Thelema has a large pantheon, with many strange gods and preternatural beings in it. It does not, however, include Satan as such, and Jesus figures as a representative of the slave gods whose worship was to be superseded. It is as if Crowley's religion helped heal the split in his own mind.

Money for the Devil

In 1983, Derry Mainwaring Knight, who was running an unsuccessful painting and decorating business, moved to the East Sussex village of Newick. His trade did not flourish there, and he was given £6,000 by kindly neighbors to pay off his alleged debts.[35]

Knight had meanwhile come to know the local rector, the Reverend John Baker. He told Baker he had been "born again" when God spoke to him as he sat on the roof of Hull Prison during a demonstration. (He had been serving a sentence for rape.) He ingratiated himself with Baker and the local congregation by handing out religious leaflets from door to door and organizing prayer meetings.[36]

About this time, Knight's wife separated from him. By February 1984, he had moved into the rectory, where he lodged in the attic.[37] He confided that he still had heavy debts and was being hounded by vicious debt collectors. Baker agreed to help him and by the following month had raised £24,925 from local Christians, which he gave to Knight.[38]

Two evenings later, Knight went into a trance in which, it seemed to the rector, he was possessed by evil spirits. He claimed that he belonged to Lucifer, had been initiated into Satanism by sacrifice at the age of eight, was a master of the occult, and held high office in a Satanic order. When he came to, Knight affirmed that these statements were true.[39] He had been too frightened to mention his Satanic connections before, because the organization had a deep hold on him, but since 1980 he had been trying to break free. It was to the Satanists that he had owed the large debts, of which there were still more.[40]

By 21 May, Baker had raised a further £18,000, which he gave to Knight in cash. But this was not the end of the matter. Knight would go into a trance whenever he saw the full moon, despite prayers being said for him. "Sometimes in the trance he would be flat out and prostrate uttering songs, or sometimes words, in the worship of Lucifer."[41]

Knight said that the trances were caused by certain items of regalia still in the possession of the Satanists, which could be used to influence him. The only way that he could finally break free would be to buy up the regalia, and this would require more money. Letters were sent out to parishioners requesting help, and these included a note from the bishop of Lewes, explaining that this was "very necessary work." Within three months, Baker had handed over £12,435 more to Knight.

These artifacts were said to include a ring, a chalice, and a sword. Eventually Knight produced some such items, and he and Baker destroyed them with the aid of a bonfire. But the full-moon trances did not finish. Knight explained that he had had two platinum disks implanted into his forehead by a Satanist surgeon. Here, at last, was something that could be tested, but instead of having Knight's head examined (or for that matter, his own head), Baker hastened to raise more money, to buy up the further regalia that was said to send the signals to the disks. By 22 October, the rector had given Knight another £34,750 in used £50 notes.[42]

On 8 November, Baker negotiated a loan of £25,000 from a Christian charity. The same day, Knight bought a £17,000 Lotus sports car. He explained to the rector that he had to convince the Satanists that he still had money and influence. If he could mislead them successfully, he might be able to break the group up altogether. For this purpose, he would also need a Rolls-Royce.[43]

So the payments continued. Most of the money came from wealthy local Evangelical Christians, including Susan Sainsbury, wife of Timothy Sainsbury, M.P., who had a mystical revelation concerning the affair in the House of Commons, which led her to hand over a total of £79,895 to Baker for him to give to Knight.[44]

Meanwhile, Knight had been introduced to many important Christians, including the bishop of Chichester, the Right Reverend Eric Kemp. The latter became suspicious when Knight told him that he had been initiated into Satanism by an "unfrocked Cardinal." It occurred to Kemp that there was no such person.[45] So he insisted that there ought to be verification that the items had in fact been bought. He was told that this might make the Satanists suspicious and jeopardize the operation.[46] Nonetheless, Kemp finally contacted the police, and on 13 March 1985, Knight was arrested and questioned for two days about the payments.

He was released on bail, and soon afterward he got the Rolls-Royce he had been after, with the help of £37,500 given by Lord Hampden.[47] All this might have gone on forever, but on 23 May, Knight was arrested again, just before £200,000 was due to have been handed over to buy a Satanic throne.[48]

The committed Christians had meanwhile been perturbed to learn that the man they had been helping had a prison record, including five years for rape, and had given venereal disease to two of his wives.[49] But they were distressed at the arrest, which they felt was interfering with the doing of God's work. They were receiving messages from God, and one of these warned them not to trust the senior investigating policeman, who was a "man with five faces."

Knight's trial began at Maidstone Crown Court on 17 February 1986 and was to last for two months. Those of the donors who were summoned into court insisted that they had been helping to stamp out evil. Michael Warren, who had donated £36,000, said that no prosecution should have been brought against Knight, because Satanism was "very much a potent source of evil in this country, and every step should be taken to stamp it out and free people from it."

The Reverend John Baker refused to name the items of regalia about which such a fuss had been made. He referred to three of them as A, B, and C, saying that several lives would be threatened if he named them.[50] "There is not the slightest doubt that anybody who gets in their way and who starts to divulge things at the top end of the organization will be shot or disposed of in some way."[51] (Later, though, another witness named some of the items, without untoward consequence.)

Confronted with evidence that Knight had spent the money donated to him on girlfriends and prostitutes, Baker said, "People who have a deep involvement in the occult don't normally get out in one, nice, neat jump—the deliverance is a process." He denied the prosecution's claim that he was a gullible fool.[52]

Another Christian witness, Randle Mainwaring, a retired bank director, said that he had met Mr. Knight at a Bible discussion group and found he had "an amazing knowledge of the Bible"; but he was incredulous when Knight had suggested blackmailing a local bank manager as a way of raising money to "buy satanic regalia." (Allegedly, one of Knight's girlfriends had secretly tape-recorded an indecent proposal the bank manager made to her.)[53]

Non-Christian witnesses testified that Knight had been spending large sums of money at the time that the Christians had been donating to him. One girlfriend said that he had spent £2,000 on her during a single day out in Southend.[54]

A tape recording narrated by Knight's mother was played. It seemed that at the age of nine, Knight had awakened in the night to see an emissary of Satan standing by his bed. From that day his troubles began. By the age of ten, he was shoplifting, "although his father was a pastor." While on national service in Germany, he had defrauded a Christian of thousands of marks, which led to a dishonorable discharge from the Coldstream Guards.[55]

Knight himself finally took the stand, refusing to swear an oath on the Bible. Before the trial he had said he was a member of the Ordo Templi Orientis (OTO), but, learning that he might be confronted with Expert testimony on that organization, he chose not to repeat the claim in court.[56] He now said that he belonged to the Sons of Lucifer (on which there could be no Expert testimony, since no one had heard of them before). While he claimed that he had wanted to get out of Satanism since he was twenty-one, he kept boasting about it. He said that he had taken nine sets of vows and that these were of "far greater importance than this court."[57]

The prosecutor, in his summing up, remarked that if what Knight had said about the Satanists were true, then he ought to be dead ten times over.[58] Knight was found guilty and sentenced to seven years, with a further two years unless he paid a fine of £50,000.[59]

No evidence was ever produced that the Satanists had any existence outside of Derry Mainwaring Knight's head. As for his statement that this head of his had two platinum disks implanted in it, this is typical of schizophrenia. So, too, are his full-moon trances. In fact, he seems to have had a classically split personality, one half a Christian, son of a pastor and well versed in the Bible, the other imagining that he was a leading Satanist who gave the other Satanists their messages from the Devil. It was in the interest of the ego of the latter personality to make the Satanists out to be as powerful as possible. Thus he told the donors that his house was bugged by the police: he knew about it because the Satanists had told him; "Satanists live and work in nearly every trade and profession." Right next to this boast came a claim that he had now accepted Jesus Christ as his savior. He claimed that the Satanists had a temple in Pall Mall, where the throne that his arrest prevented him from receiving money for was kept; that Lord Whitelaw, then Margaret Thatcher's deputy prime minister, was a leading member, along with other members of parliament; and so on.

The most significant question is why so many people were so willing to hand over so much so casually. A solution can be found in a statement issued by Bishop Kemp after Knight's sentencing. He blamed the charismatic movement, which, he said, has "brought new life to many congregations but it has also led in places to individuals and groups becoming obsessed by the thought of evil and believing that the Lord speaks to them and gives direct injunctions how to deal with it. This is extremely dangerous and needs to be carefully checked. The problem is that if someone says 'The Lord has told me' then it stops all argument."[60]

Even after the case, this faith tended to be sustained. Rather than acknowledging the hoax, subsequent Christian writers have cited Knight's conviction as yet another proof of the wickedness of Satanists.[61]

It is evident that no sane person, and few insane ones, will seriously regard him- or herself as a servant of a Christian-style principle of evil. People who become involved in Satanism regard Satan as really being the good guy; or they perceive their participation in Devil worship as involuntary; or they continually struggle and alternate between sides. Whichever way, the most common cause of involvement in Devil worship is a reaction to a repressive or hypocritical background—not, as is popularly supposed, simply a dedication to wickedness.

3

The History of Satan and the Pact

Sometime in the second millennium B.C., a Mesopotamian incantation priest named Saggil-Kinam-Ubbib wrote a dialogue between a "Sufferer" and a "Friend." The Sufferer, who has been reduced to great poverty, is told by the Friend:

> He who waits on his God has a protecting angel;
> The humble man who fears his Goddess accumulates wealth.

In other words, all things, good or bad, come from the gods, and if you are afflicted, you must have offended them in some way. But the Sufferer disputes this:

> The savage lion who devoured the choicest flesh,
> Did it bring its flour offering to appease the Goddess's wrath?
> Have I held back offerings? I have prayed to my God,
> I have pronounced the blessing over the Goddess's regular sacrifices.

They debate like this for some time without reaching a conclusion, and at the end, the Sufferer goes back to praying:

> May the God who has thrown me off give help!
> May the Goddess who has abandoned me show mercy![1]

The book of Job in the Old Testament is so similar to Saggil-Kinam-Ubbib's dialogue, both in form and content, that one must be based on the other or both on some common original. Job debates his suffering with equally unsympathetic friends:

> Why do the wicked live, reach old age, and grow mighty in power? (Job 21:7, Revised Standard Version)

At some time a prologue was added, explaining Job's personal misfortune in terms of events in heaven:

> Now there was a day when the sons of God came to present themselves before the LORD, and Satan also came among them. . . . And the LORD said to Satan,

"Have you considered my servant Job, that there is none like him on the earth, a blameless and upright man, who fears God and turns away from evil?" (Job 1:6–8, Revised Standard Version)

Satan states that this is only because he is so wealthy, with nothing to complain about.

"But put forth thy hand now, and touch all that he has, and he will curse thee to thy face." And the LORD said to Satan, "Behold, all that he has is in your power; only upon himself do not put forth your hand." So Satan went forth from the presence of the LORD. (Job 1:11–12, Revised Standard Version)

Satan then causes all kinds of trouble for Job, destroying all his property and, after further consultation with the LORD, smiting him with boils. But Job never turns from his faith in the LORD, and Satan is effectively defeated.

Job would appear to have been a "special case," but this story provided a common basis for subsequent Christian theories of suffering: that they are not necessarily caused by one's own wrongdoing but are the work of the Evil One.

All cultures have a belief in evil, or at least in chaotic spirits. As far as is known, however, the idea of a special principle of evil started with Zoroaster, a Persian prophet whose dates are uncertain. Zoroaster taught the worship of only one God, a final judgement, and other ideas that are now common but were then novelties. He believed that the supreme deity, Ahura Mazda ("Wise Lord"), created twin spirits, the beneficent Spenta Mainyu and the evil Angra Mainyu. Humans were endowed with free will that they might follow either spirit, as they chose. But, when souls of the deceased tried to climb up the Bridge of Judgment, only the followers of Spenta Mainyu would make it up to heaven. The disciples of Angra Mainyu would fall down into "a long life of darkness, bad food, lamentation."[2]

It is thought that after the Persians conquered much of the Middle East, around 500 B.C., the Jews learned these ideas and adapted them into their own religion. *Satan* was not originally a proper name but meant "the Adversary"; the word could be an ordinary noun, as in the books of Samuel, where David was a satan to the Philistines. The word could also be a verb: in Numbers 22:22, God sent an angel to *satan* (i.e., oppose) Balaam.

(A number of modern writers assert that Satan is derived from the Egyptian god Set. The trouble with this suggestion is that *set* means "throne" and is equivalent to the Hebrew *sheth*, which is spelled *shin–tau*, whereas *satan* is spelled *sin–teth–nun*; so the two words do not have one consonant or vowel in common. It would be as plausible to say that *set* was the origin of the English word *seat*. Etymological theories of this type are based on the assumption that any two words that sound similar must be the same, like the schoolboy who said: "It's fun looking through microscopes at orgasms.")

As to the *origin* of evil, there have been various legends. In Persia, Ahura Mazda had created Angra Mainyu for a purpose. Modern Jews take the same view. According to a twentieth-century rabbinical commentator, Satan is "a celestial Intelligence Officer who must report to God in the Heavenly Council. . . . His part is to oppose men in their pretensions to a right standing with God, and to test their sincerity (Job i–ii), to remind God, in no friendly spirit of their sins (Zech. iii. 1f.), and to prompt them to do acts which will bring them into disfavor with God (1 Chron. xxi 1)."[3]

In the intertestamental period, however, a completely different theory was developed: that Satan was originally a leading angel, who rebelled against God and was cast out of heaven with his followers. A passage in Genesis—"the sons of God saw the daughters of men that they were fair; and they took them wives of all which they chose. . . . There were giants in the earth in those days; and also after that, when the sons of God came in unto the daughters of men, and they bare children to them . . ." (6:2–4, King James Version)—was taken to refer to fallen angels, who came down to earth and interbred with mortals. This version was recounted in the *Book of Enoch*, a work popular at the time of Jesus but not included in the Bible, which hence is now little known.[4] It is also implicit in the New Testament, where Satan appeared transliterated into Greek letters but also translated as *diabolos*, "one who throws against" (*dia-*, "against"; *bolos*, "throw"), hence "an adversary." The *b* later softened into a *v*, hence *diavolos*, whence comes the English *devil* by way of the medieval *divel*. (Once again, despite some assertions to the contrary, *devil* is not related to the Indo-European root *div-*, the origin of the Sanskrit *deva*, a being of light.)

This legend is perhaps less satisfactory than Zoroaster's, since it does not really explain how evil began. It puzzled the French historian Gerald Massadié as a child when he was taught it by the Jesuits: if Lucifer was tempted, "then temptation must have pre-existed him, I argued, and therefore evil did too. How could that be, since he was meant to be its inventor? This line of argument annoyed one of my teachers, who in my trimester report accused me of having an evil mind."[5]

In the Dead Sea Scrolls, the word *angel* (Hebrew, *malaakh*) was more often used to mean a devil than a good spirit.[6] In the Talmud, however, *satan* (without the definite article) was the ordinary word for an evil spirit, the chief of them all being called Samael. (It should be noted that the elaborate demonologies of olden times have disappeared from modern Judaism.)

In New Testament times, the Devil, like his Persian counterpart Angra Mainyu, had the job of tempting mortals to sin. He appeared to Jesus Christ while he was fasting in the wilderness (Matthew 4:1–11; Luke 4:1–13) and made various wicked suggestions, which were, however, ignored.

In addition, it was believed that many people were possessed by devils. An ancient and universal belief was that some (or even all) illnesses were caused by evil spirits that had somehow entered the sick person's body. Much of a healer's work therefore consisted in driving these devils out. It seems to have been thought that the devils originally gained entry through the sinful conduct of the patient: hence illness and sin were identified. Thus, Jesus is reported to have said to a man with palsy, "Son, thy sins be forgiven thee" (Mark 2:5, King James Version), upon which the man recovered.

The word *demon*, which is Greek and means a spirit, came to be synonymous with *devil*. To the Pagans, a demon was usually a good spirit or even a deity. The Christians made demons evil, since they called good spirits *angels* (which means "messengers").

A later addition to the hierarchy of hell came from the book of Isaiah. While prophesying the downfall of the kings of Babylon, Isaiah declaimed: "How art thou fallen from Heaven, Hellel son of the Dawn" (14:12). *Hellel* means "shining one." Isaiah used the metaphor as one familiar to his audience, but its original signification is now lost. It may have been a version of the Canaanite legend of Ashtar, a god associated with the planet Venus as morning star, who tried to sit on the throne of Baal, proved too small for it, and so fell from heaven down to the underworld.[7]

Whatever Isaiah meant, Jewish commentators never connected this passage with the legend of the fallen angels.[8] The first person known to have made the link was the Greek Christian Origen in the second century A.D., who quoted it using the Greek equivalent of hellel, *phosphoros*, with the specific intention of refuting those who denied that Satan was once in heaven.[9]

A problem arose here, for Phosphoros, "Shining One," was the usual name for the morning star, and in the book of Revelation, Jesus states: "I am the bright and morning star" (22:16, King James Version). It may have been in reference to the latter passage that the fourth-century bishop of Cagliari took the Christian name of Lucifer, the Latin equivalent to Phosphoros. At this time the church was divided between the Arians, who held that Jesus was the first being created by God, and the Athanasians, who held that Jesus was as eternal as God. Eventually the Athanasian viewpoint was made official, and Arians were forced to recant their belief on pain of death. This was not good enough for Bishop Lucifer, who said that they ought to be put to death even if they recanted. No doubt to his astonishment as well as distress, this view was found to be a little too extreme by the church authorities, and he himself was declared a heretic.

At this time Saint Jerome, who was famous for his invective against anyone who disagreed with him, was engaged in translating the Bible into Latin. He rendered Hellel/Phosphoros as Lucifer. In a letter to Bishop Damasus he wrote, concerning the rival candidates for the bishopric of Antioch: "Now the Sun of Justice is rising in the West; but in the East that notorious Lucifer, who had fallen, has exalted his throne above the stars."[10] The "Sun of Justice" was the bishop of Rome; perhaps "Lucifer" was a snide reference to Paulinus, one of the would-be bishops, who had himself been consecrated by Bishop Lucifer. Whatever the case, the name Lucifer, which so nearly became a title of Christ, came down on the side of hell as an alternative name for Satan.[11]

Several other devil names, such as Beelzebub, Astaroth, and Asmodeus, later became common. Beelzebub, called "prince of demons" in the Gospels, is agreed by scholars to be a corruption of Baal-Zebul, that is, lord of Zebul. Though *baal*, "lord," could be a title of respect for any noble or leader, it was also used to signify a god; hence "lord of Zebul," the title of the patron god of the city of Zebul.

Though many Jews and early Christians held that the gods of the Pagans were simply nonexistent, some of them had it that the old gods were devils in disguise. Hence, the god of Zebul became the prince of demons, and in the same way the fertility goddess Ashtaroth, or Astarte, became the archdevil Astaroth, inexplicably undergoing a sex change on the way. Asmodeus seems to have been the Persian demon Asch-medai ("raging demon"), who came into Christianity by way of the apocryphal book of Tobit.[12]

Demon Lovers

Early fathers of the church who went out into the desert to live as hermits, as Saint Anthony did, often found themselves assailed by sensual visions, which they put down to the work of demons. These sex demons were termed *incubi* (when male in form) and *succubi* (female), originally the words for erotic nature spirits among the Pagans.

These beings could be fitted into biblical theology, since the sons of God (taken to be the fallen angels) "saw the daughters of men that they were fair; and they took them wives." But a problem occurred to medieval theologians. Angels are pure spirit; therefore, they would be unable to impregnate corporeal women. How, then, could the women "bare children to them"? Saint Thomas Aquinas, the official philosopher of the Catholic Church, found a neat solution: a demon would make itself a succubus, extract semen from a man, then turn into an incubus and discharge the same sperm into a woman.[13] This explanation was accepted by most subsequent demonologists.

Eventually, however, Ludovic Sinistrari spotted another difficulty here: "There were giants in the earth in those days," as a result of this crossbreeding. If the sons of God had merely used the seed of men, then the offspring should have been of the same stature as those humans already living. To explain the begetting of giants, Sinistrari proposed that the fallen angels were not pure spirit but part corporeal and so able to procreate.[14] This theory must have been too radical for his contemporaries, for it was not published until long after his death, in the late nineteenth century, an age when few people cared about the question.

Romantically inclined demons did not always have the traditional horrendous diabolical form but could take on human shape, even it was believed, convincingly imitating particular individuals. This was proved by an incident related in the *Life of Saint Jerome*. A certain devil became jealous of the holiness of Silvanus, archbishop of Nazareth. So the devil turned himself into the archbishop's form and likeness, then entered a respectable lady's bedroom at night and made amorous advances. She cried out loud, bringing others running, who found what they believed to be Archbishop Silvanus hiding under her bed. Thus was the holy man defamed, until by a miracle the devil was compelled to appear at the tomb of Saint Jerome, in his true, hellish shape, and confess his deception; after which Silvanus's holy reputation was restored. This proves that fallen angels can imitate humans—or is it the other way around?[15]

"My Name Is Legion"

Though the *Book of Enoch* said that there were only "in all two hundred" fallen angels, in human estimation evil spirits always proliferated. The Talmud gives a cautionary story about a scholar who made a talisman to banish a demon that lived in a sorb bush (rowan tree). It failed because he did not realize that sixty demons dwell in every sorb bush, and they remained unmoved, until a better scholar made a sixty-demon amulet for the bush, after which they departed. The Talmud also warns one not to go out alone on Wednesday or Saturday night, because then Igrath the daughter of Mahalath goes forth with 180,000 destroying angels.[16]

In the Middle Ages, it was calculated that God first created 399,920,004 angels, of whom exactly one-third fell and became devils, that is, 133,306,668. This figure did not become universally accepted, however. Around 1460, Alphonsus à Spina wrote that "all of the doctors agree" (a medieval theologian's way of saying, "I think") that only one-ninth of the angels fell, that is, 44,435,566 (he meant 44,435,556). Meanwhile, the Kabbalists had computed the original number of angels as 601,655,072, which does not divide by three. Others are said to have made the total of the fallen as few as 7,405,926 or as many as 2,665,866,746,664.[17] On the same theme:

> It was a smart Repartee that a *Venetian* Nobleman made to a Priest, who rallied him upon his refusing to give something to the Church, which the Priest demanded for the delivering him from Purgatory; when the priest asking him, *if he knew what an innumerable Number of* Devils *there were to take him?* he answer'd, *yes, he knew how many* Devils *there were in all: How many?* says the Priest, his curiosity, I suppose, being raised by the novelty of the answer. *Why, ten millions five hundred and eleven thousand, six hundred and seventy five Devils and a half,* says the Nobleman. *A half?* says the Priest, *pray what kind of a Devil is that? your self* says the nobleman, *for you are half a Devil already, and will be a whole one when you come there; for you are for deluding all you deal with, and bringing us soul and body into your hands, that you may be paid for letting us go again.* So much for their number.[18]

Decline and Recovery of Satan

With the rise of the Age of Reason, many theologians abandoned literal belief in devils and tried to explain the biblical references to such beings as only symbolic in meaning. Early in the nineteenth century, for instance, appeared an anonymous *Essay on The Devil; Proving a Belief in the Existence of such a Being, Contrary to Scripture, Reason, and Natural Philosophy*. The author stated that though Leviticus 17:7 says, "And they shall no more offer their sacrifices unto devils" (King James Version), the word translated as "devils," *shorim*, means "hairy," hence a goat, so that the reference was to Pan worship rather than Devil worship.[19] Other Christians, however, continued to state that the Bible was the only authority in religion and should be taken at its face value here as elsewhere.

In 1889, the Italian Arturo Graf proclaimed that the Devil had been killed off by the progress of science: "Civilization has conquered Hell and has forever redeemed us from the Devil." As Graf's English translator remarked forty-two years later, however, "That announcement may seem to some readers premature and unsubstantiated. Many Christians still regard the devil as a living entity; Billy Sunday appears to be on as intimate terms with him, in this fourth decade of the twentieth century, as was Martin Luther in the sixteenth century, or Saint Anthony in the third."[20]

Since the Second World War, Satan has definitely made a comeback: a survey in America revealed that those who expressed certainty that the Devil exists rose from 37 percent in 1964 to 48 percent in 1973; and by 1982 the figure had increased to 60 percent, though by comparison only 17 percent in France, 21 percent in Britain and 25 percent in Germany held this belief.[21]

The Sale of Souls

It is never possible to say who had an idea first,[22] but it is often suggested that the notion of the Satanic pact may have come from a misunderstanding of Saint Augustine's *On the Christian Doctrine* (late fourth century). In the second book, Augustine discussed what arts and sciences are suitable for a Christian to study. For instance, logic can be helpful for a better understanding of Christianity, but it must be used with caution, as it can lead to opinions contrary to the true faith.

Divination, said Augustine, should be totally avoided by Christians. He explained this stricture with reference to the Roman practice of augury. For example, if an eagle was seen flying from northwest to southeast, an augur might interpret this as meaning "the consul will win in battle." If it flew from southeast to northwest, then the consul presumably would lose in battle. Augustine did not deny that augury worked but said that the appearances of the omens were arranged by demons. He added that they were arbitrary: it could just as well have been that southeast to northwest meant a victory, just as the letter *X* meant something different in Latin from in Greek.

The augurs themselves would have agreed with this analysis, except that they believed the omens were sent by the gods. But the saint objected to the association between humans and the demons he thought responsible and said such society should be rejected by Christians "as the covenants [*quasi pacta*] of a false and treacherous friendship."[23]

It is not obvious, however, why an obscure passage such as this should have given rise to a detailed belief about pacts for human souls. Saint Augustine was explicit that the term *pact* was only a metaphor for an agreement that certain omens should be given particular meanings. In fact, though this passage was quoted by later demonologists, along with Isaiah 28:15—"ye have said, We have made a covenant with death, and with hell are we at agreement" (King James Version)—in an effort to justify the theory, the origins of the Satanic pact must be sought elsewhere.

It is more likely that the idea of the Satanic pact was actually derived from the pagan custom of making a vow to a god. Suppose a man was desperately in love with an uninterested lady: he might make a vow to the goddess Venus that, if he won this woman's favors, he would make some kind of offering to Venus's temple, such as sacrificing a sheep, or would perform some other service. Such a vow might have been formally written out on parchment and deposited at the temple.

This sort of practice was not likely to die out easily, even after Paganism had been made illegal. Ultimately, it was integrated into the Catholic cult of saints and has continued as such to this day. Not long ago, when a vital computer disk was lost at the head office of a business run by a Catholic family, they made vows to various saints as to what they would do if it was found again. When it turned up (having merely fallen on the floor but become almost invisible, as it was a black disk on a black carpet), the mother of the family had to refrain from buying any more jewelry until the following Christmas, and one of her daughters had to go to mass.

But there seems to have been a period when the orthodoxy tried to suppress the practice of such vows, along with other pagan remains. One can picture the preacher thundering to his flock that the old gods were nothing more than devils in disguise, so that an offering to Venus was really an offering to the Devil. If you did religious service to Venus, it was serving the Devil, who henceforth would "own" your soul, and ultimately, you would go to hell.

Accordingly, legends such as the following arose:

There was an honest worshipful man named Heradius who had but one daughter, whom he consecrated to the service of God, but the Fiend, enemy to mankind, enflamed and made one of the servants of the same to burn in the love of this maid, and when he remembered that he was but a servant, he thought it not possible that ever he should attain to come to his desire of so noble a virgin.

So he went to an enchanter, to whom he promised a great quantity of money if he would help him. To whom the enchanter answered that he could not do it, "but I shall send to the devil, who is my Master and Lord, and if you do that which he shall say to you, you will have your desire." And the young man said he would so do.

And this enchanter sent a letter by him to the devil: "My Lord and Master, by cause that I must hastily and slily draw all that I may from the religion of Christendom, and bring them to your will, to the end that your party shall always grow and remultiply, I send to you this young man, and demand that his desires be accomplished, that herein I may have glory and honor, and that from now I may gather to you and draw more."

Then he gave him his letter and bade him go. "And at midnight stand up on the tomb of a Pagan and call the devil, and hold up this letter in the air. Anon he shall come to you." And he went forth and did as he was bidden, and held the letter in the air. And forthwith came the Prince of Darkness, fellowshipped with a great multitude of fiends, and when he had read the schedule, he said to the young man: "Will you believe in me if I accomplish your desire?" And he answered that he would so do. Then the devil said to him, "Renounce your Jesus Christ." And he said, "I renounce him." And the devil said to him: "Make a book, of your own handwriting, and deliver it to me, and let it contain, that you have forsaken Jesus Christ, your baptism, and your profession of Christian religion, and that you will be my servant, and with me at Judgement to be damned."

And anon all this he wrote and took it to the devil, and put himself in his servitude. And anon the devil took with his fiends, that served fornication, and commanded them that they should go and enflame the heart of that maid in the love of that young man.

The girl persuaded her father to let her marry the young man, but her neighbors eventually pointed out to her that he was not a Christian, so she took him to see Saint Basil. The young man confessed everything to the saint, who used the gift of the Holy Spirit to annul the pact with the Devil, and they all lived happily ever after.[24]

A similar legend concerned Theophilus, a servant of a bishop, who "wisely dispensed the goods of the Church." But when a new bishop was appointed, Theophilus was, against his will, put out of his office.

In despair, he took counsel of a Jew, who was of course a sorcerer and who called up the Devil for him. Theophilus renounced God, the Virgin, and his profession of Christianity and wrote out an obligation or pact in his own blood, sealed it with his ring, and gave it to the Devil. The very next morning his job was restored to him.

But later he repented of what he had done and went and prayed to the Virgin Mary, who promptly appeared to him in a vision, rebuked him for his lapse, and commanded him to forsake the Devil. As soon as he had done so, she, by her grace, got back his pact from the Devil and gave it to him, so that he should not have to be the servant to the Devil.[25]

It is typical of the Dark Age Christian storytellers that they imagined all non-Christians openly served the Devil, even in the knowledge that they would go to hell in consequence. Yet, crude as they were, these anecdotes proliferated. The stories of Theophilus and the youth saved by Saint Basil were included in the *Golden Legend*, a medieval best-seller compiled in the thirteenth century, and hence became familiar all over Europe. It became common to accuse any successful man of having made a diabolical pact. Silvester II, a scientifically minded pope who made clocks and other mechanical gadgets, was naturally accused of a league with the Devil. So were several subsequent holders of the papal seat, and when Oliver Cromwell won the battle of Worcester, it was said that he had made a pact with the Devil on that very morning.[26]

There is an element of jealousy behind these stories. The other fellow gets the girl, the job, or the papacy. He must have had the help of the Devil!

The first historical reference to Faust is in a letter from the abbot Trithemius, the noted Kabbalist, to the astrologer Johann Virdun of Heidelberg, dated 20 August 1507. It warns Virdun against an adventurer "who has ventured to call himself the prince of necromancers," who uses the title "Magister Georgius Sabellicus, Faustus junior."

For some years after, odd references to George Faust turn up. A Georgius Faustus was at Erfurt in 1513, where he was described as a "cheiromancer." In 1520 the bishop of Bamberg paid ten gulden to a Dr. Faustus for casting his horoscope. In 1528, the town of Ingolstadt expelled a certain fortune-teller named Dr. Jorg Faustus of Heidelberg.[27]

Yet there are also mentions of a Johann Faust of Kundling. Philipp Melanchthon and other prime movers of the Reformation told unlikely stories about him: how he had flown through the air at Venice, assisted by a devil, who suddenly dropped him so that he was nearly killed; that he had eaten another magician, who yet was later found still alive. When he did finally die, he was strangled by the devil in his sleep.[28]

It looks as if the name Faustus had acquired a high magical reputation, so that more than one wanna-be immensely powerful magus took it as a surname, just as today one often meets with "Merlin." Sabellicus's title "Faust junior" implies that there had already been a "Faust senior."

There is no record of a Faust Sr., but there is an attractive theory suggested in Daniel Defoe's *The Political History of the Devil* (and in some other sources). Defoe supposed that the original of Faust was Johann Fust of Mainz, Germany. Something of the real life of this Fust is known: he was a fifteenth-century financier who advanced money to Johannes Gutenberg, also of Mainz, who had a scheme for a moneymaking gimmick now called movable-type printing. It took years for Gutenberg to get it to work, and when he was finally able to produce books, in 1455, Fust sued him over unpaid loans and seized all his apparatus.

One can imagine the mystification and bewilderment of the people of Mainz when Fust put Gutenberg's invention to work. Having had no previous talent for calligraphy, suddenly he was selling Bibles written in an impossibly neat hand. It should have taken months or years to produce just one such book, yet Fust produced them by the hundreds!

> They observ'd the exact Agreement of every Book, one with another, that every Line stood in the same Place, every Page a like Number of Lines, every Line a like Number of Words; if a Word was mis-spelt in one, it was mis-spelt also in all . . . they began again to muse, how should this be?[29]

No one knew what went on in Fust's workshop (the invention had been kept secret)—that there was a man pouring molten lead into a mold day and night. All anyone knew was that smoke and sulfurous smells issued from the place. There could be only one conclusion: he had a devil in there, writing out Bibles for him!

Defoe wrote more than 250 years after the event, and his account is unprovable. But it is certainly true that very often new and inexplicable things have been put down to the work of the Devil. The Elizabethan mathematician Thomas Allen, staying at a country house, "happened to leave his watch in the chamber window (watches were then rarities); the maids came in to make the bed, and hearing a thing in a case cry *Tick, tick, tick*, at once concluded that it was his devil, and took it by the string with the tongs, and threw it out of the window into the moat (to drown the devil). It so happened that the string hung on a sprig of an elder that grew out of the moat, and this confirmed to them that it was the devil. So the good old gentleman got his watch again."[30]

In 1587 the first "Faust book" appeared at Frankfurt-am-Main, with the title *History of Dr. Johann Faust, the notorious Magician and Necromancer, how he sold himself for a stipulated Time to the Devil, What strange Things he saw, performed and practised during this Time, until at last he received his well-merited Reward.* An English version was not long following, and this inspired the well-known play by Christopher Marlowe, since when the theme has become one of the most overworked in fiction.

Both the Faust book and the Marlowe play start off with Faust as a respected university man, of great learning yet not satisfied with all that he knows; he yearns "to know the secrets of heaven and earth."[31]

For many, this was the unforgivable sin. The quest for knowledge led to diabolical ends, they said; an explicit statement of this view is found in, for instance, Richard Boulton's *Compleat History of Magick, Sorcery and Witchcraft* (1715–16; a book that does not live up to its title): "The Devil's School is a too eager Desire and Pursuit of Knowledge and natural Causes, where, when Men begin to find themselves Proficient in some Measure . . . they are apt to advance too high; and where lawful Arts and Sciences fail of giving them Satisfaction, they are apt to apply themselves to the black and unlawful Science of Magick."[32] The reason magic is such a bad thing, Boulton says, is that it is always done by means of devils: "they flatter themselves that they are Masters, and can command the Devil; though at the same time they enter themselves as his Slaves, and lose Paradise."

With opinions like this common among the theologically orthodox, it is not surprising that the centuries when the church was most powerful were those in which there was least progress. When Christianity became the official religion of the Roman Empire, Saint Augustine and others took the chance to sneer at philosophers and scientists. Progress was thought unnecessary, since the world would end soon anyway. It did not, but Europe entered the Dark Ages.

It was only in the Renaissance, when pagan literature was rediscovered, that science began to make progress again. It is surely significant that it was just then that witch-hunting became the favorite European sport. (Contrary to what most people think, there had been little witch persecution in the Middle Ages.) Confronted with new inventions and ideas, the discovery of America, the progress of fine art, the spread of metallurgy, and the appearance of watches and spectacles, followed by telescopes, it was not surprising that some people thought that the Devil was taking over the world and hastened to kill his agents.

It is against this background that the story of Faust was spread. On the one hand, he had done the most wicked thing, given himself to the Devil, and at the end he was carried off to hell. (The Protestants were less forgiving than the medieval Catholics, who let Theophilus off as soon as he prayed to the Virgin.) On the other hand, he was depicted as a man of supreme learning. In the 1587 Faust book, he is seen expounding the nature of comets and falling stars, making correct prophecies, and going with Mephistopheles on a guided tour of the heavens, where he correctly notices that the planets turn about the sun. The section on the planets was in fact copied from a contemporary book on astronomy. The story of Faust was thus a symptom of its time, of a society trying to look both ways: backward to the age of faith, forward to an age of progress. It would be appropriate indeed if such a story had really started with a printer and a press, since the spread of books and learning changed the world so much.

The Pact in Witchcraft

Though witchcraft was traditionally done with the aid of spirits, the idea that it involved a "pact" was a legal fiction. It was not felt to be quite fair to burn somebody at the stake when their only crime might be fortune-telling or applying herbal remedies, as was often the case. But if one could say that the person had renounced the Christian faith, then she or he became a heretic and deserved no mercy. It was therefore insisted by successive witch-hunters that magical powers could be derived only from a pact with the Devil, and the pact was made by renouncing Christianity.

As time went on, other witch-finders added their own embellishments to their accounts of how a pact was made: "They must promise to sacrifice babies"; "They must renounce their baptism"; and so on. In 1603, Del Rio, author of the *Disquisitionum magicarum* (Researches into magic), threw all the different views together to make the diabolical pact a grand eleven-stage operation:

> Firstly they deny the faith, & Christianity, and the Blessed Virgin Mary. The Demon then places his claw on their forehead, to symbolically remove the Chrism.
>
> Secondly, he washes them in as it were a new Baptism.
>
> Thirdly, they renounce their old name, and are given a new one.
>
> Fourthly, they deny their godfathers and godmothers, and are assigned new ones.
>
> Fifthly, they give the devil a piece of their clothing.

Sixthly, they swear allegiance to the Demon in a circle drawn on the ground.

Seventhly, they ask the Demon to strike them out of the Book of Life, and to include them in the Book of Death.

Eighthly, they promise to sacrifice to him, and some witches vow to slay an infant every month, or every fortnight.

Ninthly, they must make an annual gift to their Demon Master.

Tenthly, he places his mark on some part of their body.

Eleventh, when they have been marked they make many vows; that they will trample on and defile and break all the relics and images of the Saints, that they will never make a full confession of their sins to a priest; and so on.[33]

On the first step, renunciation of the Christian religion, Robert Filmer justly commented: "But if this be common to all Contracts with the Devil, it will follow that none can be Witches but such as have first been Christians, nay and *Roman Catholiques*, if Delrio say true; for who else can renounce the patronage of the Virgin *Mary*?"[34] In that case, he asked, how come there are so many witches in Africa and in other pagan lands? How could anyone renounce a religion they had never heard of in the first place?

In 1608, Francesco Maria Guazzo published his *Compendium maleficarum*, the bulk of which was copied verbatim, without acknowledgment, from Del Rio's *Disquisitionum magicarum*. The *Compendium maleficarum* has generally been the better known book, partly because there is now an English translation, so that the eleven-stage pact has become attributed to Guazzo.[35]

Written Pacts

Del Rio omitted to say that the pact might be written out formally. Sometimes, allegedly, it would be for an exact number of years, usually twenty or twenty-four, at the end of which the pact maker would suddenly die. As if to prove this, some of the stories about Faust had it that on the very night when, as he had told people, his pact was due to expire, he was found strangled. The more colorful witch-hunter Pierre de Lancré said that he had seen such pacts himself, one of them written in menstrual blood. In some cases, such documents really existed and have survived to the present day.

Under severe torture, perhaps ninety-nine people out of one hundred accused of witchcraft would confess whatever was required of them. An example of the one hundredth case was Father Urbain Grandier of Loudun, who would not own to being a sorcerer, even when his legs were so badly smashed that he could never have walked again. He didn't need to, as he was speedily burned alive anyway.

Feeling, no doubt, that some kind of proof was necessary for the accusations that brought Grandier to the stake, the good priests of the town of Loudun announced that they had used their power over demons (granted to them by Christ) and had compelled Asmodeus to abstract Grandier's pact from Lucifer's private cabinet. This they printed, and they displayed copies around the town to convince the skeptical. It was in two parts. The first was an oath of allegiance signed by Grandier. The second was subscribed by a panel of devils and ran as follows:

> We, the all-powerful Lucifer, seconded by Satan, Beelzebub, Leviathan, Elimi, Astaroth, and others, have today accepted the pact of alliance with Urbain Grandier, who is on our side. And we promise him the love of women, the flower of virgins, the chastity of nuns, worldly honors, pleasures, and riches. He will fornicate every three days; intoxication will be dear to him. He will offer to us once a year a tribute marked with his blood; he will trample under foot the sacraments of the church, and he will say his prayers to us. By virtue of this pact, he will live happily for twenty years on earth, and finally will come among us to curse God.
>
> Done in Hell, in the council of the devils.
> [Signed:] Satan, Beelzebub, Lucifer, Elimi, Leviathan, Astaroth.
> Notarized the signature and mark of the chief devil, and my lords the princes of hell. Countersigned, Baalberith, recorder.[36]

This document is preserved to this day in the Bibliothèque Nationale in Paris.

Eventually, the idea of the pact became so accepted an idea that some people wanted to make one. But this caused difficulties: unless the Devil appeared brandishing the necessary documentation, what could they do? This problem is illustrated by the case of Abraham Mason, around the year 1700. Mason was a bookseller and confectioner in Chard, Somerset, who suffered from melancholy and a nagging wife. One day he told an unnamed gentleman who came looking for a book that he wished to "have some discourse with the Devil"; Mason asked his advice on how to raise the Devil and lay him again. The gentleman tried to dissuade him but, seeing him set in his intention, decided with his brother to arrange it for him.

So they Consulted together that they would get two men to assist them, and act the parts of the Devil and a Fryar; that it should be at a stone *Quarry* which was not far distant from the town.

He that was the supposed Devil, with a great Rug, with several Horse-tails fastned to it, as was most convenient to make it dreadful, and on his head a Lanthorn [lantern], fastned to a Cap, with a Hare Skin coming before his *Face*, and so tied under his *Chin*, so that the Lanthorn when he Spoak moved Forward and backward, very frightfully to the Gentleman himself.

The other like a Fryer, with Staff and Bell; and round the Pit they had scattered Gunpowder, and Brimstone, with other Ingredients, which among the dry Ferns would seem strange to any that knew not the Plot.

They having thus order the Business, and the time appointed being come, called upon the Quaker, and carried him to the place; So the Gentleman made Circles, and really to the Quaker seemed as if he Conjured the Devil indeed; then from below out of the Quarry came up the smoke of Brimstone, which Smoaked them severely; then the Gentleman spoke some more words, as if he had called the Divel, which he scarcely ended, but out of the Pit came the aforesaid Fryar, with a Bell and a Staff, and spoke in a strange note, and askt *Who it was durst disturb his Master Belzeebub, when he was buisy about his Hellish Designes?* The pretended Conjurer said, *He would speak with him, therefore I Charge thee immediately Return, Return, and tell him*; who accordingly did. Then appeared the supposed Devil, and said, *What hast thou to desire of me?* then answered the Quaker, *I have for some time sought thee, and could not before see thee.* Then answered the Divel, *What is thy Business with me?*

Quaker. I would have thee grant me four Requests.

Devil. What are they?

Qua. First, *That thou wilt give me power over all Womens Tongues.* Secondly, *That thou wilt give me power to make sick or well whom I please.* Thirdly, *That I may Command to my Bed any Woman from the furthest part of the World.* Fourthly, *That thou wilt give me the Philosopher's Stone.*

Then the Divel answered, *This is too much to give but if I grant it, What Requital shall I have from thee, O man, that desirest such difficult things from me?*

Then said the Quaker, *I who desire this of thee, will give thee my self, after such a Term of years as thou and I shall agree, and for a Token of my Reality I give thee this*; which the Conjurer bid him throw over his Left Shoulder, which accordingly he did, which was 40s. in a bag, and a Letter, which Letter was supposed to be Writ with his own Blood.

Then the Conjurer bid him pull off his left Boot, and shew the Devil his foot, but he Refused it, then they set the Gunpowder a fire below, so that the fire was on every side; then to fright him from his Devilish Intent, they

Ratled Chains, which he hearing, Ran away as fast as he could, the fire being so ordered, that it followed him a little way, and they had also Contrived to plant a man with a Coach-Whip, with Chains ratling about him, to follow him and Whip him, which so affrighted the *Quaker*, that at once he leaped over a Stile, which at other times he could hardly scramble over, and still Run till he came to the upper end of the Town, so home he went, and as he was a going to bed, his Chamber being over the Butchers, the fellow that had the Whip and the Chains fell a Ratling as if the Devil had been really there, and Roared like a Bull, and howled like a Dog, with other frantick actions, which could not but really cause fear, which so terrified the *Quaker*, that his own Wife Reported that he so shook the bed, that she thought the Devil himself had been come for him.

In the morning the Actors spent the Quaker's 40s. upon a Breakfast, to laugh at his folly, to see that he should be so willing to the damning of both Body and Soul, to throw away 40s upon the Devil, which he really thought to be so.[37]

The Pact in the Twentieth Century

Peter Haining's *Anatomy of Witchcraft* (1972), speaking of alleged contemporary Satanism, gave a list of "Satanic Oaths which the neophite is called on regularly to affirm":

1. A spoken denial of the Christian faith.
2. Re-baptism in Satan's name, the novice given a new name to replace the Christian one.
3. Symbolic removal of the baptismal chrism (consecrated oil mixed by balm) by Satan's touch.
4. Denial of godparents and gaining new sponsors.
5. As a token of submission and obedience, the novice makes a gift of his or her virginity (symbolically if necessary) to Satan.
6. While standing in a magic circle the novice pledges an Oath of Allegiance to Satan.
7. Initiate's name is included in the "Book of Death."
8. A promise to indulge in all sexual excesses with men or women.
9. Marking the initiate with Satan's "seal"—a strangely shaped mark on the skin which is concealed from view.
10. Vows of special service to Satan which include destruction of holy relics, and most importantly, not revealing the secrets of the Sabbat.[38]

Haining did not call this a pact, but careful readers will notice that his list is almost identical with the eleven-stage pact with the Devil given by Del Rio, above. Peter Haining did not claim this proved a continuity of Satanic practices through the centuries, but he did complain bitterly that most people did not take the threat of Black Magic seriously, despite all the evidence provided by reliable writers such as himself.

At the end of the 1970s appeared *Jay's Journal*, "edited by Beatrice Sparks," which was "the tragic story of a schoolboy . . . a warning to all parents!" according to the cover blurb, and has since often been quoted by Christians to warn of the dangers of the occult. It was said to be the diary of a bright American teenager who had suddenly shot himself and was found by his parents after his death.

It appeared that Jay had met a man who introduced him to "intuition, meditation, ESP, auras, life after death, the oversoul," among other things, all of which was merely cover advertising for witchcraft. He and several of his friends joined a witchcraft group, identified only as "O" (The Circle?), which was widespread in high schools all over the country, apparently. They met in covens of thirteen and practiced blood sacrifice, drug taking, levitation, and other occult arts. Within a year, he and two friends had taken part in a group ritual during which they touched their fingers to the right part of the forehead and dedicated themselves to a strange orange light that manifested in front of them. "Brad" said he would dedicate his soul if he could become the school's top basketball player. "Dell" mumbled that if he could have money he, too, would dedicate his soul. Afterward, Jay recalled touching his finger to his right temple but could not remember what he had asked for in exchange.[39]

The results were astonishing! Suddenly, when Brad was playing basketball, he couldn't miss, though he had previously been a lousy player. Dell's aunt had a heart attack and made over her fortune to him.[40]

Within three weeks, Brad and Dell were dead, killed in traffic accidents. In each case, the fatal vehicle struck the boy on the right temple of the forehead, exactly where he had touched during the ritual. A few weeks later, Jay shot himself in the same place.[41]

The strangest thing about this book was that, although purportedly by a Satanist, it had a strong Christian tone that ran all through the writing of it. Every so often Jay paused in his evil practices to reflect that his parents' religion (Protestant Christianity) was the only true one. Even the Devil, when he finally materialized in Jay's bedroom and introduced himself as Raul, took a Christian stance:

"Remember the third of the host of heaven that were cast out without bodies?" . . . Raul sat down at my desk. . . . "You've always known we existed."[42]

The sudden deaths of the three could be explained as due to the fact that they had forgotten to specify a time limit. Instead of getting twenty-four years to enjoy what they had asked for, as soon as they had it, the Devil was free to claim them. Presumably most of the many thousands of other schoolchildren in "O" took more care with their pacts, or else the whole country would have been full of teenagers suddenly dying from injuries to their right temples. If they remembered to set twenty-four-year limits, then a mass outbreak of such deaths should be occurring today, around the millennium.

4

Historical Satanism

Most modern Experts on Satanism concede that those who perished in the witch craze of the fifteenth through to the seventeenth centuries were, generally, innocent victims. Nonetheless, it is often contended that there have been a number of genuine cases of "Satanism" in history. The accounts of historical Satanism have a variety of starting points. The psychotherapist Brett Kahr, in "The Historical Foundations of Ritual Abuse,"[1] traces "infanticidal behavior" back to the Titan Cronus, father of Zeus, who ate some of his own children. Some begin with the Cathars and the Templars (to be discussed in chapter 6, below). Otherwise, the favorite examples are:

1. Georgel and Delort
2. Gilles de Rais
3. Black Masses in the south of France
4. The Chambre Ardente affair
5. The Hell Fire Club
6. The Goats
7. The mass of Saint Secaire
8. Huysmans's *Là-Bas*
9. Adriano Lemmi and Albert Pike

These are here examined in detail.

Georgel and Delort

The trial of Anne-Marie Georgel and Catherine Delort at Toulouse in 1335 is unusual in that not only did they confess to attending a sabbat, but they outlined their Satanic theology:

> Anne-Marie de Georgel, and Catherine, wife of Pierre Delort, both of Toulouse and of mature age, said, in their juridical confessions, that for

twenty years or thereabouts they have belonged to the innumerable army of Satan, giving themselves to him, as much in this life as in the next; that very often, and always in the night of Friday through to Saturday, they have assisted at the Sabbat, which is sometimes held in one place, sometimes in another; that there, in the company of men and women as sacrilegious as themselves, they give themselves up to all kinds of excess, the details of which are horrible. . . .

Anne-Marie de Georgel says that one Tuesday morning, when she was alone, washing the linen of her family, outside of the town, she saw coming towards her, over the water, a man of gigantic stature, very black of skin, whose glowing eyes resembled two burning coals, and who was dressed in the skin of a beast. This monster asked her if she would give herself to him; to which she replied that she would. He then breathed in her mouth; and from the following Saturday, she was carried to the Sabbat, simply by willing herself. There, she found a gigantic he-goat, whom she saluted, and to whom she abandoned herself. The goat, in return, instructed her in all kinds of wicked secrets: he gave her the knowledge of poisonous plants, taught her magic words, and the way to work witchcrafts on the Eves of Midsummer, Christmas, and every first Friday of the month. . . .

Interrogated on the Apostle's Creed and on the knowledge which all the faithful should have of our Holy Religion, she replied, a true daughter of Satan, that there was a complete equality between God and the Devil; that the first was King of Heaven, and the second of the Earth; that all of the souls that the latter succeeded in seducing, were lost to the Most High, and resided forever on the earth or in the air; that they went every night to visit the house in which they used to live, working to inspire in their children and relatives a desire to serve the Evil One in preference to God.

She told us moreover that the struggle between God and the Devil had been carried on for all eternity, and will continue without end; that sometimes one and sometimes the other carries the victory; that now things are turning in a manner that the Triumph of Satan seems assured.

Every Saturday night, she [Catherine Delort] falls into a strange trance, during which she is transported to the Sabbat. . . . There, she adores the goat, and gives herself to him, as do all those present at this foul festival. There they eat the bodies of new-born babies, stolen at night from the arms of their nurses; they drink all sorts of disgusting liquors; but salt is absent from every dish. . . .

Interrogated on the Apostle's Creed and on the knowledge which all the faithful should have of our Holy Religion, she replied to us that there was complete equality between God and the Devil; that the one reigned in Heaven, and the other on Earth; that the struggle between them would continue without end; that one should choose to serve the Devil, because he is wicked, that he rules the souls of the dead, and sends them against us to disturb our reason; that the reign of Jesus Christ, in this world, is passing; that it will come to an end, and that the Antichrist will not delay to come and decide the battle in favour of the Devil, etc."[2]

The Toulouse records contain no trace of this trial; so where did the story of Georgel and Delort come from? They first made their appearance in 1829 in a speech attributed to Pierre Guidonis, as Inquisitor of Toulouse, in the pages of Lamothe-Langone's *History of the Inquisition in France*. The Toulouse records reveal, however, that Pierre Guidonis was, in 1335, the prior of the Dominican convent at Carcassonne and not an Inquisitor at all. The opinion of modern historians is that Lamothe-Langone invented the story.[3]

Lamothe-Langone was best known for writing horror novels, with titles such as *The Head of Death, or the Cross of the Cemetery of Saint-Aubin* and *The Monastery of the Black Friars, or the Standard of Death*. He later turned to faking memoirs of famous historical people, his most successful production in this field being *The Memoirs of Napoleon Bonaparte* (1834), which were the Hitler diaries of the nineteenth century. The success of Juan Antonio Llorente's *History of the Inquisition of Spain* (1818) evidently inspired Lamothe-Langone to do the same for the Inquisition in France. Yet his enormous output—more than 400 volumes in all—would not have left him with much time for historical research. So it seems that, instead, he read a few standard works on the subject and filled in the gaps from his fertile imagination.

The names Georgel and Delort are rare in France; but Norman Cohn noticed that they were borne by two of Lamothe-Langone's fellow romantic authors, Jean-François Georgel and Joseph Delort. It is evident that the two oft-quoted confessions were made up as some kind of private joke. This is not a propitious start to the history of real Satanism.

Gilles de Rais

Here we have a very wicked man, who in 1440 confessed, as fans of sensational literature know, to murdering eight hundred children in the course of magical rituals. De Rais had inherited the largest estates in France, but extravagance had wasted him, and he turned to magic to make himself rich again. In the course of his rituals, so the story goes, he sodomized and murdered young boys.

On the face of it, this seems plausible. Psychotic child killers have been common in the twentieth century, but usually they are caught before they can go too far, because the disappearance of a child normally sets off a massive police search. A medieval nobleman, one might suppose, could have had the resources to get away with it for years.

From about 1300 onward, however, it was common for people to make accusations of practicing magic against their political enemies, purely because it was difficult to defend oneself against such a charge. The first victim, ironically enough, was Pope Boniface VIII, posthumously accused of having won his position by summoning demons; the reason behind the accusation was that the king of France wanted some of Boniface's papal decisions overturned by his successor.[4]

In view of this, one must carefully evaluate the evidence against de Rais. The points that can establish guilt of murder are: Was there a fair trial? Did the accused confess? Did witnesses confirm the accusations? Were bodies found? Were persons reported missing?

As to the first point, Gilles de Rais's trial by the Inquisition was a mockery of legal processes and justice.[5] The main charges against him were three: the first and most serious was heresy (that is, practicing magic, which in France had been treated as a heresy since 1320); second, that he had insulted a priest; third, that he had murdered 140 (not 800) children. The last was regarded as the least important and was dropped from the indictment for a while. Some other, lesser charges were odd: he was accused of eating rich food and drinking claret wine (the sin of gluttony), and he was also indicted as being responsible for various earthquakes and plagues that had struck the district, which were stated to be due to divine wrath at his crimes.[6]

People found guilty by the Inquisition forfeited their property, which went instead to those who had accused and tried them. Though de Rais had wasted his ancestral estates, he still owned some valuable castles, and these were seized by his accusers even before the trial had begun. "Under these circumstances, it is difficult to place any credence in the evidence against him," comments Robbins.[7]

When first brought into the court, de Rais denied everything and angrily denounced the proceedings as improperly constituted. Three days later he was brought into court again, and this time he quietly confessed to everything he was accused of, saying that he had murdered 120 children a year, boys and girls, for an unspecified number of years. (It is from this that the figure eight hundred is deduced.) Even those who think he was guilty concede that he had been tortured in the interim.[8] Clearly, this is valueless as evidence.

It was perfectly legal, in those days, for the Inquisition to torture the *witnesses*. There is no way of knowing if they did so in this case, but the Inquisitors did call alleged accomplices of de Rais to testify that they had taken part in child murder with him, then set these witnesses free afterward.

One of these accomplices confessed that he had burned dozens of children's bodies on a huge bonfire and then disposed of the remains in the castle moat.[9] The records say nothing of any bodies being found by officials, which is extraordinarily unlikely, if one thinks of the difficulty murderers usually find in disposing wholly of even one body. It is likely, then, the confession about bodies being destroyed was invented to explain the lack of them.

That leaves the evidence of the missing persons. Many people did come forward to testify that children had gone missing. It is on this that the case against de Rais must finally rest.

A total of thirty boys (no girls) were reported missing over a period of nine years: three in 1431–32, the rest in 1437–40.[10] In many of these cases, there was nothing to connect their disappearance with de Rais, and in a couple of instances, it was doubtful if there was anything mysterious about the "disappearances." A group of people from the village of Saint-Etienne-de-Montluc testified that Jamet, an orphan who used to beg in their village, had not been seen since the Feast of John the Baptist. They did not consider that he might have moved on because, say, the villagers were so mean.

The most significant cases are those where the disappearance was connected with de Rais and his men, but in these, alternative explanations to human sacrifice were given. Perrine Roundeau from Machecoul testified that Master François and the marquis of Ceva, Lombards in the service of Lord de Rais, lodged in her house. Francois had acquired a page boy from Dieppe, but after two weeks he disappeared. François told Perrine that the boy had run off with two ecus of his, which he had obtained by counterfeit signatures. The son of Jean Hubert from Saint-Leonard in Nantes was employed by Prince, one of the lord's retainers, for a week and was then dismissed and told to go back to school. He went to try another post, and his parents did not see him again. They were told that he had gone away with a Scottish knight. Another boy who was taken on as a page vanished, and it was said that he had fallen into the river from the bridge at Nantes and drowned.

When a war is going on, even quite young boys want to go away to be soldiers. In the fifteenth century their dream could come true, if they were taken on as a servant by a knight, and often this happened with their parents' knowledge and approval. If their parents did not approve, then they might run away to war anyway. In those days, even if they did not meet the enemy, there was a good chance of their army being wiped out by the plague. So, if a troop of soldiers passed through a town, often several boys would go off and never be seen again.

In short, there is nothing mysterious about these disappearances. Indeed, they do not fit with de Rais's confession that he murdered girls as well as boys. One can speculate that he was merely a handy scapegoat. Concerned parents could do nothing about the English and the plague, which were making off with their children, but they could blame an unpopular nobleman and appear to see justice done.

The description of the magical operations de Rais allegedly practiced match those in the grimoire literature, though this would not make one guilty of any crime under today's laws. These operations involved tracing circles and crosses on the floor, but there is no mention at all of black candles and inverted crucifixes, which nonetheless are found in many modern accounts of the case and must come from the imagination of the Experts who write them.

Black Masses in the South of France

Many of our Experts tell us that the oppressed French peasants of the Middle Ages turned to Devil worship as a reaction to their poverty and the corruption of the church. The Reverend Kevin Logan says that "ordinary people" in parts of France desecrated Hosts, used naked women as altars, trampled on the cross, and turned Good Friday into a day of orgies.[11] H. T. F. Rhodes and Rollo Ahmed speak with precision, as if they had a text of the rite in front of them: "Those present in the sanctuary lit their torches from the one attached to the horns of the image. The priestess then opened the office with the words: 'I will come to the altar. Save me Lord Satan from the treacherous and the violent.'"[12] Arthur Lyons considers technical points of the organization—"The methods of recruitment employed by the groups varied according to necessity. Many had been brought up into the religion from childhood by relatives or friends who were already Satanists"[13]—while Gerhard Zacharias gives a psychological analysis of the participants' mental health.[14]

What these accounts have in common is that they all ultimately derive their information from a book by Pierre de Lancré with the magnificent title *Tableau of the Inconstance of the Wicked Angels and Demons* (1612; rev. ed. 1613), which is an account of a witch-hunt that de Lancré himself conducted in the Basque area of southwest France in 1609. He offers various descriptions of the sabbat taken from various witches whom he had tortured, but there is a great deal of unity in what they said. They all flew to the sabbat on broomsticks, where they did homage to the Devil, who appeared in person and performed a parody of the mass. They then dined off the corpses of hanged men and unbaptized babies. Their sensual appetites aroused by this feast, they had sex with their favorite demons.[15] Unless one is an ultratraditional Roman Catholic, it is impossible to take what de Lancré says at face value.

But, in 1861, the French socialist historian Jules Michelet wrote *La Sorcière* (published in England as *Satanism and Witchcraft*), a romantic treatment of witchcraft, which he took to be a kind of protofeminism combined with a secret peasant revolt against the ruling classes. Carried away with the emotional appeal of this idea, he wrote an account of the sabbat based on de Lancré, ignoring some of the impossible features and giving simple, rationalistic explanations for others: the "Devil" was a statue of Pan, for example.[16] While he made it out to be all healthy fun, more recent authors have taken his outline of the sabbat and then inclined back toward De Lancré's viewpoint and made it seem very wicked.

The question is: Why believe anything De Lancré said? He remarked that one particular youth confessed freely, without torture.[17] That makes it clear that all the other confessions he quoted were made under torture. In that case, the youth who confessed freely may have done so merely to save himself a lot of bother. Furthermore, if you take away the features that most people would describe as implausible (such as sex with devils), then there is not much left. Some writers explain the flight on broomsticks as being mind traveling, perhaps stimulated by hallucinogenics. But if the flight was not physically real, then, surely, the sabbat attended after that flight was not real either.

In any case, 1609 was not in the Middle Ages. Michelet (and others), however, offer a justification for making these rites medieval. De Lancré quoted what he said were words recited by the witches in their rituals (but which, according to Spanish historian Julio Caro Baroja, were in fact political songs). These included the curse: "Ah! *Philip*, if only I had you between my hands, I would treat you the same!" De Lancré thought that "Philip" was a reference to the apostle, but Michelet speculated that it might have meant Philip VI of France, who was unpopular with the people because he was regarded as having started the Hundred Years' War. If this were true, then it would mean the rituals went back to at least the fourteenth century; but this is an exceptionally feeble argument.[18] Even assuming that these words were really part of a ritual, and assuming that they referred to a king, then "Philip" could have meant any one of a number of kings of both France and Spain, including the contemporary Spanish king. The supposed hundreds of years of medieval Black Masses rest on no more substantial foundation than this.

The Chambre Ardente Affair

One evening in 1678, a Parisian lawyer named Perrin was attending a fashionable dinner party, where the company were kept amused by a widow, Marie Bosse, who was a successful society fortune-teller. She happened to boast that many top people came to consult her, adding that only three more poisonings and she could retire.

Something about her manner made Perrin wonder if she were really joking. There were well-founded suspicions that poisoning was common in high society. So he reported the incident to a friend, Captain Desgrez, a police officer, who sent the wife of one of his men to have her fortune told by the widow Bosse and told her to say she had a husband she wished to be rid of. Sure enough, after two visits she was given a vial of poison.

Not only Bosse but several other women were arrested. They formed a loose network of fortune-tellers who also practiced poisoning and abortion. In those days, abortion was regarded as literal child murder and punished as such. Among these women was Catherine Monvoisin, commonly known as La Voisin, whose house contained a secret furnace used for burning fetuses.

Since leading people were likely to be mentioned in the confessions and the authorities did not want their names to come out publicly, they set up a special windowless tribunal room, hung with black, and lit by candles, hence called the Chambre Ardente (Burning Chamber). Many of the suspects were tortured, which casts doubt over the details of their confessions, though some of them were backed by physical evidence.[19]

A strange pavilion, set up as a chapel, was found in the grounds of La Voisin's house. Eventually, an elderly priest named the Abbé Guibourg made an astonishing confession concerning it:

EXTRACT OF THE INTERROGATION OF THE ABBÉ GUIBOURG

10 October 1680, at Vincennes

Leroy, governor of the pages of the little ecurie first spoke to him of working for Madame de Montespan, and promised him 50 pistolets and a benefice worth 2000 livres. The first mass which he said with this intention was at Menil, near to Montlhéry, on the belly of a woman who had come with another exalted lady, at the consecration he recited the conjuration:

"Astaroth, Asmodee, princes of love, I conjure you to accept the sacrifice which I offer to you of this infant, for the things which I demand of you, which are the amitie of the King, and of the Dauphin, to me, to continue, and to be honoured by the heart of princes and princesses, that I will be denied nothing that I demand of the King, as much for my parents as servants."

And naming the names of the King and of those who sacrificed at this mass, and having shed the blood of a baby, presented to him by an exalted girl, whose neck he cut with a knife, he poured it into a chalice, after which the baby was taken out and carried to another place, following which they took the heart and the entrails to him . . . he made from them a powder for the King and for Madame de Montespan; the lady for whom he said the mass always wore a veil which covered her face and a little of her bosom. He said the second mass in a derelict house on the ramparts of Saint Denis, on the same woman, with the same ceremonies, and La Pelletier was present. He said the third at Paris at the house of La Voisin on the same woman, it may have been eight or nine years ago, but later he said thirteen or fourteen years. He declares after that five years ago he had said a similar mass at the home of La Voisin on the same person, who he has always said to be Madame de Montespan, with the same intentions, and La Laporte was present; and after all was finished, wanting to retrieve his mantle which was on a chair, he found on the chair a writing which proved to be the copy of a pact, although it was only written on paper, whereas such pacts must be written on virgin parchment, in which these terms were set out:

"I . . . daughter of . . . I demand the love of the King and likewise of the Dauphin, and that I shall continue thus, and that the Queen shall be sterile, and the King shall leave her bed and her table for me, that I shall obtain all that I ask for me and my parents, that my servants and domestics shall be agreeable, kind and respectful to important people, that I shall called to the counsels of the King, and to know what happens there, and that this friendship will be double what came before, that the King shall leave and not consider La Valliere, and that the Queen shall be repudiated, that I shall be able to marry the King."

. . . At La Voisin's house, wearing the alb, the stole and the maniple, he made a conjuration in the presence of Des Oeillets which he pretended to be a charm for the King, and which was accompanied by the man who gave him the conjuration, and for which it was necessary to have some sperm of both sexes, Des Oeillets having placed some of her menses in the chalice and the man who accompanied them, having passed down the side of the bed with Guibourg, spilled some of his semen in the chalice. On top of this, Des Oeillets and the man added a powder of bat's blood and flour to give the more strength to the whole composition, and after he recited the conjuration they poured the contents into a little vessel which Des Oeillets and the man carried.[20]

La Reynie, the police inspector conducting the investigation, argued in his notes that it was unlikely two different people would have made up identical stories about such a disgusting rite, and though the same Bastille archives contain stories about pacts with devils and other implausible matters, one inclines to agree with him. Here, at last, is a genuine sexual rite including demon invocation. It should be pointed out that, according to the testimony of La Voisin's daughter, the sacrifices were actually aborted fetuses rather than live babies.

These masses are part of a long tradition, arising from the belief that the mass had magical power. There is no reason to think that the Abbé Guibourg, Madame de Montespan, and the others thought of themselves as anything but Catholics. True, it was sinful to use the mass and the sacraments for such a purpose as acquiring love, but one would have to be a Catholic to believe that it was possible.

The idea of a perverted mass with a naked woman on the altar is so appealing that it has inspired a number of modern Satanists to copy it, though without the blood sacrifice. There is, however, no reason to suppose that the practice had survived, underground, since the seventeenth century; rather, the modern Black Masses have been based on accounts of the Guibourg masses, as written up in innumerable sensational books.

The Hell Fire Club

"The infamous Hell Fire Club at West Wycombe organized black masses which were celebrated over the bodies of nude girls recruited from among the local peasantry."[21] "Dashwood, by now Chancellor of the Exchequer, set about enticing other louche aristocrats into the fraternity with the lure of enormous quantities of alcohol, drugs and free sex . . . the sex was not limited either to heterosexual intercourse or to adult participants."[22] "Sir Francis would inaugurate the Black Mass by pouring brandy laced with brimstone into glasses shaped like the Devil's horns."[23] "Mock crucifixions and incest were carried out among the inverted crosses, black candles and other trappings now commonly identified with Satanism."[24] "Dashwood claimed to have used the Black Mass to evoke the Devil in the form of a black cat or a goat-like figure."[25] Thus the Experts on Satanism would have it.

The Hell Fire Club was a Sunday drinking club established in London in 1719 by the duke of Wharton. The purpose was to enliven the dull traditional Sunday with drink and rude songs. They called it the Hell Fire Club not because they believed in hell fire but because, with the rise of the Age of Reason, they did not. The early eighteenth century saw several editions of a book titled *Of the Torments of Hell: The Foundation and Pillars thereof Discovered, Searched, Shaken, and Removed*, which argued on logical grounds that there was no such a thing as eternal punishment. (This finite globe could not contain a "bottomless pit," for example.) It is true that Thomas Lewis wrote a counterblast, *The Nature of Hell, the Reality of Hell-Fire, and the Eternity of Hell-Torments, Explain'd and Vindicated*, but it did not sell nearly so many copies.

In the same way, Bishop Francis Hutchinson's *Historical Essay Concerning Witchcraft* (1718) not only repudiated the church's traditional teaching on that topic but rejected the existence of the supernatural altogether, and this viewpoint became standard. Again, there was a reply, Richard Boulton's *The Possibility and Reality of Magick, Sorcery, and Witchcraft Demonstrated*, but this attracted no more attention than Lewis's defense of eternal torment. The supply of books on occult subjects dried up and did not restart until Victorian times.

Hellfire henceforth represented for the avant-garde no more than an inconvenient fairy tale, a myth to prevent people from enjoying themselves. So it was natural for those rakes who spent Sunday drinking instead of at church to call themselves the Hell Fire Club. According to a contemporary satire:

> Religion is their Scorn, foul Vice their Pride,
> The *Clergy* is their Subject to deride;
> *Virtue*'s discountenanced by these Beasts,

Whose revelling at *Bacchanalian* Feasts,
Makes them, when Fumes of Wine in Brains abound,
Think, like *Copernicus*, the Earth turns round.[26]

The Hell Fire Club was closed by a royal edict in 1721. If few were concerned about hell or witchcraft anymore, plenty of people were still worried about "the moral fabric of society," and the edict said that the club's members had a "blasphemous manner" and did "corrupt the minds and morals of one another." The name Hell Fire Club, however, was so potent that it survived as a floating term of abuse.

Sir Francis Dashwood, who was only twelve years old at the time of the edict, would later found a club that was not called the Hell Fire Club but would be nicknamed that by the hostile. The eighteenth century was awash with what would now be called theme clubs, the best known being the Freemasons, who put on aprons and performed what they supposed to be medieval Masons' initiation ceremonies. Dashwood founded three such clubs. The first was the Dilettantes, whose members had to have visited Italy. The president wore a toga at meetings and had a chair made in the style of those used by ancient Roman magistrates. Members took a serious interest in Roman antiquities, and the Dilettantes have survived as such to the present day. A second was the Divan Club, whose members had to have been in Turkey. They met for dinner in Turkish robes with various pseudo-Oriental observances.

So when Dashwood founded the Franciscans, as they called themselves, they probably engaged in a light-hearted parody of monastic life. He acquired an "abbey," an Elizabethan manor house, at Medmenham by the Thames. Horace Walpole, who was not a member of the club but once visited its premises, wrote: "Each has his cell, in which indeed is little more than a bed." "The habit," however, "is more like a waterman's than a Monk's, & consists of a white hat, a white jacket, & white trousers."[27] Though this is one of the few pieces of solid information about the club, it is passed over by sensational writers, since it is hard to imagine men in sailor suits performing sinister rituals.

The motto of the Abbey, carved over the doorway, was "Fay çe que voudras," that is, "Do what thou wilt," a commandment that, as Eric Towers puts it, allows salacious modern authors "spectacular flights of fancy," taking it to be "an invitation to indulge every anti-social whim, virgin-ravishing, incest, human sacrifice, devil-worship, and perhaps even cheating at whist."[28] So closely has the phrase become identified with Satanic debauchery that few people now remember it was coined by Saint Augustine, who advised, "Love, and do what thou wilt," his point being that Christians need not bother with the detailed laws of the Old Testament, as love is the only guidance one needs.

Dashwood's immediate source, however, was Rabelais's 1532 satire *Gargantua*, where a monk founds an abbey at Thélème by the Loire, which is to be the opposite of all other religious establishments. Rabelais had been a monk and knew the life as miserable and pointless. Therefore, in place of vows of chastity, poverty, and obedience, at the Abbey of Thélème all would be married, wealthy, and free. Instead of their time being constrained by a rigid schedule and the sound of a bell, they should use their own judgement and discretion. Hence, *do what thou wilt*: "Because men that are free, well-born, well-bred, and conversant in honest companies, have naturally an instinct and spur that prompteth them unto virtuous actions, and withdraws them from vice." Fixed regulations, by contrast, have the opposite effect to that intended, since it is "the nature of man to long after things forbidden, and to desire what is denied us."[29]

Though it is known that Dashwood's club included a few of his fellow members of Parliament, the only records that have survived are some uninformative lists relating to the food and drink that was consumed. The lack of any evidence has only encouraged speculation, however, the best known being as follows:

> When the brotherhood retired to their cells after dinner, as I told you, to prepare for the ceremony, [a practical joker among the members] availed himself of the office of keeper of the chapel, which he then filled, to convey [a baboon], dressed in the fantastic garb in which childish imagination clothes devils, into the chapel, where he shut him up in a large chest that stood there to hold the ornaments and utensils of the table, when the society was away.

The member arranged the lock so that he could open it by pulling on a cord.

> When they were all in the height of their mirth, on my master's kneeling down, and with hands and eye raised towards heaven repeating an invocation, in the perverted phrase of the Holy Writ, to the Being whom they served, to come among them a receive their adoration in person, he pulled the cord, and let the animal loose, who, glad to be delivered from his confinement gave a sudden spring upon the middle of the table.
>
> Terrified out of their sense by this . . . they all roared out with one voice, The devil! the devil! and starting from their seats, made directly towards the door, tumbling over one another, and over-setting everything in their way.

In the height of this uproar and confusion, the baboon, frightened at the effects of their fear, happened to leap upon my master's shoulders, as he lay sprawling on the floor, who, turning about his head at feeling the shock, saw the animal grinning horribly at him, and concluded the devil had obeyed his summons in good earnest, and come to carry him bodily away.

"Spare me, gracious devil," he said, "spare a wretch who was never sincerely your servant! I sinned only from vanity of being in the fashion!"[30]

The above, which is the only evidence that Dashwood ever worshiped the Devil, first appeared in 1765 in a novel, *Chrysal*, by Charles Johnstone. H. T. F. Rhodes and other Experts on Satanism assert that it must have really happened but do not say why. The same novel has a scene in which Jews celebrate the Passover by dining on blonde, blue-eyed Christian children.[31] It is to be hoped that no one nowadays would say the latter "really happened," so why insist that the book's depiction of Dashwood is authentic? There is no reason to believe Charles Johnstone was privy to any inside information about the order; on the contrary, according to the present-day Sir Francis Dashwood, the book's description of Medmenham is "inaccurate in almost every detail."[32]

In fact, it seems that Johnstone derived the story not from events at Medmenham but from Ned Ward's *The Secret History of Clubs* (1709) a collection of anecdotes about the "Farting Club," the "Surly Club," the "Split-Farthing Club," and many others, most if not all of which were products of Ward's imagination. Ward claimed that a meeting of the "Atheistical Club" had once been broken up by an intruder who entered dressed as the Devil and shocked the members out of their disbelief. Probably, it was just a piece of eighteenth-century urban folklore.[33]

A milder version of the proceedings appeared in an anonymous book, *Nocturnal Revels* (1779), an account of the "nunneries" (i.e., brothels) of London. The author, who has not been certainly identified, described in his introduction how a certain nobleman "thought that a burlesque Institution in the name of St. Francis, would mark the absurdity of such sequestered Societies; and in lieu of the austerities and abstemiousness there practiced, substitute convivial gaiety, unrestrained hilarity, and social felicity." He added that "no indelicacy or indecency is allowed to be intruded without a severe penalty," by which he meant indecency of language. The ladies, however, who dressed as nuns, were not expected to subscribe to an oath of celibacy. On the contrary, there were rules designed to prevent their husbands or relatives finding out that they had been there. They wore masks if necessary, except when alone with a paramour, and in case of accident, they would be able to withdraw to the Abbey to give birth discreetly. "The off-spring of these connexions are stiled the Sons and Daughters of St. FRANCIS and are appointed in due order officers and domestics in the Seminary."[34] Though the unknown author was described on the title page as "a Monk of the Order of St. Francis," he spoiled his impression of giving inside infor-mation when he said the Medmenham priory was located "upon a small Is-land in the river Thames, not far from Hampton," when in fact it was not on an island and nowhere near Hampton. Clearly, he had never been there at all but derived his remarks from hearsay and was no more an authority than Johnstone.

In 1764, after certain members had publicly fallen out over political is-sues, Charles Churchill published a satirical poem, "The Candidate," at-tacking the earl of Sandwich (the one who gave his name to the sandwich), which included the lines:

> While Womanhood, in habit of a Nun,
> At Medmenham lies, by backward Monks undone,
> A nation's reck'ning, like an ale-house score,
> Whilst PAUL *the Aged* chalks behind a door,
> Compell'd to hire a foe to cast it up;
> Dashwood shall pour, from a Communion Cup,
> Libations to the Goddess without eyes,
> And *Hob* or *Nob* in Cyder and Excise.[35]

Churchill was never a member of the club, but he had dined there at least once as a guest, so his words, unlike Johnstone's, have some weight. "Cyder and Excise" refer to Dashwood's proposal, as Tory chancellor of the exchequer, to tax cider at four shillings a barrel (for which he was heavily criticized by the Whigs, who, in the usual manner of opposition parties, suggested that so radical a measure would prove Britain's ruin). The "Goddess without eyes" is Venus (i.e., "Love is blind"). Dashwood had more than one painting made showing him in monastic garb wor-shiping Venus. It seems, then, if anyone was Dashwood's deity, it was Venus rather than the Devil. *The Dashwoods of West Wycombe* includes a photograph of a Venus de Medici statue at West Wycombe, describing it as "the figure beloved by Sir Francis."

"PAUL the *Aged*" was the club secretary, the poet Paul Whitehead, whose biographer concluded with regard to the club "that a set of worthy, jolly fellows, happy disciples of Venus and Bacchus, got occasionally to-gether, to celebrate Woman in wine."[36] Here, devotion to Venus and Bacchus referred not particularly to pagan worship but rather to debauchery and drunkenness, the usual leisure pursuits of eighteenth-century English gentlemen.

Whatever the nature of the club's activities, they were not felt to be incompatible with the practice of Christianity. In later life, Dashwood published an *Abridgement of the Book of Common Prayer* (1773), in which he gave his views on more conventional religion. "The Editor [Dashwood wrote of himself in the third person] professes himself to be a Protestant of the Church of England, and holds in the highest veneration the doctrines of Jesus Christ. He is a sincere lover of social worship, deeply sensible of its usefulness to society."

Dashwood had noticed that the prescribed services were "so long, and filled with so many repetitions" as to keep people from Church. "Many pious and devout Persons, whose age or infirmities will not suffer them to remain for hours in a cold church, especially in the winter season, are obliged to forgo . . . divine service. These, by shortening the time, would be relieved: and the younger sort . . . would probably more frequently, as well as cheerfully, attend divine service." As for the funeral service, it was so lengthy it was hazardous to the living, since they were "standing in the open air with their Hats off, often in tempestuous weather."[37]

It is significant that Dashwood cut down on the vengeance-and-damnation side of the liturgy. Benjamin Franklin, who collaborated with him, remarked that many of the psalms "imprecate, in the most bitter terms, the vengeance of God on our Adversaries, contrary to the spirit of Christianity, which commands us to love our enemies." In the same way, "all cursing of mankind, is (we think) best omitted in this Abridgement."[38]

It is evident from this that Dashwood and Franklin inclined toward Deism, then fashionable among gentlemen, which put the emphasis on a God of love and tended to reject much of the Bible as not conformable to such an image. The liturgy was to be kept because of its "usefulness to society," rather than for its importance for securing a place in heaven.

Incidentally, in the 1780s the leaders of the Episcopalian Church in the newly formed United States of America were compelled to edit the prayer book so as to omit all references to king and country. They used Dashwood's version as a prototype, and some of his amendments have been adopted by them to this day.[39]

The real Dashwood has become obscured by the legends, which have continued to grow since his death. In the 1920s, E. Beresford Chancellor, author of *The Lives of the Rakes*, lumped him together with the duke of

Wharton, since which time the Monks of Medmenham have been generally and wrongly known as the Hell Fire Club. This, along with *Chrysal's* indication that he worshiped the Devil, has allowed writers to go off into complete fantasies in which Dashwood does whatever it is they imagine Devil worshipers do, and significantly, the stories have got wilder as the twentieth century has progressed. Back in 1939, Ronald Fuller's *Hell-Fire Francis* still suffered from occasional intrusions of fact: having stated that the library at Medmenham was "stocked with pornographic tomes," he had to admit that these had "such stimulating titles as *Sherlock on Death* or *The Book of Common Prayer*."[40] No such inhibiting presence was to be found in Daniel P. Mannix's 1961 *The Hell-Fire Club*: "We do know that the chapel was draped in black and there were missals on exhibition containing obscene parodies of the scriptures. . . . The Mass was celebrated on the body of a naked woman laid out on the altar and the congregation drank the sacrificial wine from her navel. The crucifix was inverted and black candles were burnt."[41] (Daniel P. Mannix seems to have been the same person as Richard Allan, author of the "cult classics" *Skinhead* and *Boot Boys*.) Eric Maple's *Domain of Devils* (1966) added to all this that the Monks "practiced incest as a sideline," while in the same author's 1973 book *Witchcraft*, they had developed "a morbid obsession for Devil worship and human sacrifice."[42] By 1979 the Monks, as represented by such Experts, had progressed to pedophilia: "One of the more common indulgences was the sodomizing of young boys and the deflowering of young girls. These children were procured from London prostitutes."[43] It can only be a matter of time before Dashwood and his friends are accused of cannibalism.

The Goats

In the latter half of the eighteenth century the territory of Limburg [in Belgium] was terrorized by a mysterious society known as "The Goats." These wretches met at night in a secret chapel, after the most hideous orgies, which included the paying of divine honors to Satan and other foul blasphemies of the Sabbat, they donned masks fashioned to imitate goat's heads, cloaked themselves with long disguise mantles, and sallied forth in bands to plunder and destroy. From 1772 to 1774 alone the tribunal of Foquement condemned four hundred Goats to the gallows. But the organization was not wholly exterminated until about the year 1780 after a regime of the most repressive measures and unrelaxing vigilance.

All modern writers who refer to the Goats quote the preceding from Montague Summers's *History of Witchcraft and Demonology*.[44] Though Summers did not give a source, it was evidently "The Chapel of the Goats," a short story by André Van Hasselt, printed in an appendix to Collin de Plancy's *Dictionnaire infernal*. "The Chapel of the Goats" is a romance of the Romeo-and-Juliet type, a love affair between Mathilde Scheurenhof and Walter de Hegen, whose families had had a long-standing feud that was resolved only when bandits overran the district, burned down the de Hegen family mansion, and forced Walter to take refuge with the Scheurenhofs.

Van Hasselt does not say that the bandits dressed as goats, but rather the following: "It is said that the bandits have the power to transport themselves in an instant from one part of the province to another, and that a pact, made with hell, puts at their service a demon, who, under the form of a goat, carries them on its back through the air. For this reason they are given the name 'Goats.'"[45] It is evident that he did not think this story should be taken seriously. Why should anyone else do so?

The Mass of Saint Secaire

All published versions of this archetypal Black Mass are based on the account given by Jean-Francois Bladé in his *Contes populaires de la Gascogne* (1886). It is a type of cursing ritual, described as follows:

> The Mass of Saint Secaire cannot be said except in a Church where people are forbidden to meet, because it is partly fallen down, or because things happen there which Christians must not know about. In such Churches owls, screech-owls and bats make their homes, and Gypsies come to lodge there. Beneath the altar there are many toads croaking.
>
> The evil priest comes there with his mistress, who acts as his server. He must be alone in the Church, with this slut, and have had a good supper. On the first stroke of eleven, the mass starts, at the end, and continues backwards, to finish exactly at midnight. The host is black, and has three points. The evil priest does not consecrate any wine. He drinks water from a well in which a dead unbaptized baby has been thrown. The sign of the cross is always made on the ground, and with the left foot.
>
> This is how it is done by certain people, to make their enemies sicken little by little, until they die, without apparent reason, and for whom the doctors can do nothing.[46]

Contes populaires de la Gascogne is a collection of fairy stories. It tells us about "Fairies, Ogres and Dwarves," dragons, a wicked stepmother or two, "The Sleeping Beauty," and "The Sea That Sang, the Apple That Danced, and the Little Bird Who Told All."

What is the justification for putting such a legend into a modern factual work? None is offered by Montague Summers, Rollo Ahmed, Julian Franklyn (who spells it "St. Secoine" and adds a "congregation" who engage in "all kinds of orgies and excesses"), Peter Haining, H. T. F. Rhodes, Larry Kahaner (who spells it "S. Secaraire"), and the rest of the Experts.[47] They seem to assume that because it was written in a book, it must be true.

Huysmans's Là-Bas

A choirboy, clothed in red, went to the far end of the chapel and lit a row of candles. Then the altar appeared, an ordinary church altar, surmounted by a tabernacle on which stood a blasphemous satirical Christ.

The priest descended the steps backwards, kneeling on the last one, and, in a loud and big voice, cried:

"Master of Slanders, Dispenser of the benefits of crime, Intendant of delightful sins and great vices, Satan, it is you we adore, logical God, just God!

"And you, you, who in my capacity as priest, I will force, whether you will or not, to descend into this host, to incarnate in this bread, Jesus, Artisan of swindles, stealer of homage, thief of affections, hear! Ever since the day that you came forth from the womb of a Virgin, you have failed in your obligations, lied in your promises: the centuries are bloodstained, that you have overseen, fleeting God, silent God! You would redeem men, but you have not redeemed them; you would appear in your glory and you have gone to sleep! Come, liar, speak to the miserable, whom you tell: 'Hope, patience, suffering, the hospital of souls will receive you, the angels will assist you, the heavens will open.' Impostor! you know well that the angels, disgusted with your inertia, have deserted you! You would be spokesman for our plaints, Chamberlain of our tears, you would come near to the Father and you have done nothing, because no doubt this intercession would disturb your blessed eternal sleep and repose!

"And that, which we can do and will do in violating the quietude of your Body, Profaner of ample vices, Abstractor of stupid purities, cursed Nazarean, lazy King, cowardly God!"

—Amen, cried the crystal voices of the choirboys.

Durtal listened to this torrent of blasphemies and insults; the obscenity of the priest stupefied him; and silence succeeded these outbursts; the chapel was fume-filled from the incense-burners. The women, who had been silent, grew agitated, whilst the priest, re-ascending to the altar, turned to them and blessed them, with the left hand, in a grand gesture.

And suddenly the choirboys raised their voices.

As if at a signal, the women fell writhing to the floor. One was behaving like a spring, throwing herself on her belly and flailing the air with her arms; another, suddenly squinting horribly, cackling, then becoming silent, still, her jaw open, the tongue curled up, the tip on the palate; another, swollen, enraged, pupils dilated, threw back her head on her shoulders in a brusque movement, and clutched at her throat with her nails. . . .

At this, Durtal raised himself to see better, and distinctly saw and understood the Canon Docre.

He looked at the Christ which surmounted the tabernacle, and the arms spread out, screeching outrageous insults, slander, with the force of a drunken coachman. One of the choirboys knelt before him, with his back to the altar. A shiver ran down the spine of the priest. In a solemn tone, but with trembling voice, he said: "Hoc est enim corpus meum."[48]

The above is the climax to J.-K. Huysmans's *Là-Bas* (1891). In his *Anatomy of Witchcraft*, Peter Haining says that anyone who has read this "horrifying description" will know the author was "not given to flights of fancy," having apparently failed to notice that *Là-Bas* is a novel.[49] Other Experts on Satanism do concede so much but add at once that though written as fiction, the events in the book really happened. Canon Docre, the evil priest who performed the Black Mass that formed the centerpiece of the novel, is said to be "easily identifiable," though opinion is divided as to whether he is easily identifiable as the Abbé van Haecke of Bruges, Belgium, or easily identifiable as the Abbé Boullan (1824–93).

Before *Là-Bas*, Huysmans's best-known novel was *A Rebours*, which has been described by critics as "the breviary of the Decadence." It concerns the "last representative of an illustrious race, appalled by the invasion of American manners and the growth of an aristocracy of wealth," who takes refuge in solitude—not an ascetic solitude but an opulent solitude in a home filled with every excess of luxury. It was evidently part autobiographical, representing what Huysmans, an underfed writer, would have liked to have done.

In the late 1880s, the delights of mere luxury grew too tame for Huysmans, and he started taking an interest in the occult, particularly the more sensational aspects of the subject. Sinistrari's *Demoniality*, a treatise on the copulation of humans with demons, which had been recently rediscovered and published by Isidore Liseux, became a favorite. Huysmans also started to read up on Gilles de Rais, of course taking the view that de Rais had been guilty as charged.

As early as 1887, he had decided to make a novel of the subject, using the "binary form" of mixing scenes from two eras, medieval and modern. A modern writer would be seen researching the life of Gilles de Rais; interspersed with scenes of medieval child murder, the hero would get caught up with modern Devil worship. To do this properly, Huysmans had to find some real, contemporary Devil worshipers.

So, in February 1890, he wrote baldly and enthusiastically to the Abbé Boullan: "Are you a Satanist?" Boullan replied at once, denying that he was a Satanist, saying on the contrary that he was "an Adept who has declared war on all demoniacal cults"; and he added in a subsequent letter that "I can put at your disposal documents which will enable you to prove that satanism is active in our time, and in what form and in what circumstances. Your work will thus endure as a monumental history of satanism in the nineteenth century."[50]

If Boullan had declared war on the Satanists, why did Huysmans think he was one of them? Boullan's life has become overlaid with myth, but the main events are known. Joseph-Antoine Boullan was born in 1824 in a small village in the south of France. He was ambitious to become a priest and studied at Rome, where he obtained his doctorate with distinction. He joined the Missionaries of the Precious Blood and took part in several missions to Italy. From 1853 to 1856 he lived in one of the society's houses in Alsace, then went to Paris as an independent priest.

He had already acquired a reputation as an eminent theologian and was soon made the spiritual director of Adèle Chevalier, a nun who had had mystical experiences. Together they published a journal, *Les Annales du sacerdoce*, and in 1859 they founded a religious community named the Society for the Reparation of Souls, at Bellevue near Paris. It was still common, as it had been centuries before, for nuns to be molested by devils; but Boullan won a considerable reputation as an exorcist.

Soon, however, complaints about his methods were made to both the bishop of Versailles and to the police. It was said that he had engaged in "amorous intrigue" with Adèle, and that she had two children by him. He was also supposed to be supplying fraudulent medicinal remedies, namely, consecrated Hosts smeared with excrement, which he gave to possessed nuns. In 1861 the pair were put on trial for fraud and indecency. They were cleared of indecency but given three years each for fraud.[51]

In 1869, Boullan was again imprisoned, this time in Rome by the Holy

Office, as the Inquisition then called itself. While incarcerated there, he wrote out a confession, which is now in the Vatican. It is said, both by Experts on Satanism and by literary biographers of Huysmans, that he there confessed that in 1860 he had sacrificed a child born to him by Adèle, in the course of a mass.[52]

None of these writers claims to have seen the document itself. P. Bruno de Jesus-Marie, O.C.D., and Jean Vinchon, however, who contributed an article on Boullan to a volume of Carmelite studies on Satan, did obtain a photographic copy of it. They did not print it in full because, they said, it was in poor taste, but they did expound every "interesting" point in it. These included:

> He verged on sacrilege in his attempts to cure certain possessed persons.
>
> His obsession with money led him to swindle, and as a result he was sentenced to three years' imprisonment. The enquiry showed that he had taken advantage of certain revelations concerning the hereafter to exploit the credulous and induce them to give him money, that he might have the pleasure of bestowing it on others.

Also, Boullan wrote paranoically about his enemies, including "the horned ones of the priesthood"; in the prison of the Holy Office, it is not surprising that he felt that way.[53]

But of his supposed sacrifice of his own baby, no mention is made. Either Bruno and Vinchon thought infanticide too trivial to be of interest to their readers, or else all those respected academics and learned anti-Satanists who have repeated this anecdote have no better sense of historical criticism than to suppose that if a story is sensational, then it must be true.

(Inevitably, this has been another of those stories that have grown wilder in the retelling, so that by the time of Peter Haining's *Anatomy of Witchcraft* [1972], it had become a kind of fact that "dozens" of children were crucified by Boullan in front of "perverted" congregations.)[54]

In the autumn of 1869, the Holy Office rehabilitated Boullan; he returned to Paris and resumed the life a priest specializing in exorcism. (It would be quite incredible if the authorities had believed he was guilty of murdering his own child, that they should have allowed him to become a priest once more.)

Boullan, however, continued to practice irregular methods. He was frequently still employed as an exorcist for possessed nuns, but he did not content himself with using the set rite. He also "taught them how, by means of auto-hypnosis and auto-suggestion, they could dream that they were having intercourse with the saints or with Jesus Christ, and showed them what postures and occult methods they should adopt to enable supernatural entities—and more particularly his own astral body—to visit and possess them."[55] Evidently his physical desires were under control, but he could not resist the chance of astral intercourse.

This sort of thing could not go on indefinitely, and in 1875, Cardinal Guibert, the archbishop of Paris, condemned Boullan's latest journal, *Les Annales de la sainteté*, for heretical doctrines. This was no doubt true: a man like Boullan, with many strange ideas of his own, could hardly have stayed on the razor-thin path of orthodoxy. He appealed to the Vatican without success, and on 1 July 1875, he left the church.

At once he found himself another church, that of Eugene-Michel Vintras. In 1839, Vintras believed that he had had a vision of the archangel Michael, followed by appearances from the Virgin and Saint Joseph. They taught him that there were three ages of the world: the first, the Old Testament period, was the age of the Father; the second, the Christian, was that of the Son. He was given the task of initiating the third era, that of the Holy Ghost, in which divine inspiration would become a fact of daily life. He himself was the reincarnation of the prophet Elijah.

Not surprisingly, Vintras was condemned at Rome in 1848; undaunted, he formed the Church of Carmel, which established branches in Spain, Belgium, Italy, and England—Vintras was forced to live in England as an exile for a number of years. Boullan declared himself a convert to this church's doctrines, which were indeed similar to the "heretical" doctrines he had been expounding in *Les Annales de la sainteté*. Boullan and Vintras met in Brussels in August and again in Paris in October.[56]

Vintras died in December 1875, and Boullan promptly declared that he had been chosen as his successor. He claimed to be a reincarnation of John the Baptist. Most of the Church of Carmel refused to accept him as their new leader, but a few did, and headquarters were set up in Lyons.

Boullan continued to be accused of sexual irregularities by his enemies, but there is no doubt that like many magicians, his most interesting activities all took place in the astral realms. He and his followers believed that they engaged in copulation with angels, cherubim, seraphim, and historical figures such as Cleopatra and Alexander the Great.[57]

Meanwhile, there had been an occult revival going on in France, stimulated in particular by the writings of Eliphas Lévi (1810–75), whose books, though not easy to understand, were then exceptional for their belief that magic could work. Lévi was a Catholic and had at one time trained for the priesthood, and he was keen to demonstrate that he was not doing anything wicked. He therefore drew a sharp line between White and Black Magic, insisting that he practiced only the White. He was responsible for some statements about Black Magic of which there is no trace in earlier literature—for example, the belief that a pentagram with one point up is "White," whereas one with two points up is "Black" and represents the head and horns of the Devil.

Some of Lévi's disciples formed themselves into a Cabalistic Order of the Rosy Cross. To prove themselves whiter-than-White Magicians, they had to find some Black Magicians to contrast themselves with. Even before the order was formed, three of them—Stanislas de Guaita, Oswald Wirth, and Canon Roca—had contrived to infiltrate Boullan's church and witness rites normally forbidden to outsiders. When Wirth and de Guaita met in 1887, they compared notes and then set up an "initiatory tribunal" to judge Boullan. They found him guilty and communicated their verdict to him in a letter.[58]

Boullan did not take kindly to this. For a long time, his own astral activities had included doing battle with Black Magicians, and so now he declared that it was Wirth, Roca, and the Order of the Rosy Cross who were the Satanists. (The battle thus proves the old definition that "White Magic is what you do, Black Magic is what your enemies do.") Vintras had used to go off into the astral to witness Black Magic ceremonies, which not surprisingly he found to be of a wicked and disreputable nature, and Boullan had kept a large dossier of them.[59]

So, when Huysmans started his research for a "Black Magic" novel and wrote to various leading occultists hoping for admission to a Black Mass, it was to Boullan that he was directed. But when Huysmans met him, he decided he was a saintly character and depicted him as such in *Là-Bas*, in the guise of Dr. Johannes, who talks about the coming era of the Holy Ghost. When Boullan told Huysmans that he had "documents which will enable you to prove that satanism is active in our time," he was referring to the records of Eugene Vintras's astral journeys. So when *Là-Bas* finally appeared in 1891, the villains were identified as the "Rose Cross"; the evil priest who conducted a Black Mass was called "Canon Docre," who, like Canon Roca, lived at Nimes; and the mass itself was based on one that Vintras had witnessed in the astral.

This book was tremendously successful, and soon people were going around Paris pointing out disused chapels as the place "where it really happened." But did it? This depends on whether you believe that astral travelers see accurate pictures of what is happening outside their bodies or merely suffer from hallucinations.

An alternative claim is that Huysmans had attended some kind of Black Mass but did not rely on it for the novel. This is not absurd: almost certainly in the twentieth century there have been "Black Masses" put on exclusively as acts for wealthy tourists. The interest in Satanism of the "naughty nineties" of the nineteenth century might have inspired some dodgy club owner to put on spectacles of this sort. Such brief descriptions as have been published, however, suggest that these shows are as unimpressive as the fees charged for entry are excessive. As Huysmans's biographer Robert Baldick put it: "The ceremony described in *Là-Bas* was based on papers from the Vintrasian archives . . . probably because these sensational documents were more satisfying than any Black Mass which Huysmans could have witnessed."[60] Against this, Huysmans's friend Remy de Gourmont wrote later that the mass in *Là-Bas* was wholly imaginary: "It was I who hunted for details of this fantastic ceremony. I found none, for the simple reason that none exists."[61]

In January 1893, Boullan declared: "For years we have undergone attacks by means of Black Masses, and by bewitchments of every kind, by poison, by the most dangerous proceedings, and in spite of all, by the will of God, who alone is master of life and death, we are on our feet." The next day he died.[62]

Jules Bois, a friend of Boullan and Huysmans, rushed into print an article in *Gil-Blas* in which he brought accusations against de Guaita and Joséphin Peládan, the leaders of the Rosy Cross, of killing Boullan by Black Magic. Huysmans himself then gave an interview to *Figaro* in which he said: "It is indisputable that Guaita and Peládan practise Black Magic every day. . . . It is very possible that my poor friend Boullan has succumbed to their practices." De Guaita promptly challenged both men to duels: Huysmans withdrew his remarks; de Guaita and Bois fought with pistols, but neither man was injured.[63]

In 1896, Bois published *Satanism and Magic*, also based on the Vintrasian archives, to which Huysmans contributed a preface. Not wishing, one may suppose, to risk another challenge to a duel, Huysmans dropped his assertions about the Order of the Rosy Cross. He now suggested that "Canon Docre" was a Belgian priest.

A certain Baron Firmin Van den Bosch subsequently conducted a lengthy investigation into this claim. Huysmans told him that when he attended a Black Mass, he had noticed a priest dressed in a cassock and some sort of hood standing apart from the congregation, not far from the altar, watching the ceremony most attentively. Not long afterward he had seen a photograph of the same priest in the window of a bookshop specializing in works on Satanism and the occult. (This differs from the preface to *Satanism and Magic*, where Huysmans says it was a photographer's shop.) He had eventually succeeded in identifying the man as the Abbé van Haecke, chaplain of the Holy Blood at Bruges.

Assuming that this is true (which is doubtful, since Huysmans made contradictory statements at different times), then van Haecke was clearly *not* the same as "Canon Docre," since he was not performing the Black Mass but only witnessing it. Huysmans claimed that he had later visited van Haecke at Bruges, and asking him about the Black Mass, van Haecke had said: "Haven't I the right to be inquisitive? And how do you know that I wasn't there as a spy?"[64]

Herman Bossier, who attempted to confirm that the Abbé van Haecke was a Satan-pervert, learned, no doubt to his disappointment, that van Haecke was a saintly character, "held in love and respect by the good people of Bruges; and they would certainly have laughed to scorn any accusations of devil-worship."[65] Furthermore, van Haecke was known to be exceptionally inquisitive and had once attended a ceremony held by some Eastern sect, so he was the kind of person who might attend a Black Mass (in some shady Parisian nightclub, no doubt) simply out of curiosity.

Huysmans seems, in fact, to have obtained his information about van Haecke mainly from two occultist friends, Berthe Courrière and Edouard Dubus. Berthe Courrière was an unstable woman who had a history of trying to seduce priests and accusing them of ravishment if she failed. It appears she tried it on with the Abbé van Haecke, for on the night of 8 September 1890, the Bruges police found her hiding in the bushes on the Rempart des Marechaux, clad only in her undergarments. She told them that she had just escaped from van Haecke's house, where he had tried to involve her in Satanic practices. Knowing him as a well-respected priest, the police refused to believe it and arranged for her to be placed in a mental asylum.[66] This was not the only occasion in her life in which she was so incarcerated, which tends to cast doubt on her reliability. One could just as well suppose that she made up the story out of her frustration at being unable to seduce van Haecke.

Edouard Dubus, a young poet addicted to magic and morphine, also told Huysmans stories about van Haecke—how the Abbé seduced people into Satanism by means of lavish dinners, at which beautiful girls were present, and where they had their morals corrupted by means of aphrodisiacs in-jected into the brandy nuts eaten for dessert. In June 1895, Dubus was found dead in the urinal of a restaurant in the Place Maubert. It was whispered that a curse had been laid on him, either by the Rosy Cross or by Boullan's disciples, depending on which side of the controversy the rumormonger stood. But an inquest found that his death was due to the mundane cause of a morphine overdose.[67]

In view of all this, Hermann Bossier was left with only one argument that van Haecke was guilty of Satanism: when he tried to check dossiers relating to accusations made by Courrière and Dubus, he found that they were miss-ing.[68] Obviously, he thought, they were stolen to cover up the truth.

Thus, when the apparent great underground of Black Magic flourishing in Paris in the 1890s is investigated, it turns out to be (apart from what was invented by Taxil) a mass of accusations, counteraccusations, duels fought over the accusations, accounts of astral journeys, sworn statements of lu-natics and drug addicts, stories that were frequently changed, and, finally, an argument from the lack of evidence that there must once have been evi-dence in order for it to be missing. It is not possible to show that all these stories were made up, but neither can any of them be shown to be true.

Suggesting that "it really happened" has become a stock technique for marketing pulp. Robert Black's 1978 *The Satanists*, a novelization of the film, starts with the author's note: "This book is a fiction. But do not doubt for an instant that it is based upon a true story."[69] But the reader will cer-tainly doubt it, as true stories do not include every known horror-film cliché, from the near-deserted village with just a few frightened inhabitants to the human sacrifice prevented at the last minute. Likewise, *The Satan Sado-Cultist*, ("Sale to Minors Prohibited"; ca. 1971), an S/M novel in which the unfortunate heroine is forcibly inducted into the "Temple of Light," a cult making a pretense of devil worship as a cover for "unadulterated lust," notably flagellation and fellatio, is ascribed to "Peggy Torburn (as told to Kenneth Harding),"[70] so that the naive purchaser might think it was a real-life confession; though again, no cult could control its members to the ex-tent that at all times they behave like characters in porn fiction.

Adriano Lemmi and Albert Pike

Adriano Lemmi was a prominent Italian politician of the late nineteenth century. In 1895, he lived in a rented apartment in the Palazzo Borghese in

Rome. One day, so the story goes, the agents of the landlord, the prince Borghese, came around and demanded entrance to every room. They were refused entry to one of them, but as the lease had expired, the agents pointed out that they had the right to force the door unless it was unlocked.

Reluctantly, Lemmi allowed them in. "The walls were hung all round from ceiling to floor with heavy curtains of silk damask, scarlet and black, excluding the light; at the further end there stretched a large tapestry upon which was woven in more than life-size a figure of Lucifer, colossal, triumphant, dominating the whole. [Query: How did they know what size Lucifer was in life?] Exactly beneath an altar had been built, amply furnished for the liturgy of hell: candles, vessels, rituals, missal, nothing was lacking." "The decorations were extravagant, forcing the conclusion that Satan had some pretty wealthy followers in the holy city." "Cushioned prie-dieus and luxurious chairs, crimson and gold, were set in order for the assistants, and the chamber lit with electricity fantastically arranged so that it should glare through an enormous human eye."[71]

At about the same time appeared A. C. de la Rive's *La Femme et l'enfant dans la Franc-Maçonnerie*, which is now frequently quoted for the "Secret Instructions" (originally published by Adolphe Ricoux) emanating from Albert Pike, who was then the American chief of the Ancient and Accepted Rite of Freemasonry. In these instructions Pike/Ricoux states that Satan and Lucifer are not identical and should not be worshiped as if they were on a par. The true religion is the worship of Lucifer, and the worship of Satan that has crept in is a heresy. Whatever one thinks of this as a piece of theology, it was obviously shocking to learn that members of an outwardly respectable international organization were worshiping either Lucifer or Satan.

These two matters are dealt with together because they have the same origin: they are both totally fictional items put about by the nineteenth century's greatest hoaxer, Léo Taxil (one of whose other pen names was Adolphe Ricoux). Though for the most part his great Satan scam is forgotten or acknowledged for what it was, these two particular stories are still circulating as if they were true. It is now more than a century since Taxil confessed: "When I named Adriano Lemmi second successor to Albert Pike as sovereign Luciferian pontiff—for it was not in the Palazzo Borghese, but in my study that he was elected pope of the Freemasons—when this imaginary election became known, the Italian masons, including a Parliamentary Deputy, believed that it was serious."[72] Yet this libel concerning Lemmi was retold in Montague Summers's *History of Witchcraft and Demonology* (though without giving Lemmi's name), whence it has been copied by many writers who suppose that Summers is a reliable authority. The "instructions" about Lucifer were translated into English in Lady Queenborough's *Occult Theocrasy* (1933), a book purporting to expose a Jewish-Masonic conspiracy to take over the world. This received very little attention until it was reprinted by the Christian Book Club of America, a publishing house that appears to specialize in literature purporting to expose Jewish-Masonic conspiracies to take over the world. Since then, the "instructions" of "Pike" have been noticed by various Evangelical writers, who routinely repeat them in their denunciations of Freemasonry.

Thus, out of nine supposed cases of historical Satanism, two turn out to have been nineteenth-century forgeries; four are based primarily on works of fiction, with little or no reason to suppose that any true story lay behind them; and the other three are from confessions made under torture. Only one of these was backed by physical evidence.

One or two books on "historical Satanism" that are often quoted by Experts may be mentioned here. H. T. F. Rhodes's *The Satanic Mass* (1954) runs fairly uncritically through most of the cases listed above. His sixth chapter, "Sabbat of the Goat," is based on the eleventh chapter of Michelet's *Satanism and Witchcraft*, rewritten but without any new information.

Tim Tate quotes what he says is a "translation of the Guibourg Mass in the author's possession."[73] On inspection, this turns out to be *Missa Niger: La Messe Noire*, by "Aubrey Melech,"[74] which has also been quoted by other British Experts on Satanism. This book comes with "An Introductory Warning": "It is our purpose neither to shock nor to blaspheme Our Lord & Saviour Jesus Christ, but . . . [to be] an object-lesson to those who would turn from their Saviour to the worship of His ancient enemy." It gives a text of a Black Mass, apparently based on inside information, but does not specify that it was the same as that used by Guibourg.

In 1993 the publisher of this tract, Bernard King, told me that Aubrey Melech is the pseudonym of a friend of his and that the book was made possible by this friend's "contacts" within Satanism. I suggested to him that the book read like a spoof and he replied, "It's very serious," with a big grin on his face. Since then two different people have told me that King wrote the book himself. *Melech* is Hebrew for "king." Since King does not personally claim to have contacts within Satanism, it can be assumed that Aubrey Melech's contacts are as fictional as Melech himself. Despite the book's Christian pose, its author is a professed Odinist.

King's book contains a fairly crude parody of the Catholic ritual. To suggest that it was that used by Guibourg seems to involve the supposition that a standard text was issued by the Antichrist centuries ago and has been used by all Satanists ever since.

Two important points emerge. First, despite the fascination that Devil worship has always had for many people, it is surprising how rarely anything like it has actually occurred in the past. Second, it should be noted that the Experts who nowadays repeat these yarns about "historical Satanism" also quote anonymous Survivors' stories. The truth, or otherwise, of the latter cannot usually be directly investigated. It is therefore significant to note that when the same Experts relate matters that *can* be checked, they prove to have no idea of what they are writing about.

5

Satanic Crime

In July 1934, Aleister Crowley found himself in the dock at the Old Bailey. And with what crime was the "wickedest man in the world" charged? Conspiring to destroy Christianity? Dining off unbaptized babies? Practicing unspeakable perversions?

The actual charge was that Crowley had received four original letters and one copy of a letter, stolen from an artists' model, Betty May. He had wanted them to use in a libel action. Crowley was found guilty, but the judge said that as no harm had been done, the only sentence was that Crowley was to be bound over for two years and to pay fifty guineas toward the cost of the prosecution.[1]

On 18 July 1984, Anton LaVey was formally criminalized for the first time in his life. Diane, a woman he had lived with for twenty-four years, invoked a restraining order against him. He did not contest the action.[2]

It appears that leading Satanists and very wicked men do not extend their wickedness far into areas of illegality. Yet the twentieth century has, alas, been full of serious crimes, and anti-Satanists have linked many of these to Satanism. To evaluate the linkage, the crimes must be examined.

Matamoros

The border between Mexico and the United States is heavily patrolled due to all the illicit traffic passing over it: namely, Mexicans looking for work in the States and huge quantities of drugs. In April 1989, Mexican police routinely flagged down a silver Chevrolet truck at a roadblock not far from the border and were astonished when the driver went heedlessly past without stopping. They got into cars and chased him to a ranch a few miles away. Despite having blatantly ignored a roadblock, the driver seemed surprised and confused when arrested and said something about being invisible.[3]

The police quickly established that the ranch was being used by a drug-smuggling gang. But there was worse: in one of the huts they found altars and statues of Santerian and other gods, along with statues of Catholic saints. In their midst was a cauldron containing, as it proved, dried blood, parts of a human brain, and a roasted turtle. In another, smaller kettle was human hair, a goat's head, more blood, and parts of a chicken. Scattered around the area were melted candles, half-burned cigars, and garlic.[4]

Four gang members were arrested on the spot. That evening they confessed that several men had been killed on the ranch and parts of their bodies boiled in the cauldron. Among the victims was Mark Kilroy, a Texas student whose disappearance during a night out in Matamoros the previous month had been highly publicized.[5] The gang members identified their leader as "El Padrino," who was a Santerian priest.

A few days later the men were taken back to the ranch to show where the bodies had been buried. Thirteen were dug up, one of which was identified as that of Mark Kilroy. Two others were buried not far away.[6]

A month later, Saturday, 6 May, police located other members of the gang, who were living in a flat in a wealthy suburb of Mexico City. A gun battle ensued, the gang firing at police to prevent them from coming near. Bizarrely, the gang threw large quantities of paper money out into the street. People rushed to pick the bills up even as the bullets flew. The siege ended after forty-five minutes when the gang ran out of ammunition. Incredibly, no one had been killed, though one police officer was injured.

But when police entered the flat, the leader of the gang, Adolfo de Jesus Constanzo, and his gay lover Martina Quintana Rodriguez, lay dead in each other's arms. When the ammunition had run low, Constanzo had ordered one of the gang to shoot them.[7]

Many of the details behind the Matamoros killings, as they have come to be called, will never be known, but the main facts were pieced together. The previous year, the Hernandez drug family had fallen on hard times. The Mexican drug trade is incredibly brutal, with casual killings a daily fact of life, but the Hernandez family had fallen out with one another, and some members had shot their own relatives.[8]

Hoping to restore the family fortunes, Elio Hernandez, a strong believer in the power of magic, approached Adolfo de Jesus Constanzo, then a *brujo* (witch) famous in Mexico City, who was regularly consulted by the rich and famous. Elio is said to have offered Constanzo "half of the family's drug profits in return for sharing his contacts and providing protection for the family on both the material and supernatural planes of existence."[9]

Constanzo had trained in the native magical religions Santeria and Palo Mayombe, which traditionally involve blood sacrifice, usually of animals that are commonly killed for the dinner table anyway, such as cockerels. Human sacrifice is strictly forbidden. But a U.S. film released in 1987, *The Believers*, depicted an imaginary Santeria-type cult that did indeed sacrifice humans. Constanzo became fascinated by this film, and his female assistant, Sara Aldrete, used it to recruit new members.[10]

And so the gang killings, which were frequent, were made into human sacrifices. The victims were killed in the hut on the ranch and bits of their flesh offered up to the gods. Most of these killings were primarily gangland murders, but on one occasion, Constanzo demanded a blond American sacrifice: it was for this reason that Mark Kilroy was picked out at random, kidnapped, and killed.[11]

At first sight, the Matamoros killings appeared to confirm the worst fears of the Satan-hunters. Yet, on closer examination, there are several differences between these events and those popularly alleged about Satanism:

1. Child sex abuse was not even mentioned in the Matamoros case.
2. All but one of the victims was an adult, the exception being a boy of fourteen. There were no babies or small children killed, and no women were deliberately made pregnant as "broodmares."
3. The gang were not Satanists but made their sacrifices to native gods.
4. The killings took place in an area with an extremely high crime rate, among men for whom murder was an everyday fact of life. It was not the case that law-abiding citizens were turned into monsters by the influence of a cult.
5. Cannibalism does not seem to have occurred; according to Sara Aldrete, the human remains were placed in the cauldron but not eaten.
6. The gang were not skillful at covering their tracks, taking victims who would not be missed, and so on. Mark Kilroy's disappearance set off a widespread search, and their belief that magic would protect them was their undoing.
7. The gang were caught by the normal methods of law enforcement, not by means of "recovered memories," following the guidance of the Holy Spirit, or other favorite anti-Satanist techniques.

In any case, the fact that human sacrifices took place in Mexico does not prove that they happen anywhere else. In both Britain and the United States, the number of court-proven murders that were committed specifically for occult purposes is zero.

The Family

By the autumn of 1967, the "Summer of Love" in the Haight-Ashbury area of San Francisco was starting to turn sour. Bikers started using violent tactics to take over the drug market. The Haight-Ashbury Medical Clinic, which had been treating people for free, was running short of donations and found itself overwhelmed by the number of cases of venereal disease brought to them in consequence of the doctrine of free love. Petty crime became common. Flowers and incense were giving way to vomit and ugliness.[12]

Charles Manson decided it was time to move his "family," a traveling hippie community, out of the area. They acquired an old school bus, painted it black,[13] and began roaming about California.

Nearly thirty-three years old, Manson had spent more than half of his life in prison.[14] At age thirteen, he had been taken into custody for armed robbery. During his subsequent brief periods of freedom, he had committed a variety of felonies including car theft, forgery, and controlling prostitutes.

Not long after his release on parole in March 1967, Manson took LSD and became convinced he was Jesus Christ.[15] Surprisingly, he was able to convince a small band of followers of this, too. At times he would wash their feet in imitation of the gospel story.

Unlike the original Jesus, Manson took thought for the morrow. He and his followers supported themselves by drug dealing and theft, and he got those who came from well-to-do backgrounds to give him large sums of money.

While in prison, Manson had studied hypnotism and practiced manipulating his fellow inmates. He proceeded to use this talent on the Family. Susan Atkins described how they would all drop acid and sit around on the floor of the bus, listening to Charlie talk. He would tell them: "You are free. And because we are free, we can become one. The Bible says we must die to self, and that's exactly true. We must die to self so we can be at one with all people. That is love."[16] Ultimately, what he meant was that they must give up their selves to do what he wanted.

Manson also had his own philosophy, based on a combination of many of the ideas that were floating around in the 1960s—astrology, scientology, and so on—and the Bible, which he had spent a lot of time reading in prison, and particularly the book of Revelation. As well as being Christ, Manson saw himself as the fifth angel described in Revelation 9, who had charge of the abyss. The first four angels, also known as the Four Horsemen of the Apocalypse, were in his mind the Beatles. Manson was obsessed by their 1968 double LP *The White Album*, and often repeated the words to "Piggies" and "Helter Skelter." Though "Helter Skelter" is merely about a fairground ride, Manson did not know this and attributed a deep metaphysical significance to it, believing that it represented some apocalyptic catastrophe that was soon to engulf the world, starting with California.

The Family established two main bases, one at the Spahn Ranch just outside Los Angeles, which had been used to film the TV series *The Virginian*, the other in Death Valley. Here, Manson believed, existed something called the Hole, which was either an entrance to the underworld kingdom of Shambala, famous in Oriental legend, or the bottomless pit of the book of Revelation—or perhaps both, his ideas being invariably confused.

In 1967, Manson had discussed with contacts in the movie world the possibility of a film about Jesus Christ coming again as a black man and middle-class America rejecting him, just as the Romans had done. The project was dropped, perhaps as being uncommercial. Slowly Manson's ideas changed, and the coming apocalypse, which at first he had thought would be caused by Russian nuclear warheads, was replaced by one of a black uprising against the whites. He believed, or claimed to believe, that black militants were stalking him.

It is evident that the continual drugtaking in which all the Family indulged was starting to unhinge Manson. By 1969, it was common for him to threaten to kill someone over a trivial disagreement. In June he shot a black man named Bernard Crowe in the stomach, following an argument about a drug deal. Crowe survived, but Manson believed he had killed him.[17] Convinced that the apocalypse was on the way, he drew up a list of people whom he wanted to kill first.

On 25 July, during the course of another "botched drug deal," one of the Family, Robert Beausoleil, stabbed to death a certain Gary Hinman. Those who were present made an effort to clear up any incriminating traces, but Beausoleil missed a fingerprint that he had left in blood on the door. One of the Family wrote "Political Piggy" on the living-room wall in Hinman's blood. This was intended as a blind to make the police think black militants were responsible, but it failed. Shortly afterward, Beausoleil was arrested driving the dead man's car near San Francisco, and his connection with the murder was quickly established.[18]

Manson is said to have thought up a desperate rescue plan: commit some other murders similar, to Beausoleil's, and police would think that a serial killer was responsible. If Beausoleil was in custody, they would know he could not have done the later murders and so would think he was innocent of the first. Manson got this idea from an old B movie; he did not know that Beausoleil had been identified by his fingerprint. In addition, he was still expecting the "Helter Skelter" apocalypse and, by some piece of twisted thinking supposed that he should himself initiate the killing he anticipated.[19]

So on 8 August he sent a group of his followers to the house of film director Roman Polanski, who for some reason was already on his list of people to be killed. First, they shot dead a friend of the caretaker who happened to be leaving when they entered the grounds. Polanski was in London, but his wife, Sharon Tate, who was eight months pregnant, was at home with three of her friends. All were stabbed repeatedly and without mercy. Before leaving, Manson's followers wrote "Pig" on the door in Tate's blood.[20]

The next night they struck again, at the home of Leno and Rosemary LaBianca, a wealthy Los Angeles couple, stabbing them and writing "Death to Pigs," "Rise," and "Healter Skelter" on the wall in their blood.[21]

On 16 August, the Manson Family were arrested at the Spahn Ranch, not for the murders but because the police rightly believed they had been responsible for a series of car thefts. The officers seized several vehicles, but it happened that their warrant was out of date, so after seventy-two hours they had to let all the detainees go.[22]

The Family decamped to Death Valley. They could have remained undetected in the wilderness there indefinitely if they had lain low, but they continued to drive around in stolen cars. Several of them were arrested in a police raid on the night of 9 October. A further raid, on 12 October, netted Manson himself.[23]

At first the police merely thought they had broken up a gang of car thieves. But Susan Atkins boasted to two different cellmates about how she had killed Sharon Tate, and the women told the authorities. At about the same time, a Los Angeles biker told police that just after the Tate slayings he had heard Manson boasting of having ordered five murders. Soon police realized that they had caught the perpetrators of the Tate-LaBianca killings. Five of the Family were tried for murder and sentenced to death. In 1972, however, the California Supreme Court voted to abolish the death penalty, and the sentences were commuted to life imprisonment.

When the story first hit the press, it was wrongly reported that the Manson gang were known as "Satan's Slaves";[24] hence there followed headlines such as "Satan Man's Confessions" and "I Join Satan's Hippies."[25] The first book on the case, obviously put together in a hurry, was likewise titled

Satan's Slaves.[26] In fact, Satan's Slaves were a California motorcycle gang only slightly connected to the Manson Family.

Nevertheless, the Manson murders are routinely written up in books on Satanism. Apart from the horrific nature of the killings, the "Satanic" argument appears to be that Manson had read some occult literature and believed in magic. That much is true, but he was also into all of the broth of new and unusual ideas that made up the 1960s "revolution," and the influence of the occult on his private philosophy was far less than that of the book of Revelation. Obviously, no one blames the Bible for the murders.

Unlike alleged elusive Satanic criminals, the Manson Family did not display great subtlety in covering up their crimes. Two of them left fingerprints at the Tate residence. They took off their bloodstained clothing as they drove away, throwing it, along with the gun and the knives used in the murders, into a nearby canyon. The clothes and the revolver were later found and given in evidence at the trial. When they stopped to wash the blood off themselves, a man awakened by the noise wrote down their car's number, which could be traced to them since they had not taken the professional criminal's precaution of stealing a getaway vehicle. Later, both Manson and Susan Atkins bragged about the killings to others, who told the police.

It is further asserted that Manson was associated with an organization called the Process; indeed, many popular books give the impression that the Process were somehow responsible for the killings.[27]

The Process, properly called the Process Church of the Final Judgement, was founded in England and went to San Francisco in 1967. Their leader was a man variously known as Robert DeGrimston or Robert Moore. They had a kind of neo-Gnostic theology in which there was a trinity of deities, Jehovah, Lucifer, and Satan. They may have been bizarre, but they are not known to have done anything illegal. (There were reports of Alsatian dogs being sacrificed in outdoor rituals near San Francisco at this time, and it was suggested that these were connected with the Process, since they were known for keeping Alsatians; but this was never proven.)

Some investigators of the Tate-LaBianca murders, however, thought that Manson's philosophy resembled that of the Process. So the district attorney asked him a series of questions about it. He gave noncommittal answers, until he was asked if he knew a Robert Moore, at which Manson replied: "You're looking at him. Moore and I are one and the same."[28] This, thought the D.A., proved some kind of connection between Manson and the Process. In addition, Robert Moore, like Manson, became convinced that he was Jesus Christ. This was thought to prove that they belonged to the same conspiracy (of what?). Also, they both had apocalyptic views, though as the author of a study of the Process pointed out, "the Book of Revelation is available for anyone ready to open a Bible."[29]

Two members of the Process then visited the D.A. and denied that the church had had any link with Manson. Nonetheless, Ed Sanders, author of *The Family* (1972), suggested that Manson had belonged to the Process, citing as proof the fact that he had once lived in the same street as the church. The Process took legal action and compelled Sanders to remove these comments from subsequent editions of the book.[30]

A few years later the district attorny in the Manson case, Vincent Bugliosi, published his own book on the case. By this time the Process Church had split up, and he could say what he liked. He limited himself to a suggestion that they influenced Manson's philosophy. Several subsequent writers have repeated and amplified this point, implying that the Manson murders were somehow the result of a Satanic conspiracy that included the Process and taking church members' denials as suspicious.

Here we can see the logic of Satanic mythmakers at work. Accused of being involved in one of the worst crimes of the century, on such evidence as that they once lived in the same street as the perpetrator, the Process went to some length to deny it. Obviously, they must have had something to hide!

The Solar Lodge OTO

The Spahn Ranch was not the only ranch in California where nasty things were going on in the summer of 1969. Not far from the border with Colorado was the headquarters of the Solar Lodge of the Ordo Templi Orientis (OTO). Though the organizer, Jean Brayton, a woman in her forties, claimed to have been the "Southern Californian Jurisdiction" of the OTO, in fact, she does not seem to have had any real connection with any other OTO lodges; indeed the OTO was otherwise almost nonexistent in America at this time. She claimed the title of "Ipsissimus," that is, an equal of the gods.[31]

Among other ventures, Brayton had set up an occult bookstore right opposite the University of Southern California, and she used it to recruit for her lodge. She acquired about fifty followers. Like Manson, she required total obedience from them and made bizarre demands. One girl became pregnant. Brayton told her to condition herself to hate the child growing within her, and that when it was born, it would be turned over to the lodge.

The girl dutifully tried to hate her swelling belly but could not; instead, she left the cult.[32]

In pursuit of enlightenment, members took marijuana, LSD, Demerol, scopolamine, jimsonweed, datura root, ether, and belladonna. At least one of the members died of an overdose. They were reported to sacrifice cats, dogs, and chickens and to pour the blood of sacrificed animals over themselves while they practiced ritual sexual intercourse[33] (though, presumably, these statements are based on the recollections of people who had been taking marijuana, LSD, scopolamine, Demerol, jimsonweed, datura root, ether, and belladonna—not the best possible witnesses.)

Certain of the members, on Brayton's orders, went out and robbed the homes of Israel Regardie and other California occultists, taking away rare occult books and artifacts, including Regardie's Crowley collection. These were taken to the ranch, where, again like the Manson Family, the lodge were preparing for Armageddon.

Around the tenth of June, a young boy named Anthony Gibbons, whose parents belonged to the lodge, started a fire that destroyed the main ranch building and, incidentally, Regardie's Crowley collection. As a punishment, Brayton had the boy locked in a box outdoors for fifty-six days. This was in the summer, when the temperature was around 110 degrees Fahrenheit. He was given just enough air and food to stay alive. Two people, however, who had come to the ranch to look at some horses with a view to purchase, spotted the boy and went to the next town to inform the police. The ranch was promptly raided, and eleven lodge members were arrested, including Gibbons's mother, Beverly. Later they were tried for felony child abuse and all found guilty. Brayton and some other followers had escaped to a property she owned in Mexico.[34]

The Solar Lodge affair probably comes nearer than any other real court-tested case to "Satanic ritual abuse." The lodge was, apparently, part of an international organization, the members being totally obedient to the leader. There were blood sacrifices and ritual sex. Robbery and other crimes were committed, including heavy drug taking. A child was tortured.

Yet, once again, there are major differences between the Solar Lodge's practices and the ritual abuse alleged by anti-Satanists. Child *sexual* abuse was not alleged. The physical abuse of the boy was not done for any ritual or occult purpose but as a punishment. The blood sacrifices were of small animals, not humans. There was no subtle cover-up of their crimes; indeed, by leaving the boy outdoors, they gave themselves away.

It is also important to note that the Solar Lodge was not, in fact, part of any international order. Brayton got her information about the OTO from books. A number of writers in the 1970s suggested that the OTO was a wide-scale criminal conspiracy; they could do this because there were hardly any real OTO members in the United States to reply to these accusations.

What these three cases have in common, apart from indiscriminate drug use among the perpetrators, is that in each a fairly small group built up around a single charismatic leader, whom the members followed blindly. For a short time, this leader had considerable power and was able to order the commission of serious crimes. But she or he had no more skill at avoiding detection than the average criminal and so led the whole group to disaster.

This pattern is apparent in cases where there was no "occult" connection. The notorious Billionaire Boys' Club of California in the mid-1980s was grouped around Joe Hunt, who was like Manson in that he came from a relatively poor background but was able to milk disciples from well-to-do families. Hunt taught what he called paradox philosophy, a set of psychological theories that involved freeing oneself from "old values"—things like good and bad, true and false. These were held to be merely impediments that stood "between what you had and what you wanted," Hunt said. Having carefully taught all this to club members, Hunt led them through a series of unsuccessful business frauds to committing two murders, before they were finally arrested.[35]

Another example is the Russian revolutionary Sergei Nechayev. In Switzerland in 1869, he and Mikhail Bakunin sat down and wrote out a description of how a revolutionary should behave: "The revolutionist has only one idea; the revolution; and he has broken with all laws and codes of morals. He must be cold, ready to kill in himself any sentiment that interferes with his purpose. All people are to be classified in terms of their use or harmfulness to the cause of the revolutionist, and the most dangerous must be immediately destroyed., &c."

Nechayev then returned to Russia and passed himself off to the Moscow students as a member of a secret organization with iron discipline and terrible powers. (He had a paper issued by Bakunin, certifying him as leader of the Russian branch of the "Revolutionary Union of the World"—otherwise a mere idea in Bakunin's mind.) A certain student named Ivanov, who was independent minded and would not "serve as a blind tool," as Nechayev expected him to, came to doubt the reality of this organization and challenged him to prove its existence, which of course he could not. Finally, Ivanov announced his intention of founding a serious organization of his own.

Nechayev decided that Ivanov was one of those "dangerous" elements who "must be immediately destroyed" and persuaded a group of his student followers, whom he had been more successful at turning into "blind tools," to murder Ivanov. The subsequent police investigations led to the arrest of some three hundred students, eighty-four of whom were tried and nearly all of these imprisoned or exiled. Nechayev fled to Switzerland but was extradited for the murder and sentenced to twenty years hard labor. Up until his death, in 1883, he spent his time converting the prison guards at the fortress of Saint Peter and Saint Paul to his political philosophy.[36]

Clearly, then, cases like those of Matamoros and the Family are part of a criminal pattern (though Nechayev, had he been more successful, would have been remembered by history as a politician rather than as a murderer) and not a manifestation of the occult.

It should also be noted that events such as the Manson murders are used by a variety of moralists to expostulate against their pet hatred, whatever that may be. *The Longford Report* on pornography linked the murders to sex education in schools: "It was suggested that the psychological shock of sudden exposure to adult sexuality frequently resulted in a later reversion to infantile sex or even to such extremes of violent revulsion as the Manson murders in California."[37] One could equally well blame vegetarianism or the Beatles.

As a matter of fact, Manson and many other violent killers have been regular readers of the Bible. Of course, it would be absurd to blame the Bible for their crimes. The true connection seems to be that psychotic killers are deeply insecure; and deeply insecure people are drawn to reading the Bible, as offering them something hopeful to believe in.

"Say You Love Satan"

After the discovery of the body of teenager Gary Lauwers in a wood on Long Island, New York, in July 1984, and the arrest of two other teenagers for his murder, Detective Lieutenant Robert Dunn, commander of the local homicide squad, declared: "This was a sacrificial killing. It's pure Satanism." New York City's *Daily News* stated that the arrested youths, Ricky Kasso and Jimmy Troiano, belonged to the "Knights of the Black Circle," who were "a

Satanic cult with about fifteen to twenty hard-core members and up to thirty others who view the cult's sacrificial rites."[38]

Two days after his arrest, Ricky Kasso hanged himself in his prison cell. Nonetheless, the story of the murder was pieced together. Kasso was a school dropout who peddled marijuana, angel dust, and mescaline in his hometown of Northport, Long Island. Much of his supply, which he got from New York City, he took himself. He was a Satanic "dabbler" who had a copy of *The Satanic Bible*, and on Walpurgisnacht (May Eve) 1984 he took a group of friends up to Amityville's famous haunted house (as in *The Amityville Horror*), which was a few miles from his home. They tried to do a ritual outside but were stopped by the police.[39]

One evening, while Kasso slept, Gary Lauwers abstracted ten packets of angel dust from his pocket. Kasso quickly learned of the theft and demanded their return, but by now Lauwers had only five. Kasso insisted that Lauwers owed him fifty dollars in consequence. Lauwers kept saying he would pay him but never did.[40]

Evidently, this incident preyed on Kasso's mind. On 16 June 1984, he invited Lauwers to share some drugs with himself, Troiano, and another youth out in the local woods, as if he had forgotten the debt. When they were all stoned, Kasso stabbed Lauwers repeatedly, shouting at him, "Say you love Satan." The other two who were present were too shocked to do anything.[41]

Though Troiano and Kasso made a shallow pit for the body, they did nothing more to cover their traces and actually talked about the killing to friends, one of whom later called the police. Lauwers's body was found on the Fourth of July, and Kasso and Troiano were arrested on the fifth. Early on the morning of 7 July, Kasso hanged himself in his cell. Troiano was tried but found not guilty.[42]

Lauwers's murder was basically a drug-crazed killing, but insofar as there was a motive, it was his theft of five packs of angel dust. Apart from the words "Say you love Satan," there was no Satanic connection; still less was it a ritual sacrifice attended by dozens of cult members. The Knights of the Black Circle had been a gang, several years earlier, at the high school all these teenagers had attended; none of those involved with the murder had belonged to it. The New York *Daily News* story was put together from a few premature rumors. It was largely untrue, but being more sensational than the truth, it was this version that was publicized all over the world.

There have been a number of highly publicized murders with such a Satanic link in the United States: for example, the case of Joseph Bergamini of

Queens, New York, who killed his mother and wounded his father with a kitchen knife, crying, "Don't worry, I won't die, Satan," on Thanksgiving Day 1990;[43] and Phil Gamble, age fifteen, who shot and killed his brother on 2 February 1986 and in whose closet police found a pamphlet, *The Power of Satan*; a black robe; a silver chalice; a candle; and eleven heavy-metal cassettes.[44] It would be easy, but unprofitable, to give examples from the other side of the fence, such as that of James and Susan Carson, a Californian hippie couple who murdered three people in the early 1980s because, they said, their victims were "witches" and they had divine instructions to rid the world of them;[45] or Julian Dominguez of San Antonio, Texas, who killed his father and cousin in 1978 after "voices" told him he was the true Christ and his relatives were incarnations of the Devil;[46] and those (there have been several in recent years) who have been beaten to death by exorcists attempting to drive demons out of them. The real question is: Does such anecdotal evidence prove any general pattern?

Linda Blood, in *The New Satanists*, claims that "since 1984 there has been at least one sensational satanism-related murder case per year," citing Kasso's killing of Lauwers as an example.[47] Since there are more than twenty thousand murders a year in the United States, one Satanic killing a year is not much, particularly since normally the connection to Satanism is tenuous. Many American teenagers dabble in Satanism. Suppose that one person in a thousand is a Satanist of some sort; then one would expect about twenty American Satanists to commit murder annually. Unfortunately, there are no reliable figures either for the number of Satanists or for the number of "Satanic" murders, so there is no way of knowing if Satanists are more likely to kill than the average person.

Anti-Satanists sometimes show signs of desperation in this area. Michael Newton's *Raising Hell*, "An Encyclopedia of Devil Worship and Satanic Crime," contains entries like this: "DICKSON, ANTHONY. Authorities in Caddo Parish, Louisiana, officially describe twenty-two-year-old Anthony Dickson as a victim of 'ritualistic cult murder,' but they still have no idea who killed him, or why."[48] Likewise, Brian McConnell devoted a chapter of his Satanic exposé to the U.S. serial killer Coral Eugene Watts. Watts was a regular churchgoer who committed his murders on Sundays; but perhaps he was possessed by the Devil, McConnell suggested.[49]

In a horrific case in 1993, two women, Bernadette McNeilly and Jean Powell, and two men, Glyn Powell and Anthony Dudson, in Liverpool kidnapped a girl, kept her tied to a bed for six days, tortured her, and finally took her out to the country, doused her with petrol, set her on fire, and left her for dead. She nonetheless survived long enough to tell police the identity of the perpetrators.

A tabloid paper reported: "The occult dictated the drugs and car-theft dealings of Jean Powell and Bernadette McNeilly. Sex-mad Berni read the gang's fortunes by throwing rune stones. If the omens were unclear there were always the tarot cards."[50]

But was the occult really the cause of these people's criminal behavior? Regular criminals are often highly superstitious, as are those involved in dangerous professions. If you live with danger, it is natural to turn to good-luck charms and fortune-tellers, as giving a slight sense of security. This might explain why the gang used divination to plan their crimes.

But why should the converse be true? Why should reading tarot cards turn one to a life of crime? There is no reason, unless one accepts the fundamentalist theory that reading the tarot (or even one's daily horoscope) causes demon possession. If it were possible to find a cause for such a senseless crime, a more obvious factor would be the gang were amphetamine freaks.

It used to be common for psychopathic murderers to say, "God told me to do it." This was the excuse of the Yorkshire Ripper in 1981, but it did not convince the court. Since the 1970s, however, serious criminals have also often given the unlikely defense "The Devil made me do it." "In July, 1971, Kim Brown, a twenty-two-year-old avowed Satanist, rationalized her brutal murder of a sixty-two-year-old man by swearing that during a black-magic ceremony, the Devil had appeared and bidden her to commit the crime."[51] If this claim was intended as a defense, it certainly succeeded; though convicted of murder, Brown was sentenced to only seven years imprisonment.

"The neighbor's dog made me do it" does not sound like much of a defense, but that was what "Son of Sam" killer David Berkowitz said when arrested in August 1977. In eight separate attacks over a period of a year, Berkowitz had killed six people and wounded seven others. His victims were all unknown to him, mostly young women sitting in parked cars. He became known as Son of Sam from a letter he left for the police at the scene of one of the murders. Though the killings were all in New York City, Berkowitz lived in the city of Yonkers, some miles to the north.

It seemed clear that Berkowitz was a typical "lone nut" serial killer. He readily confessed to the killings but said they were ordered by his neighbor, Sam Carr: "He told me through his dog, as he usually does. It's not really a dog. It just looks like a dog."[52] Carr and his family stated that they did not know Berkowitz personally but that he had complained to them about the barking of their dog. It appeared that Berkowitz had not merely thought it noisy but believed that it was barking orders to him.

A journalist named Maury Terry, however, refused to believe in Berkowitz's insanity and became convinced that a conspiracy was involved. He suggested that Berkowitz was involved with a Satanic cult, who wanted the murders done for reasons of their own, apparently as an indirect means of making human sacrifices, in a way that could not be traced to themselves.

As proof of a conspiracy, Terry cited the fact that Berkowitz, after he had been in prison for some time, knew details of certain unsolved murders that had never been made public.[53] Unfortunately, this is a feeble argument. Before his arrest, Berkowitz had been very much a loner. After his arrest, by contrast, he was shut up with a crowd of dangerous men, some of whom would undoubtedly have known the facts behind many an unsolved crime. There is no need to postulate a national Satanic organization, only a national prison system.

In October 1979, Terry and another journalist found that a disused pumphouse in a Yonkers park had been painted with inverted crosses and pentagrams in blatant Satanic fashion. The carcasses of three German shepherd dogs had been found in the same park. Despite the lack of evidence that the Satanic graffiti was anything more than the work of disaffected teenagers, that the dead dogs were connected with the Satanic "temple," or that Berkowitz had anything to do with either (this was two years after his arrest), Terry placed them centrally in his theory of a conspiracy, connecting Berkowitz to the temple, the temple to the dog murders, the dog murders with the Process, and the Process with the OTO[54] (though the OTO had no connection with the Process except that they were mentioned alongside them in Sanders's book on Manson). By the time Terry's book came out (1987), the Process had long since ceased to exist, but the OTO had taken on a new lease of life, so they sued him and received damages and a promise to cut out all references to them in subsequent editions of his book. There was much more to Terry's argument than this—his book runs to 798 pages— but these examples are typical in that, throughout, the evidence relies on coincidence and inference rather than on anything solid.

Many supposed cases of Satanic crime fall into an "almost" category. Typically, anti-Satanist Pat Pulling quotes a Wyoming newspaper article on Satanic crime: "Police are closing in on a Satan-worshiping cult called the 'Warlocks of the Crimson Circle' that they say is behind several burglaries that have occurred in Powell [Wyoming] over the last few months, officials say . . . 12 high-school age boys are involved in the cult. . . . The group's activities have included the ritualistic mutilation of several cats and may be drug-related."[55]

It is possible that a follow-up article appeared explaining how the "Warlocks of the Crimson Circle" had been rounded up, were proven to be a branch of an international Satanic order, and were found guilty of all kinds of sinister crimes. But if so, Pulling did not quote it. One is left with the unsatisfactory end of the police "closing in" on them. In itself this would not matter, but while such articles are extremely common, subsequent reports of the Satanists being tried and convicted are not. Here is an English example, from the *Star*:

> Police were quizzing teenagers about a black magic coven yesterday after the charred remains of a cat were found on a beach. The youngsters apparently admitted to officers they dressed in cloaks for candle-lit satanic ceremonies at an Iron Age hill fort at Tickenham, near Bristol. Police confirm they have questioned eight pupils and ex-pupils of nearby Clevedon school. A spokesman said: "Practicing satanism is not a criminal offence—but sacrificing animals certainly is.[56]

Once again, any causal connection between the dead cat and the teenage Satan worshipers is obscure, except for the police's suspicion that there might have been one. As it happens, in this case the only evidence was the testimony of a teenage girl from the school, who subsequently admitted to lying. It was finally discovered that the cat had been the pet of an old lady and had died of natural causes, after which its owner had decided to give it a sort of Viking funeral.[57]

Cats often go missing, of course. Every so often a conspiracy theory develops that they are being stolen by vivisectionists, Indian or Chinese restaurateurs who serve them up to unwitting customers, or fur merchants (nearly always said to be foreigners, though one would have thought it easy enough to capture cats on one's own territory, without having to go to another country).

Early in 1998, the Royal Society for the Prevention of Cruelty to Animals (RSPCA) noted that cats in London suburbs were being found decapitated, the bodies dumped near the owners' homes. Inevitably, it was speculated that Satanists were responsible. As a matter of fact, one of the first victims had belonged to an Uxbridge, West London, witch, who was horrified and did a ritual with the intention of putting a stop to whatever was going on. There were no more mutilations in her area, but toward the end of the year, the press reported that others had occurred elsewhere in the southeast of England, notably in Tunbridge Wells, best known for its reputation as the most conservative town in Britain. At the Pagan Federation's Yule ritual, the Uxbridge witch therefore arranged for a group invocation of Bast, the Egyptian cat goddess, to "get her claws into" whoever was responsible.

By this time, some forty cats were said to have been beheaded. The newspapers, however, were cautious for once. The *Guardian* did print an interview with Gavin Baddeley of the Church of Satan, who said that he preferred cats to most people, and would much rather strangle the human population of Tunbridge Wells than the feline.[58] Three months later it was reported that police investigations had been called off because it had been concluded, after further study, that in almost all the cases the animals had, in fact, died in road accidents, further mutilations being caused by scavengers.[59]

The Satanist Connection

Sometimes crimes have been "linked" or "connected" to Satanism, but the links tend to be very tenuous. On 21 December 1996, police investigating a Belgian pedophile case raided the Institut Abrasax, which is also the headquarters of the Luciferian Initiation Order and the Belgian Church of Satan, all three organizations being run from the same semidetached house in the small town of Forchies-la-Marche. The raid was used as an excuse for sensational spreads in the Belgian press, who juxtaposed material about the pedophile case and the search for bodies with pictures of Satanic regalia and rites.

The previous August, Marc Dutroux had confessed to sexual abuse and several murders, of children and of his former accomplice, Bernard Weinstein. Among Weinstein's effects was a letter to him mentioning a "high priestess" and signed "Anubis." The police discovered that the Institut Abrasax was run by a woman known by mystical title of the high priestess Nahema-Nephthys and her partner, Anubis.

Officers found candles, chalices, ceremonial knives, inverted pentagrams, skulls, and, in the refrigerator, blood purchased at the butcher's. But they found nothing to link the couple to any crime. They were not arrested and denied having known Dutroux or Weinstein. The occult pseudonym Anubis is widely used, the title "high priestess" even more so. In an interview with *Le Soir*, "Anubis" said the letter to Weinstein was not by him and that, judging from the contents, it must have emanated from a matriarchal group.[60]

While the letter indicates that Weinstein had some kind of interest in the occult, just what would that prove? He had formerly stolen cars in company with Dutroux, who killed him because he had informed on him to the police. The only occult "connection" to Dutroux, then, is that one of his victims was an occultist.

Stories about Satanism are often illustrated with pictures of Satanic graffiti and damaged churchyards, the implication being that these things are the work of a widespread Devil-worshiping cult. In fact, on the occasions when culprits have been caught, they have usually proved to be ordinary pranksters. It should be borne in mind, first, that daubing "666" on the wall of a church is exactly the sort of thing that appeals to a vandal's mentality; and second, that some people will go to incredible lengths in pursuit of "fun." In 1974 a man confessed in court that he and five friends had taken a corpse from the vaults of Highgate Cemetery, decapitated it, and left it in a nearby parked car. He then took the head home and put it on his mantelpiece until it began to smell. He said they did all this "for a laugh."[61]

On 19 August 1987, Michael Ryan went on a shooting spree in the small English town of Hungerford in Berkshire, killing fourteen people and wounding sixteen others, as well as setting his own house on fire, before using his last bullet on himself. On the face of it, this had nothing to do with Satanism. Some weeks later, however, a Swindon man named Paul Borreson who ran a postal role-playing game called Further into Fantasy stated that Ryan had been one of his players, under the name of Phodius Tei, and that shortly before the massacre he had been given instructions to "kill his fellow Terrans." (Fantasy role-playing games are supposed to be "occult" by anti-Satanists; hence they often write this story up.) Borreson was interviewed by police but was not able to provide any proof of his claim.[62]

Gavin Sneddon, who was a player of Further into Fantasy, confirms that there had been a character called Phodius Tei, whose real identity no one seemed to know (though played largely by post, many of the players did get together on occasion), and who disappeared from the game immediately after the Hungerford massacre. He points out, however, that Borreson was "fond of manipulating other people's perception of reality," and that if Ryan had been a player, Borreson would certainly have had proof in the form of letters from him. If Borreson was telling the truth, then he must have deliberately refrained from showing correspondence from Ryan to police. In short, there is no evidence for an occult basis to this incident.

In Britain there have been some genuine, court-tried cases of child sexual abuse in which there were ritual elements. Peter McKenzie, who was sentenced to fifteen years' imprisonment in August 1989, seduced children into a "web of pedophilia with overtones of witchcraft." He had called himself "Captain Wizard" and used the occult as a bait to attract children to him, by lighting candles, teaching them to pray to Asmodeus, and so on.[63]

This is rather different, however, from what is alleged about Satanic abuse. There was only one perpetrator; there was no blood sacrifice or similar violence; and the occult appears to have been merely a device, child sex being McKenzie's real interest. Another method he used to gain access to children was offering mathematics tuition.

In the same way, in Worcester in 1990, Reginald Harris was given two and a half years' imprisonment for seducing a girl of fifteen and her younger sister. It was said that he had drawn up a Satanic contract of marriage with the elder girl. The judge described Harris as "seeking to obtain dominance of their minds by the pretense of witchcraft or black magic to continue to gratify your desires."[64] In Stafford in 1986, Shaun Wilding pleaded guilty to sexual abuse of four underage boys. It was reported that he got them to form a circle while he "chanted in a theatrical cape pretending to call up the devil."[65] There were at least six such cases (backed by courts) in Britain from 1986 to 1992, roughly one a year. It is impossible to say how far these abusers took their occultism seriously, but as Jean LaFontaine says in the British government report, in these instances the rituals were "secondary to the sexual abuse which clearly formed the primary objective of the perpetrators"[66]—as opposed to Satanic abuse, where allegedly the abuse is only a means to some obscure Satanic purpose.

J. Pengelly and C. Waredale, authors of the Pagan Federation's handbook *Something Out of Nothing*, point out: "In 1990 alone, there were no less than *eight* reported cases in Britain of Christian ministers being *convicted* of child abuse, some of them with ritualistic overtones."[67] Now, there are one-thousand child-abuse convictions a year in Great Britain, out of 45 million adults (one out of every forty-five thousand). But there are about thirty-eight thousand Protestant and Catholic priests, among which number there should be on average less than one sex offense per year. This suggests that British clergymen are almost ten times more likely to commit child abuse than the average person.

It is not possible to do a similar calculation for occultists, since there are no reliable estimates of their numbers. There would have to be fewer than fifty-thousand of them, however, for one conviction a year for child abuse

to be of significance. The anti-Satanists usually estimate the number of occultists to be much larger than fifty-thousand. It should also be remembered that while churches are meant to be self-policing bodies, "the occult"
cannot do that.

In most of the above cases, the crimes are real enough, but usually the
occult connection is tenuous. Another type of "occult crime" is where the
occultism is real but the crime proves impossible to pin down or vanishes
on examination. Andrew Boyd's *Blasphemous Rumors* states: "Disputed
sources have it that Crowley's own son died a ritual death."[68] Boyd would
appear to be implying that Crowley sacrificed his own son in some kind
of blood ritual.

The reference, however, is to a story told in chapter 14 of Dennis Wheatley's *To the Devil—A Daughter*. The hero, C.B., an Expert on Satanism, relates a story about Aleister Crowley that he says he heard firsthand.

According to C.B., Crowley attempted to raise the god Pan in an upstairs
room of a Paris hotel. Though thirteen men were present, only Crowley and
his senior disciple, "McAleister" (his "magical son"), were present at the actual evocation, the other eleven waiting downstairs. The eleven were ordered on no account to interrupt the proceedings. During the night, they
heard screams and crashes from above, which terrified them, but they followed their instructions and did nothing.

At dawn, they knocked on the door of the room but got no reply. Eventually, they broke it down. McAleister lay on his back, dead, a look of stark
horror on his face. Crowley sat naked in a corner, a gibbering idiot. He had
to be taken to a private asylum, and it was six months before he recovered
his sanity.[69]

To the Devil—A Daughter is fiction, of course; but in this case, one could
argue that it really happened, because Wheatley repeated the story in his introduction to Crowley's *Moonchild*, saying that he had heard it from one of
those present. In 1969, the Crowley biographer Gerald Suster wrote to
Wheatley asking his authority; Wheatley replied that he had heard it from a
former disciple of Crowley, who subsequently became a distinguished
Labour M.P. He declined to name him, but the only man fitting this description is the late Tom Driberg, a disciple of Crowley in the 1920s, a friend
of Wheatley, subsequently a Labour cabinet minister—and all of his life, a
notorious liar.

Crowley considered a number of men as candidates for his "magical
son," including Driberg, but never fixed on anyone. He lived in Paris on and
off from 1925 to 1929, but Gerald Yorke, who was in constant contact with

him during this period, knew nothing of the story. When Suster wrote to Israel Regardie, who was Crowley's secretary from October 1928 onward, Regardie replied: "I think Dennis Wheatley is nuts!" Subsequently Suster read through Crowley's diaries for this period and found no reference to the Pan ritual, nor any gap that would indicate a period of insanity.[70] It might be added that the idea that there must be thirteen at a ritual had no part in the ceremonial magic tradition to which Crowley belonged.

Thus, a little investigation takes us from "Crowley's own son died a ritual death" to discovering, first, that the "son" was only honorary, a title of the leading disciple; second, that he was not sacrificed but apparently died of fright; third, that the whole story was pure fiction anyway.

Brief anecdotes like that above are scattered all through anti-Satanist literature, usually with no reference given for those who might wish to know more. William J. Petersen's *Those Curious New Cults in the 80s* remarks in the chapter on Satanism: "A San Diego coed had the assignment of hacking off a limb from a male student's body."[71] Did this occur as part of an anatomy class, or in some other situation? *The Fortune Sellers*, by Gary Wilburn (an inauspicious surname for a Christian Evangelist), which tells you not to have your fortune told, has a section complaining that occultism has been admitted into some American college courses. Among these, "the University of Alabama's new experimental college encourages, in their witchcraft course, a field trip to view the Black Mass as celebrated at a nearby church."[72] That is all Wilburn relates. Surely most readers would like to know just what church it is, in Alabama of all places, that regularly celebrates public Black Masses!

We are also often told by Experts on Satanism that "Aleister Crowley . . . claimed to have murdered 150 male children every year between 1912 and 1928."[73] Tim Tate shows by multiplication that 150 children a year for sixteen years makes 2,400.[74] He does not explain why the police were never alerted.

In chapter 12 of his *Magick in Theory and Practice*, "Of the Bloody Sacrifice," Crowley wrote: "For the highest spiritual working one must accordingly choose that victim which contains the greatest and purest force. A male child of perfect innocence and high intelligence is the most satisfactory and suitable victim." He added in a footnote: "It appears from the Magical Records of Frater Perdurabo that He made this particular sacrifice on an average about 150 times every year between 1912 e.v. and 1928 e.v."[75] Frater Perdurabo was a magical name of Crowley himself.

So Aleister Crowley really did claim to have murdered 150 children a year between 1912 and 1928. The same footnote, however, goes on to give the "initiated interpretation" that "it is the sacrifice of oneself spiritually . . . what he sacrifices is not the material blood, but his creative power," suggesting that the statement was meant to be understood only metaphorically. The obvious question, then, which anti-Satanists neglect, is: Was Crowley's statement literally true?

Crowley's "Magical Records," referred to above, describe his rituals and operations in terms like this: "1 Feb [1920]. 12.30 am. Opus I, 31-666-31 poD. Opus difficult but excellent in the end. Elixir plenteous and rich. Object: That I may perform the Task of a Magus."[76]

The series 31-666-31 signifies "Alostrael," the magical name of Crowley's mistress, Leah Hirsig; "poD" is short for "per os Dominae," meaning "through the Lady's mouth." It does not take much imagination to figure out what kind of plenteous rich elixir Crowley produced with the aid of his mistress's mouth. A study of his diary for 1920 reveals 129 such workings, with a few others probably unrecorded. Thus, the total came to nearly 150 a year.

Clearly, then, when Crowley referred to the sacrifice of a "male child," he meant semen, which is a child of such "perfect innocence" that it has not even been conceived. Crowley's biographers and commentators, of whom there are many, are agreed that this was what he meant by this passage. In contrast, though Crowley's life has been researched and charted in great, often boring detail, no one has come up with the least evidence that he ever really performed a human sacrifice.

Crowley hinted that sex should be substituted for blood sacrifice elsewhere in the chapter "Of the Bloody Sacrifice," for example: "The Serpent is not really killed; it is seethed in an appropriate vessel; and it issues in due season refreshed and modified, but still essentially itself."[77] Few readers will have trouble figuring this one out.

One could fairly criticize Crowley for making a joke in such bad taste. Some people would be offended, even outraged at the fact that he made the sexual act an integral part of his magical rites. But in taking his statement about the sacrifice of the male child literally, anti-Satanists only demonstrate their unique combination of ignorance and prejudice.

It is, of course, possible that a would-be magician might take Crowley's words at face value. Just this was claimed at the trial of Rikki Neave in October 1996, on the charge of murdering her six-year-old son. The "occult-obsessed" woman was alleged to have strangled the boy, then dumped his body in a copse near their home. A copy of *Magick* was found to be in her possession. The prosecutor suggested to the jury that she may have killed him as a sacrifice as described in the book.[78]

Though the jury found Neave guilty of cruelty to her children, for which she was sentenced to seven years' imprisonment, they held her to be innocent of her son's murder, since there was evidence that his body had only been deposited some time after the police had arrived at her home. In fact, it was precisely because there was no evidence she had committed the murder that, in order to present some kind of a case, the prosecution drew attention to *Magick* and the possibility of human sacrifice.

This chapter and the preceding have shown that there is very little evidence for Satanic crime in either this century or any previous one—certainly not enough for the matter to be regarded as especially important. Yet there has undeniably been a tremendous amount of concern about Satanism over the centuries, and certainly in the last few years. If real crime is not the cause of these panics, then what is?

6

Hell on Earth

In the early Middle Ages, many people were disillusioned with the corruption of the Catholic Church. Christianity had been founded on ideals of voluntary poverty, yet the churches were the largest and best-appointed buildings. Priests often lived in great luxury, and many of them took mistresses or even wives; eventually the pope was forced to reaffirm clerical celibacy. In the south of France, many people went their own way and developed a creed known as Catharism, from the Greek *catharos*, "pure." Their theology, said to have been derived from Persia, taught that this world and everything in it were the work of the Devil. Only a human's spirit was of God. Therefore, everything of this world should be rejected.

In a way, this was a return to primitive Christianity. The high moral standards of the Cathars became well known. But the regular church objected: it was heretical to say that the Devil created this world, an act ascribed to God in the Bible. And they did not like it that the Cathars had ceased to pay church taxes.

About 1180, a cleric named Gervaise of Tilbury, in the retinue of the archbishop of Rheims, tried to persuade an attractive girl to sleep with him. She refused on the grounds that losing her virginity would certainly send her to hell. Now, fornication, in Catholic doctrine, is a sin, but not an unforgivable sin. In contrast, believing that fornication is an unforgivable sin is heresy, which *is* an unforgivable sin. So the girl was arrested, accused of Catharism, tortured, and burned at the stake. The chronicler who recorded this story calmly declared that the Cathars' high moral standards were only a cover for debauchery.[1]

To counter the Cathars, at the start of the thirteenth century Pope Innocent III arranged for the setting up of the Dominican order, of whose founder, Saint Dominic, Philip van Limborch wrote:

> His mother, before she conceived him, is said to have dreamed, that she was with Child of a Whelp, carrying in his Mouth a lighted Torch; and that after he was born, he put the World in an Uproar by his fierce Barkings,

and set it on Fire by the Torch that he carried in his Mouth. His Followers interpret this Dream of his Doctrine, by which he enlightened the whole World; whereas others, if Dreams presage any thing, think that the Torch was an Emblem of that Fire and Faggot, by which an infinite Multitude of Men were burnt to Ashes.[2]

The Dominicans were supposed at first to be preaching friars who would go around districts of heretics, converting them back to the true faith. Unfortunately, as far as the Cathars were concerned, this approach failed completely. So instead the pope decided to employ firmer means of persuasion, and in 1208 he arranged a military crusade to wipe them out completely. Uncertain who was a Cathar and who was not, the troops were told to kill everybody: "God will know his own." This ambitious project took fifteen years.

To prevent such heresies springing up again, the Council of Toulouse in 1229 prescribed death by burning at the stake for "cases of obstinacy," that is, those who refused to renounce their non-Catholic religious beliefs. By a bull of Gregory IX in 1232, Dominicans were turned from a preaching order to an investigative one, who *inquired* into people's faith. They became better known as the Inquisition.

Since it was felt a little unfair to suppress societies, with torture and execution, because they had higher moral standards than the orthodoxy, some Inquisitors found it convenient to indulge in fantasies about what they *really* got up to. Thus it was said that the Cathars held secret nocturnal orgies where Lucifer appeared in person in the shape of a cat.[3] (This detail may have been a pun on "Cathar" and "cat.") They worshiped him by kissing his anus, so the Holy Office asserted; then they put out the lights and engaged in promiscuous sex. If any children resulted, they ate them.

A set of rules were devised whereby the property of heretics condemned by the Inquisition became forfeit and went to those who had accused them and to the Inquisitors who had conducted the proceedings. This ensured that there was always a plentiful supply of suspected heretics. Accusations could be made anonymously (unlike in regular courts of law) and tended to be believed over anything the accused might say. Furthermore, it was a duty to make accusations, and one who failed to accuse even close relatives might be held to be guilty himself.

Anyone who felt doubt or uncertainty about the correctness of the Inquisition's proceedings would be well advised to keep those thoughts to herself; otherwise she might be labeled as one of the "Favourers of Heretics" or

"Hinderers of the Office of the Inquisition." A certain Friar Bernard Deliciosi of Toulouse said of some condemned heretics, "*That though they were true Catholicks, they were forced by the Violence of their Tortures to confess themselves and others guilty of Heresy, and that they were unjustly condemned*"; and he publicly asserted that "*St.* Peter *and St.* Paul *could not defend themselves from Heresy if they were alive, and had Inquisition made against them in the Manner practiced by the Inquisitors.*" For making this statement he was condemned to imprisonment in irons, to be fed only on bread and water, for life.[4]

There was always a certain delicacy felt about the Inquisition's proceedings, and many of them were concealed by euphemistic language. For example, the Inquisition never imprisoned people: rather, they "invited them" to stay at one of the Inquisition's "hotels" or "holy houses." Suspected heretics were not tortured but given "the Question" to encourage confession (with the incidental aid of racks, thumbscrews, etc.). Nor was anyone put to death, since priests were forbidden to shed blood: instead, heretics were "relaxed," that is, "handed over to the secular arm." This always meant that they were executed (by nonecclesiastics) at once, normally by burning at the stake.

It might be wondered how the general population ever tolerated all this. Sometimes they did not, and there were instances where an Inquisitor was compelled by an angry mob to leave town hurriedly. But very often the Inquisition acted with the citizens' full approval. The public burning of a heretic was always a popular spectacle in those dull days when there was no television and people had to make their own entertainment. Such "Acts of Faith" (as they were called) were always held on holy days and carried out in theatrical fashion. The victim would be suspended some way above the fire, so that death would not occur for an hour or more, prolonging the audience's enjoyment as long as possible. An English visitor to Portugal remarked that these executions were "beheld by People of both Sexes, and all Ages, with such Transports of Joy and Satisfaction, as are not on any other Occasion to be met with."[5]

Heresies sprang up all over the place. The people of Stedlinger in North Germany stopped paying taxes to the church. The Inquisition promptly dubbed them "Luciferians" and said that their master appeared in person at their meetings in the shape of a cat. Then there was Peter of Waldo, who also preached a return to simple Christianity (though without a new theology), and whose followers became known as the "Poor Men of Lyons," or the Waldensians, which corrupted in French to Vaudois. They have survived to this day, despite tremendous persecution, being accused of debauchery and all the usual things.

In 1307, Philip the Fair, king of France, arranged for the Inquisition to act against a religious-military body known as the Knights Templars. Sealed instructions were sent to law officers all over France, to be opened on the thirteenth of October. They ordered the arrest of all the Templars.

After the knights had been tortured for a while, they made a remarkable series of confessions. At their initiation ceremonies, it was said, they denied Christ, trampled on the cross, and were instructed to worship an idol in the shape of a human head, known as Baphomet. They also confessed to sodomy and that Lucifer appeared at their meetings in the shape of a cat. Later most of them retracted these confessions, saying that they had made them only because they were tortured; but in 1314, most of them were burned at the stake anyway.

What does one make of such confessions? Norman Cohn writes:

> Most people have always found it difficult to believe that even the most auto-cratic ruler could or would fabricate an entire body of accusations out of nothing, and then compel great numbers of innocent victims to substantiate them. With the example of Stalin's trials before our eyes, we should have no such difficulty . . . the charges against the Templars were absolutely without foundation.[6]

Cohn points out that the real Templar initiation ceremony has survived and is, in fact, perfectly orthodox. In any case, if a series of blasphemies had taken place at the first initiation, the young men of good family who joined in innocence would hardly have stayed when they found out what was involved. If the Templars had really corrupted their members, they would have had to have done so slowly, and not at the moment they joined.

To be fair, not all the accusations were absurd: sodomy has often been common in "celibate" orders. There are still many unanswered questions about the Templars; it is at least possible that, their minds broadened by foreign travel, they had developed unorthodox ideas about religion. But as with the other heretics, these would have been in the form of ideas about piety rather than the practice of wickedness.

The most curious confession was that they worshiped an idol called Baphomet. If this means anything, it is perhaps the Greek *bapho-metis*, "baptism of wisdom." Baphomet was usually said to be a bearded head. In the former Templar church at Templecombe in Somerset is a painted wooden board showing a bearded head; it obviously represents the head of Jesus.

A modern myth has built up about Baphomet and is so commonly repeated that its origin must be related. In the nineteenth century, the Orientalist Joseph von Hammer described various sculptured stone coffers, found in Burgundy, which he believed had once belonged to the Knights Templars. Some had inscriptions in Arabic writing, and one showed a naked figure "with a head-dress resembling that given to Cybele in ancient monuments, holding up a chain with each hand, and surrounded with various symbols, the sun, and moon above, the star and the pentacle below, and under the feet a human skull."[7] These von Hammer explained as Gnostic symbols. It does not seem to be proved that these objects ever belonged to the Templars (some writers consider them fakes), and even if they did, they might simply have brought them back from the Middle East as souvenirs and cared nothing for their mystical significance.

The French occultist Eliphas Lévi, however, who was responsible for a number of baseless assertions about Black Magic that have been repeated often enough to have acquired the status of "facts," redrew the Cybele-style image to make it look more like a conventional devil, with goat's legs and the like.[8] An engraver employed by Léo Taxil copied Lévi's "Baphomet" exactly in his illustrations of what *really* went on in Masonic lodges. Since then, the symbol has become a clichéd symbol of Devil worship; a few years ago it was reported that Anton LaVey had tried to copyright it.[9] The upshot is that many Experts on Satanism assert that the Templars worshiped an Eliphas Lévi drawing.

It may be asked: Why are modern scholars so sure that the accusations brought by the Inquisition were false? Apart from the fact that no explanation has been offered as to why large numbers of people should collectively suffer such a breakdown of normal conscience, the main reasons are:

1. Only some writers mentioned the accusations of debauchery. The more responsible Inquisitors, such as Nicolas Eymeric and Bernard Gui, gave a more or less accurate, if disapproving, summary of the Cathar and Waldensian religions. Cannibalistic orgies were described only by the fanatics, such as Conrad of Marburg, and sensationalists, such as Walter Map. It is not plausible that Gui and Eymeric, hostile as they were, would have passed over such stories if they had any reason to believe they were true.

2. There is abundant evidence that, in fact, these sects had high moral

standards. Genuine texts circulated among the Cathars have survived; the Waldensians have physically survived all attempts to exterminate them to the present day. Accordingly, much is known of what they really believed, and it is plain that, far from being engaged in Devil worship and wickedness, they were renouncers of things of the flesh. One of the more serious contemporary writers on the Waldensians, David of Augsburg, remarked that the only occasion when the allegations of sexual laxity were true was in the case of Waldensian preachers who had determined to live a celibate life but had found this too difficult a decision to keep to.

3. The stories include many absurdities, such as Lucifer appearing in the shape of a cat.
4. The proceedings were conducted in such a way as to encourage false confessions and accusations by and about innocent people.
5. No physical evidence, in the form of bodies, for instance, was ever produced to back up the stories of human sacrifice.
6. Stories about cannibal orgies belong to a literary tradition that can be traced. Back in the eighth century, John of Ojun, the head of the Armenian Church, wrote a tract condemning the Paulician heretics, whom he accused of being both atheists and Devil worshipers. Their turpitudes were perpetrated, he wrote, under cover of darkness, and at these hidden meetings they committed incest with their own mothers. If a child was born, "they throw it from hand to hand until it dies, and he in whose hand it expires is promoted to leadership of the sect. The blood of these infants is mixed with flour to make the Eucharist; and so these people surpass the gluttony of pigs who devour their own brood."[10]

Also in the literary traditions of cannibalism and infanticide, a Greek dialogue described the secrets of the Euchites, a medieval Gnostic sect, like this:

> On the very evening that we light candles to celebrate the passion-tide of our Lord savior, they lead into a prescribed house those girls who are to be initiated into their sacrilegious rites. Extinguishing the lamps, that no light may give witness to their abominable crimes, each throws himself lecherously on the girls, taking whoever comes to hand, whether she be his sister, or his own daughter, or his mother. For they believe that it is pleasing to their demons if they transgress the laws of God, which forbid marriages between blood relatives. And this ritual being done, they are dismissed from the house. Nine months later, when the unnatural progeny of unnatural union is due to be

born, they assemble in the same house, and on the fourth day after birth, they snatch the unfortunate babies from their mothers, cutting and incising their flesh with a knife, they catch the dripping blood in bowls, then, still breathing, they are thrown on a fire and burnt up. Afterwards, mixing the ashes with the blood in the bowls, they make their abominable potion, which they mix with food and drink.[11]

One of the earliest medieval heresy trials was of a group of Manichaeans burned by order of Robert I in 1022. The synod of Orleans in that year described the Manichaean's religious rites thus:

> They assembled on certain nights in an appointed house, each holding a lantern in his hand, then called out a sort of litany of demons' names, until suddenly they saw the Demon appear in their midst in the shape of some animal. Straight away, so that the vision could be clearly seen, all the lamps were put out, and as fast as they could each seized whatever woman came to hand, without respect of sin, whether he had his mother, or his sister, or a nun, considering such intercourse to be holy and religious; and if a child was conceived from that most foul intercourse, on the eighth day they lit a large fire in their midst, and they passed it through the fire like the ancient Pagans; and thus it was cremated in the fire. Its ashes were collected and kept with as great a veneration as the Body of Christ in the Christian religion, and when sick to the point of death given to them as a viaticum. There was such a diabolic fraud in those ashes that a man belonging to the heresy who once tasted them, could scarcely ever after be persuaded to abandon his heresies and walk on the true path.[12]

In the twelfth century, the chronicler Guibert de Nogent said of the Soisson heretics: "They light a great fire and all sit around it. They pass the child from hand to hand and finally throw it on the fire, and leave it there until it is entirely consumed. Later, when the child is burned to ashes, they make those ashes into a sort of bread; each eats a piece by way of communion."[13]

Among the rumors that circulated about the Knights Templar was one concerning their "cord of chastity," to which was attributed magical properties, "so powerful that as long as it was worn no Templar could abandon his errors." Also: "Sometimes a Templar who died in this false belief was burned, and of his ashes a powder was made which confirmed the neophytes in their infidelity. When a child was born of a virgin to a Templar it was roasted, and of its fat an ointment was made wherewith to anoint the idol worshiped in the chapters, to which, according to other rumors, human sacrifices were offered."[14]

In a sermon delivered by Saint Bernardin of Siena in 1427 is an account of a nocturnal meeting called the *barilotto*: "Bernardin gives the usual account of the promiscuous nocturnal orgy, of the tossing to death of the baby boy, of the making of the powders. . . . The sect which performs these rites calls itself 'the people of the barilotto.'"[15] *Barilotto* means "little barrel," that is, the flask in which the mixture of powdered ashes and wine is kept.

Saint Bernardin did not name any particular sect as being responsible; he merely hinted that "some of the people are to be found in Piedmont"—which might be a reference to the Waldensians. In 1453, however, Flavio Biondo, apostolic secretary in Rome, wrote a book called *Italy Illustrated*, in which he referred to a sect known as the Fraticelli and attributed the same *barilotto* story to them. He, too, said they had orgies with the lights extinguished:

> If a woman conceives from this coition, when the child is born it is taken to a gathering in a hidden cave where it is passed from hand to hand until all have held it and its life has departed. And whoever's hands it was in when it died becomes the highest divine pontiff, and is said to have the spirit of creation. And when otherwise one of the many depraved women offers a foetus, the priests gathering together incinerate it on the fire, and collect the ashes in a little vessel and mix them with wine, which the novitiates are given as a sacred drink at their execrable initiations; and because of this cruel superstition of drinking from a little vessel they are called by the name of Barilotto.[16]

The Fraticelli were a real sect, but their history was totally different from what Biondo suggested. They were originally a group of Franciscans who were disillusioned by how the order had moved away from Saint Francis's intentions after his death. Originally sworn to absolute poverty, the order had come to own property and was displaying signs of the same decadence that Saint Francis had objected to in the first place. They therefore secretly went back to practicing total poverty; they were kept alive by sympathizers. Though they survived as an underground order until the fifteenth century, by the time that Biondo wrote, the Inquisition was determined to quash them.

In 1466, a number of these Fraticelli, as they became known, were arrested. Under torture, the Inquisitors tried to get them to confess to having attended the *barilotto*. One or two of them did, though they retracted their confessions as soon as they were out of the torture chamber.[17]

These accounts contain no mention of bodies or other physical evidence for such child murders. Occasionally, however, evidence could be made to fit the theory. In 1454, the body of a child was found near the city of Valladolid in Spain, its flesh torn by wild dogs. There may have been a mundane cause; but the preacher Alphonsus a Spina, who was regarded as an Expert on Judaism, declared that the boy must have been murdered by Jews (who were routinely accused of child murder), who had cut out his heart, burned it to ashes, mixed them with wine, then drunk it in their secret rituals.[18]

The Fraticelli had no connection at all to any other sect; nor did the Waldensians. The link between the Euchites, the Paulicians, the Manichaeans, the Soisson heretics, and the Templars, if there was one, could only have been tenuous. And the Jews would have held aloof from all of them, if they even knew about them. Yet all these groups, from several different countries, were accused of much the same abominations, often retold in almost the same words. Physical evidence was not adduced, and confessions were made only after the Inquisition had taken to torturing suspects. The truth is not a continuity of heretical practices but a continuity of baseless accusations by persecutors who did not even have the imagination to invent some new lies.

Indeed, the slander has never stopped being used against one minority religion or another, though it is sometimes toned down a bit. In 1890 it was alleged that at a Methodist revival meeting, of all places, "in a room at the back of the chapel, the gas lights being turned down, men and women indulged freely in promiscuous sexual intercourse."[19] No doubt the cannibal feast was omitted in deference to Victorian decency.

After the suppression of the Knights Templars, the Inquisition went through a period of decline, having done their job too successfully. In 1360, Nicolas Eymeric, author of the *Directory of the Inquisition*, complained: "In our days there are no more rich heretics; so that princes, not seeing much money in prospect, will not put themselves to any expense; it is a pity that so salutary an institution as ours should be uncertain of its future."[20] Fortunately for the starving Inquisitors, a new enemy was found: the conspiracy of witches.

In theory, the Inquisition did not bother itself with secular crimes, which were beneath its dignity—a matter such as murder being considered trivial compared to the outrage to the Divine Majesty of, say, holding the wrong view about the Eucharist. But in practice, they might deal with a common criminal if he was impertinent enough to assert that what he had done was not a sin. Polygamists sometimes claimed it was lawful to have more than one wife, perhaps arguing that if Solomon had seven hundred, why should not an ordinary man have two or three? This elevated their mundane crime to the realm of heresy.

From the twelfth century onward books in Arabic began to be translated into European languages, and these included various books on magic, known as grimoires. Though their contents were of pagan origin, usually they had been rewritten to suit monotheistic magicians. Frequently the Psalms and even the sacraments of the church were used in ceremonies designed to control the spirits.

Naturally, the magicians themselves did not consider their magic sinful. A thirteenth-century handbook of angel magic, the *Sworn Book of Honorius*, even claimed that the pope and his cardinals had been deceived by evil spirits into thinking that magic was a forbidden art.[21] In truth, it said, this was a strategy of devils who wished to put a stop to everything useful to the human race.

But the church had always condemned magic, and it remained obstinate on this point. By 1398, the viewpoint of the *Sworn Book* had become common enough for the Theology Faculty of the University of Paris to feel obliged to produce a list of twenty-eight articles detailing heretical views about magic, for example:

> The first article is that, to seek the familiarity and friendship and help of demons, by magic arts and witchcraft and nefarious invocations, is not idolatry. *Error....*
>
> Sixth, that it is licit or even permitted to use witchcraft to repel witchcraft. *Error....*
>
> Eighth, that magic arts and similar superstitions and their observances have been irrationally prohibited by the Church. *Error....*
>
> Thirteenth, that through such arts the holy Prophets and other Saints made their prophecies, and worked miracles or expelled demons. *Error, & blasphemy....*
>
> Twenty-eighth, that through certain magic arts it is possible to come to a vision of the Divine Essence or the Holy Spirit. *Error.*[22]

It is not surprising that, since magicians held heretical views, they provided a fertile field for the Inquisition. The next time we hear of the subject, it has moved far:

> There are then, or were recently, as Peter the Inquisitor told me, and as is well known around the district of Bern, certain Witches of both sexes, who against the inclination of human nature, worse than every species of beast, excepting only wolves, are accustomed to devour and consume their own children. Now, in the town of Boltingen, in the diocese of Lausanne, a certain leading Witch named Stadelein, arrested by the aforesaid Peter, confessed that he had afflicted the man and wife of a certain house, killing seven successive children

in the wife's womb by his Witchcraft, so that for many years the woman always aborted. He did the same for all the offspring of the herd owned by the house, so that for years none of them were born alive.

And when the aforementioned ill-doer was asked how those crimes and others like them were done, he said: A dead lizard is placed under the doorstep of the house, and if it is removed, the fertility of the inhabitants will return. When this reptile was searched for under the doorstep, and it was not found, because it had reduced to powder, the powder or earth under there was carried away: and in the same year the fertility of the wife and all the beasts of the household returned. This confession was not revealed freely, however, but under torture; and at length he was given to the flames by the aforesaid Judge.

The aforementioned Inquisitor then told me how in the past year, in the Duchy of Lausanne certain Witches had killed and eaten their own children. The manner of acquiring this art was, he said, that the Witches gathered together to worship, and the Devil appeared among them in the assumed shape of a man. The disciples were required to deny the Christian faith, not to adore the Eucharist, and to trample on the Cross whenever possible.[23]

The above, from Johannes Nider's *Formicarius*, written around 1435, is one of the first reports of the great witch craze that went on for some three hundred years. It is apparent that witch trials must have been going on for some time when Nider wrote, though the earliest records seem to be lost. Two things stand out at once from this story. First, there was a very powerful urge to believe in a conspiracy. No evidence was offered except a confession made under torture, and when the lizard, the only thing that would have confirmed it, was not found, it was assumed to have decayed to dust. Nider and Peter the Inquisitor were also prepared to believe in witches eating their own children without, apparently, any evidence at all. Obviously, they were swayed in their belief by something other than the facts. Second, the accusations made against the witches—of worshiping the Devil, eating their own children, and trampling on the cross—are exactly the same as those which had been made about the various sects of heretics; they were made by the same people—the Inquisition—and were no doubt equally baseless.

There had always been people who blamed their misfortunes on evil spirits or curses laid by malevolent sorcerers. It was perfectly possible to take legal action in such a case: if someone died, and it was believed to be the result of a curse, then the alleged maker of the curse might be found guilty of murder.

What made the great witch-hunts possible was the idea that witches formed a *conspiracy*, so that, if one witch was caught, she (or less frequently, he) could be tortured and forced to name others. Few women could resist the effective tortures of the Inquisition, so other witches would be rounded up and made to name others still, and the whole affair could proliferate, going on, in extreme cases, until there were no more women left in the immediate area.

Various other elements were added to build up the standard picture of the witch conspiracy. At that time there seem to have been two types of real-life witches. First were the traditional village wise women, who were herbalists, healers (usually the only type of healer available), and, above all, midwives. The second, who may or may not have been the same women, were those who believed they went flying around at night, in company with a multitude of others, led by the Moon Goddess under one of her many names—Diana, Holda, or the like. The Inquisition accepted that midwives were witches but gave this the most sinister interpretation possible. If a child was stillborn (which must have been common in the Middle Ages), they asserted that the midwife had killed it. If it survived, they said that the midwife had secretly dedicated it to the Devil. And though many people might suppose that women who flew through the sky in the still hours did so merely in their minds, the learned witch-hunters insisted that they did so physically, and of course, they turned the Moon Goddess into the Devil.

Thus, within a few decades, the official belief had gone from merely asserting that it was heresy to say that practicing magic was not a sin, to belief in a vast supernatural conspiracy, whose human agents could, fortunately, be tracked down and executed by the holy men of the church. The complete picture, as the persecutors saw it, went like this: witches flew off at night to a sabbat, where they worshiped the Devil (who appeared in person), as well as making a pact with him after the manner of the *Golden Legend*. They would have sex with demons (it was another folk belief that witches derived their power from a spirit lover) or promiscuously with one another, in the latter case eating any progeny, as had been alleged of previous victims of the Inquisition. They then worked destructive magic, so that anything from a sickly child to a failed crop could be blamed on them.

The real horror, of course, was not the crimes of the witches, which were imaginary, but the appalling persecution of old women who were totally innocent or perhaps guilty only of making herbal remedies. For several decades, witch-hunting was restricted to the region of the Western Alps, but it gradually spread elsewhere. It was assisted in its outward motion by the invention of printing, which brought a fear of Devil-worshiping witches to people who otherwise might never have heard of them. The first printed book to deal exclusively with witches and how to hunt them was the notorious *Malleus Maleficarum*, written by two German Inquisitors, Heinrich Kramer and Jacob Sprenger, which appeared at Speyer in southwest Germany around 1487. The *Malleus* began by arguing that to deny the existence of witches and that they are really transported through the air (rather than only in their minds) was heresy in itself. Did witches really copulate with demons? There could be no doubt about it, since Kramer and Sprenger had burned no fewer than forty-eight women in the past five years alone for that crime.

The Inquisitors went on to suggest interesting ways of securing a conviction. Notorious evildoers and criminals should be admitted as witnesses, as well as known perjurers. If the suspect said she did not believe in witches, that would be a cause for suspicion. If witnesses against her did not agree with one another, except in the general sense that they considered her a witch, then her guilt was nonetheless manifest. If the witch was allowed an advocate, she might not choose him herself; he might not be told the names of the witnesses, and if he "unduly" defended her, he was defending heresy and liable to excommunication. If the accused demanded to know the names of the witnesses, she should be told that she knew already whom she had bewitched. The judge might tell her that her life would be spared if she told the truth and accused others, though the judge did not need to keep this promise once he had the confession. (If he was bothered at breaking his word, he might get another judge to pass the death sentence.) Legally, torture might not be repeated, but it could be "continued" for days at a time; and if the accused was still "impenitent," the judge should use devious methods, such as telling her he intended to be "merciful," meaning that he intended to be merciful to the state and burn all its witches. Kramer and Sprenger themselves had much success with these methods. Such was the interest aroused by their book that at least five other editions had been printed by the end of the century, and books on the same subject by Ulrich Molitor, Petrus Mamor, and Girolamo Visconti also appeared around 1489–90.

Once again, it may be asked: why do modern historians (or many of them) assume that all those accused were innocent? Some reasons are:

1. Most of the accusations contained absurdities: flight on broomsticks, the appearance of the Devil in person, and so forth.

2. Nearly all the accusations made against witches had previously circulated in different forms. Some were those that had been made indifferently about various heretics: kissing the Devil's anus and dining off babies, for instance. But the heretics had not been accused of magic, malefic or otherwise, and in reality, most of them practiced austere forms of Christianity; they would not have had any connection with sorcery. The real explanation must be that the conspiracy theorists of the time had combined all their favorite horror stories into one grand diabolic conspiracy.

3. Most of the confessions were made under severe torture, or at least the threat of torture. In England, where torture was not permitted, few witches confessed to anything.

4. Often there were ulterior motives for the witch-hunts. In Germany, a bad harvest would set off a hunt for the witches whose spells were presumed to have blighted the crops. In other instances, witch-hunts started from above, being initiated by Inquisitors or professional witch-finders, who had to keep finding witches in order to earn a decent living.

5. Genuine books on magic have survived from the same period, and their contents are totally different from the things alleged against witches. Far from involving Devil worship, they assume Christian belief. These represent only the learned tradition (illiteracy was then the rule), but what survives of the "unlearned" witch tradition is also quite different, being concerned with simple charms, herbalism, and divination.

The witch craze has been written up many times before, and only a few highlights need be noted here. In the first century of the persecution, witches were dealt with only by the Inquisition. When the Reformation started, witch-hunting died down, as Inquisitors had plenty of real heretics to occupy themselves with. But when Europe had settled down and the lines between Protestant and Catholic areas had become clearly defined, witch-hunting started up again. Now it was done by secular judges as well as Inquisitors. Nor did the Reformers abandon this aspect of the Catholic religion; Martin Luther himself said in one of his sermons: "Sorcerers or Witches are the wicked devil's whores who steal milk, raise storms, ride on goats or broom-sticks, travel on mantles, shoot, lame and maim people, torment children in their cradles, change things into different shapes—so that what is really a human being seems to be a cow or an ox—and force people into love and immorality."[24]

By 1598, Ludovico à Paramo, author of the laudatory *The Origin and Progress of the Holy Office of the Inquisition, Its Worthiness and Usefulness*, could write:

> Neither shall I pass over in silence, what a wonderful benefit the Holy Office of the Inquisition has brought to the human race, by the vast multitude of Witches they have burnt. Wherein is heard report, not only of vulgar and common hags, such as were found in previous years in some provinces of Spain (who are the instruments of demons, and will be cast with them into the eternal bonfire) but even that peculiar species of Witches, who in Germany and Italy, from the year 1404 gave themselves up to belief in a sort of Devil worship, against whom the Inquisition fought so hard, that in the hundred and fifty years up to the present day, at least thirty thousand Witches have been burnt, who if they had been left unpunished, could easily have brought destruction and ruin to the whole world.[25]

If his figure of thirty-thousand was approximately right, then the final total must have been much larger, as many were also burned by secular authorities, and the craze went on for a century or so after Paramo wrote.

The intensity of witch-hunting varied, however, depending on the local legal procedures. In Holland, from the 1640s onward every accused witch had the right to go to be tested at the town of Oudewater, where she would be weighed against the church Bible. In theory, she was found innocent only if she balanced it on the scales, but in practice, the good people of the town would make sure this always happened and gave her a certificate of innocence. For this reason, virtually no witches were put to death in Holland after about 1640, though hundreds had been executed in the previous century.[26] The most intensive witch-hunts occurred where the accused had no right of appeal to any higher court.

In Spain, the Inquisition was mainly interested in wealthy heretics whose riches it could confiscate. While this was hardly admirable, it did have the accidental consequence that Inquisitors could not work up much enthusiasm for finding witches, who were typically poor country women and not worth the bother. It seems that Inquisitors in Spain did not adopt the system, common in some places, of charging a flat-rate fee for each witch, payable out of public funds; nor were they inclined to press ahead with the destruction of evil if they had nothing to gain personally. In several instances, they were thus able to conclude what should have been obvious everywhere: that women who believed they flew on broomsticks did so only in their minds, their bodies remaining at home. Some witches were executed in Spain, but not many; they were more likely to be told that they were deluded.[27]

In Germany, witch-hunting was not intensive until the late sixteenth century but finally achieved such enormity as to defy belief. The laws of the Holy Roman Empire, to which all the many German states subscribed, demanded torture and death for witches. The Devil being the father of lies, his servants would not tell the truth willingly; therefore the rack was needed to abstract it from them. It was common for a priest to bless the instruments of torture before use, and because they were thus sanctified, it was supposed, they broke the power of the Devil. For the especially obstinate cases special means were invented, such as the witch's chair, a metal seat covered in spikes, under which a fire would be lit. The witch then nearly always confessed the truth within fifteen minutes.

Sometimes the torture proved fatal. In once instance, a woman was left on the rack, with heavy weights tied to her legs, while the officials of the court went to a tavern for lunch. When they came back, she was dead. They concluded she had committed suicide, at the behest of the Devil, which proved her guilt. In contrast, when a sixty-four-year-old woman in Bamberg died after application of the thumbscrew, the boot, and the rack, it was ruled that her failure to confess proved she was innocent, so she was permitted Christian burial.[28]

For some places, precise figures of the numbers of victims are known: 368 put to death in the vicinity of Treves between 1587 and 1594, two villages being completely wiped out; 77 in Burgstadt, a town of fewer than three thousand inhabitants, in a single year; 133 in one day in 1589 in the town of Quedlinberg.[29] Protestant areas adopted the Catholic practice of confiscating all the worldly goods of those found guilty of witchcraft, so that leading and wealthy citizens were often accused. The usual method of execution was burning at the stake, but an ingenious man in Neisse in Silesia devised a sort of big oven, in which forty-two women and girls were roasted to death in one year alone.

Copies of the *Malleus Maleficarum* and other such books were imported into Elizabethan England, and under their influence, witchcraft was made a capital offense in 1563. But torture was officially not permitted in England, and large-scale witch-hunts seldom occurred. Most of the witches who were executed were accused only of cursing their neighbors (rather than attendance at the sabbat). Often the only evidence presented was that a man had fallen ill or died, the presumption that this was due to malefic witchcraft by the accused being almost unargued. Execution, when carried out, was always by hanging rather than burning.

The main exception to the prohibition against torture occurred during the career of Matthew Hopkins, "Witch-Finder General," who bent the rules on what pressure he was allowed to put on the accused. He would have suspects tied up and deprived of sleep, ostensibly to encourage their familiar spirit to appear to them but incidentally to encourage confessions. Of course, when they did they named others, and in a career of less than two years Hopkins was responsible for perhaps two hundred executions. Nonetheless, the total number of condemned witches in Britain is believed to have been less than one thousand.

In Scotland, the craze started late, the first big occurrence being in 1589. *The Historie and Life of King James the Sext* relates that in that year: "Satan, with his great craft in deceiving of Christian people, did assemble certain of his supposts, some of the masculine, others of the feminine kind, in the Kirk of Northberwick at midnight, the last day of October, of whom divers were executed to the death. The cause of their assembly was to raise storms in the sea, to stay Queen Anne to come safely to Scotland."[30]

Once again, though Scotland had its own witch tradition, the malefic conspiracy theory of witchcraft was an importation. This is made clear by the book written in the wake of the above case by James VI of Scotland (later James I of England) himself, *Daemonologie*, the preface to which mentions some continental witch theorists while the body of the text reproduces their arguments.

In Scotland, torture was not permitted without a royal warrant, which was granted in only thirty-seven instances of witch-hunts, but this rule seems to have been generally ignored. (Though some delicacy was felt about it: when the legs of one suspected witch were crushed with iron weights, the court recorded this as being a "most safe and gentle" torture.)[31] Consequently, though the population of Scotland was about a quarter of that of England, the country had at least five times as many executions for witchcraft as England, most of them by burning.

Around about 1700, the dawn of the Age of Reason made people skeptical of all things supernatural, and consequently, the witch trials petered out. While the early witch trials had been imposed on the people from above, now it was the ordinary people who demanded them and the learned who were skeptical. In February 1701, Richard Hathaway, an apprentice blacksmith in Southwark, showed various classic signs of demonic possession, vomiting pins and apparently going for weeks without eating or drinking. He affirmed that the cause was a woman named Sarah Moordike (or Morduck), who had bewitched him. She was brought to trial, the mob calling out for her execution.[32] But the death sentence they expected was not forthcoming. She was found not guilty, and instead, in March 1702, Richard Hathaway was tried and convicted of the attempted murder of Sarah Moordike by falsely accusing her of being a witch.

During his trial, it was revealed that he had stayed fourteen days at the house of a Mr. Kensey, during which time he never left his room and no food or drink was brought in to him, from which he should surely have died, unless he was truly bewitched. So a hidden watch was kept on him, and it was found that a maid was secretly feeding him. He was discovered to have some packs of pins in his pocket, and when these were taken from him, he suddenly lost his ability to vomit pins.[33] It is significant that the details of this case are similar to those in earlier trials that led to executions, including the symptoms of "possession," such as the vomiting of pins. No doubt the deception could have been uncovered in the previous cases if anyone had been alert to it.

The last trial for witchcraft in England was that of Jane Wenham, "the wise woman of Walkerne," in Hertfordshire in 1712. After a girl named Anne Thorne started having fits and vomiting pins, Wenham was accused of bewitching her and having a familiar, "the Devil in the form of a cat." A local jury found her guilty, but the judge refused to believe it, and although he was obliged to pass the death sentence, he was able to arrange a reprieve for her.[34] The witchcraft laws were finally repealed in 1736, though not without objections.

A similar falling off of trials occurred in other countries. The publication of books on the demonic theory of witchcraft likewise became rare, and for a century there was, for the most part, an embarrassed silence on the whole subject. Then, from the early 1800s onward, a series of historical works began to appear, most often treating witch-hunting as a grand delusion of the superstitious past that would never be repeated.

7

Before Michelle Remembered

"Aleister Crowley's Orgies in Sicily." "Women Victims." "Black Record of Aleister Crowley." "Burnt Incense." "New Sinister Revelations of Aleister Crowley." "Scenes of Horror." "A Man We'd Like to Hang." "The Wickedest Man in the World!"[1]

So ran the headlines in the 1920s, mostly from the *Sunday Express*. Aleister Crowley ran an "abbey" in Sicily from 1920–23, in which sex—something held in apparent horror by all tabloid newspaper editors—was regarded as a religious and magical act. Furthermore, he worshiped the "old gods," particularly the Egyptian trinity of Nuit, Hadit, and Ra-Hoor-Khuit.

To describe a contemporary of Hitler and Stalin as "the wickedest man in the world" because he held sexual rites in honor of pagan deities suggests a curious set of moral priorities. Crowley was a man with many faults, who was convinced that he was chosen by the gods to transform the world, and yet whose petty selfishness invariably caused him to fall out with the few disciples he managed to attract. But this is totally different from devoting one's life to "evil for evil's sake." Such an assertion, so often made about Crowley, is born of sensationalism rather than reality.

In 1926, Britain's literati were astonished when Kegan Paul's History of Civilization series issued a volume, *The History of Witchcraft and Demonology*, by the Reverend Montague Summers, that fully accepted the old theory of witchcraft as a supernatural cult of Devil worshipers. Even for a Catholic priest, this view seemed rather too traditionalist. H. G. Wells wrote in the *Sunday Express*: "Mr Summers . . . hates witches as soundly and sincerely as the British county families hate the 'Reds.' . . . Perhaps mankind has a standing need for somebody to tar, feather, and burn. Perhaps if there was no devil, men would have to invent one. In a more perfect world we may have to draw lots to find who shall be the witch or the 'Red,' or the heretic or the nigger, in order that one man may suffer for the people."[2]

Readers of the *Sunday Express* do not appear to have found it odd to be told that while belief in witchcraft was a sad old superstition, Black Magic was a real and serious threat. People will believe they are eating a new soup if the chef has given the old one a new name.

The Reverend Summers asserted that "Satanists yet celebrate the black mass in London, Brighton, Paris, Lyons, Bruges, Berlin, Milan, and alas! in Rome itself."[3] If this were true, it would be a matter of considerable consequence; yet he offered no evidence and did not even refer to the matter again. His manner in this was followed by subsequent authors for decades. Some thirty-five years later, Monsignor L. Cristiani informed readers of his *Satan in the Modern World* that "there are at present more than 10,000 men and women addicted to a regular practice of Satanism in Paris alone,"[4] without even a pretense of having any evidence for this.

The Devil's Comeback

After the success of Dennis Wheatley's "Black Magic" thriller, *The Devil Rides Out* (1934), another publisher, John Long, asked him for a "serious" book on the same subject. He passed the request on to Rollo Ahmed, an Egyptian with West Indian blood, who obliged them with *The Black Art* (1936).[5]

Ahmed's book was largely a rehash of Montague Summers and one or two other authors, though perpetrating some almost unbelievable howlers: he located the Lancashire witches in Scotland, for instance.[6] But whereas Summers had devoted only a few lines to his claim that the Black Mass was "still" practiced, Ahmed increased this to a dozen pages. His account was confused: Léo Taxil's fictional Luciferians were jumbled up with vague rumors about spiritualist mediums.

Ahmed had to struggle for evidence: "It is less easy to prove that there are societies devoted to the black art, although there are hundreds of people who can testify to the truth of their existence."[7] It did not make any sense to claim that there were "hundreds" of witnesses yet the matter remained unprovable. In any case, Ahmed did not produce or quote any of these witnesses.

Bearing in mind this weakness, what he said about the Black Mass, in summary, was as follows:

> The would-be initiate frequently has to strip naked, drink some of the blood of the sacrifice, and sign a pact or agreement to uphold the doctrines of the Order, written in his or her own blood and signed with the new name accorded to him on this occasion. Some times it is not a name, but a number . . . such as 'beast 77.' . . . An altar is erected, dedicated to the Prince of Dark-

ness . . . adorned with tall black candles. . . . The ritual comprises vows on the part of the members to renounce all orthodox religions . . . and instead to uphold the service of evil. . . . These things having been done, a feast takes place. . . . In some societies a weird dance follows; in which all clothing is cast aside, and men and women simply, with joined hands, prance wildly, with their backs to the altar. . . . After that, animals or birds are sacrificed on the altar steps, the members drinking the blood. . . . The orgy usually ends in complete sexual abandonment.[8]

One has to ask how, if he could not even prove that such societies existed at all, he could be so sure about the details of their rituals. Mainly, it seems—as elsewhere in his book—he copied from Montague Summers. *The History of Witchcraft and Demonology* spoke of written pacts; an altar with "six black candles in the midst of which they placed . . . an image of the Devil"; dances "with their backs turned"; animal sacrifices; blood drained into chalices; feasting and sexual abandonment.[9] Summers's references, however, were all to the "witches' sabbat," that is, the fantasies of Inquisitors and witch-hunters from long ago. Ahmed merely omitted the past tense.

Soon after this book appeared, the British became concerned with real evil in the shape of Nazis and Communists. It was not until the international situation had settled down somewhat that Satanism began to be talked about again.

"Slave 62 Was Followed by the Police Last Night"

On 28 October 1951, the *Sunday Pictorial* informed its readers: "There are many men and women in Britain today who delight in wickedness and who, subscribing to the cult of Black Magic, take part in unbelievable debauchery." (Notice that, although magic need not involve sex in any way, it is taken as axiomatic that Black Magic necessarily involves debauchery.) The report went on:

1. *Black Magic is* NOT *practised by a few crazy individuals.* IT IS THE CULT OF MANY ORGANIZED GROUPS.
2. *Most of the men and women involved are not only sane*—THEY ARE HIGHLY INTELLIGENT.
3. *They include people who are nationally and internationally famous. A revival of witchcraft is sweeping the country, and people must be warned against it.*

(Notice also that, unlike the *Sunday Express*, the *Pictorial* drew no distinction between Black Magic and witchcraft.)

The article offered no names, places, or dates; nor did it identify any of the "many" Black Magic groups. Lest anyone should think this insubstantial, the reporter assured them: "I have in my possession a dossier, the result of many years' work by an investigator, a Mr A., who is out to expose these malignant people and their teachings and practices. This dossier gives the most detailed information on the activities of many well-known people."

It is evident from subsequent articles that "Mr A." was none other than Rollo Ahmed. The complete lack of any solid data in this article suggests that in the fifteen years since *The Black Art*, he still had no success in finding any evidence for his claims about Black Magic. (As to the "dossier" giving "the most detailed information" on "many well-known people," nothing was heard of it again.)

Articles of this general type appeared again at regular intervals in the 1950s. In a *Pictorial* feature of 7 November 1954. "BLACK MAGIC: 'Pic' Men Eavesdrop on the Devil," Rollo Ahmed said: "I want to prove that people in Britain are interested in Black Magic." To show the kind of things that went on in Black Magic ceremonies, he held one himself, which was secretly photographed by *Pictorial* reporters. Though he said that in Black Magic there was "a danger of exploitation, of blackmail, debauchery, fraud," nothing of the sort went on in his own rite, which was to "release a young man from a Black Magic spell." That he was able, however, to persuade some female students to come along and take part (unaware of the hidden cameras) proved that "there are adults in Britain who still wish to flirt with Black Magic." After decades of investigation, this was all he could come up with.

The obvious question—why, if such terrible things were going on, was there no evidence?—had already occurred to some people. The same year, retired Scotland Yard superintendent Robert Fabian published *London after Dark*, based on his years in the vice squad, in which he claimed to know of "a private Temple of Satanism" in Lancaster Gate:

> The room is dimly lit by wick lamps, that burn a dark green fat which smells abominable, and seems to have some stupefying power. I think the acrid smell conceals the fact that the "temple" is probably densely sprayed with ether or chloroform. At one end of the long room is an altar, exactly as in a small church—except that the altar candles are black wax, and the crucifix is head downwards.[10]

So why had the vice squad never acted against these evil cultists?

> The difficulty of the police is that, in England, it has never been the duty of the police to suppress religious sects. Nor can they easily get "spies" into the black magic orgies. For the initiates are cleverly taken, step by step, through various stages of ritual. Only by co-operating whole-heartedly in the early, trivial obscenities, can they win their way into the more vile ceremonies. . . . There is also a very real danger of police witnesses being hypnotized. Not even the London policeman or policewoman can guarantee to be immune, in an atmosphere thick with perfumed ether, throbbing with jungle drums and chants.[11]

But the following year the press were finally able to come up with up a witness. "You are about to be frightened" the *Sunday Pictorial* warned its readers on 22 May 1955 under the headline "Black Magic in Britain." There followed a lengthy preamble:

> Because devil worship is practiced in secret, because its followers look no different from the man or woman next door, this investigation has taken many months . . . enough has been discovered to prove to you that devil worship can wreck the health, corrupt the mind and degrade the body of those it ensnares. Its crimes—as we will show—include blasphemy, desecration, and moral perversion.

Four months earlier, according to the article, the *Pictorial* had learned:

> For the first time a person who had been vitally involved in a thriving black magic circle was prepared to make a full statement. . . . She told of her training, her initiation, of secret meetings at night. She told of visits to graveyards at midnight to "claim souls of the newly-buried for the devil." She told how strong men and women had been made sick by spells. How at ceremonies lasting into early dawn orgies were practiced while everything decent in life was mocked.

"How do covens get their recruits? Likely members are wooed with promises of power and thrills: too late they find they have acquired a passport to debauchery." Apparently, the editors of the *Sunday Pictorial* could not imagine that anyone might *want* a passport to debauchery. Furthermore, "in some covens each member is expected to introduce nine new initiates a year." If this were true, then simple arithmetic shows that their numbers would have increased tenfold yearly, so that within a decade there would have been more Devil worshipers than people.

"How can one get free from this evil grip? Seek out your Doctor or

Clergyman. Tell him what has happened—in confidence. Or write to us." (Why not tell the police? Or did not the evil, blasphemy, desecration, moral perversion, and debauchery involve anything illegal?)

An enigmatic anecdote was included: "An ex-black magician, interviewed by the *Pictorial*, received a phone call. Breathlessly a man's voice said: 'Do not answer me. Phone may be tapped. Slave 62 was followed by the police last night. Number One will phone you later.'"

The following Sunday the *Pictorial* produced their witness: "This is my confession," said the former witch, a Mrs. Sarah Jackson of Birmingham:

> I write it to convince you that I have been caged by fear. Fear of black magic and the Devil. Perhaps you do not believe that here in Britain, in the twentieth century, it is possible to be involved in the evils of witchcraft. I can assure you from my own terrible experiences as High Priestess in a Black Magic circle, that this is true.

Her initial lessons in Black Magic were by telephone, sometimes twice a day, and often the calls lasted one-half to three-quarters of an hour. Her instructor gave her an identifying number—448—and taught Mrs. Jackson how to call upon the elements, how to build a temple in her mind, and how to use obscene language. She learned to call on hell with the words: "Oh Hell, help me!" "Eventually I was so gripped by the voice on the 'phone that I lived only to hear it twice a day. One day in 1945 when he did not phone me as he had promised to do I even tried to commit suicide."

It was not until February 1948 that she was fit to be initiated, in a large private flat in Birmingham:

> There were about fifty people present. There was a small altar. . . . A young cockerel was killed and the blood poured into a glass to be given to those to be initiated.
>
> The candles were on a slant, almost upside-down, burning. A cross was placed upside-down in a tumbler containing water. . . . The first initiate drank the blood of the sacrificed chicken, and was informed that she had drunk the blood of the devil. Twisted prayers were said. She signed a pact bearing blood giving her soul to the devil in return for power. . . . I was initiated as a High Priestess, after my long training. Veiled, wearing my robes, I stood before the altar. Before me stood my instructor, his deputy, and a second High Priestess. . . . The ritual was a complete mockery of Christian worship.

At this time, Birmingham was not a city noted for its high life. Michael Green, who lived there in 1950-53, complained that "I was actually rebuked by a policeman for whistling a tune in the street" and noticed how women having an evening out would buy a "stick" (one-third of a pint) of mild ale and make it last two hours.[12] By contrast, the flat where this new high priestess was ordained must have had unusually tolerant neighbors: they did not complain at "the beating of drums," "twisted prayers," and mock hymns, while "drinks were given to anyone and everyone. It was right to use obscene language—the worse the better," nor at the fanatical dancing that climaxed when "men and women tore their clothes off," even though "often these meetings lasted into the early hours of the morning."

Set into this article was a warning from the Reverend Gordon P. Owen, vicar of Stopsley, Bedfordshire, saying that anyone tempted to become involved in Black Magic should "GO AND CONSULT A CLERGYMAN."[13]

The next week, in the June 5 *Pictorial*, Mrs. Jackson went into more detail about one particular Black Magic rite she had attended, on the August bank holiday in 1951.

I was ill in my bed at my home in Moseley, Birmingham. Then, just half-an-hour before midnight, I was told that someone was at the door for me. I could guess what this meant. I was wanted at a black magic meeting, to act as High Priestess. Stopping only to pull a dressing gown over my nightdress I went downstairs. A car was waiting. It drove me to the Bull Ring. . . . From there a dark-colored enclosed van took me to a house. I was ushered into a room off a dimly-lit hall. A woman in dark maroon robes stepped through some curtains. A long veil was pinned over the center of her head and draped over her face. She fetched a robe and a veil for me. . . . It was rather like a choirboy's surplice. After pinning on the veil I felt a little queer. I leaned against a wall until a man's voice called "448"—that, as I explained last week, was the number given to me at my initiation.

I walked through the curtains into a big room. The room seemed full of a sort of pink glow, and at first I could just distinguish shapes that I knew were people. Then, as my eyes got used to the lack of light, I noticed the markings on the floor. Drumming began, softly, insistently. I turned left and walked between two white lines to the corner of the room where, facing me, was a semi-circle of twelve men in masks and robes. Three women came from the bottom of the room, and walked behind me. One of them took up position with the twelve men, making a coven of thirteen—twelve men and one woman. To the beat of drums, I went to the spot where three men stood, forming a triangle. They were joined by another of the women. I stopped at the left-hand of the altar. The woman still behind me continued to the right-hand side. Facing the room now I saw, immediately in front of the altar, a star drawn on the floor and, close to it, a dragon.

Now the ritual began. Suddenly, from the door by which I had entered the room, came three men with a young girl. They led her to the point of the star nearest a statue. The men were cowled and masked. One of the girl's escorts left her and went to stand beside a kneeling man. The man spoke a parody of the Lord's Prayer, then he called on the covens. "And tonight," he said, "we have a virgin in our midst who is to be initiated." Chanting began and the young girl—she seemed about seventeen—was brought to the statue. The girl was made to repeat certain declarations. Then she was taken to the altar star, where more "vows" were made. . . . She was told to look in the mirror, to keep on looking. She remained like this for about five minutes while distortions of a Mass were carried out. One of the women stepped forward and placed a hood over the girl's head. When dancing began, everybody was served with drink—whisky, rum, gin, whatever they wanted. As soon as a glass was emptied it was refilled.

I refused a drink because I was feeling sick and worried. Because of this I was reprimanded. The drums were going. People began to be intoxicated, stamping their feet, jumping about. It became an orgy. I felt ill and leaned back against the wall for a while. I was told I could go home, but first I had to give my vow of silence to the whole room. It was then that I was told that magic was for the strong and not for the queasy. Afterwards I had to give my handprint from blood of a cockerel on a sheet of paper. I was put in a car, but the next I remember is coming to my senses at the bus terminus. *I was still in my night-dress, slippers and dressing-gown.*[14]

It may be that Birmingham was then the headquarters for Black Magic in Britain. It is very curious, however, that, though for "five months, many members of our editorial staff have worked on this probe into evil," the *Pictorial* was unable to provide any corroboration whatsoever. After all, a high priestess ought to have been able to tell them where the temples she had worshiped in were and introduced them to the people she had herself brought into Black Magic; yet she did not. So another possibility must be considered: that Mrs. Jackson was given to hallucinations. Schizoid people commonly "hear" voices and sometimes interpret them as a mysterious telephone caller. On the August bank holiday, her mind may have traveled to a Black Magic ceremony while her body sleepwalked to the bus terminal. Hallucination would explain why the neighbors never noticed anything; why Mrs. Jackson had no control over events, though she was supposed to be a high priestess; how she was able to recall an impossible detail such as candles burning upside down; the obscene language (not part of any mainstream magical tradition but used excessively by schizophrenic "voices"); and why, though supposedly dozens of others were involved, the reporters were not able to locate any of them. It is true that Mrs. Jackson's reminiscences had some resemblance to Ahmed's unsubstantiated assertions, such as the use of an identifying number, but rather than providing proof of his claims, it may merely mean she had read his book.

In view of her description of a coven of thirteen forming a semicircle facing the altar, it is likely she had also read Margaret Murray's *The Witch-Cult in Western Europe*, which introduced to England the idea of covens of thirteen and quoted the seventeenth-century witch-hunter Pierre de Lancré on the supposed parody of the mass performed at the sabbat: "Next, the whole assembly surround the altar in the form of a croissant or new moon," to hear the Devil, with the queen of the sabbat at his left hand, reciting a sermon.[15]

On 15 February 1956, the *Daily Herald* had a feature: "Police Chief Goes Back on the Witches' Sabbat." The reference was to Detective Superintendent Spooner of the Warwickshire constabulary, who every year returned to the site of an unsolved Saint Valentine's Day murder, on its anniversary. The victim had been Charles Walton, a farm laborer in the village of Lower Quinton, age seventy-four, who on 14 February 1945 was trimming a hedge on Meon Hill. When he failed to return home that evening, his niece went looking for him. She found him dead, his throat cut with his own hedging tool.

Since Walton was a harmless old man, apparently with no enemies, police were at a loss. Eventually, for want of any other lead, they thought that witchcraft might have something to do with it and went to consult various Experts. Unfortunately, there were as many opinions as Experts. Margaret Murray thought that Walton might have been a human sacrifice in a Candlemas ritual performed by traditionalist witches who still used the Julian calendar. Gerald Gardner, by contrast, said that Walton could not have been a human sacrifice, because human sacrifices had to be young and healthy. A third Expert thought it was an ordinary murder that the perpetrator had tried to make appear like a witchcraft killing, to put police off the scent. All these learned opinions notwithstanding, the police never got any closer to solving the mystery.[16]

It was discovered that, in 1875, a youth in nearby Long Compton had murdered an old woman, Ann Turner, with a hay fork, because he thought she was a witch and had cursed him. He had slashed her throat, somewhat in the manner in which Walton had been murdered. If there were any connection, someone might have thought that Walton was a witch and murdered him for it. In that case, the ultimate cause of death would not be witchcraft, but witch-hunting. (Also, police learned that Walton once saw a ghost—so what?)

Despite the lack of any suspect or established motive, this story was often written up in the newspapers as a "witchcraft murder"—indeed, it still appears regularly today. It was often stated that Walton's body was found "near a stone circle," as if to imply that it had been a Druid sacrifice. In fact, though there are hundreds of stone circles in Britain, the nearest to Meon Hill are the Rollright Stones, twelve miles away.

A few days after the *Herald* piece, 19 February, *Reynolds News* reported:

> A terrified woman, driven grey-haired by some of the most evil men in Britain, offered last night to help solve the murder of Charles Walton, who was impaled with a pitchfork in a lonely Warwickshire field on St. Valentine's Day, 1945. She will give the name of the alleged murderer to Det. Supt. A.W. Spooner, Chief of the Warwickshire C.I.D....
>
> This woman, who begged me not to reveal her name, has offered to tell Det. Supt. Spooner everything—provided she is protected from the vengeance of Britain's black magic cults....
>
> For twelve frightful years she took part with other members of the cult in grotesque rites that stem from Britain's mysterious past. Now she wants the police to stamp out these evil practices. And she wants them to solve the 11-year-old crime she claims was a ritual murder.
>
> Three or four survivors of an ancient cult live in the locality, she said, but the actual murderer was a woman who was brought by car from a different part of the country. The leader of the London cult was present.
>
> "This was revealed to me by the Midlands leader who wants Number One out of the way so that he can gain control. Their numbers are increasing in the Midlands."

The next day, 20 February, the *News Chronicle* gave further details of her story under the headline "Murder at Black Mass, Says Woman":

> A woman has come forward to say that a shepherd, killed eleven years ago, was murdered by a woman during a Black mass at midnight. She says that she was once a member of a black magic society and that she knows the name of the killer. The body of the shepherd, 74-years-old Charles Walton, was found on St. Valentine's day, 1945, in the middle of a circle of stones in a field at Lower Quinton, Warwickshire.

When interviewed by the police, this woman proved unwilling to part with specific details. They may have noticed that she knew nothing about the case other than what had appeared in the press before she made her claim, and that, furthermore she got some of the details mixed up. Walton was not a shepherd; the incorrect "near a stone circle" had become "in the middle of a circle of stones"; and she gave the time of the murder as midnight, when in fact it was about four in the afternoon.

It may be that the police and press pointed these errors out to her, for when she talked to the *Daily Mirror* on 15 March, under the title "Black Magic Murder," her story had changed:

> Thirteen people took part in the ceremony. One of them knew Walton. The rest came from various parts of the country. Walton was hedging that day in a field well away from houses and the road. The person who knew him approached him with two others. He was struck down. It was exactly midday. Rapidly they mutilated his body, soaked some robes in his blood, drove in the pitchfork, and danced round the body.

She also gave some details of her own involvement in the cult:

> People came from all over the country to attend. Animals were killed and their blood poured into goblets. The "priests" prayed to the Devil for help. The cult believes that you can get excitement and happiness from worshiping and practicing evil. The altar is a parody of a Christian altar. The Cross is placed upside down in a glass of water and the candles on a slant, almost upside down. Newcomers are initiated by being forced to drink the blood of animals. Then they all drink glasses of spirits and dance round the altar. . . . Then they have to sign a pact in blood, giving their souls to the Devil.

This paragraph makes it clear that the woman concerned was none other than Mrs. Sarah Jackson of Birmingham. She still did not have the story right—Walton was killed in the afternoon, not at midday, and the murderers could hardly have danced around his body as he was found in a ditch by the hedge he had been trimming. Nor had she yet noticed that if you turn candles upside down, they go out. Thus, though several newspapers had by now printed stories about Black Magic in the Midlands, in each instance there was only one witness, the same woman every time, and she a demonstrable liar.

It should be added that despite this woman's invaluable information, no one was ever charged with Walton's murder. *Reynolds News* also reported that a London woman, Mrs. Irene Layton, had independently gone to the police and handed over a dossier which she had compiled on Black Magic. It was the result of a probe into the subject that had lasted fifteen years and consisted of twenty-five thousand words "disclosing horrible things," but it likewise failed to lead police to the killer.[17]

If nothing else, the compiling of dossiers on Black Magic had become widespread. On 25 March, *Reynolds News*'s main front page story, headed "Black Magic: A Priest's Warning," began: "Black Magic is rife in Britain today. The cult was condemned last night by a leading churchman. And a full dossier exposing its evils is to be handed to a senior Scotland Yard official."

The leading churchman was Canon Bryan Green, who said, "I understand there has been a revival of Black Magic practices in Birmingham." (It seems that he understood this because a reporter had rung him up and told him so.) Naturally, he warned against it: "Nothing can be worse or more depraved than the deliberate distortion of the beautiful and natural gift of sex for sensuous and perverted feelings of gratification. And this is what Black Magic does."

The dossier was the work of "a student of pagan religions" who warned: "Preparations for a human sacrifice are well advanced as part of a ritual Black Mass to be performed by an unfrocked priest, regarded as world leader of the cult." He said he was "prepared to put his findings before the police," but they did not seem very interested, as it was not until 2 June, when a meeting was arranged by *Reynolds News* reporters, that the police acquired his dossier. The next day, the paper had the headline "Peers on Yard Black Magic List." The newspaper claimed: "The list reads like pages taken from Debrett! It includes two or three of the most famous names in the peerage and that of a former ambassador at the Court of St. James. It also names a number of wealthy people, including one with two country mansions and a luxurious West End flat." Where the unnamed Expert (who did not distinguish "pagan religions" from Satan worship) got his information is not known, but Scotland Yard took no action, and the paper did not refer to the matter again.

On 25 May *Reveille* turned to the subject of Black Magic, or as they titled it, "Grey Magic," focusing on Britain's second city. By now the earlier articles had done their work, and several residents had come to hear rumors about witchcraft in Birmingham, but there remained only one who claimed firsthand experience:

> Miles away, on the outskirts of Birmingham, a housewife stood at her front door and shook with craven terror when I told her I believed she had once been involved in a cult that practiced disgusting rites. "No, no!" SHE SAID. "YOU MUSTN'T MENTION ME IN THE PAPER, OR THEY'LL GET ME. . . ." Only when I promised there should be no hint at her identity would she say anything about the worshipers of Satan she claims thrive in hundreds in the Midlands.

Despite this, some readers might be able to guess her name:

> A cockerel is slain over a human altar—the unclothed body of a woman. Blood from the bird is drunk by the initiates as a sign that they partake of the body of Satan . . . there is stimulating music in the background. Under this influence, robes and black hoods—the only garments worn—are discarded and a sex orgy follows.
>
> My informant named the local Number One, a successful businessman. "He laughs at the idea of being caught," she said. "Such is the power of these devil-worshipers that nobody would dare give evidence against them."

(If this were true, why did they never manage to shut Mrs. Jackson up?)

The 1 June issue of *Reveille* repeated the mystery of the Walton murder, and 8 June the paper had an interview with the Reverend F. Amphlett Micklewright, under the headline "Underworld of Black Mass Maniacs." He "spoke of wild orgies in places where the atmosphere was drugged with ether or chloroform, the smell being camouflaged by the burning of incense." This use of ether or chloroform in Satanist temples had previously been alleged by Robert Fabian's *London after Dark*. This suggests that the minister had got his information not from any firsthand source but by reading Fabian's book, and that, like Fabian, he had not stopped to think out the plausibility of what he was saying. For, as Gerald Gardner pointed out, if worshipers had introduced burning incense into a room sprayed with ether, the result would an explosion, while "if the drug sprayed were chloroform, the most likely result would be that those who inhaled it would be very sick; circumstances which are hardly inviting for even the mildest of orgies."[18]

Meanwhile, on 3 June, the *Sunday Graphic* began a series on Black Magic by "the man who knows more than anyone about this strange, evil cult." This Expert was none other than Dennis Wheatley, whose Black Magic novels were presumed to make him an impeccable authority.

Wheatley's personal experience of organized Satan worship, however, was limited, as he admitted. He had once witnessed a nightclub compère in Nice recite the Lord's Prayer backward. Nevertheless, these limitations did not prevent Wheatley from describing the Black Mass:

> The celebrant and his assistant—who is always a woman—wear their revealing vestments back to front. The altar is furnished with a broken crucifix standing upside down, and with black candles in which brimstone has been mixed with the tallow. The ceremony opens by the congregation reciting the Lord's Prayer backwards. . . . Next, the sacrifice is offered up, the blood caught in a chalice and drunk in place of Communion Wine. Finally, after almost

unbelievable degradation between the man and woman celebrants, the congregation, made frenzied by incense containing drugs, throw themselves into a fantastic orgy.[19]

Wheatley did not explain how he knew all this. Notice one detail: the assistant was "always" a woman. Since he did not pretend to have attended so much as one Black Mass, how could he know what went on at all of them?

This particular witch craze was coming to an end, without any real harm having been done. In July, the magazine *Illustrated* published the results of its own investigations into Black Magic, which asked: "Is black magic widespread in Britain—or are a few people making a mountain out of mumbo-jumbo for the sake of the curious?" and concluded disappointingly: "Despite the headlines, solid evidence that black magic is practiced in Britain is scant indeed . . . there are not enough people in Britain who call themselves witches to form even one traditional coven of thirteen."[20]

In 1959, Mrs. Jackson gave one more interview, not to any criminological journal but to the U.S. "men's magazine" *True*.[21] Her story had changed completely: she now said that her Satanic ordeals had occurred at a house in London. At her first meeting, the ritualists decamped to a nearby churchyard, whence they had to flee when police showed up. After that, they met for orgies "every day," which, unsurprisingly, left her exhausted. This time she eventually went to the police, but after being attacked by a gang of masked men, she fled London. Without her as a witness, the police decided to drop the investigation, she said; hence the lack of any proof.

By the mid-1960s, the popular press had largely abandoned the elusive Black Magicians, mainly because there were, by now, plenty of real witches for them to photograph. From 1965 onward, Alex Sanders, the self-proclaimed "King of the Witches," regularly the permitted the press to attend his ceremonies. That Sanders was a White Witch and that his rituals did not involve anything illegal were more than compensated for, in the eyes of the sensation seekers, by the fact that naked women took part.

But the odd Satanic story still cropped up. The 1974 coffee-table *Encyclopedia of Witchcraft and Demonology*, a spin-off from the periodical *Man, Myth and Magic*, included a feature on a graveyard desecration, by persons unknown, that had occurred on the night of Halloween, 1968, at Tottenham Park Cemetery in North London:

> They arranged dead and dying flowers on the central drive in circular patterns, with arrows of blooms pointing to a new grave, which they uncovered. The coffin of a young child was thrown aside and an adult's coffin was ripped

open and the body inside disturbed. Yet another coffin was damaged before the vandals performed their most macabre act—they drove an iron stake in the form of a cross through the lid and into the breast of the corpse which lay beneath. Then they made their getaway without being seen.[22]

On 2 November 1968, the London *Evening News* had reported with regard to this incident:

> An expert in Black Magic today visited Tottenham Park cemetery . . . he said: "Black Magic is far more widespread than many people imagine. In my opinion it constitutes an evil to be compared with the taking of drugs." The expert, who declined to disclose his identity for fear of reprisals, said that he had already compiled a dossier of evidence. "As soon as I am in a position to provide definite proof I shall hand over my dossier to the police," he said. "I believe at least one person who is already in the public eye is indulging in black magic."[23]

This was at least the third dossier that, according to the popular press, named famous people as Satanists, yet still no famous person was exposed as a Satanist, even though such a story would have been a big scoop for any newspaper.

The nature of the desecration gives away its intent. It is not Satanists who drive stakes through the hearts of corpses but vampire-hunters. It may seem strange that people were staking vampires in London in the 1960s, but from 1967 onward, just a few miles away in Highgate Cemetery, there was an epidemic of vandalism that was undoubtedly caused by people endeavoring to lay the undead.[24] Whether they were ultimately inspired by Hammer Films is an interesting unanswered question; there is no reason to think that "Black Magic" was the cause.

The *Encyclopedia* also contained the Satanic reminiscences of Serge Kordeiv. Unlike most such stories, his was actually accompanied by photographs. Most of them were taken in Kordeiv's back garden and show Kordeiv, his wife, a white goat, and a cockerel—though all they prove is that the Kordeivs had a white goat and a cockerel in their back garden.

One picture, however, shows Kordeiv's wife and two other women, all naked, in front of what appears to be a stone altar with two black candles on it. There is no indication of just when or where it was taken, and it is suspiciously well lit and composed, if, as the caption suggests, it is a "snatched" shot taken during a Satanic ceremony.

As quoted in the text, Kordeiv claimed that he and his wife were invited by telephone to join a Black Magic group. A chauffeur-driven car came and took them to "a large Victorian house." In the ritual room, which was draped with red, stood an altar on which six black candles burned. "Facing us, in a half circle, were about a dozen hooded and robed figures"[25]—exactly as in the reminiscences of Mrs. Jackson. A strange incense was used, which, he suspected, contained hashish. The ceremonies were conducted by "the master," who always wore a Devil mask so that they never knew his identity.

Soon after the Kordeivs' initiation, Serge received "unexpected cheques from my agent. I was inundated with requests for work from magazines, and almost everything I touched, seemed to turn to gold." They went to several more meetings that took the same form as the first. On one occasion, a girl was accused of having betrayed the group's secrets to an outsider. So she was made to act as a naked altar while a Black Mass was said over her and a cockerel sacrificed, so as to cause the death of the man she had talked to. Kordeiv reported that the victim, a well-known businessman, had indeed expired of a heart attack that very night.

After this the Kordeivs left the group, and the run of good luck promptly came to an end. Serge was "obliged to go to law over a personal matter and was almost bankrupted by massive legal fees." One evening they returned home to find a massive toad on the doorstep. That night a poltergeist invaded the house and smashed up Mr. Kordeiv's photographic studio.[26]

Since the couple never knew the identity of the "master" or anything about the organization of the group, there was no way the story could be confirmed or checked. This kind of clever cover-up by the Satanists would become the rule in subsequent media stories about the Black arts.

Frank Smyth's 1970 *Modern Witchcraft*, another spin-off from *Man, Myth and Magic*, had a chapter titled "Modern Satanism." Much of it was taken up with Dashwood and other eighteenth-century rakes (who were hardly "modern"), but then Smyth got down to it: "Most people are familiar with the traditional 'horror story' setting for a Black mass; few people who have not attended one realize the terror and the nausea which the event can produce in real life, even in 'non-involved sightseers.'" Then he said: "A ruined or deserted church is favoured by Satanists for their rituals. . . . The Mass begins at eleven o'clock, timed so that it shall finish on the stroke of midnight . . . the host [is] often dyed red or black, and triangular in shape."[27] It is the mythical mass of Saint Secaire again, enlivened by the use of the present tense.

Smyth next quoted Sergei Kordeiv, who "attended one such ceremony." This time, Kordeiv said the participants were all naked apart from black face masks. After the priest said a mass, in the name of Satan, over the body of a girl, he proceeded to have sex with her. She started to bleed: "I am almost certain that the 'priest' was wearing some sort of spiked ring around his penis which lacerated the woman as he entered her." The evening concluded with "drunken dancing, drug taking, and general sexual activity," but Kordeiv "left early and never returned."[28]

It is quite impossible to square this account with Kordeiv's other one. Evidently, Kordeiv supposed that no one would care what he said, as long as it was sensational; and he was right. People printed his stories regardless. Given that the two different versions cannot both be true—he cannot have attended a whole series of such rituals *and* only one—he must have been lying in at least one of these interviews, which leads one to suspect he was lying both times and had never attended any Satanic ceremony.

It might be argued that the twelve people formed in a semicircle before the altar and some of the other details were so similar to those given by Mrs. Jackson in the *Sunday Pictorial* as to confirm her story. More likely what this coincidence shows is that Kordeiv had cribbed from her story to pep up his own invention.

June Johns's *Black Magic Today* (1971) started with the warning: "This book is not intended to encourage the practice of black magic." In fact, it failed to impart any information on the practice of Black Magic, the space being filled with accounts of Aztec sacrifice and the effects of LSD, combined with rumor and speculation about what Black Magic cults might be doing, unsupported by evidence. It is significant that writers like Smyth and Johns wanted to tell their readers all about the horrors of Black Magic but could find none, apart from a few very dubious stories. The implication is that there was then no real Satanism to be written about.

The same indication is provided by the dust jacket blurb of *The Satanists* (1969), edited by Peter Haining: "In the space of just a few years Satanism has become a widespread evil throughout the length and breadth of Great Britain. From being the preserve of few isolated cranks and sexual perverts, it has grown with alarming speed into a nation-wide network with members in all stratas of society. And it is not just an occasional activity—the practice of the cult's sexual and sacrificial rites occur as frequently as church services."

So what was the evidence for this claim? "Enjoy, then, this collection of stories from such notables as the Reverend Montague Summers, E. F. Benson, Algernon Blackwood, H. P. Lovecraft, August Derleth, Emil Petaja, Dennis Wheatley, Aleister Crowley, Margaret Irwin, Cleve Cartmill and Robert Bloch." There was only fiction, most of it decades old.

Around this time, it began to be hinted that although in itself Wicca was perfectly legal and acceptable to the broad-minded, there were also sinister Black Magic circles around, who used the Wiccan covens for recruitment. As if to prove this, Peter Haining's *Anatomy of Witchcraft* included an anonymous first-person narrative of a woman who had been recruited into Black Magic by way of a Wiccan coven, in Manchester in the late 1960s. Having agreed to be initiated,

> late in the evening of one August bank holiday Monday, shortly after I had gone to bed, there was a knock at the door. I pulled on a dressing gown over my nightdress, went downstairs, and found a car waiting. . . . We drove into the centre of the city where we left the car and changed into a plain van.

The van took her to a house. Here she was received by "a woman in dark maroon robes":

> A long veil was pinned over the centre of her head and draped over her face . . . she fetched a robe for me, and a veil. She told me to let my long hair fall. I slipped the robe over the top of the things I was already wearing. It was a choirboy's kind of robe with long, wide sleeves and a round neck. After pinning on the veil I felt a little queer and I leaned against the wall until someone called for me. I could hear the drums beating, quietly.
>
> I went into the other room . . . it seemed to be full of a pink glow. I could just distinguish people and that was all. It seemed very large. It couldn't have had carpets, because there were markings on the floor. I turned left through the curtains, and walked between two lines drawn for the initiated to follow. Three other women walked behind me. They joined me inside the door and had walked from the other, right-hand, end of the room.
>
> In the top left-hand corner, facing me, was a semi-circle of twelve men—hooded, masked and robed. One woman from the three behind me took up position with them to form a coven of thirteen. I turned right, and with the drums still beating, walked to the middle of the wall, where three men making a triangle were standing.[29]

Readers suffering a sense of déjà vu can be reassured that it is not their imagination. This "confession" is almost word-for-word identical with that of Mrs. Sarah Jackson published in the *Sunday Pictorial*, 4 June 1955. The setting has changed from Birmingham in the early 1950s to Manchester in the late 1960s, and—a small but significant detail—when they got to the "virgin in our midst who is to be initiated," her age had decreased from seventeen to "fourteen or fifteen." Otherwise, the world of Black Magic had become one of those fairy-tale realms where nothing ever changes.

Most of the accounts discussed thus far were the work of journalists. Yet some Christians were also interested in the subject. In April 1962, the Evangelical preacher Eric Hutchings, who was organizing a crusade at Brighton's Sports Stadium, issued a special press handout asking, "Is there evil in Britain?" and asserting that Brighton was the national center for Black Magic: "Investigators tell me that this area is a center of demon worship throughout the whole of Britain. I am no expert on these matters, but those who have studied these things report that worship of this kind is almost invariably accompanied by sexual malpractices."[30]

Confirmation of what the Experts had told him came a few years later. In June 1964, Hutchings spoke at Colston Hall in Bristol: "If you do not know the Lord Jesus Christ as your personal Saviour, you are lost. You are dead in trespasses and sins. The Bible says you are BOUND." A prostitute and drug addict named Doreen Irvine was converted at that very moment; she jumped up and shouted "He's right. I AM bound!"[31]

Later, in the "counselling room," Irvine was advised to "let Christ take over your life," then sent on her way with a copy of Saint John's Gospel and a booklet called *First Steps with Christ*. She had not gone far on her new path in life before she felt the need to call in an exorcist. Over a period of seven months a total of sixteen demons were expelled from her.[32]

Eventually Irvine became an Evangelist herself, going on crusades with Hutchings to give regular "testimony" of her conversion. Though at first she would relate "only some of the evil in my past sinful life,"[33] by the early 1970s she was speaking about past involvement in the occult, and this aroused enough interest to be written up as a book, *From Witchcraft to Christ* (1973). Though she is rather vague about dates and places in her reminiscences, it would seem to have been some time in the mid-1950s that two girls at the strip club where she then worked told her they were Satanists and, at her request, took her along to the temple of Satan for worship. Some five hundred people were present. On a throne sat the chief Satanist, robed and hooded. "Around him in a semi-circle stood some thirteen figures, also robed in black." The throned man represented Satan on earth. For two hours, the congregation chanted prayers to him.[34]

This chief took a liking to Irvine, and after some time, she was initiated at a "complicated and lengthy" ceremony attended by eight hundred people.

Two priests disappeared behind the black drapes . . . and returned with the sacred white cockerel. Its neck was broken . . . and its blood caught in a silver cup. More chants and prayers to Satan followed. . . . The chief Satanist approached me and made an incision in my left arm, and my blood was caught in the cup that contained the blood from the slain bird. . . . I dipped my finger in the mixed blood and signed a real parchment, thereby selling my soul to Satan for ever and ever. . . . The people went crazy, and all kinds of evil scenes followed. . . . To my surprise I was sworn in as High Priestess.[35]

Once again, all this is astonishingly similar to the account of Mrs. Jackson as featured in the *Sunday Pictorial*; interestingly, it was supposed to have happened at about the time her story was published. The cockerel sacrifice is there; so is the blood drinking, the semicircle of thirteen robed figures, the prayers to the Devil, and the pact signed in blood. The numbers, though, have multiplied tenfold, from fifty to five hundred ("Each member is expected to introduce nine new initiates a year"?) Even the unlikely detail of a woman being made high priestess at her first initiation is repeated.

On top of this, Irvine took up Black witchcraft (unlike most Christian writers, she bothered to make a distinction between witchcraft and Satanism, though the only difference she knew of was that Satanists met in temples, witches in covens) at an initiation in which goat's blood was smeared all over her naked body. The numbers involved here are not clear: at one point she said witches meet in groups of thirteen, but on the next page spoke of "over one hundred black witches" gathered together at one time.[36]

She developed great powers as a Black witch ("My ability to levitate four or five feet was very real")[37]—so much so that, after a meeting on Dartmoor attended by Black witches from England, Holland, Germany, France, and elsewhere, where she killed a bird in flight by using her demons, then walked into the midst of a bonfire with "flames of seven feet or more," where Lucifer materialized in person to protect her, she was elected "Queen of the Black witches."[38] She kept this post for a year, traveling the Continent, living in great style. She then willingly stepped down but continued to attend meetings. She mentions that the witches were so secretive that the man she lived with at the time knew nothing of what was going on.[39]

From Witchcraft to Christ appeared in 1973; by 1988, it had reached its eighteenth edition. In one of her subsequent books, Irvine claimed that she had learned the whole of the Satanist Bible by heart in a short time, even though it was six times thicker than the Christian Bible. (She also claimed that, when burning Christian Bibles, she had been able to hold her hands in white hot flames for half an hour without injury. How come Satanists can do all these things that Christians cannot?)[40] Yet she was able to say very little of Satanic doctrine or ritual, apart from telling her readers that Satanists teach that evil is good or that the rituals involve sexual perversions. No corroboration of her story is known, and information from other sources suggests that in the period covered by her book, the number of witches in Britain of any color, Black, White, or Green, was very small, not more than a few dozen. Yet Irvine claimed that hundreds were involved, which would also make it surprising that no one else came forward to claim they had been a Black witch at the time when Doreen Irvine had been queen of them all.

At one point, Irvine remarked that though White witches claimed never to harm people, she had known White witches who used a "fith-fath," or a doll in the shape of a person, whose lips were pinned or legs tied. One might think this referred to the period when she herself was a Black witch—before 1964—but the term *fith-fath* gives her away. It is a Gaelic term referring to invisibility. Only in the late 1960s did Alex Sanders mistakenly take it to mean a doll used in magic. In fact, her remarks on the fith-fath were cribbed, almost word for word, from June Johns's *King of the Witches* (1969).[41] This biography of Sanders described how he had been made king of the (White) witches at a massive gathering. (Johns exaggerated the numbers, Sanders in fact having fewer than forty disciples at the time.) One can thus fairly suspect that Irvine's story of being crowned and enthroned as queen of the Black witches owed a lot to Johns's book and little or nothing to real events.

It can be seen that stories about Satanism and Devil worship were common long before the 1980s. They resemble more recent stories in some respects, including the lack of physical evidence or corroboration and the failure of witnesses to remember anything in the way of esoteric doctrines. Yet, while there are serious problems involved if one tries to take such stories as records of real events, one can readily explain them as being due to a series of inventions by insecure people and hack writers, each one based on a previous story, exaggerated a little more each time.

There are, however, several differences between this material and allegations of Satanic ritual abuse:

1. Child abuse was never alleged. Unbridled sex was the usual claim, but this was always between adults. Apart from the use of vague phrases such as "evil grip," it was not even claimed that women were coerced.
2. Human sacrifice was rarely even suggested to have occurred.
3. Cannibalism never featured. At the most, a few drops of human blood were drunk, mixed with wine.

In fact, in most of these stories, witchcraft and Black Magic were taken as synonymous with sexual liberation. This used to be so shocking in itself that it was not necessary to suggest that anything else had happened.

Yet, when allegations of Satanic child abuse surfaced, it was claimed it had been going on for years, back in the 1950s, 1960s, or 1970s—depending on when the woman making the claim had been a child. It is important to note that no such stories were known at the time, even though journalists went to considerable lengths to track down stories about Satanism.

Satan Reemerges in Canada

On the night of 14 October 1972, a young British couple, Len and Sheila Olson (or Olsen), went into the Glad Tidings Church in Victoria, Canada, and told the minister they had just learned that the Devil was real. If the Devil was real, they said, then God had to be real, so they wanted to become Christians.[42]

The Olsons had just come from an occult gathering held in a back room of Diddling Metaphysical Books, run by Mark Fedoruk. During the ritual, they said, the faces of the participants had turned into those of demons. Later that same evening, the Olsons also went to the police; Len told them that three men had tried to have sexual relations with his wife while she was in the circle. No criminal charges resulted from this accusation.

Olson, however, eventually became a Pentecostal minister and director of Teen Challenge. He used his story as a "ticket to evangelical religious circles for many years."[43] In addition to the original detail of the faces of the occult participants turning into those of demons, he used to state that the witches had tried to kill them (he had not alleged this to the police) and that the couple had to fight their way out of the room. His story appeared, among other places, in *The Victorian* of 28 January 1977:

> Witches practicing black magic sound like something out of a medieval myth but they are right here—in Victoria.
> Len Olsen, now living in Vancouver but formerly of Victoria, where he says he was a member of one of five local groups of witches belonging to the Church of Satan of Canada, says the witches could live next door to anyone— undetected.

Olson repeated the story of the occultists having tried to kill him and his wife during a "sacrifice service" and added: "Every time I make a trip to Vic-

toria I see at least a dozen of the witches. Many of them are prominent business people and a substantial number are newspaper people. During the
daytime they can't be picked out from everyone else." (Query: Why only in
the daytime? Did they glow at night?)

"Olsen said he hasn't been bothered by the witches since parting company with them but 'he know he's being watched.' 'It's scary—and for anyone who thinks they're going to play around with witchcraft they're playing
with dynamite.'"[44]

On 20 November 1984, Olson told his now-familiar story in front of an
estimated three hundred thousand people on the Christian TV talk show
100 Huntley Street, in conversation with Canadian evangelist David Mainse.
The audience was shown a photograph of a bearded man in what they were
told was "the ritual room of the Church of Satan in Victoria." Some time
later, Mainse had to ask his viewers for their prayers and donations to help
him do battle with Satan, one of whose agents was suing him for libel over
this program.[45]

The case finally came to trial in June 1988.[46] The Bookstore owner Fedoruk, who had since changed his name to Lion Sun Serpent and was described as a bishop in the Holy Catholic Gnostic Ecclesia, denied that he had
ever been connected to the Church of Satan and said that in 1972 he had
been a Wiccan.[47] The ritual of 14 October that year had nothing to do with
devils or demons but had been the "Descent of the Goddess," a standard
Wiccan rite.

Lion Sun Serpent admitted that alcohol and marijuana had been freely
available at his rituals. That particular evening, Olson had started to
smoke very heavily in the circle. Others who had been there testified to
this; one said that "he had never seen anyone smoke as much pot as Olson
did that night."[48]

Not surprisingly, Olson had suddenly become paranoid. Noticing this,
Fedoruk had decided he should close the circle at once. When the group
all raised their athames (ceremonial knives), Olson started calling out,
"They're going to kill us." Fedoruk realized that this had been a mistake,
with Olson in the state he was in, so the group dispersed the energy with
their fingers instead. Len and Sheila rushed from the room, dressed hastily,
and left.[49]

Lion Sun Serpent testified that Olson had started distributing a pamphlet called *Set Free*, alleging that he had narrowly escaped from the ritual
with his life. This had caused the plantiff business problems: fundamentalist Christians would regularly harass people outside his bookstore. Some

had megaphones and would shout things like "Thou shalt not suffer a witch to live." Since 1982 he had been compelled to live on welfare. After the *100 Huntley Street* broadcast, he had been attacked in the street more than once, had lost a tooth, and had his nose broken.[50]

Carl Raschke, a professor of Religious Studies at the University of Denver, appeared as an Expert witness for the defense. He told the court that a human sacrifice might have been planned that night to celebrate the dawning of a new Satanic age. He said that each Satanic age is 666 years long. Members of the Order of the Knights Templar were arrested in France on 13 October 1307, which he said was 666 years and a day before the night of Fedoruk's ritual.[51] A number of objections could be brought to this theory, but it is sufficient to note that 1,972 minus 1,307 is only 665.

A jury decided that while Lion Sun Serpent had been a Satanist (whatever they understood by the word), he had not tried to murder Olson and therefore had been libeled.[52] He was awarded $10,000 damages, but due to a legal quirk, he had to pay half the court costs, which came to more than the award.[53]

Cannabis smoking often makes people paranoid, and one wonders how many stories about Satanism are due to this fact. In 1979 a former drug dealer told me how she and two friends had once spent an afternoon sampling a new consignment of hashish that had just arrived in town. They got into such a state that when they tried to leave the flat, they were too scared to cross the street. My informant was convinced that the supplier, an African, had put some kind of voodoo hex on the dope. It never occurred to her to blame the substance itself.

Satan Sells in the United States

In the 1960s, the novels of Dennis Wheatley were published in the United States, as well as various other European books on similar themes: Ahmed's *The Black Art* appeared as the *Complete Book of Witchcraft*, and later Doreen Irvine's *From Witchcraft to Christ* was issued as *Freed from Witchcraft*. The initial effect of these books was to inspire Anton LaVey to found the Church of Satan. But by 1970, born-again Christians had started testifying that before finding Jesus they had been involved in Satanism (though not the Church of Satan or, indeed, any other recognizable cult).

An early American Survivor of Satanism was "Coni" a twenty-four-year-old former heroin addict from Berkeley, California, who told a Christian magazine how she had been involved in "a witch thing": "Then came the day of my first black mass. It was a mockery of the Roman Catholic mass. The priest, called the goat, led the assembly in chants and meditations. People performed perverted sexual acts. A girl named Jan sacrificed her baby, burning it alive."[54] No mention of police investigation into this murder was made, and Coni was a little ahead of her time here: most anti-Satanists were then content with animal sacrifices and perverted sex.

The most successful confession by an ex-Satanist was Mike Warnke's *The Satan-Seller* (1972). In 1965, Warnke became a student at San Bernadino in southern California. According to his book, he soon started drinking heavily, then smoking marijuana, and finally injecting speed. This did not benefit his studies, and he started doing jobs outside college to fund his habits. He also did some drug dealing.[55]

A certain student, whom he came to realize was a Satanist, took to appearing in his room, taking no notice of the locked door, and disappearing just as mysteriously.[56] Once a woman materialized in front of him, gave him a message, and then vanished. Some people would take this as a sign that shooting speed is not such a good idea, but Warnke thought it proved how powerful the Satanists were. At their invitation, so he said, he started attending Satanic coven meetings. What went on there was rather mundane by the standards of later Satanists: they would pray to Satan, engage in calculated blasphemy, and maybe call up a few demons. Warnke thought it "pretty tame" at first, but after a while it got livelier, with a naked woman on the altar and curses (that succeeded) pronounced against backsliders from "the Brotherhood," as this international conspiracy was called.[57]

Warnke was soon initiated, at a rite in which he was given the Satanic name of Judas Iscariot. He also had to sign his name in blood in a vast book. He noticed that, of the earlier red names, one or two had turned green, and he was told this always happened if someone had a mind to "cop out."[58]

He progressed fast—he doesn't say how they measured his progress—and soon he had been made a "Master Counselor." Returning to his seedy apartment after the ceremony of elevation, he found that it had been fully refurbished in his favorite colors and supplied with two young women, who were eager to cater to his slightest whim.[59] Henceforth the Brotherhood paid his rent and provided him with a car and driver, and as much drink as he wanted.

As a master counselor, Warnke took charge of his area and decided to improve on the rituals. He livened one up by sacrificing a cat. The Brotherhood thought this a brilliant innovation. By clever recruiting, he was able to expand the membership of his group from five hundred to fifteen hundred. He persuaded some members to cut off one of their fingers during rituals, after which they would all nibble at it so as to make themselves cannibals. Thinking it a pity that the naked woman on the altar was always willing, one night he drove around with some heavies, picked a girl at random from the street, and got them to kidnap her. She was raped during the ritual and then released.[60]

As in the case of Doreen Irvine's story, the numbers involved are far larger than the known figures for White witchcraft in the same period. Hans Holzer's research suggests that the first Wiccan in southern California, in Los Angeles, was trained through correspondence from 1964 onward and was not able to form a coven until 1968.[61] Yet, while this woman was compelled to work alone in 1965–66, if one believes Warnke, there were hundreds of members of the Brotherhood in the smaller city of San Bernadino, fifty miles inland. This is particularly remarkable, since Warnke quoted what he said were a few lines from the Brotherhood's rituals, some of which were plagiarized from Wicca: "blessed be . . . as I do will, so mote it be," and the like.[62] (Though, by the time that Warnke's book was written, the rituals of Wicca had been openly published, they were not widely known in 1965.)

Despite being a master counselor, Warnke never knew anything about the higher levels of the organization. He was aware that the Satanist Brotherhood was vast and powerful, because he was invited to Satanist parties in wealthy, outwardly respectable homes. Occasionally he heard whispers about the "Illuminati" (who have often been accused of secretly running the world) as being a higher level of Satanism. One day he concluded that there was a massive conspiracy behind it all, responsible for the assassinations of Robert Kennedy and Martin Luther King Jr.(this showed remarkable foresight, as these murders did not occur until 1968), and to whom Hitler and Stalin were mere pawns. Satan was the true leader of this "worldwide, super-secret control group."[63]

One day Warnke tried injecting heroin instead of speed. The second time he did this, he overdosed and ended up in a hospital ward. The Satanists promptly deserted him. When he came home, his apartment was its old, dilapidated self. The people at the "hamburger joint" where he had been working refused to have him back because he had not shown up for three weeks.[64] (Why had he taken this hamburger job while the Satanists were supplying all his needs? As a blind, he said.)

Freed from drugs, in June 1966, Warnke joined the U.S. Navy and soon afterwards became a born-again Christian. He got engaged to a Christian girl, but now the Brotherhood were trying to get at him for backsliding, he believed. A black cat, clearly a demon in disguise, took to hanging around outside his front gate.[65] Due, perhaps, to the intervention of Jesus, their attempts to silence him were inept, and nothing worse happened than that his fiancée slipped in a gym class and sprained her ankle as a result of a Satanist curse.[66] Some time after their marriage, Warnke went to Vietnam, where he served in the navy's medical corps.

By 1970 he was back in the United States. His Christian friends started to persuade him that he had a mission to warn others of the perils of witchcraft. In 1972 he was, surprisingly, granted an early discharge, and he took this to be a sign from the Lord of his vocation. His account ends with him giving interviews to journalists and calling for action against the occult.

At this time, the celebrated Morris Cerullo, founder of Morris Cerullo World Evangelism, decided to add an anti-occult branch to his ministry. So he set up "the Witchmobile," a trailer displaying occult artifacts, with the intention of warning people away from the occult and toward Christianity. He hired Mike Warnke to tour with it.[67] At the Seventh Deeper Life Conference in California in 1972, Warnke and the Witchmobile were "the hit of the show."[68]

Cerullo also produced an anti-occult book, *The Back Side of Satan*. It gave several pages to reviewing Warnke's story and included the statement that at a conference in San Francisco "called by the Church of Satan in January of 1966," Warnke saw "convicted killer Charles Manson."[69] This was a truly remarkable occasion, since the Church of Satan was not founded until 30 April 1966, and Manson was not released from prison until 1967. Many of the incidents in *The Satan-Seller* were retold in *The Back Side of Satan*, but with minor differences in detail.[70]

By 1973, Cerullo had decided that the anti-occult side of his ministry was getting too much attention, and not wishing to be known just for that, he pulled out of it. This left the field open for Warnke, who became a leading Evangelist. In addition to his tales about Satanism, he used to tell a series of stories about his experiences in Vietnam and developed a comic Evangelical routine that led him to be known as "America's number-one Christian comedian." He founded Warnke Ministries, and *The Satan-Seller* reputedly sold more than 2 million copies.

Then, in 1991, two journalists from the Christian magazine *Cornerstone* decided to check out Warnke's story and went to California to track down people who had known him in the period covered by his book. Proof of its accuracy should have been forthcoming, since apart from the fifteen hundred former disciples, his fellow students must have noticed when this poor youth suddenly became rich for a while, then returned to poverty. So what were the responses? His fiancée of the period, Lois Eckenrod, told them: "I've been waiting twenty-five years for someone to ask me about Mike Warnke's story. He's a pathological liar." And Warnke's old roommate Greg Gilbert ("Herb Taylor" of the book) said: "*The Satan-Seller* is absolutely filled with lies from beginning to end."[71]

It was true that, while a student, Warnke had "dabbled" with Ouija boards and tarot cards, and some people remembered him claiming to have had his own witches' coven. But he did not invite any of these people along (despite the supposed intensive recruitment he was doing), and anyway, no one believed him even at the time, as he already had a reputation for telling tall stories. At age nineteen, he had claimed to have been a Greek dancer, a professional ambulance driver, and a Trappist monk. "Anything brought up in conversation—he'd done it."[72] None of the people who used to see him regularly had noticed the chauffeur-driven car, the redecorated flat, or the two sex slaves.

Soon after this, the charitable status of Warnke Ministries was taken away, as tax inspectors found that out of its income of over $800,000 in 1991, $303,840 went on Warnke's salary; $291,840 on his wife's salary; $214,000 to Warnke's brother-in-law; and only $900 to charitable purposes.[73]

Lucifer Unbound

Satan on the Loose (1973), by well-known Evangelist Nicky Cruz, was summed up by these words of the author: "The pendulum of history swings from one extreme to another. I'm convinced that the execution of witches three centuries ago is no more dangerous an extreme than today's permissive acceptance of them as harmless dabblers in the occult."

To demonstrate the dangers of witchcraft, Cruz repeated a story that had been told him by a girl named Olga when he had visited the church she attended in Chicago. Olga's mother, so Olga said, had started hanging out with "weird friends" who would meet with her every few weeks in the basement, which she had redecorated in a "spooky" fashion. Then one day her mother told Olga she was old enough (Cruz said she looked about eighteen) to take part. A dozen people held a "backwards" church service, praying to Lucifer while black candles burned and a cross stood upside down. Then an orgy started, and three men raped Olga with her mother's approval.[74]

There can be few mothers who would stand by and let their daughters be raped, but that in itself does not disprove Olga's story. One thing had by now become apparent however: victims of Satanism would tearfully tell their story to a church group or sell it to the newspapers, but they seldom went to the police, and when they did, no prosecutions followed.

From the early 1970s onward a number of books appeared that, although written from a variety of viewpoints (Christian, journalistic, etc.), were all of a type, so that one example will suffice. *America Bewitched* (1974), by Daniel Logan, a professional clairvoyant, stated portentously: "Black magicians and their advocates make animal and sometimes human sacrifices . . . and stop at nothing to bring about chaos and destruction to the laws of the land, the laws of nature, the laws of the universe."[75] The book gave anecdotes about LaVey's Church of Satan, the Manson murders, Aleister Crowley, the Process, the side effects of drugs, the spread of occultism, psychic experiences concerning evil spirits, a murderer who believed his victim was a witch who had put a curse on him, an off-Broadway show in which a goat sacrifice was mimed, and much more—everything, in fact, except human-sacrificing Black Magicians out to destroy the laws of the land and of nature.

Books of this sort work by a kind of psychological trick. Various unrelated things that sound strange and sinister are brought together and produce a general feeling of uneasiness, so that one may come away with the impression that there are Satanists who do all of them, despite the fact that no tangible evidence for this has been presented. (This is not to accuse the author of conscious deceit: he may have been taken in by his own rhetoric.) It must be added that neither this book nor its fellows had any idea that Satanists might practice child abuse.

The "Chick Tracts," named for their publisher, Jack T. Chick, give simple Christian messages in cartoon-strip form. Their outlook is Protestant fundamentalist—one, *Big Daddy?* criticizes the theory of evolution and suggests that the world is really only a few thousand years old, as stated in the Bible. *The Ark* argues for the reality of the biblical flood. Others attack the Catholic Church. Chick Tracts are said to have sold 300 million copies worldwide.

A couple of these tracts deal with witchcraft and Satanism (taken to be the same thing). Chick states that the "authenticity of the occult information" in them comes from "John Todd, ex–Grand Druid Priest." *The Broken Cross* (1974) starts with a virgin being sacrificed to Lucifer by figures in hooded robes. When her body is found, drained of blood, by a couple of Christian "crusaders," they decide to investigate. To their surprise, the local sheriff and the pastor (a liberal Christian) ridicule the idea that there could be Satanists in their area. Another policeman, however, Officer Bradley, takes the Crusaders seriously. After a series of further strange adventures, which incorporate a lecture on Satan and the fallen angels, in the final scene, the coven is arrested by police, led by Officer Bradley, just as they are about to sacrifice another girl; and, surprise, surprise, when their hoods come off, the sheriff and the liberal pastor are found to be among them.

Spellbound? (1978) depicts the production of a rock record by Satanic witches. The words are written by a witch and contain "coded spells or incantations," while the music comes from "an old druid manuscript." (How Druids were able to play rock music before the invention of the electric guitar is not explained.) The encoded spell would be intended, say, to increase the listeners' belief in reincarnation. A ritual would be done in the recording studio, which would repeat its effect every time the record was played, after the manner of a Buddhist prayer wheel. It is stated that all rock music is produced this way. (Steve Wilson of the Druid Clan of Dana has remarked to me that, if this is true, then by now the Druids must be owed billions of pounds in royalties.)

John Todd (a.k.a. John Todd Carr, a.k.a. John Todd Collins, a.k.a. Lance Collins, the last being his "Druid name"), the supplier of the "authentic" occult information in these comics, himself appears in *Spellbound?* as Lance Collins, a preacher who announces that all rock music is produced by Satanists and contains demonic chants, and whose congregation end up burning their rock records.

The year after *Spellbound?* came out, the magazine *Christianity Today* published the results of an investigation into John Todd's life. He first drew notice in Phoenix, Arizona, in early 1968, at age nineteen, as a "storefront preacher" with a wife named Linda. He told Pastor James Outlaw of the Jesus Name Church that he had been a witch while "in the navy" but had been converted while attending a storefront Pentecostal church in southern California.[76]

Todd then disappeared and returned months later without his wife. He explained that God had given them a prophecy to split up and seek other mates. From February 1969, he was in the army.

Todd would subsequently claim that "he joined the army to establish covens of witches, that he became a decorated Green Beret in Vietnam, and that he was later transferred to Germany, where he killed a former commanding officer in a two-hour shootout in Stuttgart. He says the Illuminati got him out of jail and that the Pentagon destroyed all his military records."

If this was true, then there would be no way of checking his story—how unfortunate! In fact, *Christianity Today* found that there *were* records of his army service, and they showed that he did not last long in the military, as he had to be treated for psychiatric problems and drug abuse. A medical report stated that "Todd finds it difficult to tell reality from fantasy."[77]

By early 1973, he had reappeared in Phoenix, where he was taken on as a worker in the Open Door Pentecostal coffeehouse. In August he was married to another Christian, Sharon Garver. Once again, Todd was claiming that he had been involved in witchcraft until his conversion to Christianity, which he now, however, dated to 1972. Ken Long, who ran Open Door, believed that Todd could work miracles and claimed to have seen him heal a handicapped youth's leg. But he started getting reports that Todd was trying to seduce teenage girls at the coffeehouse, that he had told some of them he was still involved in witchcraft, and that he wanted them to form a coven with him. He also got Sharon's teenage sister pregnant.[78]

Soon afterward Todd gave his "testimony" on a Christian TV station. He said that he was an ex-witch and gave startling revelations about secret conspiracies, such as the Illuminati, who were secretly running the world. He claimed that he had been the Kennedy family's personal warlock, remarking, "John F. Kennedy was not really killed; I just came back from a visit with him on his yacht," and that he had witnessed the stabbing of a girl by Senator George McGovern in an act of sacrifice. The result was that more than $25,000 was pledged by viewers, and he was invited to appear also on *Amazing Prophecies*.[79]

At this time there was open hostility between some charismatic and fundamentalist churches. Todd, who was taken up by the charismatics, pleased them by alleging he had proof that some of the fundamentalist churches were secret tools of the Illuminati.

By mid-1974, however, he had left Sharon and gone to Dayton, Ohio, where he met Sheila Spoonmore, who became his third wife, though only after they had lived together for two years. Never quite certain on which side of the Christian-occult fence he stood, Todd now opened an occult store named the Witches Caldron.[80] On a tape of a lecture on spells made on 3 March 1976, he said, "One reason witchcraft, I feel, is more powerful than Christianity, is it's got about 8,000 years upon it. It's got billions of people believing in it over that period of time. Christianity is a very new religion." At the end of the class, he asked two of those who had expressed interest in joining a coven to stay behind and talk to him and Sheila.[81] His initiations involved nudity and oral sex, and since some of those involved were girls of only sixteen, this got him into trouble with the law. He appealed for help to Gavin Frost of the School of Wicca in North Carolina and to Isaac Bonewitz (author of *Real Magic* and a civil rights specialist) to help with his police problems. They announced their findings on his case thus:

> We found absolutely no foundation for the charges of persecution made by the Todds; rather, we found a very negative situation conducted by an ex-Satanist, ex–Christian priest as a cover for sexual perversion and drug abuse. Todd is armed and dangerous [he always carried a .38 revolver] and any activity by him should immediately be reported to the Church of Wicca.[82]

In the end, Todd pleaded guilty to contributing to the delinquency of a minor and was given a six-month prison sentence, from which he was released after only two months for medical reasons. (He was said to be having seizures.) He was placed on five years' probation, which he promptly broke by leaving the state and returning to Phoenix. Ken Long of the Open Door got him a job as a cook in a steak house. Todd said he was out of witchcraft for good, but after only two weeks, he was talking to two girls about plans to open up an occult bookstore.[83]

He soon disappeared again from Phoenix, then showed up as a Christian preacher in California. Once again he claimed to be an ex-witch, but this time he spoke in fundamentalist churches and denounced the charismatics as agents of the Illuminati. By 1978 he was famous. Copies of tapes of his talks were widely distributed among churches and heard by many who did not listen to him in person. Here are a couple of brief extracts from one:

> The Process Church of the Final Judgement is a Church that Charles Manson belonged to and I was also a member of it and they believe in Human Sacrifice and they believe that the only answer to Christianity is to bomb the Churches and execute the Christians. . . . The Order of the Rose Cross (another word for it is Rosicrucian) they are a Human Sacrifice Order. The Holy Order of the Garter is another traditional English witchcraft Group.
>
> When I was saved I had 5,000 covens totaling 65,000 initiated Priests and Priestesses. That's just the ministers, not the congregations. So it is quite large.[84]

By 1977, the Process Church no longer existed, and they never engaged in human sacrifice. Manson never belonged to it. But anti-Satanist literature of the 1970s had given the impression that Manson had belonged to the Process and had tried to suggest the group was linked to blood sacrifice. The allegations by Todd suggest a fantasy concocted out of previous anti-Satanist literature rather than "inside" knowledge. The same is true of his other assertions. There are many Rosicrucian orders, none of whom have anything to do with human sacrifice. The Order of the Garter is a chivalric order founded in the Middle Ages; it has twenty-six members, and some modern writers such as Gerald Gardner have speculated unconvincingly that the number represents two covens of thirteen. Even if this were true, in the present day the order is composed of wholly respectable people and certainly has nothing to do with witchcraft. But Todd could easily have gotten the impression, from random reading, that the Order of the Garter was connected to witchcraft.

Todd said that he knew about all these conspiracies because he had been a leading member of the "Council of Thirteen," who secretly ran the world in collaboration with the Rothschilds (Jewish bankers who, he said, were demons in disguise). He made direct accusations against people whom he claimed he knew to be part of the conspiracy: U.S. Senator Strom Thurmond had to leave the board of Bob Jones University after Todd spread the word that he was a Freemason controlled by the Illuminati.[85]

As to the Illuminati, they were a real organization, founded in 1777, with the intention of taking over the world. Originally they had only two members, and before they could get very far with taking over the world, they were closed down by the authorities. But they did issue some propaganda that set off some kind of paranoid trigger in people's heads, and ever since it has been alleged that they survived and secretly run the world from behind the scenes. The same was said of the "Council of Thirteen" secret rulers of the world in science-fiction writer A. E. van Vogt's short story "The Rulers."[86] Jews and international bankers have also often been said to rule the world secretly. Once again, as the Christian Research Institute commented, "the information Todd asserts could easily have been obtained through reading of popular conspiracy literature rather than from his so-called 'secret firsthand knowledge.'"[87]

Eventually Todd became paranoid, convinced that "they" were after him. By the end of the decade he had crept back into the woodwork. *Spellbound?* however, has remained in print to this day and is often to be found in Christian bookshops.

Notice that many of these ex-Satanists claimed to have held leading positions within Satanism, with "high priestess" being the least of these. Irvine was "queen of the Black witches" and Warnke a "master counselor" with fifteen hundred disciples; Todd was a member of the "Council of Thirteen" rulers of the world. Also, they were fairly happy with their positions (in contrast to more recent "my rape hell in Satan's coven" type of stories); the downside was simply said to be that the gifts of Satan are not everlasting.

Not one former disciple of any of these people ever came forward to confirm their stories. Outside Irvine's book, for example, there is no evidence whatsoever that there was ever any such person as the queen of the Black witches. Furthermore, none of them were able to provide any information that would have enabled police to trace the Satanists, and in any case, none of them ever approached the police. Nor did these Satanist leaders explain anything about the practical organization of Satanism, though the Satanic orders they described would have required a great deal of organizing.

Incidentally, Warnke and Todd did not claim to have belonged to the *same* Satanist conspiracy that was secretly running the world. Nor did they cooperate in their anti-Satanist missions. In fact, it was reported that Todd attended one of Warnke's rallies, went backstage afterward and accused Warnke of "stealing his material about the Illuminati."[88]

It has become evident that the history of anti-Satanism is largely one of plagiarism. Writers on Satanism copy earlier writers on Satanism, who had copied still earlier writers on Satanism, and so on. People who claim to be Survivors of Satanism evidently repeat what they have heard or read of Satanists doing, usually the accounts of previous Survivors. Once set into motion, a sensational story about Satanism may carry on for centuries. Most of the standard features—orgies, blood sacrifices, drugs in the atmosphere, top people as members—were in place by the 1950s. By the 1970s, the same things had spread to America. Before anti-Satanism could enter its latest phase, one new input was needed: the element of child abuse.

8

Sex Slaves of Lucifer

In the summer of 1976, Dr. Lawrence Pazder, a psychiatrist in Victoria, British Columbia, was asked by a general practitioner of the city to see Michelle Smith, a twenty-seven-year-old woman who had had a miscarriage six weeks earlier and had not stopped hemorrhaging. The G.P. thought she must have some psychological complaint.[1]

Stretched out on his couch, Smith told Pazder that the week before she had had a disturbing dream. She dreamed she had an itchy spot on her hand. When she scratched it, little spiders began to pour out of her skin. Pazder recognized this as a symbolic dream, a key to something important in his patient's subconscious. Smith started seeing him regularly, but for a few months she was unable to get at whatever was bothering her so much.[2]

One day in October she snapped. She lay on his couch and screamed for twenty-five minutes. Then she appeared to revert to her childhood, so much so that she started talking in a little girl's voice. She said that a man named Malachi was hurting her, while a group of people laughed. In between coming out with these statements, she kept saying that she could not find her teddy bear: "Oh, where's my bear? I want my bear . . . I want my bear."[3]

The next week the memories became more specific. She was in a room hung with black and lit with many candles, with a group of people, "possibly thirteen," dressed in black. They were chanting in an unknown language and kept hurting her. A woman in a cape took colored sticks and kept poking her in the rectum with them.[4]

As the sessions went on, the memories—which she said were as vivid as "a rerun of a movie"—became more and more lurid. Her two chief tormentors were Malachi and a woman called "the nurse." The latter gave her an enema so that she was forced to defecate over a crucifix and a Bible. They took her to a graveyard, where a group of "ladies in black were hissing and meowing and dancing funny, like cats," and she was shut up in a grave for a while. The group were identified as the "Church of Satan," though all these events were supposed to be happening in 1954, twelve years before the Church of Satan was founded.

(A disclaimer at the beginning of *Michelle Remembers*, where all this was written up, says that this Church of Satan was not connected to the modern California Church of Satan. But no one previously had heard of any other Church of Satan.)

The climax of her memories came with the eighty-one-day "Feast of the Beast," a massive Satanic ceremony, held only once every twenty-seven years. Satan attended in person. His worshipers produced a dead baby each, piling them up before him. As a sign of homage, each cut off one of his or her fingers.[5] Satan went on to preach long sermons in verse, like this:

> Out of dark and fire red
> Comes a man of living dead.
> I only walk the earth at night.
> I only burn out the light.
> I go where everybody's afraid.
> I go and find the ones who've strayed.[6]

Stranger still, the Virgin Mary also appeared, unnoticed by the Satanists, and comforted Michelle. Eventually, Jesus himself put in an appearance. At that, Michelle stopped remembering.

Michelle Remembers is lurid, disturbing, and unforgettable. But is it plausible? Does it sound as if it all really happened as she remembered it? Take the following: "Satan took his place by the altar, flames running up and down his back—and as he did so, a red cover miraculously appeared on the stone; a monstrous spider picked its way across the cloth. A vampire bat, with pointed, rumpled squinting face and claw-tipped wings, perched on the altar's edge."[7] Does this sound like an exact memory or a hallucination?

Leaving out the question of whether or not the personal appearances at a Black Mass by Satan, the Blessed Virgin, and Jesus are plausible, the fact is that parts of the book are impossible, even if one believes in the supernormal powers of the Devil. In chapter 4, Michelle describes seeing her mother with a lump under her dress. Then she saw that "the lump had red shoes."[8] Finally the lump turned out to have been a woman, murdered by the Satanists, and the death made to appear like a road accident. Michelle was put in the car with her and taken to the hospital.[9] Obviously, a grown woman could not be a lump under another woman's dress. This is unconscious imagery, not reality.

In a number of sessions, Michelle talked about having an imaginary friend. Then, in chapter 21, the Satanists suddenly tortured this friend to death.[10] The only way this could have happened was if the Satanists, like the friend, were imaginary.

Unless reality can sometimes become as fluid as events in a dream, Michelle's memories must have been a type of hallucination. Recall the dream that started it off: spiders were coming out of her skin, and this was called a "powerful symbol." So, too, were all her later descriptions, but they were no more real. In chapter 10, the nurse threw a doll to the floor; its head broke open, and bugs crawled out. A series of other incidents with creepy crawlies followed: Michelle would be given a bowl of soup, and it would turn out to have worms in it. This kind of thing would be difficult to arrange in real life, but it is common in the dreams and imaginings of disturbed people.

Even if one were to ignore such details, the story would pose a lot of problems. The Satanists were depicted as each cutting off a finger in homage to Satan. Did no one wonder why a lot of people were suddenly going around with the same finger missing?[11]

It is also strange that the abuse of Michelle was all physical and intended to hurt and scare her. The only sexual element was when they shoved "sticks" into her anus; even this, if it happened, would be for her pain rather than for someone else's pleasure. Technically, then, the story did not include sexual abuse.

Nonetheless, at the 1980 annual meeting of the American Psychiatric Association in New Orleans, Dr. Pazder coined the phrase "ritualized abuse," which he defined thus: "Repeated physical, emotional, mental and spiritual assaults combined with a systematic use of symbols, ceremonies, and machinations designed and orchestrated to attain malevolent effects."[12]

Although Roman Catholics, Pazder and Smith divorced their respective spouses and married. This was unusual insofar as psychiatrists are normally expected not to have even social intercourse with their patients. The account of their experiences was published as *Michelle Remembers* and became an instant best-seller. It might have been made into a film but for objections and threats of legal action from Michelle's father and two sisters (none of them mentioned in the book), who all strongly denied her story. But few people heard these voices, and the Pazders have been a big hit on the lecture circuit ever since.

In the early 1980s, sexual abuse generally became a big issue for the "socially aware." Articles appeared all over the place, informing people that it was far more common than they realized. With *Michelle Remembers* floating around the edges of people's consciousnesses, it was not surprising that sooner or later the newly defined ritualized abuse would lead to legal proceedings.

The igniting spark was Judy Johnson, a Lutheran pastor's daughter who lived in Manhattan Beach, a suburb of Los Angeles. In 1983, Johnson's husband left her, leaving her to look after two sons, one an infant.[13]

At this time, the local preschool owned by the McMartin family was recognized as the best in the area.[14] When Johnson heard there was a long waiting list to get in (including children not yet born),[15] she simply deposited her two-year-old son outside the gates one day. The staff felt sorry for him and had to take him in.[16] Over a period of a few months, she left him there fourteen times.

The McMartin preschool, or day-care center, had been run since 1958 by Virginia McMartin, who, in her mid-seventies, was still in charge. It was a family business: her daughter Peggy was in charge of the day-to-day management, and her grandchildren Raymond Buckey and Peggy Ann Buckey were among the teachers. The preschool seems to have deserved its high reputation: it was spotlessly clean; school inspectors went away impressed; and Virginia McMartin won numerous civic awards, including one for "Citizen of the Year" from the local chamber of commerce.

One day, Johnson claimed, her son complained of an "itchy anus." Her ex-husband, when told of this, commented only that the child was always getting infections, implying that he thought it was his former wife's child hygiene that was at fault. The itch did not clear up, however, and after a while Johnson found that her son's anus was bleeding. On 12 August 1983, she contacted a police juvenile officer, Jane Hoag, who sent her to a hospital. A doctor pronounced that the symptoms were consistent with sodomy. (Yet sodomizing a two-year-old would cause serious injury or even death. A mere rash is hardly "consistent" with that. The doctor later admitted that "she didn't know anything about sexual abuse.")[17] So Johnson went back to the police. She said that her son had identified his abuser as "Mr. Ray," meaning Ray Buckey.

Johnson claimed that Buckey had tied the boy up, sodomized him while sticking his head in a toilet, placed an air tube in the boy's rectum, made him ride naked on a horse, and then molested him, while dressed as a policeman, a clergyman, a fireman, a clown, and Santa Claus.[18] She also mentioned the names of other children to Hoag and said that they, too, had been abused. Hoag phoned their parents asking if they had noticed anything unusual. None had.

Soon Johnson was naming other teachers, saying that Ray's fifty-seven-year-old mother, Peggy, had jabbed scissors into the boy's eyes and staples in his ears (no physical evidence was adduced for this); that Ray put her son's finger into a goat's anus; and that Peggy killed a baby and made the boy drink the blood.[19] She would later tell the district attorney's office that in addition to all of this, she had been followed by AWOL marines who had raped her son and sodomized the family dog.[20]

There was only Judy Johnson's word for all this, as her son would not talk, at all, to anyone but his mother. Her consequent central importance to the case became an embarrassment later, as in 1985 she was diagnosed as schizophrenic, and her children were put in the care of her brother. She started drinking heavily and in December 1986 was found dead of an internal hemorrhage caused by alcohol.[21]

Police searched the homes of the teachers. Nothing incriminating was found, but they took away Ray Buckey's copies of *Playboy*, photographs of children (dressed) in the playground, string (which could have been used for tying children up), Peggy Ann's graduation gown (later to be described in court as a "satanic robe"), and a rubber duck.[22] The last item was said to prove that Peggy Buckey had an "interest in children." Ray Buckey was arrested but soon released, as it was realized that it would be impossible to convict a man solely on the testimony of a two-year-old, even if they could get him to talk.

Police also seized Virginia McMartin's files of the names and addresses of the parents of four hundred current and former pupils. (She liked to keep in touch with them.) Wishing to know if other children could confirm what had happened, they sent out a letter to all of these parents:

> Please question your child to see if he or she has been a witness to any crime or if he or she has been a victim. Our investigation indicates that possible criminal acts include oral sex, fondling of genitals, buttocks or chest areas and sodomy, possibly committed under the pretense of "taking the child's temperature." Also, photos may have been taken of the children without their clothing. Any information from your child regarding having ever observed Ray Buckey to leave a classroom alone with a child during any nap period, or if they have ever observed Ray Buckey tie up a child, is important. Please complete the enclosed information form and return it to this department in the enclosed stamped envelope as soon as possible.[23]

The gossip that inevitably followed resulted in the whole town knowing about the letter within a couple of days, and a mass panic ensued. None of the children came out with stories of abuse when initially questioned by their parents, but when repeatedly questioned, some did make vague allegations. They spoke of the "naked movie star" game. This was a tag game, preceded by the rhyme "What you say is what you are, you're a naked movie star"; but none of the grown-ups knew this. Instead, they took it as evidence that pedophiles had lured children into sex acts under the pretense of playing a game.[24]

The prosecuting attorney, Jean Matusinka, then called in the help of an Expert (though unlicensed) therapist, Kee MacFarlane, who had recently been laid off in Washington and had moved to California to write a book.[25]

MacFarlane was a student of Dr. Roland Summit, who originated the dictum "Children never lie about abuse." Recently, he had published a paper on the "child abuse accommodation syndrome," which, though not recognized by the American Psychiatric Association, became instantly influential. The theory is that abuse is so traumatic for child victims that they deny it ever happened.[26]

You do not need a master's degree in Aristotelian logic to spot the problem here. According to Summit, if children say they have been abused, they are telling the truth, but if they deny abuse, it is accommodation and they have been abused. Therefore, all suspected children will have been sexually abused.

So, when children interviewed by MacFarlane (who dressed up as a clown to put them at ease) did not admit to anything, she supposed it was "accommodation" and continued to probe them. She failed to separate the interviews into "investigative" and "therapeutic." In the latter, it is considered essential for the healing process that the child admit to what has happened. Therefore, if there is proof that a child has been abused, yet they deny it, it may be acceptable for the therapist to refuse to take no for an answer. To do the same thing in an investigative interview obviously makes the result worthless.

MacFarlane asked leading questions: "Don't be afraid, [name] has already told us what happened at the school" "Somebody touched you? Well, I know it was Mr. Ray. It was Mr. Ray, wasn't it?" "If Ray touched you where would he have touched you?" She even threatened children and told them they were bad if they did not confess. If they did make accusations of abuse, she gave them presents. Over six months or more, MacFarlane thus interviewed four hundred current and former pupils of McMartin.[27]

Some of the children started to tell bizarre stories of abuse. They said that they had been tied up and given "medicines," that they had been raped and sodomized by Ray Buckey, and that some of the female teachers had inserted pencils and other sharp objects into various orifices. As well as the "naked movie star" game, they had played "the doctor game," the "horsey game," the "tickle game," and others, all involving deviant sexual practices. In some, they said, the children and teachers ran naked around the playground (which was in full view of a busy road).[28]

MacFarlane gave the children "anatomically correct dolls," which, as the name suggests, possess genitalia. The theory is that normal, unabused children will play with the dolls in a normal way but that abused children will fondle the sexual parts. The first ten children were given a "male" and told it was the "Ray doll." From their behavior with it, MacFarlane deduced that they had been abused by Ray Buckey. Then she started taking a "female" as well and saying, "Let's make this the Peggy doll," and from their responses she deduced that Peggy Buckey had been abusing the children, too. Eventually, all the McMartin teachers, right up to the elderly, wheelchair-bound Virginia McMartin, would be accused of sexual abuse.

The children's stories got progressively wilder. Some said they had been photographed naked, from which it was deduced that McMartin was part of an international child-pornography conspiracy. They said they had been abused in a store named Harry's Market and in the Red Carpet Carwash, where Ray would take their clothes off and have sex with them as the car was being washed, then quickly redress them. (The car wash in question actually washed cars in just one minute, and owners were not allowed to remain in their vehicles.)[29] Others said they had been taken down into tunnels or for flights in airplanes, or they claimed to have been abused in a hot-air balloon over the desert.

Parents and others could not understand how all this could have been going on for so long without anyone knowing. When this was put to the children, they said they had seen small animals being killed and had been told that they would be killed, too, if they talked.[30]

There was nothing Satanic, as such, in all this. The Satanism was brought into the affair by a parent, Robert Currie, who carried on his own investigation and organized the parents into a group called "Believe the Children," which came to be nationally influential. Currie offered a reward for anyone who could produce pornographic pictures of McMartin children, but though searches were conducted by the FBI and even Interpol, none were found.[31]

A ten-year-old boy said that six years earlier he and other pupils had been taken to St. Cross Episcopalian Church, where a priest flogged him with a ten-foot bullwhip, and he was abused by "atomically radiated mutants."[32] In a piece of lateral thinking that would have impressed Edward de Bono, Currie deduced that this must be the work of Satanists who were hiring churches in order to desecrate them.[33] So the American Martyrs Catholic Church invited a priest from San Francisco, who was reputed to be an Expert on Satanism, to come and speak in front of four hundred parents. Michelle Smith and Lawrence Pazder were also consulted.[34] After these allegations were repeated in the media, several other children came out with stories of abuse in the St. Cross Episcopalian Church.

The McMartin case became public in February 1984, with media trying to outdo one another in horror stories about the terrible traumas the innocent children had undergone. In March, a grand jury indicted Ray Buckey, Peggy Buckey, Peggy Ann Buckey, Virginia McMartin, and three other teachers—Mary Ann Jackson, Betty Raidor, and Babette Spitler. The D.A.'s office notified KABC-TV, so that Channel 7 was able to film Ray and his mother being arrested. All but Virginia and Mary Ann Jackson were held without bail.[35]

The pretrial hearing began in the summer. Normally such hearings last only a day or two, but this one went on for seventeen months and cost $5 million.[36] Kee MacFarlane had selected some of the more convincing children as witnesses. Those who had left McMartin and were now somewhat older were preferred, though this meant that medical examinations of them had been conducted five years after the alleged abuse. (Some of them, as it turned out, had been at McMartin only while Ray Buckey had been at college in San Diego a hundred miles away, yet nonetheless they would claim on oath that he had abused them.) Initially, forty-one children were slated to testify, though in the end twenty-eight of them were excused, so that many of the original charges had to be dropped.[37]

One boy told of being taken to a cemetery where he and other infants dug up bodies, which their teachers then hacked up. He was shown a photo lineup and asked if he recognized any of them as his abusers. He picked out the actor Chuck Norris, the newly elected city attorney James Kenneth Hahn, and four nuns in a photograph taken forty years earlier. On cross-examination, several children recanted their stories. Expert witnesses then appeared to say that it is common for sexually abused children to recant.[38]

Despite the bizarre nature of much of the testimony, and the fact that police had been unable to come up with any corroborating evidence whatsoever, most people apparently thought the case compelling, if only because so many accredited Experts said it was convincing. On 9 January 1986, all seven of the accused were ordered to stand trial on 135 counts of molestation and 1 of conspiracy. On 17 January, however, the D.A. dropped charges against all except Ray and Peggy.

One of the prosecuting attorneys, Glen Stevens, became convinced that the defendants were innocent and departed from the team. "I didn't want to send seven innocent people to prison," he explained.[39] The parents were outraged: "He has sold us out for thirty pieces of silver," said one.

The actual trial would not even begin until July 1987 and would not end until 1990, but as soon as it had been given publicity, many similar cases started to spring up.

Police in Bakersfield, Kern County, California, had recently obtained a reputation for finding out child abuse where no one would have suspected it. "Overnight, it seemed, conservative Bakersfield had become the state capital of child-sex rings, with perverted adults—frequently related by blood or marriage—swapping young victims as if they were baseball cards."[40] By 1984, they believed they had uncovered four child sex rings in the area. The "Kniffen-McCuan ring" came to light after a Bakersfield woman started examining the genitals of her two granddaughters, who visited her regularly, for signs of abuse. After some months of this, she found that one of them had indeed developed a rash around her vagina. This may have been due to her grandmother persistently poking her there, but a pediatrician to whom the girl was taken said it could have been caused by penile penetration.[41]

The grandmother claimed that the girls' step-grandfather had molested them, but when the girls were questioned—by intensive methods similar to those used on McMartin pupils—they named their own parents as abusers, and later on several other adults, including a man who had agreed to act as a character witness for their father. Four of those named were sentenced to 240 years each.[42] Proceedings against the others were dropped when it was discovered that the grandmother was insane.

Another child-sex ring, "Pitts-Dill," was unveiled in 1984. An elementary school teacher thought that a five-year-old boy was acting sexually toward a little girl and told his stepmother. It had come to be supposed that children were naturally innocent of such things, and any sexual behavior must have been learned from an adult. So the woman asked all three of her stepsons (over whom she was engaged in a custody battle) if they had been sexually molested by their natural mother and her new husband during weekend visits to them. When they denied it, she beat them, shut them in their rooms, and made them go without meals until they changed their minds.[43]

When the boys finally agreed to say that they had been abused, she went to the police. The three boys were repeatedly interviewed. Eventually, they made statements that led to eight other children being taken in by child welfare services and their parents and five other adults being charged with sexual abuse. The children described being taken to a small room filled with cameras and studio lights, given alcohol and drugs, and sexually abused in various ways. No photographs or videos were ever found to confirm this.[44] No one ever bothered to test any of the children for drugs.

Whether legal action could succeed was thought questionable, given the complete lack of physical evidence. So the sheriff's deputies went around to local churches, urging the congregations to write letters demanding prosecution, which eventually occurred. The three men and four women were in due course convicted, after the prosecutor had urged the jury to consider that Christ "took the side of children over adults in such cases," and were sentenced to a total of 2,619 years, an average of about 350 each.[45]

After allegations of Satanism at the McMartin preschool had been made public, Bakersfield investigators wondered if the rings they had discovered were likewise part of a single Devil-worshiping conspiracy. After months of further interviews, sure enough, stories of Satanism emerged—burning of black candles, sacrifices of animals and babies, and cannibalism. Here is a sample of the interviewers' technique:

> *Interviewer:* "Okay, you said that they touched the privates before they stabbed the baby? Did they take the clothes off the baby before they stabbed the baby? Did they take the clothes off the baby when they touched the privates? And then they had you go up and stab the baby? So, did the baby . . . was the baby's clothes still off after they'd taken them off and you had to stab the baby?"
> *Child:* "No."[46]

Since there were no reports of babies missing anywhere, therapists supposed the babies must have been "altar babies," that is, children bred specifically for the purpose of human sacrifice, whose births were never registered. Eventually, they concluded that a total of twenty-nine babies had been sacrificed in this way, and police dragged two lakes where the children said the bodies had been dumped. None were found. The children also described the sacrifice of older children, whom they named. Investigators found that these children were still alive.[47]

The sheriff's office concluded that the Satanists were exceedingly cunning at covering their tracks. For example, when sacrificing a child, they might have told those children who were not sacrificed that the victim was "Johnny Smith." In fact, Johnny Smith would still be alive, discrediting the children's stories.[48] After four days of unsuccessful digging on an eight-acre site where children's bodies were supposed to be buried, police had to concede that the Satanists were too clever for them and abandon the search. Eventually, the children alleged that one of the zealous social workers was herself among their Satanic molesters, as were a deputy district attorney and a sheriff's deputy. After that, investigative interviews were stopped.[49] Nonetheless, the head of the Bakersfield sheriff's Child Sex Abuse Unit gave a lecture on Satanic abuse at a conference in San Jose, bringing this new phenomenon to a wider audience of professionals. In the audience was Dr. Roland Summit, who warned that anyone who expressed skepticism might be an agent of "the other side."[50]

Where there are altar babies, there must be Satanist mothers. While the Bakersfield investigations were going on, the D.A., Colleen Ryan, was contacted by a woman named Laurel Wilson, a music teacher who was giving piano lessons to the child of one of the investigators. She claimed to be "entwined with the two women in the case." When she was interviewed, however, her testimony was found to be "useless."[51]

The same woman then met Pat Thornton, a foster mother caring for some of the children in the case. She said that she had personal knowledge of what was going on and was scared for her life. Certainly, she was hysterical and difficult to cope with, Pat found.[52]

Laurel gradually unfolded a story about having been involved in Satanism for many years. She named two leaders as Elliot and Jonathan. She talked about how her own child, Joey, had been one of the "altar babies" whose existence had been deduced by social workers: he had finally been killed in a Satanic ritual, and she said she had a cassette tape of his screams and a photograph of him taken after his death. She would not show them to Pat, as she did not want to upset her sensitive nature. Though she had tried to break away from Satanism since her father's death in 1983, even now, she said, Satanists were picking her up late at night and forcing her to watch their rituals, which included ritual child abuse. As proof, she showed scars on her arms, which she said had been caused by pornographers and Satanists torturing her.

On top of this she claimed to have inside knowledge of the Satanic group behind the McMartin case. At this time, Robert Currie was looking for an adult witness to give support to the children's testimony, so he went and made a videotape of Laurel's testimony, with only her mouth and lower jaw visible, for her own protection. She said that both of her parents were involved in the production of pornography and in Satanism, and that they had made her take part since she was small child. Later, she had spent two years in a warehouse in Los Angeles occupied by "baby breeders," that is, women deliberately made pregnant by Satanists in order to have unregistered children who could be sacrificed in Satanic rituals, without risk of discovery—just as recent publicity about the Bakersfield case had alleged. She had had two children herself, who were killed in "snuff films." She also claimed to have been present when the McMartin children were being abused and to have had a lesbian relationship with Virginia McMartin.

When Currie showed the video to other parents, however, they were unimpressed, and it was not used. One said later: "Whatever we thought was happening, she said she had witnessed it. She described most things in very general terms. The only things she described in detail were incidents that had already been described in detail on a recently aired CNN television special about our case."[53]

Currie introduced Laurel to Johanna Michaelson, the sister-in-law of Hal Lindsay, the famous Christian author. Some time afterward, her story appeared as a book, written under the pen name "Lauren Stratford" and with the title *Satan's Underground*.

Laurel—or Lauren, as she preferred to be called—was illegitimate, she wrote, and adopted by Christian parents a few weeks after birth. In contrast to what she said on the McMartin video, in *Satan's Underground* she did not claim her parents were Satanists, nor that her father was an abuser. But he left home when she was only four, and her mother started to hire her out as a child prostitute. From the age of eight she was, in addition, used in pornographic pictures.[54] More prosaically, her mother was given to the kind of temper tantrum typical of many women, such as a time when she smashed the kitchen up and then blamed Lauren for the mess.

At fifteen, Lauren ran away from home and ended up living with her father. This got her away from her mother's temper tantrums but not from the pornographers, who apparently formed a national network. They continued to take her away to studios concealed in a respectable office block, where they took perverted photographs of her, her father either not knowing or not caring what was going on. They would give her pills and injections that left her in a "relaxed, dazed state," so that she didn't care what happened, and which were also addictive, so that the pornographers could make her cooperate by threatening to remove her supply.[55] Strangely, while all this was going on, she continued to live a normal life the rest of the time, passing through college with good grades.

Suddenly, one day the pornographers took her to "The Ranch," a wealthy estate of a man named Victor, who was the mastermind of a national pornography ring. He started to use her as a prostitute as well as a model in pornography, always in degrading, violent sex. Many of his films showed "abuse, torture, and ultimate murder of humans, usually children."[56] His clients were all top people: doctors, lawyers, senior executives, judges, politicians, entertainers, and even law-enforcement personnel and clergymen. On a "typical night" she would be "used and abused by anywhere from one to ten men," many of whom were "so perverted in their sexual desires and in the kinky sex acts they demanded from the girls that some of them became nothing less than pure torture." The girls were sustained by their Christianity: "Not even Victor could take the love of Jesus away from us!"[57] Subsequently, Victor made her his personal sex slave, but his demands were so many and so perverted that she was no better off.[58]

Eventually, the delights of mere perversion grew too tame for Victor; but then he discovered Satanism. He told Lauren how he had been at a Satanic initiation of a pregnant woman: "She just held her arm out and let the high priest cut her wrists. She let the blood drain into a chalice, and then do you know what she did? She sold her soul to Satan. She used her own blood to sign her name on the pact!"[59] (Sound familiar?) "Victor would never be bored again, for Satan knows no limits in his diabolical schemes."[60]

Soon he had constructed his own Satanic temple in the basement of The Ranch.[61] Lauren was forced to take part in rituals, which she said included black robes, candles, prayers to Satan, forced sex on a stone altar, and successful summoning of demons. "Usually I heard only the voices, but on a few occasions I saw the demons materialize."[62] Often the Satanists would cut her arm to get blood to drain into the chalice, leaving the scars that were mentioned before.

In addition to the sort of stuff that appeared in Survivor stories in the 1970s, Lauren mentioned the sacrifice of babies, who were supplied by fraudulent "adoption" agencies.[63] She said that, as a punishment, she had been shut up in a drum with four dead babies who had been sacrificed. Not only that, but three of her own children—Carly, Lindy, and Joey—had been killed, two in "snuff" films and one in a Satanic ritual.[64] It was not made clear exactly how she managed to have these children without her father, with whom she was still living, knowing about them.

After her father died, she moved to another city.[65] She could not shake off the Satanists, who kept making obscene phone calls to threaten her, as well as sending a mysterious deceiving spirit guide to materialize in her room; but she did not take part in any more Satanic rituals. Years of therapy were not able to cure the neuroses that developed from her suffering, because she could not confess what had really gone on. When she saw Johanna Michaelson on television talking about Satanism and ritual abuse, however, Lauren herself was finally able to talk about it openly.

Meanwhile, accusations of Satanic child abuse had started occurring in other states. On 16 February 1985, the Department of Human Resources in El Paso, Texas, received a call from a border-patrol agent who believed that his two-year-old son was being molested. The boy initially named a baby-sitter, but his father, who had no doubt heard that sexual abuse had been uncovered at preschools in California, suspected a teacher at the East Valley Family YMCA day-care center, commonly known as "the Y." A social worker who visited them a few days later was doubtful, however, as the boy would make affirmative answers only when asked leading questions, such as "Did Miss Mickey kiss your boobies?"—"Miss Mickey" being his teacher, Michelle Noble.[66]

Agency workers interviewed people at the school (no one checked out the baby-sitter) and could find nothing wrong, so in April the investigation was closed as being inconclusive. But gossip had spread, and parents had been given lists of "indicators," that is, symptoms of abuse to look out for. In June, another border-patrol agent thought he heard his daughter, who was at the same preschool, say, "fuching." After repeated questioning, he reported, she said she had heard the word at Miss Mickey's house, where she had been taken three times with other classmates. There were people there dressed as monsters, brandishing masks and swords. Miss Mickey kissed her genitals, and a policeman chopped off a baby's head. A "Daddy monster" shampooed her hair and blow-dried it.[67]

Taken to a hospital, the little girl acted terrified when a doctor examined her and screamed, "Please don't hurt me like he did." Her hymen was ruptured, and the doctor was virtually certain that she could not have done it herself,[68] though this was later disputed. (It is well known that some girls, innocent of men, lose their badge of virginity through ballet or horseback riding.) Whoever "he" was who allegedly did it, however, was never identified, as only women would be charged in the case, and this was the only physical evidence that was found.

The Department of Human Resources reopened the case, taking advice from Experts on Satanic ritual abuse in other parts of the country. Over the summer, thirty-four children were interviewed, with the typical leading questions asked: "Did your teacher ever pull your underwear down?" "When you were at Miss Mickey's house, were there monsters there?"[69]

Most of the answers were negative, and sometimes the children seemed astonished at the questions. But they did say yes when asked if they were afraid of monsters or if they ever got nightmares. A policeman who talked to them found that they would shy away from him when he said he was a cop and displayed his gun. He told parents that the child molesters had used police uniforms to terrorize the children so that they wouldn't reveal they'd been molested.[70] Apart from Miss Mickey, another teacher, Gayle Stickler Dove, came to be implicated in the abuse.

On 31 October, appropriately, Dove was arrested at a Halloween party, and the police went on to Noble's house. She wasn't there, but the next day she turned herself in.

In 1983, the State of Texas had permitted videotapes of interviews with children in sex abuse cases to be used as evidence, instead of compelling the children to take the witness stand. This law was ruled unconstitutional in 1987, but meanwhile, videotapes of the Y children had been made—which, for the most part, showed them happily crayoning or riding toy bicycles around the interview room rather than making accusations of abuse—and were shown in court.[71]

Texas then passed another unusual law, allowing the first adult to whom a child discloses sexual abuse to testify in the child's place. This was known as the "outcry" exception. As soon as it was passed, parents of Y children started reporting a series of new "outcries" from their children. The boys were reported to have talked about having plastic syringes stuck up their penises and having to defecate in front of video cameras. It was explained that the memories of these video sessions had made them reluctant to say anything in front of the cameras in the interview room.[72]

In 1986, Noble and Dove were tried separately. Apart from the inconsequential videos, the parents appeared in person to narrate their children's outcries, bursting into tears regularly in a way that could not but help move the hearts of the jury.[73] If police had searched Noble's house, they might have found videos, monster masks, and vestiges of the children's fingerprints; or they might have found no such thing. No one knew, as the police never bothered to search. Noble was found guilty and sentenced to life plus 311 years. Dove got three life sentences plus sixty years. Her case was then ruled a mistrial; she was tried again on only one count, sticking a pencil up a boy's rectum, and was given twenty years for it.[74]

In 1985 a four-year-old New Jersey boy undergoing a medical examination for a rash had a thermometer inserted in his rectum. He told the nurse, "That's what my teacher does to me at nap time at school." The nurse asked him to explain. "Her takes my temperature."[75] In fact his teacher used the "high-tech" method of a strip across his forehead, but suspecting that his teacher was sodomizing him under the pretense of taking his temperature, the nurse told the boy's mother, who interrogated him at length and then took him to the police. When he was given an anatomically correct doll, he put his finger in its rectum.[76]

The investigation targeted twenty-three-year-old Margaret Kelly Michaels, who until a few days before had been a teacher at the Wee Care Day Center the boy attended. Police, social workers, and parents interviewed other children. Leading questions were asked, and "where children did not admit to having witnessed abuse, the interviewer would ask them to *suppose* that abuse had taken place and to demonstrate how it *might* have happened."[77]

Fairly soon, children had told investigators that Michaels would take her clothes off and play "Jingle Bells" on the piano; dress in a black robe; make children play naked pile-up games; smear peanut butter on herself and make children lick it off; make children drink urine and eat excrement; smear excrement over herself and on the children's bodies; teach children to have sex with each other; and poke knives, forks, spoons, sticks, and Lego blocks into their orifices.[78] One boy said Michaels put a tree and a car on him while she molested him. More extreme statements such as this were ignored. Only Michaels was accused, and not the rest of the staff, though it would have been rather difficult for her to have done all these things for months in a crowded facility without anyone noticing.[79]

The child who originally mentioned the temperature taking came from a family beset by marital difficulties. He had been complaining of a sore bottom for a whole year. Michaels had been at the center for only nine months.

In court, the children testified by closed-circuit television, and parents were permitted to give evidence about what their children had told them. The prosecutor got Michaels to play "Jingle Bells" on an electronic keyboard during her cross-examination. The prosecution's chief Expert witness, psychologist Eileen Treacy, told the jury that the children's symptoms were consistent with sexual abuse. As an example, she cited one boy whose parents had noticed that he was inexplicably reluctant to eat tuna fish. Treacy explained that tuna fish smells similar to women's vaginas, which proved that the boy had been made to perform cunnilingus.[80] Michaels was found guilty on 115 counts.[81] She was sentenced to forty-seven years' imprisonment, which by this time had come to be a moderate sentence in such cases.

The Cult Cops

A number of police officers in the 1980s had become concerned about cults in general and Satanic cults in particular. The first to venture into the field was Sandi Gallant of the San Francisco Police Department. As early as 1980, she put out a nationwide request for other departments who might have information on "Satanic Cults which may be involved in animal mutilations and ritualistic homicides of human beings, wherein internal organs are removed from the victims and used in church baptisms and rituals."[82]

She and another officer, Jerry Belfield, devoted a free Sunday to cult investigation. They discovered that the OTO was holding an open ritual, but Gallant thought it would be "skyclad," that is, without clothes, and she refused to take part.[83] Later, she got in touch with Dale Griffis, an Ohio police officer also interested in cults. He flew over to California to meet her. They went to an occult bookshop, drove past Anton LaVey's house, and went to some *botánicas* (shops selling traditional Santerian medicinal herbs).[84] This gives a fair idea of the depth of their investigations.

By 1984, *Crime Control Digest* could inform its readers: "Although infrequently used, human sacrifice is still an actual practice. These High Black Masses are conducted with utmost secrecy."[85] A model of cult crime was already developing, which, as Robert Hicks puts it, was "based not on criminal evidence, but rather on secondary historical sources, Christian literature, confessions of cult survivors, and pure speculation."[86] This cult crime model was quick to spread, and sacrificial masses would soon cease to be described as "infrequent."

By 1986 there were enough "cult cops" in the United States for a "seminal" conference to be held, in Fort Collins, Colorado, titled "The Emergence of Ritualistic Crime in Today's Society."[87] Speakers included Lawrence Pazder, Mike Warnke, and Sandi Gallant. A couple of quotations give the flavor of the event:

> Satanism is the worship of the Devil and of yourself. It is a self-centered, self-gratifying religious system. . . . Satan's goal is to defeat God's plan of Grace and to establish his kingdom of evil in order to ruin man. Satan needs men and women alive to accomplish his work for him, because he is a disembodied spirit. (Sandi Gallant)

> The pure group of "orthodox satanists" is never seen or identified in public, yet it is this group of invisible satanists who plant the seeds and encourage all the other more visible satanic groups. . . . Unhappily for Satan, Jesus

has authority over him. . . . It is the antithesis of Christianity. . . . For instance, satanists don't love sex, they hate it, yet they use it ritually all the time. What is good, honorable, just, worthy to us is bad, despicable, foul and unworthy to the satanist. . . . You should develop resource teams. . . . Include a knowledge-able-but-cool clergyman, an open-minded-but-stable psychologist, and a survivor who has lived through the experience and come successfully out the other side. (Lawrence Pazder)

Also present were Pat Pulling, the founder of BADD (Bothered About Dungeons and Dragons), who believed that fantasy role-playing games were part of a Satanic conspiracy to introduce teenagers to the occult; Ken Wooden, a writer and TV producer who made a highly influential *20/20* documentary on Satanic ritual abuse; and Sergeant Randy Emon, a California policeman who made various assertions, including that "persons who have signed their name in blood to Satan have suffered horrible deaths or have been killed in automobile accidents,"[88] suggesting that he had read and absorbed *Jay's Journal*.

This was the first conference of many. At these conferences, various lists of Satanic "indicators" came to be handed out, including lists of "occult-re-lated homicide clues," such as this one:

- Where the body is located: Most cult meetings or rituals are held in deserted isolated areas. Wooded areas away from people, desert areas, graveyards, abandoned buildings, churches and/or residences.
- Position of the body: Note direction of body, whether the body is formed in the shape of a circle (facing inwards or outwards), it may be nailed to a cross or formed in the shape of one, it may be hanging from something like a tree either by its feet, hands or neck. If rigor mortis is present the body may still show signs of having been tied down (bondage).
- Missing body parts or organs: In occultic blood rituals many times parts of the human body and/or organs are removed. They may have been eaten (cannibalism) or kept for use in another way.
- Body dressed or undressed.
- Stab wounds or cuts: Particularly important, the size and location of stab wounds or cuts, if done in patterns or symbols, if done to allow blood letting or draining. Incisions to the sex organs, mutilation. Note the number of cuts and/or bruises if in numbered patterns (i.e., in 3's, 6's, 7's or 13's). The location of human teeth marks or cannibalism.

- Ink marks or tattoos: Again look for patterns and/or symbols. It may even be a message written in an unknown alphabet or code.
- Painted with a substance or paint.
- Branded with a branding iron or any burns.
- Jewelry on or near the cadaver.
- Jewelry that is missing.
- Any cords or colored ropes on or near the body: Check for implements of bondage.
- Any implements near the body.
- Oils or incense on the body.
- Wax dripping from candles on or about the body.
- Signs of hands and feet having been tied or shackled, rope burns, etc.
- Semen near or inside the cadaver.
- The presence of occult ritual paraphernalia or Christian artifacts.
- Biblical verses and graffiti written in blood.
- Nondiscernable alphabets, witches' alphabet, cabalistic writings, etc.
- Animals' body parts.
- Drawings or photographs of victims.
- Photography of mock weddings, child pornography or sexual activities fixated on anal abuse.
- Marks of the beast—the alphabetical letter numbers for heaven and hell, 666, occult symbolism, etc.[89]

Virginia crime analyst Robert Hicks comments that much of this

constitutes a lesson in very basic crime-scene investigation: all but the most doltish police officers will carefully document the position and posture of a victim, the presence of wounds, what type, the presence or absence of various bodily or other fluids, whether a victim was dressed or undressed, and so on. Assuming an investigating officer encountered the candles, painted occult symbols on walls, again, only inept officers would fail to note such characteristics in a report or crime-scene diagram, much less photograph them.[90]

The presence or absence of jewelry is a catchall: it appears to mean that any jewelry on the body may have occult significance, showing that this was a ritual murder. The reference to "jewelry that is missing" presumably means that one should understand it was taken away because it had occult significance, showing that this was a ritual murder. (In fact, most people who wear occult jewelry do so because it is fashionable, and few wearers understand its significance.)

Some of the other clues suggest wishful thinking. It would make life much easier for police if murder victims had tattoos or other marks from which secret messages could be deciphered and lead them to the guilty, but it is not very likely. In practice, such things could be false leads. If it had been publicized that the words *Helter Skelter* were scrawled in blood on the wall of the scene of the Manson gang's LaBianca murders, then people who knew Charles Manson and his obsession with the Beatles' *White Album* could have pointed police to the perpetrators. If police had tried to find a kabbalistic significance in the words *Helter Skelter* they would have gotten nowhere.

A "Search Warrant Checklist" was also distributed at the Fort Collins conference. Apart from the things one would expect—altars, Satanic Bibles, and so on—officers were supposed to look out for:

- Occult games such as Dungeons and Dragons
- Ashes from fire pits, including fireplaces and wood stoves
- Mirror
- Ferns, palms
- Small animals in cages
- Posters of heavy-metal and punk-rock stars
- Paraphernalia related to the martial arts[91]

Other lists were supposed to show if children had suffered Lawrence Pazder's "ritualized abuse," now shortened to "ritual abuse." The most successful was that produced by Catherine Gould of California. A therapist who treats both children and adults, Gould had contacted a police officer in the McMartin case after hearing about it in 1984. The officer said of a preschooler Gould was dealing with: "You have Satanic Ritual Abuse." Subsequently, Gould realized she also had two adult Survivors among her patients. Her list of Satanic indicators included:

- Preoccupation with urine and feces
- Preoccupation with passing gas . . . wild laughter when the child or someone else passes gas
- Aggressive play that has a marked sadistic quality
- Preoccupation with death
- Fear of ghosts and monsters
- Fear of jail, or being caged
- Child is "clingy," demonstrates fear of being left with babysitters, particularly overnight

- Mentioning other people at school besides teachers
- Writing letters or numbers backwards in the "Devil's alphabet"
- Fear of bad people taking the child away, breaking into the house, killing the child or the parents, burning the house down
- Preoccupation with the devil, magic, potions, supernatural power, crucifixions
- References to television characters as real people
- Nightmares or dreams of any of the above[92]

This list would be used all over the world.

Prominently on display at these conferences was a book called *He Came to Set the Captives Free*, "by Rebecca Brown, M.D." (She was originally known as Ruth Bailey but legally changed her name in 1986.[93])

Rebecca had trained as a doctor in Indiana. A deeply religious Evangelical Christian, she regularly received messages from the Lord. Rather than rely on conventional methods in her medical practice, she would ask the Lord to reveal the diagnosis of obscure cases, and the Lord would not only diagnose the illness but prescribe the treatment, so that she had "never had a serious complication resulting from any procedure she has done."[94]

Despite the help of her divine consultant, she found that many of her patients were inexplicably dying. She could not understand it, but in time, an explanation was forthcoming. Rebecca converted some of the nurses to the Lord, and she held weekly Bible study groups with them. One of her converts, "Jean," told her that she had been training as a medium and had been about to be initiated into a group of Satanists. (This is another of those books that draws no distinction between Satanists, witches, and other occultists; indeed, it takes it for granted that they are all conspiring together.) Jean then revealed that several other nurses were witches, and that one of them, "Helen," was accustomed to lay her hands on sick patients, thereby sending demons into them to kill them.[95]

At the Lord's command, Rebecca bought a Bible for "Elaine" (Edna Moses), a woman who was often in and out of the hospital for a variety of causes that other doctors, not having the assistance of the Lord, could not diagnose, finally leading them to conclude that she was a "nuisance" hypochondriac. Rebecca assigned Elaine passages of scripture to read and prayed with her.[96] Neither Elaine's physical nor her mental problems seemed to go away, so Rebecca spent a whole weekend in prayer and fasting, asking for a solution. Late on Sunday evening the Lord said to her: "You have not talked to Elaine about her deep involvement in the occult."

So, on Monday, Rebecca asked Elaine about her "deep involvement in the occult."

"How did you know about that?" Elaine exclaimed.[97]

Rebecca explained that the Lord had told her. Gradually, Elaine came to trust Rebecca and unfolded her complete story, which was of a nature to make all previous Survivor stories seem mundane.

Shortly after Elaine had been born, a nurse had taken some blood from her to make her enslaved to Satan. Her childhood was friendless and unhappy. At sixteen she joined a Pentecostal church, where she made friends with a girl named Sandy.[98] When she was eighteen, Sandy invited her to come to a summer "church camp" that was, in fact, held for the purpose of Satanist recruitment. The order running it was called the Brotherhood, within which was a group of thirteen powerful witches known as the Sisters of Light. It was stated to be the same Brotherhood as that described in Warnke's *The Satan-Seller* and the American counterpart of the organization in Doreen Irvine's book.[99] One evening the Sisters suddenly demanded that Elaine sign a contract, giving herself to Satan. When she refused, the high priestess called up a menacing, eight-foot-tall demon and told Elaine that unless she signed, it would torture her to death. She signed.[100] For the next seventeen years she led a double life, outwardly a churchgoing Christian, secretly a witch and a Satanist.

Elaine was found to have unusual powers, in consequence of which she soon rose to a high position. The Sisters of Light would do magical battle with each other as a test of strength, the winner gaining the loser's demons, by which she became stronger still. Elaine soon had a whole load of captured demons and was destined for a senior position in the Brotherhood.

"My first meeting with Satan came shortly before the ceremony in which I became the high priestess. He came to me in the physical form of a man and we sat down and talked. He told me that I was to be his high priestess, that I was very special to him."[101]

Soon afterward, Elaine watched her first human sacrifice. "We were in an old barn with at least a thousand people present." (Presumably American old barns, like American automobiles, are much larger than their counterparts in Britain.) "A small baby was used. She was selected because her mother gave the child to be sacrificed and thought it to be a great honor."[102] It was explained that the births of these sacrificial babies are never registered, which is why no one had noticed babies going missing.

For her initiation as a high priestess, Elaine signed a pact in her own blood; then Satan had sex with her on the altar, followed by the high priest and many others.[103] Satan appeared at many of the rites of the Brotherhood, but this had to be carefully arranged, as, unlike God, he could not be in two places at the same time. At the big Satanic festivals the celebrations in different parts of the country were specially timed so that he could manifest at the high point of each one.[104]

Due to her success in magical competitions, Elaine rose to the national council, then to the position of regional bride of Satan, and finally to the position of top bride of Satan in the United States. Like Doreen Irvine, she had to go through many severe tests of her power to reach this position, such as changing a cat into a rabbit and back again by snapping her fingers. Finally, a man fired six shots at her from a .357 Magnum, but her demons deflected every bullet.[105] Her wedding to Satan was a relatively conventional ceremony and actually took place in a church. The groom gave her a beautiful golden ring with an inscription that read: *Behold the bride of the Prince of the world.* The happy couple took a private jet to California for their honeymoon.[106] Later, it seems, they flew to the Vatican to meet the pope (who is, of course, a Satanist).[107]

But their marriage was not a success. If she ever did something to annoy Satan, he would send around demons to beat her up. Despite all her secret airline trips and life of luxury, in her outward life she remained poor, living on welfare for much of the time. Finally she came to realize that her husband did not really love her but "that Satan was merely using my love for him to benefit himself."[108] So she readily took Rebecca's guidance and returned to the Lord.

Though all this seems far more extreme than the cult described by Doreen Irvine, there are definite similarities between the two accounts, for instance:

> A platform at the front was draped in black. On a throne-like seat sat a robed and hooded figure. . . . Around him in a semi-circle stood some thirteen figures . . . everyone bowed down and worshiped him, falling prostrate on the ground. I . . . remained standing. . . . The whole congregation was now chanting prayers to the chief Satanist in that strange rhythmic way. . . . The whole ceremony lasted some two hours.

At a later ritual, "a crown of pure gold was placed on my head."[109]

In Rebecca's account of the ritual for Elaine, the latter relates:

> I had a crown of pure gold placed on my head. . . . Satan's golden throne had been . . . set up on the platform at the front. . . . I . . . bowed down before him and did him homage. . . . Most of the ceremony was singing, chanting and

> proclaiming the praises of Satan. The Sisters of Light stood in a semicircle be-
> hind. . . . The ceremony took almost two hours, I stood the whole time.[110]

The main difference is that the chief Satanist has been replaced by Satan in person.

Though Rebecca does not mention it in her book, other doctors did not agree with the diagnoses and prescriptions made by the Lord. In 1984, consequently, she lost her license to practice medicine. Medical examiners concluded that she knowingly misdiagnosed serious ailments such as leukemia and brain tumors in patients who were not, in fact, suffering from these problems. Ruth Bailey/Rebecca Brown said that these maladies were caused by demons, devils, and other evil spirits, and that she had been chosen by the Lord as the only physician who could diagnose them. In fact, the other doctors in the hospital were themselves demons.

> As a result of these diagnoses, she prescribed her patients with massive doses
> of Demerol and the addicted patients had to undergo detoxification. Besides
> administering drugs to patients . . . she would "share" the patient's disease by
> injecting herself with "non-therapeutic amounts" of Demerol, taking three
> cubic centimeters of the stuff hourly, injecting it in the back of her hands or
> inside her thighs.

A psychiatrist who examined her said that she suffered from "acute personality disorders including demonic delusions and/or paranoid schizophrenia."[111]

After Rebecca's license had been revoked, she and Elaine moved to California and wrote *He Came to Set the Captives Free*. The book was highly successful, and ever since then, Brown has been in demand for seminars and speaking engagements as an Expert on Satanism.

This was the newest profession. For years, Christians had been warning people against involvement in the occult, but usually they could only quote Deuteronomy or relate anecdotes about demonic possession that would not convince everybody. Now they could back up their sermons with accounts of horrific crimes, and they made the most of it. Soon Experts, Rebecca and Elaine among them, were touring the country, lecturing on Satanism and the dangers of all things occult to law-enforcement seminars, social-work conferences, schools, church groups, and anyone else who would listen. Some of these Experts would begin police crime seminars by explaining how Lucifer fell from heaven. Others were secular, such as Dr. Roland Summit, whose doctrines had helped set the Satanic child abuse ball rolling. At the Eighth National Conference on Child

Abuse and Neglect at Salt Lake City in 1989, Summit began a session with the slogan: "Down with doubt!"[112]

Among these Experts was, of course, Mike Warnke, whose 1972 revelations about Satanism had not contained a word about child abuse or human sacrifice. Nonetheless, he now maintained that Satanists carried out 2 million human sacrifices a year in the United States alone[113]—a figure that, if true, ought to have been apparent even to collectors of population statistics, let alone to law-enforcement agencies.

Warnke began to introduce the "Jeffy story" into his Evangelical routine. "Jeffy," it seemed, was a boy who had been so badly abused by Satanists at his preschool that he was now a vegetable. After saddening his audience with this tragedy, Warnke would then hand out pink envelopes for their donations for a "center" to help all the children like Jeffy. The envelopes would come back with "This for all the children like Jeffy" written on them. When Warnke's affairs fell apart in the early 1990s, it emerged that the money was going to fund his third wife's spending sprees (she was fond of antiques).[114]

Survivors were now proliferating, owing to advances in psychoanalysis. It had been known for some years that people can sometimes shut out the memory of traumatic events. It occurred to therapists that, since sexual abuse of children is far more common than had been suspected, there must be many adults who had been abused as children but had forgotten it. Techniques were therefore developed for helping the emotionally disturbed to recall the sexual abuse they did not know they had undergone. In the wake of the publicity given to McMartin and other Satanic abuse cases, many patients started recalling having been made to take part in Satanic rituals—even, in some instances, having been cult leaders.

All this made for good television, and programs such as *Geraldo* and the *Oprah Winfrey* Show featured the McMartin parents, Rebecca Brown and Elaine, Lauren Stratford, and many others. The reminiscences of "breeders," women Survivors who claimed to have been made pregnant with the specific intention that their (unregistered) children would be sacrificed, were a favorite. Their psychotherapists often appeared with them.

These programs spread concern about Satanism to many more people. After Ken Wooden's 1985 *20/20* feature on Satanism, Senator Jesse Helms proposed an amendment to a Senate bill that would have eliminated tax exemptions for any religion that "has a purpose, or that has any interest in, the promoting of Satanism or 'witchcraft.'" The *20/20* report was the only source cited by Helms to support his case.[115]

Satanic panics also erupted, among other places, on military bases. As early as 1984, an army doctor at the U.S. Military Academy at West Point became concerned at the behavior of his three-year-old daughter, who (like so many other small children) suffered from nightmares and hysterical fits. Under "gentle questioning" she told her parents that she had been ritually abused by workers at the base's Child Development Center, who took her to a high school where she was pornographically photographed, married to Satan, and forced to drink urine and eat excrement, while people in costume tortured one another and killed a dog. No prosecution ever resulted from these disclosures.[116]

On 28–30 September 1986, the *San Francisco Examiner* ran a series of features on Satanic ritual abuse, which, though somewhat skeptical, nonetheless interviewed Lawrence Pazder (who "has acted as a consultant to the Los Angeles Police Department and to parents throughout the country"), Dr. Roland Summit, and Sandi Gallant (who admitted, "The problem is we are not finding any bodies"). Soon afterward, a Satanic scare broke out on San Francisco's Presidio Army Base. In November, the wife of an army captain noticed that her three-year-old son's anus "seemed a little red." When she questioned him, he supposedly said that his day-care teacher, "Mr. Gary" Hambright, had touched his penis, bitten his penis, and pushed a pencil up his bottom. His father repeated these statements to an army chaplain, Larry Adams-Thompson, on whose advice he contacted the Military Police. In turn, they brought in the FBI.

In a repeat performance of the McMartin investigation, on 15 December the army sent letters to 242 parents who had left children in the care of Hambright, saying that there had been an alleged incident of sexual abuse and asking if they had noticed anything unusual in their own children. Once again, a mass panic was set off among parents. Subsequently, sixty children would tell a therapist that they had been taken from day care to private houses, some of them off the base; that they had been touched and fondled; that they and Hambright had urinated and defecated over each other; that he had forced them to drink urine and eat feces; and that he had smeared blood and excrement over their bodies.[117] Apparently, their parents had not noticed anything odd until the army's criminal investigation unit alerted them.

On 5 January 1987, Gary Hambright was arrested. In April, however, a judge ruled that the three-year-old was too young to testify and refused to allow "hearsay" evidence from his mother and other adults to whom he had disclosed abuse.[118] Still, a parents' group continued to swap information, write letters to their congressmen, and argue that the allegations must be true, because they were so similar to what was alleged in other day-care cases.

Larry Adams-Thompson's stepdaughter, "Lisa," had been in Hambright's class from September 1986. On 14 January 1987, he and his wife, Michele, were interviewed by the FBI. Michele reported that she had asked Lisa "if Mr. Gary had been mean to her or tried to touch her," but she had "replied negatively." Nonetheless, they put her in therapy, where she was reported to have talked about people named Mikey and Shamby, though not speaking of molestation.

Satanism was not initially mentioned in all this, and it happened that Hambright was an ordained Southern Baptist minister. But the therapist introduced it into the sessions after coming across an article, "The Devil Made Me Do It." On 13 August 1987, Adams-Thompson contacted the FBI and told them Lisa had pointed out a man and a woman on the base to him and identified them as Mikey and Shamby. This couple were none other than Lieutenant-Colonel Michael Aquino, high priest of the Temple of Set, and his wife, Lilith.[119]

Lisa was shown a photograph lineup, from which she was able to pick out her former teacher, and this was taken as evidence. (Query: Of what?) She told them that "Mr. Gary, Mikey, and Shamby had abused her in a house that had a bathtub with a lion's feet. The next day, 14 August, Adams-Thompson gave them more details, saying that Lisa had been filmed with a movie camera while she bathed in a plastic lion bathtub, and that the living room had black walls and a gold cross painted on the ceiling.[120]

An investigator went with Michele Adams-Thompson and Lisa to see if she could identify the Aquinos' house. She was led past it several times but showed no reaction, not even when her mother held her up in front of it. This was recorded in the official report, but mysteriously enough, a false story got around that Lisa had, in fact, identified the house, and spontaneously at that.[121]

That midnight, police investigators, including Detective Sandi Gallant, turned up on the Aquinos' doorstep with a search warrant. They discovered that the only bathtub in the house was built into the wall, and that the living room was not painted black and did not have a gold cross on the ceiling. Nevertheless, they took away photographs, notebooks with names and addresses, a computer, and other items, none of which had anything to do with child abuse—and some of which got them into trouble later, as they had not been mentioned in the warrant.[122]

Investigators did not have an easy time preparing a case. Though Lisa claimed to have been raped, she was still a virgin; and at the time the Aquinos were alleged to have abused her, they were living three thousand miles away, in Washington, D.C., where Michael was attending classes at the National Defense University, as was proved by the daily attendance register.[123] Many of the other children in the army's day-care program also made impossible claims, such as that there were live sharks in the places where they were abused. Nonetheless, Hambright was indicted by a federal grand jury on 1 October 1987 for performing lewd acts on boys and girls from ages two to five.

Aquino was never charged, but the fact that he was suspected became public on 30 October 1987, and a huge media storm blew up. *Newsweek*'s headline "The Second Beast of Revelation" was typical of the coverage. For the first time, an actual Satanist had been named in allegations of Satanic child abuse, and journalists made the most of it, rather than focusing on the manifest impossibility of the allegations. Aquino, now stationed at St. Louis, Missouri, took the opportunity to proclaim his innocence and tried to clear up the general misconception that Satanism involves criminal acts. The army stood by him, saying they were pledged to uphold the American Constitution, which guarantees freedom of religion. "As long as an individual's religious practice remains within the limit of the law, there's no problem," a Pentagon public affairs officer told the *National Enquirer* in January 1988, adding that, since Aquino was open about his beliefs, he would not be a security risk through possible blackmail.

The Aquinos' media appearances, including on the *Oprah Winfrey Show*, made their faces famous. Suddenly, Presidio children were able to pick him out of photo lineups, and this was seized on by anti-Satanists as proof of his guilt. Furthermore, children in other parts of the country who were also being interviewed about suspected abuse (and, given the way such interviews were usually conducted, most likely being pressured to give names) saw the show and identified him as their abuser. It appeared that Aquino must have been touring the country, performing Satanic rituals at day-care centers, all the time miraculously still appearing on the daily attendance register at the National Defense University in Washington.

Meanwhile, the case against Hambright had collapsed again, without even getting to court. Undaunted, the parents filed lawsuits against the army for negligence, totaling $74 million.[124] A small team was also assigned to see if a case could be made against Michael Aquino, which, apparently, proved impossible, as he was never charged.

Aquino did his best to fight back. He tried twice to prefer formal charges against Adams-Thompson, claiming that the chaplain had made false statements with the intention of defrauding the government of the $3 million he was suing for. Both times, Aquino wrote later, the charges "were simply dismissed without proper investigation as required by law." He also complained to the commanding officer about the army psychiatrist who had examined the Presidio children, alleging, among other things, that she had "introduced references to the 'devil,' and statues of 'gargoyles,' into her sessions with the children"; "regularly introduced leading questions into her sessions"; that when she "received an 'unhelpful' answer, such as a denial of abuse, she would refuse to accept it or change the subject, and would persist in the question until receiving something she could characterize as a 'helpful' answer, i.e. supportive of a 'sex-abuse' diagnosis"; and that she had made statements about Lisa, in a sworn affidavit, that were "directly contradicted by her actual notes of the sessions." The deputy commander of her unit refused to have her investigated.

Despite these setbacks, the Aquinos were successful in legal actions against two books—Carl A. Raschke's *Painted Black* and Linda Blood's *The New Satanists*—that suggested they had been guilty. Both cases were settled out of court, and the Aquinos reported themselves "satisfied." Michael Aquino continued in the army, retiring honorably in 1994.[125]

By 1989, there had been more than fifty cases of alleged Satanic ritual abuse in the United States. It would be difficult and tedious to list them all, but a few general points may be noted.

Before all this started, some general facts about child abuse had been statistically established. The vast majority of abuse was perpetrated by relatives (98.3 percent of cases, though this is a little misleading as it includes neglect, which obviously could not be done by a stranger). Single perpetrators are far more common than pedophile "rings" or groups. Most perpetrators are men, and the victims are usually between the ages of eight and fifteen, as even among pedophiles few are sexually interested in small children.

In contrast to this, Satanic abuse in day care was allegedly carried out by groups of nonrelatives, often women, on children ranging in age from one to five years. So it was supposed that a new type of crime was emerging. Believe the Children, the group formed in October 1986 by McMartin parents and others who had "experience of ritual abuse," found in a study of thirty-six separate cases that only 2 percent did not involve women. Yet in other, nonritual cases of child abuse, only 2 percent of abusers are women.[126]

California child therapist Pamela Hudson assessed twenty-four children, whom she believed to have been ritually abused between the ages of eighteen months and three and a half years, in a Fort Bragg case in northern California. She then sent questionnaires to those involved in ten other day-care cases and published an analysis of the results. She found, for instance, that it was usual for children to say that they had been taken elsewhere to be abused: out of a sample of a dozen, "4 children reported transportation by airplane, 3 by boat, 2 by submarines, 2 by helicopter, 1 by jet." They would thus arrive at "Disneyland," "Sesame Street," "Alice in Wonderland," "the Wizard of Oz," "Santa's North Pole," or a "magic castle," where they would be abused and then returned to day care.[127]

Aware that some people might be inclined to disbelieve the truth of this transportation (remember, the parents might come at any time to collect their children), she suggested that the names of the locations might be "disinformation designed to discredit the small child's story." Likewise, rather than rejecting the "less likely modes" of transport, she would "consider the simplicity of placing a toddler inside a box or cage, draping it and putting the child into a moving vehicle, then telling the child he/she is traveling in a helicopter or submarine. Again, the more outrageous the story, the less likely it will be believed. One Fort Bragg boy called the moving vehicle a 'space ship.'"[128]

Other children said they were taken to graveyards or crematoria, and many claimed to have been taken to churches. One child claimed to have been sexually assaulted underneath a painting titled "Jesus Knocking on the Door to Your Heart." Hudson concluded that "some Satanists deliberately use Christian settings" to deceive parents and confuse investigators. "Parents in Fort Bragg were reassured by the fact that the day care operators had Bible study meetings on Saturday nights. The unaware parent believes that if a day care center is associated with a Christian church or calls itself Christian, it is actually Christian."[129]

While Hudson's interpretations of the children's stories are *possible*, they are not proven, and if it is allowed that a story must be interpreted rather than taken literally, then many other possibilities arise. If Satanists may pretend to be Christians, hiring churches and so on, then it is just as possible that Christians may pretend to be Satanists, dressing up in black hooded robes and the like, to put investigators off their trail. The stories about airplanes, magic castles, and Santa Claus, however, sound exactly like the contents of children's fantasies, and since they were recovered from children, the most obvious conclusion would be that nothing had really happened.

It is interesting to compare these allegations with the case of "Mr. Friendly," a genuine instance of classroom abuse from the same period. For four years, Friendly, a respected teacher in the small mountain resort of Big Pine in the eastern Sierras, seduced every fifth-grade boy in the town. He finally came unstuck when a nine-year-old whose family had just moved there from Los Angeles joined his class. On his first day, the boy was initiated into Friendly's "noontime club." The next day the boy told his mother, who at once contacted the authorities.

Plenty of proof was forthcoming. Many boys admitted what had happened. A search of Friendly's classroom cabinets yielded sexual devices, cameras, and large quantities of still and motion pictures of Friendly and his students having oral and anal sex. One father had found Friendly and his son in bed together partly undressed. Friendly had explained it by saying that the boy had been bullied by his classmates, so he had offered him a massage to help him get over it. The father accepted this excuse at the time. Obviously, Friendly was not a Satanist and so was not able to cover his tracks in the way that Satanists could.[130]

For the lack of solid evidence for Satanic crime was now being explained as being due to a mass conspiracy. Asked who was present at Satanic rituals, small children would sometimes mention well-known film stars or other celebrities. It was deduced from this that "top people" were Satanists and so were able to cover up their activities successfully. The most remarkable apparent proof was in the form of the "WICCA letters," whose first known appearance was in the hands of a deputy San Diego sheriff, who had "decoded" them (how or from what was not explained). They formed a simple program for taking over the world, as follows:

1. To bring the Covens, both black and white magic, into one and have the actress [Query: *Who?*] to govern all—ACCOMPLISHED
2. To bring about personal debts causing discord and disharmony within families—ACCOMPLISHED
3. To remove or educate the "new age youth" by:
   a) infiltrating boys'/girls' clubs and big sister/brother programs
   b) infiltrating schools, having prayers removed, having teachers teach about drugs, sex, freedoms
   c) instigating and promoting rebellion against parents and all authority
   d) promoting equal rights for youth
   —ACCOMPLISHED
4. To gain access to all people's backgrounds and vital information by:
   a) use of computers

b) convenience

c) infiltration

—ACCOMPLISHED

5. To have laws changed to benefit our ways, such as:

a) removing children from the home environment and placing them in our foster homes

b) mandatory placement of children in our day-care centers

c) increased taxes

d) open drug and pornography market

—NOT YET ACCOMPLISHED

6. To destroy government agencies by:

a) overspending

b) public opinion

c) being on the offensive always, opposing, demonstrating, demoralizing

—NOT YET ACCOMPLISHED

7. *Not to be revealed until all else has been accomplished*:

Target date for revelation—JUNE 21, 1986—the beginning of the summer solstice, and great feast on the Satanic Calendar.

These letters were supposed to have been compiled in Mexico City in 1983, at a conference called for the purpose of conspiring to take over the world. The final revelation was later said to be "a blatant increase in satanic activity right up till June 21, 1999, when Satan himself will establish a physical reign on earth."[131]

Other Experts emphasized that Satanism was part of an international conspiracy. The U.S. Labor Party had been promoting belief in international conspiracies for some years. Led by an eccentric named Lyndon LaRouche, the party had originally come out of the 1960s progressive student movement and at first had Maoist connections, but later it moved far to the right. When LaRouche unsuccessfully stood for the presidency of the United States in 1984, his election slogans included "Nuclear power is safer than sex" and "Feed Jane Fonda to the whales."[132]

In the 1970s the party claimed that there was a joint CIA-KGB plot to assassinate Lyndon LaRouche. "Dissident members of the group were subjected to 'debriefing' sessions, which later brought charges of kidnaping against their accusers. As a result the victims told tales, promoted by the LaRouche organization, of CIA brainwashing that involved details identical to those made later in tales of Satanic child abuse. These involved sex with animals, exposure to pornography and scatological humiliations."[133] As described in the party's official organs, such as the *New Federalist* and the *Executive Intelligence Review*, this conspiracy grew in size until it included even the queen of England, who financed the whole conspiracy means of a drug-smuggling ring that she led.

In the mid-1980s the scare came to include Satanism, and in their public handouts, the Labor Party claimed that 1.8 million children have "already disappeared in the U.S. alone." They identified as a leader "Satanist Robert McNamara, the former president of the World Bank," and claimed that the Episcopal Cathedral of St. John the Divine in New York was a center for "Satanic sexual violence."[134] Lesser fry included the OTO, Wicca, the Gnostic Church, Scottish Rite Freemasonry, and Jungian psychotherapists.

It might be objected that, far from conspiring together, most of these groups have nothing to do with one another. Scottish Rite Freemasonry, for instance, refuses even to recognize the existence of organizations such as the OTO, who make unauthorized use of their rituals, and the OTO itself is divided into competing factions, two of whom were engaged in a lawsuit during the late 1980s over who was the real OTO. (It was held to be the Caliphate OTO.) Larry Jones, founder of the Cult Crime Network, retorted to such criticisms in his *File 18 Newsletter* that this is the "horizontal conspiracy" model, whereas the true conspiracy is "vertical," that is, they all take their orders from a central source, and the rank and file might not realize that rival orders also belong to their conspiracy.[135]

It might also be asked: Why, if such a powerful cover-up is operating, are anti-Satanists able to talk about Satanism so openly? The answer, of course, is that the Lord protects his servants. In Rebecca Brown's third book, *Becoming a Vessel of Honor in the Master's Service*, she described how she, Elaine, "Esther," and "Betty" had been praying together at their home on 21 December 1988. This was Yule, and they were convinced that Satanists would come and try to sacrifice them.

Shadowy figures that looked like men with shotguns, gathered around the edge of the property. The tension grew. Everything outside was deathly still, but they could feel the demonic pressure steadily build up. Betty said it was silly for them to stand there doing nothing. "Let's do something constructive, like make chocolate chip cookies." They went into the kitchen, but as they started on the cookies, they heard thumps on the roof. Drawing on her knowledge of Satanic practice, Elaine, the former bride of Satan, suggested that the intruders were intending to light a fire above them: "That's typical for how these folks work." Rebecca told them to stand firm, though if the Satanists got into the house, "we will know that we must share the gospel with them."

Suddenly, they saw five men floundering on the ground outside. Angels of the Lord had manifested and thrown them off the roof! Half an hour later the men climbed up again, but again there was a struggle, then invisible arms grabbed them and dragged them off the property. Unable to reenter the grounds, eventually the Satanists gave up and drove off. "The girls ate cookies and praised the Lord for His wonderful deliverance from their enemies."[136]

Blonde, Blue-Eyed Virgins, Beware!

Rumors about Satanism (as opposed to the pronouncements of clergy and journalists) had been circulating in the United States at least since the 1970s. A favorite described how a woman driving alone late at night, in some remote area, encountered a group of robed and hooded figures. They formed a chain, with linked arms, across the road, blocking her path. Rather than stopping, she accelerated and hit one of them, the rest of them scattering. Later, blood was found on her bumper, but when sheriff's deputies visited the scene, they found nothing.[137] This story was of the "foaf" variety, that is, the woman concerned is not named but is most often identified as a "*friend of a friend*" (hence *foaf*) of the narrator. In general, foaf stories prove impossible to pin down.

In February 1974, this rumor, which circulated, among other places, in the town of Missoula, Montana (population 38,000), was picked up by the media in neighboring Spokane, Washington. Then, in April a Missoula woman, Donna Pounds, was found murdered in her basement. She had been raped, bound, and then shot in the head. Her murderer was never caught.[138]

Within a few days a rumor had gone around Missoula that she had been sacrificed by a Devil-worshiping cult. Unlike most such rumors, this one was monitored by sociologists from the University of Montana. They found widepread belief that "devil signs" had been cut into Pound's body, that a pentagram had been painted on the wall in her blood, and that a Satanic book describing a sacrifice ritual had been found in a trash can nearby.[139] (None of this was true.) It was also believed that there were going to be three murders in all, "a Christian woman, a virgin, and a betrayer." A five-year-old girl had been stabbed to death a couple of months earlier (these were the first murders in Missoula for two years); she was the virgin, and Pounds the Christian woman. The murder of the betrayer was uneasily anticipated, though fortunately, it never occurred.

Jeffrey S. Victor, professor of sociology at Jamestown Community College in Jamestown, New York, recorded details of thirty-one separate rumor-panics that occurred in the United States over 1987–89. He noted that about 65 percent involved the kidnapping and ritual sacrifice of children, and that "about 40 percent of these kidnapping stories specifically mention blond, blue-eyed children or virgins—cultural symbols of innocence and purity." Another interesting detail was that they nearly always occurred in small towns and rural areas, not big cities.

He was able to chart in detail a panic that occurred in his own town. The first incident to set people talking was on 31 October 1987, when about sixty teenagers held a party at "the warehouse," a disused factory that had become a rehearsal place for local rock bands. Many of the guests had punk hairstyles or wore Halloween costumes. Jamestown being a somewhat out-of-the-way place, punk styles were thought (in 1987) to be "new" and "strange." Rumors started to circulate among those not involved about sex and drug orgies at the warehouse.[140]

On 19 November, the *Geraldo* show had a feature on "Satanic Cults and Children," making all the allegations that had by now become usual nationwide: "There are over one million Satanists in this country . . . they have attracted police and FBI attention to their Satanic ritual child abuse, child pornography, and grizzly Satanic murders. The odds are that this is happening in your town." By January, several concerned parents had become convinced that it was indeed happening in Jamestown and had called a Catholic priest to suggest that Satanic rituals were taking place at the warehouse.[141] It is typical of Satanic panics that people's first instinct is to contact the church rather than law enforcement, but later the police started to receive calls, too—by May, they had "hundreds."

By April, rumors specified that Satanists killed cats at their meetings. From 16 April, the Humane Society began to receive phone calls about the killing of cats, which grew progressively more frequent, though no bodies of slain cats or dogs were found.[142]

On the weekend of 16–17 April, two out-of-town Experts on Satanism spoke at a local fundamentalist church and afterward went to a wooded area behind Jamestown Community College known as "the hundred acre lot," where there was a purported ritual site. They ran into the police, who were themselves investigating the spot. Together they found a fire, around which trees were marked with graffiti slogans such as "Get Stoned." When the college authorities went to the site on the Monday, they found twenty-five anti-Satanist Chick Tracts (specifically, *Pity the Poor Witch*) in plastic envelopes. Rumor soon turned them into pro-Satanist propaganda.[143]

By May the rumors had come to include planned violence by "the cult." The most common version was that they planned to sacrifice a blonde, blue-eyed virgin on Friday the thirteenth. (No one seems to have wondered how it was that the secret plans of a secret cult were so generally known.) At least one mother was sufficiently concerned to dye her blonde daughter's hair brown.[144] After Friday the thirteenth had been and gone, the panic subsided. It should be added that many other panics centered on Friday the thirteenth, and that between 1984 and 1989, sacrifices of blonde, blue-eyed virgins were expected in Arkansas, South Carolina, Kentucky, West Virginia, Montana, Virginia, Indiana, Wisconsin, Kansas, Wyoming, Pennsylvania, North Carolina, Texas, New Mexico, and Georgia, though in no known case did one actually occur.

Three states eventually produced laws against "ritual crime." The Idaho legislature did so only after hearing the testimony of "Anne," a Survivor of Satanism. She said that her parents and grandparents all belonged to one of twelve covens, the high priests of which formed a thirteenth coven, led by a man called the Supreme. "The Supreme had ultimate control over every member of every coven."

Anne declared that she was dedicated to Satan at the age of three. At age five, as a ritual test, she had to drink the blood of two sacrificed girls and kill a kitten. She passed and was chosen to train as a priestess for the coven. For twelve years, "I was forced time and time again to eat flesh and drink blood of both animal and human sacrifices. I was also forced to drink urine, eat feces, and to eat bugs."

The most traumatic sacrifice for her was that of a friend named Jenny. "She had beautiful long, blonde hair and blue eyes . . . my hands were on the knife under the hands of the high priest when Jenny died. . . . I never mentioned Jenny to anyone until I told my therapist a couple of years ago."[145] No supporting evidence for Anne's testimony was presented.

By the end of the 1980s, the scare was beginning to lose its impetus. Robert Hicks, a criminal justice analyst in Richmond, Virginia, described the law-enforcement model of cult crime, as presented at seminars all over the country, as "ill-considered, based on non-documented secondary sources or other unsubstantiated information, and . . . rife with errors of logic." He argued this point at length in articles and eventually a book, *In Pursuit of Satan* (1991).

A 1989 report for the Committee for Scientific Examination of Religion, *Satanism in America*, produced serious objections to the pronouncements of anti-Satanists:

> Where are all the bodies? Where are the rituals held? Where are the blood, the bones, the teeth, the hair, the fibers from the victims' clothes? . . .
>
> In fact, not a single arrest, let alone conviction, has resulted from the testimony of the 'survivors'. . . . The breeders' stories are bizarre and inconsistent. Lauren Stratford, for example, is not even consistent from interview to interview on how many of her children were murdered—she claimed to have given up three on the *Oprah Winfrey Show* but only one on the *Sally Jessie Raphael Show*.[146]

Other problems soon arose concerning Lauren Stratford. In September 1989, she was booked as a star speaker at an anticult weekend, the Rockford Conference on Discernment and Evangelism, scheduled to take place in Rockford, Illinois. Three weeks beforehand one of the organizers, Eric Pement, editor of *Cornerstone* magazine, received a phone call from another anticultist, Kurt Goedelman of Personal Freedom Outreach. Goedelman expressed doubts about the validity of Stratford's reminiscences, mentioning that her real name was Laurel Wilson and giving Pement the phone numbers of her mother and sister. From her book it had appeared that her mother was dead, and no sister was mentioned at all. Pement thought that Stratford was "credible," but nonetheless he made some phone calls that tended to confirm Goedelman's cautions. So he told Stratford that she could not appear at the conference unless she provided other witnesses or evidence for her story. She refused to do so and her name was pulled, but she turned up in Rockford anyway and gave a presentation on Satanic ritual abuse at a Pentecostal church.

Meanwhile, Pement had assigned one of his journalists, Jon Trott, to check out Stratford's story, in which task he was soon joined by anti-occult writers Bob and Gretchen Passantino. They were able to contact a number of people who had known Wilson/Stratford well and quickly found that, instead of years of active Satanism, she had a long history of involvement in Christianity and a record of persistently making false accusations of sexual abuse. At various times over the years, she had claimed to have been raped by her own father, assaulted by her brother-in-law, molested by several teachers, sold into prostitution by her "step-mother" (there was no such person), and seduced by lesbian members of the Assembly of God Church. More than one person had observed her cutting her own arms, creating the scars that she would later blame on Satanic cultists. She was accustomed to go to great lengths to get attention: though never a drug user, she had once pretended to be an addict and gone through a drug-abuse program at Teen Challenge in Los Angeles. While staying with an Evangelical couple, she had even pretended to be blind, but when she accidentally gave away that she could see, she admitted to faking it so as to win sympathy. In the mid-1970s she had told a friend a series of stories about abuse by her mother, mentioning enemas, penetration by sharp objects, and other details that the friend finally realized were identical to those related in Flora Rheta Schreiber's *Sybil* (a book about an adult recalling child abuse, published in 1973). It was only in 1984, after stories of Satanic abuse had started to be made public, that she had introduced Satanism into her routine. This contradicted all her previous stories of abuse, and even her stories about Satanism changed a few times before she settled on the version given in her book.[147]

Her father, the *Cornerstone* journalists discovered, had died in 1965. She was born in 1941, so according to her chronology, she would have been forced into all kinds of sex acts for twenty years. In 1966 she married the son of a Pentecostal minister. (This is not mentioned in her book.) The marriage lasted only two months, but Trott and the Passantinos traced her ex-husband, who, in the face of her allegations of two decades of Satanic abuse and of three children born before that date, confided an intimate fact: on their wedding night, she had still been a virgin.[148]

So the journalists asked Harvest House, Stratford's publishers, what proof they had of her testimony. They offered three things: (1) several staff members who had talked with Laurel were impressed by her sincerity; (2) Experts had confirmed to them that the kind of things described in her book really happened;(3) they gathered character references for her from her supporters. As to direct proof, they had none. After *Cornerstone* published their findings, Harvest House dropped the book, which in two years had sold 133,409 copies; but it was promptly reissued by another publisher.[149]

"Lauren Stratford" then faded from public view, to reappear a decade later as "Laura Grabowski," in whose guise she claimed to have been a child survivor of Auschwitz. She was now dying of a rare blood disease, she said, as a result of experiments performed on her by Dr. Josef Mengele. She told her new story convincingly enough to be given money by a Holocaust victims' fund and a Jewish care organization in Los Angeles.[150]

Gradually, too, some of the convictions for Satanic ritual abuse began to be overturned. In 1988, both Michelle Noble and Gayle Stickler Dove were given retrials on the grounds that the original proceedings had been flawed, and both women were acquitted.

As early as 1986, the California attorney general's office issued a highly critical report on the investigation into the Pitts-Dill case in Bakersfield. The sheriff's department in general showed "inexperience and lack of training." They had not had the training in child sexual abuse that is mandatory in California, though the deputies had found the time to attend a Satanic crime seminar in Nevada. The principal therapist had no training in sexual abuse investigation either. It noted that despite all their unsuccessful efforts to find bodies, they had not made obvious checks, such as medical tests on children who claimed to have been drugged by the Satanists. Leading questions had been asked of the children.

The report ignored the question of the convictions. In November 1990, however, they were all overturned on the grounds of prosecutorial misbehavior, after the seven accused had spent five years in prison.[151] Margaret Kelly Michaels's sentence would be overturned in 1993. Even the Bakersfield "Kniffen-McCuan ring" were released on 13 August 1996, after twelve years behind bars. The children who had accused them had since grown up and now said that they had claimed to be molested only because "they were pressured by social workers, sheriff's deputies and prosecutors" to say so. On the basis of their new testimony, a judge threw out the convictions.[152]

A two-day law-enforcement seminar on Satanism given by Lyle J. Rapacki in 1989 in Anchorage, Alaska, arranged by the Alaska Peace Officers for Christ, did not impress the officers attending, who found it to be a "fundamentalist Christian sermon." Subsequently, the Alaska Police Standards Council decided that Rapacki was "unqualified to teach the subject." They found that "Rapacki had perjured himself in an Oklahoma trial where he served as expert witness on Satanism, and that he had publicly lied about the death of a teenage girl. In a televised interview, Rapacki had described her murder at the hands of Satanists. He later admitted that the girl was not dead."[153]

In 1990, Ken Lanning, an FBI agent who specialized in child abuse, stated that he had investigated three-hundred cases of Satanic child abuse and found no evidence in any of them. In an official FBI report of January 1992, he wrote: "A satanic murder should be defined as one committed by *two or more* individuals who *rationally* plan the crime and whose PRIMARY motivation is to fulfill a prescribed satanic ritual calling for the murder. By this definition, I have been unable to identify even one documented satanic murder in the United States."[154] Some of the original Experts, notably Sandi Gallant, concurred with Lanning and withdrew their earlier conclusions.

In January 1990, verdicts were finally delivered in the McMartin trial, by which time it had become the most expensive in American legal history. All the children, parents, and Experts who had testified notwithstanding, there were a lot of problems with the case. Staff at the Red Carpet Carwash, Harry's Market, and St. Cross Episcopalian Church all testified it would have been absolutely impossible for children to have been abused on the premises without them noticing.[155] The number of child witnesses had been finally reduced to nine, those with the more extravagant stories not being called, so that more charges had to be dropped. Weeks spent looking at blown-up color slides of children's anuses established little, since Experts could not agree about them. A doctor called by the prosecution said of Judy Johnson's son, whose "itch" had started the whole Satanic abuse charade, that it proved he had been sodomized. A doctor called by the defense said, on the contrary, that it showed a rash consistent with infection caused by diarrhea.[156]

A great deal of fuss had been made about the fact that Ray Buckey did not wear underwear. When he finally took the witness stand, he explained that it was because he used to get wet when playing volleyball on the beach, and that underwear took longer to dry than shorts, giving him rashes, so he had stopped bothering with it. It was proved that once or twice he had unwittingly exposed his genitals in consequence. But this did not prove he was a member of an international conspiracy of Satanists who abused children in bloody rituals, any more than his collection of *Playboy* magazines proved anything other than a normal sexual desire for adult women.

On 18 January it was announced that the jury had deadlocked on thirteen counts and found the defendants not guilty on the other fifty-two. On every one of the deadlocked counts, at least seven jurors had been against conviction; but incredibly, a retrial of Buckey on these counts was called.[157] It was much shorter than the original, and on 27 July it was announced that the new jury was likewise deadlocked on all counts.[158] It would have been possible to try him yet again, but the state had already spent $16 million, and that was held to be enough. So, after seven years and the most expensive trial in American history, no one was found guilty of anything. Buckey had spent five years in prison, which leads one to query the old saying that "an innocent man has nothing to fear."

Yet certain events provided anti-Satanism with a new impetus. When the Matamoros killings were discovered, Pat Pulling and reporters from the *Oprah Winfrey Show* rushed enthusiastically down to Mexico to view the crime scene. Experts on Satanism appeared on television, saying that similar finds would soon be made in the United States. This prophecy has yet to be fulfilled. As the McMartin jury started to consider their verdicts, 27 million people watched a made-for-television CBS film, *Do You Know the Muffin Man?* concerning a case very similar to McMartin's, except that at the end, it turned out the day-care teachers really were Satanists, concerned parents finally discovering a robed ritual in a room full of child pornography. This film led to a number of new day-care Satanic abuse accusations. In South Carolina, several teachers at a preschool were accused of abuse, the man who ran the school, Bob Kelly, being accused among other things of sacrificing children in a spaceship and throwing others into a swimming pool full of sharks. The investigators did not find a swimming pool full of sharks—or for that matter, a spaceship—or any physical evidence whatsoever, apart from a single Polaroid photo, in a woman defendant's home, of her having sex with her (adult) fiancé;[159] but Kelly was nevertheless found guilty and given twelve life sentences, to be served consecutively.

And by now, the idea of dangerous criminal Satanic cults was spreading, like ripples from a disturbance in a pond, to the farthest parts of the world.

9

Is *Your* Vicar a Witch-Hunter?

On 14 April 1988, the Right Honorable Geoffrey Dickens, Conservative member of Parliament for Littleborough and Saddleworth, surprised the House of Commons by calling for a debate on witchcraft. He warned M.P.s that witchcraft was "sweeping the country" and said it was "common knowledge" that witches abused children, so there ought to be a law against them.[1] He was subjected to immediate derision, but nevertheless he was able to get a brief adjournment debate on the subject on 27 April 1988.

On that occasion Dickens said:

> First, I wish to warn parents to be vigilant and to impress upon their children the dangers of dabbling in black magic and other obscure occults. Secondly, I wish to call on all Christians to unite in prayer, word and deed to condemn Satanism and to provide kind and special support for those possessed by the devil who turn to the Church for help. Thirdly it is necessary to ensure that the Home Office is aware of and alert to the rapid growth in the United Kingdom of black witchcraft and Satanism.

He went on:

> This black magic influence is so strong and dangerous that the power and command over adults and children is total. Disgusting ceremonies are held, in which children are sexually abused by Satanists. Paedophiles are joining such groups because they have found yet another way to get their hands on children whom they know will be too terrified to talk.

Dickens, it must be said, had been involved in alerting the public and the House of Commons to the problem of child abuse for a number of years.

After giving vague reports of graveyard desecrations, child abuse, and the spread of occult shops, he warned that "we could soon follow the path of the United States of America." He concluded by stating: "It is my intention in a few weeks' time to hand a dossier to the Home Office, compiled by Childwatch and me," presumably giving details of these matters.

The reply of John Patten, the home secretary, was quite balanced:

It is a basic tenet of an open society such as ours that a person must be free to hold the beliefs that he or she wishes, as I am sure that my honourable friend agrees, but that principle is certainly modified by a clear requirement that any acts arising from such beliefs must be within the bounds of the criminal law, and I know that I have my honourable friend's agreement on that point.[2]

On 3 January 1988, the *Sunday Sport*, a journal famous for headlines like "World War II Bomber Found on Moon" and "Vampire's Bizarre Three-in-a-Bed Sex Romp," had quoted Dickens under the headline "Evil . . . Satanic Guides Are Sold to Kids." The story was that "an occult shop in Leeds" was selling copies of Anton LaVey's *The Satanic Rituals*. Dickens did not, in fact, have any evidence that children were buying it but assumed that they might do so, as it was not labeled "Not for sale to persons under 18 years of age." He said, "We are living in a mad society when perverted cults which worship the devil can freely publish guides on how to dabble in the occult. The Home Office must act."

This might not seem to amount to much—certainly it was not "news," since the book had been on sale in Great Britain for over a decade. But many more stories were to follow. On 13 March, the *Sport*'s "News Extra" section included "I Was Satan's Virgin Sacrifice": "Evil devil-worshipers turned a 20-year-old girl into a virgin sacrifice in a depraved sex ritual. Brainwashed Audrey Harper was cruelly raped by a top witch in a sick initiation ceremony." The article described how poor Audrey had met Satanists at a "drink and drugs party" and, within weeks, had been persuaded to attend a ritual at a house near Virginia Water in Surrey, to which she was "driven blindfolded," where there "were 13 women and one man—the high priest."

The story that followed was faintly familiar:

There were black candles burning and they were laced with heroin so everybody in the room became like zombies as they burnt. I was led in and made to lie down on the altar. Then the high priest slit the neck of a cockerel with a special dagger and daubed its blood over my breasts and thighs.

Audrey stayed in this cult for five years before she was able to break away by turning to God.

The next week, 20 March, the *Sport* had an interview with the Reverend Kevin Logan of St. John's Church near Blackburn, Lancashire, who claimed there were more than fifty witches' covens operating between Blackburn and Manchester. He was said to be planning a book "listing 30 murders committed in Britain during the past ten years as a direct result of witchcraft." Logan said, "I'm not launching a witch-hunt, but I'm begging people to be on their guard."

In August, the *Sunday Sport* launched a midweek edition called simply *The Sport*. The second issue had a spread: "'Please Save My Baby from Satan': The Sport exposes evil cult that threatened every child in Britain." It showed photographs of a pregnant woman in a churchyard, who was said in the text to be scared that Satanists wanted to kidnap her unborn child for the purposes of human sacrifice.

Who were these Satanists? They were the "Scorpio cult, which operates a worldwide web of evil and depravity." A certain Alan Blunden had been arrested and charged with criminal damage to business premises. His defense was that the business in question was run by Scorpio members.

The article quoted Dianne Core, the founder of an organization called Childwatch, who said of Scorpio that "some of them have scorpion belt buckles or badges. If you meet someone with a scorpion symbol anywhere on their person, look out. This is one of the most evil, disgusting societies I have ever come across." *The Sport* must have had a witty gremlin in its sub-editors' office, for on the page opposite this assertion was an advertisement for Zodiac jewelry.

As well as Scorpio, the anti-Satanists quoted in this article discussed the OTO. The Reverend Kevin Logan offered the Expert opinion that "the disciples of OTO are not harmless weirdos. They are very dedicated disciples of the occult. You will find them in business, the professions and in the Civil Service."

As evidence, *The Sport* produced Geoffrey Dickens, M.P., who remarked: "The problem is that people with real knowledge of the organization are just too frightened to speak out." The OTO was said to "include top politicians and generals among its members." The spread also agreed with Lyndon LaRouche's "influential" *Executive Intelligence Review* to the effect that "high-ranking NATO officials are involved."

Why were these sinister conspirators at large, undetected? A possible explanation appeared: "A DOSSIER naming perverted members of a sinister Satan Cult . . . has gone missing on its way to the House of Commons." Dianne Core had sent it to "the office of Witchfinder General MP Geoffrey Dickens at Westminster. But the package—whose full contents could have blown British society apart—never arrived." Having mail go astray is a depressingly familiar experience for many people nowadays, but Ms. Core seemed to think a conspiracy was to blame. "The OTO are a sinister and secretive sect with tentacles everywhere. Their influence even extends to the establishment." Nonetheless, readers were assured that Geoffrey Dickens, M.P., was himself compiling a dossier about the activities of Scorpio, "which he will soon be presenting to Home Secretary Douglas Hurd."[3]

What should one make of these claims? In 1995 I talked with the former head of the London OTO, who at the time was a fire-prevention officer with Camden Council. He said that at the organization's height they had about fifteen members, but they later went into decline, ceasing to meet in 1992. It would be difficult for fifteen people to extend their sinister tentacles everywhere, even if they wanted to; and there is, in any case, no reason to think they were engaged in anything criminal. The beliefs and rituals of the OTO are openly published, and though bizarre by most people's standards, there is nothing illegal about them. I cannot comment on Scorpio, as I have never met any members, nor have I ever met anyone who claims to have met any members; in contrast to the OTO, whose history has been written up in tedious detail, no one had heard of Scorpio before 1988, when the name suddenly appeared in the press like a rabbit from a hat.

The statement that Dickens was preparing a dossier to send to the home secretary was repeated in a number of popular newspapers. The following spring, Chris Bray of the Sorcerer's Apprentice (the occult shop in Leeds that Dickens had been complaining about) wrote a query on it to the Home Office. He received a reply stating that, despite press reports that Dickens had sent a dossier of child abuse allegedly connected with witchcraft to the home secretary, this dossier had not been received. They added that they had no other evidence of a problem of the kind he described, and that, in any case, existing laws would be adequate to deal with any such cases if they did occur.[4]

Some of these things, such as statements that witchcraft was sweeping the country and dossiers that were going to expose famous people as Satanists but never materialized, had been heard of in Britain back in the 1950s. Dickens's statements that "children are sexually abused by Satanists," however, were new to this country but astonishingly similar to what had been asserted in America for the previous few years. One has to conclude either that Satanists of the child-abusing type had extended their sinister conspiracy across the ocean from the United States or that the panic about child-abusing Satanists had been imported, as evidenced by *The Sport*'s quotation from a LaRouchist journal.

As to the first possibility, there is no evidence for it, not even of the kind that would convince an anti-Satanist. Jacquie Balodis, an American Survivor and founder of Overcomers Victorious, claimed to have been taken to many far-flung places by the Satanists, including Britain.[5] But that is the only piece of evidence offered by believers for the international nature of criminal Satanism.

What about the possibility of the importation of the scare? All through the 1980s it was common, every summer, to see young American Evangelicals on the heathen streets of London, asking complete strangers: "Have you heard?" Around 1987, I watched a group of these Americans lay hands on one of their fellows, who was babbling "in tongues." I supposed this was meant to be the gift of the Holy Spirit, but when I asked, one of them informed me that he was possessed by a demon. Most of these Evangelicals would have been aware of the American Satanism scare, and some would probably have talked about it. Christian bookshops always have a certain amount of imported American stock, and this has included *He Came to Set the Captives Free* and other titles promoting the Satanic child abuse scare.

The first hint of things to come was in the autumn of 1987, when the Evangelical magazine *Prophecy Today* told its readers: "Britain is under siege from the Satanists. . . . Information we are presently receiving suggest the reintroduction of infant sacrifice into Britain that is a throw-back to the pre-Christian era of paganism. The repeal in 1951 of the 1735 Witchcraft Act opened the door to blood sacrifice. It underlines the seriousness of the Satanic attack." As proof of all this, the magazine pointed out: "The marriage breakdown rate in Britain today is nearly one in every two marriages." In case any reader should fail to spot instantly the connection between Satanism and the divorce rate, the editors also included an interview with a Christian ex-witch, who claimed: "Witches also pray for the breakdown of Christian marriages; I used to take part in that."[6]

In addition to this, a supplementary insert, *NOW!* had a headline "Occult Menace to World Finance," though the article underneath was less sensational than one might think, merely noting that share traders had taken to consulting astrologers. Another headline, "Devil Worshipers Double" topped an article that claimed the number of Satanists in the United Kingdom had "more than doubled in five years to an estimated 15,000, meeting in thirty-one groups across the country." Unfortunately, the writers did not explain who had made this estimate or how.

The year 1987 also saw the appearance of Toyne Newton's *The Demonic Connection*, a book that suggested the existence of large and powerful Devil-worshiping cults with rich and powerful members, including unnamed television personalities. Unfortunately, the only evidence provided was a journalist's interview with a man who claimed to represent the "Friends of

Hekate," a vast and powerful and sinister occult organization. The reporter did not seem to realize that this sort of claim is routinely made by would-be Satanist leaders who do not have so much as one disciple.

It is certain that British social workers, who often take their lead from the United States, imported American Satanic abuse Expertise. Pamela Klein, one of the original American Experts on Satanic ritual abuse, resided in England from July 1985 to January 1986. While in the country, she set up a business with an English social worker, Norma Howes, as a consultant for cases of child sexual abuse.

In 1988, a two-year-old boy in Kent was showing signs of disturbed behavior: "He kept wanting to take his clothes off, would laugh hysterically, and told about strange drinks that made him feel funny." Norma Howes was called in as a consultant, and she, in turn, took advice from her old colleague Pamela Klein, who offered a diagnosis of Satanic abuse over the telephone. Klein sent over a list of "Satanic Indicators," apparently a version of Catherine Gould's, including "an unusual preoccupation with urine and feces, fear of ghosts and monsters, aggressive play, and the child being 'clingy,' reciting nursery rhymes with indecent overtones, suffering from nightmares and bed wetting, preoccupation with 'passing gas,' using mouth to make 'gas sounds' and wild laughter when the child or someone else 'passes gas.'" Not surprisingly, the child concerned was found according to these tests to have been Satanically abused. When it came to a hearing, however, the judge did not believe the boy had been abused but maintained that his mother, who was divorced from his father, had put him up to making the allegations.[7]

Stories about Satanism and children started to appear in other papers in late 1988. The front page of the *Daily Mirror* on 10 November stated that a "blue-eyed" four-year-old girl and her two-year-old brother had been "rescued from a sect of devil worshipers." Their mother had discovered, with the help of social workers, that they had been "sexually abused by their father and other evil members of a nationwide satanistic cult." Dianne Core, founder of Childwatch, said that the family were "in danger." Needless to say, "a dossier on the coven—including sex acts with animals—has been compiled by Mrs Chris Strickland who runs a support group in Cumbria called Mothers of Abused Children."

The article went on to explain how the mother had no idea what was going on, except that she had noticed her son was bruised. But after her husband was jailed for assaulting her, she and the social workers had found that they had been made to take part in rituals involving sexual abuse and human sacrifice. A follow-up article on 11 November added that police were searching for someone known to children as "the Bugs Bunny Man" or "the Vicar," who would get them to chant, "Oh Lord, Prince of Darkness," as they danced around a fire. "The man has also turned up in other parts of the country, Childwatch founder Dianne Core said yesterday."

On 27 January 1989, the *Colchester Evening Gazette* had an article by Gordon Thomas describing the work of Sandi Gallant: "They call her Satan's Cop, ten years ago fellow officers laughed when she said the devil was on the rampage. Now, thousands of demon related crimes later, they listen when she says 1989 could be a particularly bad year for satanic crime—not only in the USA but also in Britain." The "most conservative" estimate of the number of Devil worshipers in America was "more than four million," and Susan Davidson of the Adam Walsh Center "says there could be as many as 500,000 active satanist cults in Britain alone." (Unless "satanist cults" is a mistake for "Satanic cultists," these cults could not be very large; otherwise there would not be enough people in Britain to go around.) "Through Interpol, [Gallant's] advice is available to police forces in Britain. She has a package of tapes that provide a unique series of guidelines on how to investigate satanic crimes."

On 21 May 1989, the front page of the *Sunday Mirror* had a picture of a toddler with the headline "Saved from Devil's Cult Sacrifice." It appeared that someone in Kidderminster had told Social Services in Nottingham that a child in Crawley had been marked out as a human sacrifice. The report was passed on to the police, in consequence of which the parents kept an all-night vigil, accompanied by two C.I.D. officers. Nothing untoward happened.

Nonetheless, the paper was able to cite several Experts as to the dangers of Satanism. Roger Cook, of the television show *The Cook Report*, told them: "Satanism is spreading in the UK. It isn't illegal. But many Satanists commit illegal acts, some on young children, which are sickening and repugnant." Geoffrey Dickens, M.P., who "has compiled a dossier on Satanic cults," said: "I am satisfied beyond any shadow of doubt that human sacrifices and cannibalism takes place in Britain today." And Audrey Harper, "a committed Christian who urges children not to dabble in the occult," estimated: "In just one area of Surrey there must be 30 live human sacrifices a year."

Then there were the victims. Maureen Davies, a director of the Reachout Trust, told the *Mirror* the story of "Penny," who had been made pregnant five times by a coven to which her parents had introduced her. "Penny's life is at risk. If the Satanists knew she was going to spill the beans, they would stop at nothing to shut her up." (Query: Did she not think there was any chance that the Satanists might read the *Sunday Mirror*?) She added that the abortions were performed by "a doctor who is a member of the coven," and so, as there was no evidence, the police had not been called in.

The police had, however, been involved in the case of "Samantha," who claimed to have been used as a "broodmare" by a Satanic cult and made pregnant no fewer than eight times between the ages of eleven and fourteen, the child in every case being aborted for use in Satanic rituals. "Some of the aborted foetuses were put in a freezer, to be eaten later at disgusting ceremonies." Her story had led to a prosecution, which had been dropped: "A spokesman for the Crown Prosecution Service explained: 'Because of the nature of the evidence by the principal witness, we considered that it would be unsafe and unsatisfactory to be put before a jury.'"

More about Samantha's story was later revealed by Dianne Core and Tim Tate (who called her "Teresa" and "Natalie," respectively). A product of a broken home, she was sent to live with her grandmother in Suffolk for some years. In January 1988, however, when she was fourteen, she turned up at her mother's home in Sussex and pleaded to be taken back. Her mother agreed.[8]

In February 1988, Lauren Stratford appeared on the *Oprah Winfrey Show*, speaking of her Satanic cult experiences.[9] She told viewers how she had watched children being murdered and had herself been made to breed babies for human sacrifice. Shortly afterward, Samantha started to tell her mother that her grandmother was a priestess of a Satanic cult and had taken her to a country house where rituals were held, where Lucifer was present in person, and where she had watched children being murdered and had herself been used as a "breeder."[10] Altogether, she had been raped and made pregnant eight times. Seven of these pregnancies had been aborted at the fifth month, sacrificed, and eaten, but the eighth had miscarried in a toilet at school. She showed her mother the tiny fetus, which she had taken home with her in a pencil case.[11] Soon she was telling her story to the metropolitan police.

Corroborative evidence was hard to come by. A medical examination showed that Samantha had certainly been pregnant at least once (the fetus proved this anyway). But most women who have successive abortions become infertile after the third or fourth, and eight amateur abortions ought to have left distinctive marks on her womb, even if they were possible. It was suggested that she had been brainwashed by the cult to make her think there had been more pregnancies than there really were, in order to discredit her story if she talked. Police drove her through the countryside in search of the house where the rituals had taken place, and where presumably there were still mutilated children. She claimed to have been forced to attend three ceremonies a week for ten years, suggesting that she had been to this house fifteen hundred times, yet she could not locate it. It was supposed that the Satanists had given her drugs to stop her from remembering properly.

Seven men named by Samantha were arrested and charged with rape, and her grandmother was charged with aiding and abetting rape and procuring an illegal abortion. Prosecution lawyers, however, insisted there be no mention of Satan worship, murder, or cannibalism.[12] (To claim that murders had happened, without any corpses or missing persons, would invite ridicule.)

Meanwhile, Samantha was put in therapy with a counseling teacher, who encouraged her to write down her experiences in a notebook. A few days before the trial was due to start at the Old Bailey, the counselor gave the book to prosecution lawyers. She did not realize that they would be obliged to disclose it to the defense, and that they had already decided they would have no chance of winning if the whole of Samantha's story was told in court. So when the trial was due to start, they announced that they would offer no evidence, and the case was dropped.[13]

It may be that Britain harbored a secret cult very similar to those alleged to exist in America, particularly in their remarkable ability to cover their tracks. In view of the fact, however, that the police were unable to find any corroboratory evidence at all, one has to consider another possibility; that Samantha had concocted a fantasy based on the *Oprah Winfrey Show* and a grudge against her grandmother. Notice that the medical examination proved only that she had been pregnant once. A thirteen-year-old girl becoming pregnant once is not such an unusual event that a Satanic conspiracy is needed to explain it.

Horror stories about Satanism nevertheless grew more frequent. "Children Sacrificed to Satan," proclaimed the July–August issue of *NOW!* citing Geoffrey Dickens; the Reverend Kevin Logan ("30 murders committed in Britain in the last ten years were the direct result of witchcraft"); Dianne Core ("pedophiles . . . are joining witch covens in their droves . . . because of their reputation for easy child sex"); Doreen Irvine ("a Christian exorcist cast out 48 demons from her"); and a "reformed black witch" who seems to have been Audrey Harper. They concluded: "Witchcraft is no longer illegal in Britain. *It should be.*"

A *Cook Report* special on Satanism was transmitted on 17 July 1989, following a considerable amount of tabloid hype. The *Report*'s researcher, Tim

Tate, had first learned about Satanic abuse from American Experts, some of whom were featured in the program, along with the Reverend Kevin Logan and Audrey Harper. "Samantha," filmed in silhouette, described what happened at Satanic rituals: "They used to talk about Lucifer. He used to appear and be there, and they used to say it was for him. And I thought he was a normal person, you know, just another person who was there. But now I know that he was a spirit or something."

The makers had less success in finding Satanists to interview. Perhaps in desperation, they included shots of an Ozzy Osbourne concert, followed by an interview in which Osbourne concluded, "It takes me all my time to conjure myself out of bed." To be able to film a genuine Satanic ritual, they had paid for Michael and Lilith Aquino to come over from America to initiate David Austen as the British head of the Temple of Set, in front of their cameras. Central TV provided them with a ritual site by a lake on a golf course near Birmingham and enlivened the ceremony with dry-ice smoke effects. (This greatly annoyed Dianne Core, who complained to the *Star*: "It is horrendous that Roger Cook brought him into this country when we are fighting to keep him out."[14] In consequence, she had been dropped as a consultant for the program.)

Cook also tried to "doorstep" Chris Bray of the Sorcerer's Apprentice in Leeds. Bray locked the shop up, and when the camera crew would not go away, he called the police and he and his staff departed wearing Halloween masks.

A "help line" that was open after the program and staffed among others, by Maureen Davies received nine hundred telephone calls. The next day, most of the newspapers were cynical. More than one viewer had been irked by the way in which Audrey Harper casually lumped together homosexuals, lesbians, and pedophiles. *The Times* commented that it had become difficult to distinguish comic parodies of television journalism from the real thing. But somebody must have taken the program seriously, as a month later, in the early hours of 13 August, someone broke into the Sorcerer's Apprentice, piled up witchcraft and Aleister Crowley books, and set fire to them. The conflagration caused serious damage to the shop, but fortunately, it was spotted by a passerby who called the fire brigade.

Chris Bray then set up the "Sorcerer's Apprentice Fighting Fund" (SAFF), with the hope of preventing this sort of behavior from spreading. They sent out information bulletins to all interested parties, which did something to counteract the Christian propaganda that was also being sent in all directions. The Broadcasting Complaints Commission eventually produced a report in which they admitted that the program had been "unfair" to Bray, though they, too, insisted that as a whole it had been a serious investigation into Satanism.[15]

On 25 March 1990, under the headline "I Sacrificed My Babies to Satan," the *Sunday Mirror* reported that a twenty-three-year-old woman, Caroline Marchant, had committed suicide at the Reverend Kevin Logan's vicarage. Marchant was a Survivor of Satanism, and it was supposed that she had killed herself from fear that the Satanists would "get" her for her disclosures.

While still a teenager, it was reported, Caroline had met a boy named Danny in a village in Norfolk, whose parents were Satanists who lured her into their coven. The mother, "a high priestess who served her Master at the altar," initiated her. Caroline had recalled:

> I was a very keen candidate to join Satan's kingdom. The ceremony was very long and many people attended. When the time came I stepped forward to the altar. An incision was made in my arm and some of the blood caught in a cup. I drank from the cup and sealed my life over to Satan forever, rejoicing that I was now a bonded child of Satan. Much sexual perversion went on that night. Later I learned more of Satan and practiced my arts calling on the power of darkness. Satan had really become my Lord and Master.

Careful readers will have already noticed that this confession is very similar, sometimes word for word, with that of Doreen Irvine in *From Witchcraft to Christ* (1973); which was itself extraordinarily similar to that of Mrs. S. Jackson, made to the *Sunday Pictorial* in 1955; whose story was itself derived from the writings of Rollo Ahmed; which, in turn, were largely based on Montague Summers's resurrection of the old witch-hunters' manuals. Caroline's version does, however, have new details not found in Jackson's and Irvine's accounts, primarily the ritual slaughter of newborn babies, including a couple of her own. Caroline had said that "snuff" videos had been made of these sacrifices: "'She told me they are still available on the black market,' said Maureen Davis [*sic*], who runs Reach Out, a Christian sanctuary for reformed Satanists." Caroline had even claimed that Danny had eventually been sacrificed by his own father. Scars and burns on Caroline's body were said to have been inflicted by Satanists.

In December 1990, the *Independent on Sunday* produced the results of their own inquiry into Marchant's case.[16] The reporters had carefully investigated her life and found that she had always lived with other people, none of whom knew anything of any Satanic involvement. They learned that in the spring of 1985, while she was living with a girl she had met through a

Baptist church, she used to scratch herself compulsively until the blood ran. This was the source of her "Satanic" scars.

The same friend, Sarah Pollard, recalled that "Caroline first claimed to have been involved in Satanism some time after she read a book called *From Witchcraft to Christ*. I loaned her my copy of it while we were on a visit to Cirencester in the summer of 1986. She began to hear voices and believe she was possessed by demons."[17]

In the summer of 1987, Caroline rowed with Sarah, and for the next three years she lived in various Christian Evangelical centers and moved around in an "informal network of Christian households." Eventually she produced her "diary," actually an autobiography dealing with events supposed to have taken place years earlier. She met Doreen Irvine while being counseled at the Zion Christian Temple at Yate, near Bristol.

Though Caroline claimed in her autobiography that, while she was a teenager, the Satanists had made her pregnant, the *Independent on Sunday* journalists found close friends of hers from that time who were certain she had never been pregnant. One said, "If Caroline had even missed a period she would have told us about it." Another pointed out that she had been an enthusiastic dance pupil and could not have hidden a pregnancy, even one that was aborted, while wearing a leotard. (Apparently, the *Sunday Mirror* had not tried to interview any of these people but relied instead on information given to them by the Reverend Kevin Logan and Maureen Davies.)

She had indeed known a youth called Danny in Norfolk. He was not murdered in a Satanic ritual but killed in a motorcycle crash in 1983. Everyone who knew him rejected Caroline's claims as preposterous.

By early 1990, Caroline was suicidal. Walking on Brighton Promenade, arms linked with those of two women counselors, she tried to hurl herself and them into the path of a car. A few hours later, in a nearby vicarage, she slashed one of her wrists.[18]

On 15 February 1990, she arrived at the Reverend Kevin Logan's vicarage. She told him (as he would later report on a television program) that she had been recruited into Satanism when she had been hanging around a railway station in London.[19] This completely contradicted the story told in her "diary."

She was shortly to undergo a "debriefing," in which she was expected to reveal information about Satanic "recruitment, snuff videos, political hierarchy systems, Satanic financing . . . the IRA, Baader-Meinhof, Libyan connection," and so on. None of this interesting material would ever be known, because the next morning she took a whole bottle of amitriptyline, after leaving Logan a suicide note. When he realized what had happened, he drove her straight to Blackburn and Lancashire Royal Infirmary (rather than risk waiting for an ambulance), but she had gone into a coma and died on 5 March.

The journalists' conclusion was that her suicide was due not to fear of Satanist retribution but to fear that the anti-Satanists would find out she had been fibbing all along.[20] It is only fair to add that the Reverend Kevin Logan did not think so, and he later wrote movingly of his memory of her and his distress at being unable to save her.[21]

Readers will have noticed by now that the same names crop up again and again in these articles: Geoffrey Dickens, M.P., the Reverend Kevin Logan, Maureen Davies, Dianne Core, and Audrey Harper. Who were these people?

Geoffrey Dickens (1931–95) worked his way up from a deprived background. In 1972 he was awarded the Royal Humane Society's Testimonial on vellum for saving the lives of two boys and a man who had tried to rescue them from drowning, off the coast of Majorca. Eventually, he became "one of the most colorful figures to have graced the Tory backbenches since the Second World War."[22] He was vocal on a wide range of subjects: he called for the outlawing of crossbows and dangerous teddy bears; he was against homosexuality, particularly in the church; he urged the chemical castration of a rapist, in one case, and electric fences to control misbehavior at football matches; in 1988, he warned of a threat of locusts being borne on grains of sand blown from the Sahara; another time he urged that seals should be put on contraceptive pills to ease their plunder of the nation's fishing stock. He suffered from the afflictions of Dr. Spooner and Mrs. Malaprop, on one occasion referring heatedly to "these Fidopiles" and on another shouting, "Many lives have been saved by the Prevention of Television Act!" (He meant Terrorism.)

He was active in campaigns against pedophiles and rapists (for both of whom he suggested, at the 1991 Tory Party Conference, the solution "Castrate the buggers!" to enormous applause), and he "cultivated a network of anti-paedophile vigilantes who fed him with information."[23] It was these people who, in 1988, got him to extend his attack on pedophilia to include the network of child-abusing Satanists.

One of Dickens's regular informants was Dianne Core, the founder of Childwatch, an independent child welfare organization who have helped bring about the prosecution of a number of pedophiles. After the death of the Reverend Jan Knos, who was awaiting trial on several charges of indecent assault on children at his vicarage, the *Telegraph* reported: "Childwatch, the children's protection group . . . is compiling a dossier on 10 clergymen, five of whom are said to be currently involved in sexual abuse. The others have had allegations made against them in the past. Mrs. Dianne Core . . . alleged that some church leaders were attempting to 'cover up the scandal' which was linked to a severe problem of homosexuality in the Church."[24] A few days later, *Today* reported: "Church leaders will be urged today to crack down on pervert clergymen who prey on young children. Officials from the charity Childwatch will present the Archbishop of Canterbury's office with a 'disturbing' dossier. The meeting follows accusations by Childwatch founder Mrs. Dianne Core and MP Geoffrey Dickens, a trustee, that homosexuality is rife in the Church of England."[25] It seems the cover-up was successful, as nothing came of all this. Notice that Core and Dickens did not bother to distinguish homosexuals from pedophiles.

Like many social workers, Core tries to stay informed of American developments, and in 1987, she acquired some of the anti-Satanist material produced in California by Sandi Gallant. Soon afterward, Core was uncovering evidence of child-abusing Satanic cults in Hull. A teenage rent-boy (male prostitute) claimed to have been sexually abused by a cult named Scorpio, though he refused to give names or any other details that would enable his abusers to be identified.

One of Core's regular contacts was Dr. Kenneth McAll, a Christian psychiatrist who had claimed, in the early 1980s, that some mental illnesses were caused by demonic possession. McAll had also been finding evidence of Satanic abuse and estimated that Satanists carried out four thousand human sacrifices a year in Britain. This figure was frequently repeated by Core in media interviews.

Both McAll and Core were somehow linked to the Lyndon LaRouche organization, who arranged for them to go on lecture tours. In early 1989, Core spoke at a LaRouche conference in Rome and subsequently in the United States. Her speech in Atlanta, Georgia, was printed in the *New Federalist* under the title "We Are in the Middle of Spiritual Warfare." She claimed that, according to "information that we are getting from all over the British Isles," there are women "born to families within the cult, or chosen by the cult, to have babies. The babies aren't registered, and in fact what happens is they sometimes go the full pregnancy, then the baby is taken off them, and is sacrificed at one of the big Satanic feasts." She gave a list of indicators of Satanic abuse in children: "Crying for no apparent reason. Inordinate fear of adults. Nightmares. Appetite changes. Conversation about bizarre foods. Acting-out behavior which is not common. Strange language forms or content." Finally, she stated enigmatically that St. John the Divine Cathedral in New York was full of unspecified "Satanic activities" that "need to be taken in hand by the people of America and stopped."[26]

Kevin Logan, born in 1943, was brought up a Catholic but lapsed as an adult. He began a career in journalism but was later converted to the Church of England and went to theological college. He was ordained in 1975 and in 1982 became vicar of St. John's Church in Great Harwood, Lancashire,[27] not many miles from Pendle, famous for the 1612 mass execution of nineteen residents for witchcraft. Logan admits, "As an over-zealous convert from Roman Catholicism, I have identified my fair share of Antichrists in the past—all centered on Rome and the Pope."[28] Around 1987, he took part in a campaign by local churches who wanted to erect a twenty-foot-high rolled-steel cross atop Pendle Hill. They pointed to the fact that it was there George Fox had the vision that led him to start the Quaker movement. At the same time, Logan started complaining about forces of darkness in the area and declared the existence of thirty local witch covens. (There was some fitness in this, as George Fox had devoted twenty pages of one of his religious tracts to attacking witchcraft: "But every child of God, born of the spirit of God, judgeth the Adulterer and Witch. Arise children of God, and judge, and not suffer the Witch to live."[29] Ironically, the early Quakers were regarded with so much suspicion that some of them were accused of witchcraft.) In the end, the council vetoed the giant cross on aesthetic grounds.

Logan's 1988 book, *Paganism and the Occult*, did not have the promised list of thirty murders caused by witchcraft but was rather, as its subtitle said, "a manifesto for Christian action." He had noticed that devotees of Paganism and the occult were increasing in numbers, while attendances at some churches were declining, and addressed the question of how Pagans could be made to share in the gifts of the Holy Spirit. He included a list of indicators, compiled by a Christian woman, "by which we may recognize those who are involved in the occult"; they included "a lack of humour and common sense."[30]

He also gave a page or so to a discussion, in vague terms, of Satanic abuse, for which one of his informants was an "associate" in "the Hull area"—no doubt, Dianne Core: "In some instances, a woman will be ordered to become pregnant and the resulting baby will then be sacrificed. Male children are sacrificed by females and vice versa. When adults break a coven's sexual rules, the punishment can be death."[31] If this kind of thing were true, why did he give it so little space?

In the mid-1980s, the Evangelical Alliance set up the Reachout Trust, a

"Christian Ministry to Cults and Occult," whose stated purpose is "to promote a bible based Christianity by any means expedient." A lot of their publications are concerned with theologically correct answers to Jehovah's Witnesses and Mormons, but they also have an anti-occult ministry. This was headed by a North Wales woman named Maureen Davies, daughter of an Anglican clergyman, who at one time flirted with spiritualism but later became a born-again Christian.[32]

In 1989 she wrote an article on "Satanic Ritual Abuse"[33] in which she stated: "A year ago I was introduced to my first case of ritual child abuse. Since then I have been involved in or contributed to helping over 15 situations of satanic abuse." She stated that children were being recruited into Satanism in large numbers: some through "Generational Witchcraft or Satanism" (i.e., by their families), some lured by occult magazines, and others by parties at which drugs were available and perverted sex took place, after which they would be blackmailed. For example: "A 15 year old was recruited through the tarot cards, enticed back to a house and drugged. Perverted sex then took place. The subject was then blackmailed and then subjected to black magic rituals." Davies claimed that rituals involved drugs, perverted sex, and blood sacrifice. "In the temples or covens they have young girls or older women that they call 'Brood Mares,'" who would be made pregnant in order to supply unregistered babies for human sacrifice, though older children and adults were also killed.

In September 1989, Davies went on a trip to America to learn from the Experts there. She appeared on a Christian television show in Chicago, then attended the Rockford conference (the one from which Lauren Stratford was barred). Among others, she met Larry Jones, who was delighted to hear that Satanic ritual abuse was now being reported from Britain, as this would confound the skeptics. What could they say "in the light of international confirmation that the same satanic crime problems exist across the globe?" he asked in the October 1989 edition of his *File 18 Newsletter*.

Audrey Harper's story is told in her 1990 book, *Dance with the Devil* (with a forward by Geoffrey Dickens, M.P.). She had been converted to Christianity early in 1967 after attending a meeting at the London Metropolitan Tabernacle led by the Reverend Eric Hutchins,[34] the very same preacher responsible for saving Doreen Irvine three years earlier, though he had somehow lost the *g* in his surname. An orphan who had been brought up in a Dr. Barnardo's home, Harper had—again like Irvine—become a prostitute and drug addict in early adult life.

Her life also resembled Irvine's in that, while a junkie, she had been involved a Satanic witch coven. As she told it in the book, once, when she was down and out, she had been approached by two women in a West End pub, who invited her to come to one of their monthly parties at Virginia Water in Surrey. She was taken to a large house, and the next thing she knew, she was being initiated. As usual in such stories, a semicircle of robed figures stood facing the altar: eleven of them, with a gap for Audrey, who, with the "master" warlock, made up thirteen. Other hooded figures formed a congregation. She had to sign, in her own blood, a parchment declaring, "I am no longer my own. Satan is my master. I live to serve him only."[35]

Then, a nine-day-old baby was brought forward as a sacrifice. The master cut its throat and poured the blood into a chalice. He then daubed the blood all over Audrey and raped her.[36]

The curious thing here is that, when she had told the story of her initiation to the *Sunday Sport* for the 13 March 1988 edition, the blood sacrifice was merely a cockerel, though its blood was smeared over her in the same way. Either the *Sunday Sport*—which included in the same issue as her interview a story headlined "Giant Jellyfish Ate My Family"—thought her tale of infanticide too extreme for their readers and toned it down, or Harper decided that a cockerel sacrifice was not sensational enough.

After the ritual, the cult members returned Audrey to the streets of London. She continued her uneasy existence as a starving heroin addict, but from now on she had a double existence. Every so often she would be summoned to a coven meeting, sometimes by telephone but usually by a direct telepathic message from Satan.[37] She was also given lessons in Satan worship, during which she learned how to levitate.[38] In addition, the Satanists got her to recruit children—mostly runaways who were hanging around cafés or amusement arcades—and take them to parties, where the Satanists would abuse them. At these meetings, black candles laced with heroin were burned and photographs were secretly taken, as the coven made its money from pornography.[39] At other times they would desecrate churches, tearing up Bibles and prayer books and splattering blood and excrement around.

Audrey Harper's trips to Satanic coven meetings stopped at the end of 1966, around the time that she kicked her drug habit and shortly before her conversion to Christianity. She was not able to talk about what had happened to her for twenty years, but she continued to suffer nightmares as a result of Satan's influence. In 1986 she went for help to a minister named Roy Davies, who, inspired by God, said, "You've been involved in witchcraft, haven't you Audrey?"[40] She told him everything; he exorcized her, and that night she slept peacefully for the first time in years. Her tongue loosened, she made up for lost time. In 1987 the Evangelical Alliance's anti-Halloween handout, *Doorways to Danger* (the "doorways" in this title appear to derive from Rebecca Brown's *He Came to Set the Captives Free,* which has a chapter of that title, which states that all occult activities lead to demonic infestation), quoted her as saying that she had "made a blood covenant with Lucifer" and used to "take part in the desecration of Christian churches."

By late 1988, she was able to talk about having seen the sacrifice of a baby. She never approached the police, but after making this claim on the TV program *After Dark*, two detectives from Virginia Water came and interviewed her. They do not appear to have taken any action in consequence.[41]

All of the people described here had been involved in campaigning against the occult as un-Christian. A 1988 Halloween feature in the *Independent*, "The black magic games that turn into terror" (31 October), quoted a Christian psychiatrist as saying that "the symptoms of occult involvement . . . include loss of control, hallucinations, and a variety of psychotic symptoms." There was nothing about Satanic crime here, but, as the same article said, "Geoffrey Dickens MP, is currently campaigning to combat the threat to children posed by black magic and the occult. . . . According to Maureen Davies . . . occultists are currently carrying out an extensive recruiting campaign." The article also featured a born-again Christian named Ian Thain, who "believes that the Witchcraft Act should be reinstated." Obviously, things like "loss of control" were not nearly as powerful bogeymen as sex crimes and murder.

Social Services: Is Your Family Safe?

In 1973, a seven-year-old girl, Maria Colwell, was battered to death by her stepfather. What made the matter worse was that Maria was known to be at risk and had been removed from her home for fostering, but she was subsequently—and fatally—returned. Inevitably, there was heavy criticism of the social workers concerned.[42]

This case led to increased public awareness of the problem of "child abuse," as the standard phrase became, which, in the 1970s, was usually taken to mean physical abuse. Child protection committees were given considerable powers to take children into care if they were believed to be in danger. In the 1980s, further public concern was aroused by child *sexual* abuse, which was recognized to be widespread and, rather uncomfortably, to be most often perpetrated by fathers against their own children.

In 1987 came a backlash. It was revealed that Drs. Marietta Higgs and Geoff Wyatt of Cleveland in north Britain had diagnosed 121 children as being victims of abuse during just five months. Some of these children had been referred by their parents for physical problems such as constipation and asthma, but most of them were, without warning, taken into care, and a scandal arose. It became clear that some people had become over-zealous in their urge to protect children.[43]

It must be said at once that social workers were put in a nearly impossible position: publicly castigated if they failed to act, publicly castigated if they did act. But it was nonetheless obvious that methods being used to evaluate child sexual abuse were flawed. Dr. Higgs had relied heavily on the reflex anal dilation (RAD) test to diagnose abuse. This technique, imported from America, is supposed to detect anal damage and hence anal abuse. The theory is that an anus that has been penetrated will expand when touched, which a healthy anus should not. But other studies show that small children who are sexually abused are seldom, if ever, anally raped. This suggests that the test may give positive results on children who have *not* been penetrated. In fact, in 1988 a California pediatrician did what had not, apparently, occurred to anyone before and checked the anuses of nonabused children: he found that the anuses of about half of them "winked" when touched. Clearly, the test had always been valueless.[44]

For the social services to be able to take custody of a child, they must prove the child is "at risk," but the standards of proof are lower than those in criminal cases. Apart from questionable tests such as RAD, accusations can be made anonymously, the parents not being told who has accused them or what they are accused of. This, of course, encourages malicious people to make baseless accusations. In fact, the rules are very like those used by the Inquisition in cases of heresy. It is not surprising, then, that, as during the Inquisition, social workers started to find evidence of witchcraft.

So far, most of what has been discussed with regard to Satanism in Britain was a "paper scare," having little connection with the real world. Yet, with anti-Satanism, things often happen backward: normally, an event occurs, and then it is written up in the papers; in the British Satan-hunts, the newspaper features came first, to be followed by real events.

Nottingham

Between 1986 and 1987, social workers in Nottingham took eight children from an extended family on the Broxtowe Estate into care. Eventually, in February 1989, ten adults would plead guilty to fifty-three charges, including incest, cruelty, and indecent assault. The main basis for the charges was that they had held noisy, drunken parties where they had sex with each other and the children. No mention of Satanism or rituals was made in court.

Yet, well before the outcome, the social workers had decided that something more than just sexual abuse had been going on. After the children had been made wards of the court, the judge had ruled that, in the wake of Cleveland, the children should not be further interviewed by social services or police, but he asked the foster parents to keep diaries of anything they said.[45]

One boy, only three when taken into care, started talking at the age of four about witches, monsters, and clowns. He said that his family held witch parties, where they killed a sheep. On one occasion, he was afraid to get into the bath because it might be full of sharks.[46]

This was passed on to Nottingham Social Services. At this time, word of the American Satanism scare was beginning to filter into Britain. One of the social workers later said, "There was a buzz of excitement around. There was no doubt some people realized that if they could prove Ritual Abuse existed in Britain, they could publish, give lectures, and generally become eminent in their field."[47]

In February 1998, two Nottingham social workers, Chris Johnston and Judith Dawson, traveled to Birmingham to see Ray Wyre of the Gracewell Clinic. He gave them a list of Satanic indicators, which had been given to him by a researcher for the *Cook Report*, who had, in turn, acquired them from an American Expert on Satanism.[48] After this, other children were questioned about witch parties and came out with a fantastic string of disclosures: "babies being shot and put in the garages"; "a naughty policeman killing babies"; "babies being stabbed in a balloon and cooked in the oven"; "Jesus being chopped up and eaten off a silver pad"; "an uncle killing a man, cutting him up and putting him in a bag after going to a fantastic castle in a boat with Mr. Pooh Pants and the local vicar"; "the witches killing a baby taken out of a female member of the family's tummy and then making it better"; and much more.[49]

Three young adult women from the family were also questioned, and they, too, talked about Satanic rituals. One made statements like this: "We'd have parties, with a table, and it used to have a red cross on it, and candlesticks, and goblets, and they'd cut whatever it was up . . . if it was a certain day in the month, it would be an animal, other times it would be children."[50]

An apparently detailed picture was built up and passed on to the police, who, however, decided that the allegations of rituals were false and likely to discredit the real evidence. But social services continued to insist they were true, and the gulf between the two agencies became so wide that it was decided an inquiry should be held, by a joint unit staffed by police officers and social workers who had had no involvement with the evidence gathering.

The Joint Enquiry Team set about their work with a degree of common sense not usually found in Satanism investigations. They began by noting that it was not always possible to "believe the children," since they had said things like "They throw lots of babies in the bins. I was murdered when I was a baby and shoved in the bin," so that, if true, "most of the children disclosing would actually be dead." This was apart from remarks such as "My mum flies on a broomstick."[51]

It came out that the police had good grounds for their doubts. In early 1988, children had spoken of having seen a sheep sacrificed, specifying the house and the room in which this took place. This room was twice searched by police. Even if it had been cleaned up, there should have been forensic evidence in the form of traces of sheep's hair and blood. They found none.

A police interview with one of the adult witnesses, held on 22 August 1988, went as follows (with the names omitted):

> I have been interviewed on numerous occasions about sexual offences I have seen occur against children in the family and adults. I have made statements regarding these matters and these things I have described are true. Since all the adult members of the family were arrested I have been interviewed by the Social Services on a number of occasions. I have 3 children of my own and they are all in care, and I have been known to the Social Services for some time.
>
> When this case was in full swing, [my social worker] started interviewing me and asking me questions about parties involving witches. The first time she asked me about these things I told her that the only parties of any kind I had been to were at [the family house]. She interviewed me twice when I told her I didn't know anything about any other houses. On the third time she started asking me over and over again whether I'd been to any other big houses where witch-parties had taken place. I kept saying I hadn't but in the end I just got fed up with being asked so I just said "Yes." She asked me to describe the houses. I told her I couldn't so she said she would take me round to see them in the car. I got in her car and she drove me to two houses. The first was a big house, white colored near the Nottingham Knight pub. There were sheep in the fields around it. She pointed out the house and asked me if that was the house. I said "Yes."

She asked me what happened while I was there. I told her there were video cameras there and children being abused. I made it all up. I had never been to that house before in my life. I made up a description of the inside of the house. She took me to another house near Wollaton Park. It had a big black gate. She asked me whether this was another house I'd been to. I just said "Yes." I agreed with whatever she'd said.

I have been interviewed about 20 times by [my social worker] about these houses but all I do is just keep saying yes. Whenever I see [her] she buys me dinner and gives me coffee and ice creams. I have never been to any of these houses in my life. I am aware that [a teenage girl] is a regular visitor to the Social Services office. I have seen [her] many times over the past few months and she's told me she's been telling the Social Services about witch parties. I know she's telling lies. She goes up to the Social Services offices because she gets her dinners free and [another social worker] gives her money. [She]'s told me that if I tell the Social Services about witch parties at big houses I might have a chance of getting my daughter back. [My social worker's] told me if I tell the truth I could get [her] back.

There is one other house [my social worker] has took me to. It's miles away. [She] was driving me around all afternoon and I got really fed up. We were up near some Park somewhere, Clumber Park I think. I wanted to go home and I just pointed to a house standing on its own. When I told her this was a house I'd been to where witch parties had happened she brought me a coffee and a cornetto.

I have never been to any of these houses and everything I have told [her] is lies. I've told her the truth more than once but she wouldn't believe me so I just said anything. At one stage I have pointed these houses out, that [she] had showed me, to police officers but I was too frightened to tell them that I'd made it up. I thought I'd get into trouble. The only things I know about witch-craft and magic are the things I've seen on telly.[52]

Part of an interview with the teenage girl who was getting free meals and money and who came out with detailed descriptions of witch parties went like this:

Your father's killed a baby more than once. We know that your father delivered a foetus and aborted it—he drank the baby's blood.

I didn't know anything about that.

You tell us about things that happened when you were there.

I ate the stomach, my dad ate the head.

What part of the head? What's special about the stomach? . . . You had to eat babies more than once.

I can't remember.

We think you did. Whose baby? Who brought it? A name? Difficult to remember who asked you to kill the baby?

I didn't kill it.

Who told you to? Did she give you a knife?

No.

I think she did.[53]

After three months of this therapy, the girl alleged witnessing seven murders with cannibalism.

The Joint Enquiry Team examined how the children had been interviewed and noted that their stories could have origins other than in fact. Two of them had undertaken play therapy using witch costumes, monsters, flowing gowns, rubber snakes, plastic spiders, small unclothed baby dolls, toy syringes, masks, and Mr. Pooh Bear, which may have influenced their responses. There were suggestions of contamination and leading questions. The boy who had talked of seeing Jesus chopped up and eaten off a silver plate "could just as easily be thinking of the Communion." The same boy had seen the film *Jaws* before expressing fear of sharks.[54] The children had spoken of witch parties only at places other than their home, "in July 1988 when the foster parents had been asked to take the children around to identify locations."[55]

The family were under constant surveillance from the authorities and also attracted the attention of their neighbors, which would have made it difficult to perform blood sacrifices unnoticed. "Outside of the babies and the children, sheep are large, noisy, difficult animals and when one was slaughtered by an Indian on a council estate in Leicester it hit the national newspaper headlines the following day. In our view another explanation has to be sought."[56]

The second approach the team employed was to check the reliability of the general information on Satanic abuse "that had been presented to us and which we had initially accepted in good faith." They quickly concluded that "historical Satanism" was not a reality, nor did the like seem to be a fact in the present day. "We were aware that the books we were using might be an apologia or propaganda but we were fortunate to obtain the unpublished and private papers of a probable member of OTO and a former member of a Hampshire coven and these appeared to corroborate that neither organization was involved in sacrifices, or the abuse of children."[57]

They were suspicious of the American list of Satanic indicators, as its author advised police who were investigating day-care centers to assume that "all kids are victims and all teachers are perpetrators until your field is narrowed." So the Joint Enquiry Team asked the British Embassy in Washington to research this Expert's background. They received the reply "that he had no medical background (despite his claim to be a medical consultant) and that he was a social worker who was unpublished, had no educational pedigree and that he was not taken very seriously by the FBI."[58] They also noted that many U.S. cases of alleged Satanic abuse had collapsed, and that doubt had been cast on others.

The team then made inquiries with regard to Experts elsewhere in Britain:

We have met with a Chief Inspector from Humberside who has told us that after a national "Evangelical" proponent of Satanic abuse spent many hours with two 11 year old boys at her home they eventually alleged Satanic abuse. A well respected school master was arrested but intensive police investigations found that none of these allegations against the school master were based on reality. As a consequence of the discrediting of the witnesses due to the improper intervention of this person the Prosecution had to drop serious charges of rape and buggery against two men.[59]

In summary, the report suggest that a witch-hunt had been going on, and this was reinforced by a list of Satanic indicators, compiled by the Americans Maribeth Kaye and Lawrence Klein, which had been used by social services. It included a section "How to Become a Satanist" that was, in fact, a slightly modernized version of Guazzo's eleven-stage pact with the Devil, taken, as Kaye and Klein acknowledged, from the *Compendium maleficarum*.

The Joint Enquiry Team finished with this recommendation:

The use of the current information on "Satanic" ritualistic abuse/witchcraft should be stopped immediately in the absence of any empirical evidence to support it. Presentations using this material, which in our view has no validity, should also cease immediately as it is contagious.[60]

This advice would not be followed.

An important way in which social workers keep up with developments in their field is by attending conferences. In September 1989, Pamela Klein and her colleague Robert "Jerry" Simandl of the Chicago Police Department were the star speakers at a conference in Reading, west of London. Simandl, who spoke of four babies cooked in a microwave (one week later, a Nottingham boy who was still being interviewed by the social services spoke of seeing a baby cooked in a microwave), defined "ritual abuse" as "repeated physical, emotional, mental and spiritual assaults on children, combined with a systemized use of symbols and ceremonies and the use of evil designed and orchestrated to attain harmful effects—to turn the victims against themselves, society, and God." This, it should be noted, is almost word for word identical to Dr. Lawrence Pazder's original definition of "ritualized abuse."

According to the *Independent*'s account of the conference, Chris Johnston said of the Nottingham case:

> "At first we didn't believe the children. . . . Finally the sheer force of numbers convinced us that they were telling the truth." Eventually she had contacted Maureen Davies. . . . Davies confirmed that what the children described corresponded with stories elsewhere. Now Ms. Johnston receives calls from other social workers seeking advice on satanic rituals. "There seems to be a national network." Ms. Davies has a dossier on ritual sexual-abuse cases and says that satanists carry out murders as part of their rituals.[61]

In December 1989, the newsletter *Community Care* printed an article on Satanic child abuse with the title "Facing the Unbelievable." It admitted that "some organizations have been described as 'unhelpful,' amid claims that they are simply sensationalising the situation for their own ends." They described the Reachout Trust, however, as "a reliable source of information," specifying the work of Maureen Davies. A list of Satanic indicators was given: "odd chantings," "obsessions with urine and feces," "aggressive play," and so on. Jerry Simandl and Pamela Klein were quoted, as well as Audrey Harper, who said, "If in doubt, get in contact with someone in a better position to know." The article added, "At the moment the only way social workers can get in touch with someone in such a position is through the Reachout Trust," and gave Maureen Davies's telephone number. In consequence, some fifty social workers contacted her.

Similar claims continued to be put before the general public. On 17 March 1990, the news broke that the National Society for the Prevention of Cruelty to Children (NSPCC) had dealt with some cases of Satanic abuse. In fact, the subject had received just a few sentences in an NSPCC press release:

> The NSPCC has voiced its increasing concern as evidence is mounting of child pornography, ritualistic abuse and sex rings involving children. . . . Ritualistic abuse—physical, sexual and emotional abuse of children in bizarre

ceremonies. An increasing number of NSPCC teams are working with children who have been ritualistically abused. A great deal more needs to be found out about the scale of the problem.

This aspect of the release filled the press: "Ritual Killing in Child Sex Rings"; "Hell's Depraved Doctrine Makes Children the Tragic Victims"; "Children as young as five are being forced by devil-worshipers to join in vile sex orgies"; "Foetuses are being killed by paedophiles during satanic rites, senior social workers believe." For the first time, the broadsheet papers gave the subject as much space as the tabloids. (This is an interesting sequence: from *Prophecy Today* to *Sunday Sport* to general tabloids to *Community Care* to the broadsheets.) The *Independent* interviewed Audrey Harper on the subject of baby sacrifice: "Sometimes killing will be done by stabbing through the heart. Bits of the body are taken out. . . . Sometimes they will melt down the fat for candles and bones are used for aphrodisiacs."

Rochdale

Among those who contacted Reachout were Rochdale Social Services, in the Manchester area. A six-year-old boy had been behaving strangely, and when, in November 1989, his headmaster found him hiding in a cupboard, he referred the boy to social services. The boy told social workers that he had been taken away from his home by an entity who had come in at his bedroom window and given him a liquid like fizzy tea. When he drank it, the being grew to be over nine feet tall. He spoke of ghosts, of stabbing babies, and of being held prisoner in wooden cages.[62]

The boy and his three siblings were taken into care. Medical examinations showed no trace of abuse. It was discovered, however, that in 1985 the parents had complained that their home was haunted and had called in a priest to perform an exorcism, after which the haunting stopped. This was taken as proof that the parents had an interest in the occult. Police searched their house but found nothing incriminating except a wooden cross in a cupboard, which, they had to admit, could have had an innocent explanation.

The boy's eleven-year-old sister claimed to have witnessed abuse "in dreams." During weeks of interviews, the siblings named other children, cousins and friends who lived on the same council estate. At the beginning of June, some Rochdale staff attended a conference at Cardiff, where Nottingham social workers "shared their experience of Satanic child abuse" (their findings, that is, not their interviewing methods). A week later, twelve more Rochdale children were taken into care in dawn raids, and later on four more were brought in, making twenty in all. These children, too, were interviewed intensively. One boy said he had eaten a cat. Another claimed to have watched "the Black Master of Huddersfield" stab a man to death and drive off in a black Ford Escort. The rest of his family failed to see this happen because they were at the chip shop at the time.[63]

American social workers had claimed that Satanists could program children to respond to coded messages, which might be hidden in innocent-seeming greeting cards. To prevent this from happening, all contact between the children and their parents was cut off. As the parents of the original boy were wrapping presents to give to him on his seventh birthday, the telephone rang and a social worker informed them: "You are a danger to your children. You can no longer see them. We have obtained a court order."[64]

After three months of police investigation, Manchester chief constable James Anderton announced that no evidence had been found and that therefore no prosecutions would be made. Rochdale Social Services Department then issued a statement pointing out that there are different standards of proof involved in criminal and wardship cases.[65]

Meanwhile, "Sara," an adult undergoing therapy at Rochdale's Birch Hill Hospital, started disclosing to her psychiatrist, Dr. Victor Harris, that at the age of four her grandfather had introduced her to a Satanic coven in which she was repeatedly raped, compelled to obey the "masters," forced into a grave full of snakes, and made to watch animal and human sacrifices. Her parents never knew what was going on.[66] According to the *News of the World*: "Dr. Harris says the satanists manage to keep the murders a secret because they only use babies born to members of the coven. The parents do not register the births, so there is no record they even existed." Dr. Harris said that he had three other patients who had also undergone Satanic abuse and who told similar stories.

In a refreshing reversal of the usual circumstances: "frightened Sara was also warned that the sinister Satanists had compiled a DOSSIER on Dr. Harris. 'They warned me that they'd get his children,' she says."[67] As usual, however, the Satanists' cover-up was patchy: they were able to prevent any physical evidence or confirmation of Sara's story from being found, but they did nothing to stop Dr. Harris and Sara from talking to the newspapers and appearing on television programs.

In the late summer of 1990, the first real skeptical note entered some press reports. Barbara Amiel commented in *The Times*, "On average, almost a decade elapses before fashions in social issues cross the Atlantic," and as it was now ten years since the publication of *Michelle Remembers*, the ritual abuse scare had thus reached Britain "on schedule." She also pointed out, "Actual evidence of ritual abuse is in short supply on either side of the Atlantic."[68]

It has subsequently been claimed that cynical journalists simply rejected stories of Satanic child abuse out of hand. In fact, a study of old papers shows that for two and a half years they did nothing but uncritically repeat the stories fed to them by the Satan Squad. In March 1990, Rosie Waterhouse coauthored an article for the *Independent* that featured the claims of the Reverend Kevin Logan, Maureen Davies, and others, appearing to accept them (though with some caution); she also quoted Eileen Barker, who spoke of "gross exaggeration." It was not until September 1990 that Waterhouse was to be found asking questions like: "Is there a single shred of real evidence to show a cult of devil worship?"

Yet believers remained widespread. On 12 October 1990, the bishop of Oxford stated on BBC Radio 4: "By the year 2000 Satanists will be sacrificing one baby per minute." He had this information from a "reliable friend."[69] An international conference on incest in August 1990 was reported by the *Guardian* on 8 August, under the headline "Child abuse 'linked to satanic cults'": "The London conference heard that covens habitually sexually abuse children or make them take part in acts of bestiality during satanic rituals. Human sacrifices included babies induced and then killed, while sometimes foetuses were eaten in ceremonies." The principal informant was Sue Hutchinson, the founder of SAFE, a telephone help line "for victims of ritual or satanic abuse," founded six months earlier. "Ms. Hutchinson said that she had no evidence to substantiate her claims, but insisted the practices were widespread." In addition, a psychotherapist named Norman Vaughton said that "in America there were an estimated 10,000 human sacrifices a year."

On 17 December, Mr. Justice Hollings ordered some of the Rochdale children to be returned home. He said social-service investigators were "obsessed with the belief" that they had uncovered a Satanic abuse group, but it was obvious there was a "great deal of fantasy" in the children's stories because of how they were questioned. Social workers had failed to follow the guidelines laid down in the report on the Cleveland affair; interviews were carried out too quickly and were not properly recorded, while the children were told what other children had been saying.

On 7 March 1991, ten more children were returned by Mr. Justice

Douglas Brown, leaving only the original four in care. Justice Brown also heavily criticized the proceedings. He said that the original boy had been watching *The Evil Dead* and other "video nasties" immediately before telling stories about Satanic rituals. It emerged that the boy who had said he had eaten a cat had been referring to a bowl of soup containing pasta animal shapes. The next day, the Social Services chief of Rochdale resigned.[70]

Orkneys

Not long before the Rochdale children had been returned, on 27 February, the news broke of the seizure of nine children from four Orkney families. This particular outbreak did not last long, however. At the proof hearing in Kirkwall (a sheriff's courthouse) on 3 April, Sheriff David Kelbie ruled that the proceedings for custody were "fundamentally null and void" and dismissed them. He went on to say that proper tapes and transcripts of many of the interviews had not been made, and where they had been, the interviews had "amounted to repeated coaching." Despite this, most of the children had emphatically denied that anything had happened to them. Those who had spoken of rituals had depicted events similar to Christmas and Halloween parties, as well as a wedding described by the other children, and there were significant discrepancies among their accounts. The grounds of referral mentioned "ritualistic music," but it was not clear if this was Kylie Minogue, Michael Jackson, Andrew Lloyd Webber, "Strip the Willow," or "The Grand Old Duke of York." (Query: What part do these play in traditional Satanism?) As to the Satanic regalia recovered—a cloak, masks, crosses, and so on—they had "little evidential significance, unless one had started off to see it." The sheriff did not have the power to send the children home but suggested that this be done as soon as possible.[71]

The Orkney Social Work Department was promptly besieged by angry parents, followed closely by journalists, and things nearly turned nasty. Eventually it was agreed that the children would be returned home at once from the Scottish mainland, and they arrived on the morning of the 4 April, to a mass celebration.

An inquiry into the affair, headed by Lord Clyde, lasted 135 days and cost £6 million. The final report contained more than a hundred criticisms, including that the social workers failed to give sufficient thought to whether it was necessary to remove the children, and that they and the police failed to distinguish between taking allegations of abuse seriously and accepting them as fact. It was recommended that, in future, children should not be taken into care without clear evidence, and that parents should have the immediate right to challenge any protection order. The report did not, however, consider the question of whether abuse had really taken place.

Nevertheless, some exceedingly odd details emerged. It was related that in a session with one girl "she had been told to draw a picture of a circle with her family in it. There had to be a man in the middle, and she had to add herself and her best friend. This was later to be described as a picture of a ritual."[72]

The aftermath dragged on for years. In 1993, the chief of social services finally resigned. Around the same time, two of the girls gave details of how they had been investigated: "I was put in a room with a piece of paper and a pen and told to write down what had happened, and if I didn't write it down I wasn't coming out," one said. "I got bribed with a new pair of shoes. I was told that if I said something more I could have two pairs."[73]

In March 1996, the parents were finally vindicated by an official apology from the council. A joint statement said: "Orkney Islands Council fully accepts the criticism contained in Lord Clyde's report and asks all members of the four families to accept this wholehearted apology. The four families accept Orkney Islands Council's apology."[74] Damages were awarded, undisclosed but believed to have been £10,000 for each child and £5,000 for each parent.

There was a curious postscript to the affair. In 1999, it was announced that Dr. Avril Osborne, who had been appointed as the replacement head of social work, was taking early retirement following a hate campaign against her, "which included poison pen letters and phone calls and which culminated in blood being smeared on her doorstep." Dr. Osborne is a lesbian, and though said to be "exceptional" at her job, she was "a victim of small-community intolerance."[75]

Liverpool

The Reverend Kevin Logan's antics came back to him in a remarkable way. Two teenage girls in Liverpool started going around Evangelical churches giving "testimony" about how they had been made to take part in Satanic rituals. Eventually, they ended up in council care, and their allegations were taken seriously, with the result that in the summer of 1990, eight other children were taken into care, homes were searched, and seventeen adults interviewed by police.[76]

The adults were soon freed, but in the home of one woman, police had found letters concerning involvement in witchcraft. Her two children, in consequence, were not returned to her. Now, it happened that although this woman had been a Wiccan, she had since become a born-again Christian and had been counseled by the Reverend Kevin himself. After a year, Logan was compelled to appear in court as an Expert witness and testify that "every Wiccan witch whom I had ever known in a long evangelistic ministry to those in the occult would have run a million miles before wilfully abusing a child."[77] At the end of the hearing, the allegations were dismissed and the children returned home.

Ayrshire

On 19 May 1990, a "Mrs. F." went to her doctor in Ayr, Scotland, and told him that she suspected her husband of sexually abusing their three sons, who were aged five, three, and ten months. The F. family were "periodic nomads" who had comfortable permanent homes, but toured Scotland and northern England in caravans between April and September. Two days before, at a caravan site at Ballarat on Royal Deeside, she had found their eldest son lying on his front with his pajama trousers down, and this had aroused her suspicions.

The police were called in. A surgeon and a pediatrician examined all the F. family children and found no trace of sexual abuse. But two Strathclyde social workers attended the examination. They persuaded Mrs. F. to take the children to a refuge. Elaborate allegations of abuse were quickly made, and the children's cousins from the "H." and "L." families, who were also part-time travelers, were implicated. Mrs. F. was quickly told that if she returned home, she could not take the children with her. On 18 and 19 June, the four children of the H. family were taken into care. Mr. L. was asked if his daughter, aged ten, could be taken for tests for a few days. He agreed—and did not see her again for five years.

At a hearing that August the families

> were accused of Satanic sexual abuse, which was supposed to have taken place in haunted castles, among skeletons in graveyards and in a hot-air balloon over Strathclyde. They were accused of dressing up as clowns, of wearing cloaks, hoods and masks or nothing at all. . . . It was said one man could, on

occasion, turn into a spider and a mouse. A woman was said to have been murdered as a sacrificial offering after intercourse with a Satanist, though no body was ever found.[78]

Mr. H. was incredulous: "They asked us if we drink blood, because one of the other children had said we did. Another boy of three had said we smeared human feces all over ourselves. . . . The boys were saying that we dressed up as Santa Claus. We were meant to have a big sled that flew out of the living room window."[79] The couple were so stunned that they were unable to defend themselves properly.

On 17 August 1990, Sheriff Neil Gow took the rare step of making a public statement, after eleven days of hearing evidence in camera. He said there was evidence that "there has been systematic sexual abuse and corruption of a number of young children in Ayrshire over a period of up to 18 months."[80] The only physical evidence, however, was that a dentist had found that some of the teeth of one boy showed "clean and neat" cut marks. This was said to be due to the grandmother having pried open the child's mouth and scraped the enamel off his teeth with a pair of pliers.

In May 1992, Mrs. F. retracted all her allegations of sexual abuse, which, she said, had never been anything more than suspicion. The parents made various efforts to appeal, and on 12 August 1993, three judges ordered a fresh hearing before a new sheriff. It began on 6 December and was heard by Sheriff Colin Miller, who decided that the press should not be admitted.[81]

The hearing lasted more than a year. The final report accused social workers of "unplanned, inco-ordinated, and obsessive interviews with the children, in which 'facts' were planted." The general behavior of the original accuser, Mrs. F., was described as "bizarre and disturbed." The one boy's bad mouth "was just the victim of natural decay."[82] After this, judges ordered that the children should be returned to their parents, five years after they had been taken away.

The L. girl, now fifteen, told journalists how she had first been taken to a local authority assessment center, where she was kept in a "tiny attic room with just a bed." Most days, for almost two months, social workers took her to a special interviewing bungalow. "They would come for me in the morning and put me in the car. I dreaded it," the girl said. "I told them I didn't want to go, but they said it was for my own good. . . . They kept saying the same thing: 'We know you've been hurt at home. Tell us what happened. We know you've been hurt.' I said: 'Nothing has happened. I want to go home. It's not true.' But they did not stop." The chief interviewer had been the same chief interviewer as in the Orkneys case.[83]

Epping Forest

In November 1991, a case of Satanic ritual abuse finally led to a prosecution. The accusations were brought by two girls, ages ten and fourteen, against their parents and three other adults. The girls had started talking of indecent assault in February 1990, but in September, after a lot of publicity had been given to the Rochdale case, the older girl started disclosing that they had been taken from their home at night to a stone monument decorated with a black cross, candles, and stars. People would arrive dressed in black, light a bonfire, and read from a book. She spoke of being given a strange drink that made her feel "sexy" before falling asleep. She later awoke feeling sore. She had heard the "devil names" Lucifer and Lucillus.[84]

In court, the younger girl said they had been taken to Epping Forest on Monday, Wednesday, and Friday evenings. (It is interesting to compare this allegation with the 1613 statement of the witch-hunter Pierre de Lancré: "The normal meeting place is called the Goat's Heath, and the Witches go there on three nights, that is Monday, Wednesday and Friday.")[85] Sometimes they would sacrifice rabbits, on other nights babies. The prosecution admitted that there was no evidence for these killings other than the girls' testimony. The girls reported that they would dance naked and be raped and buggered by several men. The meetings took place at a Gypsy memorial stone in the forest, which commemorated the grandfather of one of the accused. This stone is only a few yards from a main road.

On the third day of the trial, the younger girl admitted under cross-examination that she had made up the list of names and addresses she had given to social workers. The defense counsel pointed out that the girl's evidence did not match that given to a magistrates' court eighteen months earlier. On the fourth day, the judge ruled that the girls' testimony was "uncertain, inconsistent and improbable" and directed the jury to find the defendants not guilty.

Outside the court, the girls' father said, "We have lost our home, our jobs and been to prison. They believed the word of children, never questioning it. We are Christians, not devil worshipers." The mother—the parents had separated since the affair began—added, "The girls made it all up. They learned about the Satanic things in horror films and videos."[86]

Beginnings of a Backlash

In the midst of the furor over ritual abuse, new books started to appear. *Witchcraft: A Strange Conflict* (1991), by Peter Hough, a member of ASSAP (the Association for the Scientific Study of Anomalous Phenomena), was open-minded but largely skeptical. Hough included interviews with both occultists and anti-Satanists, among the latter Maureen Davies, who made the interesting remark "When you've got a child or an adult being sexually molested by an incubus, then you know it's not imagination." Hough concluded that "for future cases of alleged Satanic ritual abuse, objectivity is needed all round."[87]

Chasing Satan (1991), by Dianne Core, and *Children for the Devil* (1991), by Tim Tate (who had been the researcher for the *Cook Report* on Satanism), endeavored to prove that Satanic ritual abuse really happened. They were hampered by the problem of still being unable to quote any case of alleged sacrifice backed up by physical evidence. Tim Tate complained that the skeptics had not bothered to study Satanism, which he himself had done by reading Peter Haining's 1972 *Anatomy of Witchcraft* and one or two similar works. He suggested that the trial of Gilles de Rais vindicated recent similar stories, overlooking the most obvious resemblance: that de Rais was accused of murdering hundreds of children, yet no bodies were found.[88] Tate's remarks on the Nottingham case infuriated Detective Superintendent Peter Coles, who sued. The book was withdrawn from sale.

In due course, the Department of Health commissioned Professor Jean LaFontaine to do a study of ritual abuse, which finally appeared in 1994. "Official: Satanic Abuse a Myth" the London *Evening Standard* told its readers on 2 June 1994.

Professor LaFontaine had studied eighty-four cases in which there were allegations of ritual abuse. She concluded that in three of those cases rituals had taken place but were subordinate to the abuse, which was the real motive of the perpetrators. In the other eighty-one cases there had been no ritual; and if ritual abuse is defined as abuse that is "part of rites directed to a magical or religious objective," then it had not happened in any of them.

Not surprisingly, the report produced a reaction from anti-Satanists. The Reverend Kevin Logan responded that year with *Satanism and the Occult*, a book that showed some signs of hasty composition, as when he wrote that 1966 was declared "Anno Santanas"[89]—meaning, apparently, the first year of Santa's kingdom on Earth. He attempted to show that ritual abuse really happened, but unfortunately, he was only able to cite cases where the importance of alleged ritual elements was specifically disavowed—such as that of Reginald Harris, whom the judge described as making a "pretense of witchcraft" to get power over children—and that had collapsed altogether, such as the case in Holland's Oude Pekela (discussed below). Nevertheless, Logan seems to have proved to his own satisfaction that the occult is the cause of all the world's problems, for at one point he notes that fortune-tellers sometimes have stalls at charity fetes, commenting: "Odd, isn't it, how society raises money for its vulnerable members by using the very thing which is causing them so much damage!"[90]

The publication of *Treating Survivors of Satanist Abuse*, edited by Valerie Sinason of the Tavistock Clinic in London, was timed to coincide with the LaFontaine report. In the first chapter, Sinason tells how "Ingrid," a severely mentally handicapped Swedish woman, was found to be severely bruised and hallucinating. Ingrid described, in halting language, how an "Evil devil" had tied her up, taken her out at night "cold in the moon," and abused her. "Devil women watched films with me," she said. "They had black dog. Gave us shit to eat." Since good care for the mentally handicapped is a matter of pride in Sweden, this seemed impossible; but according to Sinason, "Ingrid's limited cognitive abilities meant she could not lie or fantasize."[91] Perhaps not; but equally, she might be unable to distinguish hallucination from reality. Presumably, for a book like this, writers will pick their most compelling cases, yet none of those Sinason presented were any more convincing than Ingrid's. No doubt it is distressing to work with numbers of disturbed children, but that does not mean one should automatically believe them when they say they were abused by clowns, conjurers, and Santa Claus.[92] And the citation in Sinason's collection of the spurious *Missa niger: La Messe noire*, by "Aubrey Melech," along with *Michelle Remembers* and *Satan's Underground*,[93] does not inspire confidence.

Since the LaFontaine report, public and media sympathy has shifted from the Survivors of Satanism to the victims of the anti-Satanists. In January 1995, when it was announced that the Crown Prosecution Service had dropped all charges against four couples in Bishop Auckland, County Durham, who had been accused of abusing their children in rituals involving Devil worship, blood sacrifice, and drug taking, *Today* greeted the news with the front page headline "Witch Hunt of the Innocents." Other papers gave the views of the parents, who claimed that some of the children's stories were based on videos (which, ironically, have themselves been a target for anti-Satanists): "One of the children's statements concerned fish hooks, similar to a scene in Hellraiser where they are used to mutilate a man."[94]

One couple, it was noted, spent four months in custody, during which time they lost their homes and their jobs.[95]

The reporting on the Dallimore case, which was made public soon afterward, was similarly skeptical. The Dallimore family had moved to the village of Hockwold in Norfolk in 1991. They had hoped the move would be good for their daughter Rebecca, nineteen, who had been sexually assaulted by a stranger some time earlier and was nervous of going out alone. Rebecca suggested that she make friends through the parish church. Her mother was not a churchgoer, but had no objections, since "of all the things youngsters can get involved in these days, the local church seemed the most harmless of places."

The local vicar, the Reverend Arthur Rowe, had introduced the church to "charismatic" Christianity, where congregants become inspired by the Holy Spirit, which leads them to writhe about and utter incomprehensible "tongues." This brought in worshipers from surrounding communities, but not all the local villagers approved. One old woman later told *Today*:

> I've never seen anything like it in the Church of England. The vicar kissed the carpet in his sitting room. There was strange chanting and someone collapsed on the floor twitching. The vicar then said I'd received the most terrible message from the Lord. I was later told that I was riddled with the devil and they wanted to exorcize me. It was terrifying.

Rebecca Dallimore took to all this, however, and started attending special healing sessions as well as the regular services. At one, in the summer of 1993, a woman approached Rebecca with a message inspired by the Holy Spirit. The woman told her that she knew Rebecca had been sexually abused.

About three weeks later, Rebecca asked her mother if she could go away for the weekend to stay with two friends from a neighboring village. She never came back. Her parents discovered her at the home of a couple who belonged to Rowe's congregation. She screamed at them: "I hate you both, I'm finished with you." They did not see her again.

A week later they received a letter from a lawyer, warning them to stay clear of their daughter, who did not wish to see them again "for reasons you are well aware of." Rev. Rowe then preached a sermon in which he said the church was giving shelter to a girl who had been abused by her family for seventeen years. Her mother, Valerie, found no one to help her. "Try telling anyone your daughter has been taken by a cult called the Church of England and they'll laugh in your face."

Months later, the Dallimores were interviewed by the police, and they finally learned what they were supposed to have done. Rebecca had made a statement that the entire family had taken part in Satanic rituals—that she had been raped by her father and her brother, abused with inverted crucifixes, and daubed with animal blood. At one of these rites, the body of her dead grandmother was on the altar. The police did not appear to take this too seriously, as there was no substantiation for her claims, and her story changed at different meetings with them. Nonetheless, the Dallimores' home was searched, without success, for Satanic paraphernalia. Charges were brought against them but later dropped. In June 1995, a few days before a BBC *Everyman* documentary featuring the case was due to be screened, the vicar resigned.[96]

The Satan-Hunt in Other Countries

International Satanic orders are mythical, but Evangelical churches, social work departments and the *Oprah Winfrey Show* extend their influence to the furthermost parts of the earth. It is not surprising, then, that Satanism scares have occurred in many far-flung places, which may be briefly noted here.

Canada

On 7 February 1985 a woman named Sharon Wells, of Hamilton, Ontario, phoned the Children's Aid Society and asked them to take her children into care. A highly unstable woman, by her own admission, she was afraid that she was going to hurt them. So "Janis" and "Linda," both under eight years of age, were put into the care of a foster mother, Catherine McInnis.[97]

McInnis thought that the girls had a "sexual odor" when they arrived at her home; she noticed that their vaginas were inflamed and that they complained of sore bottoms. So she concluded that they had been sexually abused. Soon the girls were "making disclosures" about ritual abuse, alleging that they had eaten excrement and drunk urine, and that a girl called "Elizabeth" had been killed.[98] Then, McInnis saw a TV program from the United States on ritual abuse,[99] and suddenly she thought she could make sense of what she was hearing. After that, the girls' stories started to incorporate Satanism. Eventually, one of them would claim that her own father had killed two children and her mother, seven; the other said that each parent had killed five children. They had seen these children killed in grave-yards; they had been made to dismember chickens; and pornographic films had been made of them in the studios of CHCH-TV Channel 11 in Hamil-ton. When McInnis was given two unrelated girls to foster, they, too, started alleging that they had been ritually abused by their parents' Satanic cult.[100]

Police attempts to find corroborating evidence were unsuccessful. They looked at the children's old backyard, where the bodies of three children were supposed to be buried, and concluded that the earth beneath the paving stones had not been disturbed. No evidence was found that the Channel 11 studio had been used by unauthorized persons, though it was said that the building was unused for long periods and that security was lax. Photographs of both girls were shown to the Toronto police task force on pornography, but they did not match the girls in any child pornography they had seized. The home of Wells's boyfriend, who was named in the girls' allegations, was searched: no evidence of pornographic, Voodoo, or Satanist material was found, though there were several hours of videotape record-ings of Christian religious services. The police took the girls out in a car to search for the graveyard where the rituals had taken place, but they refused to cooperate, because, they said, they had not been allowed to go on the rides at Canada's Wonderland.[101]

No criminal charges were brought, but after a long and expensive hear-ing, Wells, her estranged husband, and her boyfriend were held to be guilty of sexual abuse and refused access to the children.

Holland

In May 1987, a four-year-old boy in the town of Oude Pekela, near the German border, came from a play area with a bloody anus. He was exam-ined by doctors familiar with American anti-Satanist literature, who con-sidered that he had been sexually abused. The affair quickly escalated, and soon ninety-eight children ranging in age from four to eleven told authori-ties that they had been enticed into buses by German pornographers dressed as clowns, abducted, molested, tortured, and filmed (and then re-turned before anyone noticed they were missing). It was said that the leader of the cult was known as the "master." Alleged incidents included a naked girl tied up, with knives thrown at her; a cat dismembered with a chainsaw; and crosses cut into the backs of live babies. A number of arrests were made, but no convictions followed. After a year, officials concluded that the origi-nal child had been poked with twigs while playing with another infant.[102]

South Africa

In May 1990, Captain Leonard Solms, the head of the Child Protection Unit in Cape Town, a "Bible-thumper" who described himself as an Expert on Satanism, held a media conference at which he declared that police had been investigating claims made by "10 self-confessed satanists," a number of them children who were undergoing counseling. He said that parents had allowed their children to be raped and sodomized by fellow Devil worshipers in "macabre initiation ceremonies"; that children were forced into sex acts with dogs and goats; that the blood of sacrificial animals was drunk; that "a number of public figures and professional people" whose names he knew had taken part in Satanic ceremonies; and that, in the past five years, eleven babies "bred" for the purpose had been murdered by Satanists, who had torn the infants' hearts out and eaten them. No mention was made of bodies being found, and he admitted that he had not been able to identify the parents of any of these sacrificial babies.[103]

Only one court case seems to have arisen from this investigation, that of Rene Tupper, a thirty-six-year-old widow of Fish Hoek, Cape Town, who was accused of abducting an eighteen-year-old girl, subjecting her to "satanic torture," and cutting her breasts and inner thighs for ritual purposes. She was alleged to have had two accomplices, but they could not be found.

In due course, however, the case against Tupper collapsed. It seems the girl had made these accusations only when interviewed by Captain Leonard Solms, but eventually he accused her of lying to him.

Outside the court, Mrs. Tupper said that her life had been ruined by the captain's "witch-hunt." She had been financially wrecked by the cost of the defense and was forced to flee to Port Elizabeth with her two daughters because of harassment by her neighbors and former friends.[104]

Australia

In April 1989, the U.K. Survivor "Samantha" told viewers of the Australian Broadcasting Corporation's *60 Minutes* how she had been raped and made pregnant in order to produce babies for Satanic sacrifice. (It will be recalled that Samantha had made these allegations only after Lauren Stratford had appeared on the *Oprah Winfrey Show* saying much the same thing.) Since then, as Dianne Core puts it, "[Samantha's] disclosures are consistent with what victims from Sydney to Melbourne and Perth are now revealing."[105]

Here is one example: in 1991, TV Channel 10 broadcast an investigation into alleged sexual abuse, child sacrifice, and cannibalism at a nursery school in the small community of Nar Nar Goon, forty-four miles southwest of Melbourne. Children were supposed to have been lured into a Devil-worshiping cult whose members included doctors, lawyers, journalists, university professors, and police. One woman, filmed in silhouette, claimed that her daughter had been made to eat one of her school friends, and another woman said that she had "had babies for the cult." Detectives were investigating the allegations, but the only physical evidence reported was that medical examinations showed at least one child had been sexually abused.[106]

New Zealand

Early in 1991, soon after lectures were given by American Experts on ritual abuse, the country's first Satanic day-care case emerged. A child at the Christchurch Civic Childcare Centre told his father that he did not like his teacher's "black penis." Questioned, he said this was "just a story," but his concerned parents turned to a "community consultant" for help. The boy's teacher, Peter Ellis, was suspended and the child interviewed three times, without making any specific allegations of abuse.

But concern had now spread, as other parents had found out about the story. A team of social workers interviewed 116 children, and about 50 made allegations of abuse. One six-year-old was very forthcoming: he said that Ellis had abused him in the toilet, made him eat excrement, dressed as a witch, and threatened to turn him into a frog if he told what was going on. In a subsequent interview, he said that Ellis had put him through a trapdoor into an underground maze, and that children from the day care had been made to stand naked in a circle, around which slit-eyed adults dressed as cowboys played guitars. Afterward, the children were put into ovens and told they would be eaten. Asked why he had not said all this before, he replied, "Oh, I just remembered today."[107]

In September 1992, Ellis was arrested, and forty-two charges of indecent assault were brought against him. In November, four of his female coworkers were also arrested and charged. At the pretrial hearing, charges against the women were dropped, but Ellis still faced twenty-five charges, all of which he denied. In the actual trial, the prosecution maintained that "no toddler could have made up" such details. Ellis was found guilty of sixteen charges out of twenty-five, and sentenced to ten years' imprisonment.[108]

10

I'm Not Paranoid, There *Is* a Conspiracy

Witchcraft and Satanism have always been regarded, by the hostile, as conspiracies rather than merely criminal acts; and conspiracy theorists tend to suppose that the conspiracies they believe in embrace everything they dislike. The Roman Church lumped witchcraft together with heresy, including that of Protestantism; thus it was widely believed by Catholics that the storms which dispersed the Spanish Armada in 1588 were raised by two Lapland sorcerers, sent to Queen Elizabeth's aid for the purpose by the Protestant kings of Scandinavia.[1]

In Reformation England, by contrast, witchcraft was taken to be more or less identical with popery. One of the first British tracts published on the subject began thus:

THE PRINTER TO THE CHRISTIAN READER

Here hast thou (gentle Reader) the examination of John Walsh of Netherbury in Dorsetshire, touching Sorcery and Witchcraft, which he learned (as hereafter is shewed) of a certain Priest named Sir Robert of Drayton. Wherein thou mayest see the fruits of Papists and papistry, and their ill exercises of their idle lives. . . . For hereby not only the simple people have been falsely seduced and superstitiously led: but all estates have been sore grieved and troubled by these their practices of Sorcery and Witchcraft . . . [which] not only the fat belly fed Monks, flattering Friars, and idle lusty Priests practiced and used: but also the holy fathers themselves, Popes, Cardinals, and Bishops were chiefly and wholly given to the study and exercise of these most wicked and devilish sciences, and by these means did work to come to the Papal seat, high dignities, and great wealth. Which was (as the histories declare) with the murdering and poisoning prively one of another.

As first Pope Alexander the sixth, having society with wicked Spirits and Devils, gave himself body and soul unto them, upon condition he might attain to the Pope's seat . . . Platina also writeth the like of Pope John 8, Pope Silvester, Pope Benedict 8. . . . Pope Clement 8 was also of this fraternity, as in the Commentaries upon the Articles of the Doctors of Paris is declared: where his style is thus set forth: that he was a Bastard, Empoisoner, Homicide, Bawd, Simoniac, Sodomite, Perjurer, Whoremaster, Nigromancer, Church robber, and a practiser of all kind of wickedness.

. . . their inferior sort, as Monks, Friars, and Priests also used, and would teach the same witchcrafts and Sorceries to such men and women, as they had committed evil with. As of late was confessed of a woman which used Witchcraft and Sorcery, that she learned the same of a priest, whose harlot she had been many a year.[2]

Many of today's Evangelicals likewise hold the Catholic faith to be nothing more or less than Devil worship. Rebecca Brown complains that due to the popularity of films like *The Exorcist* "people are turning to the Catholic priests everywhere for help in dealing with the raging giant of Satanism in our country today. Catholic priests are completely helpless to deal with any witchcraft because they themselves are serving Satan."[3]

In 1594 the exiled English Catholic Thomas Stapleton delivered a dissertation to the University of Louvain titled *Cur magia pariter cum haeresi hodie crererit* (Why magic today flourishes equally with heresy), stating: "Magic flourishes alongside heresy, and heresy alongside magic," referring heresy especially to Martin Luther and the Lutherans. Thirty years or so later, the same dissertation was delivered to a German Protestant University: "Luther" and "the Lutherans" had been changed to "the Pope" and "the Jesuits"; otherwise it was unaltered.[4] Readers will recall that the words *Satanist* and *Satanism* were first recorded in the sixteenth century, where they were used by adherents of different brands of Christianity to describe the others.

The Jewish Peril

The Edict of Faith used by the Spanish Inquisition listed a series of symptoms of possible heresy or conversion to Judaism, Islam, or Protestantism, all of which had to be reported to the Inquisitors. Among the Judaic "indicators" were:

- eating flesh in Lent
- going out on Saturday without shoes
- reciting the Psalms of David without the Gloria Patria

- giving children Jewish names
- saying that the Messiah has not yet come
- celebrating the Passover (rather a giveaway, that one)
- "if they have recommended their Children either to Witches or Magicians."[5]

What has the last one to do with traditional Judaism? Absolutely nothing; but in the Middle Ages, it was widely believed that Jews practiced both sorcery and human sacrifice. Indeed, they were sometimes supposed to be part of the witchcraft conspiracy: to underline the point, witches' gatherings were called *sabbat(h)s* or *synagogues.*

Additionally, Jews were frequently accused of kidnapping Christian children in order to feast on them at the Passover. No evidence in the form of leftovers was produced (quite apart from the fact that Christian children would not be kosher), but it did give people the excuse to go out and massacre Jews from time to time.

In fact, the rabbis were just as much against magic as anyone else; they had, in a sense, started the whole thing with their dictum "Thou shalt not suffer a witch to live." The medieval codifier Maimonides, commenting on this sentence, noted that the word translated as "witch," *mekashephah*, (perhaps better rendered as "sorceress"), is feminine. Why? Because people are naturally inclined to mercy when a woman is to be put to death. Moses therefore said "a sorcer*ess*" to make sure that the women would be executed as well as the men.[6]

The Masonic Threat

The Freemasons are a conspiracy theorists' delight, with all the appeal of secret rituals and "top people" as members. The belief, however, that Freemasons are secret Devil worshipers was struck a mortal blow by the confession of Léo Taxil, from which it has never really recovered—notwithstanding the ingenious suggestion of a certain Father E. Cahill that the Taxil affair was itself a Masonic conspiracy, intended to discredit anti-Masonry.[7]

Nonetheless, the question is often asked: Should a Christian be a Freemason? Since Freemasonry has always numbered many Church of England bishops among its initiates, there can be no doubt at all that it is compatible with Anglicanism. It is quite possible, however, that the Masonic principle of tolerance is incompatible with certain types of Christianity. The Reverend C. Penney Hunt, author of *The Menace of Freemasonry to the Christian Faith*, quoted the handbook for the Second Degree as saying: "Therefore it is that we find among Mohammedans, Buddhists, Jews, Hindoos and Christians, men who, while they often employ different symbols, use them to describe precisely the same spiritual experiences." Rev. Hunt asked, apoplectic: "Then why waste money on Missionary Campaigns?"[8] Why, indeed?

Another Christian anti-Mason wrote, with regard to Masonic charity:

> The great purpose in giving charity to the needy should be to bring them to Christ; the meeting of their temporary necessities is the smallest object; and unless the charity is given in the name of Christ, it not only fails to bring those helped to own Him, but HARDENS THEM AGAINST HIM because benefit is received from this non-Christian Order. *Every cent that a Christian gives through a* NON-CHRISTIAN ORDER *is therefore so much money put into the campaign against Christ.* You may not yet be aware of the fact that the devil is a close COUNTERFEITER of Christ's work . . . and that he maintains charitable institutions in OPPOSITION to Christ, as if he were more charitable than Jesus Christ and His people.[9]

The same author also complained that Masons spend far more on their expensive lodge furnishings and jewelry than they do on charity, though one would have thought he would be grateful for this, as it meant less money put into the campaign against Christ.

It is not, of course, obvious to the ignorant multitude that a charitable organization may be doing Satan's work. In the same way, outsiders who chance to read copies of Masonic rituals are normally surprised, and sometimes disappointed, to discover how Christian they are in content. It takes the discernment of a fundamentalist to tell that they are the work of Satan.

A favorite anti-Masonic target is the "long-lost" secret of the Royal Arch. Those (only a minority of Masons) who are "exalted" to this degree used to be informed that the "Sacred and Mysterious Name of the True and Living God Most High" is "JAH-BUL-ON." JAH is, of course, the short form of Jehovah. According to the best-selling anti-Masonic book of recent years, Stephen Knight's *The Brotherhood*, "BUL = Baal, the ancient Canaanite fertility god," and "ON = Osiris, the Ancient Egyptian god of the underworld."[10]

Knight did not think up these interpretations; they have become absolutely standard in attacks on the Craft, and in February 1989, the Supreme Grand Chapter bowed to the pressure and decided to cut out all reference to "the Name" from the ritual. It is worth pointing out, belatedly, that these names had nothing to do with the above interpretation.

The eighteenth-century devisers of the Royal Arch were struck by the way in which contemporary Masons of different races worshiped the same God by different names: Dieu, Gott, Theos, and so on. They supposed that the same was true in the Middle East thousands of years ago and tried to express this with a divine Name that was a combination of names of God from the ancient languages—Chaldee, Hebrew, Syriac, and Egyptian—which might have been spoken by the builders of the temple of Solomon. Unfortunately, at that time nothing was known about the Egyptian language, and little (in Britain) about Hebrew, Chaldee, and Syriac. So these Masons simply looked through the Bible and guessed. The book of 1 Kings (6:38) related that the temple of Solomon (on which the Masonic legends are based) was finished "in the month Bul." For some reason, the devisers of the Royal Arch thought this was a name of God; in fact, it was simply the name of the eighth month, meaning "rain" (i.e., the rainy season).

They found "On" in Genesis 41:45, where the patriarch Joseph married "Asenath the daughter of Poti-pherah priest of On" and bore him two sons. They thought this must be a name of God, but in fact it meant Poti-pherah was the priest of the *city* of On.

"JAH-BUL-ON" was laid out on an altar that also displayed the Hebrew letters *aleph, beth,* and *lamed* (A, B, L). The Working Group established by the Standing Committee of the Church of England to address the question "Freemasonry and Christianity: Are they compatible?" complained that these letters can be used to form "BAL, the name of a Semitic deity bitterly opposed by Elijah and the later Hebrew prophets."[11] Unfortunately for this notion, the middle letter of Baal is *ayin,* not *aleph*; and the middle letter of Bul is *waw,* so that neither Bul nor Bal is equal to Baal. Evidently, the devisers of Masonic rituals had not, generally, read the Bible carefully; yet neither have their subsequent Christian critics read the Bible carefully. Thus, an intended expression of monotheistic unity has been taken to be proof of secret polytheism.

Though Masonic lodges do not admit women, in some countries wives and daughters of Freemasons may join the Order of the Eastern Star, whose ritual is based on the stories of five biblical women—Jephthah's daughter, Ruth, Esther, Martha, and Electa—and is intended to inculcate five moral virtues. Consequently, they take as their symbol a five-pointed star. Some Evangelical writers state that this Star of the Order "represents Satan-worship." In fact, as noted previously, the "inverted" pentagram was associated with the Devil only by Eliphas Lévi in 1861, whereas the Order of the Eastern Star dates from 1778. so its symbol cannot have been chosen with any Satanic intention.

Clearly, Freemasonry must be viewed through hellfire-tinted spectacles to see any Satanism in it. John Lawrence, author of *Freemasonry—A Religion?* (who thought it was, which made it a dangerous rival to Christianity), noticed in a lucid moment that Masonry is a religion in the sense that, for some people, their garden is their religion, and for others, football or stamp collecting.[12] The only reason, then, for dealing with Freemasonry is that it has a poor reputation already, and that such titles as *Football: A Religion?* or *Christianity and Stamp Collecting: Are They Compatible?* would not have the same impact.

It is a case of the shifted argument: Freemasonry is compatible with Christianity but not with fundamentalism. When fundamentalists ask, "Should a Christian be a Mason?" and answer in the negative, what they are really saying is: "A Christian ought to be a fundamentalist."

Left-Right

The Christian Exorcism Study Group, who reported in *Deliverance*, edited by Michael Perry, that they had been monitoring Satanism, included in their findings the assertion that "Satanists seek to wield political and financial power. . . . Satanists are at work in some of the more extreme forms of left-wing and right-wing political activity."[13] If this were true, it would be a gross tactical error by the Satanists, as in Great Britain, at least, extreme left- and right-wing parties have no real chance of getting any political power. It is likely that this is another case of people lumping together all the things they fear.

"Were the Nazis Satanists?" has been a popular journalistic theme for years. The idea has a macabre romantic appeal, but despite the appearance of a series of titles such as *Storm-Troopers of Satan* (by Michael Fitzgerald), there is still no evidence that the Nazis were Devil worshipers. Trevor Ravenscroft's *The Spear of Destiny* appears at first sight to produce such evidence, but on closer inspection, his primary sources prove to be clairvoyant investigations, documents seen only by initiates, and other unverifiable materials.

Many of the Nazis were dabblers in occultism, but this is not necessarily a matter of consequence. In the 1930s, Germany's astrologers were rounded up and put in concentration camps. Those responsible must have had some kind of belief in astrology to have thought that astrologers were potentially dangerous; indeed, one of these astrologers, Wilhelm Wulff, was released in 1941 on condition that he cast horoscopes for the SS leaders. But one hardly needs to rewrite history because of this, any more than one can say that America in the 1980s was run by Nancy Reagan's astrologer.[14]

Another point of which much has been made is that Hitler was familiar with Theosophical literature, probably Madam Blavatsky's *The Secret Doctrine* or its imitators. But *The Secret Doctrine* is full of warnings against involvement in Black Magic, and in any case, what appealed to Hitler was undoubtedly Blavatsky's theorizing that the Aryans represented the peak of evolution. Hitler was also fond of Hegel, Nietzsche, Houston Stewart Chamberlain, and other writers who said that the Germans were an inherently superior race.

At the opposite end of the political spectrum, in the 1970s Richard Wurmbrand, who had spent many years in prison in Communist Romania for distributing Christian literature, asked *Was Karl Marx a Satanist?* Here are some of the reasons Wurmbrand thought so:

Marx's writings were full of verbal inversions. He answered Pierre-Joseph Proudhon's book *The Philosophy of Misery* with another titled *The Misery of Philosophy*, and he was inclined to use sentences like: "We have to use instead of the weapon of criticism, the criticism of weapons." Such inversions, says Wurmbrand, are a peculiarity of Black Magic.

"All active Satanists have ravaged personal lives. This was the case with Marx, too."

Marx's wife once addressed him in a letter as "high priest and bishop of souls." Wurmbrand asks, "Of what religion? The only European religion which has high priests is the Satanist one."[15]

The reader may assess the validity of his arguments from these samples, which go on for seventy-five pages, after which Wurmbrand says, "I do not claim to have provided undisputable proof that Marx was a member of a sect of devil-worshipers," but "I believe there are sufficient leads to imply this."[16]

He omits to mention that there is no evidence for *any* sect of Devil worshipers having existed anywhere in the nineteenth century. Indeed, while his statements about Marx are fully referenced, he gives no authority for his assertions about Satanism, and one would love to know his sources. Passing over the claim that in the Black Mass, "black candles are put in the candlestick upside down," he says, for instance, that "in the rites of higher initiation in the Satanist cult an 'enchanted' sword which ensures success is sold to the candidate. He pays for it by signing a covenant, with blood taken from his wrists, that his soul will belong to Satan after death."[17]

One might think from the precision of this statement that Wurmbrand knew what he was talking about; but that is doubtful. At the University of Paris during the riots of 1968 he saw a poster saying, "It is forbidden to forbid," which horrified him, as he saw it as a simplification of the oath for the seventh degree of Satanic initiation, "Nothing is true and everything is permitted."[18] Now these two slogans are not particularly alike, but in any case, "Nothing is true and everything is permitted" is not a Satanic statement at all. It came from the seventh degree of the Ismaili Order, a branch of Shia Islam. How Wurmbrand came to confuse a medieval Muslim sect with a Satanic church remains one of the unsolved mysteries of anti-Satanist literature.

Black and Blue

Satanists are routinely said to finance their organizations by dealing in pornography, specifically "hard-core" or "child" pornography. This is another error of judgment by the Satanists, as there is far more money in "soft-core" pornography (because it sells in much larger quantities). But it does fit in neatly with the moral crusaders' beliefs. For one thing, it provides another reason why people should not buy the filthy stuff: if they do, they will be financing Satanism. Then again, one of the favorite arguments against soft-core pornography—that people who read it "graduate" to hard-core or even child pornography—is suspiciously like the argument that people who start reading tarot cards or using Ouija boards will end up cutting up children in Satanic rituals (and is equally unconvincing).

The extent of child pornography is disputed. It is agreed that it hardly existed before the 1960s (another reason for disbelieving Stratford's *Satan's Underground*, whose authoress claimed that such pictures were taken of her in the 1940s). In the 1970s a Danish company, Rodox, made thirty ten-minute films of children having sex with adults. Apparently, these are the only commercial child sex films ever made.[19] If one hears about child porn videos being seized by police, it seems they are always either copies of the original Rodox films or home video material, taken by abusers themselves. Likewise, child pornography magazines used to be sold in Amsterdam and a few other places, but due to police actions, the supply dried up in the mid-1980s. Of course, there is nothing to stop pedophiles from taking photographs or making homemade magazines, which may be circulated to a few like-minded friends. But they could not do so on a large scale without discovery. It is believed that the biggest distributor of child pornography in the United States is the FBI, in the course of entrapment operations against pedophiles.

Not all such material may be illegal. It is said that pedophiles' collections contain things like the schoolgirl publication the *Jackie* annual. (Query: Should such items be labeled "Not for sale to persons over eighteen years of age"?)

Since the 1970s, or perhaps earlier, it has been rumored that some murders in films or "video nasties" are not staged but that the victims were really killed. In 1990 it was widely reported that there were pedophile "snuff" films going around in which children had been murdered on camera. It is interesting to note that the 1990 snuff scare was promoted by Geoffrey Dickens, Dianne Core, and others who had also been peddling fear of Satanism; and that Satanists are alleged to make snuff films, presumably of their human sacrifices.

In 1976, an American film producer offered a prize of $20,000 to anyone who could provide evidence that anyone had really been killed in this way. Twenty-five years later, the money has yet to be claimed. A 1979 film was actually called *Snuff*, and the advertising suggested that the woman murdered in the final scene had really been killed. Police investigated and found that the actress concerned was still alive.[20] Those responsible deserved an award for all-time bad taste in advertising, but they were not criminals.

There are logistical problems with the idea of snuff movies. No doubt there are people who would sink that low if they could get away with it; but could they get away with it? The natural instinct of any murderer is to cover up the crime. The last thing anyone would want to do would be to make the evidence public, and of course, it would be astonishing never to have had a prosecution if a film of the crime was available for all to see. There is the further problem that key scenes in films often need to be reshot several times. Why go to such difficulty and risk, when a fake murder would probably look gorier anyway?

Part of the reason for the persistence of this myth is that there are certainly many films of gratuitous violence, and some of these are actually nicknamed "snuff," perhaps because it gives viewers a bigger kick to imagine that it really happened. Thus the films of Linnea Quigley have been dubbed snuff movies, even though she has been "murdered" in a whole series of them.

The Federal Bureau of Investigation (FBI)

When the FBI's specialist in the sexual victimization of children, Kenneth Lanning, announced that he had investigated three hundred alleged cases of Satanic child abuse and found no evidence in any of them, to anti-Satanists the explanation was obvious: the FBI had been infiltrated and taken over by Satanists.

Pamela Harris, a worker at the Adam Walsh Child Resource Center in Orange County, California, interviewed a boy, "Charlie," who told her how his pastor had asked him and some other boys to remain behind after Sunday school. In the sacristy, he showed Charlie a skeleton and a freshly dismembered cat. This was to scare the boy into silence. The children were taken to a van, given drugged lemonade, and driven out into the desert. Charlie was too scared to say aloud what happened next, but instead of speaking, he drew pictures of monsters abusing children.

Harris concluded that Charlie had been taken to the same Ranch described by Lauren Stratford. She gave all the information she had to police and the FBI, but they did nothing. Her conclusion was that "high-ranking government, military and civilian officials" were Satanists and had sent word to law enforcers that the Ranch was not to be investigated.[21] It may simply be, however, that these trained investigators thought it implausible that numbers of children should return from Sunday school several hours late, having been drugged and violently abused, without any of their parents noticing.

The Central Intelligence Agency (CIA)

No conspiracy theory is really complete without the CIA. Recently, some Experts have concluded that Satanism is only a "blind," a cover for CIA experiments in mind control. If children are sexually abused at preschool, so the theory goes, then it will be easy to program them to become CIA agents in adult life: "CIA controllers sometimes dressed up in Satanic costumes to further traumatize the children, this also provided a cover that wouldn't be believed if the children ever talked about their experiences.[22]

General Xenophobia

Many people get their ideas about Satanism from the novels of Dennis Wheatley, and indeed, their author claimed that the kind of things he described in them really went on.

The opening of *The Devil Rides Out* reveals more about Wheatley's mind than he can have been aware of. The heroes, Rex Van Ryn and the Duke de Richleau, become concerned about their friend Simon Aron, who has started keeping strange company. They meet a group of his new friends, all of whom are either foreign or deformed. From this it follows that they are all Satanists: "A native of Madagascar . . . A grave-faced Chinaman . . . A fat, oily-looking Babu . . . a red-faced Teuton . . . The Albino, the man with the hare-lip, the Eurasian who only possessed a *left* arm. They're Devil Worshipers all of them."[23]

This being fiction, de Richleau is right. As an English Catholic, Wheatley admired some West Europeans (hence his French- and Dutch-named heroes) but was suspicious of most other peoples. Simon Aron, an English Jew, was "one of us" but capable of going over to the other side. In Wheatley's subsequent Black Magic novels, everyone from the Communist Party to an American Indian medicine man were added to the Satanist conspiracy.

Taking physical deformity as a sign of Satanic allegiance has a long history. In 1610, the witch-burner Pierre de Lancré interviewed a seventeen-year-old girl who had a cast in one eye. She confessed to him (on the rack, doubtless) that her mother had taken her to the sabbat, where Satan had poked her in that eye with his horn; hence its irregularity.[24]

There are other forms of aberrance. Wheatley's later novel *The Satanist* featured the Brotherhood of the Ram. Once again, at a typical meeting, "among the women there was an enormously fat negress and a young Chinese girl; among the men, two negroes, one of whom had white hair, an Indian and two who looked like Japanese . . . the majority were far from attractive."[25] The black woman turns out to be a lesbian who uses her evil powers to make girls fall in love with her.

That lesbians are common in Satanism is also asserted in nonfiction books, though no evidence is offered. The underlying assumption is that "perverts" are capable of doing anything, though actually, this is not true. Kitty, the lesbian occultist mentioned in chapter 1, used to belong to a witch coven but left because she was expected to have sex with the high priest. In fact, it is unlikely that lesbians would be attracted to Satan worship, for the simple reason that, traditionally, Satan is male. If there was a lesbian sect devoted to the practice of evil, they would more likely choose a destructive goddess, such as Kali or Lilith, as their patron deity.

The End Is Nigh!

In July 1987, a Congress on the Holy Spirit and World Evangelization, held in New Orleans, declared that 1990–2000 would be the "Decade of Evangelism." Their stated goal was to convert 20 million people to Christianity by the year 2000. Part of the reason for this sudden enthusiasm was a belief that the world would end at the turn of the century, so they needed to get as many Christians as possible for the fateful day.

In such a millennial atmosphere, it is easy to believe that Satan is alive and well and living on planet Earth, probably down your street. A 1970s Christian apocalyptic book, Basilea Schlink's *Countdown to World Disaster*, has chapter headings such as "Abortion?—Mass Murder!" "Sexual Emancipation?—Sexual Perversion!" "The Relevant Gospel?—Blasphemy!" It is not surprising to find also "Religious Tolerance?—Satanism!" which asserts: "Satanists murder their victims and then offer parts of the body for ceremonial sacrifices in the black masses. Such atrocities and sacrilege can only mean that the hour of greatest judgment is about to strike."[26] In a later book she amplified this, saying that since the Antichrist is coming, "demons are deluging the earth. At the bidding of Satan, their master, they perform signs and wonders, also using his servants in the many Satanist brotherhoods as tools to this end."[27] She gave her authorities, and unsurprisingly, they were Doreen Irvine's *From Witchcraft to Christ* and Mike Warnke's *The Satan-Seller*.

These views also came together in an earlier generation. In 1597, Florimond de Raemond published *L'Anti-christ*, which tried to prove that the Antichrist was coming soon:

> All those who give signs of the times of the arrival of the Antichrist, write that Witchcraft will spread everywhere. Has it ever been so popular as in this wicked age? . . . Our prisons are overflowing, and not a day passes that our judgements are not bloodstained, and we do not return to our houses horrified by the hideous and frightful things they have confessed. And the Devil is such a good master, that we cannot send a large enough number to the fire, that from their ashes will not arise other, new ones.[28]

In the same way, Alexander Roberts's *Treatise of Witchcraft* (1616), began: "In these last days, and perilous times, among the rest of those dreadful evils, which are foretold should abound in them . . . be Sorcerers, Wizards, Witches, and the rest of that rank and kindred: no small multitude swarming now in the world."[29]

Eventually the witch craze came to an end; but the world did not.

Liberals

For fundamentalists of all kinds, intolerance is the highest virtue. It follows that liberalism is the greatest sin. It is no surprise that the following should be found on a Christian Internet bulletin board:

> Satan and his fallen angels are spiritual beings so they're unable to act physically in this realm. This is where the need for human organization comes in. . . . Satan has found he can use the liberal media very effectively to manipulate the affairs of mankind. The liberal media is not only the devil's best device for corrupting and controlling human society, it's his most diabolical. . . . When the Antichrist finally arise to power, the liberal media will be tripping over themselves while trying to report his every word. . . . When Jesus Christ returns to earth, he'll cast the liberal media into the pit of darkness.[30]

The Black Kabbalah

The Kabbalah of the Jews is based on mystical interpretation of the Old Testament. The rabbis of the Middle Ages supposed that since it was all the word of God, an infinite number of divine mysteries were hidden therein and could be recovered by allegorical interpretation, seeking anagrams and acronyms, and similar methods.

The "Black Kabbalah" is when people use the same sort of methods to find evidence and information relating to Satanism, often in innocent-seeming things. The exemplar of this method was the nineteenth century archbishop Leon Meurin, whose *Freemasonry, the Synagogue of Satan* had the basic thesis that Freemasonry is based on the Kabbalah, and the Kabbalah is Jewish, therefore Freemasonry is a conspiracy to take over the world. It would be tedious to go through the details of his method, but one gets an idea of them from the outburst that the usually dry occult historian Arthur Waite wrote in response, pointing out that by such means one can prove anything about Freemasonry:

> It is well known that the Fraternity makes use of mystic numbers and other symbols. Take, therefore, any mystic number, or combination of numbers, as *e.g.*, 3x3=9. You will probably be unacquainted with the meaning which attaches to the figure of the product, but it will occur to you that the 9 of spades is regarded as the disappointment in cartomancy. Begin, therefore, by confidently expecting something bad. Reflect upon the fact that cards have been occasionally denominated the Devil's Books. Conclude thence that Freemasonry is the Devil's Institution. Do not be misled by the objection that there is no traceable connection between cards and Masonry; anticipate an occult connection or secret *liaison*. The term last used has probably occurred to you by the will of God; do not forget that it describes a questionable sexual relationship. Be sure, therefore, that Freemasonry is a veil of the worst species of moral licence. You have now reached an important stage in the unmasking of Masonry, and you can sum it as follows:—Freemasonry is the cultus of the Phallus.
>
> . . . recollect that our first parents went naked till the serpent tempted them, and then they wore aprons. Hence the apron, which is a masonic emblem, has from time immemorial been the covering of shame. Should it occur to you—vide *Genesis*—that God made the aprons, dismiss it as a temptation of the devil, who would, if possible, prevent you from unveiling him.[31]

Maury Terry is a modern Satan-hunter who has liberally applied the Black Kabbalah to his subject. He carefully analyzed a letter sent to the police by David Berkowitz, "Son of Sam":

> I am deeply hurt by your calling
> me a wemon hater. I am not.
> But I am a monster.
> I am the "Son of Sam." I am a little
> "brat.". .
> "Go out and kill" commands
> Father Sam. . .
> I am the "monster"—
> "Beelzebub"—the
> "Chubby Behemouth."
> I love to hunt. . .
> Police: Let me
> haunt you with these

words:
I'll be back!
I'll be back!
To be interrpreted
as—bang, bang, bang,
bank, bang—ugh!!
    Your in
    murder
    Mr Monster[32]

Most people would conclude only that the writer was a psychopath, but to Terry, hidden messages appeared. The odd spelling "wemon" was, he said "as in demon," and brat is "as in imp or little devil." The letters thus have occult significance. Likewise, "the hunt" refers "to the goddess Diana, queen of the Black Sabbath and leader of the Wild Hunt," and the words "I'll be back, I'll be back" are the same as those spoken by Satan in James Blish's novel *Black Easter*.

"Beelzebub" and "Behemouth" are the names of demons. Terry noticed that Behemoth was once drawn as an elephant-headed figure, and the next shooting after police had read this letter occurred outside the Elephas disco. Furthermore, Eliphas Lévi was the author of *Transcendental Magic* (Dogme et rituel de la haute magie, 1855–56), which has an illustration of a "Goetic Circle of Black Evocations and pacts" around which are the names of four demons, including Amasarac and Berkaial. "Berk" is short for Berkowitz, and read backwards, Amasarac yields the name Sam Carr, the man whose dog, Berkowitz claimed, had ordered him to kill. How this coincidence came about (since the names Berkaial and Amasarac were far older than Berkowitz and Carr) Terry did not explain. Out of such coincidences, Terry constructed a national Satanic conspiracy, then made it international by noting that Berkowitz spelled *honour* in the British way (rather than the American *honor*), thus proving that his conspiracy was linked to the Process, who were British—and so on.[33]

The problem with this method of investigation is that it can be used to show that anyone at all is a Satanist—even the anti-Satanists. Kahaner's *Cults That Kill* was published by Warner Books of New York, whose address was 666 Fifth Avenue. The *Evangelical Dictionary of Theology*'s dismissive article on "Satanism and Witchcraft" ("relatively innocuous" it considered) was signed "I. Hexham"![34]

In fact, apparent Satanic indicators often form by pure chance. On a certain railway station in Norway is a sign reading:

HELL

GODS EXPEDITION

Hell is the name of the town and means "luck." *Gods Expedition* is Norwegian for "freight" (literally, "Goods Traveling").

After the death of former French president François Mitterand, the celebrity fortune-teller Jacques Bois declared that Mitterand "could have been a secret devil worshiper."[35] As evidence, he cited the fact that Mitterand's hearse had the numbers "666" on its registration; from this, it seems, one is supposed to deduce that the former president belonged to a secret conspiracy that practiced perverted sex and ate babies.

The Beast 666 is first found in the prophecies of the end times in the book of Revelation: "And I stood upon the sand of the sea, and saw a beast rise up out of the sea, having seven heads and ten horns." Another beast then appeared, who "causeth all, both small and great, rich and poor, free and bond, to receive a mark in their right hand, or in their foreheads: And that no man might buy or sell, save he that had the mark, or the name of the beast, or the number of his name. Here is wisdom. Let him that hath understanding count the number of the beast: for it is the number of a man; and his number is Six hundred threescore and six" (Revelation 13:1, 16–18, King James Version). (The Beast is *not* called the Antichrist; this is a word that occurs only in the epistles of John, where it refers to anyone who rejects the doctrine of Incarnation.)

The prophecy of the number of the Beast has been partly fulfilled: bar codes, which are now a standard part of buying and selling, have three separate sixes among the numerical code. Perhaps the system was devised by an agnostic with a twisted sense of humor. Some Christians expect the rest of it to come true. In 1983, Roy Livesey, who identified the "ten horns" with the ten countries that then formed the European Economic Community (EEC), published a pamphlet *Beware! "666" Is Here* with a picture on the front of a man with a bar code embossed on his forehead. The text contained the following allegation:

> In July and August 1980 the IRS [U.S. Internal Revenue Service] mailed Social Security checks with the following instructions on the back: "The proper mark is in the right hand or forehead." The IRS admitted their mistake: "These government checks requiring a mark in a person's right hand or forehead are not to be put into use until 1984.[36]

In 1992, Caroline Robertson, a London businesswoman, was informed by a "young, intelligent" Evangelical Christian (whose remarks she later repeated to the author); that the firm of Proctor & Gamble was founded by "Alex Crow," who was "a major 20th century Satanist," and that all of its profits go to the international Satanic conspiracy. Indeed, this has been a persistent rumor for some fifteen years.

The first major company alleged to donate a portion of their profits to the Church of Satan was McDonald's, back in 1977. The rumor had it that the company president had actually appeared on the *Phil Donahue* program and admitted it. No one had seen this startling confession, of course, but few people watch every episode of a regular program. From about 1981 onward, the same rumor transferred itself to Proctor & Gamble.

The trademark of Proctor & Gamble shows a bearded man facing a moon and thirteen stars. This was alleged to be a Satanic symbol, and it was said to be possible to see three 6s in the curls of the man's beard. Once again, it was said that the president had appeared on some major network show and admitted the firm's Satanic connection. At the height of the rumor, in June 1982, Proctor & Gamble had to assign fifteen telephone operators simply to answer all the calls received about it.[37]

The story goes through regular revivals. In 1994, a letter was sent by the Internet to Christian bulletin boards internationally:

> The president of Proctor & Gamble appeared on the Phil Donahue show on March 1, 1993. He announced that due to the openness of our society, he was coming out of the closet about his association with the CHURCH OF SATAN. He states that a large portion of the profits of Proctor & Gamble products go to support the SATANIC CHURCH. . . . Below are a list of Proctor & Gamble products. . . . Christians should remember that if they purchase any of these products, they will be contributing to the support of the Church of Satan. Inform other Christians about this![38]

The UFO Menace

Toyne Newton's *The Demonic Connection* (1987), claimed that a dangerous Satanic cult met in the vicinity of Clapham Wood in Sussex. As proof of the sinister nature of the area, he mentioned various sightings of UFOs—unidentified flying objects—in the wood, failing to explain what the connection was between UFOs and Satanists, other than that they both seem sinister. Yet he could have cited, had he wished, a widespread theory that UFOs are demons in disguise. As early as 1954, Gordon Cove's booklet *Who Pilots the Flying Saucers?* took this line:

What we are suggesting is the possibility that Satan has seized one of the planets as his base of operations to attack the earth. . . . The first thing a military general seeks, when war is declared, is a convenient headquarters. Satan is the cleverest military genius ever known. Is it feasible that Satan, along with his principalities and powers, would continue to float airily around in the atmosphere for thousands of years, when there are literally millions of planets which would be well adapted for a headquarters?[39]

Since UFOs appeared to be more solid and tangible than devils, who are spirit beings, Cove also suggested that Satan might have taken control of beings on other planets, taught them how to build spaceships, and sent them off through the universe to do his bidding. The saucers were thus piloted by demon-possessed Martians and Venusians.

On 18 March 1978, Bill Herrmann, a thirty-year-old truck driver of Charleston, South Carolina, saw a "slick metal disc, about sixty feet in diameter," maneuver in the sky near his home. Suddenly it came down right in front of him; green and blue light was all around him, and the next thing he knew, he was in a field miles away, with a diminishing orange light visible as the spacecraft skittered away.

As is now routine in such cases, Herrmann was hypnotically regressed and recalled an examining table, flashing lights, and creatures resembling human fetuses, with overlarge heads and eyes, spongy white skin, and wearing rust-colored jumpsuits. Unlike most abductees, who think they have been taken off by space aliens, Hermann, who was a fundamentalist Baptist, was convinced that his experience was a "Satanic delusion." Since then, whenever he sees a UFO—and he has had several more encounters—he renounces it in God's name. This apparently works very effectively.[40]

A letter received by the U.S. Air Force in the 1960s purported to reveal the truth, although the writer's source of information was not given:

The "beings" that captain these saucers number 79, and each of the 79 has his own saucer. The 79 pass as earth men in the sense that no human could tell one of the 79 from an ordinary fellow human. . . . These 79 are not of human origin. They are fallen angels. They have murdered 79 men and have commandeered their bodies. . . . They are evil . . . in fact their leader is the inventor of evil . . . Satan.

The writer cautions that UFO pilots will teach that there is no God, which will be a ploy. "Beware, there is a GOD in Heaven . . . the proof that this country of ours exists is certification. Without GOD there would be no reason for

America. This is the great Christian bastion of the world. The U.S. is the major target to be destroyed by the 79."

That the public has not been told the truth about UFOs is due to a cover-up in the highest places:

> The denials of existence of flying saucers is not your fault. You have orders that come down from your so-called seniors. If this was traced all the way up it would show that Robert McNamara is the issuer of the flying saucer secrecy order. He denies they exist and has told his commanders to deny their existence. This is most interesting because Robert McNamara, Secretary of Defense for the U.S., knows more about flying saucers and the authenticity than anyone in the whole U.S. military—*Robert McNamara is a captain of a flying saucer. He is a fallen angel in the murdered body of Robert McNamara.* This took place in 1959. He is a very evil and dangerous man. His total dedication is to obey Satan and destroy the United States.[41]

This is the same Robert McNamara who, twenty years later, would be identified as a leading Satanist by LaRouchist propaganda. Other fallen angels masquerading as humans were, the letter writer asserted, Gerald Ford, Ronald Reagan, Chou En-lai (China), Leonid Brezhnev (Russia), and George Brown (England).

More than one prominent anti-Satanist inclines toward the demonic theory of UFOs. Religious radio broadcaster Bob Larson, author of *Satanism: The Seduction of America's Youth* and founder of Bob Larson Ministries, in his *Larson's New Book of Cults* (in which he describes himself as "one of the world's foremost experts on New Age thought") rejects the possibility of life on other worlds because it is not mentioned in the Bible: "If extraterrestrial beings do exist, surely the Lord would have told us without equivocation. It seems that such a crucial matter would be discussed somewhere in the Word of God."[42]

Instead, Larson considers that UFOs may be of angelic origin, but with caution, for there are two types of angels, fallen and not fallen:

> When God intervenes supernaturally, it is to bring comfort and peace, unless there is a clear reason for his wrath to be exhibited. What can be said of blips disappearing from radar screens and flashing oval objects floating through distant skies? While neither God nor Satan can be positively identified as the source, the latter seems a far more likely culprit . . . do UFOs serve a unique role in the master plan of Satan to deceive mankind?[43]

Hal Lindsey, in his *The 1980's: Countdown to Armageddon*, pointed out that the Bible warns that in the last times "fearful sights and great signs shall there be from heaven" (Luke 21:11, King James Version), which is fulfilled by the appearance of demonic UFOs:

> I believe these demons will stage a spacecraft landing on Earth. They will claim to be from an advanced culture in another galaxy. They may even claim to have "planted" human life on this planet and tell us they have returned to check on our progress. . . . If demons led by Satan, their chief, did pull off such deception, then they could certainly lead the world into total error regarding God and His revelation. They could even give a false explanation for the sudden disappearance of all the world's Christians—which will happen in the final days.[44]

We are still awaiting the "sudden disappearance of all the world's Christians."

Send Your Check to the Enlightened Master

In America in the 1930s, a certain Godfré Ray King was informed by the Ascended Masters of the Inner Planes that gold had mystical properties and, used correctly, could literally bring about a golden age. It accordingly became the sacred duty of his followers to provide Godfré Ray King with as much gold as possible. In 1994, the leaders of the Order of the Solar Temple announced to their members that they were going to collectively make the "push to Sirius," achieved by committing ritual suicide, which they all duly did. Incidents such as these have given legitimate cause for concern about "fringe" religions.

The majority of anticultists, however, are Evangelical Christians, and evidently motivated by rivalry. Decades ago, Horton Davies's *Christian Deviations* (2d ed., 1961) made the issues clear. According to Davies, while the ecumenical movement (meaning the modern harmonious relationship between Protestant and Catholic) was bringing churches together, the "sheep-stealing" of sects from "other folds of the Christian Church" was "a scandal—a tearing of the seamless robe of Christ" and constituted a "challenge and menace," even a "great danger."

Yet, by the middle of his first chapter, Davies had noticed the reason for the growth of sects: that the regular churches were congregated by the comfortable middle classes, whose social life was usually outside their church, whereas sects were "consciously established as the refuges of the poor" and often supplied all the members' friends and activities.[45] Thus, sects feed their sheep when the churches do not.

The only remedy Davies could offer was to explain the cults' theological errors. Since he himself stated, "The appeal is rarely to the reason, almost always to the emotions," this approach was obviously weak. In any case, it is not easy to prove the superior merits of one religion over another by reason alone. Another anticultist of the same time, J.-P. Krémer, provided readers of his *False Cults and Heresies Exposed* with biblical texts to be used to refute the doctrines of more than a dozen sects. For rebuttal of those who consider that the Bible itself was not divinely dictated but the work of fallible mortals, Krémer cited 2 Timothy 3:16: "All scripture is given by inspiration of God."[46] Arguments such as this tend to impress only those who already believe. My friend Gavin Sneddon has suggested starting a "Campaign for Joined-Up Thinking."

It will be recalled that the Inquisition was set up to deal with the new religious movements of the Middle Ages, and that when they ran short of heretics to persecute, they turned to witch-hunting. In the same way, the spread of interest in the occult from the 1960s onward was soon noticed by these anticultists. Alistair Forrest and Peter Sanderson's *Cults and the Occult Today* (1982) stated that "witchcraft is openly satanic, with sexual perversion, sadism, animal sacrifices and the desecration of Christian symbols."[47] Their authorities were not given but were evidently Doreen Irvine and *Jay's Journal*. More recently, the Reachout Trust, which originally specialized in literature warning against the Jehovah's Witnesses and the Moonies, spawned the anti-occult ministry of Maureen Davies.

A curious thing is that anticultists lump all "fringe" religious groups together. Whereas most people acknowledge a difference between, say, Judaism and Islam, anticultists suppose that all "cults" pursue the same ends with the same methods. Jean Ritchie begins her *The Secret World of Cults* by stating that cults practice "mind control" in the form of "love-bombing," that is, a large amount of attention and approval that is always given to the new recruit but withdrawn when he or she shows any resistance to the cult's ideas. This is supplemented by "a form of hypnosis": the members take part in chanting and meditation, along with a low-protein (usually vegetarian) diet and little sleep, not to aid their spiritual development but to put them into a trance, in which they become receptive to the cult's ideas. "Exclusivity is an important hook. Members of the cult are told that they are only ones who will be saved."[48] After chapters devoted to the Children of God, the Unification Church (the Moonies), the Hare Krishnas, the Mormons (whom some writers have the decency to recognize as a religion rather than a cult), Scientology, the Central London Church of Christ, the Rajneeshis, the Jehovah's Witnesses, therapy cults, and the New Age, Ritchie turns to Satanism and Satanic child abuse as being the most sinister cultism of all.

At this point a doubt may enter the reader's brain. How would the aforementioned mind-control techniques work in a Satanic order? Excessive indulgence in the pleasures of the flesh would have the opposite effect to meditation and dieting. It would be a strange Satanic cult that practiced "love-bombing." And could they control their recruits by assuring them that they were the only ones certain of damnation?

The real reason for this approach is polemical practicality: despite all the carefully reasoned arguments of the Evangelicals, new religions have continued to grow, whereas attendance at established churches has consistently declined. Scare tactics are obviously more effective than theological posturing. "Cult mind control" and, better still, "Satanic child abuse" will certainly gain attention. And whether or not they frighten people back to church, they always make good journalistic copy.

In 1993, William Shaw decided to investigate cults firsthand by joining a few. When he explained his intention to Ian Howarth of Britain's secular Cult Information Centre, he was told this was "foolhardy." Howarth claimed to have "identified twenty-six separate techniques of mind-control which cults use over their victims" and assured Shaw he would succumb to them if he got involved.[49]

In 1994, however, Shaw concluded: "After a year watching people join cults I have yet to see anyone lured in by anything other than their own hunger to believe."[50] Such a conclusion cannot appeal to anticultists, as it means that cult followers are merely exercising their right to freedom of religion, so that there is nothing anticultists can do about it.

The Inquisition often claimed that heretics' enthusiasm for their particular sect was caused by drinking some special liquid, usually wine mixed with the ashes of a cremated baby. The underlying presumption was that no sane person would ever reject the doctrines of the Catholic Church, so the heretics must have had their minds invaded by a supernatural force. The assertion that cults brainwash their followers has ultimately the same basis: a refusal to accept that people may sincerely believe in unorthodox creeds.

The Enemy Within

It is not common to meet someone possessed by an evil spirit, but strangely enough, it occurs often in Evangelical and charismatic churches. To judge from writers expounding this type of Christianity, every other Christian they meet is suffering possession. Thus, Bill Subritzky, author of the international best-seller *Demons Defeated* (1985), describes how he was once at a church convention where so many of those present had some kind of demon in them that he had to exorcise them ten at a time.[51]

Why should demons possess only Christians? Subritzky lists numerous methods by which demons can enter, a favorite being sex:

> In the act of sexual intercourse outside of marriage, demonic activity can occur readily as demons are transferred from one body to another. . . . Other forms of sexual perversion are demonic. For example, there are various forms of oral sex. . . . Similarly, masturbation can become demonic . . . people who have been involved in masturbation for any length of time have the utmost difficulty in giving it up . . . they have surrendered themselves to the demon of masturbation.[52]

The theory of Sexually Transmitted Demons, however, does not solve the problem, as there is no reason to think that Christians are more given to masturbation, adultery, and sexual perversions than non-Christians. The same is true of other occult checklists of things to be avoided as tending to lead to demon possession. Subritzky warns against:

- punk rock music
- chain letters
- martial arts (judo, karate, etc.)
- yoga ("involves Eastern demon worship")
- reincarnation (can one avoid it?)
- self-hypnosis
- significant pagan days (Observing them, presumably—no one can avoid them.)
- concept therapy
- dream interpretation
- Gypsy curses (Again, how does one avoid them?)
- horoscopes
- Dungeons and Dragons
- Japanese flower arranging ("sun worship")[53]

One also has to stay away from the more obvious things such as witchcraft and Satanism. Since most of these things are likely to be avoided by Christians anyway, why is it the Christians who become possessed?

Diagnosis of psychological problems seems to depend on what kind of therapist you go to. In January 1995 it was reported that Margeaux Hemingway, granddaughter of Ernest Hemingway, had been committed against her will to a psychiatric clinic in Idaho by her family. Her stepmother explained, "She was hearing voices. She thinks she can heal people, and take the devil out of them. She literally sees the devil coming out of their heads."[54] Under different circumstances, no doubt, she might have become a healer rather than a patient. (She died of uncertain causes the next year.)

To get an alternative to the Christian analyses of demonic problems, I sought out Jocelyn Chaplin, a leading Jungian psychotherapist. She told me:

> It's well established that this is a projection of the unacceptable side of the person, if they're brought up in a very strict Christian home for example, there's a split between sin and goodness, and so thoughts, sexual desires, or aggressive feelings against one's parents or friends have to be suppressed, in order to feel acceptable. And so they split off, and can take the character of an external voice or an external person. Hospitals are full of people who have done this. Psychotherapy is concerned with helping people not to see as sinful, unacceptable, very human feelings, such as anger toward one's parents, sexual desires towards an inappropriate object, and acknowledge those feelings, and integrate them into the whole personality. But when they're split off, they can take the form of voices, or belief that the devil or Satan is trying to attack them. So if you're a Christian, particularly in a charismatic church, it becomes a demon's fault, whereas in another subculture you might blame your mother.

If what Chaplin says is true, then it would explain why sex is a good entry point for demons. Christians may not do it more than other people, but they often feel a lot more guilty about it. But then, exorcism will not do any long term good in such cases, since the "split" parts of the personality will not go away. Indeed, books on exorcism mention cases where demons come back again and again, remarking that this proves how powerful demons are.

Actually, these lists of demonic entry points form a control mechanism. If people engage in things you disapprove of—perverted sex, hypnotism, and the like—threaten them with hellfire. If that fails to work, then threaten them with the more immediate danger of demonic possession. And if they are still unconvinced, then say the forbidden things lead on to Satanism and eating children.

Also, any obstacle to the progress of the gospel can be explained as due to demonic infestation. A Birmingham minister, the Reverend Tom Walker, warns of the "spirit of laughter," an evil entity that causes people who are, say, listening to an Evangelical preacher to "laugh out loud in an uncontrollable way." This is "a sign of direct Satanic attack," thinks Walker, who has apparently often encountered people with this form of possession during the course of his ministry.[55]

The long lists of "doorways," or entry points for demons, make daily life awkward for Christians. Members of one North London Church have to avoid, among other things, Care Bears (because they do rituals for healing without invoking the name of Christ), the film *E.T.*, Captain Beaky (whose creator was a spiritualist), Cabbage Patch Dolls (because they encourage people to treat toys as human), figurines of unicorns (mythological), and frogs ("And I saw three unclean spirits like frogs come out of the mouth of the dragon, and out of the mouth of the beast, and out of the mouth of the false prophet"; Revelation 16:13, King James Version). One woman owned a china tea set, passed down in the family as an heirloom; she was persuaded to smash it by another church member, who noticed there was a Chinese dragon in the pattern. A woman who looked after the church child care was found to be teaching the children relaxation exercises; she was thrown out. All these things, the church elders suppose, might bring demonic influence into the congregation's lives.

While exorcisms would seem to be, at worst, a harmless fad, on occasion they have had disastrous consequences. On the night of 5–6 October 1974, Michael Taylor, a Yorkshireman who had recently taken up charismatic Christianity, underwent an all-night exorcism at a local church. He then went home and murdered his wife, strangled the family poodle, and was found in the street by a policeman, naked and covered in blood. The exorcists subsequently explained that although they had driven forty evil spirits out of Taylor, a few remained, including the demon of murder.[56]

Fortunately, it is very rare for a possessed person to go crazy like this. Many other exorcisms have gone wrong, however because of an extraordinarily widespread and venerable belief that a demon can be driven out of a body by physical torture. Though few people have expressed concern at the spread of "Christian ritual abuse," that is just what exorcisms often amount to. The victims, mostly women and children, have been forced to take part in ceremonies where they were savagely beaten, often fatally. Exorcists have gouged a woman's eyes out;[57] held a three-year-old girl over a fire, onto which her favorite doll had been thrown, so that she would "feel the heat of Hell," and later murdered her; placed a baby in an oven;[58] forced a crucifix up a girl's nose so that it entered her brain; and forced two steel crucifixes down a woman's throat. Other children have met death by being strangled, being forced to drink a poisonous potion, or being hit repeatedly over the head with a concrete block.[59]

To be fair, this folly is by no means exclusive to Christianity, and in recent years people have died at the hands of Muslim, Santerian, and Chinese and Japanese exorcists, and even a Thai female shaman who beat her client to death with a dried stingray tail.[60]

In many cases, demonic possession has been a prelude to Satanic scares. Once exorcists are called in, the possessee will either accuse someone of having sent the demons into them by witchcraft or, after exorcism, suddenly remember that he or she was involved in Satanism for years. Either way, wherever exorcism has been a common practice, stories about witchcraft and Satanism have followed.

Other Demonic Activities

Demonic possession of animals does not appear to be a serious problem, but there are occasional reports of it. According to Charles H. Kraft's *Defeating Dark Angels*, "The danger exists of satanists demonizing and selling or giving pets to people they seek to infect." As evidence he reports: "I've heard of a woman who suspected her baby parakeet to have a demon and tested the theory by commanding it to perform a trick it had never been taught. It complied immediately and a demon was later cast out of it."[61]

An American minister named Brett Norton is reported to specialize in the treatment of canine possession. He has published a list of indicators to show whether or not a pooch may really be a hellhound in need of exorcising rather than exercising, including: "Does your dog desecrate holy monuments? One way might be to urinate against a relic such as a gravestone or church wall. This proves that Satan has turned him against the church."[62]

Allied to theory of possession is the theory that a class of demons known as "territorial spirits" haunt particular places. In West Africa, so the story goes, a pastor ordered a tree that was known as "the devil's tree" to be cut down: "The second the tree was felled, the pastor dropped dead."[63] The existence of such spirits could explain other tough questions: "Why, for instance, has Mesopotamia put out such a long string of tyrannical rulers? . . . Why is there so much overt demonic activity in and around the Himalayan mountains? Why has Japan been such a hard nut to crack with the gospel?"[64]

Evangelists are now advised to take up "smart-bomb praying": that is, instead of sending prayers off in the general direction of the enemy, their demonic adversaries should be carefully identified. This can be done in various ways, through historical research into the "old gods" of a country or by inquiry of the Holy Spirit. Thus, during a lecture on "How to Destroy Satan and His Clan," in Bolton Library in 1990, the Reverend David Stanley, an Essex vicar, informed the audience that demonic "Princes of the Air" had settled on England: his own town of Basildon, for example, had been seized by Jezebel, "a lustful spirit," while Bolton itself had been taken by "a spirit of control."[65] Armed with such information, the Christians' prayers can be precisely targeted, like cruise missiles, and hence are far more effective.

In 1972, Dr. Kenneth McAll (a Christian psychiatrist who would later estimate that there were four thousand human sacrifices a year in Britain alone) and his wife were sailing in the area known as the Bermuda Triangle and were caught in a storm for two days, during which they continually heard a strange dirge. They concluded they were hearing the restless spirits of African slaves who had been thrown overboard by traders who considered them unsalable, and that this was the cause of all the mysterious disappearances in the zone.

Some years later, McAll joined forces with the Anglican exorcist the Reverend Dr. Donald Omand, who had had a remarkably similar experience in the Triangle in the 1950s. Along with the bishop of Bermuda and others, Omand (who had previously exorcised Loch Ness) held exorcism rituals around the points of the Triangle in January 1978, while special services were said in other parts of the world. According to McAll's book *Healing the Haunted*, "Ten and a half years later the Australian Broadcasting Corporation researched through their library for a program and found that there had been no more unexplained disasters within the Bermuda Triangle."[66]

Whatever one may think of the territorial-spirits theory, in practice, the exorcism of places has not so far had any disastrous outcomes such as has happened with the exorcism of people.

The Devil Has the Best Tunes

Rock records have been a fruitful field for the Black Kabbalists. Pastor Jacob Aranza, author of *Backward Masking Unmasked: Backward Satanic Messages of Rock and Roll Exposed*, states that Led Zeppelin's "Stairway to Heaven," when played backward, yields the message "There's no escaping it. It's my sweet Satan"; though, as Timothy d'Arch Smith points out, when Led Zeppelin's records are played in the more usual, forward direction, there is "practically no reference to the occult in their lyrics."[67] It is presumed that such messages are intended to brainwash the listeners into becoming Satanists, though so far there is no evidence that people can be affected by messages heard backwards. (The late Roger Sandell asked, pertinently: "If it was possible to influence people in this way, why are there no messages like 'Buy our next album'?")[68]

Many Evangelicals go further and maintain that *all* rock music is the work of Satan. Rebecca Brown's friend Elaine told her that when she was a bride of Satan, she met many of the big rock stars, who had all agreed to serve Satan in return for wealth and fame.[69] One need not take her word for it, as proof is apparent—at least, to the anti-Satanists.

Take Live Aid, for instance. Jeff Godwin, a Christian Expert on rock music, who wrote that Live Aid was "the brain-child of an Englishman named Bob Geldolf [*sic*]," found plain signs of the presence of Satan in the words to "We Are the World." "The world must come together as one"; no, says Godwin: on the contrary, "Suppose ye that I am come to give peace on earth? I tell you, Nay; but rather division" (Luke 12:51, King James Version). "We are all a part of God's great big family"; but not according to Jesus, who, as Godwin points out, said, "Ye are of your father the devil" (John 8:44, King James Version). Accordingly, "We are the ones to make a brighter day" is "referring to Lucifer."[70] The other lines reveal the same message, as do the lyrics and packaging of all other rock music studied by Godwin. Paul McCartney's *Pipes of Peace* album shows him holding a syrinx, also called a panpipe, the instrument of the god Pan, who for some Christians is none other than the Devil. Nina Hagen has sung about UFOs, which, the reader will recall, are demons sent by Satan to deceive. Though Godwin stops short of identifying individual musicians as Satanists, he does specify that Stevie Nicks will burn in hell forever.[71]

Given the litigious nature of American society, it is not surprising that these assertions have given rise to lawsuits. In 1990 the British heavy-metal band Judas Priest were sued by the families of two Nevada teenagers who shot themselves after listening to their album *Stained Class*. It was claimed that, played backwards, the record contained the message "Do it," and that this had caused the suicides.[72] (The families could not sue over the overt contents of the songs, which a judge ruled were "free expression" protected by the U.S. Constitution.)

Among the Expert witnesses called by the families was a Las Vegas salesman who claimed that hidden messages on recorded material had supernatural powers. His Ph.D. credentials turned out to have come from a mail-order firm, and the judge dismissed his evidence. Out, too, went the theories of a probation officer who published a handbook, for schools and police forces in California, on the dangers of heavy metal-music and how to "de-punk" fans. The principal Expert was Dr. Wilson Key, author of a best-selling paperback, *Subliminal Seduction*.[73] Dr. Key believes the word *sex*, and depictions of skulls and penises occur in almost all advertising materials, and in many other places too. He has observed them in Ritz crackers, Rembrandt paintings, and Abraham Lincoln's beard on five dollar bills.[74]

The producer of one of the songs, James Guthrie, cross-examined by one lawyer, was asked, "Just what does C-90 mean here?"—the insinuation being that it contained a Satanic message. Guthrie had to explain that "C" stood for "cassette," and "90" signified a playing time of ninety minutes.[75]

The defense's argument was that the boys came from a disturbed background and that this, combined with a drink-and-drugs binge, had caused their suicides—not the music they had listened to. This was accepted by the jury, and the action against the band failed.

There is nothing new in all this. In the 1930s, Montague Summers stated that "some acute observers have shrewdly scented the devil's own orchestra" in jazz music, and he quoted a certain Father Philip De Ternant, who

> "condemns the 'Voodoo Cult imported into our Dance Halls without protest,' and points out how young people are being corrupted by 'the roll and the thump of the Voodoo Drum' which 'responsive to subtle manipulation not far removed from black magic, plays a most hypnotic part' in the obscene, murderous, and wholly diabolical Voodoo cult. Quite unwittingly, no doubt, to-day many dancers are exercising their steps to the music of the witches."[76]

Four centuries ago, when the waltz (then called *La Volta*) was introduced to France, some witch-hunters claimed it had been originally taught by the Devil to his witches and had spread from them to the rest of the population. Thus Bodin: "But the dances of the Witches make men frenzied, and cause the women to miscarry, such as that which is called the Waltz, that the Witches brought to France from Italy, where the movements are so insolent and wickedly outrageous, that innumerable homicides and abortions are the result."[77]

The Ouija

Christian writers routinely list the Ouija board as a doorway to the occult. Usually they illustrate this claim with an anecdote such as the following: a family started playing around with a Ouija board. It spelled out the names of families who, it said, had previously lived on the site of their home. They checked with the local history library and found that the names were correct! Horrified, they went to the local vicar for spiritual help. They are now all "lovely Christians."[78]

If this kind of incident is common—many such are told, and there is no reason to think they are all made up—then there must by now be hundreds of Christians who became converted after being scared by a Ouija board. It may then be argued that the Ouija is thus a doorway to Christianity, and one would think that the Christians would be grateful for it rather than complaining.

The Christian argument, however, seems to be that because, undoubtedly, many people have been scared by the Ouija, it must be dangerous and evil and work by demon power. That it can be frightening does not prove it is dangerous, and anyway, dangerous things are not necessarily evil. Electricity is dangerous and should not be played with by children, but that does not make it inherently evil; still less does it mean that electrical appliances work only by means of indwelling demons.

Can Your Dreams Become Reality?

One of the most dangerous doorways to the occult, according to anti-Satanists, is fantasy role-playing, particularly Dungeons and Dragons (D&D). Joan Hake Robie, founder of Joan Robie Ministries, has said D&D "is not a game" but a "teaching on demonology, witchcraft, voodoo, murder, rape, blasphemy, suicide, assassination, insanity, sex perversion, homosexuality, prostitution, Satan worship, gambling, Jungian psychology, barbarism, cannibalism, sadism, desecration, demon summoning, necromantics, and divination."[79] All of these, she said, are forbidden in the Bible, though one wishes she had given chapter and verse for the scriptural ordinance against Jungian psychology.

In the United States there used to be a tax-exempt organization named BADD (Bothered About Dungeons and Dragons), founded by a woman named Pat Pulling, whose gifted teenage son committed suicide in 1982. He was a regular D&D player at school, and his mother blamed his suicide on the game.

Pulling linked D&D to Satanism, serial killers, heavy-metal music, ritual child abuse, and the like and said that the game's symbols "are used in real sorcery and conjuration of demons."[80] The argument seems to be that because D&D turns the mind to violence and occult practices, it will encourage teenagers to do the same things in the real world. Why, then, it could be asked, do responsible parents permit teenagers to read the Bible, which contains scenes of adultery, murder, infanticide, necromancy, demonic possession, suicide, assassination, harlotry, coprophagy (feeding on excrement), human sacrifice, rape, cannibalism, and incest, with instructions on how to carry out blood sacrifices and cursing rituals?[81]

Pulling has an unusual approach to statistics: she once stated to the press that 8 percent of people in Richmond, Virginia, were involved in some kind of Satanism. When challenged as to her derivation of this figure, she explained she had arrived at it by adding an estimated 4 percent adult involvement to 4 percent teenage involvement.[82] Apart from this, in 1987 she produced a list of some seventy suicides, and a similar number of teenage murders, that she related to D&D.

Michael Stackpole, who analyzed her data, found that in most cases, the only provable connection was that the teenager concerned was a D&D player: in itself, that does not prove D&D was responsible for the suicide or crime, and in most cases, Pulling offered no evidence that it was so. After at least two of the suicides, the parents of the deceased actually stated to the press that they did not consider D&D was the cause.[83]

The first suicide linked to Dungeons and Dragons was James Dallas Egbert III, generally known as Dallas. A superbright sixteen-year-old, Dallas had entered Michigan State University in East Lansing at only fourteen years of age. Overwhelmed by an urge to disappear, on 15 August 1979, he went down into the heating tunnels beneath the campus and took an overdose of quaaludes. They only made him sleep for twenty-four hours. When he awoke, still wishing to disappear, he went and stayed with some gay men he knew in the city for a couple of weeks. He then took a train to New Orleans, bought some chemicals, mixed up what he thought was a lethal poison, and drank it. He was merely sick.

Meanwhile, his parents had hired a leading private detective, William Dear, to find their son. Dear had discovered that college D&D players, Dallas among them, had sometimes illegally used the heating tunnels for live role-playing. He went down there, and from the food remains, he was able to identify the spot where Dallas had slept. The boy's disappearance had created national media interest, and this Dungeons and Dragons connection was highly publicized.

In the end, Dallas simply telephoned Dear and told him where he was. He was reunited with his family and started at another college, but in August 1980, he put a gun to his head and this time succeeded in leaving the world. Dear's subsequent book on the case was called *The Dungeon Master* and went into detail about the game. Since then, the story has been routinely listed in anti–D&D writing.

That highly intelligent young people are liable to self-murder is well established. In Britain, for instance, it is believed that the highest suicide rates are found among Oxford and Cambridge undergraduates (as has been the case since before Dungeons and Dragons was invented). There are several reasons for this tendency: the very bright are often very emotionally sensitive; usually, going to college marks the first time they have lived away from their families; they will have left behind all their friends and have to make new ones (at which they may not succeed); it is an age at which one is often disappointed in love; and all the while there is intense work, with regular assessments and examinations to wrack the nerves. Dallas had the further problems of being forced to recognize that he was gay (at least most students are spared that) and being much younger than all those around him.

Dallas told Dear he had "three different reasons for wanting to disappear": he always felt pressured to get good grades; he could not face telling his mother he was gay; and he had been unable to make friends. When Dear asked him about Dungeons and Dragons, he said, "When I played a character, I *was* that character. Didn't bring all my problems along with me. It's a terrific way to escape."[84] In short, there does not appear to be the least reason to blame his death on fantasy role-playing.

Pat Pulling has claimed that role-playing involves 4 million young Americans. If this is roughly true, and given that the suicide rate for fifteen- to twenty-four-year-olds in the United States is something like one in ten thousand annually, then just by the law of averages, one would expect at least four hundred fantasy role-players a year to commit suicide. Since the seventy on Pulling's list covered a period of more than a decade, if anything it would seem that fantasy role-playing decreases one's likelihood of killing oneself.

One or two teenage murderers have taken up Pulling's line, no doubt aware that any excuse is better than none ("I did it, but Dungeons and Dragons was to blame"). Murderers, however, are hardly the best witnesses, particularly as they may be desperate for "mitigating circumstances" to help them avoid the death penalty. Statistically, the same problem occurs: with more than twenty thousand murders a year in the United States, one would expect perhaps two hundred or more annually to be committed by people who had played D&D.

Professor Carl A. Raschke cites two murders where the *victims* were Dungeons and Dragons enthusiasts. In one, a girl was killed by a drug ring who believed she was a police informer. In the other, both motive and killer were unknown.[85] Professor Raschke does not say what these cases are supposed to prove about D&D. No doubt many murder victims are smokers, but not even the most extreme health fanatics would say *this* is proof that smoking kills.

Pulling also quoted a couple of cases where adults held D&D parties and subsequently abused children who came along to them. But as the late Roger Sandell pointed out, "these fall into a long established pattern of paedophiles cultivating activities and interests liable to bring them into contact with children,"[86] the most notable of which is becoming a Boy Scout leader.

As to the "authentic occult information" in Dungeons and Dragons, here is an example of a Second-Level Wizard Spell: "Tasha's Uncontrollable Hideous Laughter." "The victim of this spell perceives everything as hilariously funny," and this affects the "strength points" for a round. "The material components are a small feather and minute tarts. The tarts are hurled at the subjects, while the feather is waved in one hand."[87] If this is "real sorcery," then *Thomas the Tank Engine* was written as a manual for British Rail workers.

At the Gen Con in Kent in 1994, a competition was held to find the top fantasy role-player in Europe. In second place came Debbie Gallagher, a London woman who is also a leading occultist, which would seem to prove the anti-Satanists' case. In March 1995, Gallagher kindly agreed to be interviewed for this study:

Isn't it true that in your case fantasy role-playing was a "doorway" to the occult?

No, I was interested in the occult from a very early age, from about nine upwards; I had my first pack of tarot cards at the age of eleven, I played my first game of Dungeons and Dragons when I was seventeen.

Then did the occult lead you to Dungeons and Dragons?

No, my brother led me to Dungeons and Dragons.

There's this boyfriend of yours who's . . .

. . . completely anti the occult. He's made, and most role-players have to make, a very sharp differentiation between what they think is real and what isn't. He will not believe that anything to do with the occult is anything other than irrational and ridiculous. But he enjoys a good fantasy film, he enjoys a good fantasy book, he enjoys role-playing. He expresses the view of most of the role-players that I've met, and I've met a lot. I'm an occultist who likes to role-play, I was an occultist first. I'm interested in role-playing because it's drama, it's theater, not because of its occult content, and that is the case for something like 99 percent of players. Occultists I know tend to look at fantasy role-players and see them as failures who can't face reality. The role-players say exactly the same about the occultists. Both sides see each other as washed-out losers who cannot cope with the real world.

Do you get people in role-playing who can't distinguish fantasy from reality?

In every area of life, in every single profession, there will be some strange people, they would have been a bit strange whatever pastimes they had engaged in. You will find strange people role-playing, a lot of inadequate people role-playing, but you don't get out-and-out crazies who really believe that they are Frongar the mighty Mage.

The inadequate people—what effect does fantasy role-playing have on them?

When it began, what you used to get was a whole load of thirteen-year-old boys, virgins, covered in spots, full of fantasies, the kind of kids who maybe weren't particularly good in school, maybe more easily bullied. They found this world in which they could become the Grey Mouser, a clever, roguish thief, or Ningauble, a wizard, or Fathd, a great fighter, just with the roll of a dice. It got rid of their feelings of inadequacy, it didn't turn them into occultists, not even inept ones.

Were they "sucked into a vortex of undesirable real-life behavior"?

No more than your average university student. They drank a lot of beer, and ate a lot of pizza, when they reached the age that they could afford beer and pizza. They didn't get laid any more often because very few girls actually role-played at the time.

Exorcists like Bill Subritzky list fantasy role-play as a means by which demons can enter humans to possess them. You've met a lot of role-

players; have you ever noticed that they have a tendency to be demon-possessed?

Curiously enough, no. I've noticed a lot of spotty young boys being possessed by the demon of lust, as they imagine themselves grappling with a large-breasted female fighter who eventually succumbs on the field of battle.

It's claimed that fantasy role-playing games encourage Devil worship, suicide, and murder.

I think you can safely call that a pile of dogs'-dos. I think it's nonsense. And I'd be very surprised if independent figures can be found to substantiate that claim.

Isn't it true that in certain role-playing games you decide the character by throwing three six-sided dice?

There are about five different ways of using between three and five dice, and deciding a character through that. Nowadays most role-playing systems don't create a character through dice. A points system is used.

But in the case of three six-sided dice, doesn't the "6-6-6" prove that the Antichrist is behind it?

I've got nothing to say in response!

Ms. Gallagher was unable to refute the Evangelical argument . . . ?

That's right, stunned into silence by the logic behind it!

The Advanced D&D manuals, they list the goddess Kali and mention that sometimes human sacrifices are performed to her. Pat Pulling takes this as evidence that players might go out and do it for real.

It certainly isn't. I know the AD&D manuals extremely well, where any god is mentioned, any demon, any entity of any kind, they'll give them a label, good, neutral, or evil; it's made completely clear which they are and what you are to expect from them. Most role-playing games emphasize the battle between good and evil, in a very Christian way. It's Darkness versus Light.

How far is fantasy role-playing based on real occultism?

With Advanced Dungeons and Dragons, which is the most popular, you will learn precisely nothing about any existing form of the occult whatsoever. There is no crossover between that and any occult history, any occult background; it is just an excuse for creating Terry Pratchett–type Mages, that's all they are, they wear a hat and they throw a spell. When you deal with better systems, *Ars Magica*, *Mage*, you find yourself dealing with historical fact; there will be more truth about history, about the kind of armament people wore, about the way they got about the countryside, about percentages of people who could read and write, and about how people really felt about religion, and therefore about all aspects of spirituality, including magic.

A few months back you wanted to know who was pope in the year 1230. What was that for?

This was for a game of *Vampire*, and *Vampire*, quite apart from being about vampires, is also historical because vampires live for a long time. The idea behind the game is that most vampires were wiped out by the Inquisition, so the problem is working out, for the benefit of the game, precisely when the Inquisition in the relevant part of the world was strong. If I get it wrong in my game, there are people who will pick up on it and say: "That's not right!"

It is remarkable that, for role-playing purposes, you're learning about the papacy of Gregory IX, and another time you were going up to the British Newspaper Library looking for material about Springheel Jack. Now, if the average spotty teenagers were asked to find out these things for a school project, they would probably get a massive attack of inertia, but if it's for fantasy role-playing, they're really keen.

It is very educational, what does happen is, for example, someone creates an Assyrian campaign, with Assyrian, Mesopotamian, and ancient Egyptian ideas. They may throw them all in for a bit of Hollywood glamor, and people start learning about the Egyptian laborers, and what they earned, and so on, you have to go away and find out things. It's educational, it's education without teachers, it makes people learn for themselves.

Debbie Gallagher, thank you.

Do children who play Monopoly all grow up to be property speculators? Does chess foster racial disharmony by setting up white against black? Because anti-Satanists cannot distinguish fantasy from reality, does that mean the rest of the population are similarly afflicted?

11

"Thou Shalt Not Suffer a Witch . . ."

Gerald Suster is the author of around thirty books, his main subjects being sex, magic, novels, biography, and boxing. He is an earnest disciple of, and the leading authority on, Aleister Crowley. He contributed the article on Crowley to the supplement to the British *Dictionary of National Biography* and has written a full-length study on Crowley, *The Legacy of the Beast* (1988).

In 1989, Suster was a tutor at a private sixth-form college in Sussex. After a meeting of the Society, an occult discussion group that used to be held at The Plough in Bloomsbury, a man came up to him and asked him to talk about Crowley's *Book of the Law*. Unbeknownst to Suster, the man was a freelance journalist and was secretly tape-recording the conversation.

The next thing Suster knew, two journalists from the *News of the World*, to whom the freelancer had sold the tape, turned up at the school, showed him a transcript, and asked to talk to him. He agreed but was subsequently "flabbergasted when they proceeded to misquote me in every possible way."

When I talked with Suster, over a generous helping of whiskey, in February 1995, he recollected their conversation as follows:

> "Have you ever taken drugs, Mr Suster?"
> "At University I tried marijuana, like a lot of people."
> "Funny how everyone says that, isn't it, Mr Suster?"

This turned up in the paper as "I advocate the use of drugs. I have taken marijuana and speed."

The freelancer had asked Suster about the Cakes of Light, the Thelemic sacrament that, according to the *Book of the Law*, should include blood. Suster told me "I have indeed eaten Cakes of Light made with animal blood, it's no different from having black pudding. I get the blood from the butchers." But according to the *News of the World*, "Suster admitted GORGING himself on human blood."[1]

As Suster told me, "Again, according to the *News of the World* I'm supposed to attend kinky group sex sessions. I never have, I'm not really into that sort of thing. If other people want to, that's up to them."

Above the caption "Sick Books Of Evil" in the tabloid was a photograph showing Suster's *Legacy of the Beast* next to Israel Regardie's *The Law Is for All*; the latter was published by Thorson's, a subsidiary of Collins, owned, ultimately, by Rupert Murdoch, the proprietor of the *News of the World*.

What was the school's reaction to this article? "I was, quite properly, asked to resign." Though the headmaster considered Suster an excellent teacher (and was already well aware of his occult interests), schools of this type could be ruined by a scandal, so Suster had to go. "It was a bit difficult for me at first. I lost my job, my home, my salary, and my job satisfaction."

Suster sued for libel and eventually received five-figure damages. "Since then my career's taken off." In the long run, he thinks the paper did him a good turn.

The Reverend Kevin Logan's *Satanism and the Occult* describes Suster as a "Caliphate OTO leader."[2] "I'm not a Caliphate OTO leader," he responds. "I joined in spring 1986, and in spring 1987 I accepted the job of secretary of the London OTO. I resigned from the Caliphate OTO about two and a half years ago. I wasn't a leader, I was a secretary."

Didn't the Caliphate OTO use the twenty-six separate techniques of cult mind control to prevent him from resigning? "No." What about LaRouche's claim that the OTO is supplied money by a drug ring run by the queen? "Now I've heard everything!" Suster also ridiculed the suggestion that senior NATO officers were members and all the other absurdities that have been printed about the OTO in the tabloid press.

Once again we have the basic issue of freedom of religion, guaranteed by the eighteenth article of the Universal Declaration of Human Rights, to which the British government is a signatory but not the *News of the World*. The paper would not attack Jews or Catholics, but followers of "way-out" belief systems such as Thelema are regarded as fair game.

While there is a great deal of amusement to be had from the posturing of the Satan-busters, not all their activities are harmless fun. Virgin 1215's radio phone-in at Midsummer 1994 included the following dialogue:

Caller: Tonight we're going devil-worshipper-hunting.
Nick Abbott: What are you going to do when you find them?
Caller: Kick the shit out of them.

The largest real Satanic order in Britain (as opposed to the vast number of imaginary ones) is the Temple of Set, currently with seventy to eighty members. Though its activities are perfectly legal, joining nonetheless brings danger: not from demonic powers and principalities but from tabloid journalists.

Applicants normally first have an individual meeting with a senior Temple member on neutral ground, such as a wine bar. On one occasion, in 1989, against the advice of British chief David Austen, a priest arranged to meet a man and a woman at the same time. This was indeed a grand error, as the woman was, in fact, a journalist for the *News of the World*. Worse still, the man was a nursery-school assistant who was hoping to do a master's degree in "New Religious Movements." The journalist quickly discovered this, and he was promptly featured in an article headlined "Child Care Man to Join Sex-Orgy Witches."[3] The man lost his job. Ironically, even before the article appeared, the Temple of Set had rejected his application for membership.

The next summer, the same reporter turned up at the home of another Temple member, a secretary at Sussex police headquarters who sometimes used the name Carol De'ath. Asked about Satanism and her sex life, De'ath obligingly told her all about them. Her story appeared as "Exposed: The Wicked Witch from Police HQ."[4] The same day the *Sunday Mirror* also printed an interview with her, "Police Girl's Sex Romps with Satan Lover," subheaded "Exclusive"[5]—and soon afterward, another Satanist had joined the unemployment statistics.

Pagans are often regarded as somewhat less than human. In March 1996, the bishop of Bath and Wells was due to lead an interfaith service at Newbury, "to mourn the destruction caused by the road scheme," which Catholics, Buddhists, Hindus, Jains, Jews, and Hare Krishnas were to attend. After a BBC reporter told him that Pagans would also be present, he pulled out. "Pagans are not believers in anything [!]—they are nature worshipers," said the bishop. "I had to explain that I have taken a solemn oath personally to the Queen to uphold the Church of England. I cannot take part in a service where Pagans are specifically welcomed."[6]

The Satanism scare has added to these problems. Though some anti-Satanists admit that the revival of Paganism and witchcraft is something quite different from the Satanism they are purporting to expose, others deliberately try to blur the distinction, and this tends to confuse the general public.

In 1986, Zsuzsanna Budapest, a well-known Dianic witch from San Francisco, was asked to speak about witchcraft at the St. Theresa Library in San Jose. Books on witchcraft were checked out more than any other type there, and some teenagers had asked if they could hear a talk by a real witch.

A leaflet advertising the talk came into the hands of a local church. Members of the congregation protested to the city council that for such a talk to be sponsored by public money would violate the First Amendment (separating religion and government). The deputy attorney ruled that the talk could go ahead. So the congregation organized mass protests. Budapest listened to her answering machine one morning and found messages such as the following:

> The Lord despises Witches. You are evil, and you don't even know it. Give up your evil intent and leave the little children alone.

> "Thou shalt not suffer a witch to live," remember that, Witch.

> The Lord told me to kill you. He talked to me last night, and he told me to kill you.

The police advised her to cancel the speech. She did not, instead asking them for protection. They provided her with fifteen officers and four snipers. She had to be escorted into the library past hundreds of protestors, many of whom came from out of town and had been given free bus rides in by the 700 Club. So her talk went ahead, the hall filled with fundamentalist Christians, who kept praying to drown her voice out, and Pagans, who had come along to show her support. Apparently, there wasn't room for the original teenagers who had requested the talk.[7]

A. J. Drew once ran a bookshop in Obetz, Ohio, but by now events probably have driven him out. The shop stocks books on astrology for love and sex but keeps them under glass and does not sell them to minors. A local pizza-parlor owner suggested in council that this shop be firebombed, which amused the local police chief. A firebombing was called for in at least three council meetings, with no response from the police. The mayor, an attorney, refused to shake the hand of Drew's attorney—a Wiccan.

The local fire department also joined in. They decided that candles in the shop constituted a bonfire and contravened fire regulations.

Pagans are not the only people to suffer harassment in Obetz. A local Jewish woman told Drew that a swastika had been burned into her front yard, sixty "For Sale" signs had been put on her lawn, and the side of her house had been burned. The swastika burner was sentenced to just two weeks' community service. Her children were told in school that Jews have tails and green blood and eat their first young.

Though the Constitution of the United States is meant to separate government and religion, the school in this Ohio town violates the First Amendment by having children recite the Lord's Prayer. The city council likewise start all their meetings by joining hands and reciting the same prayer. Despite the obvious breaches of the Constitution, the local branch of the American Civil Liberties Union (ACLU) (equivalent to Liberty in Great Britain) showed no interest in the case. Drew would win easily if he took his case to the Supreme Court, but this would cost about $3 million.[8]

In the above cases, the victims of prejudice were witches or Pagans of some kind (except for the Jewish woman in Obetz), so they should at least have expected the trouble they got. But harassment of this kind has afflicted those who are not occultists at all, and who are often practicing Christians. In the village of Irvine, Kentucky, in September 1988, a photographer working on a grant from the Kentucky Arts Council to take pictures of schoolchildren was accused by local rumors of photographing "blond, blue-eyed" potential child victims for ritual sacrifice by Devil worshipers. She was forced to leave town hurriedly after a school principal, with whom she had arranged a meeting, chased her out of the school, shouting insults and threats at her.[9] The Church of Fire in Pharr, Texas, burned to the ground after a rumor said a "blonde-haired blue-eyed child" was to be sacrificed there.[10]

The Sunday after the not-guilty verdicts were delivered in the McMartin trial in California, the minister of St. Cross Episcopalian Church, John D. Eales, announced that he had been forced to seek disability retirement due to the extreme stress that fallout from the case had put him under. Neither he nor anyone else at the church was formally charged with anything, but the church was unable to shake off the allegation of a McMartin pupil that he and other students had been forced to witness animal sacrifices and satanic rituals at the altar of St. Cross. Though investigators using "sophisticated equipment" checked the altar and found no trace of blood, attendance dropped drastically at both the church and the church-run preschool, which closed soon afterward.

Periodically over the years, Eales said, he would receive threatening phone calls at the church and rectory, and the harassment increased as the McMartin case drew to a close. Twice in December, the church and rectory were pelted with bottles and rotten eggs. In a note left in the rectory driveway after the second attack, the vandals, who identified themselves as "the Beach Cities' Conscience," warned that "there is simply no place for Satan worship in this town." Eales said his doctors had told him that "the kind of stress you have been under kills."[11]

People wrongly accused of child abuse can easily lose their jobs and their homes, even if, ultimately, charges are dropped, as in the Epping Forest case. Often they lose their friends as well or otherwise suffer disintegration of their lives. In 1990, Mark Ye Morris, a folk musician from South London, was stuck in "a crap marriage" and had trouble finding work. His children, a boy of four and a girl of six, had behavior problems at school.

One day, his daughter came to school with ring marks around her wrists, which were due to her sleeping in a dressing gown that she'd had since she was three, and which had become too tight. The school called in social services, however, who suspected Morris of abusing her.

"They didn't find anything wrong," Morris recounted to the author in 1999; "we were okay parents." Social services did notice, however, that he had an interest in stone circles, astrology, and morris dancing. Since this was at the height of the ritual abuse panic, they were suspicious of these "occult" activities. "That was February 1990. About May or June the team leader said, there's only a slight doubt, but she was going to seek advice from an Expert in these things." The Expert was a woman from the Reachout Trust, who apparently concluded that Mark might be a member of an international Satanic conspiracy. In any case, in early August social services got an order to come around and take the children away. "I think the children thought we didn't love them any more. The foster home was shitty, apparently."

"The marriage was crap anyway, this helped break it up. Social Services wouldn't give the children back to both of us, so my wife decided to divorce me and have the children back. The court hearing was March 1991, I was given just a week to clear out, I was homeless for two months. I fought for access, I was given only supervised contact for one or two hours every two or three weeks. Satanic abuse was eventually knocked on the head, but they still didn't rule out sexual abuse, which upset me." Mark Ye Morris learned that police surgeons had strip-searched the children. They didn't find anything, but another Expert pointed out that oral sex does not leave any marks. It was years before Mark was allowed full access to his children once again.

Yet those who are merely suspected are relatively lucky. It is hard to imagine the horror of ordinary, middle-class people, often women, who may have devoted their lives to looking after small children and never have been in trouble for so much as a parking offense, upon suddenly finding themselves in prison as "child abusers," regarded as scum even by rapists and murderers.

Peggy Buckey, "a trusting, gentle, kind woman," typically had her life threatened two or three times a day during her two years in a California jail. Once, other prisoners set her hair on fire. The guards often beat the prisoners, and though, since she was in a high-publicity case, it did not happen to her, she saw them do it to other women. Prison officers often watched and did nothing when girls were raped by other inmates. Handcuffs were put on Buckey so tightly that she developed arthritis. The female prisoners were often ordered to strip, open their vaginas, and cough. When Buckey asked why, guards told her they were looking for concealed guns. Two expensive diamond rings, taken off when she entered the jail, were not returned to her on her release.[12]

But at least Buckey *was* released. One would not expect this to happen to Bob Kelly, who was given twelve consecutive life sentences for such offenses as abusing children in a spaceship. How does one serve *consecutive* life sentences? It was explained that in North Carolina a lifer cannot be considered for parole until at least 20 years have been served; so Kelly could not be set free in less than 240 years.

The Organization of Prejudice

What literature is right and proper for children has long been a heated topic. Recently, material on witchcraft has been under pressure for reasons unconnected with anti-Satanism: a while ago, a teacher at a politically correct North London school got into trouble for telling his class a story about the "Witch of Edmonton" (Elizabeth Sawyer, hanged in 1621 for selling her soul to the Devil). It is not known what he said about her, but it seems that he propagated sexist stereotypes instead of explaining that she was a victim of patriarchal oppression.

From the mid-1980s, concern about the involvement of children in the occult has led to a series of pamphlets such as the Scripture Union's anti-occult tract for children, *Danger! Open Mind* (1986), which warns against involvement with Ouija boards, astrology, levitation, and so on. "Keep an open mind—and you may find it is filled with the wrong things."[13]

Quantities of advice have also been printed for Christian parents, such as this from Maureen Davies: "If we come at it as a Christian and, 'Deuteronomy says this and this,' you will switch these people off because they don't believe the Bible to be the word of God anyway." ("There shall not be found among you any one . . . that useth divination, or an observer of times, or an enchanter, or a witch, or a charmer, or a consulter with familiar spirits, or a wizard, or a necromancer. For all that do these things are an abomination unto the LORD"; Deuteronomy 18:10–12, King James Version.) "So you've got to get a listening ear before you start spouting scripture and usually come in as a parent or a concerned individual."[14]

Maureen's advice to Christians to pose as "a parent or concerned individual" is repeated by Rev. Kevin Logan, who advises them to "present yourself as a polite and sensitive concerned parent; better still, a group of concerned parents,"[15] and has had some success. The title of Teresa Tomlinson's *Summer Witches* had to be changed to *The Secret Place* when issued in paperback, because, as Rev. Kev himself puts it, "pressure was applied by concerned parents."[16] Parents have come to be concerned by the use of the word *witch* in any children's book. With incredible irony, in America, one of the victims has been C. S. Lewis's *The Lion, the Witch and the Wardrobe*, a book consciously and deliberately written as Christian propaganda.

In this as in other matters, the British anti-Satanists have been following the American lead, where such protests have become almost routine. As an example, Citizens for Better Education was started by a woman in Plymouth, Michigan, who considered that there was too much occult material in her local schools, citing a six-part animated film, *Tales of Winnie the Witch*, which was shown to all kindergartners. In a Plymouth school library was a copy of *Witches and their Craft*, by Ronald Seth, in which, she complained, "goats have sex with girls, people swear allegiance to Satan, animals are sacrificed," and so on.[17]

Witches and their Craft, it must be noted, it not a "how-to" book on witchcraft but a historical survey, stopping at around 1700. The author certainly repeats lurid stories from the witch-craze era, but he expresses skepticism about their authenticity and also describes the tortures and punishments meted out to alleged witches. In effect, the complaint is that books of historical information are available. It could be asked: Why stop there? So much of history is a list of wars, massacres, assassinations, executions, plagues, famines, and so on, any of which might affect sensitive children, that one might as well ban the subject altogether.

The enthusiasm of some Christians for battling such a tangible enemy as an occult bookshop is shown by the protests that occurred in Teddington, Middlesex, against the opening of an occult shop in their town. At the invitation of the local M.P., the Reverend Kevin Logan traveled down from Lancashire to address a meeting of three hundred "concerned" citizens. The fuss was unnecessary, as no such shop was even planned. A humorist had simply phoned up the local newspaper and asked how much it would cost to advertise an occult shop he was opening. As he intended, the paper scented a news item and phoned local clergy for comment, which was disapproving. That autumn the same trick was pulled off successfully in more than a dozen towns.[18]

But the same prejudice can also be applied to real targets. The first such recent big campaign, started in 1988, was against the Sorcerer's Apprentice shop in Leeds, probably because it was the best known. Apart from the arson attack (of which the Reverend Kevin Logan said afterward that those responsible were "by definition" not Christians), the shop suffered a great deal of vandalism and other harassment.

The campaign against The Bridge of Dreams, an occult shop in Lincoln, showed signs of careful planning. A few days after it first opened, on 1 December 1990, a forged version of one of their leaflets was produced, with "The Sorcerer's Apprentice" at the top. Copies of these were sent to the real Sorcerer's Apprentice, with the intention of making them think someone had stolen their name. Fortunately, the proprietors of The Bridge of Dreams got in touch with Chris Bray and sorted the matter out, after which SAFF took their side in what followed.

The Lincoln press started running features attacking The Bridge of Dreams, and the local radio station had a phone-in about it, featuring a Reachout Trust director. The proprietors were not told of this program in advance. They began to receive hate mail and threatening phone calls. Christians would picket the shop and harass people going in.

By May the proprietors had decided to close the shop and instead started a stall at Corby. A new set of protests started up against them there, orchestrated by the Christian Rescue Service. They returned to Lincoln and opened a new Bridge of Dreams in December 1991. On 28 January 1992, it was gutted by an arson attack.[19] Whether those responsible were Christians, concerned parents, or lager louts, it is certain they would not have acted as they did but for the Evangelical campaign.

In some places, people are fighting back. In response to censorship demands by religious groups, in 1992, Gene Kasmar of Brooklyn Center, Minnesota, petitioned the Brooklyn Center Independent School District to remove the Bible from school libraries, saying, "The lewd, indecent and violent contents of that book are hardly suitable for young students." The school board of Brooklyn Center unanimously voted down his petition on

9 November, but perhaps he had made his point.[20] Likewise, in Concord, California, in 1992, the high priestess of the Oak Haven Coven asked the Mount Diablo School Board to ban the story of Hansel and Gretel from school libraries, saying, "This story teaches that it is all right to burn witches and steal their property."[21]

In Bedford, New York, two women, Mrs. Di Bari and Ceil Di Nozzi, founded Concerned Parents: Citizens and Professionals Against the Seduction of Children in February 1995, after learning that before- and after-school clubs allowed pupils to play Magic: The Gathering, a card game in which players take on fantasy roles and cast spells. "It's black magic and mind control," Mrs. Di Bari said of the game. "It uses incantations to the devil, contact from below. It is a real belief in a real bad religion." Concerned Parents also considered that Fox Lane High School was spreading Satanism in its science lessons, reading lists, social studies classes, and relaxation exercises. Di Bari cited the fact that a lesson on the Aztecs mentioned they used to perform human sacrifices. "They call it diversity," she said. "I call it perversity. It's total immersion in paganism. If you want to teach about Mexico, why not give us modern religion?"

In September, Concerned Parents sponsored a gathering at which four hundred people turned up to denounce this spreading of occultism. Bedford's school superintendent, Bruce Dennis, described it as "the most manipulated public event I've seen in my 27 years in public education." He suspected that the crowd was dominated by Christian Coalition militants who did not live in the district. (Christian Coalition had been campaigning against Magic: The Gathering in several states.)

So Dennis called a second meeting in November, this time checking identifications so that only residents of the Bedford Central School District were admitted. This time one thousand people turned up, bearing placards such as "Bedford Parents Against Intolerance and Censorship." A lawyer said, "It is unbelievable that we have to come here—in Bedford, the most educated community in America—and listen to this." A teacher, criticized for having her children "make idols of a Hindu god, Ganesha," held up a child's simple paper elephant mask and said, "This is the Ganesha which was referred to, and I think this speaks for itself." Fewer than five people spoke in favor of the Concerned Parents' agenda. Dennis said he hoped this would settle the debate: "I think the amount of time and attention we've given to these two women was adequate and sufficient, and now it's time to move on."[22]

A central feature of all these anti-occult movements is the suppression of books. Evangelicals insist that all "occult literature," from Erich von Däniken to Dennis Wheatley, should be burned, "regardless of cost."[23] In the United Kingdom, one of their successes is preventing Penguin Books from reissuing Aleister Crowley's *Magick*.

When the Nazis came to power in 1933, one of the first things they did was to arrange public burnings of books they disapproved of. It was remarked at the time that those who began by burning books would end by burning people, and so it proved. The current anti-occult campaign has not gone nearly so far, but its chosen direction is unmistakable.

A favorite Evangelical Christian target is Halloween, because it is the most visible and obvious occult festival and, though adopted by the church (Halloween is short for "All Hallows' Eve," the feast of All Saints or Hallows being on 1 November), has kept its pagan roots. In their leaflet *Halloween*, the Association of Christian Teachers complained, "Paganism is hardly a cultural mainstay of all that is best in our society"[24] (which is however a matter of opinion), and to help move the waverers, cautionary booklets have since been brought out in October each year as advance defenses.

In 1987, the Evangelical Alliance issued *Doorways to Danger*, the occult being the danger and Halloween the major doorway. As proof of their assertion, they quoted Audrey Harper, who described how she had made a blood covenant with Lucifer and desecrated Christian churches. (This was before she started talking about seeing a baby sacrificed.)

Various publications advise Christians to use the holiday as an opportunity to warn their children of the dangers of the occult. "Visit your children's head teacher and explain how, as a parent, you do not wish to see emphasis placed on either Halloween or witchcraft within the school curriculum." Parents also are urged write to the newspapers, putting the anti-Halloween case. To stop children from celebrating Halloween, alternative festivals are suggested, such as One World Week (23–30 October) or the traditional Christian All Saints' Day.[25]

This is not appreciated by everybody. In 1990, parents in West London were reported to be "angry" when a primary school banned Halloween "because of its supernatural implications" and instead gave the children a "Hallelujah party" on the evening of 31 October. "Parents claimed the school deliberately misled pupils by giving the party such a similar name." One mother said, "It's all been very confusing and upsetting for the children. They weren't allowed to make masks or do the traditional Halloween things."[26]

Incidentally, I have never known any occultist to say that his or her interest was initially aroused by childhood celebrations of Halloween. Nor do Survivors of Satanism claim this. The whole campaign thus is misplaced, even from the anti-Satanists' viewpoint.

A more recent anti-Halloween production is *The Thin End of the Wedge*, issued by the Christian Publicity Organisation, which cites *Doorways to Danger* and Irvine's *From Witchcraft to Christ* as authorities. "It is believed that what begins as just a flirtation with 'horror' can sometimes be the first step on a slippery slope to other more sinister activities. . . . Witchcraft, once illegal, is now achieving a degree of respectability in the UK." To show readers what a witch looks like, included in the publication is an illustration of fashion designer Gaile McConaghie wearing one of her "Medieval Magick" outfits. This is based on a picture that once appeared in the *Daily Mail*. McConaghie is quoted, by way of the *Mail*, as saying she had been interested in witchcraft since the age of thirteen, and in addition, remarks on the possible dangers of witchcraft that she denies ever having said are attributed to her.[27] The leaflet also has photographs of innocent-looking children, who are suggested to be at risk from all this.

Hounding Out

In 1979, following information given them by psychics, Andy Collins and Graham Phillips dug into the foundations of an old stone bridge in Worcestershire and found a short ceremonial sword concealed there. This started the craze for "psychic questing," that is, going around the countryside searching for buried magical artifacts.[28]

In 1987, Collins wrote in the paranormal journal *Anomaly*:

> For many years I wrote up lengthy reports of paranormal occurrences and edited journals on the same subjects. It got me nowhere; only perhaps the frustration of seeing my research, investigations and theories being ripped off in coffee table books by armchair authors of the subject. From now on, I intend to market my material to the widest possible audience, in a style that the public like, when writing up my psychic questing material.[29]

The first fruit of his new approach was *The Black Alchemist* (1988). Collins described how a psychic named Bernard had led him to various sacred sites around southeast England, where they found that various objects such as stones inscribed with magical symbols had been planted, apparently quite recently. They concluded they were the work of a mysterious character they dubbed the "Black Alchemist," who had sinister but obscure motives.

This Black Alchemist soon became aware that they were on his trail and counterattacked. In the churchyard of Runwell in their home county of Essex, Andy and Bernard found not only one of the now-familiar inscribed stones but also a black envelope addressed to "Andrew Brian Collins." When they examined it later, in the Downham Arms, they found it to contain a curse suggesting they would both be dead in nine days.[30] Fortunately, this proved untrue. The book came to no dramatic climax, only expressed a hope that the mystery would one day be cleared up (which, so far, it hasn't been).

There were varied reactions to the book. Some complained at the "horror-story" style, though as anticipated, it sold far better than his more academically presented efforts. Some people took it to be proof of an international Satanic conspiracy, which is something Collins specifically denies, saying it is rather the case that a few individuals are manipulating the energy matrix of the landscape for their own selfish purposes. Unfortunately, "various sensation-seeking newspapers hijacked the book's findings to print grossly inaccurate stories suggesting that the south of England was rife with black magic rings and human sacrifice."[31]

More surprisingly, Collins found himself assailed by born-again Christians who accused him of arousing interest in the occult among young people. When he attempted a lecture tour, they came out in force.[32]

A talk was announced at a restaurant in Brentwood High Street. The manager received a number of threatening telephone calls, one saying that the windows would be smashed and warning of major demonstrations outside. He decided to cancel the event, saying, "We felt we really could not have that sort of thing outside a restaurant." Under the heading "Church Slams Powers of Darkness," the *Brentwood Gazette* then quoted some local vicars who were "united in their fight against the forces of evil." "I have had personal experience in my ministry of lives severely affected or completely ruined by involvement with the occult, and ruined in a particularly evil and horrid way," said one. "There is no way that anything to do with the power of darkness and Satan can be compatible with Christianity," warned another, though one wonders if they thought smashing other people's windows compatible with Christianity.

The venue was moved to an open air site nearby. About sixty people gathered to hear the talk, but it never happened. Police and a council official appeared, told Collins he was in contravention of a bylaw, and urged him to leave the town, amid cries from the would-be audience of "Where's democracy gone?" and "What about free speech?" In the end, the police actually escorted Collins's car to the town boundary.[33]

A Colchester Scripture Union worker led a campaign against another of Collins's scheduled talks, at the county library. The library received one hundred letters and a five-hundred-signature petition in protest but nevertheless allowed the talk to go ahead. Eastbourne library chiefs, however, did decide to ban Collins's "controversial black magic lectures." When he put up posters advertising an "Occult All-Dayer" in Chalkwell, near his home, Christians tore some of the posters down and pasted rival posters for a forthcoming Billy Graham tour on top of others.[34] They started to send death threats to Collins's home, having taken his address from the telephone book. Unfortunately, Collins is ex-directory, and the hate mail was received by another man of the same name living nearby, who was so alarmed that he sought police protection.[35] The all-day event went ahead as planned but was picketed by a large number of demonstrators, who sang hymns and prayed for those going in.

The campaign extended over a period of two years, and though Collins gave many talks around the south of England, he was banned from giving many others. Bookshops were forced to remove *The Black Alchemist* from display after receiving complaints from customers. "In my home town of Leigh-on-Sea I was threatened by an obviously disturbed born-again Christian who claimed he would carry out God's work and kill me if I did not cancel an up-coming conference."[36]

The irony is that while the born-again Christians declared that "God, truth and light will all win in the end. We have nothing to worry about," Andy Collins had depicted himself as doing battle with the forces of darkness, and the headline describing him as a "Black Magic Man" was a classic of misleading ambiguity. In a subsequent book, *The Second Coming*, he speculated that it was because he had made it easy and "hip" to be a psychic: "It is this that poses a major threat to world religions. Suddenly people are once again thinking for themselves."[37]

Genesis P-Orridge (born Neil Megson) is a multimedia artist, musician, and video maker. Like many others nowadays, he tried to get audiences' attention by shock effects. He first made headlines in 1976 with the notorious "Prostitution" exhibition at the Institute for Contemporary Arts. More fuss was created when he released a short film that appeared to show a young woman cutting his penis off. He is best known for playing with the rock bands Throbbing Gristle and Psychic TV. He is also a practicing occultist and has often been featured by the press as such. In the early 1980s some of his fans and followers formed the Temple Ov Psychick Youth (TOPY), which has done performances of its own as well as practicing occult ritual. Two London members, the "enigmatic duo" John and Paul, were responsible for the 1996 mass attempt to levitate the Houses of Parliament in protest against the Criminal Justice Act. (Though Parliament did not rise into the air, a fortnight later it was discovered that Big Ben was leaning by three millimeters, for which some of the levitators claimed responsibility.)

Much of Genesis's artwork lies on the borderline between art and obscenity and for a long time attracted the interest of the Obscene Publications Branch. It would have been difficult, however, for them to secure a prosecution by the present laws, under which artwork of any kind can usually be defended as being in the "public good." In such cases, the police's normal tactic is simply to confiscate the offending material and not return it. This is most effective against small-scale dealers in erotic literature, who are often not able to afford the legal costs necessary to get their stock back.

So it was not too surprising when, on 15 February 1992, the police raided Genesis's home and took away two tons of videos, photographs, and artwork—his whole life's work.[38] At the time Genesis, his wife, and his two daughters were in Nepal, helping out at a soup kitchen for refugees.

The next day, an *Observer* headline asserted: "Video Offers First Evidence of Ritual Abuse." The article claimed that a video showing "sex and blood rituals" had been given to Channel 4 by "a therapist caring for a cult survivor." They had incorporated it into a *Dispatches* program made by Andrew Boyd, which was being shown that week, to coincide with the publication of Boyd's *Blasphemous Rumors*. They then passed it on to the police, and "Scotland Yard's Obscene Publications Branch believes the video is authentic."

Accompanying this was the account of "Jennifer," a Survivor who was to be featured in the *Dispatches* program and who claimed to have been ritually abused by the group who made the video. Ensnared into Satanism by astrology and tarot cards, she was drugged, initiated, and raped; then a baby aborted. Subsequently, she was forced to take part in the murder of her own baby daughter and witness the murders of four other children.

Dispatches was shown at 10.30 P.M. on 19 February and quickly provoked a number of phone calls of complaint. While the promised ritual abuse video did indeed show a naked man being cut and having the blood smeared over his body, it was obvious that he was a willing participant, rather than having been forced into it. Moreover, the video in question had been well known to some viewers for years, having been made by Genesis P-

Orridge and TOPY in the early 1980s and regularly shown as a backdrop at Psychic TV concerts. In fact, part of it had previously been shown on Channel 4 in 1985 as part of a series on performance art videos! The makers' of the *Dispatches* program's depth of knowledge of Satanism was indicated by their description of Aleister Crowley as a "Scottish Satanist."

The next weekend's *Independent on Sunday* featured Derek Jarman, the film director, who had introduced the original video (a brief long shot of him had been shown in *Dispatches*), who told the newspaper, "At first I was horrified and then very, very angry that they had so misrepresented scenes from the Topy video." Michael Hames, head of the Obscene Publications Branch, said that since the statements made by "Jennifer" to the *Observer* and *Dispatches* included allegations of murder, the police wished to interview her. But Channel 4 refused to identify her, on the usual grounds that journalists have to protect their sources.[39]

By the following weekend, however, the *Mail on Sunday* had tracked her down. She revealed that for years she had not known that she had been involved in Satanism and forced to sacrifice her own baby. She had remembered these facts only while attending Ellel Grange, a healing center run by charismatic Christians. One day, one of the prayer team "had seen a mind-picture of me standing over a tiny baby, helping a devil priest to wield a knife. We cut into the baby's chest and the blood was collected and we drank it. The baby's body was a sacrifice to Satan." The Christians got her to confess that this vision had been of a real event, and that she had been blocking the truth from her mind for years.[40]

Not surprisingly, a number of Christians have suddenly remembered that they are ritual abuse Survivors while staying at Ellel Grange. In the case of Jennifer, it is not clear how she went from being told about abuse she had no recollection of, to giving apparently detailed (but totally wrong) information about an art-rock video. The *Mail* also alleged that of the other two women Survivors interviewed for *Dispatches*, one was a "professional victim," the other a long-term patient of a mental hospital.

Several question marks still hang over this affair, but one thing is certain: Genesis P-Orridge and his family have not set foot in Britain since. They are afraid that, if they come back, their children might be taken into care, and so they have settled in California. In the summer of 1995, after proceedings by his lawyers, Genesis finally got his property back from the police. It does not appear that he will be charged with any crime, but a combination of prejudice and trial by media have driven him from his own country.

At the start of 1995 it was stated by Genesis P-Orridge: "The Temple Ov

Psychick Youth was voluntarily terminated by its SOURCE with ex-dream prejudice on 3rd September 1991 in accordance with their original intents."[41] But this came as news to surviving members, and John and Paul have responded with a new periodical, *Turbulent Times*, detailing their current activities and publications. They have also set up the mysteriously titled Association of Autonomous Astronauts ("travel through space by means of concepts, at an infinite speed of thought"), which, by a curious coincidence, has the same acronym (AAA) as Accuracy About Abuse, an organization for believers in the reality of Satanic abuse.

Incidentally, TOPY, or its remnants, is not Satanist. Indeed, one of the group's recent publications, "Blood and Fire," is a short, critical essay on Satanist thought, which they dismiss as nothing more than a juvenile "let's shock them" stance: "The Church of Satan's 'eternal values' are just another way of saying that their philosophy hasn't progressed one iota in 30 years. . . . Anybody with any real experience of Satanists loses the initial 'crikey—these chaps worship The Devil!' shock value and just wants them to get out of the way to the bar."[42]

The final word on this affair must go to the occultist Giles Patrick:

> I once had a chilling conversation with a fundamentalist Christian Vicar. He was defending the "set-up" Dispatches TV program which perpetuated the satanic abuse blood-libel. He claimed that it didn't matter if the contents of the program were true or not, as long as it turned people away from the occult. When I pointed out that some of the greatest minds ever in this country (and Ireland) were occultists—from Dr. John Dee to W.B. Yeats, he said that the root of evil was the intellect, the thing good Christians should fear most. He said that education led minds to question, and that an open mind was a slippery slope. The world would be a better place, he said, if the only book available was the Bible. And he wasn't joking.[43]

12

How?

"Brother Hugues de Beniols became, in 1275, the supreme chief of the Toulouse Inquisition," wrote E. L. Lamothe-Langone.

> By the order of this monk, that year a general investigation into heretics, magicians and witches was made: the latter were pursued most vigorously. Conspicuous amongst the number of ill-doers who were caught was the *donna* Angele de la Barthe. This foolish creature, aged fifty-six, imagined herself to have had congress with demons; she told some of this fantasy to certain of her neighbors, who hastened to denounce her to the Holy Office. Summoned before the judges, she averred that a demon had visited her every night for a large number of years: she added that as a result of this congress she brought forth a monster, which had the head of a wolf and the tail of a serpent; it would only eat human flesh. To satisfy his appetite, his mother would go out nightly to steal babies, which he devoured. After two years, this monster disappeared without leaving a trace. Hugues de Beniol did not inquire if it was true that for two years a large number of babies had disappeared, which could not have happened anywhere without causing a great terror in the land; he contented himself with delivering the usual sentence. The *donna* Angele, after her condemnation, was delivered to the Seneschal, who had her burnt alive in the Place Saint Stephen, at Toulouse.[1]

It is fairly certain that Angele de la Barthe never existed; in 1275, congress with demons was not yet a crime, and the story of her trial, Norman Cohn has shown, was concocted by a fifteenth-century chronicler.[2] But if she had existed, Lamothe-Langone's comment would have been perfectly valid: Why did people not notice babies going missing, indeed, why was the thief never caught in the act? And the same question applies to all such stories, old and new.

One early allegation of child murder by witches was made by John of Salisbury (ca. 1120–80), who described how women gathered under the patronage of the Moon Goddess and added: "It is further believed that babies are sacrificed by Witches, being cut up into small pieces and greedily devoured. Subsequently they are vomited up and the presiding deity takes pity on them, and returns them whole to the cradles from which they were snatched."[3]

This fascinating and original explanation as why no children were missed did not catch on. Instead, the authors of the *Malleus Maleficarum* played on a reasonable fear, that of infant mortality, which was then extremely high. They stated that children who died in infancy were in fact killed by witches' spells, and that subsequently, the witches would dig up their bodies for magical and culinary purposes. They then quoted the convincing confession of a witch to this effect:

> We set our snares chiefly for unbaptized children, and even for those that have been baptized, especially when they have not been protected by the sign of the Cross and prayers. And with our spells we kill them in their cradles or even when they are sleeping by their parents' sides, in such a way that they afterwards are thought to have been overlain or to have died some other natural death. Then we secretly take them from their graves, and cook them in a cauldron, until the whole flesh comes away from the bones to make a soup which may easily be drunk. Of the more solid matter we make an unguent which is of virtue to help us in our arts and pleasures and our transportations; and with the liquid we fill a flask or skin, whoever drinks from which, with the addition of a few other ceremonies, immediately acquires much knowledge and becomes a leader in our sect.[4]

Due to the wide influence of Kramer and Sprenger's treatise, it became a stock accusation that witches had killed children by spells and then secretly dug them up again. In one case the matter was put to the test, in Lindheim in 1663. Under torture, a midwife confessed that she and six other people had killed, by witchcraft, the child of Johann Schüler, a local miller (whose wife had indeed had a stillbirth the previous year), and that later they exhumed the infant's body and cut it up to make a witches' ointment. The Schülers demanded, however, that the grave be opened for proof. In the presence of the father, the judges found the corpse unviolated.[5] (Nonetheless, the midwife and the other six she had implicated were burned at the stake, because "confessions made under torture must be true." The next year Frau Schüler was also burned as a witch, and her husband would have met the same fate had not a timely popular uprising against the witch-hunters forced them to leave town hastily.)

At the present time, every so often there is a public alert after a baby has been snatched from its carriage or stroller, or even from the maternity hospital. Invariably, the culprit turns out to be a woman frustrated at her inability to have a child of her own.

Yet babies today are supposed to be suffering the same sort of appalling ends as those described in the *Malleus Maleficarum*: "It is cut up into pieces and rendered down, and the fat is used to make the candles for the Satanic mass. The bones are ground up and drunk as an aphrodisiac by the high priest, because they are the bones of an innocent baby."[6]

So where do the Satanists get their babies from? Since it is obvious, even to most anti-Satanists, that people would notice if quantities of babies were going missing, they have devised the "broodmare" theory: that the babies are bred specifically for sacrifice, their births never being registered. But this creates problems of its own. Does no one think it odd when a woman keeps getting pregnant, yet no baby appears? This particularly applies to Lauren Stratford, the original baby breeder, who was living with her non-Satanist father at the time she was supposed to have had her three unregistered children. Pregnancies leave very distinct marks apparent to a gynecologist, amateur abortions still more so (if, indeed, they do not kill the mother).

But this is only the first problem. A far bigger one is the question: How do the Satanists dispose of the evidence? Few ordinary murderers can entirely dispose of a body, and modern forensic science can detect even tiny traces of blood and flesh. Satanic ritual murders ought to be the easiest crimes to prove, since they are supposedly performed in front of a large number of witnesses, under circumstances that ought to send blood flying all around, which could not be cleared at once; and there would be much secondary evidence in the form of temples, robes, ceremonial implements, and so on.

Evidence has been sought hard in several countries around the world. In the McMartin case alone, police searched twenty-one residences, seven businesses, thirty-seven cars, three motorcycles, and a farm; eighty-two locations were photographed and a church investigated; thousands of pornographic photographs and magazines were examined for pictures of the McMartin children; and laboratory tests were performed on twenty blankets from the school, children's clothing, sheets, rags, mops, notebooks, soil, sponges, quilts, underwear, and the altar of the suspected church.[7] Five hundred square feet of woodland near Toledo, Ohio, were dug up in 1985 after an Expert on Satanism had declared that a piece of red thread hanging over a branch of a tree was an indicator that a human sacrifice had taken place there.[8] Police in Evansville, Indiana, staked out both schools and houses with blue fronts after rumors that school kids were being taken from their classes to a "blue house" for ritual abuse.[9] Mason County, Washington, was combed by aircraft and helicopter patrols looking for Satanic rituals, while heat-seeking devices were used to find decomposing corpses and likely grave sites dug up by enthusiastic amateurs.[10] Dozens of homes in Britain have been searched for Satanic regalia, and in lieu of Satanic regalia police have taken away detective novels, videotapes of television programs, crosses (surely *Christian* indicators?), and other odds and ends.

The end result has been nothing. Digs for human sacrificial victims have sometimes turned up animal bones, which have proved to have died of natural causes; nighttime aircraft patrols have spotted the bonfires of outdoor beer-drinking bashes; and at least one Halloween party has been interrupted by a force of armed police.[11] But of Satanic rituals there is still no evidence, and as for human remains, none have been uncovered.

Now, it could be quite reasonably argued that, although many stories about Satanism have proved to be untrue, this does not mean they are all false. Undoubtedly some women make false accusations of rape, for example, but this does not mean real rape is not common. The kind of practices alleged about modern Satanism, however, ought to leave a great deal of physical evidence behind; yet, notwithstanding all the hundreds of child and adult witnesses who claim to have seen babies sacrificed, in *no* case has this been backed up by either a missing baby or a found corpse. Murderers might be able to cover their traces completely in a few cases. It is unlikely that they could do so in a *majority* of cases, but even that is not alleged: we are expected to believe that in *every* case of Satanic child murder both the corpse and the disappearance of the victim were covered up to the extent that the police could find no evidence at all.

It should be added that even if no crimes had been committed, Satanism would leave a lot of evidence. Enter the home of the average occultist, and you will see books on astrology and witchcraft, statues and figurines of deities, candles, an altar, and a variety of paraphernalia. Satanists, in real life, tend to convert their homes into Satanic temples, for instance, painting the walls black, and they could hardly hide all this at short notice, even if they knew in advance they were going to be raided. That the police have not found such things proves that those accused of criminal Satanism are not only not criminals but not even engaged in any kind of occultism.

A number of writers have drawn a parallel between Survivors of Satanism and the incidence of people claiming to have been abducted by aliens. In both cases, usually the alleged victim had a traumatic experience at the hands of mysterious unearthly beings, aliens or Satanists, and then forgot about it until treated by a therapist specializing in recovering such memories. Both experiences apparently involve fetuses being aborted, whether for sacrifice or for alien genetic experimentation. In both cases, believers claim that there is no hard evidence because the Satanists or the extraterrestrials are so exceptionally skillful at covering their tracks. Thus, skeptics argue, the important thing is not anything that happened to the victim but what kind of therapist he or she went to.

There is probably substance to this argument, but there are significant differences between the two types of alleged experience. For one thing, believers in alien abduction are not wasting large quantities of taxpayers' money and ruining lives by false accusations. Also, the "cover-up" argument is not easy to disprove in the case of space beings. Since we cannot know anything about them, it is undeniably possible that they might be so efficient as to be capable of secretly experimenting on humans without leaving any physical evidence behind them. This is not the case with putative Satanists, however: since they are human beings, we know a great deal about their limitations. Unless one argues that Lucifer goes around covering up his disciples' traces, the lack of evidence for Satanic murders is conclusive.

And where do Satanists get those children who are not sacrificed but sexually abused, then set free to tell their stories to child therapists or, as adults, to church groups and tabloid journalists? Some are said to be generational Satanists; that is, Satanism has been practiced in their families for many generations. Nongenerational children are acquired through mysterious recruitment programs.

There are logical difficulties in the very concept of "generational Satanism." If Satanists were in the habit of sacrificing some of their children, then their numbers would continually decrease until they died out. It is argued that those who are abused as children will grow up to be abusers themselves. There is no evidence for this claim (which is suspiciously like the old allegation that witches brought up their children to be witches, so that if your mother was burned for witchcraft, the same was likely to happen to you), and in general, one would expect people who were abused by their parents to make a deliberate break from their parents' lifestyle, rather than continuing in it. Children of abusing Satanists would surely not stay in Satanism, even if they grew up to be abusers.

In cases of "nongenerational Satanism," where children are ritually abused by outsiders, they apparently have astonishingly negligent parents who, when their little offspring regularly go missing for many hours and return having been drugged, tied up, raped, sodomized, flogged with bullwhips, cut with knives, smeared with blood and excrement, and other things that should have left obvious signs, fail to notice anything amiss, until a child therapist or Expert on Satanism informs them of what has been going on.

There are many other reasons for general disbelief. If human sacrifices were carried out during well-attended rituals, as is usually alleged, then there ought to be many witnesses. One would expect that, at least in some instances, several ex-Satanists would testify to having seen a particular sacrifice, agreeing as to date, place, and details, and this would provide definite proof. Yet this has never happened. Survivors of Satanism all tell similar kinds of stories, but there is no agreement in the sense of any two describing the same particular ritual or even the same temples.

Then again, police are often able to investigate criminal organizations at source. After the 1999 terrorist nail-bomb attacks in London, it was revealed that the far-right group Combat 18, who were among the suspects, "has been heavily infiltrated by Scotland Yard's special branch." It was, however, thought most likely that a small cell was responsible: "The real difficulty for the MI5 and police is that it is difficult to infiltrate groups with as few as two or three people."[12] It is now known that the bombs were the work of one man, and in such cases, of course, infiltration is impossible. Infiltration of Satanist groups numbering in hundreds or even thousands, and who are supposed to recruit intensively, should be fairly simple; yet, apparently, no security agent has succeeded in gaining entry to any cult of this sort.

Satanists are often alleged to hold their rituals outdoors, yet there is no known instance of them being caught in the act. Most readers will never have tried to hold a ritual outdoors, but they can be assured that to do so without interruption is not easy. In the Epping case it was alleged that rituals involving animal and human sacrifice were held in Epping Forest from 1982 until 1990. Toward the end of this period, at Beltane 1989, a group from North London Paganlink did go to Epping Forest to hold an outdoor ritual. Some of them later told me how, ten minutes after arriving, they were stopped by two forest rangers who asked what they were doing. The group told them. The rangers explained that two days earlier a group of Hell's Angels had held a noisy party in the forest that had provoked complaints. Satisfied that they were not Hell's Angels, the rangers permitted them to continue.

At Lammas 1995, the Pagan Federation arranged an indoor ritual at a hired hall in North London. About sixty people attended. It was interrupted by a neighbor protesting at the noise. Another Lammas ritual, held in a nearby back garden a couple of days later, was not only watched at a distance by more than a dozen neighbors but provoked telephone calls to the council, the fire brigade, and the police. Interestingly, one of the callers claimed there was nude dancing, though in fact no one was even partially naked. (The author was present at both.) These examples, a few among many, prove that it is quite impossible to hold regular outdoor rituals unobserved, and it is not easy to hold indoor rituals unnoticed either. For those trying to exercise their right to freedom of religion, this is a nuisance; but for anyone engaged in criminal Satanism, it would be disastrous.

Supposing that a Satanic temple was fully soundproofed: even so, if hundreds turned up, as is routinely alleged, neighbors would still notice them arriving. And where would they all park their cars? It should be borne in mind that Britain is so thickly populated that there are few houses out of sight of any other house, even in the Orkney Islands.

Satanists are often alleged to take photographs or videos of their perverted rituals and then sell them as pornography. Alternatively, they are said to use these to blackmail members into obedience. Either way, if this were true, then since so much pornography ends up being seized by the police, and since, for blackmailers to succeed, they must sometimes carry out the threat to expose their victims, by now one would expect solid proof of the reality of Satanic abuse. Yet there is no such evidence. As long ago as 1963, A. V. Sellwood and Peter Haining reported how they had followed up a rumor that a film made at a Black Magic rite was being sold in Soho sex shops, and indeed they discovered one showed naked people dancing in a circle. Unfortunately, they then met the brother of one of the women in it, who informed them that it was taken at a nudist colony and had no "occult" connections.[13] (Having admitted this in their book *Devil Worship in Britain*, Sellwood and Haining hastily changed the subject.)

Blackmail is always a risky crime, as the intended victim may refuse to give in to it and go to the police. In recent years it has been alleged that even children have been photographed in compromising situations, so as to force them to stay in a Satanic cult; but obviously, no one who had taken pornographic photographs of children would dare send them to noninvolved people. In the case of adults, it must further be asked how often blackmail is actually possible nowadays, when the media are already full of the sex (one can hardly say "private") lives of everyone from factory workers to high government officials. I know a respectable man, one of whose—let us say, unusual—hobbies was featured on the TV sex program *Eurotrash*, and whose only concern was that his mother might accidentally see it. It did not bother him whether anyone else learned about his particular peccadilloes.

Since sensational newspapers and books like to illustrate their stories, this absence of visual material is a problem for them. Sometimes they use artists' impressions of Satanic rituals; they may exploit the fact that the public does not usually distinguish between different types of occultism and show archive pictures of non-Satanic rituals; or they may use photographs specially created in order to show the kind of things that Satanists do. Professor Raschke's book on Satanic crime, *Painted Black*, had three shots of "a recent satanic ritual" that nonetheless quite clearly showed the Thelemic Mass of the Phoenix, which is not Satanic (or illegal). Peter Haining's *Anatomy of Witchcraft* included a photograph of a semiclad woman reclining to form a "Black Magic Altar." Haining omitted to mention that the woman in question was a waxworks exhibit.[14]

Religions, cults, sects, and the like rely for much of their appeal on their doctrines, which normally form a complete mental world of their own. Modern witchcraft, for example, has its own theology, sayings, texts, sacred days, specialized terminology, and rituals, just as the Catholic Church does.

Occult doctrines are seldom simple. Here is a typical sentence from Aleister Crowley's *Magick*: "As the Wand is Chokmah, the Will, 'the Father,' and the Cup the Understanding, 'the Mother,' Binah; so the Magick Sword is the Reason, 'the Son,' the Six Sephiroth of the Ruach, and we shall see that the Pantacle corresponds to Malkuth, 'the Daughter.'"[15] Anyone who has been involved in Thelema will be able to spout a whole load of this stuff.

It is perfectly possible for people to recall details of rituals they did not understand. Consider the case of Betty May, who lived for some months at Aleister Crowley's Abbey of Thelema in Sicily in 1922–23, having been taken there by her husband Raoul Loveday, who subsequently died of dysentery after unwisely drinking local spring water.

> When we were all assembled, the Mystic [Crowley] rose from his seat, and taking one of the swords from the side of the brazier, held it pointing towards the altar while he intoned an invocation in a language with which I was not familiar. From hearing it every day, however, the sounds remain fixed in my memory:
>
> > *Artay I was Malcooth—Vegebular*
> > *Vegadura, ee–ar–la—ah moon.*[16]

This is a good enough recollection to be sure that what she heard was a modified form of the Golden Dawn's Cabalistic Cross: *Ateh Aiwass Malkuth, ve-Geburah, ve-Gedulah, le-Olam, Amoun,* which is Hebrew meaning "Thine, Aiwass, are the Kingdom, and the Power, and the Glory, forever, Amoun [Amen]."

If ritually abusing Satanists were a cult like any other, it should be expected that a body of doctrine and ritual could be recovered from the Survivors. In fact, nothing of the kind has emerged, and its absence is conspicuous. When Richard Ofshe interviewed Ericka Ingram, who claimed to have been forced to attend eight hundred and fifty Satanic rituals, he asked her what went on during these rituals. "They chant," Ericka said. What were the words? She couldn't remember. Did you sit or stand? he asked her. She couldn't remember that either. Who were the other people and what were they like? It was too stressful to talk about.[17]

In the few cases where a Survivor has claimed a recollection of a Satanic prayer, what they have reproduced is not suggestive of esoteric doctrine or ritual but, on the contrary, sounds as if they had made it up themselves, and lacked imagination at that. Typical is that of former Birmingham high priestess Mrs. S. Jackson in 1955, who said she was taught to call upon hell with the words "Oh Hell, help me!" A Nottingham boy told his foster mother, "You walk round the bonfire saying 'witchy, witchy, witchy.'"[18]

Believers in Satanic abuse think that credibility is added to the accounts of child and adult Survivors because they say the same things, suggesting that the rituals have not changed through the years. But this is not necessarily sustained by examination. There are many accounts of a ceremonial "marriage to the beast Satan," but the act varies: Katchen and Sakheim write that typically "the young woman is raped by the men of the group and tortured."[19] By contrast, Survivor M. Reynolds says that her marriage to the Evil One was consummated by the high priestess using a U-shaped dildo.[20] Others, like Rebecca Brown's friend Edna "Elaine" Moses, report that Satan himself materialized to wed his bride.

Other accounts mainly reiterate the usual details of blood sacrifices and scatology. This leaves a great deal unanswered. Is there a set liturgy? If so, why has it not been reconstructed from the memories of various Survivors? What are the words of consecration? What are the names of power? Are astrological times observed? Is the temple oriented to the points of the compass? Do the officers have set positions to stand? How is the circle opened? Are the quarters invoked? Are elemental pentagrams traced? Do the participants visualize the Watchtowers (the symbolic ends of the earth)? Are the Qlippoth (spheres of evil) called on? Are tables of correspondences employed, and if so, do they use Crowley's *Liber 777* or some other system? Are ritual dramas performed? Is energy raised by dancing? Do the rites end with banishing? On all these questions, the Experts on Satanism are silent.

Survivors and Experts do not even seem to know much about perverted sex. The reminiscences of brothel girls usually include semicomical anecdotes about clients with bizarre and irregular requests. Yet nothing of that kind was related by Lauren Stratford, who claimed to have been forcibly prostituted for years; she merely moaned about being "used and abused," without giving details. She made no mention of those men, who are always numerous, who want to be used and abused by the girls rather than vice versa. In fact, this whole section of *Satan's Underground* reads like a recycling of a feminist antiporn essay, rather than a real memoir.

A contribution to *Out of Darkness*, Katchen and Sakheim's "Satanic Beliefs and Practices," states that Satanists use all the major published grimoires, listing *The Sacred Magic of Abramelin the Mage*, the *Goetla* (*sic*), *The Necronomicon*, and Eliphas Lévi's *History of Magic* and *Transcendental Magic*.[21] Now, *The History of Magic* is what it says, and not a grimoire at all; *Transcendental Magic* is full of warnings against Black Magic. The *Goetia* gives instructions on how to call up evil spirits but assumes that the operator is a Christian. *Abramelin* purports to be the work of a more or less orthodox Jew and is concerned with attaining the knowledge and conversation of the holy guardian angel, though if achieved, this is incidentally supposed to give one power over evil spirits. That leaves *The Necronomicon* (1977 version), which is a modern fake, though the Satanists might not be aware of that (none of the anti-Satanists are); like an extreme form of the *Goetia*, it is concerned with how to conjure up abominations. None of these books gives instructions on abusing children or carrying out human sacrifices. The anti-Satanists, then, cannot cite any published works advocating or detailing the kind of activities that they say are widespread.

"In addition, as noted above, each cult or coven maintains its own 'book of shadows' or grimoire, in which it codifies its rituals, often in secret languages or alphabets such as Theban or Enochian." Katchen and Sakheim do not quote any such book, but an appendix gives three "Alphabets Used by Satanic Groups": Runic, Enochian, and Theban.[22]

These alphabets are neither Satanic nor secret. Runic is the ancient alphabet of the northern races, superceded by Latin in the early Middle Ages. Enochian, as already noted, is supposed to be the alphabet used by angels. Theban first appeared in Cornelius Agrippa's *Occult Philosophy*, where it was attributed to Honorius the Theban, whose name is also attached to a book of angel magic. All three are widely reproduced in popular books on the occult.

Thus, such details of Satanic theory and practice as are produced at all are evidently derived from easily available books on non-Satanic occultism. There is no trace of any secret Satanist doctrine or ritual.

Catholic priests have often been accused of abusing choirboys or debauching nuns. In some cases, this has undoubtedly happened; in others, the accusations were quite certainly fabricated. In no case, however, has the accuser, while claiming to have been a choirboy or a nun, proved to know nothing at all of Catholic doctrine or ritual beyond a vague idea that Catholics worship God and meet in churches; and if such a situation were to happen no one would take it seriously. Yet this is the equivalent of the claims of Survivors of Satanism.

Real-life occultists, like everyone else, address each other by their names, using titles (if at all) only at solemn moments in rituals, for instance, "I call upon the Priestess of Inanna." Yet ex-Satanists generally report that cult leaders were known only as "the Master" or "the Overseer" or "the Abaden," titles that are not even used by known magical or Satanic orders. The reason is fairly obvious: it enables Survivors to say they have no idea of the leader's real identity. Often, indeed, they cannot name any of their fellow cultists. This is in sharp contrast to members of real cults, whose social life usually revolves around the sect. (This is a genuine reason that some people find it difficult to leave religious cults: if they do so, they may lose all their friends.)

Another minor but significant point is that, in the reminiscences of adult Survivors, Satanism appears to have "more officers than men." Survivors, from Mrs. Jackson onward, have claimed to have been made high priestess without even a period as an ordinary priestess. Further, they often graduate to "master counselor," "bride of Satan," "queen of the Black witches," or some other exalted title. If a real cult were being exposed, then, by the law of averages, the majority of ex-members would merely have held ordinary posts.

All human organizations are susceptible to internal bickering. There is no reason to doubt the former Satanist who told the Reverend Kevin Logan that he had left because of a disagreement with the way that women were selected for sexual initiation: "It wasn't fair," he complained. "The high priest got all the young good-looking ones while I was left with the old fat ones."[23] Yet one never hears of anyone leaving Satanism because "the high priestess got to eat all the plump babies and I got left with the ones which were all bone and gristle."

Though Satanic child abuse would have had to have been happening for decades to produce adult Survivors of a wide variety of ages, no one in Britain had heard of it before 1988. "In my thirty years in journalism," wrote John Parker, "I can honestly say I had never previously encountered a single case involving it."[24] The detective who investigated the claims of "Samantha," first made in 1988, said, "In all my 18 years in the Force, I had never heard a story like it."[25] Maureen Davies has stated that she was introduced to her first case of ritual child abuse in 1988.[26]

In many cases there are more direct objections to the allegations than their implausibility and the lack of evidence. In 1991, a twenty-eight-year-old Kent woman went to police with a series of allegations about her father that she had recalled during therapy. She claimed he had molested her from the age of three, sold her into prostitution at sixteen, and made her take part in Satanic rituals during which twenty men had raped her. She was persuaded to undergo a medical examination. It showed that she was still a virgin.[27] Conspiracy theorists could take this in their stride—"The Satanists repaired her hymen!" or "The doctor who examined her was a Satanist!"— but the authorities rightly lost interest.

The consultant pediatrician in the Orkney case, Dr. D. H. S. Reid, gave a whole series of reasons that the accusations had to be false, including:

- The quarry where the abuse was supposed to have taken place proved, when he examined it, to be deep and filled with water.
- The low temperatures and high winds of the Orkneys made it physically impossible for anyone to go around naked at night.
- The landscape is treeless and everyone knows everyone else's business. When a local resident once accidentally left his light on at night, a neighbor assumed that something was wrong and called the district nurse. Car lights going to the quarry at night would have been seen.
- The terrain was such that cars would probably have broken their axles, and the ritualists their ankles.
- The Reverend Morris McKenzie was elderly and for medical reasons would have been quite unfit to take part in strenuous Satanic rituals.
- Perpetrators of child sexual abuse start their activities at an early age, yet not one of the eleven middle-aged or elderly accused had any previous record of abusing.

All this was apart from the lack of medical or other physical evidence, and the fact that he found the interviews with the children had been improperly conducted.[28]

Karyn Stardancer, a California Survivor-turned-therapist, claims that, when she was a child in the 1940s and 1950s, her intergenerational abusers belonged to five separate cults who were secretly in league with each other: a Satanic cabal, which used a fundamentalist church as a cover and for recruitment; a Dionysian cult, which had survived underground since the time of the Roman Republic; a feminist pagan coven, whose matriarchal leader was secretly having an affair with the chief Satanist; a youth gang who used Satanic imagery; and military mind-control experts affiliated with the Dionysians, the Masons, and other conspiracies.[29]

Passing over the issue of whether or not a fundamentalist church would be a fertile recruiting ground for Satanism, this alleged conspiracy is highly anachronistic. On the one hand, feminist witchcraft was a by-product of the feminist revolution of 1968; such covens simply did not exist in the 1940s and 1950s. The use of Satanic imagery by youth gangs seems to have become common only in the 1980s. On the other hand, it would have been incredible for the Dionysian cult to have survived in secret, unsuspected, for more than two thousand years, particularly since it is doubtful if it ever existed in the first place. The Roman historian Livy said that the Senate had to suppress the Dionysians because the cult, originally only for women, had started initiating men, after which its nocturnal rites became more sinister. Young people were recruited and corrupted. Drunkenness and debauchery led on to many other crimes, and those reluctant to take part were used as human sacrifices. This sounds very similar to modern ritual abuse allegations, but when Livy also says that the sacrifices were somehow carried out so that afterward the bodies could not be found, one suspects the affair was actually an early example of a moral panic.[30]

Thus, it is hard to accept the existence, circa 1950, of such a conspiracy as Stardancer describes. By contrast, in 1980s California, when Stardancer started "recovering" her memories, feminist covens were commonplace; the use of Satanic imagery by youth gangs was widely discussed in anti-Satanist literature, as was military mind-control and the possibility that some churches were Satanic fronts; and Livy's account of the Dionysian cult was being cited as an example of "historical Satanism." Thus, Stardancer's recollections can be best explained as a confabulation made decades after the nonevents.

In the 1970s many sensational books ran thorough accounts of Aleister Crowley (sexual rites), Anton LaVey (worshiping Satan), and Charles Manson (drug orgies and murder). Put all these things together, and the resulting cocktail would be a Devil-worshiping cult that practiced sex, drug taking, and murder. Such cults could be flourishing secretly in our midst, it was suggested. Common sense says that if any such cult existed, it would not remain secret, or even active, for very long. But this type of writing defied common sense and responded to the nonappearance of evidence by growing more extreme.

It will be recalled that, in 1955, Mrs. Jackson described the initiation of a virgin of seventeen, and that when the same story was told by Peter Haining in 1972, the girl's age was reduced to "fourteen or fifteen." Then, the first mention of outright child abuse by Devil worshipers occurred in 1979, in William R. Akins's essay on the "Hell Fire Club," where, after repeating all the familiar fables about Francis Dashwood and his friends, Akins added the new one that they had sodomized and raped young boys and girls.[31] That was supposed to have been two centuries earlier, but 1980's *Michelle Remembers* presented "ritualized abuse" as having occurred fewer than three decades before. Finally, in 1984, Satanic abuse of children was suddenly believed to be current. This pattern is not one of progressive development of Satanic practices but a progressive development of collective paranoia.

Satanic Statistics

Many figures for Satanism, sorcery and even human sacrifice have been regularly repeated in the media, but their origins may be hard to discover. On the audio-tape *How to Tackle the Occult in Your Area*, Maureen Davies asserted that the number of "registered witches in this country" was eighty thousand,[32] and around the same time, the *Independent* quoted her as giving the same figure as the number who belonged to "official covens." In 1995 various issues of *Alpha News*, a magazine full of articles and features extolling the usefulness and necessity of Alpha courses (on Christianity), contained a box giving some of the reasons Alpha courses were needful, including the assertion: "Although there are 30,000 Christian clergy in Britain, there are more than 80,000 registered fortune-tellers and witches."

In November 1995, Peter Ward, a barrister who has made an (unpublished) study of Satanism allegations, rang Maureen Davies and asked for her authority for the figure of eighty thousand registered witches in Great Britain. She denied ever having made such a statement. So Ward contacted the offices of Nicky Gumbel, the founder of Alpha. A courteous woman told him that the figure came from a leaflet that was once dropped through Nicky Gumbel's door. She didn't know where it was now but said that it, in turn, gave its source as the annual Her Majesty's Stationery Office (HMSO) publication *Social Trends*, 1992 edition. Ward then informed me, and asked me to check this book. I found that it says nothing whatever about witches or fortune-tellers. It does give figures for clergy: 31,400 Protestant ministers and 7,600 Catholic. Presumably, the author of the leaflet did not consider Catholic priests to be "Christian clergy."

There is, of course, no register of witches or fortune-tellers in Britain, but in bureaucratic countries such as France and Germany, fortune-tellers (who may also be witches) are indeed required to be registered for tax purposes, and in the early 1980s, the number may have stood around eighty-thousand. Possibly at that time some English Christian read a translation of a French or German sermon that mentioned "eighty-thousand registered witches and fortune-tellers in this country," took "this country" to mean Britain, and repeated it, leaving it circulating ever since.

The most common estimate of the yearly number of human sacrifices in the United States is fifty-thousand. This figure seems to be derived from the frequently quoted fact that fifty-thousand children are reported missing to the FBI every year, the assumption being that missing children must have been sacrificed by Satanists. In one sample studied by Joel Best, however, 97 percent of the missing children were found again within twenty-four hours.[33]

The various figures and related claims do not necessarily agree with one another. When one Expert says that there are ten thousand human sacrifices a year in the United States alone, and another Expert says that there are 2 million human sacrifices a year in the United States alone, one starts to wonder if, in fact, there are any human sacrifices a year in the United States, or anywhere else. A doctor who was interviewed on British television in 1993 stated that no less than 10 percent of the population are practicing Satanists.[34] By contrast, Jim Perry, a born-again Christian ex-Satanist, says that any real Satanist lives in a mansion and drives a Rolls-Royce.[35] If both were correct, this would mean that one Briton in ten lived in a mansion and drove a Rolls-Royce, which is obviously not the case.

The Right to Reply

In the early sixteenth century, more than a hundred women were put to death for witchcraft in Piedmont in northern Italy. Andreas Alciatus, the humanist, was sent by his bishop to investigate the matter independently.

He found that some of the husbands of the accused women, men of honest reputation, had sworn that at the very time their wives were supposed to have been dancing under a great tree at the witches' sabbat, they were, in fact, lying by their sides, and some had talked with them or made love. The Inquisitor declared that it was not really the wives who lay there but devils who took on their form, to deceive the husbands. To which Alciatus asked why the Inquisitor did not, rather, presume that it was the devils who were seen dancing under the tree, in the shape of those women, and that the women themselves were with their husbands and so should be discharged on their testimony.[36] The Inquisitor's reply is not recorded; but arguments like this could, and did, go on for centuries.

It is only fair to note that anti-Satanists have replies to most of the objections made to their case, some of which are noted here, though many of these replies deserve themselves to be responded to.

A father who claimed Satanists had put his son in a cage with a live lion "to instil fear" approached Arthur Lyons and asked him what part lions played in traditional Satanic ritual. Lyons replied none, so far as he knew, and pointed out that, in Africa, he had known a lion roaring three hundred yards away to make his tent shake; so if the Satanists had a lion, why didn't the neighbors hear it roaring? The father suggested: "What if the lion's vocal cords were surgically removed?"[37]

According to the FBI's Kenneth Lanning, one police Expert on Satanism "told a therapist that a patient's accounts of satanic murders in a rural Pacific Northwest town were probably true because the community was a hotbed of such satanic activity. When the therapist explained that there was almost no violent crime reported in the community, the officer explained that that is how you know it is the satanists. If you knew about the murders or found the bodies, it would not be satanists."[38]

The "Devil" is the chief Satanist dressed up

This possibility was suggested as long ago as 1818, by Jules Garinet in his *History of Magic in France*:

> The monks, who abused public credulity, to divert themselves in their idleness, could have taken on ridiculous disguises, and done all the extravagances that they attributed to devils. One thing is certain and incontestable, that in the criminal trials of wizards and witches, the place of the scene of the Sabbat is always indicated to be in the neighborhood of some Abbey.[39]

The trouble is that no such human devil was ever found out or identified at the time. There were a few cases, during the witch-hunting era, in which someone successfully impersonated the Devil, but always in the course of a practical joke or confidence trick; none of Satan's many alleged appearances at sabbats was ever explained this way.

In contemporary times, both adults and children have reported seeing Satan in person at Satanist meetings. Now, the homes of accused Satanists have frequently been searched by the police, and if these people had been accustomed to dress as the Devil, then surely, in at least some cases, their Satan outfits would have been recovered. This has not happened.

Children could not make up stories like this

The suggestion is that the details are too authentic to have been created by toddlers. Apart from the fact that not even the adult Survivors have produced any authentic details about Satanism, such a claim is at best tenuous. Children can easily hear about witches and Satanists from older children or adults, and every grown-up has heard about the Satanism scare. Unless one lives as a hermit, cut off entirely from the media, one will have read newspaper stories, seen documentaries, watched horror films and possibly "video nasties," all on the themes of Devil worship and human sacrifice. Churchgoers in America and England may have heard talks by Mike Warnke or Doreen Irvine. Most people who read books at all will also have taken in a few novels and short stories on the subject. This material is part of contemporary life, and it will filter down to small children as it touches everybody else. As for children who have barely learned to talk, before they can talk, they have to be able to understand what is said to them, and one of the ways in which children are encouraged to learn to speak is by reading them fairy stories, from which they will learn about witches, evil spirits, bad fairies (and perhaps the mass of Saint Secaire?). To say that a child couldn't make up remarks about witches, one would have to prove the child had never heard a fairy story and had had no contact with children who had. (Also, often adults who would not talk about certain things in front of children will say them in front of infants, assuming that they cannot yet understand, not realizing that children often understand what is said before they can speak.)

Besides this, the images of devilry are not only potent but "archetypal," as Jocelyn Chaplin pointed out to me, part of Jung's "collective unconscious" of material that turns up in the dreams of people everywhere. Small children are likely, then, to have dreams about witches and other supernatural figures, and this would continue to be the case even if they were read Malinowski instead of the Brothers Grimm at bedtime.

The similarity between children's stories in different parts of the world is often mentioned by anti-Satanists: "There were other indicators which Hudson and other American experts would have recognized: the children's unshakeable belief in aspects of the abuse which could not possibly have been true—a live shark at one of the parties—was a recurring feature of the Nottingham disclosures."[40] Surely, this proves not only that the children's recollections were not reliable but that they were all tapped into the same "collective unconscious," rather than that their abusers all belonged to the same international conspiracy. The same comment applies to identical children's stories about witches floating in the air, Devil worship in spaceships, naked nuns, demonic dogs, satanic Santas, and perverted clowns.

As an example of an authentic detail that an older child "could not have known about had he not read occult books," Pat Pulling cites a teenager who wrote that an evil spirit woke him one night, told him that he was sent by Satan, and ordered him to start misbehaving at school. The spirit said his name was "Cali in Calcutta."[41] Kali is the Indian goddess who gave her name to the city of Calcutta and is well known to (for example) viewers of *Indiana Jones and the Temple of Doom*. It is not an arcane name that one could learn only from occult books. In fact, the boy most likely learned it from the Christian anti-occult book *Three Habitations of Devils*, which describes how a missionary exorcised a woman in India and was told by the spirit possessing her: "I am from Cali in Calcutta."[42] (In any case, if one took his story at face value, there would be no reason to think he had read occult books, since it was the evil spirit himself who told him this name.)

A major cover-up is operated by the Satanists, many of whom are "top people" in society

This falls down where most conspiracy theories fall down: if there is such a powerful cover-up in force, why don't the Satanists shut the anti-Satanists up, rather than allowing them to expound their claims on television and in all the national newspapers?

The bodies are not found because the Satanists have eaten them

Do they eat the bones as well?

Satanists use portable crematoria to dispose of the bodies

Aside from the question why, in that case, no search has turned up a portable crematorium, it has to be asked: Is there such a thing as a "portable crematorium"? To cremate a human body fully requires a temperature of perhaps two thousand degrees centigrade for more than an hour. An industrial oven could achieve this, but one large enough for a corpse would weigh at least a few tons—not very portable—and require a large mobile generator to power it. A small lorry with a crane would be needed to transport such equipment to and from a ritual site.

Satanists send fire demons to police evidence lockers to burn up the contents

Have police stations reported outbreaks of mysterious fires?

The power of Satan causes the bodies to disappear

Once again: Why doesn't the power of Satan make the anti-Satanists vanish?

The media are interested in sensation rather than truth

This is the argument of Tim Tate's contribution to *Treating Survivors of Satanist Abuse*, in which he cites the press rejection of Satanic claims in the Nottingham case. Yet anyone who followed the Satanism scare in Britain would have noticed that, from 1988 until 1990, scarcely a skeptical word was printed, except in a few little-known pagan and occultist journals. For a couple of years, at least, anti-Satanist claims were simply uncritically repeated. It was only when several cases had collapsed, and none had stood up, that some papers (and only some) took notice and started criticizing belief in Satanism. In fact, the media's interest in sensation played a big role in propagating the scare.

Rosie Waterhouse reported how, in the same spirit, the Survivor-therapist Sue Hutchinson "has appeared on several TV programs, talking about how survivors had told her of foetuses being induced and sacrificed, children being hung up by their feet and suspended over electric saws and suffering sexual abuse including rape, buggery and bestiality. She refused to give me details about her own background, saying the press always sensationalised stories."[43]

*People simply reject stories about Satanism out of hand, because
they are too shocking to accept*

I can only say that this is certainly not the case with the present study. I
have attempted to follow up scare stories about Satanism since the 1970s, always with no result. In 1979 a woman hinted to me that she was a member
of a Black Magic temple. I tried to draw her out, with the vague intention of
infiltrating this sinister cult, but she would not talk about it unless she was
drunk, and when drunk, she made no sense. I was never invited along. This
kind of experience was repeated a number of times, but for years I continued to take it as possible that criminal Satanists were real and potentially
dangerous, though good at covering their tracks. It was not until 1987, when
a born-again Christian woman informed me that regular human sacrifices
were carried out in the House of Commons by Satanist M.P.s, that it occurred to me that, rather than trying to investigate such claims, it might be
more fruitful to study the people who made them. Even so, what is truly implausible is not the allegations themselves but that, if true, so little evidence
is found.

The skeptics are Satanists themselves

This is a very old line, and it has sometimes led to persecutions of its
own. In the mid-fifteenth century Guillaume Edelin, a doctor of theology
in France, declared that it was impossible for witches to make pacts with
the Devil and fly on broomsticks. In consequence, for a number of years
no witch trials occurred in places where his opinion had influence. In
1453, Edelin was arrested and in due course confessed that he had himself
flown on a broomstick to the witches' sabbat, where he made a pact with
the Devil in which he agreed to pretend publicly that witchcraft was a
phantasm. This document was produced in court, making his guilt apparently undeniable, though, since he was a cleric, he was sentenced only
to life imprisonment. Petrus Mamor, who related the story of Dr. Edelin,
commented that it showed that to deny the reality of the witch cult was
"perilous." He meant "perilous to the Catholic faith,"[44] but it could also
be perilous for the skeptic.

"The Devil's best trick is to convince us that he does not exist."
                                                                —*Baudelaire*

This saying was coined by a Satanist!

13

Why?

In alleged cases of criminal Satanism, there are no missing persons, no bodies, no bones, no blood, no temples, no altars, no robes, no rituals, and no Satanists. In the face of this complete lack of evidence, the question we should be asking ourselves is: Why the revival of witch-hunting? What inspires people to chase their own shadows?

The idea that witch-hunting was an unrepeatable folly of the past is a by-product of the naive optimistic rationalism of the eighteenth century. Once it had been decided that religious experiences were merely a result of epilepsy, then it was supposed that, in time, a cure could be found, and that would be that. The terror that comes by night was to be banished by artificial lighting. Satan existed only as part of Christian doctrine, which was thought to be in irreversible decline.

Of course, before the twentieth century was half run, it had become obvious that a society that does not believe in witches can commit equally great or worse atrocities in a struggle against communists, fascists, Trotskyists, anarchists, capitalists, Jews, blacks, or any other minority, real or imagined. Since recent years have seen a big revival of the occult and Paganism on the one hand and Evangelical Christianity on the other, some kind of new Satan-hunt was inevitable.

There are differences between the old and the modern witch scares, but they can generally be explained by legal and social conditions. The most obvious is that child abuse, the centerpiece of recent allegations, was hardly met with in the old witch trials. Margaret Murray remarked: "Among the witches there appears to have been a definite rule that no girl under puberty had sexual intercourse with the Devil," citing the confession of Jean Hervillier in 1578, who said that her mother had vowed her to the Devil in infancy, but that it was not until she was twelve (then the age of consent for girls in Catholic countries) that she was presented to him and he "slept with her carnally."[1]

On the few occasions that child sex was then alleged, it was always in the form of sex with devils, not adult humans. The most notorious instance was the confession of the children of Elfdale and Mohra in Sweden in 1669: they said they would go to a crossroad and call on the Devil, who would appear and carry them through the air, over churches and high walls, to the fairy kingdom of Blockula. There, they dined on broth with colworts (cabbages) and bacon in it, oatmeal, bread and butter, milk and cheese. After eating they got up and danced, swearing and cursing all the while. The Devil would play on a harp, then "all confessed, that he had carnal knowledge of them, and that the Devil had sons and daughters, which he did marry together, and they did couple, and they brought forth Toads and Serpents." The lords commissioners asked the children to demonstrate their witchcraft powers, but they said that since they had confessed, their powers had deserted them. Nonetheless, fifteen children and twenty-three adults whom they had accused of being witches were executed, and thirty-six other children, in view of their youth, were sentenced only to be flogged outside the church every Sunday for a year.[2] Notwithstanding that "children never lie about abuse," most of what they confessed to was physically impossible, and it is clear that, under pressure, they had made up stories based on what they had heard witches did.

The reason for the change in emphasis on children's experiences is that until recent times, the sexual abuse of children was simply not a problem that concerned people. In England, the legal concept of an "age of consent" was not created until 1576; it was set at ten, and applied only to girls.[3] In 1580 the witch-hunter Bodin remarked, after defining incubi and succubi, that there were also "Devils in the shape of children, who copulate with the nurse-maid witches,"[4] as if he thought such relations usual, or even natural, provided that the children really were children.

In witch trials, the most important point was usually to establish that the accused had made a pact with the Devil, since this was regarded as so abominable that, if proved to the court's satisfaction, other charges hardly mattered. Today, making a Satanic pact is not a crime (leaving aside the question of whether a modern jury would be convinced by a parchment signed "Beelzebub"), but child abuse is regarded as exceptionally serious, and in such cases it is often possible to bend the rules of evidence in the same way that witch hunters did.

Then again, a few hundred years ago, there were innumerable theological axioms that no one dared dispute. In 1505 a certain Brother Samuel Cassini of Pavia in Italy issued a pamphlet, *The Question of the witch*, in which he challenged the belief that witches could really fly. Now, the educated men of the time had pointed out that, since the sun, moon, planets, and stars were kept in motion by angels who pushed them around the sky, it would be a small matter for demons, who were fallen but still angels, to carry witches through the air. Indeed, according to the Catholic Bible, an angel of the Lord carried the prophet Habbakuk from Judea to Babylon by a hair of his head, and in the Gospels of Matthew and Luke, the Devil took Jesus up to a high mountain. Cassini could not deny any of this, so he was reduced to arguing that such a miracle could not be worked for a sinful purpose.[5]

In modern Britain, and in the United States, at least, you are free to follow your own beliefs about religion (however much some people would like to prevent you), and this makes it harder for the Christian theory of Satanism to become established. In particular, in the witch craze it was generally accepted that the Devil appeared in person at the sabbats. Satan has also been alleged to have put in personal appearances in most of the best-known modern Satanism cases, but the believers do not stress this point, as it would tend to undermine their credibility with the general public.

It is clear that, despite differences in detail, the same psychological forces were at work in the witch craze as now, and in considering the motives of those involved, cases from present and former times will be considered together, that they may shed light on each other.

Why Should People Make Untrue Confessions?

There is no doubt that people confess to things they have not done. Sometimes, after publicity is given to an unsolved murder, two or three different men will come forward and say that they did it. At most, only one of them could be telling the truth.

In April 1652, a certain Giles Fenderlin was tried in London for the murder of his wife. He told the court, presumably by way of defense, that they had never actually been married. He then went off into a story about how, when he had been a soldier in the Netherlands, he had sold his soul to the Devil. Desiring magical immunity from bullets, he had approached a Jesuit. (As a Protestant, he naturally supposed a Jesuit was the obvious person to get one in touch with the Devil.) The method of magical shielding was first demonstrated on a cat, which was tied up and had several bullets fired at it, receiving no more injury from each than a small blue spot. In exchange for such protection, however, Fenderlin was eventually persuaded to sign a diabolic pact:

> Whereupon the Jesuit drew a covenant and delivered it to him in Latin, and also presented him with a Ring of Inchantment, with a stone in it, that had this efficacy and power, that by it if he came to any house where there was money buryed, or conveyed into any private place, that he could by the direction of that Ring find it out.
>
> And further the said *Giles* saith, That when he was in the face of his enemy, or in any other place of danger, that having the said Ring upon his hand, if he did but turn the stone of the said Ring downward, that formerly was upward, he could convey himself away undiscovered into any remote place 40 or 50 miles distance from the said place; *for* which Ring and Covenant, he gave the said Jesuit 3l. 17s. Also, he said, That he was to make use of that Ring but for 5 years, & that it was fetcht away from him again in 1648. But affirmed, that if he could have procured money to renew his Covenant for that Ring, he had never come to this unhappy end; but by the power and efficacie thereof, had been secured from all men living; by reason no power of man could have either try'd him, or condemned him, much less to have made him suffer as a Malefactor.[6]

It is hard to say what Fenderlin hoped to gain by this story, unless it was to draw attention away from his real crime. But the sworn statements of murderers are not good evidence. Knowing that he had nothing to lose, he may have decided to take the chance to indulge in a favorite fantasy to a captive audience of learned men.

Torture

The effects of torture do not need to be pointed out, but they were not wholly apparent to those responsible for the witch trials. In Germany, it was believed that the instruments of torture were innately holy: they would often be blessed by a priest before use, and this meant they would compel even the most villainous person to tell the truth. Indeed, since the Devil is the "father of lies," it was pointed out, a voluntary confession by a witch could not be trusted. Similarly, it does not seem to occur to modern Experts, in their accounts of "historical Satanism," that confessions made under torture, such as that of Gilles de Rais, might not have been absolutely accurate.

"Without Torture"

Friedrich von Spee, a Jesuit who observed the progress of early seventeenth-century German witch trials with skepticism, heard it frequently said by judges that the accused confessed without torture and thus were undeniably guilty. He wondered at this, made enquiries, and learned that in reality they had been tortured, in an iron vice with sharp-edged bars in which their shins were crushed, bringing blood and causing intolerable pain; but since this was mild compared to what their Inquisitors *could* have done, it was technically called "without torture," deceiving those who did not understand the special phrases of the Inquisition.[7]

Self-Destructive Urges

Someone might confess to a crime carrying the death penalty, not because they did it but as an elaborate way of committing suicide. Reginald Scot noticed that if a witch's confession

> be voluntary, many circumstances must be considered, to wit; whether she appeach not her self to overthrow her neighbor, which many times happeneth through their cankered and malicious melancholic humor: then; whether in that same melancholic mood and frantic humor, she desire not the abridgement of her own days. . . . I myself have known, that where such a one could not prevail, to be accepted as a sufficient witness against himself, he presently went and threw himself into a pond of water, where he was drowned.[8]

It is common for people who take to drink or drugs to do so out of a self-destructive impulse (which is why campaigns warning that drugs are harmful tend to fail in their effect). But those who take up Satanism out of a self-destructive urge are likely to be disappointed, unless they succeed in calling up an abomination without proper protection and get destroyed by it. Perhaps this explains the following incident: on 13 June 1971, at a pregraduation party at Vineland High School, New Jersey, a twenty-year-old student named Andrew Newell, who had previously attempted suicide, asked two friends to kill him. The reason given was: "He had convinced them that he belonged to a sect of Satan worshipers and had to die violently before his soul could be put in charge of 'forty leagues of demons.'" Foolishly, his friends agreed, taped his feet and hands together, and then threw him into a pool, where he drowned.[9]

Drugs

The effects of hard drugs are well known. Many ex-Satanists are also former heroin addicts, and though heroin is not a hallucinogen, it can make it hard for a user to distinguish fantasy from reality. Audrey Harper's Satanic involvement exactly coincided with her heroin use—when the drugs stopped, so did the Black Magic. Her book reported events, such as levitation, that can be explained only by the exercise of very remarkable paranormal powers or as drug delusions. Dr. Kenneth McAll told Andrew Boyd that all eight of the Satanic abuse Survivors he had treated had been taking heroin,[10] McAll assumed that the Satanists had got them addicted so as to have a hold over them, but obviously, another explanation is possible.

Plea Bargaining

In 1459, the Inquisition began a series of witch trials in Arras, France. On a single day, five people made a public confession that they had worshiped the Devil, flown on broomsticks to the sabbat, trampled on the cross, and so on. The confessions made, the Inquisitor "handed them to the secular arm" to be burned. At once the confessed witches shouted out that they had been deceived, that they had been told that, if they confessed, they would be let off with the penance of performing a short pilgrimage. They could still be heard protesting their innocence as the flames rose to consume them.[11]

One of the first successful prosecutions for ritual abuse was in Miami, Florida. In 1984, the proprietor of the Country Walk preschool, Illeana Fuster, and her husband, Frank, were accused of giving children mind-altering drugs, sodomizing them, wearing Dracula and Frankenstein masks, praying to Satan, and chopping the heads off blue parakeets to scare the children into silence. Videos were supposed to have been made of the proceedings, though none were found by police. The couple denied the charges.[12]

In the United States there is a procedure known as plea bargaining, something like the British "turning Queen's evidence," in which one accused person will confess and give evidence concerning the others in exchange for a shorter sentence. After a year in prison during which she refused to acknowledge any wrongdoing, shortly before the trial, Illeana suddenly confessed to the charges. She stated that the videotapes had not been found because a confederate of Frank's had taken them away the day before their arrest. In consequence, Frank Fuster received six life sentences plus 165 years.

Illeana was given a sentence of only ten years and released on parole after three, then deported to her native Honduras.

After her release, Illeana recanted her "confession." She said that she had spent most of the year before the trial in solitary confinement, except for visits by attorneys and therapists. They had persuaded her that she must have shut out of her mind what had been going on and put her through "therapy" sessions to make her recall it. She finally made a confession because her attorney said that a plea bargain was the only way she could avoid getting a life sentence herself. Her sworn statement has been used by lawyers in their attempt to get Frank Fuster's sentence overturned, but the prosecution argued that it could not be used unless Illeana returned to the United States, and if she did so, she might be charged with perjury.[13]

Craving for Attention

The Satanist *poseur*, who typically says he holds a leading position in a vast and powerful international Satanic order, is often frustrated to find that no one takes much notice of him. "My real name is Baphomet Damon Shub-niggurath Morloch p'tah p'tah Wormwood." "Yes, Dave, have another drink." But if he becomes a Christian ex-Satanist *poseur*, he can gain a large, receptive audience and may even be able to make a living by going around lecturing on the horrors of Satanism. "I used to be known as Baphomet Damon Shub-niggurath Morloch p'tah p'tah Wormwood," he will say, and jaws will drop.

There are other advantages: a Satanist who gains one or two disciples will have to keep inventing explanations as to why they never meet their fellow members of the vast and powerful international Satanic order; the ex-Satanist has no such problem. Anyone who claims the ability to curse enemies with sudden death may end up being put to the test and failing. The ex-Satanist has merely to say that she *used* to have this ability, name a sudden death (after the event, of course), and claim responsibility. Tell a group of people in a corner of a nightclub how Satan materialized in your bedroom, and they will most likely sneer. Tell it to an Evangelical congregation, and they will hasten to make a donation to your Mission to Victims of the Occult.

On the principle of "more joy in heaven," churches of this type encourage members to stand up and give "testimony" of how sinful their lives were before they found Jesus. The greater the sin, the greater the present joy; hence former Satanists are particularly welcome.

*

False accusations are easier to understand than false confessions. (Survivors' stories may include both.) Obviously, someone may bring an accusation out of sheer malice; but there are several other possibilities.

More Torture

When the unfortunate old woman suspended from the ceiling by her elbows admitted that, yes, she was a witch, they would not at once stop hurting her. She was also expected to name her accomplices. Since witches were always supposed to have attended sabbats, they were assumed to be able to name several others. Sometimes they were even given a list of names of persons to accuse.

Cajoling of Children

After repeated investigative interviews, children may confess simply because they are so fed up with being asked questions. In some cases, children have been offered presents if they confess or have even threatened by interviewers, if they won't. Jean LaFontaine reported:

> To the extent that the children are not allowed to leave the room or the building where they have been taken for interview, they are under duress. In transcripts of interviews, children are recorded as asking if they may leave or if the interview is over. For a few children the detention implicit in an interview is acutely distressing. . . . The interviewers may be driven to use permission to play with the toys as a reward for answering questions. In other cases, questions designed to elicit information may convey information about what is required. There is evidence in the transcript that in the course of repeated interviews children learn what it is that the adults want to hear.[14]

Leading Questions

Historians of the witch craze have been aghast at how suspects were asked direct questions, such as these demanded of women on the rack in Franconia: "When did the Devil solemnise his wedding with you? What was the name of this Devil? Have you had children by him? How often have you ridden on the fork [equivalent to the broomstick] and what persons have been with you at the witch-dances? How many tempests and hailstorms have you raised?"[15]

A modern counselor, the Reverend David M. Woodhouse, warns other counselors: "It is very important that you do not ask leading questions at any time."[16] His section on obtaining information from clients includes various questions that he, presumably, does not regard as leading, for instance: "Where are your three books of Shadows? Where is your human bone, usually a finger bone? What are your astral or psychic numbers?"[17] Some of the questions asked of the teenage girl in the Nottingham case were more in the nature of affirmations: "You were asked to kill the baby"; "Mum put the knife in and made you do it"; "You quite like drinking blood and that made you guilty"; "She made you eat him"; "You were told the Devil would be pleased."[18] Smaller children have been asked: "Did she put the fork in your butt?" (asked of a five-year-old); "Does daddy touch you with his pee-pee?" (asked of a two-year-old).[19] Is any comment necessary?

Faulty Reporting

When we are told that a girl of three said her abuser "put his penis into her bottom, mouth and vagina,"[20] we are entitled to question whether a girl of that age really used such adult words, and if not, whether, in fact, she made any accusation at all. Even where interviews have been recorded, the transcripts may not be accurate, and it is the transcripts that are used as a record. In one case, where they were double-checked, "errors included a child reported as saying 'yes' when (s)he said 'no,' or vice-versa; when, in one instance 'it took considerable discussion to produce one name,' the child was reported in the transcript was having produced a list of names; however, the 'list' was not a list of people involved in abuse but, as the child clearly said, a list of members of his family."[21]

Interpreted Answers

Cory Hammond is a psychologist on the medical school faculty of the University of Utah. He has a national reputation as an authority on clinical hypnosis. Some years ago, he attended a conference in which he heard a case study of Satanic cult abuse described. Since then, he has specialized in helping patients to remember the Satanic cult abuse they have forgotten.

Hammond asks Survivors what he calls "non-leading" questions, one of which is: "If there were a doctor associated with your cult programing, and that name was a color, what would the color be?" A common answer is "Green." From this Hammond has developed an elaborate theory: the leading Satanic cult brainwasher is Dr. Green, whose real name is Dr.

Greenbaum, and he is a European Hasidic Jew. As a teenager he was rounded up by the Nazis, but he escaped the gas chambers by agreeing to cooperate with Nazi scientists in mind-control experiments. Greenbaum had a tremendous knowledge of the Kabbalah, which integrated well with the Nazis' Satanic beliefs, and was of invaluable use in cult mind control. After the Second World War, the U.S. government smuggled this team to America, where their experiments were taken up by the CIA. Dr. Greenbaum (now Dr. Green) and the Nazis began torturing and brainwashing children on army bases, supported by CIA funding. The whole thing was sponsored by an international Satanist conspiracy. Subsequently, the conspiracy has come to include the National Aeronautics and Space Administration (NASA), the Mafia, big business, government leaders, and the entertainment industry. Their ultimate aim is to take over the world. Horror films are all made by Satanist producers in Hollywood and incorporate subliminal signals that will program the viewers to obey when the time comes.

For some time Cory Hammond kept these discoveries quiet, but in 1992 he presented them to the Fourth Annual Regional Conference on Abuse and Multiple Personality Disorder, prefaced with the philosophical consideration: "I've finally decided—to hell with it, if the cults are going to kill me, then they are going to kill me." This bravery won him a round of applause. Readers will be relieved to learn that the Satanic cults did not kill Hammond; indeed, since then he has traveled all over the United States, lecturing on his findings.[22]

Hidden Motives

"A Dallas woman told police that she was kept captive for three months during which time a man and woman (wearing black robes) visited her in a windowless, candle-lit room and read her materials related to Satanism two times per day. The story was later discovered to be a hoax. Apparently, she lied to hide the fact that she had had a baby."[23] In the case of "Samantha" already noted, a real teenage pregnancy was explained as one of many caused by repeated rapes in the course of Satanic rituals.

Though Audrey Harper is a firm believer in stories of Satanic abuse (including, presumably, her own), she does admit that not all Survivors tell the truth. She once accompanied a social worker to an interview with a girl who claimed to have been ritually abused but whose story was actually quoted from Harper's own book *Dance with the Devil*. In another case, a girl named

Emma rang her up, said that she had been involved in witchcraft and Satanism, and told Audrey she needed a safe house to live in. When Audrey made inquiries, a minister told her that Emma was desperate to find somewhere to live away from home, where relationships were strained. Her story about Satanism was merely intended to secure new accommodations.[24]

Buried Desires

Moyshe Kalman is a Merseyside psychiatrist who controversially specializes in hypnotic regression of people who believe they have been abducted by aliens. In a recent book, he comments on the similarities of some of the claims of Satanism survivors and those of alleged abductees. While he is inclined to believe the latter, he questions the truth of ritual abuse stories and illustrates his doubt with a significant case history.

A twenty-three-year-old woman named Zoe, who was suffering from phobic attacks, came to Kalman for help. She did not want to be hypnotized, but in fact, she did not need to be, as she would slip into trance spontaneously during sessions. The Rochdale case was then in the news, and Zoe expressed concern that she might remember having been subjected to sexual or even Satanic abuse.

After some weeks, she suddenly began to recall how, as a child, a neighbor named Bill had taken her to a disused warehouse furnished with "altar, inverted cross, chalice and dagger—the usual trappings of Satanic worship." With terrible emotion she would relate how he had dressed all in black and had ceremonially raped her to the accompaniment of chanting, incense, candles, and the forced imbibing of "blood and human body products."

After several more weeks, however, Zoe began to doubt her memories. Finally she concluded they were false, and moreover, she found an explanation for them. She was the child of communist parents who had taught her to think that sex was "materialistic" and "bad." She had thus grown up to repress her sexual feelings and had never had a date. The truth was not that Bill had abused her but that she had found him sexually attractive. "Zoe could allow herself an erotic fantasy only if she were the victim. After all, if you are the victim, you are not responsible; it is not your fault, no one can blame you and you just might as well enjoy the experience that is being forced on you." Having recognized all this, her phobias disappeared. As Kalman ominously comments, "If Zoe had left analysis before its completion, still believing that she had been the victim of ritual abuse, the outcome would have been rather different."[25]

The related issue of Satanic violence is (unwittingly) explained in Jacqui Saradjian's *Women Who Sexually Abuse Children*, which includes a chapter on ritual abuse. It features four women who all claimed to have belonged to Satanic cults in which children were "caged, hung, chained, whipped, burnt, tortured, drowned, buried alive, and strapped to inverted crosses and assaulted," and in which, in addition, participants had sex with demons.[26]

Saradjian notes that all four women were turned on by the idea of inflicting pain. One, when asked what thoughts sexually excited her, started to talk about performing sadistic acts on children and got so "highly physiologically aroused" as to make the interviewer change the subject.[27] Though Saradjian evidently believes their stories about Satanism, given that she does not report any corroborating evidence for the existence of the cults that the women claimed to belong to (though all had talked to police), it is more likely that their stories of ritual torture were simply fantasies about what they would have liked to have done.

Presumably, those who have such fantasies get an additional kick from pretending that they were real events. This is also probably the rationale behind the belief in snuff movies: viewers who enjoy gratuitous violence will enjoy it even more if they can convince themselves that "they really did it."

Moreover, whereas the women apparently felt they had little control over their lives, their Satanic tales gave them the illusion of empowerment: "All four women explicitly described feelings of importance within the groups that they had experienced in no other aspects of their lives. When they described this aspect of their experiences, in every case the women's demeanor changed to being more upright, commanding, in posture and attitude, and their tone became more animated, bordering on excited."[28]

Holy Spirit

In 1704, many sermons were preached against witchcraft by the minister of Torryburn, Scotland, the Reverend Allan Logan (why are so many anti-Satanists called Logan?), who could pick out witches by divine inspiration. At the administration of communion, he would cast his eye along, point to some unfortunate woman, and say: "You witch-wife, get up from the table of the Lord," at which she would rise and depart, perhaps to be later accused of witchcraft in court.[29]

The guidance of the Holy Spirit is regarded as the only reliable authority by many of the Christians engaged in battle with Satan, as seen in the unusual medical practices of Dr. Rebecca Brown. When a church member receives a direct message that another member has (unknowingly) been the victim of sexual abuse, it is called the Word of Knowledge, a piece of divinely inspired information, which no true Christian should doubt.

For We Are Many

In November 1990, Mark Peterson, age twenty-nine, was tried for rape in Oshkosh, Wisconsin. The case presented an unusual legal problem: the victim, "Sarah," was reported to suffer from multiple personality disorder (MPD). One of her personalities, "Jennifer," had agreed to sex with Peterson. Some of her other personalities, however, considered that they had been raped. Eventually, Peterson was found guilty of having sex with a mentally ill person, a crime in Wisconsin. Since then, there have been at least two similar cases. There was also a report of a French lawyer, Jean-Luc Pollard, who tried to sue his six alter personalities for ruining his life. At last report, a judge had yet to decide "whether to allow the case of Pollard v Pollard, Pollard, Pollard, Pollard, Pollard and Pollard."[30]

A meeting of RAINS (Ritual Abuse Information and Network Support) on 7 February 1992 was told by psychiatrist Joan Coleman that cults have learned how to induce multiple personality disorder in their victims. According to American Experts on MPD, this makes the victims forget the cult abuse. Therefore, MPD sufferers should be hypnotized or otherwise encouraged to remember the cult abuse they have forgotten.[31]

Multiple personality disorder is a scientific form of demonic possession. James Noblitt and Pamela Perskin, authors of *Cult and Ritual Abuse*, found fourteen points of similarity between the two conditions, including: both are more frequent among females; both often occur after trauma, ordeals, and the like; both have been associated with cults; one entity or personality may be amnesiac about what another has done; in both, the regular personality is called the "host"; the entities may be characterized as animals, spirits, demons, or deities; sufferers may defy "recognized physical limits"; and a disproportionate number of both types believe they have psychic powers.[32] They could have added that, with both, the condition manifests mainly during exorcism or therapy and seems therefore to be largely an act put on for the exorcist or therapist. Indeed, in 1993 medical insurance firms in Idaho demanded the return of payments made to psychologist Terry Clapp for treatments of people with MPD, since it was revealed that his preferred treatment was exorcism, which the insurers said they did not cover.[33]

False Memory

It must be said at once that severe moral problems are raised by the suggestion that human memory is not reliable. If we are to discount people's memories because, for whatever reason, we cannot believe them, then we are one step nearer to the state George Orwell described, where the government dictates to the people what they are to remember.

Nevertheless, in at least some cases this conclusion has become inescapable. Therapist Colin A. Ross, who has treated many alleged Survivors of ritual abuse, thinks that at least some of their memories are accurate but confesses that many cannot be: "I talked with a woman who had a clear, fully formed memory that seemed absolutely real to her . . . of having her head cut off" in a sacrifice ritual.[34] Two other women patients told him details about treatments for cancer that, it turned out, they had never had. A woman who believed she had been raped by Satanists "countless times" was shown to have an intact hymen.

> Another woman claimed that her children had recently been murdered by a Satanic cult, that the FBI had confirmed the murders in person to her, and that she had talked on the phone with the morgue that was holding the bodies; however, the children were still alive, as proven by the therapist's conversation with them on the phone. This woman also claimed that her husband was in prison on charges of sexually abusing his daughters, which was disproved by a phone conversation with the husband.[35]

Many of these memories are "recovered memories," that is, memories of things that, for years, the victims did not know had happened to them. The subject is controversial. Though amnesia is a recognized condition, it is disputed whether people can forget traumatic events yet otherwise have normal memories of the rest their lives.

Some therapists take it for granted, however, that "buried memories" are the usual cause of whatever emotional problem or addiction has brought a client into therapy. Much of the treatment, therefore, consists of encouraging patients to recover their lost memories of abuse. Various methods are employed: they are asked to record vivid dreams and to regard them as clues to the truth. If, in art therapy, a client starts drawing in black and red, this is a sign of the reality trying to break through: "The black represents the robes. The red represents blood."[36] Clients then may start to have "flashbacks," in which static visual scenes may suddenly appear in their minds. These are often of a gruesome nature, such as "a baby being fed a bottle of blood." The woman who saw this also found that hearing the phrase "running around like a headless chicken" brought to her mind a vision of "a ceremony in which blood from a headless chicken was spilled over a plain white dress she was wearing; she was in a horseshoe of adults dressed in robes."[37]

At this stage, say the therapeutic Experts, to help clients understand what is happening, they should be given literature on Satanic ritual abuse.[38] After this, they may start having longer and more unpleasant flashbacks and will be ready to integrate them into a coherent narrative.

It will be observed that these methods may well bring up unconscious images that are not memories at all. If so, then the coherence of clients' final narratives will depend on their ability to visualize, not on anything that really happened to them. If a group of people have strong visual imaginations, then the outcome can be disastrous.

In August 1988, Karla Franko, a charismatic Christian from California, spoke to a group of sixty teenage girls at a two-day retreat near Olympia, Washington, organized by the local Church of Living Water. Inspired by the Holy Spirit, Franko announced that someone in the audience had been molested, as a young girl, by a relative. Not one but several girls announced that they had indeed been abused, while for some reason a deaf girl rushed out and tried to drown herself by shoving her head into a lavatory.[39]

Later, after most of the girls had left, Franko was asked to pray over Ericka Ingram, a twenty-two-year-old counselor who was sitting in the hall sobbing. The word of the Lord came to Franko, and she declared: "You have been abused as a child, sexually abused." She added that it was Ingram's father who had done it.[40]

Ericka, who had recently been reading Lauren Stratford's *Satan's Underground*, moved out of her parents' house soon afterward, followed six weeks later by her eighteen-year-old sister, Julie. A short while later, both girls started claiming that their father had molested them as children.[41]

Their accusations were soon passed on to the police, to whom they were something of an embarrassment, as their father, Paul Ingram, was a deputy in the county sheriff's office. On 28 November he was arrested. He stated officially that he could not remember having abused his daughters, but that he believed the allegations: "My girls know me. They wouldn't lie about something like this."[42] He supposed he must have "repressed" the memory, and the next day, a psychologist told him that it was not uncommon for sexual offenders to bury the memories of their crimes. Once he confessed, he was assured, the memories would come flooding back.

Ingram was encouraged to practice visualization, letting scenes form in his mind and come to life. Soon he was seeing the kind of sexual abuse that he had been accused of. In addition, he started to see robed figures kneeling around a fire, the sacrifice of a cat, and other Satanic sequences. Subsequently, Ericka also spoke of Satanic rituals, where babies were sacrificed. She even indicated the spot where they had been buried, which was excavated without success.

Ingram's son Chad was also interviewed. At first he denied ever having been abused, though by now his father had remembered, or visualized, Chad being sodomized. He was encouraged to discuss dreams he'd had as a child and was told: "You want to believe it's dreams," but "it was real, Chad." In one of his dreams, a witch with long black hair and a black robe came in through the window and sat on top of him. "That's exactly real," police exclaimed.[43] Chad could not recall more, however, so the psychologist concluded he must have been "programmed not to remember anything."

Dr. Richard Ofshe, a psychologist from the University of California who was called in as a consultant, in the hope that he could help unblock the Survivors' remaining memories, became suspicious of the process of recovery. So he told Ingram that he had also been accused of making one of his sons and one of his daughters have sex with each other. No such allegation had been made, nor would it ever be made; yet nevertheless, Ingram was able to recover a memory of having done this.[44]

Inevitably, several other adults were implicated, but owing to the lack of evidence, charges were not pressed. On 1 May 1989, Paul Ingram pleaded guilty to sexual abuse and was sentenced to twenty years' imprisonment. Some time after starting his sentence, he retracted his confessions but was told that he could not appeal against his conviction since he had pleaded guilty.

Self-Justification

Therapists report that Survivors of Satanism often exhibit deviant behavior as a consequence of their abuse. One Survivor took up a career as an exotic dancer because, she said, she was accustomed to Satanic orgies, where exhibitionism was the only way to get attention. Some may get involved in sado-masochistic encounters, taking the slave role, since their ritual sufferings have left them unable to get sexual pleasure except in this way. Others are said to be drawn to promiscuity or hard-core pornography.[45] These are activities that society normally frowns on, yet therapists, even Christian therapists, here treat them sympathetically, because they are supposed to be a response to severe trauma. Masturbation is regarded as an un-Christian habit, yet in the case of Survivors, the Reverend David M. Woodhouse says, the problem "needs sensitive handling."[46] Obviously, believing that one is a Survivor of Satanism can be a big help for anyone with a guilt complex (of whatever real cause). Even routine problems can be blamed on Satanic cult abuse: men with premature ejaculation can say that they wish to get the act over with as soon as possible, because their experiences in Satanism put them off sex.

Psychotherapy is a difficult process that does not always produce the desired results. The failure of patients to get better or even to recall the Satanic abuse that the therapists believe they have undergone can be blamed on the power of Satanist mind control. Similarly, the Reverend Woodhouse warns that clients in Christian therapy may still be under the influence of the Satanists: "Some Counselors have not discovered the commission given by a coven to cause havoc through the Client and this has led to disaster. Several Christian marriages have been severely affected by Clients who have had intercourse with their Counselor thus bringing Christian therapy into disrepute."[47] The stratagems of Satan are subtle indeed!

Gold Digging

The earliest trial for sorcery of which there is a detailed record was of Apuleius in about the year 150. He was accused of using magic to make a wealthy widow fall in love with him. As proof, it was said that he had been seen examining various fishes (with the intention of using them in spells), and that a certain boy had thrown a fit when Apuleius was standing near to him. In his defense speech, which still survives, Apuleius stated that his accusers were in-laws of his new wife who had hoped to get her fortune for themselves. Since he had committed no crime in reality, the accusation of using magic was the only one they could make. He added that he had been examining different species of fish because he was writing a book on natural history, and the boy who had thrown a fit in his presence was an epileptic who threw fits regularly.[48]

At the present time *any* Survivor of Satanism is a potential gold digger, at least in the United States. Anyone who can convince a civil court that she or he has been sexually abused as a child can sue for substantial damages from the parent or other "abuser."

Breaking Up Is Hard to Do

Many allegations of Satanic child abuse have first appeared in the course of divorce proceedings, from the Bakersfield case onward. One of the *Geraldo* shows on Satanism featured Louis Behr and his four sons, aged two to nine, who stated that the boys' mother and her boyfriend had made them take part in Satanic rituals involving bizarre sexual games, ritual baby killings, and blood drinking. Subsequently, the FBI established that the eldest son had persuaded his brothers to make up these stories, because their mother had been given custody of them and he wanted to live with his father.[49]

Satanic Indicators

Various peculiar means were formerly used to detect witches. The suspect might be tied up and thrown naked into a river: if she floated, she was a witch; if she sank, she might well drown, but she was thereafter held to have been innocent. Others were tested as to whether they could recite the Lord's Prayer correctly, which not all could. Jane Wenham, the last woman to be convicted as a witch in Britain, would say, "Lead us not into Temptation, but deliver us not from evil."[50] Another method was to prick the woman with a needle and see if there was a spot where she felt no pain; if such was found, this was taken to be the Devil's mark. When a Scottish witch-pricker arrived in Newcastle in the 1650s and agreed to find witches for twenty shillings each, thirty suspected witches were brought before him, and he picked out twenty-seven of them. Fifteen of these were executed. Over the course of his career, this witch-pricker (who himself ended his life on the gallows) was said to have been responsible for the deaths of two hundred women.[51]

Modern methods of detecting sexual abuse are scarcely less unusual. Any behavior at all out of the ordinary, and even quite normal behavior ("Child destroys toys"),[52] may be taken as an indicator of abuse, even of Satanic abuse. Children's anuses may be touched to see if they dilate, though this has no bearing on abuse and 50 percent of healthy children's anuses dilate anyway. A test that may be used on a boy is for a female examiner to touch his penis, the theory being that abused boys will get erections more easily. On one occasion, this was tried on a boy of *fourteen*.[53] It had not, apparently, occurred to those responsible that a fourteen-year-old boy will be close to his natural peak of potency, and that it would be more a matter for concern if he did *not* get an erection easily. (Yes, the age of consent is sixteen, but nature inconveniently ignores the law.) If the children have not previously been abused, they will have been by the time the authorities have finished poking their private parts.

Children Coached by Adults

In 1696, a stir was made in Dublin by the claim of a boy named James Day, a blacksmith's apprentice, to be in league with the Devil. According to his story:

> He went on *Saturday* the 8th day of *June*, into a Field near St. *Patricks Well*, and writ in his own Blood these Words; *In the Name of the Devil, I command you to appear*; and that immediately there came to him a Tall Slender Black Man . . . [who] made him great Offers of Money, and Worldly Goods, if he would become his Servant; particularly, That he should win at all sorts of Game; and that after they parted, he went immediately by some secret Direction, to the Lottery on *Essex-Bridge*, where he won that evening Eleven Shillings and Four pence.

The following Saturday, the fifteenth of June, Day met the Devil again, who had a document that he wanted him to sign:

> The Devil carry'd him that afternoon to a House that lookt like a Tavern, he knows not where, but that they had there Sack and March Beer sugar'd, with other Liquours; and that all the while they were drinking, they sat one on each side of a Table hand in hand, the devil pressing him all the time to sign the said Leafe; and that they had no Drawer, or Attendant to supply them with Drink, but that notwithstanding, they drank plentifully, the Cups were always full.

On Wednesday the nineteenth of June, while visiting his uncle Patrick Dawson, Day met a mysterious old woman,

> who told him, That she had been Dead, and was Risen from the Dead, and that while she was Dead, she was in Heaven, where she saw and convers'd with God, and Christ, the Angels, the Virgin Mary and Saints, and that they all told her, there was no Salvation any where but in the Church of *Rome*; and that she saw King *Charles* II in Heaven, and that the reason of his being there was his dying a Papist; that there was great Virtue in Holy Water. . . .
> . . . on *Friday* the 21st day of *June*, the Boy disclosed the Whole Plot, and gave his Confession: That his Uncle *James Tuit*, and *Patrick Dawson*, with their Wives, being all Papists, had frequently Advis'd and Press'd this Boy their Nephew, to come over to their Religion; and that on the 8th day of *June*, the

said *James Tuit* did first put the fore-going Story in the Boys Head; and that afterwards the same day, his Aunt *Joan Tuit* did carry him to the Popish Chappel at St. *Audoen's* Arch, where the doors being shut, and none present besides her and one Man; two supposed Priests, or Fryars, repeated to him the very same Story and caused him to swear by the *Mass Book* to related and stand by it, and they themselves swore by the same Book, as also *Joan Tuit* and the other man, never to discover the secret.[54]

Nowadays, we are told, "Children never lie about abuse," as if this principle were as incontrovertible as the law of gravity. (Indeed, more so, since some children have spoken of Satanic abusers levitating.) In April 1993, two eight-year-old boys suffered burns while playing in a park in South London. They told police that a man of distinctive appearance had poured petrol on them from a can, set it alight, and then run off. Other people who had been in the park at the time remembered seeing a man who matched the description. After hunting this maniac for two days, police discovered that, in fact, the boys had set themselves on fire while playing with matches and a stolen can of petrol. They made up the story to avoid getting into trouble.[55] Since they accused someone who had really existed and been in the area, an innocent man could easily have been arrested.

Granted that such incidents are rare, "Children seldom lie about abuse" still needs qualification. First, children do not always distinguish fact from fantasy. "This is a spaceship," a boy will say, holding up a plastic squeeze-bottle. Normally, this does not matter; but if a therapist is listening for evidence of abuse (they do not even expect to hear coherent stories), then a description of a game of witches and Wizards may be interpreted as an account of a Satanic ritual.

Second, children often tend to say what they think adults want to hear. If they are repeatedly asked about ritual sex, they may finally get the impression that they are naughty if they do not give affirmative answers. When continually asked things like "Which parts of the baby did you eat?" eventually they will oblige and start talking about cannibalistic ceremonies. But to present this end product as "what the children say" is outrageously misleading.

Other Ways Untrue Stories Circulate

John Parker's *At the Heart of Darkness*, "an investigation of the Occult," described how Phil Hine, for some years the editor of *Pagan News*, had admitted in *Chaos International* to having vampiric tendencies. His craving had started after a minor childhood accident: "Red droplets misted across my face and in the long, frozen moment that followed I licked a bright bead of blood from the back of my hand." As an adult, he would drink not only his own blood but other people's. Parker's comment was: "Mr. Hine was apparently telling his readers that he possessed an insatiable desire to drink blood."[56] Parker had failed to notice that this piece was a fictional vampire story that happened to be written in the first person.

On 1 July 1989, the *Star* quoted an Expert on Satanism as believing that "Roman Polanski's cult horror film Rosemary's Baby—where a child is deliberately conceived to be sacrificed to the Devil—is more fact than fiction." Actually, the story is rather different from this (anyone who has not seen *Rosemary's Baby* and wishes the plot to remain a surprise in the event that they ever do, please skip the rest of this paragraph): the heroine comes to believe that her next-door neighbors are Devil worshipers and are planning to sacrifice her unborn child. In the final scene, it is revealed that they are indeed Satanists but that her child is honored by them, as he is the Antichrist, fathered by the Devil (who raped her as she lay in a drugged sleep).

Once again, anti-Satanists prove incapable of stating a straightforward fact correctly. But it is interesting that they often mention this film. If a number of them misunderstood the plot (perhaps they stopped watching before the end), then might not this have given birth to the legend of "baby-breeders"?

Likewise, the foundation of the Church of Satan is said to have been inspired by the American release of the film of Dennis Wheatley's *The Devil Rides Out* and the simultaneous publication of several of his "Black Magic" novels. Since anti-Satanists are always far more numerous than Satanists, might it not have also started off the search for dangerous Satanic cults? "The Brotherhood of the Ram," the Satanic conspiracy in Wheatley's *The Satanist*, could have been the original of Mike Warnke's "The Brotherhood."

Certainly, the horror film industry has familiarized everyone with the notion that there are people out there who dress up in robes to perform sinister rituals involving human sacrifice and the like, and this must have made it easier for allegedly true stories about Satanism to be believed. And while it would be difficult to prove that Survivors of Satanism actually borrow their stories from popular fiction and fantasy, there are indications of this in some instances. A Survivor who appeared on the *Oprah Winfrey Show* claimed he had taken part in a Satanic ritual where there was a human sacrifice: "The High Priest brought out these seven daggers and they impaled him in the form of a cross with the seven daggers."[57] Challenged by Michael Aquino, who was also on the program, to name the Satanist leader responsible, the Survivor said: "I don't remember his name," adding, "I have partial amnesia, specifically about that night." Perhaps if his full memory was restored, he would merely recall watching the *Omen* films.

In a child-access case in New Zealand, a four-year-old boy who was undergoing sexual abuse interviews told his mother, one breakfast time, that he had dreamed about his father's new girlfriend being dressed as a witch. The story then changed from a dream to something believed to have really happened. The witch costume was described in detail and was later recognized by the father and his girlfriend to be that of *Bad Jelly the Witch*, whom the children had watched on television during one of their visits.[58]

Jay's Journal relates how he mentioned to his Devil-worshiping girlfriend how he would like the lead role in the school play, but it was already cast and into rehearsals. That very night, the lead boy suffered a ruptured appendix, obviously as a result of the girlfriend's evil spells, and Jay was offered the part instead.[59] That this incident is almost identical to one in *Rosemary's Baby* cannot be coincidence.

That the Devil worshipers are depicted as in the ascendancy at the end notwithstanding, *Rosemary's Baby* presents an essentially Christian view of witchcraft. The same is true of the other film that anti-Satanists most often blame for spreading interest in the occult, *The Exorcist*. In fact, the real effect of this film was not to spread Satanism but to encourage Christians to become possessed. Not long after it was screened in the Wurzburg region of Germany, a twenty-two-year-old student at Wurzburg University, Anneliese Michel, started throwing fits, speaking in tongues, and displaying other symptoms that her Catholic parents took to be signs of demonic possession. Two priests were assigned to exorcise her. She was flogged, encouraged to fast, and, in between sessions, kept tied to her bed. After several months of this treatment, she died. Her weight had gone down to seventy pounds, and a doctor said she died of starvation. The parents commented piously that Anneliese was now at peace, but the priests were prosecuted and convicted of negligent manslaughter.[60]

This leads to another point. The Devil worshipers in *Rosemary's Baby* were not accused of doing anything worse in their rituals than taking off their clothes and playing the recorder. In *The Devil Rides Out*, the main concern is that anyone, once initiated into Black Magic, will certainly go to hell forever. As with the early Inquisition, mundane crimes hardly entered into it. But since the 1960s, filmmakers have tended to become as extreme as censorship will permit, and horror films have to be quite lurid if they are to be a success.

In the same way, postwar Britain was very straitlaced and could be shocked by Mrs. Jackson's stories of fanatical dancing to the rhythm of repetitive drums; but within a few years the discotheque craze had started, and this was no longer newsworthy. Society changed almost beyond recognition after the 1950s. Nowadays—when genital torture is done as a stage act in some nightclubs, when cannibalism has been regarded as an avant-garde art form, and when perverted sex is shown on television—it takes a great deal to outrage the public. Accordingly, the recent stories about Satanism have been extreme.

Another indicator of the changing times is found by comparing two films, both called *The Witches*. In the 1960s version, apart from the usual plot device of a human sacrifice prevented at the last moment, the main activity of the witches was having an orgy, of exceptional torridness considering that due to censorship, they could not actually take their clothes off. In *The Witches* of the 1980s, the "Royal Society for the Prevention of Cruelty to Children" turned out to be run by witches, who used it to get hold of children in order to eat them. This, curiously, prefigured subsequent events.

You Cannot Be Serious!

Many of today's Pagans have a macabre sense of humor, and stories about Satanic crime have inspired a good deal more; for instance, "The trouble with human sacrifice is it makes an awful mess on the carpet." At a Pagan conference held near Leicester in 1989, a woman was wearing a badge that read, "I like babies but I've never been able to eat a whole one."

Remarks of this sort have sometimes been taken seriously by anti-Satanists. Tim Tate quotes a patently spurious "study program" for the Twelfth Degree of the OTO (there is no such grade), which included instructions such as "Take hostage a busload of Libyan terrorists" and "Design and perform a ritual of human sacrifice. Cannibalism . . . optional."[61]

Overreaction

Insofar as Satanic crime actually exists, it is usually the work of teenage dabblers. Public imagination, however, tends to go to excess over their activities. Not long ago there was an outbreak of animal mutilations, accompanied with the daubing of Satanic symbols, in the Sussex town of Lewes.

Locals thought there must be a large-scale Satanic cult in their midst. But it all stopped when the police arrested one teenager.[62]

In other cases where speculation has run wild, the real explanation has proved to be quite innocent. "Police Watch Temple of Devil Worship," reported the *Daily Sketch* on 3 December 1956, after the summer house of a disused mansion at Chigwell Row, Essex, had had unknown intruders: "A heavy table had been moved into the center of the tumble-down building. On it were ringed 15 heavy stones. In the center of this ring were three smaller stones surrounding some feathers, sprigs of laurel, holly, acorns and chestnut leaves." A local vicar said: "If it is proved to be for black magic rituals I would be willing to ask my bishop whether the place should be exorcised."

This was not necessary. Two days later the *Daily Mail* interviewed the culprits, a group of secondary school boys who had been on a nature ramble. They told the paper, "We have never heard of Black Magic. But as it seemed to scare you so much we thought it would be better to explain."

It's My Own Invention

In October 1996, Brent Garner, a detective in Palmerston North, New Zealand, reported that he was receiving threats from a Satanist. He moved his wife and two children from the family home to a secret location for their protection. On the eighteenth of October, police found him outside his burned home, covered in petrol and with crisscross knife wounds on his back. He told them that a masked intruder had tied him up and set fire to the house, but he managed to escape by rolling through a window.

Inevitably, the press coverage of the case discussed Satanism generally. The inevitable clergyman, Father John Moss, national chaplain of the Catholic Church's Charismatic Renewal, stated that Satanism was widespread in New Zealand, and that, in particular, Satanists were actively recruiting young people. He knew this because people came to his church to escape the cults. The inevitable female Survivor, a woman identified only by the name "Talisman," was quoted as saying from her insider knowledge that there were a dozen Satanic orders in the country, but the attacker in this case had "no contact with any of the official organizations."

On 23 November, Detective Brent Garner himself was arrested on charges of forgery, arson, and false pretenses. It appears that he invented his Satanist assailant and set his own home alight, presumably to claim the fire insurance.[63] This is an extreme case, but only in the lengths that the "victim" took his invention.

Anyone who has worked with emotionally disturbed people should be aware that they often physically injure themselves. In particular, many women cut their own arms with knives. Anti-Satanists, however, do not seem to have noticed this: they often cite scars, typical of self-mutilation, as proof that a woman's stories of Satanic abuse are true.

Vain Repetition

The *Daily Express*, 28 December 1934, reported: "Four active 'occult magic circles' are at present operating in London. Each has an initiated membership of thirty or forty men and women. One of the 'circles' is run in a studio in Chelsea and is attended chiefly by artists." This must have been the Golden Dawn, founded in 1888 for the study and practice of ceremonial magic. Due to various schisms, by the 1930s there were four rival lodges in London, one of which indeed met in a studio at Clareville Grove, off Old Brompton Road, between Kensington and Chelsea.

Now, the members of the Golden Dawn were not Satanists. Their rituals were both verbose (for which reason they are seldom nowadays performed) and conducted with Victorian decorum. Montague Summers, however, reproduced almost the whole of this article in his *Witchcraft and Black Magic* (1946) in the middle of a discussion of Satanism (or what he understood Satanism to be), so that the incautious reader would think these unnamed "occult magic circles" engaged in blood sacrifices, Black Masses, and the like.

One reader so deceived was Edward Podolsky, M.D., author of an *Encyclopedia of Aberrations*, "a psychiatric handbook" (1953), who included a section on "Devil Worship," largely based on Summers's book. He went beyond Summers's words, however, stating that, in England, "the Black Mass is still celebrated in the drawing-rooms of Mayfair and in Chelsea studios under conditions of almost absolute secrecy. There are at least seven active chapters of Satanists, each with an initiated membership of nearly fifty men and women."[64] He clearly had no justification for increasing both the number of these societies and their membership. Podolsky's book was subsequently cited by the authors of *Cult and Ritual Abuse*, as if it proved Satanic cult abuse went back decades.

Nor did the increase end there; for in 1962, the U.S. "men's magazine"

Taboo ("Gnostics," vol. 1, no. 2) ran a piece on Devil worship that said, "London's 'Daily Express' recently stated that "Four active 'occult magic circles' are at present known to be operating in London. Each has an initiated membership of about two hundred men and women."[65]

In 1984, a Devonshire Christian who had discovered that his wife was pregnant by another man attacked her paramour with a chainsaw, severing a testicle. In the course of the ensuing media publicity, it was revealed that other members of the husband's charismatic Church had told the wife she was bearing "the Devil's child." In the *Tatler*'s review of that year, this turned into an assertion that she "had been told by local black magicians that she was expecting the Devil's child."[66] Was this deliberate, or a Freudian error?

Probably, word-of-mouth stories about Satanism circulate and multiply in a similar way, but it is impossible to trace their origins. When I have tried, I have gotten nowhere, except to be warned that, if I probed too far, the Satanists would kill me. So far, they haven't.

It is possible, however, to make a few observations about "urban folklore," to which class such tales belong. These are frequently passed around in casual conversation, but usually without it being said exactly when or where they happened. A favorite from the 1970s concerned a hippie babysitter who got stoned and put the baby in the oven, thinking it was a roast. Later, when microwaves became common, it was said he put the baby into a microwave. Then, in the mid-1980s, the same kind of story was told of Satanist baby-sitters who *deliberately* roasted or microwaved the baby. An anti-Satanist California police sergeant related the yarn in a monograph ("When the parents came home, they found the young couple, who belonged to a satanic cult, had roasted the baby on a gridiron"), but, as Robert Hicks observed, "the lack of a citation prevents the reader from verifying the story."[67]

Psychologist George B. Greaves rejects the "urban legend hypothesis" as an explanation of stories of Satanic cult activity because of the differences between the two. For instance, Satanism stories are told as first-person accounts—unlike the folkloric "it happened to a friend of a friend" scenario—and "unlike 'urban legends' there is no measure of fun or delight in them. There is no punch line, no 'gotcha!' outcome."[68]

Yet some people, having heard a good story, will claim, "It happened to *me*," when they retell it. A Nottingham boy spoke of seeing a woman who "killed a baby and placed it in a microwave. . . . At his Police interview he did not retract his story but went on to say that babies were cooked for six hours and came out black."[69] (The social workers appeared to accept this; it was left to the Joint Enquiry Team to argue that if, in fact, this had been done, the babies would have exploded.) Urban folktales are simply a part of the disparate materials from which confabulated stories of Satanic abuse may be compiled.

Nearly every Christian claiming to be an ex-Satanist tells a story about having tried to put a curse on a Christian and finding that, for the first time, the power failed to work. Rebecca Brown's friend Elaine told her that, when she had been the bride of Satan, her husband came to her demanding that she kill, by her dark arts, a doctor at a nearby hospital. Elaine did the necessary incantations, but "after about six months, I began to realize that every time I did an incantation in the direction of that doctor the demons came back to me unable to get through."[70] The doctor in question was, of course, Rebecca Brown herself, Satan's failed campaign against her being proof of her holiness.

This narrative has a venerable pedigree. According to the "Life of Saint Ambrose" (333-397): "It happened that one enchanter called devils to him and sent them to Saint Ambrose for to annoy and grieve him. But the devils returned and said that they might not approach to his gate, because there was a great fire all about his house"—this being a divine fire that protected the holy man.[71]

Exaggerated Language

The first thing to notice is that anti-Satanist writing sometimes uses unnecessary adjectives (that is, one might speak of a "black dog," because dogs come in a variety of colors, but not "black coal," because no one expects coal to be otherwise). Phrases such as "evil Devil worshipers" and "sinister Satanists" imply that there also exist good Devil worshipers and mundane Satanists, which cannot be the intention.

Christian opponents of spiritualism have often dubbed it "necromancy." This is technically correct, since necromancy means "divination by the dead," but it is patently dishonest: the word *spiritualism* makes one think of an eccentric old lady wearing a multicolored head scarf, whereas *necromancy* conjures up an image of hooded figures digging up a corpse at midnight.

Emotive but vague terminology is a traditional weapon in the rhetorician's armory. The word *pervert* can mean many things; it is often taken to refer to child molesters, but it is also applied to homosexuals, as a way of trying to establish the quite unproven supposition that homosexuals are more likely to abuse children than heterosexuals.

Exorcists and anti-Satanists make frequent reference to "perverted sex" as a "Satanic doorway." Yet it is clear that many of those engaged in battle with Satan consider anything other than a married couple in the missionary position to be "perverted sex." Thus, a man who goes down on his wife is a sexual pervert and hence, by implication, a child molester, possessed by an evil spirit, and a practicing Satanist.

> EXERCISE: *Translate the following passage into anti-Satanist jargon:*
> Pupils from the primary school danced around the maypole with colored ribbons. The vicar, a folklore collector, says parish records indicate these customs go back to the Middle Ages. The May Queen was crowned on the village green, then everyone joined in the traditional Lovers' Dance through the woods.
>
> ANSWER:
> Children as young as five had to cavort around a phallic symbol during a sick ceremony celebrating one of the major Satanic festivals. A local clergyman, who has compiled a dossier on the cult's activities, believes that generational Satanism has flourished in the area for centuries. After the initiation of a high priestess, all of the sinister Devil worshipers engaged in mass open-air perverted sex rites.

Seeing More than Is There

"Once I went toward evening to H.," wrote a Heidelberg professor in 1597, "and walked across the bridge. There I saw a crowd of people staring at the mountain and making a great outcry. I asked what was the matter. 'Look,' said one of them, 'how the witches are dancing up there.' When I looked up I could see nothing more than that the wind was blowing in the trees and agitating them. This, for the people, was a witch-dance. Such is the power of superstition and imagination."[72]

A few years ago, as a mutual friend informed me, an anti-Satanist in Shepherd's Bush, West London, found an oven glove dropped through the letter box of her apartment. She was terrified, taking it to be a curse object posted to her by a witch. Her mother had to explain to her that it was her own oven glove, which she had lent to a neighbor, who had just returned it.

But Satanists seemed to be extremely common in this particular block: when residents of another flat painted their front door red, the same woman insisted they must have mixed the paint with the blood of a sacrificed baby.

Christian demonologists are prone, like all other occultists, to giving a supernatural interpretation to events that may have mundane causes. Consider an incident that is often cited as proof of the "territorial spirits" theory: in 1983, an American missionary told an Evangelical magazine how he was once handing out tracts in a town that lay on the border of Uruguay and Brazil, the frontier actually running down the main street. He noticed that no one would accept his tracts on the Uruguay side of town, but many took them in Brazil, sometimes even the same people who had ignored him in Uruguay. He attributed this to a demonic cover of darkness enshrouding Uruguay, the demons being respecters of national boundaries, presumably.[73]

A more obvious explanation is that, as Dr. Rose Lopes points out, "Uruguay is much more conservative and repressive than Brazil," and that "political repression in Uruguay was very strong from late 1970s to mid 1980s."[74] In any police state, people will pretend to ignore a foreigner handing out subversive tracts, even if they are secretly interested. Probably the missionary concerned was simply lucky not to get arrested on the Uruguay side of the main street.

There is reason to suspect that this kind of thinking is behind many reports of Satanism. In her 1988 program on "Satanic Worship," Oprah Winfrey reported, "We hear of day-care horror stories of how children are writing the satanic alphabet before they can even do their ABCs."[75] Now, Catherine Gould's list of Satanic indicators explains the "Devil's alphabet" as "writing letters or numbers backwards." Of course, a common mistake of children who have not mastered their ABCs is to write letters backward.

Related to this is the anti-Satanist habit of lumping all occult things together. According to the LaFontaine report: "It was stated in one affidavit that a little boy had 'talked of ghosts' in an interview. The transcript of the interview showed an hour in which the interviewer had asked 33 questions on the subject of ghosts, to which the child had given a few short, and apparently reluctant answers."[76] Yet, even had the boy "disclosed" spontaneously, what would that prove about Satanic abuse? I have known a Satanist who was afraid of ghosts, and for all we know, there may be ghosts who are afraid of Satanists; but otherwise, they are unconnected.

Black Propaganda

On 5 April 1640, a parchment was found affixed to the door of the Council Chamber of Granada in Spain: it praised the Law of Moses (as opposed to the New Testament) and commended the sect of the Protestants; it attacked the Catholic faith; it denigrated virginity and chastity, to the extent of praising prostitution; and above all, it threatened the destruction of a marble statue of the Virgin, popularly known as the Lady of Triumph. This statue stood on an open plain outside a gate of the city and was the particular object of devotion of a hermit who was consecrated to her.

The parchment was handed to the Inquisition, who compared it with specimens of the handwriting of every literate person in the city. The astonishing conclusion was that it was the work of that holy hermit who so adored the Lady of Triumph. At length, he admitted he had done it because he thought the people did not sufficiently revere the Lady of Triumph and had been too slow to build her own church. So he invented this threat to her to press them into action, and to draw attention away from himself he praised the Mosaic Law—as people were always willing to distrust the Jews—and also the sect of Protestants—since as a Catholic, he thought it natural that Jews and Protestants would conspire together.[77]

Early in 1989, Cynthia Angell, a San Francisco attorney, was acting in a custody case for the father of children who were alleged to have been abused at the Presidio day-care center. Just before the case was due to start, she was asked to meet a "key witness" in the parking lot of a local restaurant.[78] When she arrived, a man opened the door of her car and stuck a gun in her side. He got into the passenger seat and compelled her to drive to a remote spot outside the town, where they met up with a second kidnapper. The men showed her a photograph of a partially skinned infant, then played a tape of adults chanting while children screamed. They said this was a Satanic ritual and advised her not to talk about it. They then let her go, and she went straight to the police.

At first sight, this appears to be a singularly inept attempt at a cover-up. Not only did the kidnappers fail to scare her off the case, but they even offered proof that Satanic child abuse was really happening. On reflection, this was more likely their intention, the event being actually the work of someone's dirty-tricks department.

A few months earlier, a woman driving along a local highway had seen what appeared to be a dead infant hanging from a sign by the road. As she slowed down, two armed men pulled up behind her and told her to move on. From the description she gave to police, they may have been the same men who kidnapped Angell.[79] Since child murderers do not deliberately display the evidence of their deeds where it will be seen, it can be safely assumed that this was another publicity stunt by anti-Satanists.

In 1974, Colin Wallace was a senior information officer with the British army in Northern Ireland. His main job was, in fact, spreading disinformation. When the Irish Republican Army (IRA) acquired a consignment of Russian rocket launchers, some of the rockets failed to explode. The British army believed the reason for this was that the terrorists had not properly understood the instructions, which were in Russian, and fired several rockets with the safety pins still in. They did not, of course, announce this; instead, Wallace leaked a story to the press that the rockets had failed because they were old, and the explosive charges had deteriorated with age. It was hoped this would confuse the bombers and make them less ready to trust the Soviets.

Among Wallace's successes was the creation of a witchcraft cult. Equipped with black candles and chicken feathers and instructions on how to draw magic circles, "covens" of army officers set up "Satanic sites" in derelict houses in Republican areas. The press got wind of this and gave it a lot of space, glad of a distraction from the sectarian troubles.

The purpose of this disinformation was twofold: to make people believe that paramilitary organizations were secret Devil worshipers and to make people scared to go where witches were believed to be. This could have backfired—in some places, it might have led to an invasion of would-be Satan-hunters or men hoping to see nude women dancing—but in Northern Ireland, it worked. "Children were ordered home early and forbidden from areas where the 'witches' pranced at night. These areas were carefully selected by the Army so that they could be kept clear. The witchcraft craze proved the most effective method yet discovered by the British Army for clearing an area of human beings."[80]

Dream Demons

Therapists dealing with adult Survivors encourage them to take some of their dreams as literal memories of abuse. Early in his career Freud considered, on this basis, that it was common for fathers to seduce their daughters. He later realized that if this were so, a majority of Viennese fathers would have to be having intercourse with their daughters. So instead he decided this was the "Electra complex": that girls had unconscious desires toward their own fathers. In the same way, at a certain point in adolescence boys would experience a desire for their mothers, the "Oedipus complex."

No one appears to have collected any figures on this—Freudians are not interested in statistics—so, as an experiment, I asked ten men if they had ever dreamed of having sex with their own mothers. Four said yes. (While some may have had such a dream and forgotten it or not wished to admit it, there is no obvious reason why anyone should falsely say yes.) This is too small for a proper sample, but unless these answers were an exceptional fluke, the inference is clear: such dreams are far more common than consummated mother-son incest can possibly be.

Expertise

In 1958, a Catholic priest wrote:

> On December 2nd, 1947, there died in Brighton, England, at the age of over seventy, a certain Aleister Crowley, who was reputed a master of black magic. He was the founder of two periodicals specializing in satanism: *Gnosis* and *Lucifer*. He had opened a satanic temple in London which is still used, and a satanic cult is practiced there. Hymns composed by Crowley are sung there, and the titles of these are significant: 'Hymn to Pan,' 'Collects for the gnostic mass.' Crowley's disciples recite them over their master's tomb.[81]

Now, it is not hard to discover that Aleister Crowley died in Hastings; that he had nothing to do with the periodicals *Gnosis* and *Lucifer*, which, in any case, specialized not in Satanism, but in Theosophy; and that his disciples could not recite any hymns over his tomb, since he was cremated. Conversely, it would be very difficult to find evidence that Crowley founded any temple in London, Satanic or otherwise, that was still active in 1958.

Other Experts on Satanism inform us that Aleister Crowley was a "Scottish Satanist"; that he had the numbers 666 tattooed on his forehead; that he founded the Golden Dawn and the OTO, as well as Proctor & Gamble; that he wrote some of the rituals for the Ancient and Accepted Rite of Freemasonry; that Benito Mussolini's government investigated his Abbey of Thelema and discovered that human infants born to the disciples were being killed in rituals, after which they expelled him from Italy; and that the Hell Fire Clubs were formed by Crowley's ex-disciples. They attribute to him such books as *The Kabbalah Unveiled* and *The Manual of Magic*, all the while giving his name as Aliester Crowley, Alastair Crowley,

Aleister Crawley, or even Alex Crow. In short, the Experts know less about Crowley than anyone who has read even one of the readily available standard biographies.[82]

Some Experts state that the number of Crowley's followers cannot be known, as they dare not admit to their allegiance publicly. A little observation ought to convince the Experts that, on the contrary, most Thelemites, like Crowley himself, are obsessed with self-advertisement; in consequence, it is possible to trace the history of the movement in full, boring detail. Whatever the source of these Experts' assertions, they are not derived from observation of the real world.

More than one glossary of the occult printed by American anti-Satanists contains the term *Belomanay*, explained as divination by arrows.[83] A moment's thought shows that this must be a mistake for *Belomancy*. That the error is perpetuated from one Expert to another proves that they merely repeat each other's pronouncements, without giving them even one moment's thought.

Many of these Experts are clergy, or at least born-again Christians. Since their religion forbids them to be involved with the occult, most of them are ignorant of the subject. In the Derry Mainwaring Knight case, several Christian Experts were consulted, yet not one of them was well-enough informed to realize that no large Satanist organization such as Knight described even existed, and therefore, he must have been lying.

Another curious thing: most therapists and clergy do not have any ex-Satanists among those they help. By contrast, Andy Arbuthnot of the London Healing Mission in Notting Hill Gate has had many former Satanists in his congregation. Jim Perry, who started attending Arbuthnot's mission in 1984, was soon telling of his initiation in Uxbridge into "the Brotherhood" (presumably the same Brotherhood immortalized in the books of Mike Warnke and Rebecca Brown), along with all the other classic anti-Satanist clichés—for instance, that his group was led by a wealthy local businessman known as "the master."[84] Arbuthnot explained, "The Lord, in His wisdom, has chosen to send to this mission for ministry a succession of people who . . . have been actual leaders of quite large Satanic groups, if not leaders of Satanism internationally."

One inevitably wonders if there is something in the therapy or healing given by such people that encourages memories of having been Satanist leaders. Arbuthnot was a regular exorcist, and in 1995, he resigned after newspaper articles attacked his methods. One Christian woman related how Arbuthnot had persuaded her that she had been a high priestess of

Satan but had suppressed the memory. She could be cured if she could be rid of the demons that, he said, lurked in her genital area. So he gave her regular "internal ministry," in which he doused his fingers with consecrated Dubonnet and pushed them into her vagina and anus.[85]

Rank-and-file Christians rely on their Experts for information, which can have curious results. An Evangelical preacher who reads even a little genuine occult literature may discover, for instance, that spiritualism, witchcraft and Satan worship are very different things. This may annoy him, and, citing the text "He that is not with me is against me" (Matthew 12:30), he may declare in his next sermon that, since all three are against Christ, all are really the same thing. An attention seeker in his congregation may take this as a cue and later give testimony, "I was a spiritualist Satan-worshiping witch," under the impression that this is authentic occultism. Many Survivor stories read as if they had origins of this nature.

Confessions of a Teenage Satanist

Jules is a strikingly attractive photographer in her mid-twenties. Her disclosures, which she made to me in the summer of 1995, reveal the reality of Satan worship among today's youth.

> When I was a small child I found that I was psychic, I could see things that weren't there, and I could tell what was going to happen to animals. I lived in a tiny mining village, there was no room for behavior like that. At school one day I said to a girl, "I'm sorry to hear that your cat died." She said, "My cat hasn't died." The next day she came to school, and her cat had died, and she said, "You Witch!"
>
> And when I got to a comprehensive school, one day I overheard a conversation in the staff room, talking about banning "supernatural" books from the library. I made sure I speedily procured such books. (I nicked them.) One was *The Satanist* by Dennis Wheatley, and I later got things like *The Black Arts*. Because I was confused about my psychic abilities, and I didn't know anything about magic, I assumed that I must be a Satanist. When I read *The Satanist*, I saw the characters in the book, the "Brotherhood of the Ram" as like-minded beings, and (in my foolish youth) I wondered how I could join.
>
> So then I developed the idea that the Archangel Lucifer was the true God, that God made the Archangel Lucifer as the perfect being, then God realized that Lucifer was more perfect than he was, so he got jealous and banished Lucifer, and called him the Devil. The Archangel Lucifer also had the secrets of magic, and this was what really scared the shit out of God.

So I thought, if I was a Satanist and worshiped Lucifer, I was worshiping the true God, and if he did regain his rightful position, he would reward me in some way. Also he knew the secrets of magic, and he'd teach me, and explain how I could use my magical abilities. No one else could, including a string of child psychologists who wanted to put me in hospital and experiment on me.

What sinister activities did Jules engage in?

I used to read Anne Rice novels by candlelight, and listen to Wagner records, chanting "Lucifer, Lucifer." Then I read somewhere that I should sell my soul, so I bought some parchment, cut my ring finger, and wrote on the parchment, "I do sell my soul to Satan up until the age of thirty." At fourteen, I thought everything stopped when you got to thirty anyway. I signed it, rolled it up, and took my ring off, and slid my ring over it to hold it.

And I would draw pentagrams on pieces of parchment, and put various names that I'd read in books in each point of the pentagram, and I would chant them, and stick them around my room. And if there was something I wanted, I would make a pentagram and write my will, what it was that I wanted, in the center. I would chant and I would burn it, yelling out at the top of my voice whatever it was that I wanted.

One evening I persuaded a friend with a car to drive me to an old derelict castle, there were rumors it was haunted, that a group of Satanic monks had once worshiped there. I went into the courtyard, it was about half nine in the evening, I couldn't do it at midnight because I wasn't allowed out at midnight. My friends wouldn't come in, they were too scared. I removed one of the stones from the wall, and I hid the parchment with my ring around it in the wall. Then I stood in the courtyard, and in all four directions made some kind of speech about how I was going to worship Satan. Then, I was convinced that I saw a huge black figure, maybe two feet off the ground, in front of me. I was scared, but I felt really honored as well. Then I left.

A couple of weeks later, I went to check on the parchment, and it had gone. I think, perhaps, one of my friends had watched from the gateway and had removed it later, but I don't know.

After this I thought I was the all-knowing, all-powerful being. There would be things that irritated me, like the sound of metal scraping on metal, and I said, I can cope with this sound because Satan will give me the power to cope with this sound.

Then I started persuading other people at school that they should become Satanists as well. They tried, but they were either too sensible or too scared. Then they would mention something to their parents, the parents would complain to the school, and the school spoke to my mother about it. She was very worried about me, but she didn't tell me off.

Then, when I got to sixteen, for some reason I panicked. And I was seeing a guy at the time who was a born-again Christian, so he said I should go to his Church, but everything prevented it from happening. For example, one Sunday morning I woke up, I went to have a shower to get ready to go to Church, and discovered my voice had gone completely. So my mum telephoned someone who was going to pick me up, to say I couldn't go. As soon as she'd made the phone call my voice came back. Or I'd oversleep, or the person that was picking me up, their car would break down. Eventually I got there, I tried to fit in, but it didn't happen. Everybody thought I was weird, they tried to get my boyfriend to get rid of me. His mother said, "You're doomed, but they can save you." I confessed to my lover about my "Satanic" past, and he told the rest of the Church.

They all said they were my only salvation, they were going to save me. They insisted that I must destroy, by fire, all my "occult" literature. I was at a vulnerable point in my teens, and sadly I listened to what they said. Lots of books went, including harmless "horror" literature, e.g. James Herbert. Basically, the books which I had once saved, with a passion, from the school, I came regrettably to destroy. I actually cried as I made the bonfire in my back garden, and I did try to grab books back out of the fire, but my mother stopped me, purely to prevent me from getting burned. (My mother was totally disgusted that I had been influenced to burn such sacred things as books.)

Then one day after the service suddenly they all pounced on me and tried to exorcize me. They held me down and spoke in tongues over me, and shouted and screamed a lot. "Lord, save her soul, for she is the spawn of Satan, the Devil's child!" And I shouted and screamed too because I didn't want to be held down. Then I realized, they're not going to let me go until I shut up, so I shut up. Then, as I was still, they let me go, then as I was going, I said, in a deep and strange voice, "You shouldn't have done that," as if Satan was speaking through me. Some of them looked shocked, some of them looked frightened and screamed, then they all started to pray. After that, they wouldn't have me back in their Church.

Here, at last, we have a genuine instance of attempted Satanist recruitment among teenagers, although one fourteen-year-old girl hardly constituted the threat to civilization we have been led to believe in. There is no point trying to debate the nature of Jules's psychic experiences; this is a subject on which, for instance, members of the Society for Psychical Research, the Committee for the Scientific Investigation of the Claims of the Paranormal, and the Inquisition have all expressed firm but radically different views. Yet there is no doubt that some people believe they have such experiences, and this leads to sequences of events like that described above, eventually forcing people into opposing camps. As soon as she was old enough to leave home, Jules moved to a big city and became a chaos magician. The members of the church where she used to live are probably still telling people how they once had a Devil worshiper in their midst.

Who Believes All This?

Janice Hellary, a former Evangelical from North London, told me that she was once lent a copy of *He Came to Set the Captives Free* by a fellow Christian. Her friend believed it all, but Janice's reaction was "Which century are we living in?" Not everyone accepts the claims of the anti-Satanists without question. Who are those who do?

Concerned Parents

During World War I, many women went out to work for the first time, keeping the factories running, and doing jobs that had never been done by women before, such as driving buses. In May 1915, three Irish sisters in Blackpool, Emmeline, Flora, and Ruth Flaherty, spinsters all and trained nurses, offered to look after children whose mothers were working and war orphans. After the war, many of the mothers stayed in work, particularly those whose husbands did not return, and so the Flahertys' child care continued to be valuable to the community.

But strange stories began to circulate about these sisters. Decades later, Alan Robson collected the same legend concerning them from three different people, "so [it] is likely to have some truth to it." During the General Strike of 1926, a protest march went past the Flahertys' house, and two men saw the three sisters "physically abusing a tiny blonde-haired girl." They broke into the house and snatched the child. The sisters responded angrily that they had merely been disciplining the girl for being naughty.

The two men then heard crying coming from a back room. Investigating, they found to their horror, so the story goes, a dozen children chained up naked, their bodies mutilated with razors. One had his eyes cut out of his head.

The pair rushed from the house, returning soon afterward with a group of policemen. There was now no sign of the unfortunate youngsters, and investigations turned up no evidence. But it was widely supposed that, while those children who were collected at the end of the day were well cared for by the Flaherty sisters, the orphans who would not be missed were tortured and eaten.

The next year, Ruth Flaherty had her handbag snatched in a park by a fifteen-year-old boy. When he took it into some bushes and searched it for money, so he later told his father, he found a pickled human hand. The father took him to the police station (after beating him for stealing) to repeat his story. He was able to lead the police to the spot in the bushes where he had left the handbag. It was still there, but there was no sign of any hand. The police took him seriously and searched the Flaherty house once again. This time, they took away meat for analysis. It proved to be pork and veal.

At the end of the 1930s, after the Flahertys had returned to Ireland, their old house was demolished. The builders found teeth and other human remains, but because of the war, nothing could be done about it. Later still, in the 1950s, an American magazine published what they said was the confession of one of the Flaherty sisters, which someone had found in a greenhouse in Ireland. In it she admitted that for years she and her sisters had sacrificed children to Satan.[86]

Here we have most of the classic features of baby-eating witch stories: a "tiny blonde-haired girl" at risk, orphans whom no one would miss, a youthful thief who draws attention from his crime by accusing someone else of something much more serious, repeated police investigations that find nothing, implausible explanations as to why nothing was done (World War II did not affect everyday life so greatly that murders went uninvestigated), a document of obscure origins that is supposed to prove it all really happened, and a lack of any motive except "Satan."

There is a glimpse too, however, at the motives of the believers. Because women were going out to work, against the Protestant tradition, they must have felt guilty at leaving their children. All parents sometimes worry unnecessarily about their children: these working mothers must have been prone to baseless fantasies.

Small children commonly tell each other horrible stories about unpopular adults. Usually their parents ignore them or tell them to stop telling lies. The working mothers of Blackpool were a special case, and three foreign spinsters, stereotypical witches, were readily to be defamed.

In present day America, many mothers work, simply to keep ahead in the rat race, and many of them must feel guilty about it. Consequently, it is not surprising that stories about Satanic ritual abuse have cropped up mainly in the day-care centers where those working mothers leave their children.

To judge from anti-Satanist literature, many parents are concerned about ordinary enough things. "Talking about toilets" is standard behavior for small children, yet excessively concerned parents may regard it as so abnormal as to be evidence of Satanic abuse.

Journalists

In May 1995, following the murder of the son of a vicar, Caroline Wise of the Atlantis Bookshop in London received a telephone call from a provincial newspaper. To the best of her recollection, as told to me later that day, the conversation went as follows:

It's about this murder of a vicar's son. He was rumored to be gay, and he had books on astrology in his room, so it must have been a ritual killing.

Why must it be a ritual killing? I don't see the connection.

Because obviously these things go on.

They don't. There has never been any evidence for a "ritual killing."

But I read in the News of the World *that a man sacrificed a virgin!*

Don't worry, I won't tell anyone you read the *News of the World*. But it isn't very helpful to the police, putting all this nonsense around.

The police have been very cagey, they won't give out any details.

They have to be reserved, they can't give out the clues they've got until they've caught the man who did it.

Astrology might be all right, but would it be fair to say that it leads on to more sinister stuff?

Everything occultists do is legal, everything in this shop is within the law. Never, in twenty years I've been involved in the occult have I come across anything like you're suggesting, nor have any of my predecessors, who had many years more experience than me.

Are you telling me these things don't happen?

Yes, you find me one case of it really happening!

It's a shame.

What's a shame?

That these things don't really happen.

What do you mean?

It's quite exciting, the idea of ritual murder.

On another occasion, she told me, a journalist from the national media phoned her and asked for "the names and addresses of all the child-abusing Satanists that you know." She replied, "If I knew any such people, I'd have told the police."

Wise comments: "I find that sort of journalism totally irresponsible, making a sordid story seem exciting, that's what I find disturbing. These people are so callous. They don't consider the feelings of the family of the victim, they don't consider the feelings of occultists, they don't consider the needs of the police."

Christians

In the late seventeenth century, belief in both Christianity and witchcraft was declining, and Joseph Glanvil had no doubt that the two things were connected: "The Question, whether there are *witches* or not, is not matter of vain Speculation . . . on the resolution of it . . . our *Religion* in its main Doctrines is nearly concerned. . . . If such there are, it is a sensible proof of Spirits and another Life." On which account, he said, atheists "labour with all their might to perswade themselves and others, that *witches* and *Apparitions* are but Melancholick *Dreams*, or crafty Impostures . . . when they have once swallowed this Opinion, and are *sure* there are no *witches* nor *Apparitions*, they are prepared for the denial of *Spirits*, a *Life to come*, and all the other Principles of *Religion*."[87]

One of the leading American Experts on Satanism is Thomas W. Wedge, a former deputy sheriff in Logan County, Ohio, who has led "Satanic Crime" seminars all over the United States. In an 18 April 1989 article, "Blue Knights and the Black Art," in the *Washington Post* Marjorie Hyer described a three-day seminar on "Cults and the Occult," sponsored by the University of Delaware, that Wedge presented for law enforcement officers and that Hyer had attended:

> Wedge began his seminar with the fundamentals—"Theology 101," he calls it, starting with the Bible. "Satan wanted to become God, he wanted other angelic beings to worship him," Wedge said. God punished the rebellion by casting him out. "One third of the angels chose to follow him," he said. It is these fallen angels that Satanists try to conjure up, he said.

Unlike some Christians, Wedge did draw a distinction between Satanists and Pagans: "Pagans are fascinating people. You can learn so much from them." But he added, "Don't misunderstand me. They're still Pagans." Wedge is a "conservative Baptist."

Not all Christians believe in the reality of Satanic abuse. As the Reverend Woodhouse has so wisely put it: "Many deny that anything evil is happening, as so many Christians live in an unreal world divorced from reality."[88] Conversely, not all Satanic believers and Experts have a Christian stance; some have a genuinely secular outlook, and Pat Pulling and Valerie Sinason are Jewish. But there are too many Christian anti-Satanists for their religious affiliation to be coincidence, indeed, there are more of them than is evident at first sight. Andrew Boyd's *Blasphemous Rumors* featured Ruth Zinn of the Earls Court Project, who claimed to have firsthand experience of twenty cases of Satanic ritual abuse. What Boyd did not mention is that the Earls Court Project is a Christian organization set up by Holy Trinity Brompton, one of Britain's leading Evangelical churches.

An incidental consequence of Satan-hunting is that it enables some Christians to indulge in semipornographic writing, which they likely would never do for its own sake. This was equally true centuries ago. Some sixteenth-century theologians stated that the Devil could turn himself into animal form to have sex with women, quoting as proof a convent at the diocese of Cologne in 1566, where a dog lifted up the robes of the nuns in order to abuse them and was assumed to be a devil in animal form. For some reason Bodin did not agree but argued, "I think it was a real dog," citing proven cases where women had sex with dogs: "At Toulouse there was a woman who abused herself in this way: and in front of everybody the dog tried to mount her. She confessed the truth, and was burnt. . . . At the convent of Mont de Hesse in Germany, the nuns were demoniacs: and one could see the dogs impudently waiting on their beds."[89] In other circumstances, passages like this would have got a book destroyed.

There is a psychological phenomemon called projection, that is, seeing one's own faults in others. In recent years Evangelicals have often claimed that Satanists are engaged in intensive recruitment campaigns. Ask yourself: How many times has anyone tried to recruit you into Satanism? And how often has someone tried to convert you to Christianity?

Paradoxically, Satanic activity has become an advertisement for Christianity. The blurb to Bob Larson's latest offering, *Larson's Book of Spiritual Warfare* (1999), promises that by the end of the book, the reader will be convinced, among other things, that "the Bible is truly God's infallible, inspired Word." It attempts this not by examining the Bible but by giving anecdotes about exorcism, psychopathic killings, rock music, Dungeons and Dragons, horror films, drugs, Satanic abuse, Aleister Crowley, witchcraft, Voodoo, New Age therapies, parapsychology, divination, and more exorcism. It is the wartime mentality: having a powerful collective enemy brings people together.

Evangelical books on Satanism always end by concluding that you can be saved only through Jesus. Actually, all Evangelical books, no matter what the ostensible subject, tend to the conclusion that you can be saved only through Jesus. But this message perhaps sounds a bit more plausible in the context of Satanism than of children's toys or television programs.

Another advantage of belief in Satanism is that it appears to make life easier. Consider the Chick Tract *The Curse of Baphomet*. It begins with a middle-class American couple learning that their son Tommy has shot himself and, though alive, is unconscious and has no will to live. Three days later a friend, Ed, tells them Tommy's attempted suicide may be their fault, for belonging to Freemasonry. (The wife belongs to the female counterpart, the Order of the Eastern Star.) Masonry, says Ed, is witchcraft in disguise.

The couple cannot at first accept this, so as proof, Ed quotes the "instructions" of Albert Pike on the worship of Lucifer (it is only a century since these were boasted to have been a hoax) and points to what he calls the "symbol of Baphomet" (actually the Cross of Salem, a Christian emblem adopted by the Knights Templars and many other esoteric societies), which, as he proves with photographs, is common in Masonic decor and regalia. Clearly, their Freemasonry has let a demonic influence into their home, provoking their son's suicide.

Convinced, the couple go home and burn all their Masonic regalia. At once the phone rings, and it is the hospital, telling them that Tommy is awake and even his depression is gone. "Praise God!"

It would be wonderful if everyone's problems had such a simple solution. Actually, there is very little that concerned parents can do about the teenage suicide rate; but who wants to acquiesce in such a situation? Hence, a spurious theory about the cause may come to be believed as at least indicating a possible course of action. In the same way, German farmers of the sixteenth century could do nothing about the hail and blight that ruined their crops, causing poverty and potential starvation. So they became convinced that it was due to witches using evil spells against them and went out and burned some witches. It may not have done their crops any good (it certainly didn't do the witches any good), but it made the farmers feel better.

Dr. Thomas E. Radecki, research director of the U.S. National Coalition on Television Violence and an opponent of Dungeons and Dragons, cited this case from his own psychiatric practice: a twelve-year-old boy "underwent a personality change after getting involved with the Dungeons and Dragons game. He became too aggressive for his single mother to handle and had to be placed in foster care."[90] This is suggested to be typical of the effects of Dungeons and Dragons. Now, it is completely normal for children to undergo personality changes at puberty; indeed, it would be unnatural if they did not. At the same time, they stop playing with dolls and train sets and develop new interests, possibly more adult games such as D&D. The only exceptional thing here is that the boy became too aggressive to handle, but even that is not particularly unusual, though it may be impossible to cure. Since he came from a single-parent family, it is possible that his disturbance stemmed from the trauma of his parents' split, or the lack of a male role model. Yet the unargued assumption is that the Dungeons and Dragons caused the aggression, and it implies a simple solution: ban D&D, and teenagers will stop being troublesome.

Then again, the high failure rate of marriages in Britain today has affected even the Royal Family. What can be done? Well, according to the common opinion of Evangelicals, it is caused by Satanists praying for the breakup of Christian marriages, so you can start by calling for Halloween to be banned in your children's school, writing to the papers saying that Dungeons and Dragons leads to Devil worship, and burning down your local occult bookshop.

Notice that these theories are usually constructed in a way that suits the conservative worldview. The reason that witches were supposed to dine off unbaptized babies was not that babies lose their flavor after baptism but to make sure that parents made their children Christian "or else the Witches will get them!" The WICCA letters, reproduced in chapter eight, imply that the Satanist conspirators are responsible for everything that middle-class America is afraid of: increased taxes, youth rebellion, personal debts, drugs, pornography, removal of prayers from school, invasion of privacy by computer databases, and so on. If only the conspiracy could be uprooted, then all of their problems would be solved!

The irony is that the libel about cannibalistic orgies is first known to have been told about the Christians themselves. To become a Christian, the Romans said, the new convert was first required to stab a baby, after which the assembled company tore it limb from limb and ate it. The lights were then put out and an incestuous orgy followed. When the women became pregnant, their progeny were used to initiate more Christians. Thus the cult was spreading and threatened to undermine the very fabric of pagan society (as indeed it did, though for different reasons).

At the present time, attendance at established churches is in steady decline, whereas new religions are growing. For want of a legal inquisition, the orthodox can counterattack only by devious means such as the spreading of scare stories. Basilea Schlink's outburst, "Religious Tolerance?—Satanism!" gives it away that the underlying motive, conscious or otherwise, is not to stamp out Satanism but to stamp out religious tolerance.

Mind Healers

Mental-health professions are often sharply divided on the question of cause. While there is no known physical reason for schizophrenia, for example, neither can it readily be shown to arise from psychological trauma. Usually, psychiatrists believe the true cause is purely medical, whereas psychoanalysts think it is purely mental. Since evidence of "suppressed trauma" supports the latter group's theory, they have a strong incentive to believe in it. So they are likely to accept the reality of "recovered" memories, even in cases where there are severe logical difficulties in taking them as literally true.

Many therapists, accordingly, believe in Satanic child abuse, but by no means all. Jocelyn Chaplin, a Jungian, author of *Love in an Age of Uncertainty*, came out as a doubter in conversation with the author:

> On the whole it seems to me, and this is my opinion only, that it's the anti-Satanists who've got the serious psychological problems, and are suffering from a form of delusional paranoia, and that the problem is theirs, and that on the whole, it is a purely imaginary phenomenon.
>
> The Shadow, in a Jungian sense, is everything both in individuals and in society that is unacceptable, all put into the sort of dark corners of the shadow of the psyche, shadow of the soul, and a lot of this Satanism and so on is actually the Shadow of a society that has become wedded to science and to reason. Because it's been so imbalanced in the area of reason, there's these completely irrational Satanistic ideas that are part of the Shadow. Also, the Shadow contains all the unacceptable feelings of people like fundamentalist Christians who can't accept their own negative emotions. And of course it's also the Shadow in a way of society. The image is certainly around in the collective unconscious, it's a powerful image; it's also in the movies.
>
> There's a very strong force, particularly in the States, of positive thinking:

if you think positively about everything, everything will be alright, if you really want to be president of the United States you can be. There's a lot of positivity, which is overbalanced, it's not balanced with an honest looking at the other side of things. If you can just simplify and split and talk about sin, and Satan, and split off all the unacceptable bits and dump them on to the Devil, it makes life much easier for people. Life today is very complicated and full of uncertainty.

It's the way a child would cope with reality, to split things very simplistically, Good and Bad. This is very normal for children, it's not normal for responsible adults; children will often create witches and bad women, because they can't bear the thought that their own mother is a mixture—one of the things human beings can't bear is ambivalence—so they split, my mother is good and perfect, but there's a bad witch around. But of course there's Good witch, Bad witch, all sorts of splits. Melanie Klein talks about the Good Breast and the Bad Breast, so even tiny babies start having a split. This whole idea of Satanism is very childish and regressed.

Many therapists nowadays insist it is their duty to believe the patient. People who have experience of working with the severely disturbed may well query this. Should one, for instance, automatically believe a man who insists that his father is the pope? Or a woman who says she is the Mother of God and everybody else is a CIA agent? When a patient tells a psychiatrist that all psychiatrists are conspiring to take over the world, must the psychiatrist believe it?

One morning in the early sixteenth century, a girl from Bergamo in North Italy was found naked in the bed of her brother-in-law at Venice. Asked by her relatives what she was doing there, she told them:

> Last night I was lying in bed awake and saw my mother, who thought I was asleep, rise from her bed and take off her vest and anoint her body with an unguent from a pot which she took from a secret place; and then she mounted a staff which was at hand as if it were a horse, and rose up and was carried through the window, so that I could no longer see her. Then I also rose from bed and anointed my body as my mother had done, and was at once borne through the window and brought to this place, where I saw my mother threatening with horrid gestures the boy lying in this bed. I was frightened at this, and saw that my mother also was disturbed by my appearance and began to menace me; so I called upon the name of the Lord Jesus and of His Mother, and then I no longer saw my mother, and was left here alone and naked.[91]

It might not be supposed that anyone would accept this excuse; but, on the contrary, the authorities had the girl's mother interrogated, and sure enough, under torture she confessed. The story was repeated in Bartolomeo Spina's 1525 book *De Strigibus* (On witches) and repeated by several later writers who took it as convincing proof of the reality of the Devil's servitors. What has to be asked in such cases is: Why do some people have such a powerful urge to believe that it overwhelms their reasoning powers?

Perhaps the question is unanswerable; but it may be speculated that, everything that electric lighting and materialist philosophy have done for the world notwithstanding, people retain somewhere a morbid horror of the unknown; education and skepticism fly from the face of primordial fear. What ought to be sought out is not, then, an objective Satanic conspiracy but the subjective source of the ancient terrors that have been reawakened.

What of the Future?

The creation of the crime of ritual abuse by five states of the United States is potentially dangerous. Human sacrifice is now a felony whether done "actually or in simulation." If it was actually done it would be murder anyway, without these new laws; but what about "in simulation"? A simulated human sacrifice is often enacted by pagan groups at Lammas. Usually it is crudely done: a priestess waves a dagger or scythe at the "victim," who falls down and plays dead, then a few minutes later gets up as if nothing had happened, as indeed it hasn't. But if this was done in Idaho, it could lead to fifteen years' imprisonment for a first offense and life imprisonment for a second or subsequent offense.

What can be done with all these people who invent stories about Satanism? It is evident that they have sad and tedious lives, and that their Satanic reminiscences, however unpleasant, are, like those of Madame Bourignon's girls, a kind of wish fulfillment. The best cure, then, would be for them to take up Satanism: not joining an international Satanic conspiracy (because such doesn't exist) or doing anything illegal but dancing around a bonfire in a black cape chanting, "Hail Satan!" which would certainly brighten up their lives. They could then tell Satanic tales in all honesty, and, if, in the end, they decided to go back to Christianity, they would have a genuine but harmless sin to confess to in their testimony.

As to the question of demonic possession, whether it can occur or not is more a matter of religious faith than anything else. I cannot agree, however, with the Evangelical Christian assertion that the usual cause of such possession is involvement in the occult. Over the years I have met a very large number of occultists, but the only person I have ever seen possessed by an irremovable demon was a born-again Christian.[92] Most cases cited by exorcists likewise involve regular churchgoers. It would appear that the normal cause of demon possession is involvement in Christianity.

Then there is the inspiration of the Holy Spirit. Anti-Satanists have claimed that the Lord has told them, by way of the Holy Spirit, to kill witches, to give the wrong treatment to hospital patients, and to accuse innocent people of serious sexual abuse. They really ought to ask themselves if they are sure they have heard their divine instructions correctly.

Whether Lucifer and his diabolic cohorts really exist or not is another question that belongs in the realm of personal belief and conscience. Having presented so many Christian opinions, however, it will not be amiss to quote a couple of alternative views.

Denis de Rougemont wrote that the Devil is "a mythical being, therefore he exists and remains ever-active. A myth is a story that describes and illustrates in dramatic form certain fundamental structures of reality."[93]

The Buddhist writer T. Lobsang Rampa once received a Canadian Evangelical tract with a request for a donation of money that would "help wipe out Satan." He commented:

> There must be negative or there cannot be positive. There must be opposites or there is no motion. Everything that exists has motion. Night gives way to day, day gives way to night; summer gives way to winter, winter gives way to summer, and so on. There just has to be motion, there just have to be extremes. It's not bad to have extremes, it just means that two points are separated from each other as far as they can be. So, good old Satan, keep him going for a time because without Satan there could be no God, without God there could be no Satan because there wouldn't be any humans either. The worst "Satan" is the awful driveller who tries to ram some religion down the throat of a person of another religion.[94]

On the subject of cults generally, it might be helpful if writers would essay intelligent analysis rather than simply pouring scorn on them all. Any nonmainstream religious body is now liable to be denounced as a cult and lumped together with many unrelated groups. I write here from personal interest, as the religious organization that I belong to, the Fellowship of Isis, is sometimes included in lists of cults. These lists are normally accompanied by remarkable generalizations: that all cults teach that their scriptures are infallible, that members believe nonmembers of the cult are all doomed to hell, and that cults place a heavy emphasis on recruitment. Not one of these things is true of the Fellowship of Isis, but all of them are true of Evangelical Christianity, the main force behind distrust of cults.[95]

Religious movements could be classified according to their beliefs and practices. Three distinctions are noticeable:

1. Those that center on a charismatic founder or leader, and those that do not.
2. Those that encourage members to live communally, and those that do not.
3. Those that believe in a coming apocalypse, and those that do not.

It is not possible to state these distinctions precisely. All groups have leaders of some sort; in the case of Findhorn, for example, the founders presented themselves as basically ordinary people who succeeded by applying divine laws to their lives, implying that anyone could do the same. This contrasts with, say, the founder of the Hare Krishnas, whose writings are regarded by followers as the only books anyone needs to read.

In the case of Scientology, some members live communally, but many do not. It is uncertain whether the communal livers form a high enough percentage to make it characteristic of the movement, and they are therefore omitted below.

The three differences produce eight permutations, illustrated here with many of those groups commonly listed in anticult writing (though probably none of them appreciate the "cult" label):

Charismatic leader, communal, apocalyptic
Unification Church (Moonies), David Koresh's Branch Davidians, Children of God, Aum (Tokyo subway bombers), Solar Temple, Jim Jones's Peoples Temple (Jonestown), Manson Family, Heaven's Gate

Charismatic leader, communal, nonapocalyptic
Rajneeshis, Hare Krishnas

Charismatic leader, noncommunal, apocalyptic
Six O'Clock Service (Chris Brain), Armstrongism

Charismatic leader, noncommunal, nonapocalyptic
Aetherius Society, Est, School of Economic Science, School of Transcendental Meditation, Satanism

No charismatic leader, communal, apocalyptic
Central London Church of Christ, Jesus Army

No charismatic leader, communal, nonapocalyptic

Findhorn Community

No charismatic leader, noncommunal, apocalyptic
Jehovah's Witnesses

No charismatic leader, noncommunal, nonapocalyptic
Unitarianism, spiritualism, Nichiren Shoshu Buddhism, Paganism,
Fellowship of Isis, Wicca

The most striking thing is that those cults that have been responsible for
multiple deaths—the Manson Family, Jim Jones, David Koresh and the
Branch Davidians, the Solar Temple, the Tokyo subway bombers, and
Heaven's Gate—all fall into the same class: apocalyptic communal cults
with a charismatic leader. Nor is this particularly surprising: people living
communally are continually exposed to the influence of a charismatic
leader (and no alternative views), making them ready to do anything he
says, while believers in the apocalypse incline toward drastic action. If the
authorities feel it necessary to keep on an eye on possible dangerous organizations, it is this sort they should look out for.

Satanism, it should be noticed, is not in this dangerous category. Indeed,
it is not even entirely fair to say that it focuses on charismatic leaders.
Though the Church of Satan would have amounted to little without Anton
LaVey, no one hung onto his every word, and church members are allowed
considerable autonomy.

The lists of Satanic indicators that have circulated so widely have caused
nothing but trouble. Instead, the following might be useful:

Satanic Bullshit Indicators

- If it is said that the cult leader is known as "the Master"
- If it is said the Satanists meet in groups of exactly thirteen
- If the only witness was a drug addict at the time
- If the only witness has a history of schizophrenia
- If the only witness is a demon-possessed charismatic Christian
- If the witness is a "friend of a friend" of the narrator
- If a Survivor of Satanic crime tells her or his story to a church but does
  not go to the police
- If a Survivor of Satanic crime sells her or his story to the media but
  does not go to the police
- If a Survivor tells contradictory stories on different occasions
- If a Survivor's story gets more extreme with each retelling

- If parts of a Survivor's story are verbally identical to an earlier Survivor's story
- If Devil worship is the only motive offered for crimes
- If it is implied that most of the participants were unwilling
- If a lecturer on Satanic crime begins by explaining how Lucifer fell from heaven
- If children say they were abused by clowns, spacemen, and Santa Claus
- If it is said children could not make up such details
- If it is said the cult earns money through pornography and drugs
- If it is said members are photographed, then blackmailed into obedience
- If someone has compiled a dossier naming famous people as members
- If stories about Satanism are identical to scenes in Dennis Wheatley novels or *Rosemary's Baby*
- If a witness cannot locate the Satanic temple
- If no evidence is found at an alleged ritual site
- If no forensic evidence is found for blood sacrifice
- If it is said hundreds attended Satanic gatherings but the neighbors did not notice
- If witnesses report that Lucifer was present in person

Most of these items are self-explanatory. Covens of thirteen are easy to imagine but hard to arrange. For over forty years, popular press articles have stated that "dossiers" prove that top people are Satanists, but no such dossier has ever been made public or led to a prosecution.

As an example of how this list could be used, in the mid-1980s BBC Radio 1's *Newsbeat* had a brief interview with a Survivor of a Devil-worshiping cult who met out of doors in the West Country. I quote from memory, but the exchange went something like this:

Q: There are two hundred members?
A: It's more than that.
Q: They were taking drugs?
A: No, what happened was, you have to do everything the Master tells you. I was ordered to do things I didn't want to do, and when I refused he flogged me. I started taking heroin for the pain.

There is not much to go on, but some of the indicators are present. By her own admission, the witness was taking hard drugs. Large numbers of people were meeting out of doors, which should have attracted attention, particularly since police always keep a lookout for "raves." I forget if the term for the cult leader was "the Master" or some other pompous title, but either way, it may have been a cover for the fact that she couldn't say what his name was. This "Master" (or whatever) was alleged to be guilty of inflicting grievous bodily harm, and if he had ever been prosecuted the papers would surely have noted the fact. There was no explanation as to why people should want to join a cult where they would have to obey every order, with severe punishment for failure. One could even speculate that the interviewer gave the figure "two hundred" based on her previous statements, suggesting that her story got more extreme with each retelling.

This woman may have been the same as "Nicky" who was featured in the *Daily Mirror* at about the same time. If so, there are some other indicators: Nicky's claims were believed by her vicar, but "police are skeptical." She gave a different version in the newspaper of how she became a junkie, saying it was a response to her father's death. Also, some of her quoted words were almost identical to those of Doreen Irvine's *From Witchcraft to Christ*: "My blood was mixed with that of a cockerel and I had to drink it . . . I became queen of the black witches."[96]

Finally . . . ?

One thing we may be sure of is that this is not the end. In America, though Michael Aquino says that only lunatics now believe in the reality of Satanic abuse,[97] many such lunatics are employed in positions of responsibility. Charismatics continue to receive information on Satanism from the Holy Spirit, while exorcists still cast out demons. Those who have publicly challenged belief in the existence of ritual abuse have been ostracized by social workers, showing that they are willing and able to start all over again. The necessary theology has not changed. The epitaph on Satan-hunting must be: "Not dead, just sleeping."

Appendix
The Black Mass

Early witch trials did not include the accusation that witches performed a parody of the mass, nor is this allegation found in the *Malleus Maleficarum*, or in the descriptions of the sabbat given by the *Errores gazariorum* (1450?), Mamor (1462), Dodus (1506), or in the accounts of the crimes of witches in Nodé (1578) and Bodin (1580). Grilland (1536) gave a hint when he said that "Satan would be worshiped like God,"[1] but he did not specifically mention a Devil's Mass.

In 1594, however, the Parliament of Bordeaux tried a young woman named Jeanne Bosdeau, who confessed that she had been introduced to witchcraft by an Italian who led her into a field, traced a circle on the ground, and read an invocation from a black book. Suddenly a black goat appeared, with a black candle burning between its horns, accompanied by two women. The goat asked the Italian who the girl was, and he replied that she had come to enroll among his subjects. On the goat's instructions, she made the sign of the cross with her left hand and kissed him under the tail in homage. The next time the Italian took her to the same place, the goat had sex with her. Subsequently, she would go to the sabbat every Wednesday and Friday, where there were more than sixty others, each carrying a black candle:

> In this assembly the Mass was said in their own way, with their backs to the altar. He who performed the office, whom she named, was dressed in a black cope with no cross, he held up a segment or round of turnip stained black in place of the host, everyone crying at the elevation, *Master, help us.* Water was put in the chalice instead of wine: and to make the holy water, the goat would piss in a hole in the ground.[2]

Three years later, Florimond de Raemound published Bosdeau's story in his *L'Anti-christ.* Quite suddenly, a parody of the mass came to be commonly mentioned in witch trials. In 1598 the Bordeaux Parliament accused Pierre Aupetit, curé of the village of Pageas in the province of Limousin, of being a witch. Aupetit persistently denied it, but under torture he made a full confession, including that for twenty years he had celebrated masses in honor of Satan at the sabbat.[3]

Theorists of witchcraft hastened to include this new feature in their accounts of the evils of the sabbat. Del Rio repeated Florimond de Raemound's account of Jean Bosdeau; Boguet generalized it:

> Sometimes they say Mass at the Sabbat . . . he who is to say the office is clothed in a black cope, with no cross upon it, and after putting water in the chalice he turns his back to the altar, and then elevates, in place of the Host, a round of turnip colored black, and then all the witches cry aloud "Master help us" &c.[4]

Evidently, Boguet assumed that if a mass was done at one sabbat, it must be done at many. In the south of France in 1609, Pierre De Lancré found that it was the Devil himself who performed the Satanic Mass. All of the many witches who were put to death in the Bamberg district in 1612 had confessed that, at their gathering, some of the devils went through a mock celebration of the sacrifice of the mass, handing around to the witches a Host made of burning pitch and a chalice of liquid brimstone, which, not surprisingly, "burnt like Hell-fire through their entrails."[5]

It can be seen that the Black Mass is on a par with Satanic child abuse: for years and years, no one suspected that Devil worshipers did such a thing, but once someone had the idea, it became a stock accusation. These accounts say nothing about Satanism; they show only that anti-Satanists, old and new, lack originality.

The ancient priesthood of France, the Druids, claimed to have magical powers. In time, they were supplanted by the Catholics, but the common people still tended to believe that their priests were magicians. Theoretically they were not, but official theology seldom makes any impression on the popular mind. Folklorists collected amazing beliefs from the peasants: in one district it was believed that every curé was accompanied by a black dog, which was a demon in disguise.

Since the priests were magicians in the popular mind, their principal ritual, the mass, took on magical powers. The priests did not necessarily discourage such beliefs, and they might hold, for example, that consecrated Hosts had medicinal properties. Hence, events like the following occurred:

> In *Gelderland* a priest persuaded a sicke woman that she was bewitched; and except he might sing a masse upon hir bellie, she could not be holpen. Whereunto she consented, and laie naked on the altar whilest he sange masse, to the satisfieng of his lust; but not to the release of hir greefe.[6]

A number of magical books were written specifically for the use of priests and incorporated the use of the sacraments for magical ends, as in the following:

> Aosel giver of treasure
> Acozas giver of gold & silver
> Almazin & Elicona

> By vertue of this blessed sacrifice & of ye body & blood of our Lord Jesus Xpt therin contained I command you & also any other spirit whatsoever at the calls of F[athe]r {name} which are conteyned in this booke to appeare vissibly in this glasse [crystal] in ye forme of a man."[7]

The Guibourg masses, assuming that they really happened, were probably a combination of these ideas. It was supposed by the common people that the sacraments were magical; it was supposed by the theologians that they were desecrated by witches. Guibourg would not have thought of himself as a witch, but he may have borrowed ideas from what he thought witches did, remaining at root a Catholic.[8]

According to the doctrine of apostolic succession, the making of priests and bishops is irreversible: that is, if a priest becomes sinful or even a heretic and is expelled from the church, he is still a priest and able to perform the mass. (There are even "wandering bishops" who have formed continuous schismatic lines of succession, giving rise to fringe churches whose priests are real priests in Catholic eyes.) Thus, it is often said, the Black Mass requires an unfrocked priest to celebrate it.

One might suppose that Satanists would find it difficult to get an unfrocked priest to perform Black Masses for them, since such men are rare and by no means all of them can be devoted to Devil worship. Surprisingly, what one finds is the opposite: there have been twentieth-century Catholic priests who have dedicated themselves to Lucifer, but they have lacked congregations.

The earliest Black Mass for which there is reliable evidence was conducted on Boxing Day in 1918 at Eton Road, Hampstead, by no less a person than the Reverend Montague Summers. An actor called "Anatole James" watched Summers perform "a debased form of the Roman Mass," accompanied by homosexual acts with a youth named Sullivan. Being an atheist,

James was "bored to tears." The circumstances under which Summers became a Catholic priest are obscure. His biographer considered that he might have obtained his orders abroad or from a schismatic bishop or both; but either way, according to the theory of apostolic succession, he was still capable of performing the mass and, hence, a legitimate Black Mass. He confided to a friend that he could be sexually aroused only by corrupting young Catholic men.[9]

At some point, Summers abandoned black magical practices and instead wrote the series of books for which he was most famous, denouncing all magic and witchcraft as the greatest of evils. Both his biographer and his bibliographer consider that he must have at some time received a "psychic kick-back" through dabbling unwarily. There is some slight evidence for this—one of his few attempts at fiction, *The Grimoire*, concerns a man who unwittingly calls up a devil and cannot get rid of it again.

Summers's *History of Witchcraft and Demonology* and its successors not only revived the traditional view of witchcraft as a criminal cult of Devil worship but embellished the original sources. Thus, with regard to the Black Mass, Summers wrote that the curé Jean Belon was condemned to death in 1597 "for desecration of the sacrament and the repeated celebration of abominable ceremonies." As authority for this he cited Baissac, *Les Grands Jours de la sorcellerie*;[10] but in fact, Baissac said he did not know for what charges Belon was condemned. The details Summers gave he must have invented.

"The officiant nowadays . . . cuts and stabs the Host with a knife, throwing it to the ground, treading upon it, spurning it."[11] One can only speculate whether these details likewise came from Summers's own imagination, or whether he was describing what he had formerly done himself. He made another, minor contribution to the mythology of Satanism by repeating Margiotta's story that Adrianno Lemmi had a Satanic temple in his Rome apartment—a totally false story that otherwise might have been unknown to the English-speaking world, but which has been repeated from Summers by Dennis Wheatley, Richard Cavendish, and several other Experts on Satanism.

Incidentally, Summers indicated a motive for Christians to believe in the Black Mass: "It is plain the witches are as profoundly convinced of the doctrines of Transubstantiation, the Totality, Permanence, and Adorableness of the Eucharistic Christ, and of the power also of the sacrificing priesthood, as is the most orthodox Catholic. Indeed, unless such were the case, their revolt would be empty, void at any rate of its material malice."[12] What better argument can there be for the truth of Catholic doctrines than that even the deadly enemies of the church believe them?

In the 1930s, Pierre Geyraud met a priest who told Geyraud that he had, while at Seminary, become disillusioned with the pettiness and hypocrisy of some of his superiors and found his affections insensibly turning toward Satan. Yet he did not decline to take the minor orders or, in due course, to become ordained.

When Geyraud met him, he had left the church and taken a job in commerce. Yet he continued to say the mass, since once a priest, always a priest. The difference was that he now dedicated it to Lucifer. Geyraud was permitted to watch and later printed some of it:

—*In nomine Domini Dei nostri Satanae Luciferi Excelsi. Amen.*

The Latin prayers followed, in the order of the Catholic mass, the only difference being that they were directed to the Devil rather than to God. Translated, they included:

—Receive, Lord Satan, Father and magnificent Redeemer, this immaculate host. . . .
—O Satan, you who are the glorious rebel against Adonai and his Christ, we adore you. . . .
—Deliver us from the damnable servitude of Adonai and his cursed Christ, and admit us to the rank of your elect. . . .[13]

It is unlikely, however, that priests who are also Satanists are very numerous. Twenty years ago, I have been told, one young Satanist went to study theology at a London college, with the specific intention of becoming ordained so that he would be able to perform the Black Mass. Not, perhaps, being able to take much interest in topics such as New Testament Greek and the doctrine of the Incarnation, he missed so many lectures and got so far behind in his course work that he was thrown out.

Meanwhile, however, the idea remained popular with non-Satanists. H. T. F. Rhodes's *The Satanic Mass* (1954) was able, by careful selection of material, to establish an apparent historical continuity of Black Masses stretching back to Gnostic heretics in the Dark Ages and off into prehistory. According to Rhodes and the various writers who copy from him, the Black Mass derived from the dualist religion, which placed God and Satan on a par.

The term *dualism* was coined by nineteenth-century academics to describe religions they did not understand. Persian Zoroastrianism is dualist in the sense that it admits of two primordial spirits (both created by the supreme God), Good and Evil. The Manichaeans seem to have taken this one step further and effectively believed in two gods, a god of Good and a god of Evil. This belief should be termed *dyotheism*. The word *dualism*, however, has persistently been used to mean dyotheism, and people have concluded that the Zoroastrians themselves believe in two gods. A modern Zoroastrian states firmly: "Zoroastrians do not believe in two Gods and thus are not dyotheists."[14] The Manichaeans apparently did believe in two gods, but the Zoroastrians regarded them as heretics. To accuse the Zoroastrians of believing in two gods is on par with confusing the Protestant and Roman churches and saying that the fundamental Catholic heresy is their denial of the existence of purgatory.

The word *dualist* implies a belief that good and evil are equally powerful, and some people take it to mean just that. There is an old story of a Catholic woman who was lighting a candle before a statue in church, when the priest came up and pointed out that the statue was of Beelzebub. "But Father," she pointed out, "isn't it good to have friends on both sides?" Aside from this, there is no real evidence that anyone has ever held that God and Satan are equal or to be treated the same way. In any case, *dualism* is a word that no group applies to themselves, only to other creeds they disapprove of.

This nonreligion was, however, believed by Lamothe-Langone to have existed among the Cathars, and he accordingly put a dualist confession into the mouths of the nonexistent witches Anne-Marie Georgel and Catherine Delort. Rhodes jumped from this to assuming that their religion must have had some sort of Black Mass as its central ritual, ignoring the fact that the Black Mass was not heard of until 250 years after the supposed date of Georgel and Delort's trials (quite apart from the fact that they never existed anyway).

In the case of Jean Bosdeau, who may be said to be the true inventor of the Satanic Mass, Rhodes suggests that "the goat was no supernatural and infernal appearance but a human being beneath a goat's skin." The Parliament of Bordeaux, who certainly believed in the unseen world—ten years later they sentenced Jean Grenier to life imprisonment for being a werewolf—might have supposed that a man dressed as a goat was really the Devil, but equally, they might have accepted a totally false story if it confirmed their prejudices.

The medieval heretics whose rituals were supposed to be the ancestors of the Black Mass were rather different from what Rhodes suggested. He points out that the Bogomils were called "the Children of Satanael," failing to notice that this was an insulting term fixed on them by their enemies in the Orthodox Church. They themselves accused the Orthodox Church of being "filled with demons."[15] If the balance of religious power had chanced to go differently, then modern historians would be writing that the Orthodox Church was a demon-worshiping order. In short, Rhodes derived a nonexistent rite from a nonexistent theology.

Since this book had an air of historical objectivity, the Satanic Mass took on a kind of reality. Seven years later, Daniel Mannix wrote that Sir Francis Dashwood's rituals (of which, in fact, nothing is known) "followed the general lines of the traditional Black Mass." In the same spirit, Francis King's glossy coffee table book *Witchcraft and Demonology* (1987) included a nineteenth-century engraving of a naked woman lying on her front on an altar, with the Devil at one end overseeing the proceedings while a mitred figure performed a rite with a chalice on her bottom; King's caption commented that "more conventionally" the woman lay face upward.[16] He omitted to say whether or not it was conventional for the Devil to be present in person at the Black Mass.

(While I was working on the final draft of this book, a woman informed me that she was in contact with "traditional Satanists" via the Internet. When I queried this, she admitted that she could not say how traditional Satanism might differ from nontraditional Satanism, Reformed Satanism, or whatever.)

So what happens in the "traditional Black Mass"? Jeremy Kingston insists, "The Black Mass is always said on the naked body of a woman, preferably a virgin."[17] As if to prove it, this statement is accompanied by a photograph of a naked woman.

Likewise, according to Julian Franklyn: "The first requirement in the celebration of the Black Mass is a virgin, naked, spread-eagled on the 'altar' and the climax is reached when the officiating priest performs the sexual act with her."[18] If this is true, then it is unlikely that the Black Mass is often performed. Virgins, it is said, are hard to find; virgins willing to take their clothes off and have a Black Mass said over them must be *rarissime*. And if one could be procured, then, since the ceremony involves her defloration, the search would have to be made all over again before the Black Mass could be done a second time!

It is hard to see why a naked virgin on the altar was thought, by the 1970s, to be part of the tradition of the Black Mass. The Black Masses witnessed by James and Geyraud did not feature women at all. In the legendary mass of Saint Secaire, the woman is not naked, or on the altar, or a virgin; neither are those in Huysmans's fictional Satanic Mass. The Guibourg masses had Madame de Montespan naked on the altar, and Maria de Naglowska herself formed the naked altar in her Mass of Gold; these women, however, were anything but virgins. In fact, the naked virgin was a new development: the only source one can imagine is that some of the classic grimoires insist on the use of virgin parchment. This has nothing to do with human females, of course, but clearly, many anti-Satanist writers are unable to see or hear the word *virgin* without thinking of a naked woman.

When Anton Szandor LaVey wrote his own Black Mass, he did not think it necessary for the celebrant to be ordained, no doubt because he had no faith in the Catholic apostolic succession to confer miraculous power anyway. But he was influenced by Huysmans's *Là-Bas* to the extent of making the prayer of Canon Docre the centerpiece of his own rite, which he called Le Messe Noir. It also featured "holy water" made by a "nun" urinating in a font, a detail perhaps derived from the original Jean Bosdeau account of the Black Mass.

Aubrey Melech (a.k.a. Bernard King) suggested that LaVey's Black Mass could not be authentic, as the word *Messe* (mass) is feminine, so it should have been called *La* Messe *Noire*. Melch/King then perpetrated the same kind of mistake himself, calling his own version—which was fairly similar to LaVey's and included the same prayer from *Là-Bas*—Missa Niger, which should, of course, have been Missa *Nigra*.

The Black Mass has not occurred so much in stories about ritual abuse. This may be because these allegations by and large originate with Evangelical Protestants, for whom the mass is nothing but popery. Since Catholic ceremonial is, in strict Protestant belief, a type of Satanism in itself, they would see no reason for Satanists to parody it.

The general idea of a Black Mass is so appealing, however, that there can be little doubt that nowadays it does happen, on a small scale commensurate with the actual number of Satanists. One group in a wealthy district of London is said to perform it regularly. The celebrant has never been a Catholic priest, but since those concerned do not believe in transubstantiation anyway, this does not matter. A typical recent example, on Halloween 1996, commenced with a form of Mass said on the belly of a naked woman and ended with group sex. My informant, being a married man, discreetly left at this point. Thus, the end result of the exposure of nonexistent Black Rites is that they have come to occur in reality.

These ceremonies are not normally open to the public. I was able to attend a memorial Black Mass for Anton LaVey, however, that was held in a

London nightclub on 23 April 1998. (Probably this was the nearest date to May Eve for which the organizers were able to hire the venue.) As punters entered, they were greeted by a cute girl in a black robe who cried, "Hail Satan!" as they passed her. The Black Mass itself was held on a stage that was not really large enough. A naked woman, who I strongly suspect was not a virgin, lay on a table to form the altar. A man in a black and red leather harlequin outfit opened the ritual by intoning one of the Enochian keys. Two women, one in a black dress, the other clad in red rubber, read out parts of LaVey's own *Messe Noir*. Then the woman in black took a Host—I wonder how many of the audience even knew what it was?—which she rubbed into the vagina of the altar-woman before she dropped it on the floor and trod on it. Black-robed worshipers in the front row—there wasn't room for them on the stage—shouted, "Hail Satan!" wherever appropriate. At the climax, a man walked on dressed as Santa Claus and passed around a ceremonial drinking horn. Presumably, he represented his anagrammatic counterpart, but it is curious that Santas are associated with Satan worship by Satanists and anti-Satanists alike. No orgy ensued.

Since someone is sure to ask: no, there were no blood sacrifices or other illegal acts; no, there were no children present—nightclubs do not admit anyone under eighteen—and no, Lucifer did not materialize in person at the center of the stage.

Notes

As per standard British usage, only titles and dates are given for contemporary accounts in newspapers.

NOTES TO THE INTRODUCTION

Translations of passages from foreign works are by the author unless otherwise indicated.

1. Boguet, *Discours des Sorciers*, chap. 1.

2. Boguet, *Discours des Sorciers*, chaps. 2 and 3.

3. Boguet, *Discours des Sorciers*, chap. 5.

4. Black, *Orkney: A Place of Safety?* p. 27.

5. Black, *Orkney: A Place of Safety?* pp. 27–28.

6. Black, *Orkney: A Place of Safety?* chap. 1.

7. Ludovico Maria Sinistrari, *De delictis, et poenis*; these are the chapter headings of Titulus IV, "De delictis contra castitatem."

8. Boguet, *Discours des Sorciers* (1610), chap. 21; (1970), chap. 20.

9. Del Rio, *Disquisitionum Magicarum*, bk.2, q. 16. Caro Baroja, *World of the Witches*, p. 120, has "two children" for "their own children"; he must have been misled by the obvious misprint of *duos* for *suos* in the 1616 Venice edition.

NOTES TO CHAPTER 1

1. Taxil, *Confessions d'un ex–libre–penseur*, pp. 237–38, 251–53. On pp. 364–65, he dates his conversion to 23 April 1885. There is a convenient summary of this book in Rhodes, *The Satanic Mass*, chap. 23.

2. Taxil's reception by Leo XIII is mentioned in a letter to the pontiff prefixed to his *Les Conversions célèbres*.

3. Taxil, *Révélations complètes sur la Franc–Maçonnerie: Les Frères trois–points*, vol. 2, pp. 109–11.

4. Taxil, *Y–a–t–il des femmes dans la Franc–Maçonnerie?* p. 264.

5. *L'Existence des loges de femmes*, not seen. It is discussed in F. Legge, "Devil Worship and Freemsasonry," *Contemporary Review* (October 1896), and Waite,

Devil-Worship in France, pp. 77–81, both of whom comment on the similarity of Ricoux's style to that of Taxil. Extracts are given in Meurin, *Lu Franc–Maçonnerie synagogue de Satan*, pp. 209–10, 215–16, 433–34, 450, 456–59.

6. English translation in Lady Queenborough, *Occult Theocrasy*, p. 220.

7. Translated by Mark McCann, *Talking Stick Magickal Journal* 2, 2 (1999): p. 186.

8. English translation in Lady Queenborough, *Occult Theocrasy*, p. 220.

9. Dr. Bataille [pseud.], *Le Diable*, vol. 1, pp. 7–20.

10. Dr. Bataille [pseud.], *Le Diable*, vol. 1, pp. 115–55.

11. Dr. Bataille [pseud.], *Le Diable*, vol. 1, p. 224.

12. Dr. Bataille [pseud.], *Le Diable*, vol. 1, chap. 17.

13. Dr. Bataille [pseud.], *Le Diable*, vol. 1, chap. 15.

14. Taxil wrote a book, *Monsieur Drumont: Étude psychologique*, attacking an anti–Semitic contemporary.

15. See Cohn, *Warrant for Genocide*, particularly chap. 3.

16. Lillie, *The Worship of Satan in Modern France*, pp. xviii–xxi. Only the preface to this book actually deals with the worship of Satan in contemporary France, the rest being a reprint of Lillie's *Modern Mystics and Modern Magic*.

17. Margiotta, *Adriano Lemmi*, p. 336.

18. *La Palladium régénéré et libre*, which can have had only a small circulation, is described by Henry Charles Lea, "An Anti–Masonic Mystification," *Lippincott's Monthly Magazine* (December 1900): 955.

19. Vaughan [pseud.], *Mémoires d'un ex–Palladiste*, pp. 18–29, 33–48, 109–10.

20. Comte C. H., *Mémoire à l'adresse des membres du Congrès antimaçonnique de Trente*, pp. 34, 20–22.

21. Waite, *Devil–Worship in France*, passim. *Blackwood*'s story in Meurin, *La Franc–Maçonnerie synagogue de Satan*, pp. 218–24. Vaughan [pseud.], *Mémoires d'un ex–Palladiste*, pp. 420–2. In fact, Waite was not then a Freemason, though he became one in 1901 and wrote a number of works on Masonry. See R. A. Gilbert, *A. E. Waite* (London: Crucible, 1987), chap. 14.

22. *Verité*, 6 November 1896, quoted in Godré, *Diana Vaughan et ses répondants*, pp. 41–2.

23. Abridged from Fry, *Léo Taxil et la Franc–Maçonnerie*, pp. 145–47, 153–56. Fry reprinted the whole confession from *Le Frondeur*, 25 April 1897.

24. A Toulouse priest who was present, "L'Abbé de la Tour de Noé," responded with a pamphlet, *La Vérité sur Miss Diana Vaughan*, arguing that it was Taxil's confession that was fraudulent.

25. Bourre, *Les Sectes Lucifériennes*, p. 86.

26. Mariel, *Dictionnaire*, s.v. "Naglowska."

27. Geyraud, *Les Petites Églises*, pp. 148–53.

28. The authorized biography is Blanche Barton, *The Secret Life of a Satanist*,

which contains a detailed bibliography. The sketch in Burton H. Wolfe's introduction to LaVey's *Satanic Bible* gives an adequate picture.

29. Temple of Set, "General Information and Admissions Policy" (1996), P.O. Box 470307, San Francisco, California 94147.

30. Graham Harvey, "Satanism in Britain Today," *Journal of Contemporary Religion* 10, 3 (1995): pp. 283–96.

31. Long, *Diablerie*, n.p.

32. Copy in author's possession.

33. de Guiata, *La Clef de la magie noire*, vol. 2 of *Le Serpent de la Genèse*, which is part 2 of *Essais de sciences maudites*, 1897, p. 397; Bessy, *Pictorial History of Magic and the Supernatural*, p. 198.

34. E.g., Boyd, *Blasphemous Rumours*, p. 144. Others supplement the list with additions of unknown origin, e.g., Sakheim and Devine, *Out of Darkness*, p. 37, which includes dates such as 1 July, "Demon Revels."

35. Wheatley, *Satanism and Witches*, p. 138.

36. However, it was occasionally used much earlier, e.g., "the unlawful Art of *Black Magic*," in Hale, *Collection of Modern Relations*, p. 10.

37. Cigogna, *Magiæ Omnifariæ*, p. 459.

38. Gillett, *The Occult*, p. 22.

39. Good historical surveys of the genre are Butler, *Ritual Magic*, and McIntosh, *The Devil's Bookshelf*.

40. Crowley, *The Goetia*, p. 18.

41. *Key of Solomon*, London: S. L. MacGregor Mathers, edition, 1888, p. 119.

42. Recently, books on Enochian have proliferated. In terms of fidelity to Dee's originals, the best are by Robert Turner: *The Heptarchia Mystica* (London: Aquarian, 1986) and *Elizabethan Magic* (London: Element, 1989).

43. When I showed this passage to Kitty, she denied wearing an anorak, saying, "This is a country jacket"—though it looked like an anorak. She had no other objection to my description of her.

44. The word translated here as "unguent–jar," *bouëtte*, is obscure and omitted from most dictionaries; however, Randle Cotgrave's *Dictionarie of the French and English Tongues* (1611; reprint, Columbia: University of South Carolina Press, 1968) has "Bouëtte: f. A little box," and Bodin describes how a woman "print vne bouëtte & s'oignit, puis auec quelques paroles elle fut transportee" (*De la démonomanie*, bk. 2, chap. 4, f. 81ᵛ), which makes it clear that it referred to a container of flying ointment.

45. Perreaud, *Demonologie*, pp. 110–112.

46. Perreaud, *Demonologie*, pp. 107–8.

47. Kramer and Sprenger, *Malleus Maleficarum*, Speyer, 1487, part 2, q. 1, chap. 4.

48. Boguet, *Discours des sorciers*, chap. 18, 1610 ed.; chap. 17, Montague Summers ed.

NOTES TO CHAPTER 2

1. *Apology for M. Antonia Bourignon*, p. 264. The biographical part of that book is based on Bourignon's own books of reminiscences, *La Parole de Dieu* and *La Vie exterieure*.

2. *Apology*, pp. 264–65.

3. *Apology*, p. 270.

4. *Apology*, pp. 281–82.

5. *Apology*, pp. 282–83.

6. *Apology*, p. 284.

7. Hale, *Collection of Modern Relations of Matters of Fact*, p. 23. This section of Hale's book is also based on Bourignon's own memoirs.

8. *Apology*, pp. 285–86.

9. *Apology*, p. 287.

10. *Apology*, p. 288.

11. *Apology*, pp. 288–89.

12. Hale, *Collection of Modern Relations of Matters of Fact*, p. 35.

13. Quoted by Coulange, *Life of the Devil*, pp. 158–59.

14. Quoted by Robbins, *Encyclopedia*, p. 316; and Huxley, *Devils of Loudun*, p. 188.

15. Aubin, *Cheats and Illusions*, pp. 4, 20–21.

16. *Confessions of Madeleine Bavent*, pp. 1–2.

17. *Confessions of Madeleine Bavent*, p. 7.

18. *Confessions of Madeleine Bavent*, p. 7.

19. *Confessions of Madeleine Bavent*, pp. 27–28.

20. *Confessions of Madeleine Bavent*, p. 37.

21. *Confessions of Madeleine Bavent*, pp. 38–40.

22. *Confessions of Madeleine Bavent*, p. 49.

23. *Confessions of Madeleine Bavent*, p. 52.

24. *Confessions of Madeleine Bavent*, pp. 50–51.

25. *Confessions of Madeleine Bavent*, p. 60.

26. See Robbins, *Encyclopedia*, s.v. "Louviers Nuns." Contemporary discussions of the case include Esprit de Bosroger, *La Pieté affligée*; Delangle, *Procez verbal*; and Le Gauffre, *Recit veritable*.

27. Crowley, *World's Tragedy*, pp. xi–xii, the relevant section reprinted in his *Confessions*, pp. 63–66, and in his *Crowley on Christ*, pp. 132–38.

28. Crowley, *Confessions*, p. 54.

29. Crowley, *Confessions*, p. 67.

30. Crowley, *Confessions*, p. 67.

31. In fact, the sin against the Holy Ghost seems to have referred to the alleged blasphemy of the Pharisees in declaring that Jesus cast out devils by the aid of Beelzebub—an easy enough sin to imitate.

32. Crowley, *Confessions*, p. 68.

33. Crowley, *Confessions*, p. 58.

34. Crowley, *Confessions*, pp. 124–26.

35. *The Times*, 18 February 1986.

36. *The Times*, 18 February 1986; *Brighton Evening Argus*, 18 February 1986.

37. *Telegraph*, 18 February 1986; *The Guardian*, 20 February 1986.

38. *The Times*, 26 April 1986.

39. *Brighton Evening Argus*, 19 February 1986; *Daily Mail*, 20 February 1986.

40. *The Times*, 20 February 1986.

41. *Brighton Evening Argus*, 24 February 1986; *The Times*, 25 February 1986; *Daily Mail*, 25 February 1986.

42. *The Times*, 26 April 1986.

43. *The Times*, 19 February 1986.

44. *The Times*, 1 March 1986.

45. *The Guardian*, 26 April 1986.

46. *The Times*, 4 March 1986.

47. *Daily Express* 19 February 1986.

48. *The Times*, 26 April 1986.

49. *Brighton Evening Argus*, 21 March 1986; *The Times*,22 March 1986; *Daily Mail*, 22 March 1986.

50. *The Times*, 20 February 1986; *Telegraph*, 20 February 1986.

51. *The Times*, 26 February 1986.

52. *The Times*, 25 February 1986.

53. *Brighton Evening Argus*, 17 March 1986; *The Times*, 18 March 1986.

54. *The Times*, 27 February 1986.

55. *The Times*, 27 March 1986.

56. *The Times*, 26 April 1986.

57. *The Times*, 10 April 1986.

58. *The Times*, 19 April 1986.

59. *Brighton Evening Argus*, 25 April 1986; all the British daily papers carried stories on the outcome on 26 April 1986. The case is also described in McConnell, *The Possessed*, pp. 183–87. Also, the anonymous "Mother's Story" in Logan, *Paganism and the Occult*, chap. 8, exactly corresponds to the Knight affair.

60. *The Times*, 26 April 1986.

61. E.g., Logan, *Satanism and the Occult*, pp. 36, 173.

NOTES TO CHAPTER 3

1. D. Winton Thomas, *Documents from Old Testament Times* (New York: Harper & Row, 1961) pp. 97–103; James B. Pritchard, *Ancient Near Eastern Texts* (Princeton: Princeton University Press, 1955), pp. 438–40.

2. The doctrine is stated in briefly in the Gathas, the oldest portion of the

Zend Avesta, *Yasna* 30:3–6. See William W. Malandra, *An Introduction to Ancient Iranian Religion* (Minneapolis: University of Minnesota Press, 1983), pp. 19–20, 39–40; and Farhang Mehr, *The Zoroastrian Tradition* (London: Element Books, 1991), pp. 71–89.

3. Rabbi Dr. Victor E. Eichert, commentary to *Job*, Soncino Books of the Bible (Hindhead, Surrey: Soncino Press, 1946), pp. 2–3.

4. *The Book of Enoch*, trans. by R. H. Charles (London: Society for Promoting Christian Knowledge, 1982), particularly chaps. 6–8.

5. Massadié, *History of the Devil*, p. 5.

6. Gobey, *Terminology for the Devil*, p. 13.

7. Pritchard, *Ancient Near Eastern Texts*, p. 140.

8. E.g., Davidson, *Dictionary of Angels*, s.v. "Lucifer."

9. Origen, *On First Principles*, trans. by G. W. Butterworth (London: Society for Promoting of Christian Knowledge, 1936), bk. 1, chap. 5, 5, pp. 49–50.

10. Jerome, *Letters*, vol. 1, Ancient Christian Writers 33 (London: Longmans, 1963), letter 15 (p. 70).

11. Most books ignore the question of how Lucifer became identified with Satan; the suggestion made here is only a hypothesis.

12. See, e.g., Davidson, *Dictionary of Angels*, s.v. "Asmodeus"; for Beelzebub, see almost any Bible dictionary.

13. Thomas Aquinas, *Summa Theologica*, part 1, q. 51, art. 3, ad. 6.

14. Sinistrari, *Demoniality*, particularly secs. 30–34.

15. *Lyf of saint jerom*, sig. Ciii^v–Cvi^v.

16. Talmud, *Pesachim*, 111b, 112b.

17. The figure 399,920,004 is derived from assuming nine orders of angels, each of 6,666 legions of 6,666 angels each. It is quoted by several medieval theologians. Davidson, *Dictionary of Angels*, s.v. "Fallen Angels," attributes the original calculation to the cardinal–bishop of Tusculum in 1273, presumably Peter of Spain (later Pope John XXI), who took this post in 1273. The figure, however, is not to be found in Peter's *Commentary on the Pseudo–Dionysus* (Pedro Hispani, *Exposiçao sobre os livros do beato Dionisio Areopagitica*, ed. P. Manuel Alonso [Lisbon 1957]), where one might expect it; in fact he says only that the angels are "innumerable" (p. 102.) The figure 7,405,926 is 1,111 times 6,666; 2,665,866,746,664 is 399,920,004 again multiplied by 6,666, but who made this latter calculation is, again, unclear. Several writers, notably Roskoff, *Geschichte des Teufels*, p. 380, attribute it to Martin Borrhaus, in Feyerabend, ed., *Theatrum Diabolorum*, but this is totally wrong: on the contrary, Borrhaus there says it is a "great temerity" for mortals to attempt to number the angels, knowledge belonging to God alone (f. XVI^v).

18. Defoe, *The Political History of the Devil*, p. 87 (bk. 1 chap. 7, but chap. 6 in some editions).

19. *Essay on The Devil*, p. 4. *Shorim* would be better transliterated as *seirim*.

20. Graf, *Story of the Devil*, pp. 265, v.

21. Lyons, *Satan Wants You*, rev. ed., pp. xiii–xiv.

22. The obscurity surrounding the origin of the idea of pacts with the Devil is not illuminated by Rudwin, *Devil in Legend and Literature*, pp. 169–70, who says: "This notion of a bargain with Beelzebub . . . is traceable as far back as the Persian sacred writings," specifying that in the *Shah–Nameh* of Firdusi (medieval but based on much older legends) Zohak makes a pact with Iblis (Satan). This is untrue—Iblis helps Zohak gain the throne, in the knowledge that Zohak will turn out to be a tyrant, but there is nothing in the nature of a pact; see *Shah–Namah*, translated into English by Arthur George Warner and Edmond Warner, vol.1 (London: Kegan Paul, 1905, pp. 135–37)—yet this statement is repeated by other writers who have presumably read Rudwin but not Firdusi. Rudwin goes on: "This Persian belief in a devil–compact forced its way into the religions of the Jews during the period of their Babylonian captivity under Zoroastrian rulers, and was transmitted by the Jews to the Christians. The devil–compact is clearly mentioned in the Book of Enoch, the Talmud and the Kabbala and is besides evident from a number of biblical passages. . . . St. Augustine treats the notion at great length. St. Basil . . . tells us in his *Dialogues* of a compact which his own servant Proterius closed with the Fiend." As far as I can discover, not one of these statements is true, though it would be impractical to go through all of the literature of the Kabbalah in search of a doctrine that is probably not there.

23. Augustine, *De Doctrina Christiana*, bk. 2 chap. 23.

24. Voragine, *Legenda Aurea*, f. liii.

25. Voragine, *Legenda Aurea*, f. clx.

26. *A True and Faithful Narrative of Oliver Cromwell's Compact with the Devil for Seven Years*, pp. 3–7.

27. These sources and others quoted in the Rose edition of *History of . . . Doctor John Faustus*, pp. 6–7.

28. Palmer and More, *Sources of the Faust Tradition*, pp. 99–101.

29. Defoe, *Political History of the Devil*, bk. 2, chap. 11.

30. John Aubrey, *Brief Lives*, ed. by Richard Barber (London: Boydell Press, 1993), p. 17.

31. *History of . . . Doctor John Faustus*, chap. 2 (p. 68, Rose ed.).

32. Boulton, *Compleat History of Magick, Sorcery and Witchcraft*, vol. 1, p. 7.

33. Del Rio, *Disquisitionum magicarum*, bk. 2, chap. 4. This section first appeared in the expanded 1603 edition.

34. Filmer, *Advertisement to the Jury–Men of England, Touching Witches*, p. 6.

35. The eleven–stage pact in Guazzo, *Compendium maleficarum*, bk. 1, chap.6. Del Rio's book was popular with plagiarists: Philip Ludwig Elich's *Daemonomagia, siue de daemonis cacurgi* (Frankfurt, 1607) is likewise, for the most part, copied straight from the *Disquisitionum magicarum*.

36. Robbins, *Encyclopedia of Witchcraft*, s.v. "Pact with the Devil."

37. *A Strange and Wonderful, (Yet True) RELATION Of the Cursed and Hellish*

Design of Abraham Mason, a Pretended Quaker, to give himself to the Devil, with the manner how he would have done it; and how strangely he was prevented, a broadsheet (ca. 1700).

38. Haining, *Anatomy of Witchcraft*, p. 64 (page references are to the 1974 ed.).

39. Sparks, *Jay's Journal*, particularly pp. 34, 77, 147.

40. Sparks, *Jay's Journal*, pp. 148–49.

41. Sparks, *Jay's Journal*, pp. 157, 161, 176.

42. Sparks, *Jay's Journal*, pp. 155–56.

NOTES TO CHAPTER 4

1. In Sinason, ed. *Treating Survivors of Satanist Abuse*, chap. 5.

2. Lamothe–Langone, *Histoire*, vol. 3, pp. 235–40.

3. The forgery is exposed by Cohn, *Europe's Inner Demons*, chap. 7.

4. Cohn, *Europe's Inner Demons*, pp. 180–82.

5. The trial documents published by Bossard, *Gilles de Rais*; in French by Bataille, *Le Procès de Gilles de Rais*; in English by Hyatte, *Laughter for the Devil*.

6. Hyatte, *Laughter for the Devil*, pp. 59, 61; Summers, *Geography of Witchcraft*, p. 395.

7. Robbins, *Encyclopedia of Witchcraft and Demonology*, p. 404.

8. Summers, *Geography of Witchcraft*, p. 394, euphemistically says he was at this point cast "out of the bosom mercy of Mother Church," which is Summers's way of saying that merciful Mother Church permitted him to be tortured.

9. Hyatte, *Laughter for the Devil*, p. 55.

10. Depositions made 18 and 27–30 September 1440, in Hyatte, *Laughter for the Devil*, pp. 129–50.

11. Logan, *Satanism and the Occult*, p. 127.

12. Rhodes, *Satanic Mass*, pp. 53–54; also Ahmed, *Black Art*, part 2, chap. 4.

13. Lyons, *Satan Wants You*, chap. 3.

14. Zacharias, *Satanic Cult*, chap. 5.

15. de Lancré, *Tableau*, various passages; also the famous engraving by Spranger, which illustrated all these things.

16. Michelet, *Satanism and Witchcraft*, p. 84.

17. de Lancré, *Tableau*, p. 148.

18. de Lancré, *Tableau*, p. 137; Michelet, *Satanism and Witchcraft*, p. 86.

19. King, *Sexuality, Magic and Perversion*, pp. 65–66; general discussion of the affair in Johnson, *Age of Arsenic*.

20. Ravaisson, *Archives de la Bastille*, vol. 6, pp. 335–37.

21. Maple, *Domain of Devils*, p. 167.

22. Tate, *Children for the Devil*, p. 84.

23. Raschke, *Painted Black*, p. 84.

24. Boyd, *Blasphemous Rumours*, p. 166.

25. Cawthorne, *Satanic Murder*, p. 21.

26. *Hell–Fire Club*, p. 19. This pamphlet also reproduced the king's edict.

27. Horace Walpole, *Journal of Visits to Country Seats* (Oxford: Walpole Society, 1928), pp. 50–51.

28. Towers, *Dashwood*, p. 148.

29. Rabelais, *Gargantua* (London: Everyman's Library, 1932), chap. 57.

30. Johnstone, *Chrysal*, vol. 3, bk. 2, chap. 17, pp. 240–42.

31. Johnstone, *Chrysal*, vol. 2, bk. 1, chap. 23.

32. Dashwood, *Dashwoods of West Wycombe*, p. 42.

33. Ward, *Secret History of Clubs*, pp. 68–78.

34. *Nocturnal Revels*, sig. A4ᵛ–A7ᵛ.

35. Charles Churchill, *Poems* (London, 1764), p. 33.

36. Thompson, "Life of Paul Whitehead," xxxviii.

37. Dashwood, *Abridgement of the Book of Common Prayer*, pp. iii–iv.

38. Dashwood, *Abridgement of the Book of Common Prayer*, pp. v–vi.

39. Kemp, *Sir Francis Dashwood*, p. 148.

40. Fuller, *Hell–Fire Francis*, p. 89.

41. Mannix, *The Hell–Fire Club*, p. 27.

42. Maple, *Domain of Devils*, p. 167; Maple, *Witchcraft*, p. 94.

43. Ebon, *World's Weirdest Cults*, p. 169.

44. Summers, *History of Witchcraft and Demonology*, p. 136.

45. Collin de Plancy, *Dictionnaire infernal*, p. 553. Presumably Summers did not give his source because it was so obviously silly.

46. Bladé, *Contes populaires de la Gascogne*, vol. 2, pp. 246–50.

47. Summers, *History of Witchcraft and Demonology*, pp. 156–57; Ahmed, *Black Art*, pp. 257–58; Franklyn, *Survey of the Occult*, p. 79; Haining, *Anatomy of Witchcraft*, p. 125; Rhodes, *Satanic Mass*, pp. 61–62; Kahaner, *Cults That Kill*, pp. 54–55.

48. Abridged from Huysmans, *Là–Bas*, pp. 369–78 (chap. 19).

49. Haining, *Anatomy of Witchcraft*, pp. 133–34.

50. Baldick, *Life of J–K Huysmans*, pp. 160–61.

51. Baldick, *Life of J–K Huysmans*, pp. 154–55.

52. E.g., Cassiel [pseud.], *Encyclopedia of Forbidden Knowledge*, p. 56. The story seems to have first appeared in Bricaud's 1913 *J.–K. Huysmans et le Satanisme*, pp. 74–76, twenty years after Boullan's death and half a century after the alleged event.

53. P. Bruno de Jesus-Marie and Jean Vinchon, "The Confession of Boullan," in *Satan*, p. 265.

54. Haining, *Anatomy of Witchcraft*, p. 126.

55. Baldick, *Life of J–K Huysmans*, p. 156.

56. Baldick, *Life of J–K Huysmans*, p. 156; also Laver, *First Decadent*, pp. 135–38; King, *Sexuality, Magic, and Perversion*, pp. 155–58.

57. King, *Sexuality, Magic, and Perversion*, pp. 158–59.

58. Baldick, *Life of J–K Huysmans*, pp. 157–58.

59. Many were published in Bois, *Le Satanisme*. One, which was supposed to have happened in the thirteenth century, is translated in Rhodes, *Satanic Mass*, pp. 172–73, part of which is reproduced by Raschke, *Painted Black*, pp. 90–91, with the odd assertion that Bois had himself "witnessed" it.

60. Baldick, *Life of J–K Huysmans*, p. 163.

61. Baldick, *Life of J–K Huysmans*, p. 149.

62. Laver, *First Decadent*, p. 141.

63. Laver, *First Decadent*, pp. 142–43.

64. Baldick, *Life of J–K Huysmans*, pp. 149–50.

65. Baldick, *Life of J–K Huysmans*, p. 150.

66. Baldick, *Life of J–K Huysmans*, p. 150, also p. 138.

67. Baldick, *Life of J–K Huysmans*, pp. 151, 211.

68. Baldick, *Life of J–K Huysmans*, p. 151.

69. Black, *The Satanists*, p. 7.

70. Torburn [pseud.], *Satan Sado-Cultist*.

71. Summers, *History of Witchcraft and Demonology*, p. 152; Lyons, *Satan Wants You* (1972 ed.), p. 72; Wheatley, *The Devil Rides Out*, p. 27.

72. Fry, *Léo Taxil et la Franc–Maçonnerie*, p. 159.

73. Tate, *Children for the Devil*, p. 76 and note 9 on p. 360.

74. Melech [pseud.], *Missa Niger*.

NOTES TO CHAPTER 5

1. Symonds, *King of the Shadow Realms*, pp. 498–99.

2. Barton, *Secret Life of a Satanist*, p. 198.

3. Linedecker, *Hell Ranch*, pp. 61–62; Provost, *Across the Border*, pp. 59–60, 71–73.

4. Linedecker, *Hell Ranch*, pp. 62–63; Pulling, *Devil's Web*, chap. 1.

5. Provost, *Across the Border*, pp. 23–58; Linedecker, *Hell Ranch*, pp. 1–17.

6. Provost, *Across the Border*, pp. 83–86.

7. Provost, *Across the Border*, pp. 219–24; Linedecker, *Hell Ranch*, pp. 135–38.

8. Linedecker, *Hell Ranch*, pp. 44–49.

9. Linedecker, *Hell Ranch*, p. 49.

10. Provost, *Across the Border*, chap. 5; Linedecker, *Hell Ranch*, chaps. 3, 6.

11. Hicks, *In Pursuit of Satan*, p. 79.

12. Sanders, *The Family*, p. 34 (page references to the Panther ed. throughout).

13. Sanders, *The Family*, pp. 37–38.

14. Bugliosi, *Helter Skelter*, pp. 184–98.

15. Sanders, *The Family*, p. 32.

16. Atkins, *Child of Satan, Child of God*, p. 90.

17. Sanders, *The Family*, pp. 166–72; Bugliosi, *Helter Skelter*, pp. 122–23, 139–42, 380–81.

18. Sanders, *The Family*, pp. 201–3, 211–13.

19. Manson's prosecutor Bugliosi stated flatly that the "copycat" motive "wasn't true" (*Helter Skelter*, p. 573), but he was obliged to take this stance because of the progress of the court case: the defendants had tried to get Manson let off by claiming that Family member Linda Kasabian, who had become the chief prosecution witness, had herself masterminded the murders. Though this was ridiculous, the suggested motive was not; after her repentance (she was "born again" in her prison cell), Susan Atkins wrote that "to the best of my understanding, the copycat plan was the primary motive" (*Child of Satan, Child of God*, p. 134). Of course, Manson had already become set on mass murder, and in any case, no one can be sure of the precise motivations behind psychopathic atrocities.

20. Sanders, *The Family*, chap. 16.

21. Sanders, *The Family*, chap. 18.

22. Sanders, *The Family*, pp. 288–93.

23. Sanders, *The Family*, pp. 318–24.

24. E.g., *The Sun*, 3 December 1969.

25. *News of the World*, 7 December 1969; *People*, 7 December 1969.

26. Taylor, *Satan's Slaves*, with a preface dated December 1969, only shortly after the Manson gang were charged and well before their trial. A French book on the murders, Demaix, *Les Esclaves du diable* (1970), was evidently based on the same mistake.

27. E.g., Newton, *Raising Hell*, pp. 298–99.

28. Bugliosi, *Helter Skelter*, p. 635.

29. Bainbridge, *Satan's Power*, p. 120.

30. Carlson and Larue, *Satanism in America*, p. 97.

31. Sanders, *The Family*, p. 129; King, *Sexuality, Magic and Perversion*, p. 138, where he refers to the group as the Lunar Lodge.

32. Sanders, *The Family*, p. 130.

33. Sanders, *The Family*, pp. 129–30.

34. Sanders, *The Family*, pp. 132–33; Tate, *Children for the Devil*, pp. 132–35; Lyons, *Satan Wants You* (1988 ed.), p. 94.

35. Randall Sullivan, "The Billionaire Boys Club," *Tatler*, February 1986.

36. David Shub, *Lenin* (London: Pelican, 1966), pp. 23–25.

37. *Pornography: The Longford Report* (London: Coronet, 1972), p. 69.

38. St. Clair, *Say You Love Satan*, pp. 14, 315, 328–29.

39. St. Clair, *Say You Love Satan*, pp. 197–207.

40. St. Clair, *Say You Love Satan*, pp. 189–90, 193–96, 208.

41. St. Clair, *Say You Love Satan*, pp. 228–45.

42. St. Clair, *Say You Love Satan*, pp. 255–78, 322, 405.

43. *New York Times*, 23 November 1990.

44. Lane, *Encyclopedia of Occult and Supernatural Murder*, p. 121; Newton, *Raising Hell*, pp. 137–38.

45. Lane, *Encyclopedia of Occult and Supernatural Murder*, pp. 48–50.

46. Lane, *Encyclopedia of Occult and Supernatural Murder*, p. 106.

47. Blood, *New Satanists*, p. 82.

48. Newton, *Raising Hell*, p. 125.

49. McConnell, *The Possessed*, chap. 14.

50. Logan, *Satanism and the Occult*, p. 25, quoting *Today*.

51. Logan, *America Bewitched*, p. 156.

52. Terry, *Ultimate Evil*, p. 201.

53. Terry, *Ultimate Evil*, chaps. 16–18.

54. Terry, *Ultimate Evil*, chap. 9.

55. Pulling, *Devil's Web*, p. 47, quoting *Casper State Tribune*, 12 February 1987.

56. "Kids 'Link' to Coven," *The Star*, 6 February 1990.

57. "Animal Sacrifice Scares," *Pagan News*, 36, p. 3.

58. *The Guardian*, 17 December 1998; other articles in *Independent on Sunday*, 22 November 1998; *The Independent*, 27 November 1998; Mark Pilkington, "Fortean Bureau of Investigation," in *Fortean Times* 120 (March 1999), pp. 22-23.

59. *The Times*, 25 March 1999; "Animal Madness," *Magonia* 67 (June 1999).

60. *Le Soir*, 24 December 1996; *La Libre Belgique*, 24 December 1996.

61. McConnell, *The Possessed*, p. 179.

62. Borreson's claim first appeared in the *Daily Mail*; repeated by Logan, *Paganism and the Occult*, pp. 21–22; Logan, *Satanism and the Occult*, pp. 90–91.

63. *The Independent*, 8 August 1989; *Daily Mail*, 8 August 1989; Logan, *Satanism and the Occult*, pp. 35–36.

64. *The Independent*, 9 August 1990.

65. Logan, *Satanism and the Occult*, p. 53.

66. LaFontaine, "Extent and Nature of Organised and Ritual Abuse," p. 30.

67. Pengelly and Waredale, *Something Out of Nothing*.

68. Boyd, *Blasphemous Rumours*, p. 127.

69. Wheatley, *To the Devil—A Daughter*, pp. 213–16.

70. Suster, *Legacy of the Beast*, p. 88; conversation with the author, February 1995.

71. Petersen, *Those Curious New Cults in the 80s*, p. 94.

72. Wilburn, *Fortune Sellers*, p. 180.

73. Sinason, ed., *Treating Survivors of Satanist Abuse*, p. 52.

74. Tate, *Children for the Devil*, p. 101.

75. Crowley, *Magick*, pp. 219–20.

76. Crowley, *The Magical Record*, p. 93.

77. Crowley, *Magick*, p. 222.

78. *The Times*, 4 October 1996; *Telegraph*, 4 October 1996; *The Sun*, 4 October 1996.

NOTES TO CHAPTER 6

1. *Chronicle of Ralph of Coggeshall*, extracted in Kors and Peters, *Witchcraft in Europe*, pp. 44–47.

2. van Limborch, *History of the Inquisition*, vol. 1, p. 61. After three centuries, this book remains the best general survey.

3. E.g., Walter Map, *De nugis curialium*, translated into English by Frederick Tupper and Marbury Bladen Ogle (London: Chatto & Windus, 1924), p. 72.

4. van Limborch, *History of the Inquisition*, vol. 2, pp. 52–53.

5. van Limborch, *History of the Inquisition*, vol. 2, p. 301.

6. Cohn, *Europe's Inner Demons*, p. 86.

7. Joseph von Hammer, *Mémoire sur deux coffrets gnostiques du Moyen Age* (Paris, 1832).

8. Lévi, *Transcendental Magic*, p. 186.

9. "My God!" *Fortean Times* 64 (August–September 1992): 20.

10. Conybeare, *Key of Truth*, p. 153; Cohn, *Europe's Inner Demons*, p. 18.

11. Psellus (though his authorship has been disputed), *De operatione daemonum dialogus*, pp. 20–23.

12. Text in Summers, *History of Witchcraft and Demonology*, p. 48 (quoted from Charles Schmidt, *Histoire et doctrine des Cathares ou Albigeois* [Paris, 1849]; Summers's translation pp. 25–26.

13. Quoted by Cohn, *Europe's Inner Demons*, p. 49.

14. Lea, *History of the Inquisition*, vol. 3, p. 264.

15. Quoted by Cohn, *Europe's Inner Demons*, pp. 49–50.

16. Flavio Biondo, *Italia illustrata* (Basel, 1531), vol. 1, p. 338.

17. Cohn, *Europe's Inner Demons*, pp. 42–54.

18. Alphonsus a Spina, *Fortalitium fidei*, bk. 3, 7th consideration, 11th cruelty.

19. Olliver, *Handbook of Magic and Witchcraft*, p. 151.

20. Quoted by Robbins, *Encyclopedia of Witchcraft and Demonology*, p. 271.

21. *Sworn Book of Honorius*, English version in British Library, Ms. Royal 17.A.XLII, f. 2.

22. The twenty-eight articles are prefixed to Bodin, *De la démonomanie*. Arguments similar to these were made by Basin in *De magicis artibus*.

23. Nider, *Formicarius*, bk. 5; see pp. 715–16 in the 1582 Frankfurt ed. of Kramer and Sprenger, *Malleus Maleficarum*.

24. Jansen, *History of the German People*, p. 272.

25. Paramo, *De origine et progressu officii sanctae inquisitionis*, p. 296.

26. Bekker, *World Bewitched*, pp. 217–19; Gijswijt–Hofstra and Frijhoff, *Witchcraft in the Netherlands*, pp. 86–89.

27. Plaidy, *Spanish Inquisition*, chap. 10.

28. Jansen, *History of the German People*, p. 424.

29. Summers, *Geography of Witchcraft*, pp. 486–88.

30. *The Historie and Life of King James the Sext* (Edinburgh, 1825), p. 241.
31. *Trial, Confession and Execution of Isobel Inch*, p. 11
32. *Full and True Account of the Apprehending and Taking of Mrs. Sarah Moordike.*
33. *Tryal of Richard Hathaway*, passim.
34. See, e.g., Robbins, *Encylopedia of Witchcraft and Demonology*, pp. 536–37.

NOTES TO CHAPTER 7

1. These articles reprinted in Stephensen, *Legend of Aleister Crowley.*
2. H. G. Wells, "Communism and Witchcraft," *Sunday Express*, 21 August 1927; reprinted in H. G. Wells, *The Way the World Is Going* (London: Ernest Benn, 1928), pp. 94–102.
3. Summers, *History of Witchcraft and Demonology*, p. 151.
4. Cristiani, *Satan*, p. 180.
5. Wheatley, introduction to the 1971 paperback reprint of Ahmed, *Black Art.* Page references given here are to this edition.
6. Ahmed, *Black Art*, p. 224.
7. Ahmed, *Black Art*, p. 278.
8. Ahmed, *Black Art*, pp. 269, 273–74.
9. Summers, *History of Witchcraft and Demonology*, pp. 141, 151, and passim.
10. Fabian, *London after Dark*, p. 76.
11. Fabian, *London after Dark*, p. 77.
12. Michael Green, *The Art of Coarse Drinking* (London: Hutchinson, 1973), p. 70.
13. *Sunday Pictorial*, 29 May 1955.
14. *Sunday Pictorial*, 5 June 1955.
15. Murray, *Witch-Cult*, p. 149, quoting de Lancré, *Tableau*, p. 402.
16. Fabian, *Fabian of the Yard*, chap. 16, "Under the Shadow of Meon Hill"; McCormick, *Murder by Witchcraft*, passim.
17. "Black Magic Killer—Woman Talks," *Reynolds News*, 19 February 1956.
18. Gardner, *Meaning of Witchcraft*, p. 247.
19. Quoted here from the reprint in Wheatley's *Satanism and Witches*, pp. 148–49.
20. *Illustrated*, 7 July 1956.
21. *True*, undated clipping, probably late 1959.
22. *Encyclopedia of Witchcraft and Demonology*, p. 118.
23. "Black Magic Expert Visits Cemetery," London *Evening News*, 2 November 1968.
24. The story of the Highgate vampire has been written up many times, notably by Sean Manchester, "President of the British Occult Society," in *The Highgate Vampire*, which includes an attack on one David Farrant; and in *Beyond the Highgate Vampire*, by David Farrant, "President of the British Psychic and Occult Society,"

which includes an attack on Sean Manchester. Brian McConnell's *The Possessed*, chaps. 15 and 16, is nonpartisan. Carol Page's *Bloodlust* has a critical chapter on Sean Manchester.

25. *Encyclopedia of Witchcraft and Demonology*, p. 135.

26. *Encyclopedia of Witchcraft and Demonology*, p. 136.

27. Smyth, *Modern Witchcraft*, p. 92.

28. Smyth, *Modern Witchcraft*, pp. 92–93.

29. Haining, *Anatomy of Witchcraft*, pp. 58–59.

30. Quoted in the *Daily Mail*, and "Evangelist and that Old Black Magic," *Brighton Evening Argus*, both 27 April 1962.

31. Irvine, *From Witchcraft to Christ*, p. 114.

32. Irvine, *From Witchcraft to Christ*, pp. 115–16, 143.

33. Irvine, *From Witchcraft to Christ*, p. 165.

34. Irvine, *From Witchcraft to Christ*, pp. 88–90.

35. Irvine, *From Witchcraft to Christ*, p. 94.

36. Irvine, *From Witchcraft to Christ*, pp. 97–98.

37. Irvine, *From Witchcraft to Christ*, p. 99.

38. Irvine, *From Witchcraft to Christ*, pp. 101–2.

39. Irvine, *From Witchcraft to Christ*, p. 106.

40. Irvine, *Spiritual Warfare*, p. 95.

41. Johns quotes an interview with Alex Sanders in which he says that a White witch "must not even harm his enemies." Asked if the use of the fith–fath harms enemies, he replies: "We fashion a doll in wax or plasticine, fasten its lips together with a safety pin, bind its limbs together. . . . No harm is wished her, beyond the impulse to keep her mouth shut" (*King of the Witches*, p. 127). Compare Irvine, who says that although White witches "claim never to harm anyone, I can say that I've known white witches who did so . . . [they] use 'fith–fath,' a doll made of clay. . . . They use a pin on this image to seal the lips of the person represented. They tie a cord to the legs of the image to inflict pain in the persons' legs" (*From Witchcraft to Christ*, p. 105).

42. Marron, *Witches, Pagans and Magic in the New Age*, p. 149.

43. Marron, *Witches, Pagans and Magic in the New Age*, p. 143.

44. "'Witchcraft in City' Claim," *The Victorian*, 28 January 1977, quoted in Smith and Pazder, *Michelle Remembers*, pp. 289–90.

45. Marron, *Witches, Pagans and Magic in the New Age*, pp. 142–43.

46. *Canadian News Index* (covers seven major newpapers), 1988, "Satanic libel case."

47. Marron, *Witches, Pagans and Magic in the New Age*, p. 142.

48. Marron, *Witches, Pagans and Magic in the New Age*, p. 148.

49. Marron, *Witches, Pagans and Magic in the New Age*, pp. 148–49.

50. Marron, *Witches, Pagans and Magic in the New Age*, pp. 150–52.

51. Marron, *Witches, Pagans and Magic in the New Age*, pp. 152–53. Raschke briefly mentions the case in *Painted Black*, p. viii.

52. "Satanist wins $10,000 in libel case," *Montreal Gazette*, 21 July 1988.

53. Marron, *Witches, Pagans and Magic in the New Age*, pp. 154–55.

54. *Focus on Youth* 4, 2 (Summer 1970), a journal put out by Young Life, Colorado Springs, Colorado; quoted by Wilburn, *Fortune Sellers*, pp. 155–56.

55. Warnke, *Satan-Seller*, pp. 18–9, 22–24.

56. Warnke, *Satan-Seller*, p. 87.

57. Warnke, *Satan-Seller*, pp. 33–34.

58. Warnke, *Satan-Seller*, pp. 40–44.

59. Warnke, *Satan-Seller*, pp. 58–61.

60. Warnke, *Satan-Seller*, pp. 101–12.

61. Holzer, *Truth about Witchcraft*, pp. 162–63.

62. Warnke, *Satan-Seller*, p. 60.

63. Warnke, *Satan-Seller*, pp. 93–94.

64. Warnke, *Satan-Seller*, pp. 112–18.

65. Warnke, *Satan-Seller*, p. 142.

66. Warnke, *Satan-Seller*, p. 139.

67. Hertenstein and Trott, *Selling Satan*, pp. 142–44.

68. Hertenstein and Trott, *Selling Satan*, pp. 146–47.

69. Cerullo, *Back Side of Satan*, pp. 170–71.

70. Warnke claimed in Cerullo's *Back Side of Satan* that he set a building on fire by witchcraft to impress his stepbrother; in *The Satan-Seller*, it was to impress an "old buddy" from school days. In *The Satan-Seller*, the Satanists burned an "inverted cross" onto a professor's lawn (p. 78); in *Back Side of Satan*, they "branded a star into the wooden front door of the professor's home" (p. 169). In *Back Side of Satan*, the altar "stood before an inverted cross" (p. 168); in *Satan-Seller*, the inverted cross stood at the end of the altar (p. 33).

71. Hertenstein and Trott, *Selling Satan*, pp. 54–5.

72. Hertenstein and Trott, *Selling Satan*, pp. 58–59.

73. Hertensten and Trott, *Selling Satan*, p. 305; Victor, *Satanic Panic*, p. 230.

74. Cruz, *Satan on the Loose*, pp. 3–4; also Cruz, *Devil on the Run!* pp. 103–6.

75. Logan, *America Bewitched*, pp. 49–50.

76. "The Legend(s) of John Todd," (*ORCRO*, Occult Response to the Christian Response to the Occult) 6, May/June 1990, p. 51 (reprinted from *Christianity Today*, 2 February 1979).

77. "The Legend(s) of John Todd," p. 53.

78. "The Legend(s) of John Todd," pp. 51–52.

79. "The Legend(s) of John Todd," p. 51.

80. "The Legend(s) of John Todd," p. 52.

81. "The Legend(s) of John Todd," p. 44.

82. "The Legend(s) of John Todd," p. 53.

83. "The Legend(s) of John Todd," p. 52.

84. "The Testimony of John Todd Collins," tape transcript in *ORCRO* 6, May/June 1990, pp. 42–43.

85. "The Legend(s) of John Todd," p. 53.

86. A. E. van Vogt, "The Rulers," in *Destination: Universe* (London: Panther, 1960).

87. "The Legend(s) of John Todd," p. 57.

88. Hertenstein and Trott, *Selling Satan*, p. 164.

NOTES TO CHAPTER 8

1. Smith and Pazder, *Michelle Remembers*, pp. 3–4.

2. Smith and Pazder, *Michelle Remembers*, pp. 4–5.

3. Smith and Pazder, *Michelle Remembers*, pp. 17–19.

4. Smith and Pazder, *Michelle Remembers*, pp. 24–29.

5. Smith and Pazder, *Michelle Remembers*, pp. 237, 242, 266.

6. Smith and Pazder, *Michelle Remembers*, p. 222.

7. Smith and Pazder, *Michelle Remembers*, p. 243.

8. Smith and Pazder, *Michelle Remembers*, pp. 35–36, 39.

9. Smith and Pazder, *Michelle Remembers*, pp. 52–54.

10. Smith and Pazder, *Michelle Remembers*, pp. 189–91.

11. This practice was first found in Warnke, *Satan-Seller*, pp. 100–101.

12. Pazder, quoted in Kahaner, ed., *Cults That Kill*, pp. 200–201.

13. Nathan and Snedeker, *Satan's Silence*, p. 69.

14. Tate, *Children for the Devil*, p. 271.

15. Paul Eberle and Shirley Eberle, *The Abuse of Innocence*, p. 17.

16. Hicks, *In Pursuit of Satan*, p. 187.

17. Mary A. Fisher, "A Case of Dominoes?" *Los Angeles* magazine, (October 1989).

18. Nathan, *Women and other Aliens*, p. 149; Nathan and Snedeker, *Satan's Silence*, pp. 83–85; Hicks, *In Pursuit of Satan*, p. 188.

19. Hicks, *In Pursuit of Satan*, p. 188.

20. Nathan, *Women and Other Aliens*, p. 149.

21. Newton, *Raising Hell*, p. 252; Hicks, *In Pursuit of Satan*, p. 188.

22. Fisher, "A Case of Dominoes?"

23. Hicks, *In Pursuit of Satan*, p. 189.

24. Nathan and Snedeker, *Satan's Silence*, p. 74.

25. Tate, *Children for the Devil*, pp. 276–77.

26. Roland Summit, "The Child Abuse Accommodation Syndrome," *Child Abuse and Neglect* 7, 1983.

27. Hicks, *In Pursuit of Satan*, pp. 191–92.

28. Carlson and Larue, *Satanism in America*, p. 64; Kahaner, ed., *Cults That Kill*, p. 222.

29. Eberle and Eberle, *Abuse of Innocence*, pp. 172–73, 181.

30. Carlson and Larue, *Satanism in America*, p. 64; Tate, *Children for the Devil*, p. 281.

31. Hicks, *In Pursuit of Satan*, p. 190.

32. Eberle and Eberle, *Abuse of Innocence*, pp. 171, 355.

33. Interview on the television show *Geraldo*, 25 October 1988, episode on "Devil Worship: Exposing Satan's Underground"; quoted by Carlson and Larue, *Satanism in America*, pp. 67–68.

34. Nathan, *Women and Other Aliens*, pp. 161–62; Nathan and Snedeker, *Satan's Silence*, p. 89.

35. Eberle and Eberle, *Abuse of Innocence*, pp. 20–21.

36. "Molestation Hearing is California's Longest, Costliest," *Washington Post*, 12 January 1986; "Child Molestation Case Finally Comes to Trial in Los Angeles," *Christian Science Monitor*, 20 April 1987; Tate, *Children for the Devil*, p. 286.

37. "Most Charges Dropped in McMartin Case," *Washington Post*, 13 June 1985.

38. "The Terrible Puzzle of McMartin Pre-School," *Washington Post*, 17 May 1988; Eberle and Eberle, *Abuse of Innocence*, p. 22.

39. Eberle and Eberle, *Abuse of Innocence*, p. 31.

40. Newton, *Raising Hell*, p. 36.

41. Nathan and Snedeker, *Satan's Silence*, p. 55.

42. Nathan and Snedeker, *Satan's Silence*, p. 65.

43. Nathan and Snedeker, *Satan's Silence*, p. 94.

44. Hicks, *In Pursuit of Satan*, p. 261.

45. Hicks, *In Pursuit of Satan*, p. 268.

46. Hicks, *In Pursuit of Satan*, p. 267.

47. Nathan and Snedeker, *Satan's Silence*, pp. 100–101.

48. Newton, *Raising Hell*, pp. 39–40.

49. Wexler, *Wounded Innocents*, p. 144.

50. Nathan and Snedeker, *Satan's Silence*, p. 103.

51. "Satan's Sideshow," *Cornerstone* 18, 90 (early 1990), p. 26.

52. *Cornerstone* 18, 90, p. 27.

53. *Cornerstone* 18, 90, p. 27.

54. Stratford, *Satan's Underground*, pp. 22, 34–36.

55. Stratford, *Satan's Underground*, pp. 53–54.

56. Stratford, *Satan's Underground*, p. 67.

57. Stratford, *Satan's Underground*, pp. 69, 75.

58. Stratford, *Satan's Underground*, pp. 76–78.

59. Stratford, *Satan's Underground*, p. 83.

60. Stratford, *Satan's Underground*, p. 79.

61. Stratford, *Satan's Underground*, p. 84.

62. Stratford, *Satan's Underground*, p. 87.

63. Stratford, *Satan's Underground*, p. 95.

64. Stratford, *Satan's Underground*, pp. 105–6, 142–48.

65. Stratford, *Satan's Underground*, p. 117.

66. Nathan, *Women and Other Aliens*, pp. 125–26.

67. Nathan, *Women and Other Aliens*, p. 130.

68. Nathan, *Women and Other Aliens*, p. 130.

69. Nathan, *Women and Other Aliens*, pp. 131, 128.

70. Nathan, *Women and Other Aliens*, p. 131.

71. Nathan, *Women and Other Aliens*, pp. 134–35.

72. Nathan, *Women and Other Aliens*, pp. 139–40.

73. Nathan and Snedeker, *Satan's Silence*, p. 208.

74. Nathan, *Women and Other Aliens*, p. 131; Newton, *Raising Hell*, p. 276.

75. Hicks, *In Pursuit of Satan*, p. 196.

76. Hicks, *In Pursuit of Satan*, p. 197.

77. Hicks, *In Pursuit of Satan*, p. 198.

78. Hicks, *In Pursuit of Satan*, pp. 200–202.

79. Nathan, *Women and Other Aliens*, p. 164.

80. Hicks, *In Pursuit of Satan*, pp. 202–203.

81. Nathan, *Women and other Aliens*, p. 165.

82. Quoted in Kahaner, *Cults That Kill*, pp. 16–17.

83. Kahaner, *Cults That Kill*, pp. 4, 18–19.

84. Kahaner, *Cults That Kill*, p. 23.

85. Hicks, *In Pursuit of Satan*, p. 33.

86. Hicks, in Best, Richardson, and Bromley, *Satanism Scare*, p. 176.

87. Hicks, in Best, Richardson, and Bromley, *Satanism Scare*, pp. 176–78.

88. All these speakers are quoted by Hicks, in Best, Richardson, and Bromley, *Satanism Scare*, pp. 177–78.

89. Quoted by Hicks, *In Pursuit of Satan*, pp. 65–66.

90. Quoted by Hicks, *In Pursuit of Satan*, p. 66.

91. Reprinted in various places, e.g., in Cruz, *Devil on the Run!* pp. 147–48.

92. Widely reproduced, for instance, in Hicks, *In Pursuit of Satan*, pp. 245–246; a longer version in Sakheim and Devine, p. 210.

93. Robert Hicks, "None Dare Call It Reason: Kids, Cults and Common Sense" (talk prepared for the Virginia Department for Children's Twelfth Annual Legislative Forum, Roanoke, Virginia, 22 September 1989); reprinted in *ORCRO* 6 (May–June 1990): 7.

94. Brown, *He Came to Set the Captives Free*, pp. 12–13.

95. Brown, *He Came to Set the Captives Free*, pp. 17–18.

96. Brown, *He Came to Set the Captives Free*, pp. 83–85.

97. Brown, *He Came to Set the Captives Free*, pp. 88–89.

98. Brown, *He Came to Set the Captives Free*, pp. 25–28.

99. Brown, *He Came to Set the Captives Free*, pp. 29–30.

100. Brown, *He Came to Set the Captives Free*, p. 39.

101. Brown, *He Came to Set the Captives Free*, pp. 48–49.

102. Brown, *He Came to Set the Captives Free*, p. 49.

103. Brown, *He Came to Set the Captives Free*, pp. 50–51.

104. Brown, *He Came to Set the Captives Free*, p. 49.

105. Brown, *He Came to Set the Captives Free*, pp. 55–56.

106. Brown, *He Came to Set the Captives Free*, pp. 59–61.

107. This incident is cited by Hertenstein and Trott, *Selling Satan*, apparently from the original ChickPub edition of *He Came to Set the Captives Free* (1986); it is not in the Solid Rock Family Enterprises reprint, which seems to have been slightly toned down.

108. Brown, *He Came to Set the Captives Free*, p. 59.

109. Irvine, *From Witchcraft to Christ*, pp. 89–90, 102.

110. Brown, *He Came to Set the Captives Free*, pp. 59–60.

111. Hicks, "None Dare Call It Reason," reprinted in *ORCRO* 6 (May–June 1990): 7.

112. "Think Tank," *ORCRO* 8 (December 1990): 17.

113. Carlson and Larue, *Satanism in America*, p. 22.

114. Hertenstein and Trott, *Selling Satan*, p. 301.

115. Carlson and Larue, *Satanism in America*, pp. 85-86.

116. Blood, *New Satanists*, pp. 163–65.

117. Blood, *New Satanists*, p. 167; Tate, *Children for the Devil*, p. 161.

118. Blood, *New Satanists*, pp. 167–68.

119. Blood, *New Satanists*, p. 170; Tate, *Children for the Devil*, p. 154.

120. Blood, *New Satanists*, p. 171; Tate, *Children for the Devil*, p. 166.

121. Michael Aquino, "Comments Concerning *The New Satanists* by Linda Blood," (pamphlet), Temple of Set, 2 February 1995.

122. Aquino, "Comments Concerning *The New Satanists*"; Michael Aquino, letter to the author, 4 June 1996.

123. Aquino, "Comments Concerning *The New Satanists*"; Aquino, letter to the author, 9 April 1996.

124. Aquino, letter to the author, 4 June 1996, citing a letter from the U.S. Army Claims Service to Aquino, dated 27 November 1989.

125. Aquino, "Comments Concerning *The New Satanists*."

126. Tate, *Children for the Devil*, p. 13.

127. Hudson, *Ritual Child Abuse*, p. 20.

128. Hudson, *Ritual Child Abuse*, p. 20.

129. Hudson, *Ritual Child Abuse*, p. 21.

130. Roland C. Summit, "Hidden Victims, Hidden Pain," in Wyatt and Powell, *Lasting Effects of Child Sexual Abuse*, pp. 41–43.

131. Johnston, *Edge of Evil*, pp. 14–15.

132. *The Times*, 12 August 1986.

133. Roger Sandell, "Desperately Seeking Satan," *Magonia* 42 (March 1992): 10.

134. Carlson and Larue, *Satanism in America*, pp. 22, 93.

135. Quoted in Carlson and Larue, *Satanism in America*, p. 264.

136. Brown, *Becoming a Vessel of Honor in the Master's Service*, chap. 1.

137. Robert W. Balch and Margaret Gilliam, "Devil Worship in Western Montana: A Case Study in Rumor Construction," in Best, Richardson, and Bromley, *Satanism Scare*, p. 257.

138. Balch and Gilliam, "Devil Worship in Western Montana," p. 249.

139. Balch and Gilliam, "Devil Worship in Western Montana," p. 252.

140. Victor, *Satanic Panic*, p. 32.

141. Victor, *Satanic Panic*, p. 33.

142. Victor, *Satanic Panic*, p. 34.

143. Victor, *Satanic Panic*, pp. 34–35.

144. Victor, *Satanic Panic*, p. 43.

145. *File 18 Newsletter* 5, 90 (April 1990), published by The Cult Crime Impact Network, Boise, Idaho.

146. Carlson and Larue, *Satanism in America*, pp. 35, 78.

147. "Satan's Sideshow," *Cornerstone* 18, 90, p. 25.

148. *Cornerstone* 18, 90, p. 25.

149. Hertenstein and Trott, *Selling Satan*, p. 278.

150. *Daily Mail*, 25 October 1999.

151. Hicks, *In Pursuit of Satan*, p. 268.

152. *San Francisco Chronicle*, 14 August 1996.

153. Hicks, *In Pursuit of Satan*, p. 321.

154. Lanning, *Investigator's Guide*, p. 31.

155. Eberle and Eberle, *Abuse of Innocence*, pp. 231, 236–37.

156. Eberle and Eberle, *Abuse of Innocence*, pp. 142–44, 200, 308–9.

157. Nathan, *Women and Other Aliens*, pp. 150–51, points out that retrying someone when most jurors have found them not guilty is unheard of.

158. Eberle and Eberle, *Abuse of Innocence*, pp. 359–413.

159. Nathan, *Women and Other Aliens*, p. 166.

NOTES TO CHAPTER 9

1. *Hansard Parliamentary Debates* (14 April 1988), col. 348. Reported in *The Times*, *The Sun*, *Daily Mail*, *The Star*, all on 15 April 1988.

2. *Hansard Parliamentary Debates* (27 April 1988), cols. 485–86.

3. *The Sport*, 17 August 1988.

4. *Pagan News* (April 1989); Ruthven, *Malleus Satani*, p. 32.

5. *Sunday Mirror*, 30 October 1988; a brief account of Balodis's claims overall appears in Hicks, *In Pursuit of Satan*, p. 139.

6. "Britain Under Seige," *Prophecy Today*, 3,5 (1987): 17.

7. *Independent on Sunday*, 16 September 1999.

8. Tate, *Children for the Devil*, p. 51.

9. *The Oprah Winfrey Show*, 17 February 1988, transcript by Journal Graphics. *The Oprah Winfrey Show* was then available in Britain only to cable subscribers.

10. Tate, *Children for the Devil*, pp. 52–56.

11. Core, *Chasing Satan*, pp. 91–94.

12. Tate, *Children for the Devil*, p. 219.

13. Tate, *Children for the Devil*, p. 222; Core, *Chasing Satan*, p. 95.

14. "Go To Hell!" *The Star*, 3 May 1989. Further information from David Austen, conversation with author, June 1995.

15. Hough, *Witchcraft*, p. 134.

16. David Hebditch and Nick Anning, "A Ritual Fabrication," *Independent on Sunday*, 30 December 1990.

17. Hebditch and Anning, "Ritual Fabrication."

18. Logan, *Close Encounters with the New Age*, p. 24.

19. *Kilroy* (television program), 31 October 1990.

20. Hebditch and Anning, "Ritual Fabrication."

21. Logan, *Close Encounters with the New Age*, pp. 18–27.

22. Obituary of Geoffrey Dickens, M.P., *The Times*, 18 May 1995.

23. *The Guardian*, 18 May 1995; *Telegraph*, 18 May 1995.

24. *Telegraph*, 20 April 1987.

25. *Today*, 28 April 1987.

26. Diane Core, "We Are in the Middle of Spiritual Warfare," *New Federalist*, April 1988.

27. *Crockford's Clerical Directory* 1998-1999; Logan, *Close Encounters with the New Age*, pp. 39–40, 44–45.

28. Logan, *Paganism and the Occult*, p. 111.

29. Fox, *Declaration of the Ground of Error*, p. 24.

30. Logan, *Paganism and the Occult*, p. 99.

31. Logan, *Paganism and the Occult*, p. 84.

32. Maureen Davies, interview in Hough, *Witchcraft*, p. 119.

33. The essay "Satanic Ritual Abuse" was circulated as a set of loose photocopied sheets. It is here quoted from an unauthorized reprint in *ORCRO* 6 (May/June 1990): 14-19.

34. Harper, *Dance with the Devil*, pp. 140–44.

35. Harper, *Dance with the Devil*, p. 52. Her account of her involvement begins on p. 44.

36. Harper, *Dance with the Devil*, pp. 54–56.

37. Harper, *Dance with the Devil*, p. 71.

38. Harper, *Dance with the Devil*, p. 67–68.

39. Harper, *Dance with the Devil*, pp. 71–73.

40. Harper, *Dance with the Devil*, pp. 181.

41. "Police Quiz TV Witch!" *Lightning Flash* 15 (Winter 1988–89): 5; *Heart of the Matter*, on BBC1, 22 July 1990; also Hough, *Witchcraft*, pp. 105–6.

42. Often written up, e.g., in Margaret Jay and Sally Doganis, *Battered* (London: Weidenfeld and Nicolson, 1987), pp. 14-16.

43. Stuart Bell, *When Salem Came to the Boro* (London: Pan Books, 1988).

44. Nathan and Snedeker, *Satan's Silence*, pp. 196-97.

45. *Joint Enquiry Team Report*, June 1990; short version published by Nick Anning, David Hebditch, and Margaret Jervis, May 1997 (hereafter cited as *JET Report*), pp. 9–10.

46. *JET Report*, pp. 18–19; foster mother interviewed on *Dispatches*, October 1990.

47. *Mail on Sunday*, 21 October 1990.

48. Tate, *Children for the Devil*, pp. 306, 309; *JET Report*, p. 23

49. *JET Report*, pp. 16–17.

50. *Dispatches*, Channel 4, October 1990. Though this was not recorded until a couple of years later, it was presumably similar to her earlier statements.

51. *JET Report*, p. 18.

52. Photocopy of statement appended to the full version of the *Joint Enquiry Team Report*.

53. Transcript in the full version of the *Joint Enquiry Team Report* (unpaginated).

54. *JET Report*, p. 24–25.

55. *JET Report*, p. 18.

56. *JET Report*, p. 19.

57. *JET Report*, pp. 26–27.

58. *JET Report*, p. 28.

59. *JET Report*, p. 35.

60. *JET Report*, p. 41.

61. *Independent on Sunday*, 20 September 1989; see also *Mail on Sunday*, 16 September 1990.

62. *Telegraph*, 8 September 1990.

63. Mike Dash, "Satan and the Social Workers," *Fortean Times* 57 (Spring 1991): 47–48.

64. *The Observer*, 23 September 1990.

65. *The Observer*, 23 September 1990.

66. *The Independent*, 15 September 1990.

67. *News of the World*, 5 August 1990. Sara's story is also related in Hough, *Witchcraft*, pp. 110–14, and *The Independent*, 5 September 1990. The story of "Tess" in Boyd, *Blasphemous Rumours*, chap. 16, corresponds exactly to this case.

68. *The Times*, 21 September 1990.

69. Quoted in Gilbert, *Casting the First Stone*, p. 107.

70. *Daily Mirror* and all other daily papers, 8 and 9 March 1991.

71. Black, *Orkney: A Place of Safety?* chap. 10.

72. Black, *Orkney: A Place of Safety?* p. 135.

73. Mike Dash, "Bedevilled," *Fortean Times* 72 (December 1993–January 1994): 49.

74. *The Times*, 5 March 1996.

75. *Diva* (June 1999): 28.

76. Reported in various papers, e.g., *Express*, 15 September 1990.

77. Logan, *Satanism and the Occult*, pp. 39–40, 42–44.

78. *The Independent*, 14 April 1991.

79. *Sunday Times*, 24 May 1992.

80. *The Guardian*, 18 August 1990; *Telegraph*, 18 August 1990.

81. *The Herald*, 13 August 1993; *The Scotsman*, 7 December 1993.

82. *The Guardian*, 28 February 1995 and 1 March 1995.

83. *Independent on Sunday*, 5 March 1995.

84. *The Times*, 14 and 15 November 1990; *The Independent*, 15 November 1990. Lucillus was an ancient Roman personal name. If it was ever a Devil name, it did not find its way into Collin de Plancy's *Dictionnaire infernal*, Davidson's *Dictionary of Angels, Including the Fallen Angels*, Julien Tondriau and Roland Villeneuve's *Dictionary of Devils and Demons*, or any other standard work on demonology.

85. de Lancré, *Tableau*, p. 398.

86 Mike Dash, "Satanic Ritual Abuse in Epping?" *Fortean Times* 61, pp. 34–5.

87. Hough, *Witchcraft*, p. 121.

88. Tate, *Children for the Devil*, pp. 66-68.

89. Logan, *Satanism and the Occult*, p. 139.

90. Logan, *Satanism and the Occult*, p. 98.

91. Sinason, ed., *Treating Survivors of Satanist Abuse*, pp. 15–17.

92. Sinason, ed., *Treating Survivors of Satanist Abuse*, p. 248.

93. Bibliography to Joan Coleman's "Satanic Cult Practices," in Sinason, ed., *Treating Survivors of Satanist Abuse*, p. 253.

94. *The Times*, 14 January 1995.

95. *Daily Mail*, 13 January 1995.

96. *Today*, 18 and 19 July 1994; *Telegraph*, 19 May 1995; *Everyman* (television documentary show), BBC, 21 May 1995.

97. Marron, *Ritual Abuse*, pp. 46–47, 51–52.

98. Marron, *Ritual Abuse*, pp. 56–59.

99. Marron, *Ritual Abuse*, p. 101.

100. Marron, *Ritual Abuse*, pp. 72–79, 128–29.

101. Marron, *Ritual Abuse*, pp. 124, 139, 148.

102. F. Jonker and P. Jonker–Bakker, "Experiences with Ritualist Child Sexual Abuse: A Case Study from the Netherlands," *Child Abuse and Neglect* 15 (1991): 191–96; Tate, *Children for the Devil*, pp. 223–28; Nathan, *Women and Other Aliens*, p. 153.

103. "Satanic Ring Killing Babies," *Johannesburg Sunday Times*, 20 May 1990.

104. Bob Richard, "Satanic Round-Up," *Fortean Times* 60 (December 1991–January 1992): 35.

105. Core, *Chasing Satan*, pp. 91–92.

106. *The Star*, 29 October 1991, *The Guardian*, 30 October 1991.

107. Mike Dash, "Bedevilled," *Fortean Times* 72 (December 1993–January 1994): 47.

108. Goodyear–Smith, *First Do No Harm*, p. 82.

NOTES TO CHAPTER 10

1. de Raemound, *L'Anti–christ*, p. 398.

2. *The Examination of John Walsh* (1566). The pope Clement VIII mentioned was the "anti–Pope" of that name, not the Clement VIII who was pope from 1591 to 1605, which was, of course, after the date of this pamphlet.

3. Brown, *Prepare for War*, p. 170.

4. Hauber, *Bibliotheca, acta et scripta magica*, vol. 2, p. 506.

5. Quoted by van Limborch, *History of the Inquisition*, vol. 2, p. 114.

6. Maimonides, *Guide to the Perplexed*, trans. Shlomo Pines (Chicago: University of Chicago Press, 1963), p. 542 (3.37).

7. Cahill, *Freemasonry and the Anti–Christian Movement*, p. 70.

8. Hunt, *Menace of Freemasonry to the Christian Faith*, pp. 11–12.

9. McCormick, *Christ, the Christian, and Freemasonry*, p. 57, quoting George L. Hunt, *Secret Societies*. The capitalization and italicization are probably McCormick's.

10. Knight, *The Brotherhood*, p. 236.

11. *Freemasonry and Christianity*, p. 29.

12. Lawrence, *Freemasonry—A Religion?*, p. 113.

13. Perry, ed., *Deliverance*, p. 62.

14. There is too great a literature to review properly here. King, *Satan and Swastika*, and Suster, *Hitler and the Age of Horus* (recently reissued as *Hitler: Black Magician*), are well researched and argued, but their conclusions are open to question. James Webb's *The Occult Establishment* (London: Richard Drew, 1971), is very well researched but badly written and reaches no clear conclusion. The best study is Nicholas Goodrick–Clarke, *The Occult Roots of Nazism* (London: Aquarian, 1985), which describes the more sensational writings as a "modern mythology."

15. Wurmbrand, *Was Karl Marx a Satanist?* pp. 21, 26, 27–28.

16. Wurmbrand, *Was Karl Marx a Satanist?* p. 75.

17. Wurmbrand, *Was Karl Marx a Satanist?* pp. 10, 12.

18. Wurmbrand, *Was Karl Marx a Satanist?* p. 62.

19. Tate, *Child Pornography*, pp. 41–50.

20. See for instance "Flesh on Film," *Time Out,* (23–30 March 1988): 20.

21. Thomas, *Enslaved*, pp. 50–52.

22. "Commander X," *Mind Stalkers: UFOs, Implants and The Psychotronic Agenda of The New World Order* (New Brunswick, New Jersey: Global Communications, no date, late 1990s), pp. 30-31.

23. Wheatley, *Devil Rides Out*, pp. 10, 14, 15, 27.

24. de Lancré, *Tableau*, pp. 192–93.

25. Wheatley, *The Satanist*, p. 82.

26. Schlink, *Countdown to World Disaster*, p. 34.

27. Schlink, *Escaping the Web of Deception*, p. 44.

28. de Raemond, *L'Anti–christ*, pp. 102–3.

29. Alexander Roberts, *Treatise of Witchcraft* (London, 1616), sig. A2^r–A2^v.

30. Rapture index web pages, quoted in *The Pagan Prattle* (Winter 1996–97).

31. Waite, *Devil-Worship in France*, pp. 91–92.

32. Terry, *Ultimate Evil*, pp. 83–85.

33. Terry, *Ultimate Evil*, pp. 266–69.

34. *Evangelical Dictionary of Theology*, (London: Marshall Pickering, 1985).

35. *The Star*, 18 January 1996.

36. Livesey, *Beware! "666" Is Here*, unpaginated.

37. Brunvand, *Choking Dobermann*, pp. 169–86; *Church Times*, 16 October 1998.

38. "Let Sleeping Myths Lie," *Pagan Prattle* (Summer 1994).

39. Quoted in *UFOs—Where Do They Come From?* pp. 64–66.

40. *UFOs—Where Do They Come From?* p. 67.

41. Bill Adler, ed., *Letters to the Air Force on UFOs* (New York: Dell Books, 1967), pp. 116–90.

42. Larson, *Larson's New Book of Cults*, p. 348.

43. Larson, *Larson's New Book of Cults*, p. 348.

44. Lindsey, *The 1980s,* pp. 32–33.

45. Davies, *Christian Deviations*, pp. 11, 17, 21, 25.

46. Krémer, *False Cults and Heresies Exposed*, unpaginated.

47. Forrest and Sanderson, *Cults and the Occult Today*, pp. 69–70.

48. Ritchie, *Secret World of Cults*, pp. 4–6.

49. Shaw, *Spying in Guru Land*, p. xvi.

50. Shaw, *Spying in Guru Land*, p. 185.

51. Subritzky, *Demons Defeated*, chap. 5.

52. Subritzky, *Demons Defeated*, pp. 109–10.

53. Subritzky, *How to Cast Out Demons*, pp. 62–68.

54. London *Evening Standard*, 20 January 1995.

55. Walker, *Occult Web*, p. 38.

56. See, e.g., McConnell, *The Possessed*, chap. 12.

57. "Eyeless in Arcadia," *Fortean Times* 80 (April–May 1995): 13.

58. Watkins, *Real Exorcists*, pp. 131–32, 134–35.

59. "Fatal Exorcisms," *Fortean Times* 123 (June 1999): 40.

60. "Fatal Exorcisms," *Fortean Times* 123 (June 1999): 123.

61. Kraft, *Defeating Dark Angels*, p. 234.

62. Quoted by Tony Lee, "World Link," *Burnt Offerings* 1, 2 (Spring Equinox 1997): 5.

63. Wagner, *Territorial Spirits*, p. 39.

64. Wagner, *Breaking Strongholds in Your City*, pp. 36–37.

65. *Guardian*, 20 September 1990.

66. McAll, *Healing the Haunted*, pp. 34–36; also McAll, *Healing the Family Tree*, pp. 60–61, and Alexander, *Devil Hunter*, chap. 15.

67. Aranza, *Backward Masking Unmasked*, p. 60; d'Arch Smith, *Books of the Beast*, p. 121.

68. Roger Sandell, "Desperately Seeking Satan," *Magonia* 42 (March 1992): 9.

69. Brown, *He Came to Set the Captives Free*, p. 63.

70. Godwin, *Dancing with Demons*, pp. 203, 205–6.

71. Godwin, *Dancing with Demons*, pp. 3, 217–18, 115.

72. *Sunday Times*, 29 July 1990; *Time*, 30 July 1990.

73. Dr. Wilson Key, *Subliminal Seduction* (1973; reprint, New York: Signet, 1981).

74. *Guardian*, 13 August 1990.

75. *Guardian*, 13 August 1990.

76. Summers, *Popular History of Witchcraft*, p. 153.

77. Bodin, *De la démonomanie des sorciers*, f. 88ᵛ (bk. 2, chap. 4).

78. Sparkes, *It's No Laughing Matter*, p. 10.

79. Robie, *Reverse the Curse in Your Life*, p. 54.

80. Pulling, *Devil's Web*, passim.

81. For example: adultery, 2 Samuel 11:1–5; murder, Genesis 4:8; infanticide, Matthew 2:16; necromancy, 1 Samuel 28:7–25; demonic possession, Mark 5:1–20; suicide, Matthew 27:5; assassination, Judges 4:21; harlotry, Proverbs 7:6–27 and Hosea 1:2–3; coprophagy, 2 Kings 18:27; human sacrifice, 2 Kings 3:27; rape, 2 Samuel 13:14; cannibalism, 2 Kings 6:26–29; incest, Genesis 19:30–38; blood sacrifices, Numbers 19:1–10; cursing rituals, Numbers 5:17–24 and Deuteronomy 27:11–26.

82. Carlson and Larue, *Satanism in America*, p. 258.

83. Michael Stackpole, "The Truth about Role Playing Games," special appendix to Carlson and Larue, *Satanism in America*.

84. Dear, *Dungeon Master*, p. 381.

85. Raschke, *Painted Black*, pp. 180, 182.

86. Sandell, "Desperately Seeking Satan," p. 9.

87. *Advanced Dungeon and Dragons Player's Handbook* (Cambridge: TSR Incorporated, 1989), p. 146.

NOTES TO CHAPTER 11

1. *News of the World*, 16 April 1989.

2. Logan, *Satanism and the Occult*, p. 168. On the same page, Logan wrongly attributed to Suster an article on the Caliphate O.T.O. that had appeared, anonymously, in *Pagan News* (August 1989), and also gave an incorrect reference. Following a complaint from Suster, Kingsway Books have agreed to amend any future edition.

3. "Child Care Man to Join Sex Orgy Witches," *News of the World*, 8 October 1989.

4. "Exposed: The Wicked Witch from Police HQ," *News of the World*, 22 July 1990.

5. "Police Girl's Sex Romps with Satan Lover," *Sunday Mirror*, 22 July 1990.

6. "Pagans Banned by Boorish Bishop," *That's Magick!* 3 (Summer 1996): 32, quoting *Newbury Weekly News*, 21 March 1996.

7. Zsuzsanna Budapest, *Grandmother Moon* (San Francisco: Harper San Francisco, 1991), pp. 94–105.

8. "Mayor Invites Klan to Burn Witches," *Pagan Prattle* (Summer 1994): 6.

9. Victor, *Satanic Panic*, p. 177, quoting an Associated Press (AP) news release, 3 October 1988.

10. Carlson and Larue, *Satanism in America*, p. 83.

11. *Los Angeles Times*, 22 January 1990, B1.

12. Eberle and Eberle, *Abuse of Innocence*, pp. 126–27.

13. *Danger! Open Mind*, (unpaginated).

14. Maureen Davies, "How to Deal with the Occult in Your Area," transcript in Occult Response to the Christian Response to the Occult (*ORCRO*) 7 (September 1990): 21.

15. Logan, *Satanism and the Occult*, p. 286.

16. Logan, *Satanism and the Occult*, p. 213.

17. Johnston, *Edge of Evil*, pp. 109–10.

18. Logan, *Satanism and the Occult*, pp. 99–100.

19. Gilbert, *Casting the First Stone*, pp. 4–5.

20. *Plain Truth* (July 1993), quoting *Chicago Star Tribune*, 23 September 1992; 10 and 11 November 1992.

21. "My God!" *Fortean Times* 64 (August–September 1992): 20.

22. "Satan Hunters Condemned in Westchester," *New York Times*, 22 November 1995, p. A11.

23. Subritzky, *How to Cast out Demons*, p. 66.

24. *Hallowe'en* (unpaginated).

25. *Doorways to Danger* (unpaginated).

26. *Kensington and Chelsea Times*, 2 November 1990.

27. *Thin End of the Wedge* (unpaginated); Gaile McConaghie, conversations with the author, December 1995.

28. See, e.g., Graham Phillips and Martin Keatman, *The Green Stone* (London: Granada, 1984); and Andrew Collins, *The Seventh Sword* (London: Century, 1991).

29. Andrew Collins, "Green Stone," *Anomaly*, journal of record for the Association for the Scientific Study of Anomalous Phenomena, no. 4 (October 1987): 35.

30. Collins, *Black Alchemist*, pp. 108, 125–30.

31. Collins, *Second Coming*, p. 11.

32. Andy Collins kindly sent me a photocopy of a collage of newspaper clippings about this campaign, though unfortunately, date and title are not visible in every case.

33. "Church Slams Powers of Darkness," *Brentwood Gazette*.

34. *Southend Evening Echo*, 22 May 1989.

35. *Southend Yellow Advertiser*, 9 June 1989.

36. Collins, *Second Coming*, p. 9.

37. Collins, *Second Coming*, p. 11.

38. *Star*, 17 February 1992. I am grateful to John and Paul of the Association of Autonomous Astronauts for background information about the affair. It is also discussed in *Pagan Prattle* (Summer 1994): 12–13, and *Fortean Times* 64 (August–September 1992): 50–51.

39. *Independent on Sunday*, 23 February 1992.

40. *Mail on Sunday*, 1 March 1992.

41. *Talking Stick* 18 (Spring 1995): 25.

42. Temple Ov Psychick Youth, "Blood and Fire" (no date or pagination).

43. *Occult Observer* 2, 4.

NOTES TO CHAPTER 12

1. Lamothe–Langone, *Histoire de l'Inquisition en France*, vol. 2, pp. 614–15.

2. Cohn, *Europe's Inner Demons*, pp. 126–28.

3. John of Salisbury, *Policraticus*, Leyden, 1639 (written 12th century), p. 83 (2.17).

4. Kramer and Sprenger, *Malleus Maleficarum*, Speyer: 1487 part 2, qn. 1, chap. 2.

5. Robbins, *Encyclopedia of Witchcraft and Demonology*, s.v. "Schüler"; also Summers, *Geography of Witchcraft*, pp. 497–99.

6. Dianne Core, "We Are in the Middle of Spiritual Warfare," printed in *New Federalist* (March 1989).

7. Paul Eberle and Shirley Eberle, *The Abuse of Innocence*, p. 42.

8. Kahaner, *Cults That Kill*, chap. 10.

9. Anson Shupe, "The Modern Satanist Scare in Indiana: A Case Study of an Urban Legend in the Heartland, U.S.A." (paper presented at the 1991 Annual Meeting of the North Central Sociological Association, Dearborn, Michigan).

10. Wright, *Remembering Satan*, pp. 179–80.

11. Victor, *Satanic Panic*, p. 177.

12. *The Times*, 1 May 1999.

13. Sellwood and Haining, *Devil Worship in Britain*, pp. 13–15.

14. Raschke, *Painted Black*, plates; Haining, *Anatomy of Witchcraft*, plates.

15. Crowley, *Magick*, p. 87

16. May, *Tiger Woman*, p. 177.

17. In Wright, *Remembering Satan*, p. 139.

18. Tate, *Children for the Devil*, p. 22.

19. Martin H. Katchen and David K. Sakheim, "Satanic Beliefs and Practices," in Sakheim and Devine, *Out of Darkness*, p. 35.

20. Reynolds, *The Reality*, p. 40.

21. Katchen and Sakheim, "Satanic Beliefs and Practices," p. 34.

22. Katchen and Sakheim, "Satanic Beliefs and Practices," pp. 34, 40.

23. Logan, *Paganism and the Occult*, p. 89.

24. Parker, *At the Heart of Darkness*, p. 286.

25. *Sunday Mirror*, 21 May 1989.

26. Davies, in *Satanic Ritual Abuse* (1989), says her first case was "a year ago."

27. "It Happens in the U.K. Too," *Fortean Times* 71 (October/November 1993): 28; further information from Margaret Jervis.

28. Reid, *Suffer the Little Children*, pp. 45–49.

29. Karyn Stardancer, presentation at RAINS [Ritual Abuse Information and Network Support] conference, "Better the Devil You Know?" (Warwick University, Friday, 13 September 1996); summary in "It Never RAINS But It Pours," *Magonia* 59 (April 1997): 8-9.

30. Livy, *Rome and the Mediterranean*, trans. Henry Bettenson (West Drayton, Middlesex: Penguin Classics, 1976), pp. 401–13 (bk. 39, chaps. 8–18).

31. William R. Akins, "Hell-Fire Club," in Ebon, *World's Weirdest Cults*, p. 169.

32. "How to Deal with the Occult in Your Area," *ORCRO* 7 (September 1990): 14.

33. Best, *Threatened Children*, p. 52.

34. "In Satan's Name," *Viewpoint '93*, ITV, 29 June 1993; also *News of the World*, 27 June 1993.

35. In Storm, *Exorcists*, p. 48.

36. Alciatus, *Parergon iuris*, pp. 75–76.

37. Lyons, *Satan Wants You* (1988 ed.), pp. 156–57.

38. Lanning, *Investigator's Guide to Allegations of "Ritual" Child Abuse*, p. 35.

39. Garinet, *Histoire de la magie en France*, p. liii.

40. Tate, *Children for the Devil*, p. 27.

41. Pulling, *Devil's Web*, pp. 39–41.

42. Sumrall, *Three Habitations of Devils*, p. 37.

43. Rosie Waterhouse, "A Modern Witch Hunt," *The Oldie*, no. 1 (21 February 1992): 13.

44. Mamor, *Flagellum maleficorum*; both editions of this book (ca. 1480) are unpaginated.

NOTES TO CHAPTER 13

1. Murray, *Witch-Cult*, p. 175; her source was Bodin's *Le Fleau des demons et sorciers*, which was merely a reissue (1616) of the *De la démonomanie des sorciers*; see, in the latter, preface (1580 ed.), sig.aiii^v, f. 212^v (bk. 4, chap. 5).

2. Summary of the case in Glanvil, *Saducismus Triumphatus*, appendix.

3. Goodyear–Smith, *First Do No Harm*, p. 65.

4. Bodin, *De la démonomanie des sorciers*, f. 106^v (bk. 2, chap. 7).

5. Cassini, *Questione de le strie*, passim. This essay set off a minor pamphlet war; see the entries under Cassini and Dodus in the bibliography.

6. *The Witch of Wapping*, passim.

7. von Spee, *Cautio criminalis*, p. 119-20.

8. Scot, *Discoverie of Witchcraft*, bk. 3, chap. 7.

9. Logan, *America Bewitched*, pp. 154–56; Newton, *Raising Hell*, pp. 271–73.

10. Boyd, *Blasphemous Rumours*, p. 75.

11. See, e.g., Cohn, *Europe's Inner Demons*, p. 231.

12. Tate, *Children for the Devil*, pp. 247–49.

13. Nathan and Snedeker, *Satan's Silence*, pp. 169–77.

14. LaFontaine, *Extent and Nature of Organised and Ritual Abuse*, p. 27.

15. Jansen, *History of the German People*, vol. 16, p. 421.

16. Woodhouse, *Rebuilding the Ruined Places*, sec. 3, p. 2.

17. Woodhouse, *Rebuilding the Ruined Places*, sec. 1, p. 5.

18. *Joint Enquiry Team Report*, June 1990; short version published by Nick Anning, David Hebditch, and Margaret Jervis, May 1997 (hereafter cited as *Jet Report*), p. 30.

19. Nathan and Snedeker, *Satan's Silence*, pp. 141, 209.

20. Tate, *Children for the Devil*, p. 166; Blood, *New Satanists*, p. 171.

21. LaFontaine, *Speak of the Devil*, p. 130.

22. Ofshe and Watters, *Making Monsters*, pp. 187–91; Victor, *Satanic Panic*, pp. 294–95.

23. Carlson and Larue, *Satanism in America*, p. 31.

24. Harper, *Deliverance Means Love*, pp. 105–6.

25. Peter Hough and Moyshe Kalman, *The Truth about Alien Abductions* (London: Cassell, 1997), chap. 6, "The Devil in Our Midst."

26. Saradjian, *Women Who Sexually Abuse Children*, p. 183.

27. Saradjian, *Women Who Sexually Abuse Children*, p. 174.

28. Saradjian, *Women Who Sexually Abuse Children*, p. 165.

29. Chambers, *Domestic Annals of Scotland*, vol. 3, pp. 298–99.

30. McConnell, *The Possessed*, pp. 277–78; "Miss Personality 1990," *Fortean Times* 56 (Winter 1990): 19; and "Officer, You've Got The Wrong Person," *Fortean Times* 79 (February/March 1995): 14.

31. Rosie Waterhouse, "A Modern Witch Hunt," *The Oldie*, no. 1 (21 February 1992).

32. Noblitt and Perskin, *Cult and Ritual Abuse*, p. 37.

33. *Pagan Prattle* (Summer 1994), citing *American Medical News* (25 October 1993): 3.

34. Colin A. Ross, *Satanic Ritual Abuse*, p. 56; also p. 96.

35. Ross, *Satanic Ritual Abuse*, p. 57.

36. Ryder, *Breaking the Circle of Satanic Ritual Abuse*, p. 55.

37. Phil Mollon, "The Impact of Evil," in Sinason, ed., *Treating Survivors of Satanist Abuse*, p. 143.

38. Ryder, *Breaking the Circle of Satanic Ritual Abuse*, pp. 89–91.

39. Wright, *Remembering Satan*, pp. 24–25.

40. Wright, *Remembering Satan*, pp. 25–26.

41. Wright, *Remembering Satan*, pp. 26–27, 82.

42. Wright, *Remembering Satan*, p. 8.

43. Wright, *Remembering Satan*, pp. 62–63.

44. Wright, *Remembering Satan*, pp. 136–39; and Ofshe and Watters, *Making Monsters*, pp. 166–75.

45. Ryder, *Breaking the Circle of Satanic Ritual Abuse*, pp. 63–64.

46. Woodhouse, *Rebuilding the Ruined Places*, sec. 2, p. 12.

47. Woodhouse, *Rebuilding the Ruined Places*, sec 1, pp. 7–8.

48. Apuleius, "A Discourse on Magic" (text of his defense), in *Works of Apuleius* (London: Bohn's Libary, 1902).

49. Hicks, *In Pursuit of Satan*, pp. 230–31.

50. Bragge, *Defense of the Proceedings against Jane Wenham*, p. 34.

51. Gardiner, *England's Grievance Discovered*, pp. 107–100.

52. Catherine Gould, "Diagnosis and Treatment of Ritually Abused Children," in Sakheim and Devine, *Out of Darkness*, p. 215.

53. *Mail on Sunday*, 23 September 1990.

54. *The Detection of a Popish Cheat*, broadsheet.

55. *The Times*, 16 and 17 April 1993; "Hoaxed Crimes," *Fortean Times* 71 (October/November 1993): 24.

56. Parker, *At the Heart of Darkness*, pp. 146–47; conversation with Phil Hine.

57. Journal Graphics transcript of *The Oprah Winfrey Show*, 17 February 1988.

58. Goodyear–Smith, *First Do No Harm*, p. 100.

59. Sparks, *Jay's Journal*, pp. 164–65.

60. Sebald, *Witch–Children*, pp. 58–60, 206; McConnell, *The Possessed*, chap. 14.

61. Tate, *Children for the Devil*, p. 133.

62. "The Devil in Lewes," *Guardian*, Weekend magazine, 12 April 1997, p. 26.

63. "Letter from New Zealand," *False Memory Society Journal*, (1996): 26.

64. Edward Podolosky, *Encyclopedia of Aberrations*, (London: Arco, 1953), p. 186.

65. *Taboo,* vol. 1, no. 2, September 1962.

66. *Tatler* (December 1984): 110.

67. Robert Hicks, "The Police Model of Satanic Crime," in Best, Richardson, and Bromley, *Satanism Scare*, p. 178, citing Sgt. Randall S. Emon, "Occult Criminal Investigation," *Baldwin Park* (California) *Police Department Training Bulletin* 86, 2 (1986).

68. George B. Greaves, "Alternative Hypotheses Regarding Claims of Satanic Cult Activity: A Critical Analysis," in Sakheim and Devine, *Out of Darkness*, pp. 61–62.

69. *JET Report*, p. 38.

70. Brown, *He Came to Set the Captives Free*, p. 79.

71. Voragine, *Legenda aurea*, f. lxiii^r.

72. Lercheimer, *Christlich bedencken und erjnnerung von Zauberen*, not in the original 1585 edition, but included in the 1888 reprint (which was based on the revised 1597 version, not seen), p. 132 (chap. 20).

73. Wagner, *How to Have a Healing Ministry*, p. 201; also, Wagner, ed., *Territorial Spirits*, pp. 47–48.

74. Rose Lopes, letter to the author, February 1996.

75. Journal Graphics transcript of *The Oprah Winfrey Show*, 17 February 1988.

76. LaFontaine, *Extent and Nature of Organised and Ritual Abuse*, p. 28

77. van Limborch, *History of the Inquisition*, vol. 2, pp. 190–92.

78. Interview for the *Cook Report*, May 1989, printed in Tate, *Children for the Devil*, pp. 162–64; also Journal Graphics transcript of *Geraldo Rivera Show*, 13 November 1990. Angell's statements in these two interviews were not entirely consistent, however. Tate quotes her as saying the case was due to start on 1 February, and that she received the call asking her to go to the restaurant the night before. On *Geraldo* she said that the kidnapping happened on "February second, 1989," and that this was "the day the trial was to begin." She told the *Cook Report* that "before I could even get out of the car two men got in through the passenger side," but she told the audience of *Geraldo* that "one man got into my car" and implied that the second appeared later. In the earlier interview she said, "I made formal enquiries about issuing a subpoena to get Michael Aquino in court and on the stand," but she did not say that she had actually obtained a subpoena. Yet, on *Geraldo,* she claimed that the kidnapping occurred "Shortly after I issued a subpoena for Michael Aquino." On 19 November 1990, Michael Aquino's lawyer sent Angell a letter pointing out that Michael Aquino had never received any subpoena from her and asking that she either provide proof that she had issued this subpoena or cease from repeating this

statement, which was defamatory in that it implied Aquino was responsible for her kidnapping. No reply was received.

79. Blood, *New Satanists*, p. 16.

80. Paul Foot, *Who Framed Colin Wallace?* (London: Macmillan, 1989), pp. 100–101.

81. "Nicolas Corte," *Who Is the Devil?* (1958), p. 98.

82. Misinformed writing about Crowley is too extensive to list, but see, for instance, Baskin, *Dictionary of Satanism*, s.v. "Crowley"; Sellers, *Web of Darkness*, p. 41; Logan, *Satanism and the Occult*, p. 73; Anderson, *Satan's Snare*, p. 63.

83. E.g., Pulling, *Devil's Web*, p. 172; Paul Banner, "Introduction to Satanism," South Carolina Criminal Justice Academy, quoted by Hicks, *In Pursuit of Satan*, p. 69.

84. Storm, *Exorcists*, pp. 41–56; and Logan, *Satanism and the Occult*, pp. 113–16.

85. McConnell, *The Possessed*, pp. 274, 283–84, 297–98; *News of the World*, 17 September 1995; *Express*, 19 January 1999.

86. Robson, *Nightmare on Your Street*, pp. 58–61.

87. Glanvill, *Saducismus triumphatus*, part 2, pp. 1–3.

88. Woodhouse, *Rebuilding the Ruined Places*, sec. 1, p. 7.

89. Bodin, *De la démonomanie des sorciers*, f. 162^r (bk. 3, chap. 6.)

90. Quoted by Robie, *Reverse the Curse in Your Life*, p. 53.

91. Spina, *De strigibus*, c.xviii.

92. Spiritualists and other mediums do, of course, become, or appear to become, temporarily "possessed" by nonphysical entities, and I have seen this happen. But it seems to be a quite different phenomenon from the possession alleged by Christians: mediums become possessed only briefly, under controlled conditions; Christians are supposed to have demons inside them permanently, which can be moved out only by exorcism.

93. Rougemont, *Talk of the Devil*, p. 18.

94. T. Lobsang Rampa, *Feeding the Flame* (London: Corgi, 1971), pp. 27–28.

95. Perhaps the nadir was reached with Forrest and Sanderson's *Cults and the Occult Today*, which claimed, "Some [cults] go so far as to say that all other groups are Satanic counterfeits" (p. 17), and then went on to denounce all cults as Satanic counterfeits.

96. *Daily Mirror*, 16 and 17 September 1985.

97. Michael Aquino, letter to the author, 18 May 1999.

NOTES TO THE APPENDIX

1. Grilland, *Tractatus de hereticis et sortilegiis*, bk 2, chap. 3, n. 6.

2. de Raemound, *L'Anti–christ*, pp. 103–4.

3. de Lancré, *Tableau*, p. 180.

4. Boguet, *Discours des sorciers* (1610), chap. 21, (1970) chap. 20.

5. Jansen, *History of the German People*, vol. 16, p. 423.

6. Scot, *Discoverie of Witchcraft*, bk. 4, chap. 6.

7. British Library ms. Additional 36,674, f. 66r.

8. This point is argued by Gardner, *Meaning of Witchcraft*, chap. 13.

9. d'Arch Smith, *Books of the Beast*, pp. 56–57.

10. Summers, *History of Witchcraft and Demonology*, pp. 149, 170; see also Baissac, *Les Grand Jours de la sorcellerie*, p. 395.

11. Summers, *History of Witchcraft and Demonology*, p. 156.

12. Summers, *History of Witchcraft and Demonology*, p. 147.

13. Geyraud, *Les Petites Églises*, p. 141.

14. Fahrhang Mehr, *The Zoroastrian Tradition* (Shaftesbury, Dorset: Elements Books, 1991), p. 37.

15. Rhodes, *Satanic Mass*, p. 77; Anna Comnena, *Alexiad*, trans. by E. R. A. Sewter (London: Penguin Books, 1969), p. 498.

16. Mannix, *The Hell-Fire Club*, p. 27; King, *Witchcraft and Demonology*, p. 107.

17. Kingston, *Witches and Witchcraft*, p. 110.

18. Franklyn, *Death by Enchantment*, p. 262.

Bibliography

This list comprises books, seen by the author, that primarily concern the Devil or Satanism or are quoted several times. Some works that are not directly related to the subject and cited only once or twice are not included here but have full publication details given in the notes.

Abbé de la Tour de Noé [pseud.]. *La Vérité sur Miss Diana Vaughan*. [Paris?], 1897.

Ahmed, Rollo. *The Black Art*. 1936. Reprint, Arrow, 1971.

Alciatus, Andreas. *Parergon iuris*. Lyons, 1554.

Alexander, Marc. *The Devil Hunter*. London: Sphere Books, 1981.

Alphonsus a Spina. *Fortalicium Fidei*. Strasbourg, 1467.

Anderson, Neil T. *The Bondage Breaker*. Tunbridge Wells: Monarch, 1993.

Anderson, Peter. *Satan's Snare: The Influence of the Occult*. London: Evangelical Press, 1988.

Anglo, Sydney, ed. *The Damned Art*. London: Routledge & Kegan Paul, 1977.

Antebi, Elisabeth. *Ave Lucifer*. Paris: J'ai Lu, 1970.

Apology for M. Antonia Bourignon. London: 1699.

Aranza, Jacob. *Backward Masking Unmasked: Backward Satanic Messages of Rock and Roll Exposed*. Shreveport, La.: Huntingdon House, 1983.

Ashe, Geoffrey. *Do What You Will: A History of Anti-Morality*. London: W. H. Allen, 1974.

Ashley, Leonard R. H. *The Complete Book of Devils and Demons*. London: Robson Books, 1997.

Ashton, John. *The Devil in Britain and America*. London, 1896.

Atkins, Susan, with Bob Slosser. *Child of Satan, Child of God*. London: Hodder & Stoughton, 1977.

Aubin, Nicholas. *The Cheats and Illusions of Romish Priests and Exorcists discover'd in the History of the Devils of Loudun*. London, 1703.

Augustine, Saint. *De doctrina christiana*. Cologne, 1930. Translated by the Reverend Professor J. F. Shaw in *A Select Library of Nicene and Post Nicene Fathers*. Vol. 2, Buffalo, NY, 1887.

Bainbridge, William Sims. *Satan's Power*. Berkeley: University of California Press, 1978.

Baissac, Jules. *Le Diable*. Paris, [1882].

Baissac, Jules. *Les Grands Jours de la Sorcellerie*. Paris, 1890.

Baker, Roger. *Binding the Devil: Exorcism Past and Present*. London: Sheldon Press, 1974.

Baldick, Robert. *The Life of J-K Huysmans*. London: Oxford University Press, 1955.

Baron, Frank. *Faustus on Trial*. Tübingen: Max Niemeyer Verlag, 1992.

Barstow, Anne Llewellyn. *Witchcraze*. London: Pandora, 1994.

Barton, Blanche. *The Secret Life of a Satanist*. Los Angeles: Feral House, 1990.

———. *The Church of Satan*. New York: Hell's Kitchen Productions, 1990.

Basin, Bernard. *De magicis artibus*. N.p., 1482.

Baskin, Wade. *Dictionary of Satanism*. London: Peter Owen, 1972.

Bataille, Dr. [pseud.]. *Le Diable au XIXe siècle*. 2 vols. Paris, 1892–95.

Bataille, Georges. *Le Procès de Gilles de Rais*. [Paris], 1965.

Batstone, Patricia, and Margaret Oxenham. *Occult: The Hidden Dangers*. Cullompton, Devon: Cottage Books, 1991.

Baudelaire, Charles Pierre. *Les Fleurs du mal*. Paris 1857; reprint, n.d.

Bekker, Balthasar. *The World Bewitched*. London, 1695.

Bergeron, Richard. *Damné Satan*. Montreal: Centre d'Information sur les Nouvelles Religions, 1988.

Bernard, Richard. *A Guide to Grand-Iury Men . . . in cases of Witchcraft*. London, 1627.

Berry, Harold J. *Examining the Cults*. Lincoln, Neb.: Back to the Bible, 1977.

Bessy, Maurice. *A Pictorial History of Magic and the Supernatural*. London: Spring Books, 1964.

Best, Joel. *Threatened Children*. Chicago: University of Chicago Press, 1990.

Best, Joel, James T. Richardson, and David G. Bromley. *The Satanism Scare*. New York: Aldine de Gruyter, 1991.

Black, Robert. *The Satanists*. London: Futura, 1978.

Black, Robert. *Orkney: A Place of Safety?* Edinburgh: Canongate Press, 1992.

Black, S. Jason and Christopher S. Hyatt. *Pacts with the Devil*. Phoenix, Ariz.: New Falcon, 1993.

Bladé, Jean-François. *Contes populaires de la Gascogne*. 3 vols. Paris, 1886.

Blatty, William Peter. *Before the Exorcist*. Eye, Suffolk: ScreenPress Books, 1998.

Blood, Linda. *The New Satanists*. New York: Warner, 1994.

Bodin, Jean. *De la démonomanie des sorciers*. Paris, 1580.

Boguet, Henri. *Discours des sorciers*. 3rd Lyons ed., 1610. Montague Summers ed., London: Frederick Muller, 1970.

Bois, Jules. *Le Satanisme et la magie.*, Preface by J.-K. Huysmans. Paris, 1895.

Bossard, Eugène. *Gilles de Rais*. Paris, 1886.

Bossier, Herman. *Geschiedenis van een Romanfiguur, de "Chanoine Docre" uit "La-Bas" van J.-K. Huysmans*. Brussels, 1942.

Boulton, Richard. *Compleat History of Magick, Sorcery and Witchcraft*. 2 vols. London, 1715–16.

———. *The Possibility and Reality of Magick, Sorcery, and Witchcraft demonstrated.* London, 1722.

Bourre, Jean-Paul. *Les Sectes Lucifériennes aujourd'hui.* Paris: Pierre Belford, 1978.

Boyd, Andrew. *Blasphemous Rumours.* London: Fount Paperbacks, 1991.

———. *Dangerous Obsessions.* London: Marshall Pickering, 1996.

Bragge, Francis. *A Defense of the Proceedings against Jane Wenham.* London, 1712.

Bricaud, Joanny. *J.-K. Huysmans et le Satanisme.* Paris, 1913.

———. *Huysmans, occultiste et magicien.* Paris, 1913.

Brown, Rebecca. *He Came to Set the Captives Free.* 1986. Reprint, Springdale, Pa: Solid Rock Family Enterprises, 1992.

———. *Prepare for War.* 1987 rev. ed., Springdale, Pa: Solid Rock Family Enterprises, 1992.

———. *Becoming a Vessel of Honor in the Master's Service.* 1990. Reprint, Springdale, Pa: Solid Rock Family Enterprises, 1992.

Brown, Rebecca, with Daniel Yoder. *Unbroken Curses.* Springdale, Pa: Whitaker House, 1995.

Brown, Robert. *The Personality and History of Satan.* London, 1887.

Brunvand, Harold. *The Choking Dobermann.* London: Penguin, 1987.

Bugliosi, Vincent, with Curt Gentry. *Helter Skelter.* 1st ed. *The Manson Murders.* 1974. Reprint, London: Arrow, 1992.

Burman, Edward. *Inquisition, The Hammer of Heresy.* Wellingborough, Northampton: Aquarian Press, 1984.

Butler, E. M. *Ritual Magic.* Cambridge: Cambridge University Press, 1949.

C., Comte H. *Mémoire à l'adresse des membres du Congrès antimaçonnique de Trente.* Paris and Vienna, 1897.

Cahill, the Reverend E. *Freemasonry and the Anti-Christian Movement.* 2d ed. Dublin, 1930.

Carlson, Shawn, and Gerald Larue. *Satanism in America.* El Cerrito, Calif.: Gaia, 1989.

Caro Baroja, Julio. *The World of the Witches.* Translated by Nigel Glendinning. London: Weidenfeld and Nicolson, 1964.

Carus, Paul. *The History of the Devil and the Idea of Evil.* London: Kegan Paul, 1900.

Cassiel [pseud.]. *Encyclopedia of Forbidden Knowledge.* London: Hamlyn, 1990.

Cassini, Samuel. *Questione de le strie.* [Pavia], 1505.

———. *Contra fratrem Vincentium or. predicatorum qui inepte et falso impugnare nititur libellum de lamijs editum a.f. Samuele.* [Pavia], 1507.

Cavendish, Richard, *The Black Arts.* London: Pan, 1969.

Cawthorne, Nigel. *Satanic Murder.* London: True Crime, 1995.

Cerullo, Morris. *The Back Side of Satan.* Carol Stream, Ill.: Creation House, 1973.

Chambers, Robert. *Domestic Annals of Scotland.* Vol. 3. London, 1861.

Chancellor, E. Beresford. *The Lives of the Rakes.* Vol. 4: *The Hell-Fire Club.* London: Philip Allen, 1925.

C[hick], J[ack] T. *The Broken Cross*. Chino, Calif.: ChickPub, 1974.

———. *Spellbound?* Chino, Calif.: ChickPub, 1978.

———. *The Trick*. Chino, Calif.: ChickPub, 1986.

———. *The Curse of Baphomet*. Chino, Calif.: ChickPub, 1991.

Cigogna, Strozzi. *Magiæ Omnifariæ*. Cologne, 1606.

Clapton, Gary. *The Satanic Abuse Controversy*. London: University of North London Press, 1993.

Cohn, Norman. *Warrant for Genocide*. London: Pelican, 1970.

———. *Europe's Inner Demons*. London: Paladin, 1976.

Collection of Rare and Curious Tracts on Witchcraft and Second Sight. Edinburgh, 1820.

Collin de Plancy, J. A. S. *Dictionnaire infernal*, 3d ed. Paris, 1844.

Collins, Andrew. *The Black Alchemist*. Leigh-on-Sea: ABC Books, 1988.

———. *The Second Coming*. London: Century, 1993.

Confessions of Madeleine Bavent. 1652, Translated by Montague Summers. London: Fortune Press, 1933.

Constantine, Alex. *Psychic Dictatorship in the U.S.A.* Portland, Ore.: Feral House, 1995.

Conway, Moncure Daniel. *Demonology and Devil Lore*. 2 vols. London, 1874.

Conybeare, Frederick. *The Key of Truth*. London, 1908.

Cooling, Margaret. *Hallowe'en in the Classroom?* St. Albans: Association of Christian Teachers, 1988.

Cooper, Thomas. *The Mystery of Witch-craft*. London, 1617.

Core, Dianne, with Fred Harrison. *Chasing Satan*. London: Gunter Books, 1991.

Corte, Nicholas [pseud.]. *Who Is the Devil?* London: Burns and Oates, 1958.

Coulange, Father Louis. *The Life of the Devil*. Translated from the French by Stephen Haden Guest. New York: Alfred A. Knopf, 1929.

Cristiani, Monsignor L. *Satan in the Modern World*. Translated by Cynthia Rowland. London: Barrie & Rockliff, 1961.

Crowley, Aleister. *The Goetia*. London: Foyers 1904.

———. *The World's Tragedy*. Paris, 1910.

———. *The Equinox of the Gods*. London, 1936.

———. *Moonchild*. 1929. Reprint, London: Sphere Books, 1972.

———. *The Magical Record of the Beast 666*. 1914–20.Reprint, London: Duckworth, 1972.

———. *Magick* [incorporating Bk. 4, parts 1 & 2, and *Magick in Theory and Practice*]. London: Routledge & Kegan Paul, 1973.

———. *Crowley on Christ* [original title: *The Gospel According to Saint George Bernard Shaw*]. London: C. W. Daniel, 1974.

———. *Confessions*. London: Routledge & Kegan Paul, 1979.

———. *Gilles de Rais*. London: Society for the Propagation of Religious Truth, 1982.

Cruz, Nicky. *Satan on the Loose.* 1973. Reprint, Basingstoke: Lakeland, 1985.

———. *Devil on the Run!* Rev. ed. Eastbourne: Kingsway, 1990.

Dalton, Michael. *Countrey Justice.* 5th ed. London, 1635.

Daneau, Lambert. *A Dialogue of Witches.* London, 1575.

Danger! Open Mind. London: Scripture Union, 1986.

d'Arch Smith, Timothy. *Montague Summers: A Bibliography.* London: Aquarian, 1983.

———. *The Books of the Beast.* London: Crucible, 1987.

Dashwood, Sir Francis. *Abridgement of the Book of Common Prayer.* London, 1773.

Dashwood, Sir Francis. *The Dashwoods of West Wycombe.* London: Aurum, 1987.

Davidson, Gustav. *A Dictionary of Angels, Including the Fallen Angels.* New York: Free Press, 1967.

Davies, Horton. *Christian Deviations.* 2d rev. ed., London: SCM, 1961.

Davies, Maureen. *Satanic Ritual Abuse.* [Self published, 1989].

Davies, R. Trevor. *Four Centuries of Witch Beliefs.* London: Methuen, 1947.

Dear, William. *The Dungeon Master.* London: Sphere Books, 1985.

Dearing, Trevor, with Dan Wooding. *Exit the Devil.* Ongar: Logos Publishing International, 1976.

Defoe, Daniel. *The Political History of the Devil.* London, 1727.

de Grimston, Robert. *Jehovah on War.* London, [1968].

de Guaita, Stanislas. *Essais de sciences maudites.* 3 vols. Paris, 1890–97.

de Lancré, Pierre. *Tableau de l'inconstance des mauvais anges et démons.* Rev. ed. Paris, 1613.

Delangle. *Procez verbal de monsieur le penitencier d'Evreux.* Paris, 1643.

Del Rio, Martin. *Disquisitionum magicarum libri sex.* Expanded ed. Mainz, 1603.

Demaix, Georges J. *Les Esclaves du Diable.* Paris: J'ai Lu, 1970.

de Raemound, Florimond. *L'Anti-christ.* Lyons, 1597.

de Rougemont, Denis. *Talk of the Devil.* Translated by Kathleen Raine. London: Eyre & Spottiswoode, 1945.

Detection of a Popish Cheat or a True Account of the Invention and Discovery of the Story of a Boys conversing with the Devil. Broadsheet. London and Dublin, 1696.

The Divels Delusions. London, 1649.

The Doctrine of Devils. London, 1676.

Dodus, Vincent. *Apologia Dodi. Contra li defensori de le strie. Et principaliter Contra questiones lamiarum fratris samuelis de cassinis.* Pavia, [1506].

———. *Elogium in materia maleficarum, Ad morsus: fugas: et errores Fra Samuelis Cassinensis contra Apologiam Dodi.* Pavia, 1507.

Drahcid, C. R. [Bernard Wilets]. *The Dark Arts.* [Long Beach, Calif., 1956?].

Eberle, Paul and Shirley Eberle. *The Abuse of Innocence.* Amherst, N.Y.: Prometheus, 1993.

Ebon, Martin. *The World's Weirdest Cults.* New York: Signet, 1979.

———. ed. *Exorcism: Fact Not Fiction.* New York: Signet, 1974.

Ellis, Roger. *The Occult and Young People*. Eastbourne: Kingsway, 1989.

Encyclopedia of Witchcraft and Demonology. London: Octopus, 1974.

Ericsson, Eric. *The World, The Flesh, The Devil*. London: New English Library, 1981.

Esprit de Bosroger, Père. *La Pieté affligée ou discours historique et theologique de la possession des religieuses . . . de Louviers*. Rouen, 1652.

Essay on The Devil; Proving a Belief in the Existence of such a Being, Contrary to Scripture, Reason, and Natural Philosophy. London, [1815?].

Evangelical Alliance. *Doorways to Danger*. London, 1987.

Ewen, C. L'Estrange. *Witch Hunting and Witch Trials*. London, 1929.

Examination of John Walsh. London, 1566.

Fabian, Robert. *Fabian of the Yard*. London: Naldrett Press, 1950.

———. *London After Dark*. London: Naldrett Press, 1954.

Farrant, David. *Beyond the Highgate Vampire*. London: British Psychic and Occult Society, 1992.

Feyerabend, Sigmund, ed. *Theatrum Diabolorum*. Frankfurt-am-Main, 1569.

[Filmer, Robert]. *An Advertisement to the Jury-Men of England, Touching Witches*. London, 1653.

Finch, A. Elley. *Witchcraft, Conjuration, Exorcism, and other assumed dealings with the Devil*. London, 1887.

Finkelhor, David, and Linda Meyer Williams, with Nanci Burns. *Nursery Crimes*. Newbury Park, Calif.: Sage, 1988.

Fitzgerald, Michael. *Storm-Troopers of Satan*. London: Robert Hale, 1990.

Forrest, Alistair, and Peter Sanderson. *Cults and the Occult Today*. London: Marshall, Morgan & Scott, 1982.

Fouquet, L. *Luciferianism or Satanism in English Freemasonry*. Montreal, 1898.

Fox, George. *A Declaration of the Ground of Error*. London, 1657.

Franklyn, Julian. *A Survey of the Occult*. London Arthur Barker, 1935.

———. *Death by Enchantment*. London: Sphere Books, 1975.

Frederickson, Bruce G. *How to Respond to Satanism*. St. Louis, Minn.: Concordia, 1988.

Freemasonry and Christianity: Are They Compatible? London: Church House Publishing, 1987.

Friesen, James G. *Uncovering the Mystery of MPD*. Nashville: Thomas Nelson, 1991.

Fry, L. *Léo Taxil et la Franc-Maçonnerie*. Chaton, 1934.

A Full and True Account of the Apprehending and Taking of Mrs. Sarah Moordike. London, [1701].

Fuller, Ronald. *Hell-Fire Francis*. London: Chatto & Windus, 1939.

Garçon, Maurice, and Jean Vinchon. *The Devil*. Translated by Stephen Haden Guest. London: Victor Gollancz, 1929.

Gardiner, Ralph. *England's Grievance Discovered*. London, 1655.

Gardner, Gerald. *The Meaning of Witchcraft*. London: Aquarian Press, 1959.

Garinet, Jules. *Histoire de la magie en France*. Paris, 1818.

Gastineau, Benjamin. *Monsieur et Madame Satan*. Paris, 1864.

Gaule, John. *Select Cases of Conscience Touching Witches and Witchcraft*. London, 1646.

Geyraud, Pierre. *Les Petites Églises de Paris*. Paris, 1937.

Gijswijt-Hofstra, Marijka, and Willem Frijhoff. *Witchcraft in the Netherlands*. Rotterdam: Universitaire Pers, 1991.

Gilbert, Robert A. *Casting the First Stone*. London: Element, 1993.

Gillett, David. *The Occult*. London: Church Pastoral Aid Society, 1974.

Glanvill, Joseph. *Saducismus triumphatus*. London, 1681.

Gobey, the Reverend Francis X. *The Terminology for the Devil and Evil Spirits in the Apostolic Fathers*. Catholic University of America Patristic Studies, vol. 93. Washington, D.C.: Catholic University of America Press, 1961.

Godré, L. Nemours. *Diana Vaughan et ses répondants*. Paris, [1897].

Godwin, Jess. *Dancing With Demons*. Chino, Calif.: Chick Publications, 1988.

Godwin, William. *Lives of the Necromancers*. London, 1834.

Goldstein, Eleanor, and Kevin Farmer. *True Stories of False Memories*. Boca Raton, Fla.: Social Issues Resources Series Publishing, 1993.

Goodyear-Smith, Felicity. *First Do No Harm: The Sexual Abuse Industry*. Auckland: Benton-Guy, 1993.

Gostick, Jesse. *Who Is the Devil?* London, 1872.

Graf, Arturo. *The Story of the Devil*. Translated from the Italian by Edward Noble Stone. London: Macmillan, 1931.

Grand Grimoire. Paris, 1845.

Greenwood, Benjamin I. *Slogans of Satan*. London: 2d ed. Page & Thomas, 1930.

Grilland, Paul. *Tractatus de haereticis et sortilegiis*. Lyons, 1536.

Gruss, Edmond C. *The Ouija Board: A Doorway to the Occult*. Phillipsburg, N.J.: P&R, 1994.

Guazzo, Francesco Maria. *Compendium Maleficarum*. Milan, 1608. Montague Summers ed., New York: Dover, 1988.

G'Zell, Otter, ed. *Witchcraft, Satanism and Occult Crime*. 4th ed. Ukiah, Calif.: Green Egg, 1991.

Haack, Annette, and Friedrich-Wilhelm. *Jugendspiritismus und satanismus*. Munich: Münchener Reihe, 1990.

Haack, Friedrich-Wilhelm. *Satan-Teufel-Luzifer*. Munich: Münchener Reihe, 1989.

Haining, Peter. *Anatomy of Witchcraft*. London: Souvenir, 1972; London: Tandem, 1974.

Hale, Matthew. *A Collection of Modern Relations of Matter of Fact, Concerning Witches and Witchcraft*. London, 1693.

Hallowe'en. St. Albans: Association of Christian Teachers, [1982?].

Hanna, David. *Cults in America*. New York: Tower Publications, 1979.

Hannah, Walton. *Darkness Visible*. London: Augustine Press, 1952.

Hansen, Joseph. *Quellen und Untersuchungen zur Geschichte des Hexenwahns.* Bonn, 1901.

Harper, Audrey, with Harry Pugh. *Dance with the Devil.* Foreword by Geoffrey Dickens, M.P. Eastbourne: Kingsway, 1990.

———. *Deliverance Means Love.* Foreword by Doug Harris. Eastbourne: Kingsway, 1992.

Hauber, Eberhard David. *Bibliotheca, acta et scripta magica.* 3 vols. Lemgo, 1738–45.

Hayden, Torey. *Ghost Girl.* London: Macmillan, 1991.

The Hell-Fire Club: kept by a Society of Blasphemers. London, 1721.

Hertenstein, Mike and Jon Trott. *Selling Satan.* Chicago: Cornerstone, 1993.

Hickey, Marilyn. *Satan-Proof Your Home.* Denver: Marilyn Hickey Ministries, 1991.

Hicks, Robert A. *In Pursuit of Satan.* Buffalo, N.Y.: Prometheus Books, 1991.

The History of the Damnable Life and Deserved Death of Doctor John Faustus. 1592. Edited by William Rose. London: Routledge, 1926.

History of the Witches of Renfrewshire. London: Paisley, 1877.

Holzer, Hans. *The Truth about Witchcraft.* London: Arrow, 1971.

Hopkins, Matthew. *The Discovery of Witches.* London, 1647.

Hough, Peter. *Witchcraft, A Strange Conflict.* Cambridge: Lutterworth, 1991.

Hudson, Pamela H. *Ritual Child Abuse* Saratoga, Calif.: R&E, 1991.

Huegel, F. J. *That Old Serpent—The Devil.* London: Marshall, Morgan & Scott, [1937].

Hunt, the Reverend C. Penney. *The Menace of Freemasonry to the Christian Faith.* 4th ed. Derby: Freedom Press, 1930.

Hutchinson, Francis. *An Historical Essay Concerning Witchcraft.* London, 1718.

Huxley, Aldous. *The Devils of Loudun.* London: Penguin, 1971.

Huysmans, Joris-Karl. *Là-Bas.* Paris, 1891. Reprint, London: Sphere Books, 1974

Hyatt, Victoria, and Joseph W. Charles. *The Book of Demons.* London: Lorrimer Press 1974.

Hyatte, Reginald. *Laughter for the Devil.* London: Associated University Press, 1984.

Hyperius [Antonius Gerardus]. *Two Common Places.* London, 1581.

Irvine, Doreen. *From Witchcraft to Christ.* London: Concordia, 1973.

———. *Spiritual Warfare.* Basingstoke: Marshall Pickering, 1986.

James I of England. *Daemonologie.* Edinburgh, 1597.

Jansen, Johannes. *History of the German People after the Close of the Middle Ages.* Translated by A. M. Christie. Vol. 16. London, 1910.

Jenkins, Philip. *Intimate Enemies: Moral Panics in Contemporary Great Britain.* New York: Aldine de Gruyter, 1992.

Jennings, Gary. *Black Magic, White Magic.* London: Rupert Hart-Davis, 1967.

Jerome, Joseph. *Montague Summers.* London: Cecil and Amelia Wolf, 1965.

Jewett, the Reverend Edward H. *Diabology.* New York, 1889.

John of Salisbury. *Policraticus.* Ca. 12th century. Leyden, 1639.

Johns, June. *King of the Witches*. London, 1969.
———. *Black Magic Today*. London: New English Library, 1971.
Johnson, W. Branch. *The Age of Arsenic*. London, 1931.
Johnston, Jerry. *The Edge of Evil*. Dallas: Word, 1989.
Johnstone, Charles. *Chrysal*. Expanded ed, 4 vols. London, 1764-65.
Kahaner, Larry, ed. *Cults That Kill*. New York: Warner, 1988.
Kemp, Betty. *Sir Francis Dashwood: An Eighteenth Century Independent*. London: Macmillan, 1967.
King, Bernard. *Blood Circle*. London: Sphere Books, 1990.
King, Francis. *Sexuality, Magic and Perversion*. London: New English Library, 1972.
———. *The Secret Rituals of the O.T.O.* London: C. W. Daniel, 1973.
———. *Satan and Swastika*. London: Mayflower, 1976.
———. *The Magical World of Aleister Crowley*. London: Weidenfeld & Nicolson, 1977.
———. *Witchcraft and Demonology*. London: Hamlyn, 1987.
Kingston, Jeremy. *Witches and Witchcraft*. New York: Doubleday, 1976.
Kirban, Salem. *Satan's Mark Exposed*. Chattanooga, Tenn.: AMG International, 1978.
———. *Satan's Angels Exposed*. Chattanooga, Tenn.: AMG International, 1980.
Knight, Stephen. *The Brotherhood*. London: Panther, 1985.
Kors, Alan C., and Edward Peters. *Witchcraft in Europe, 1100–1700*. London: Dent, 1973.
Kraft, Charles H. *Defeating Dark Angels*. Tunbridge Wells: Sovereign World, 1993.
Kramer, Heinrich, and Jakob Sprenger. *Malleus Maleficarum*. ca. 1487. More than thirty subsequent editions, including Frankfurt, 1582; Lyons, 1669; Montague Summers ed., London: Arrow, 1971.
Krémer, J.-P. *False Cults and Heresies Exposed*. London, [ca. 1960].
LaFontaine, Jean. *The Extent and Nature of Organised and Ritual Abuse*. London: Her Majesty's Stationery Office, 1994.
———. *Speak of the Devil*. Cambridge: Cambridge University Press, 1998.
Lamothe-Langone, E. L. *Histoire de l'Inquisition en France*. 3 vols. Paris, 1829.
Lane, Brian. *The Encyclopedia of Occult and Supernatural Murder*. London: Headline, 1995.
Langton, Edward. *Satan, A Portrait*. London: Skeffington, [1946].
Lanning, Kenneth V. *Investigator's Guide to Allegations of "Ritual" Child Abuse*. Quantico, Va.: National Center For The Analysis of Violent Crime, FBI Academy, 1992.
Larson, Bob. *Larson's New Book of Cults*. Wheaton, Ill.: Tyndale House, 1989.
———. *Satanism: The Seduction of America's Youth*. Nashville: Thomas Nelson, 1989.
———. *In the Name of Satan*. Nashville: Thomas Nelson, 1996.
———. *Larson's Book of Spiritual Warfare*. Nashville: Thomas Nelson, 1999.

Laver, James. *The First Decadent, Being the Strange Life of J. K. Huysmans.* London: Faber, 1954.

LaVey, Anton. *The Satanic Bible.* 1969. Reprint, London: Star, 1977

———. *The Satanic Rituals.* New York: Avon, 1972.

———. *The Satanic Witch.* Los Angeles: Feral House, 1989.

———. *The Devil's Notebook.* Portland, Ore.: Feral House, 1992.

Lawrence, John. *Freemasonry—A Religion?* Eastbourne: Kingsway, 1987.

Lea, Henry C. *A History of the Inquisition.* 3 vols. London, 1888.

———. *Materials Toward a History of Witchcraft.* Philadelphia: University of Pennsylvania Press, 1939.

Lee, Robert, with David Lee. *Beware the Devil.* Basingstoke: Marshalls, 1983.

Le Gauffre. *Recit veritable faict a la Reyne.* Rouen, 1643.

[Leloyer, Pierre]. *A Treatise of Specters.* London, 1605.

Lercheimer, Augustin [Hermann Witekind]. *Christlich bedencken und erjnnerung von Zauberen.* Heidelberg, 1585. Edited by Carl Binz. Strasbourg, 1888.

Levack, Brian P. *The Witch–Hunt in Early Modern Europe.* London: Longman, 1987.

Levenda, Peter. *Unholy Alliance: A History of Nazi Involvement with the Occult.* New York: Avon, 1995.

Lévi, Eliphas. *Transcendental Magic.* 1855-56. 2 vols. Translated by A. E. Waite. London: Rider, 1976.

———. *The Key of the Mysteries.* 1861. Translated by Aleister Crowley. London: Rider, 1971.

Levin, Ira. *Rosemary's Baby.* London: Pan, 1968.

Lewis, [Thomas] *The Nature of Hell, the Reality of Hell-Fire, and the Eternity of Hell-Torments, Explain'd and Vindicated.* London, 1720.

Life and Death of Lewis Gaufredy. London, 1612.

Lillie, Arthur. *The Worship of Satan in Modern France.* London, 1896.

Lindsey, Hal. *Satan Is Alive and Well on Planet Earth.* London: Lakeland, 1973.

———. *The 1980's: Countdown to Armageddon.* New York: Bantam, 1981.

Linedecker, Clifford L. *Hell Ranch: The Nightmare Tale of Voodoo, Drugs, and Death in Matomoros.* Austin, Tex.: Diamond, 1989.

Livesey, Roy. *Beware! "666" Is Here.* Kidderminster: Bury House, Clows Top, 1983.

———. *Beware Alternative Medicine.* Kidderminster: Bury House, 1983.

———. *Understanding the New Age.* Chichester: New Wine, 1986.

Logan, Daniel. *America Bewitched.* New York: William Morrow, 1974.

Logan, the Reverend Kevin. *Paganism and the Occult.* Eastbourne: Kingsway, 1988.

———. *Close Encounters with the New Age.* Eastbourne: Kingsway, 1991.

———. *Satanism and the Occult*, Kingsway, Eastbourne, 1994.

Long, Anton. *The Book of Wyrd: The Black Book of Satan.* Church Stretton: O.N.A., 1984. New ed., *Codex Saerus.* Shrewsbury: Thormynd Press, 1992.

———. *Diablerie.* Shrewsbury: Thormynd Press, 1991.

———. *Satanism—A Basic Introduction for Prospective Adherents.* Shrewsbury: Rigel Press, 1992.

Lyf of saint jerom. "Printed by Caxton." London, [ca. 1490?].

Lyons, Arthur. *Satan Wants you.* London: Mayflower, 1972. Rev. ed., New York: Mysterious Press, 1988.

MacDougall, Curtis D. *Hoaxes.* New York: Dover, 1958.

Mackay, Charles. *Extraordinary Popular Delusions and the Madness of Crowds.* New York: Farrar, Straus & Giroux,, n.d. [1980s], from the editions of 1841 and 1852.

Mackenzie, Sir George. *Laws and Customs of Scotland in Matters Criminal.* Edinburgh, 1678.

Maldonat, Juan. *Traite des anges et demons.* Translated by Francois de la Borie. Paris, 1605.

Mamor, Petrus. *Flagellum maleficorum.* 1462. [Lyons, 1490].

Manchester, Sean. *The Highgate Vampire.* London: British Occult Society, 1985.

———. *From Satan to Christ.* London: Holy Grail, 1988.

Mannix, Daniel P. *The Hell-Fire Club.* London: 4-Square, 1961.

Maple, Eric. *The Domain of Devils.* London: Pan, 1966.

———. *Witchcraft.* London: Octopus, 1973

Margiotta, Domenico. *Le Culte de la nature dans la Franc-Maçonnerie universelle.* Grenoble and Bruxelles, [1895].

———. *Adriano Lemmi, chéf Suprême des Franc-Maçons.* 7th ed. Paris and Lyons, 1896.

Mariel, Pierre, ed. *Dictionnaire des sociétés secrètes en Occident.* Paris: Grosset, 1971.

Marillac, Alain. *Le Baphomet idéal templier.* Verdun: Louise Corteau, 1988.

Marron, Kevin. *Ritual Abuse.* Toronto: Seal, 1988.

———. *Witches, Pagans, and Magic in the New Age.* Toronto: Seal, 1989.

Marshall, David. *The Devil Hides Out.* Grantham: Autumn House, 1991.

Martin [later Marthin-Chagny], Louis. *L'Anglais est-il un Juif?* Paris, 1895.

———. *L'Angleterre suzeraine de la France par la F.M.* Paris, 1896.

Massadié, Gerald. *The History of the Devil.* Translated from the French by Marc Romanu. London: Newleaf, 1996.

Matson, William A. *The Adversary—His Person, Power, and Purpose: A Study in Satanology.* New York, 1891.

May, Betty. *Tiger Woman.* London: Duckworth, 1929.

McAll, Kenneth. *Healing the Family Tree.* London: Sheldon Press, 1982.

———. *Healing the Haunted.* London: Darley Anderson, 1989.

McConnell, Brian. *The Possessed.* London: Headline, 1995.

McCormick, Donald. *The Hell-Fire Club.* London: Jarrolds, 1958.

———. *Murder by Witchcraft.* London: John Long, 1965.

McCormick, W. J. *Christ, the Christian, and Freemasonry.* 3d ed. Belfast: Great Joy Publications, 1987.

———. *Out of the Devil's Parlour.* 2d ed. Belfast: Great Joy Publications, 1987.

McDowell, Josh, and Don Stewart. *The Occult*. Amersham: Scripture Press, 1992.

McIntosh, Christopher. *Eliphas Levi and the French Occult Revival*. London: Rider, 1972.

———. *The Devil's Bookshelf*. London: Aquarian, 1985.

Melech, Aubrey [pseud.]. *Missa niger: La Messe noire*. Northampton: Sut Anubis, 1986.

Meurin, Leon. *La Franc-Maçonnerie synagogue de Satan*. Paris, 1893.

Michaelis, Sebastian. *Admirable Historie of a Penitente Woman, and A Discourse of Spirits*. London, 1613.

Michelet, Jules. *La Sorcière*. Paris, 1861. Translated as *Satanism and Witchcraft* by A. R. Allinson. London: Tandem, 1965.

Molitor, Ulrich. *De laniis et phitonicis mulieribus*. N.p., 1489.

Monsters and Demons in the Ancient and Medieval Worlds. Mainz: Philipp von Zabern, 1987.

Montgomery, John Warwick. *Demon Possession*. Minneapolis, Minn.: Bethany House, 1976.

More, Henry. *An Antidote against Atheisme*. London, 1653.

Mossiker, Frances. *The Affair of the Poisons*. London: Sphere Books, 1975.

Murray, Margaret. *The Witch-Cult in Western Europe*. London: Oxford University Press, 1921.

Nathan, Debbie. *Women and Other Aliens*. El Paso, Tex.: Cinco Puntos, 1991.

Nathan, Debbie, and Michael Snedeker. *Satan's Silence*. New York: Basic Books, 1995.

Neil-Smith, Christopher. *The Exorcist and the Possessed*. St. Ives: James Pike, 1974.

Newton, Michael. *Raising Hell*. New York: Warner, 1994.

Newton, Toyne. *The Demonic Connection*. Poole: Blandford Press, 1987.

Nider, Johannes. *Formicarius*. 1435. [Book 5 reprinted with editions of the *Malleus Maleficarum* from 1582 onward.]

Noblitt, James Randall, and Pamela Sue Perskin. *Cult and Ritual Abuse*. Westport, Conn.: Praeger, 1995.

Nocturnal Revels: or, the History of King's-Place, and other Modern Nunneries. 2d ed. London, 1779.

Nodé, Pierre. *Declamation contre l'erreur execrable des malificiers, sorciers, Enchanteurs, Magiciens, Devins, et semblables observateurs des superstitions*. Paris, 1578.

Nomolos, the Reverend Yaj. *The Magic Circle*. Toluca Lake, Calif.: International Imports, 1987.

Notestein, Wallace. *History of Witchcraft in England*. Washington, D.C., 1911.

The Occult Census. Leeds: Sorcerer's Apprentice Press, 1989.

Ofshe, Richard, and Ethan Watters. *Making Monsters: False Memories, Psychotherapy and Sexual Hysteria*. New York: Scribner's, 1994.

O'Grady, Joan. *The Prince of Darkness*. Shaftesbury, Dorset: Element Books, 198.

Olliver, Charles W. *Handbook of Magic and Witchcraft*. 1928. Reprint, London: Senate, 1996.

[Ormiston, the Reverend. James]. *The Satan of Scripture*. London, 1876.

Page, Carol. *Bloodlust*. London: Warner, 1993.

Palmer, Philip M., and Robert P. More. *The Sources of the Faust Tradition*. New York, 1936.

Paramo, Ludovico à. *De origine et progressu officii sanctae inquisitionis, eiusque dignitate et utilitate*. Madrid, 1598.

Parker, John. *At the Heart of Darkness*. London: Sidgwick & Jackson, 1993.

Parker, Russ. *The Occult, Deliverance from Evil*. London: Inter-Varsity Press, 1989.

Passantino, Bob, and Gretchen Passantino. *When the Devil Dares Your Kids*. Guildford: Eagle, 1991.

———. *Satanism*. Carlisle: OM Publishing, 1995.

Pelton, Robert W. *The Devil and Karen Kingston*. New York: Pocket Books, 1977.

Pengelly, J., and D. Waredale. *Something Out of Nothing: The Myth of "Satanic Ritual Abuse."* London: The Pagan Federation, 1992.

Perkins, William. *A Discourse of the Damned Art of Witchcraft*. Cambridge, 1608.

Perreaud, François. *Demonologie*. Geneva, 1653.

Perry, Michael, ed. *Deliverance: Psychic Disturbances and Occult Involvement*. London: Society for Promoting Christian Knowledge, 1987.

Peters, Alexander. *The Devil in the Suburbs*. London: New English Library, 1972.

Petersen, William J. *Those Curious New Cults in the 80s*. New Canaan, Conn.: Keats Publishing, 1982.

Petitpierre, Dom Robert. *Exorcism*. London: Society for Promoting Christian Knowledge, 1972.

Plaidy, Jean. *The Spanish Inquisition*. London: Robert Hale, 1978.

Porter, David. *Children at Risk*. Eastbourne: Kingsway, 1986.

———. *Children at Play*. Eastbourne: Kingsway, 1989.

———. *Hallowe'en: Treat or Trick?* Tunbridge Wells: Monarch, 1993.

Praz, Mario. *The Romantic Agony*. 1933. Reprint, London: Fontana, 1960.

Prieur, Jean. *Hitler et la guerre luciférienne*. Paris: J'ai Lu, 1992.

Provost, Gary. *Across the Border: The True Story of the Satanic Cult Killings in Matamoros, Mexico*. New York: Pocket Books, 1989.

Psellus, Michael. *De Operatione daemonum Dialogus*. [ca. 1050?] Paris, 1615.

Pulling, Pat, with Kathy Cawthon. *The Devil's Web: Who Is Stalking Your Children For Satan?* Milton Keynes: Word Publishing, 1990.

Queenborough, Lady (Edith Starr Miller). *Occult Theocrasy*. Abbeville, n.p., 1933.

Raschke, Carl A. *Painted Black: From Drug Killings to Heavy Metal—The Alarming True Story of How Satanism Is Terrorizing Our Communities*. San Francisco: Harper & Row, 1990.

Ravaisson, François. *Archives de la Bastille*. Vol. 6. Paris, 1873.

Ravenscroft, Trevor. *The Spear of Destiny*. London: Corgi, 1974.

Reed, Robert D., and Danek S. Kaus. *Cults: How and Where to Find Facts and Get Help*. Saratoga, Calif.: R&E, n.d.

———. *Ritual Child Abuse: How and Where to Find Facts and Get Help*. Saratoga, Calif.: R&E, 1993.

Regardie, Israel. *The Eye in the Triangle*. London: Falcon Press, 1982.

Reid, D. H. S. *Suffer the Little Children*. St. Andrews: Napier Press, 1992.

Relation Of the Cursed and Hellish Design of Abraham Mason, a Pretended Quaker, to give himself to the Devil. London, ca. 1700.

Relation of the Devill Balams Departure out of the Body of the Mother-Prioresse of the Ursuline Nuns of Loudun. London, 1636.

Remy, Nicholas. *Demonolatry*. Lyons, 1595. Montague Summers ed., London: Frederick Muller, 1970.

Reynolds, M. *The Reality: The Truths about Satanic/Ritualistic Abuse, and Multiple Personality Disorder*. Portland, Ore.: n.p., n.d.

Rhodes, H. T. F. *The Satanic Mass*. 1956. Reprint, London: Arrow, 1974.

Richards, John. *But Deliver Us from Evil*. London: Darton, Longman & Todd, 1974.

Ritchie, Jean. *The Secret World of Cults*. London: Angus & Robertson, 1991.

Ritual Abuse. King's Cross, New South Wales: NSW Sexual Assault Committee, 1993.

Robbins, Rossell Hope. *Encyclopedia of Witchcraft and Demonology*. London: Peter Nevill, 1959.

Robie, Joan Hake. *Reverse the Curse in Your Life*. Lancaster, Pa.: Starburst, 1991.

Robson, Alan. *Nightmare on Your Street*. London: Virgin, 1993.

Roskoff, Gustav. *Geschichte des Teufels*. Leipzig: Zweiter Band, 1869.

Ross, Colin A. *Satanic Ritual Abuse: Principles of Treatment*. Toronto: Toronto University Press, 1995.

Rudwin, Maximilian. *The Devil in Legend and Literature*. Chicago: Open Court, 1931.

Russell, Jeffrey Burton. *Satan: The Early Christian Tradition*. Ithaca, N.Y.: Cornell University Press, 1981.

Ruthven, Suzanne. *Malleus Satani*. London: Ignotus, 1994.

Ryder, Daniel. *Breaking the Circle of Satanic Ritual Abuse*. Minneapolis, Minn.: CompCare, 1992.

St. Clair, David. *Say You Love Satan*. London: Corgi, 1990.

Sakheim, David K., and Susan E. Devine, eds. *Out of Darkness: Exploring Satanism and Ritual Abuse*. New York: Lexington, 1992.

Sanders, Ed. *The Family*. London: Rupert Hart-Davis, 1972; London: Panther, 1972.

Sanford, Doris. *Don't Make Me Go Back, Mommy: A Child's Book about Satanic Ritual Abuse*. Pictures by Graci Evans. London: Multnomah Press, 1990.

Saradjian, Jacqui. *Women Who Sexually Abuse Children*. Chichester: John Wiley, 1996.

Satan. Translated from a volume in the series *Collection de psychologie religieuses études carmelitaines*. London: Sheed & Ward, 1951.

Schlink, Basilea. *The Unseen World of Angels and Demons*. 1972. Reprint, Basingstoke: Lakeland, 1985.

———. *Countdown to World Disaster*. Basingstoke: Lakeland, 1974.

———. *Escaping the Web of Deception*. 1975. Reprint, Darmstadt: Evangelical Sisterhood of Mary, 1989.

Schnoebelen, William and Sharon Schnoebelen. *Lucifer Dethroned*. Chino, Calif.: ChickPub, 1993.

Scot, Reginald. *Discoverie of Witchcraft*. London, 1584.

Scott, A. F. *Witch, Spirit, Devil*. London: White Lion, 1974.

Seabrook, William. *Witchcraft*. 1942. Reprint, London: Sphere Books, 1970.

Search, Gay. *The Last Taboo: Sexual Abuse of Children*. London: Penguin, 1988.

Sebald, Hans. *Witch-Children*. Amherst, N.Y.: Prometheus Books, 1995.

Sellers, Sean. *Web of Darkness*. Foreword by Bob Larson. Tulsa, Okla.: Victory House, 1990.

Sellwood, A. V., and Peter Haining. *Devil Worship in Britain*. London: Corgi, 1964.

Seth, Ronald. *Witches and their Craft*. London: Tandem, 1970.

Shaw, William. *Spying in Guru Land*. London: Fourth Estate, 1994.

Sheed, F. J. *Soundings in Satanism*. London: Mowbrays, 1972.

Sinason, Valerie, ed. *Treating Survivors of Satanist Abuse*. London: Routledge, 1994.

Sinclair, George. *Satan's Invisible World Discovered*. Edinburgh, 1685.

Sinistrari, Lodovico Maria. *De delictis, et poenis*. 1700. Reprint, Rome, 1754.

———. *Demoniality*. Ca. 1700. Montague Summers ed. New York: Dover, 1989.

Sipe, Onjya, with Robert L. McGrath. *Devil's Dropout*. Milford, Mich.: Mott Media, 1976.

Smith, Margaret. *Ritual Abuse*. San Francisco: Harper San Francisco, 1993.

Smith, Michelle, and Lawrence Pazder. *Michelle Remembers*. London: Sphere Books, 1981.

Smyth, Frank. *Modern Witchcraft*. London: Macdonald, 1970.

Sparkes, the Reverend Don. *It's No Laughing Matter—A Look at the Present Occult Explosion*. Kettering: Norheimsund, 1987.

Sparks, Beatrice. *Jay's Journal*. London: Corgi, 1981.

Spencer, Judith. *Suffer the Child*. New York: Pocket Books, 1989.

Spina, Bartolomeo. *De strigibus*. Venice, 1525. Reprint, 1581.

Stapleton, Thomas. *Cur magia pariter cum haeresi hodie crererit*. [1594]. In *Opera*. Vol. 2 Paris, 1620.

Stephensen, P. R. *The Legend of Aleister Crowley*. London: Mandrake Press, 1930.

Storm, Rachel. *Exorcists: The Terrifying Truth*. London: Fount Paperbacks, 1993.

Stratford, Lauren. *Satan's Underground*. 1988. Gretna: Pelican, 1991

Subritzky, Bill. *Demons Defeated*. 1985. Reprint, Chichester: Sovereign World, 1986.

Subritzky, Bill. *How to Cast Out Demons and Break Curses*. Auckland: Dove Ministries, 1992.

Summers, Montague. *The History of Witchcraft and Demonology*. London: Kegan Paul, 1926.

———. *The Geography of Witchcraft*. London: Kegan Paul, 1927.

———. *The Grimoire*. London: Fortune Press [1935].

———. *A Popular History of Witchcraft*. London: Kegan Paul, 1937.

———. *Witchcraft and Black Magic*. London: Rider, 1946.

Sumrall, Lester. *Three Habitations of Devils*. Springdale, Pa.: Lester Sumrall Evangelistic Association, Whitaker House, 1989.

Suster, Gerald. *Hitler and the Age of Horus*. London: Sphere Books, 1981.

———. *The Legacy of the Beast*. London: W. H. Allen, 1988.

Symonds, John. *King of the Shadow Realms*. London: Duckworth, 1989.

Tannahill, Reay. *Flesh and Blood*. London: Hamish Hamilton, 1975.

Tate, Tim. *Child Pornography*. London: Methuen, 1990.

———. *Children for the Devil*. London: Methuen, 1991.

Taxil, Léo. *Révélations complètes sur la Franc-Maçonnerie*: 4 vols. Paris, 1885–86.

———. *Confessions d'un ex-libre-penseur*. Paris, [1887].

———. *Monsieur Drumont: Étude pschyologique*. Paris, [1890].

———. *Les Conversions célèbres*. Paris, [1891].

———. *Y-a-t-il des femmes dans la Franc-Maçonnerie?* Paris, [1891].

Taylor, James. *Satan's Slaves*. London: New English Library, 1970.

Taylor, Mike R. *Do Demons Rule Your Town?* London: Grace, 1993.

Terry, Maury. *The Ultimate Evil*. London: Parragon, 1993.

The Thin End of the Wedge. Worthing: Christian Publicity Organisation, [1995].

Thomas, Gordon. *Enslaved*. London: Bantam, 1990.

Thompson, Edward. "Life of Paul Whitehead." Prefixed to Paul Whitehead, *Poems*. London, 1777.

Tondriau, Julien, and Roland Villeneuve. *A Dictionary of Devils and Demons*. London: Bay Books, 1972.

Torburn, Peggy [pseud.]. *The Satan Sado–Cultist*. N.p. [United States, ca. 1971].

Towers, Eric. *Dashwood*. London: Crucible, 1986.

Trevor-Roper, H. R. *The European Witch-Craze*. London: Peregrine, 1978.

Trial, Confession and Execution of Isobel Inch, John Stewart, Margaret Barclay and Isobel Crawford, For Witchcaft, at Irvine Anno 1618. Ardrossan, [ca. 1855].

Trinkle, Gabriele, with David Hall. *Delivered to Declare*. London: Hodder and Stoughton, 1986.

A True and Faithful Narrative of Oliver Cromwell's Compact with the Devil for Seven Years. London, 1720.

Tryal of Richard Hathaway. London, 1702.

Turney, Edward, *Diabolism*. London, 1872.

UFOs—Where Do They Come From? Vol. 12, of *The Unexplained*. London: Orbis, 1984.

van Limborch, Philip. *The History of the Inquisition*. Translated by Samuel Chandler. 2 vols. London, 1731.

Vaughan, Diana [pseud.]. *Mémoires d'une ex-palladiste*. Paris, 1896.

———. *La Restauration du paganisme*. Paris, [1896].

Viator, E. *Les Suites de la conversion de Miss Diana Vaughan*. Paris, 1896.

———. *La Vérité sur la conversion de Miss Diana Vaughan*. Paris [1896].

Victor, Jeffrey S. *Satanic Panic*. London: Open Court, 1993.

Villeneuve, Roland. *Satan parmi nous*. Paris and Geneva, 1961.

———. *Dictionnaire du Diable*. Paris: Pierre Bordas, 1989.

von Spee, Friedrich. *Cautio Criminalis*. Rinteln, 1631.

Voragine, Jacques. *Legenda aurea* (The golden legend). Ca. 1270. London, 1503.

Wagner, C. Peter. *How to Have a Healing Ministry without Making Your Church Sick*. Eastbourne: Monarch, 1988.

———, ed. *Territorial Spirits: Insights on Strategic-Level Spiritual Warfare from Nineteen Christian Leaders*. Chichester: Sovereign World, 1991.

———, ed. *Breaking Strongholds in Your City*. Tunbridge Wells: Monarch, 1993.

Waite, Arthur Edward. *Devil-Worship in France*. London, 1896.

———. *The Book of Black Magic*. London, 1898.

Walker, Charles. *The Devil's Disciples*. Worthing, Sussex: published by the author, 1990.

Walker, Tom. *The Occult Web*. Rev. ed. Leicester: Universities and colleges Christian Fellowship, 1989.

Wall, Charles J. *Devils*. 1904. Reprint, London: Studio Editions, 1992.

[Ward, Ned]. *The Secret History of Clubs*. London, 1709.

Warnke, Mike, with Dave Balsiger and Les Jones. *The Satan-Seller*. Plainfield, N.J.: Logos International, 1972.

———. *Schemes of Satan*. Tulsa, Okla.: Victory House, 1991.

Watkins, Leslie. *The Real Exorcists*. London: Futura, 1984.

Weber, Eugene. *Satan Franc-Maçon*. Paris, 1964.

Weldon, John, with Zola Levitt. *UFOs: What on Earth Is Happening?* New York: Bantam, 1976.

Wexler, Richard. *Wounded Innocents: The Real Victims of the War against Child Abuse*. Buffalo, N.Y.: Prometheus Books, 2d ed. 1995.

Weyer, Johann. *De Praestigiis Daemonum*. Basel, 1583.

Wheatley, Dennis. *The Devil Rides Out*. 1934. Reprint, London: Arrow, 1964.

———. *The Haunting of Toby Jugg*. 1948. Reprint, London: Arrow, 1973.

———. *To the Devil—A Daughter*. 1953. Reprint, London: Arrow, 1973.

———. *The Satanist*. 1960. Reprint, London: Arrow, 1964.

———. *Satanism and Witches*. London: Sphere Books, 1974.

Wilburn, Gary. *The Fortune Sellers.* London: Scripture Union, 1972.

Wilkes, Carl A. *Satanism: The Dark Doctrine.* London: Karpatenland, 1994.

The Witch of Wapping. London, 1652.

Woodhouse, the Reverend David M. *Rebuilding the Ruined Places: Caring for the Severely Abused.* Stourbridge: Oakland Christian Ministry, 1994.

Wright, J. Stafford. *Christianity and the Occult.* London: Scripture Union, 1971.

Wright, Lawrence. *Remembering Satan.* London: Serpent's Tail, 1994.

Wurmbrand, Richard. *Was Karl Marx a Satanist?* Rev. 5th ed. Diane Books, n.p., 1979.

Wyatt, Gail Elizabeth, and Gloria Johnson Powell *Lasting Effects of Child Sexual Abuse.* Newbury Park, Calif.: Sage, 1988.

Wyre, Ray. *Working with Sex Abuse.* Oxford: Perry Publications, 1987.

Young, the Reverend Joseph. *Demonology: or, the Scripture Doctrine of Demons.* Edinburgh, 1856.

Zacharias, Gerhard. *The Satanic Cult.* Translated by Christine Trollope. London: George Allen & Unwin, 1980.

Index

About the Author

Gareth J. Medway studied physics at Imperial College, University of London and has since been a freelance writer specializing in comparative religion and the history of occultism. His writing has been published in numerous specialist journals and magazines including *Fortean Studies*, *Magonia* (which awarded him the Roger Sandell Memorial Prize), and *Pagan News*.